WILLIAM SHAKESPEARE

WILLIAM SHAKESPEARE: THE FLOWER PORTRAIT

WILLIAM SHAKESPEARE

A Biography

By A. L. ROWSE

HARPER & ROW, PUBLISHERS
NEW YORK AND EVANSTON

FIRST EDITION

LIBRARY OF CONGRESS CATALOG CARD NUMBER: 63-16517

Preface

IT is usual to preface a book on Shakespeare with an apology for adding to the number, and I had every intention of adhering to the custom. My hope was, as an historian, to be able to illuminate at least the history plays, the inspiration and treatment of England's past, by the most historically minded of dramatists.

But this approach to Shakespeare's life and work, and their relation to the age, has produced discoveries that have astonished me, shed light upon problems hitherto intractable, produced results which might seem incredible, if it were not for the consideration that this is the first time that an historian of the Elizabethan period has tackled them.

It stands to reason that someone who has spent a lifetime studying the period and the social life of Shakespeare's time should have something to contribute, and for a number of years I have had this book in mind in my researches. All the same, I am overwhelmed by what historical investigation, by proper historical method, has brought to light.

It has enabled me to solve, for the first time, and definitively, the problem of the Sonnets, which has teased so many generations and led so many people into a morass of conjecture. The key to the resolution of their problems, all of which are now cleared up — except for the identity of Shakespeare's mistress, which we are never likely to know — has been to follow strict historical method and establish a firm dating and chronology. This is an indispensable foundation for the structure of any biography of Shakespeare, and it is precisely here that an historian has most to offer.

But the establishment of a firm chronology, with a close study of what was happening at the time, year by year, has resulted in an unhoped-for enrichment of the contemporary content and experience that went into a number of the plays, particularly of the earlier and more obscure period. I have, for the first time, been able to establish the date and the occasion of *A Midsummer-Night's Dream*, with what follows as to the conception of the play. *Love's*

Labour's Lost has hitherto been a play to which the key has been missing ; a flood of light pours in, when one realises that an important element of it is a skit on the Southampton circle by an intimate member of it. The environment of feud and duelling in *Romeo and Juliet* has its contemporary connotations very close to this same circle. The relation of *The Merchant of Venice* to the Lopez affair is well known. But it is not only with regard to the early plays that a knowledge of the circumstances and events of Shakespeare's time has yielded results — the same holds good for such a problematical play as *Troilus and Cressida*, or such a political play as *Coriolanus*.

The historian is deeply indebted to the work of the literary scholars — we each have the strengths and the defects of our respective disciplines : our work is complementary. I am immensely indebted, as all who tackle the subject must be, to the indispensable work of Sir Edmund Chambers, most massive (though not the most perceptive) of Shakespearean scholars, to the expertise and detective genius of Sir Walter Greg. What giants they were ! But to these I should like to add the name of the admirable antiquarian, Edgar Fripp, who added so much to our knowledge of the Stratford and Warwickshire background, whose love gave him perceptive insights often denied to the more academic, and these much outweigh the *naïveté* of some of his judgments.

My obligations are numerous : first and foremost to the Huntington Library in California, and to All Souls College, Oxford. The Huntington Library exemplifies that marriage between history and literature which I strongly hold by myself, and which can be so fruitful. Some part of what I owe to the companionship there I express in my dedication ; but I should like to thank Dr. John E. Pomfret and Professor Allan Nevins for their constant encouragement and support. I am especially indebted to Professor Richard Hosley's discriminating judgment and expert scholarship on the Elizabethan stage.

In England I am grateful to Professor F. P. Wilson for his Elizabethan conversation over the years, and for so kindly submitting to hear read the crucial chapters on the Sonnets and the surrounding plays ; and to my old friend John Garrett, for his invitations year after year to lecture at the Anglo-American summer conferences at Stratford, from which I much profited, in seeing the plays, and getting to know that endearing town and countryside with fair familiarity. All English folk of my generation owe a great obligation to our Shakespearean actors, above all to Sir John Gielgud for his inner understanding of Shakespeare, and to Sir Laurence Olivier and Dame Edith Evans ; in addition I am indebted to the perceptive conversation of Robert Speaight.

I am greatly obliged to the Duke of Portland for all the trouble he took over his portraits of the Earl of Southampton and his mother, and for so generously having them photographed for me. And to Mr. Robert Wark, Curator of the Huntington Art Gallery, for his help over locating these portraits.

A chief obligation over this book is to Professor Jack Simmons of the University of Leicester, who, amid the pressure of many duties, found time to read my manuscript. I cannot sufficiently express what my book owes to his critical acumen, his forceful judgment, the admirable suggestions of his combined scholarship and sensibility.

A. L. ROWSE

THE HUNTINGTON LIBRARY
  SAN MARINO, CALIFORNIA
    4th December 1962

CONTENTS

ILLUSTRATIONS

William Shakespeare

The Swan Theatre
C. Walter Hodges, M.S.I.A.

An Elizabethan Player
Dulwich College Picture Gallery

Southampton as a Young Man
The Duke of Portland. Welbeck Abbey

Southampton in the Tower

The Earl of Essex as Lord General
The British Museum

Where Shakespeare Lodged with the Mountjoys
From Fripp: Shakespeare. Man and Artist

Engraved Portrait of Shakespeare by Droeshout
From Fripp: Shakespeare. Man and Artist

Shakespeare's Monument in Stratford Church
Walter Scott

The Gild Chapel and the site of New Place
W. A. Clark, F.R.P.S.

WILLIAM SHAKESPEARE

CHAPTER I

Elizabethan Warwickshire

WARWICKSHIRE is the heart of England, and it was by one of those historic proprieties that illuminate things that Shakespeare, in whom the English people are most fully and faithfully mirrored, should have been born there in the Elizabethan age. These things, place and time — the very dates 1564–1616 — are significant : if he had been born twenty years earlier or later, his achievement would not have been what it was. The time would have been not ripe, or it would have been overripe, for him and his work as we have it. His career and his work, what he made of his opportunity and his providential good fortune, provide a signal example of the fruitful marriage of the right moment with the man.

His native Warwickshire lies before us in Dugdale's map as it was in Shakespeare's day — for Dugdale was working in the next generation only after him : a lozenge-shaped county, with the River Avon running through the midst roughly dividing Arden from Feldon, the remains of the old forest from the open fields and wide pastures of the south. Watling Street, the ancient Roman road across England from London to Shrewsbury, runs along the county's north-eastern border. To south and east it is bounded by the rolling country of Northamptonshire and Oxfordshire ; on the west by the woodlands of Worcestershire, to the south-west by the Cotswolds — from Stratford one looked across the Vale of the Red Horse up to those hills over which lay the road to Oxford and London.

In the centre of the county, Coventry is depicted with its three big spired churches : the busiest industrial town, hub of the cloth-making industry, in particular of cap-making. Neighbouring Warwick is shown on the Avon, with the castle exposing a proud front to the river. There is Kenilworth with its large lake embracing the castle, upon which were held the splendid water-festivities the Earl of Leicester laid on to entertain the Queen in 1575. Up in the north-western corner is Birmingham, a small township but already beginning to show evidences of its prodigious industrial expansion : Camden found it 'full of inhabitants and resounding with hammers and anvils, for most of them are smiths'.¹ On the south-eastern border is the little town of Southam that leads to Banbury and thus to London. From the River Anker in the north, the countryside where the poet Michael Drayton was born and brought up, to Barton-on-the-Heath in the extreme south — where Shakespeare's uncle and aunt lived, Edmund and Joan Lambert, and that creation of his early fancy, Christopher Sly, 'old Sly's son of Barton Heath' — it was some forty miles. A small world, but teeming with life, excitement, adventure.

From early times, and right through the Middle Ages, the primary division in this landscape was that made roughly by the River Avon. The north was a countryside of scattered farms and hamlets in the woodland ; the south was more populous, with large villages and open fields, plenty of arable, richer. This was reflected in the social structure.² Warwickshire in general was a county of landowners of middling status, where the gentry ruled, not great baronial families — not even after 1560, when Elizabeth I replanted the Dudleys at Warwick and at Kenilworth : they had merely a social pre-eminence, no stranglehold on this free shire. Throughout Arden there was a large number of free tenants, with their small holdings and enclosed fields ; in the south the manorial system was more complete, society richer and more complex. Shakespeare's were Arden folk on both sides, both on his father's and his mother's, who indeed bore the name of Arden.

There was something exciting to the imagination in the very situation of Stratford-upon-Avon, on the threshold of the Arden country, from which Shakespeare's father and mother had come to live in the comfortable town. Their son did not hesitate when he came, years later, to write *As You Like It* to make the Duke and his fellow exiles from the painted pomp of Court life seek rustic solitude in the Forest of Arden :

> Are not these woods
> More free from peril than the envious Court ?
> Here feel we not the penalty of Adam,
> The seasons' difference ; as the icy fang
> And churlish chiding of the winter's wind.

Here he found

> tongues in trees, books in the running brooks,
> Sermons in stones, and good in everything.

When John Leland was riding about the country, making notes, in the sad years immediately after the Dissolution of the Monasteries, he came into the county from Banbury and made for Warwick, 'twelve miles by champaign ground, fruitful of corn and grass, barren of wood, and two miles by some enclosed and woody ground'.³ At Warwick he was much impressed, as well he might be, by the splendid tomb of Richard Beauchamp, Earl of Warwick, in his chapel : 'there he is entombed right princely, and portrayed with an image of copper and gilt, hooped over with staves of copper and gilt like a chariot'. The scene is not much changed, except that there came to join him, in Shakespeare's lifetime, Ambrose Dudley, Earl of Warwick, his brother Robert, Earl of Leicester, and his beautiful termagant Countess Lettice, and across from them their little boy Robert, 'the noble imp', heir to all these glories, who perished before them. There they all are, lying on their tombs.

Leland noted that, though the castle keep was in ruins, Henry VIII was now building fair lodgings for occupation on the south side. Among chief features of the town was the High Street running from east to west, with another from north to south crossing it, 'with a right goodly cross in the middle of it'. The north gate of the town had fallen down ; beyond it was a suburb with a hospital of St. Michael much in ruin. On the south the fine bridge of twelve arches served for a gateway. Over the east gate was a chapel of St. Peter, on the north side of the west gate was a fraternity of St. George. When this was swept away by the Dissolution of the Chantries, Leicester acquired the property and turned it into an almshouse, conferring the mastership on the egregious Puritan, Cartwright. This too, with tower and court-yard, half-timbered gables and balconies, remains little changed.

But Leland becomes quite lyrical about the sequestered spot of Guy's Cliff, further up-stream, devoted to the cult of the legendary Guy of Warwick, whose story Elizabethans continued to read avidly along with *Amadis of Gaul*, *Bevis of Southampton* and similar romances. 'It is a place of pleasure, an house meet for the Muses ; there is silence, a pretty wood, *antra in vivo saxo*, the river rolling with a pretty noise over the stones', and much more in Latin to the same effect.

Leland continued his perambulations noting that a Compton had recently razed the remains of the castle in Fulbrook park, which had been an eyesore to Warwick castle, and took the stone to build his fine house at Compton Wynyates. The bridge over the Avon at Bidford had lately been amended with stone from the dissolved priory at Alcester. Sudely castle — shortly to come to Queen Catherine Parr — had been built by the Butlers, 'western men'. At Toddington were the Tracys, of the family that provided one of the knights who murdered St. Thomas Becket : they are still there. Leland came round by Stratford, of which he gives us a full description, and then rode away by champaign ground, that is, open arable, and by a bridge over the Alne to Coughton of the Throckmortons.[4]

When Camden came to visit the county a generation later, early in Shakespeare's lifetime, he began by noticing the visible contrast between Arden and Feldon. 'The Feldon lieth on this side Avon southward, a plain champaign country, and being rich in corn and green grass yieldeth a right goodly and pleasant prospect to them that look down upon it from an hill which they call Edghill.'[5] It still does. One looks out over the green and elmy Vale of the Red Horse, called after 'the shape of an horse cut out in a red hill by the country people hard by Pillerton'. (One sees that red tinge in the stone of which the church of the Holy Trinity at Stratford is built, by the waters of the Avon, where Shakespeare and all his family lie.) Little Compton was then called Compton in the Hole, 'so called for that it lieth hidden in a valley under the hills, yet hath it delights and pleasure about it'. The Compton family originated here, of whom Sir Henry Compton was made a baron in 1572 ; his light-headed son married the richest heiress in London, daughter of 'Rich Spencer', Lord Mayor, on whose death the young man went mad with joy, until a spell in the Tower restored him to his senses. Wormleighton was the residence of another rich Spencer, ancestor of the Althorp line, whose wealth was founded on sheep, on those wolds 'so highly commended and notorious for good sheep pasture'.

At Leamington 'there boileth out a spring of salt water' — hence the later spa. Rugby then was but a market, chiefly of butchers. Camden, too, was touched by the charms of Guy's Cliff at Warwick, but after reciting the exploits of the legendary Sir Guy, he adds, 'howbeit, wiser men do think that the place took that name of later time by far, from Guy Beauchamp, Earl of Warwick'. This is half a century later than Leland, and exemplifies a more critical spirit ; this is progress.

On his way at Charlecote, Camden paid tribute to 'the renowned ancient family of the Lucys, knights', who had been there four hundred years then — and are still there. And so into Stratford, 'a proper little market town, beholden for all the beauty that it hath to two men there bred and brought up' : Archbishop John de Stratford and Sir Hugh Clopton. One of the Clopton coheiresses was married to Sir George Carew, 'whom I am more willing to honour in this respect, if there were none other, for that he is a most affectionate lover of venerable antiquities'. There he lies in the Clopton chapel at Stratford in all the panoply of war : drums, flags, cannon — for he was Master of the Ordnance and Lieutenant-General in Ireland. There is no reference on the part of Camden, Ben Jonson's schoolmaster, to the living Shakespeare already shedding more lustre on the scene.

'Now let us enter into the woodland, which beyond the River Avon spreadeth itself northward much larger in compass than the Feldon, and is for the most part thick set with woods, and yet not without pastures, cornfields and sundry mines of iron.' On the River Arrow near Alcester lay Beauchamp's Court, residence of Sir Fulke Greville, the father of Sir Philip Sidney's friend : him also we can still see in full armour and ruff on his tomb in Alcester church. 'Whose only son carrying likewise the same name hath consecrated himself so to true virtue and nobility, that in nobility of mind he far surmounteth his parentage and unto whom, for his exceeding great deserts toward me, yet will I ever render thanks.' A great many were under obligation to Sidney's Fulke Greville, grasping as he was, Camden among them.

Alcester itself was much decayed now and only a small market of wares, though much frequented at the time of its corn fair. At Henley-in-Arden scant remains were to be seen of the castle of the Montforts. But Kenilworth, 'where wild brooks meeting together make a broad pool among the parks', had been re-animated and made magnificent by Leicester to whom the Queen had granted it : 'who to repair and adorn it spared no cost : in so much as if a man consider either the gallant building or the large parks, it would scorn (as it were) to be ranged in a third place amongst the castles in England'. To Leicester's elder brother, Ambrose, whom the Queen made Earl of Warwick regranting to him the Warwickshire estates of his father, John, Duke of Northumberland, Camden paid a warmer tribute : 'a most worthy person, both for warlike prowess and sweetness of nature'. That was true :

the most popular of the Dudleys. He died in 1590, and his widowed Countess became the closest confidant of the Queen, remaining with her to the end.

At Solihull was nothing to be seen but a fine church. Sutton Coldfield, standing on a churlish hard soil, had been revivified by John Veysey, Henry VIII's bishop of Exeter, who spent his wealth gained from that see on raising up buildings, founding a grammar school, making a park, gaining privileges for his native town. Coventry was wealthy and prosperous : 'a city very commodiously seated, large, sweet and neat, fortified with strong walls and set out with right goodly houses : amongst which there rise up on high two churches of rare workmanship, standing one hard by the other, and matched as it were concurrents' — Holy Trinity and St. Michael's. The third, the medieval monastic cathedral, had been destroyed by the Dissolution, and Camden saw but the ruins, as we see today. He owed his account of Coventry's history to the antiquary Henry Ferrers of Baddesley Clinton : 'a man both for knowledge of antiquity very commendable and my especial friend'. The medieval house of which he was the owner for seventy years he enlarged with an Elizabethan banqueting-room, towered porch, panelling and pilasters, armorial glass in the hall : there it still remains, with arched bridge and gabled wings reflected in the quiet waters of the moat.

Up on the Cotswolds, looking out over south Warwickshire, were the Rollright stones, a prehistoric circle then complete. 'The common people usually call them rollrich stones and dreameth that they were sometimes men, by a wonderful metamorphosis turned into hard stones.' The large stone they called the King — who should have been king of England — the five close together were knights on horseback, the rest were the army. Such was the mind of the country people of the time.

When we come to Drayton, that other Warwickshire poet of the age, the picture is corroborated in verse. It is Drayton who first calls his native county the heart of England, and all his days he was devoted to it, had in his mind its pastoral scenes, its rivers and streams by which he spent much of his life, was inspired by it in his work. He was born at Hartshill near Atherstone, at the opposite end of the county from Stratford, a year or so before Shakespeare.[6] In his later years he used to come frequently to spend the summers at Clifford Chambers, a couple of miles from

Stratford, by the little River Stour that runs through those meadows into the Avon :

> dear Clifford's seat, the place of health and sport,
> Which many a time hath been the Muses' quiet port.

This house too, half-timbered and gabled, remained right up to the first of the two German wars that have ruined England in our time ; but still the poet's kind patrons, Sir Henry Rainsford and his wife Anne Goodere — whom Drayton loved from her child-hood days and celebrated in his sonnets, *Idea's Mirror* — are depicted kneeling face to face on their monument in the church there.

Michael Drayton was a patriotic soul, and he expressed the inspiration he owed to his country background directly and simply :

> My native country then which so brave spirits hast bred,
> If there be any virtue yet remaining in thy earth
> Or any good of thine thou breathed'st into my birth,
> Accept it as thine own whilst now I sing of thee,
> Of all thy later brood th' unworthiest though I be.[7]

An Arden man, he begins his description of the county with the forest and the songs of all the different birds haunting those wood-lands. From that he proceeds to a lively account of hunting the deer in the glades, while a marginal note informs us that 'the hart weepeth at his dying : his tears are held to be precious in medicine'. He goes on to sing the hermit's life in forest solitude and describes him seeking through the rides for simples to heal ills :

> And in some open place that to the sun doth lie
> He fumitory gets and eye-bright for the eye,
> The yarrow wherewithal he stops the wound-made gore . . .

There follows a charming passage of country-lore about the herbs and plants that are specifics for different ailments. In short, the best part of his song of Warwickshire in *Polyolbion* is devoted to the forest :

> Fair Arden, thou my Tempe art alone,
> And thou sweet Anker art my Helicon.

He follows the course of the rivers flowing out of the wood-land, now much reduced, when once it extended from the Trent to the Severn. And so to the towns, like Coventry, whose legends of St. Ursula and the Lady Godiva he celebrates, as also the story of Warwick castle, and the Beauchamps. Out of the county he jogs, once more across the Vale of the Red Horse and up into the Cotswolds, of which he offers 'a nice description' with praise of its white-woolled sheep :

> As white as winter's snow when from the river's side
> He drives his new-washed sheep ; or on the shearing day,
> Whenas the lusty ram with those rich spoils of May
> His crooked horns hath crowned . . .
>   there the shepherds' king
> Whose flock hath chanced that year the earliest lamb to bring
> In his gay bawdrick sits at his low grassy board
> With flawns, curds, clotted cream and country dainties stored ;
> And whilst the bagpipe plays, each lusty jocund swain
> Quaffs syllabubs in cans, to all upon the plain
> And to their country girls whose nosegays they do wear,
> Some roundelays do sing, the rest the burden bear.

We may set this beside Autolycus's sheep-shearing in *The Winter's Tale* : we recognise the common inspiration.

If Shakespeare could return to his native south Warwickshire he would find it not greatly changed, all very recognisable still. True, the immense open fields have been enclosed, making a smaller, more interesting pattern of quickset hedges and ditches in low-lying country, the woodland and wild much reduced. But there is the landscape, and, among the works of men's hands, above all the churches — like his own, raising its noble tower and clerestory above the Avon that washes the churchyard. Or there is Snitterfield on its hill a few miles to the north of Stratford : thither his grandfather came in the reign of Henry VIII ; the old church still has its fine Renaissance stalls with elaborate traceries and poppy heads of vines, the font with clumsy big medieval heads supporting the bowl in which many of the family were baptised. From the churchyard on its knoll one looks out over much of the hundred of Barlichway, which from early times had its meeting place at the Gospel Oak in the lane leading up from the road to Stratford.

Charlecote church was unfortunately rebuilt by the Victorians, but we can see there on their tombs all three Sir Thomas Lucys who ruled there in Shakespeare's time. Nearer Stratford, in fact, now within the borough, is the old manor house of Alveston with Elizabethan wing, panelling and staircase : the manor belonged to the eccentric Grevilles of Milcote. They sold it in 1603 to Nicholas Lane, whose clumsy, rustic effigy, padded sleeves and long hair, is in the little shut-up church. Or there is the church of Rowington, where there were earlier generations of Shake-speares, with its Elizabethan altar-table, old oak chests and alms-box : *disjecta membra* of the age. Or Aston Cantlow, with fine west tower and more woodwork from timbers of the Forest — an oak pulpit, chests, a candelabrum of the time : here Shakespeare's parents would have been married, for Mary Arden's home at Wilmcote was in this parish.

Or among the houses he would recognise is Charlecote, not much disturbed in shape in spite of the Victorian interference with the fenestration. The broad gate-house remains as it was, and much of the diapered brickwork. The core of Clopton House, on the gentle slope northward from Stratford and looking down across the meadows to the spire of Holy Trinity, dates from the sixteenth century. Though much altered later, it has its original porch with Renaissance arch, and in an attic upstairs painted texts and the adjuration :

> Whether you Rise yearlye or goe to bed late
> Remember Christ Jesus that Died for your sake

The Cloptons remained true to the old faith and were Catholic Recusants ; at the time of Gunpowder Plot in 1605 it was rented by one of the conspirators, and, when searched, Popish relics and mass-vestments were found there. The Underhills of Idlicote were Catholics also : it was from this William Underhill that Shakespeare bought New Place, the best house in the town, in 1597. That same year Underhill was poisoned by his son and heir Fulke, who was executed at Warwick for the murder in the year following. So that the deed of purchase of New Place had to be confirmed when the second son, Hercules, came of age.[8]

Claverdon, near Henley-in-Arden, formed part of the Dudley estates Ambrose got back from the Queen. A few years later, in 1568, he sold it to rich Sir John Spencer of Wormleighton, whose eldest son was buried here in a grand tomb in 1586. Billesley Hall, a few miles west of Stratford, remains with its gabled and many-windowed front reflected in the pond before the house. In Shake-speare's day it was owned by Thomas Trussell, who conveyed it away in 1585 and in that summer took to highway robbery on the old Kent Road by Bromley, and for this Falstaffian exploit was attainted and sentenced to death in Armada year. Beautiful Bidford bridge over the Avon remains much as it was when Leland saw it. The manor here was sold in 1568 to Lodowick Greville of Milcote, who shortly sold it again to Lady Griffin for her son, Rice Griffin, still a minor. On attaining his majority he wasted his estate, encumbered it with debt and had to sell land to John Combe, Shakespeare's crony of Old Stratford, who left the poet £5 in his will.

This Lodowick Greville was a horrid case : a homicidal type. When his younger son shot an arrow which fell and killed his elder brother, the father 'made a jest of it, telling him it was the best shoot he ever shot in his life'.9 In 1579 he was imprisoned for attacking Sir John Conway of Arrow in the streets of London. He came to a bad end. He had designs on the property of a well-to-do old bachelor, a tenant of his, Thomas Webbe, whom he inveigled over from Oxfordshire to make merry at a feast. Afterwards he had Webbe strangled in his bed, got a servant to impersonate him dying and called in a parson to make the 'will' in favour of Greville. The story was blurted out by one of the servants involved, 'in his cups at Stratford', upon which Greville had him murdered by his fellow. This man was arrested and confessed. Greville was imprisoned for nearly a year in the Tower, but nothing could be got out of him ; standing mute in order to save his estates for his son, he was pressed to death, in accordance with the law, on 14 November 1589.

It cannot be said that life in the neighbourhood of Stratford in those years was without its excitements.

Or we may take the villages round about, without going far : the evidences remain, the picture holds. Shottery, the village where Anne Hathaway was brought up and from which she was married to Shakespeare, has several ancient timber-frame cottages, in addition to that which was her home and goes now by her name : in her day it was known as Hewlands farm. We may take the road out to Wilmcote, through gently rolling country-side and up a hill from which one sees the blue sickle of the Cots-wolds on the south-west horizon ; the wheatfields tawny towards harvest, the arable extending in wide swathes down the gentle slopes towards Stratford. In the village is the Tudor house known as Mary Arden's : admirable example of a prosperous yeoman's house of the time : stone foundation and timber frame — it is no mystery that so much timber was used when they had so much woodland around them. In the attics one sees the rough-cut trees that still hold up the roof as they have done for four hundred years, the timber floors uneven now with age ; in the living-room the open hearth, ingle-nook in the corner, the winged settle to shut out the draughts.

One need go no further out than the little market town of Henley-in-Arden. In the sixteenth century it was within the large parish of Wootton Wawen, where one sees the manor house going back to that time, an Elizabethan wing with friezes and fluted pilasters. In 1559 the manor was bought by the widow of Sir John Smith, a Baron of the Exchequer, for the son and heir Francis. Though the family had Catholic sympathies, Francis went like a sensible man to church, where he is buried under a grand Renaissance tomb. Henley itself is still one long street of half a mile, the broad church tower with medieval gild hall beside it in the middle. Behind their later fronts are a good many Tudor houses, especially the inns, the Blue Bell, Three Tuns, White Swan. In 1609 and 1610 the manor court laid it down, sad to say, that 'neither Master Bailiff nor any other inhabitant shall licence or give leave to any players to play within the town hall upon pain to forfeit 40s.' Nevertheless, happily, in 1615 a troupe did visit the town and other neighbouring places.[10]

As for the Warwickshire clergy, we are fortunate in possessing an amusing, if uncharitable, report of them from the sour Puritans in 1586.[11] The lower parish at Warwick had Humphrey Waring for vicar : 'some knowledge, little discretion, he preacheth sometimes, but negligently ; he is thought to be unsound in some parts of Christian religion, loveth the ale-house well, and very much subject to the vice of good fellowship'. (Which they certainly were not.) Martin Delaine was vicar of the upper parish, 'a preacher and learned in the tongues, yet the people profit not'. (Well, what did they expect ? These were persons who would not take 'yes' for an answer.) At Snitterfield was a hireling, Henry Flatche : 'he is dumb and unlearned, and yet thought to be honest, but far unfit for the ministry ; he teacheth to play on instruments and draweth wrought works'. Poor old Flatche had to make do on £15 a year. At Wootton Wawen, Mascall was a preacher, 'though he be grown idle, negligent and slothful ; a man deformed and of tainted life. He hath two charges besides Wootton, namely, Henley and Ullenhall, which he supplieth by his hirelings, whereof one, upon a rumour of a change in religion in Monsieur's days, did shave his beard.'[12] At Temple Grafton, John Frith was 'an old priest and unsound in religion, he can neither preach nor read well ; his chiefest trade is to cure hawks that are hurt and diseased, for which purpose many do usually repair to him'. This useful old person lived passing well on £20 a year. At Baddesley Clinton was William Shaw, 'dumb, unlearned and idle, unsound in religion and a secret persuader of the simple to popery, one that prayeth for the dead, a blasphemer of the name of God, vicious and licentious of life, a companion at all games, an alehouse haunter'. Nothing was too bad to be believed of him evidently. The vicar of Honiley 'could not one day read the commandments for want of his spectacles. An old pardoner in Queen Mary's time and yet remaineth popish. A woolwinder and girthmaker by his usual occupation' — the poor old priest needed another trade, for he had only £5 a year to live upon. The parson of Lapworth, for a similar reason, some time played the serving man in a livery coat, some time the minister ; while the vicar of Packwood was 'an old priest and a mass-monger, a drunkard and dumb and, as it is thought, a sorcerer'. We know what that was intended to imply.

We do not have to take this biased and bileful view *au pied de la lettre*, but it adds a few strokes to the picture. Some ministers, like vicar Barton of Stratford, met with approval ; but they were a minority. While a few 'godly' ministers had been suspended for refusing to subscribe Whitgift's articles and making trouble : they, of course, were virtuous.

All in all we may take Warwickshire to be more representative of the life of Elizabethan England than any more eccentric county in the north, west or even east. It exemplified a characteristic Midlands balance of arable and woodland, sheep pasture and water-meadows ; it was well-watered and fruitful, beautifully served by its rivers and streams. There was the life of nobles, occasional as it was, at lordly castles like Kenilworth and Warwick. Everywhere in the countryside there were the gentry — Lucys at Charlecote, Cloptons at Clopton, Grevilles at Milcote and at Beauchamp's Court, Catholic Throckmortons at Coughton, Protestant — indeed Puritan — Throckmortons at Haseley, Gooderes at Polesworth, Ferrers at Baddesley Clinton. The towns were little hives of trades, crafts, industry — mostly reflecting the dominant agricultural life of the countryside round about : clothiers, drapers, butchers, tanners, glovers, shoemakers, carpenters, wheelwrights, coopers, smiths. On the dominant issue of the age, religion, the country was prettily divided, with a strong Catholic minority opposed to the Protestants, who won out with the

Queen's accession.[13] There were Catholic Throckmortons, Comptons, Underhills, Somervilles, Ardens, to oppose Protestant Dudleys, Grevilles, Lucys, Throckmortons. We might say that Warwickshire was a perfect microcosm of inland England.

The achievement of this little cosmos, its contribution to the larger world of England, gives us much to reflect on. Perhaps we can hardly claim for it the works, for the state no less than for themselves, of the grand Dudleys. But there is the political importance of Sir Nicholas Throckmorton, first of Elizabethan diplomats, Leicester's adviser ; and his nephew Job Throckmorton, Puritan orator and pamphleteer, who had more than a hand in the Martin Marprelate tracts. Sir Fulke Greville was almost as distinguished a figure in government and administration as he was a poet and writer. And Holinshed, the chronicler, came to rest there and died as steward to Thomas Burdett of Bramcote up in Drayton's native countryside.

With Drayton and Shakespeare this little county produced from her ordinary folk, one country bred, the other from the town, two men of genius very true to herself. Is it altogether fanciful to think of Drayton, the pastoral writer, meditative and slow-moving over the country scene, as the poet of Arden, and of Shakespeare, passionate and quick, mercurial and mimetic, the dramatist profoundly concerned with people, the life of the town, with country always near at hand, as the poet of Feldon ?

CHAPTER II

Stratford Town

STRATFORD too is very recognisable, strangely unspoiled, in spite of the horror of the age we live in. The layout of the town has hardly changed since the Middle Ages : three streets running parallel with the River Avon, one of them open to the river, where in Elizabeth's days there were archery butts by the bridge — now laid out as grounds, presided over by the *Genius Loci* — three streets at right angles to the others, running roughly east and west. The boundaries of the little borough remained the same from 1591 to three hundred years later ; at the earlier date it had just over two hundred houses and it grew hardly at all till 1800.[1] This meant that within the town boundaries there was a good deal of open space unbuilt on, orchards and groves of trees. In 1582 there were nearly a thousand elms in and about the town, so it was bowered in trees, full of birdsong and the sound of water, for two brooks flowed through the streets to the Avon. An Elizabethan town would be no less full of smells, pungent and acrid, or pleasant and sweet. One characteristic of Shakespeare's we can detect for ourselves : he had a very sensitive nose and ear.

Let us perambulate.

We come into the town over the fine stone bridge that so much impressed Leland : it is much as it was then. It was built just before 1500 by Hugh Clopton, a Stratford boy who went to London and made a fortune in trade ; 'having neither wife nor children', he was able to devote part of it to good works which were the pride of the town. The main street of Stratford was, and is, the street ahead of us, Bridge Street, running up to the old market cross at the intersection with the High Street and Henley Street : in Shakespeare's day the cross was replaced by a more useful covered structure, under which his father had his standing on market days along with the other glovers of the town. In Bridge Street were the three chief inns, the Bear, the Swan, the Angel — only the last remains, much translated. The Bear and the Swan were at the bottom on opposite corners, and they probably enjoyed the patronage of opposite parties in religion, over which Stratford was strenuously divided ; for we find the Earl of Warwick staying at the Swan in 1583, while the landlord of the Bear married two wives in succession who were staunch Catholics and thus compounded with his conscience.[2]

A half turn to the right at the top takes us along Henley Street to the house where Shakespeare was born. Here on the right stand a couple of houses isolated now, somewhat altered in configuration with time though much is recognisable within. One of these houses Shakespeare's father occupied as his shop, the premises he needed for his trade as a glover and wool-dealer, the other was the family home. At the back of what is known as the Middle house there extends a pretty wing, with separate kitchen and stairs, into the close — now a garden filled with the son's favourite flower, roses. It would have made a convenient little home to bring his wife to, under the paternal roof in the Elizabethan manner. In those days people managed to crowd into small space — needs must — and lived their lives the more gregariously, the more intensely and briefly. The living-room on the street is not severely changed : open fireplace of brick and stone, raftered ceiling and broken flagged floor. At the back is the kitchen with wide open hearth for all the cooking-pots and pans : upstairs the big family bedroom dominating the house, the place of birth and death.

It is touching to stand there looking at the scene, simple and intimate. As a devoted custodian of the place writes : in the imagination 'it gathers memories and fancies. Shadows and weird noises are in the rafters, the wind is in the chimney, crickets are on the hearth, fairies glisten in the light of the dying fire, through the casement-window shines the moon, from without comes the "to-whit, to-whoo" of the owl.'[3] With so many trees about, and barns, it must have been a fine place for owls ; the upper end of Henley Street was then open country, orchards and a grove of elm and ash. At any rate here was Shakespeare's home, until he bought New Place in 1597. And the fact is that, though he needed to earn his living in London, he was unusually attached to his native-place, coming back there often for the summer. In that so true to his nature, the loyalties and affections so obvious all through his writing, the ties acknowledged in his life.

In Henley Street were gathered John Shakespeare's friends and neighbours. Next door on the east was William Wedgwood, tailor, a not very respectable Wedgwood, who had been banished from Warwick by the Earl and had his livery plucked from him. 'Leaving his wife he went to Stratford and there married another wife, his first wife yet living; besides that he is a man very contentious, proud and slanderous, oft busying himself with naughty matters and quarrelling with his honest neighbours.'[4] And so he went to Stratford. Alderman Whateley, draper, was very respectable, though there were skeletons in the family cupboard: two brothers, fugitive Catholic priests who lurked about Henley, whom their prosperous brother helped to support. Whateley had beehives in his garden, 'wax, honey and other things in the apple-chamber'. There are Whateleys still among the shop-keepers of Stratford. A few doors away was another glover, Gilbert Bradley, for whom Shakespeare's bachelor brother Gilbert would have been named. A stream flowed across the street into Rother Market and thence down Chapel Lane and by New Place to the river. Below the stream was Hornby's smithy. When Shakespeare came to write *King John*, he wrote:

> I saw a smith stand with his hammer, thus,
> The whilst his iron did on the anvil cool,
> With open mouth swallowing a tailor's news;
> Who, with his shears and measure in his hand,
> Standing on slippers — which his nimble haste
> Had falsely thrust upon contrary feet.

It is an authentic portrait; that observant mind, which registered and stored up everything and forgot nothing, must often have seen such a one.

Back down Henley Street now to the High Street where lived the most prosperous shopkeepers and principal burgesses, leading people in the town: Quineys, Rogerses, Sadlers, Walkers, Woolmers. Adrian Quiney, mercer, was a colleague of John Shakespeare on the town council. His son Richard was several times bailiff of the borough and for years the most active spirit in its affairs; he died in 1602 as the result of a head-wound he received in trying to quell a brawl raised at fair-time by the followers of the injurious lord of the manor, Edward Greville of Milcote. Quiney's son Thomas, who as a grammar-school boy could write his father a good Latin letter, was to marry Shakespeare's daughter Judith.

On one side of the Quineys was Baynton's shop with wares ranging from sugarloaves to gunpowder ; on the other John Smith's tavern whence he furnished cakes and ale, and wine for Sir Fulke Greville and the Earl of Warwick. When he came to be bailiff in 1598, Quiney's friend Sturley wrote that he 'doth baily it exceeding many of his predecessors beyond all expectation well'.[5]

In High Street, too, lived Shakespeare's friend Henry Walker, mercer, whose son William was his godson, to whom he left a gold sovereign in his will. Here were Hamnet and Judith Sadler, after whom Shakespeare's twins were named. Philip Rogers, the apothecary, sold confections of roses, liquorice, aniseed, sarsaparilla, and the new specifics coming from the New World, sassafras, guaiacum and 'tobecka', against which Sturley so rightly warned Quiney.[6] After the fires of 1594 and 1595, which did much damage in the centre of the town, the houses in the High Street had to be rebuilt, some of them on a grander scale. Two of them that remain are Tudor House at the corner of Ely Street, a three-storeyed building with overhanging frontage and decorative timber-work — the Woolmers were here for generations ; and Harvard House, with the best wood-carving in the town — grotesques, bull's head, the Dudley cognisance of bear and ragged staff — so called because the daughter of Alderman Rogers, who built it, married a Harvard of Southwark and became the mother of the founder of Harvard College.

Or from Henley Street we could follow the stream into Rother Street, where the cattle-market has always been held —

It is the pasture lards the rother's sides.

Here on the south side remains part of the large house built by prosperous Abraham Sturley, plaster ceilings and friezes within.[7] Most fascinating is the White Swan Hotel of the fifteenth century and later, for in the big panelled room downstairs is a section of frescoed Elizabethan wall, three scenes from the Book of Tobit, contemporary figures in conversation, Tobias and his dog, the angel Gabriel half hidden by the drapery, all in colour with swags of fruit, frieze and texts from the Bible. The inn was known as the King's house and was then owned by a rich brewer, Robert Perrott, who much objected to his granddaughter marrying young Richard Tyler, a schoolfellow of Shakespeare. Perrott cut her out of his will, with warning to her sisters not 'to match themselves without consent of their parents'.[8] To the offspring of this marriage, a young William, Shakespeare left 26s. 8d. for a ring to remember him by.

And so down the lane to the heart of the town for us, the nexus of buildings dominated by the grey-stone tower of the Gild-Chapel built by Hugh Clopton, and within the precincts the Gild-hall, where the 'halls' or meetings of the council took place, the almshouses, grammar school, and little houses for both schoolmaster and the vicar. Externally there is not so much changed here, though the whole area was then more heavily overhung by trees. When Leland was here, 'about the body of this chapel was curiously painted the Dance of Death'.⁹ The interior was sadly ravaged by the Reformation, the rood loft and screen pulled down, the images defaced and broken up, paintings white-washed. In our day we have with much effort recovered something of the painted Doom upon the chancel-arch and even a few of the frescoes on the walls. 'This Clopton builded also by the north side of this chapel a pretty house of brick and timber, wherein he lay in his latter days.' This was New Place : a five-gabled house built somewhat back from the street with a little court before it, barns and garden at the back. Shakespeare bought it in 1597 and lived here during his later prosperous years : now, nothing left of it but the foundations, brick-walls of the cellars, the two wells. For an odious eighteenth-century clergyman who owned it, already irritated by the number of sightseers, quarrelled with Stratford and revenged himself by pulling the house down.¹⁰

Adjoining it on the street is the attractive house of Thomas Nash, who married Shakespeare's granddaughter, Elizabeth Hall. Next to it remains Julian Shaw's house, a neighbour who witnessed Shakespeare's will. Then comes the house, now part of the Shakespeare Hotel, in which lived friend Thomas Reynolds and his son William. This family also occupied a farm near the church and were the largest household in the town, altogether with their servants some twenty-two persons. They were obstinate Catholics, who paid their heavy fines for recusancy, rather than go to church. Not so William Shakespeare, who left young William Reynolds 26s. 8d. 'to buy a ring'. On the opposite corner of the street the Falcon Hotel remains recognisable, a Tudor house subsequently enlarged. It seems that in front of the chapel was another cross, the third in the town, for on market days the dealers in butter, cheese and white meats had their pitch here after

1608, while the country butchers had their place in Chapel Street. From New Place Shakespeare looked out on all that chaffer — 'market folks that come to sell their corn', 'the vulgar sort of market men . . . at wakes and wassails, meetings, markets, fairs'. The ringing of the market-bell from the chapel told them when the time for their chaffering was up.

We follow the road down which they were carried at the beginning of their lives to christening in the church, and at their end for burial in church or churchyard.

> Now it is the time of night
>> That the graves, all gaping wide,
> Every one lets forth his sprite,
>> In the churchway paths to glide.

As one goes up the churchway path under the limes, one has the sense that it is haunted : it *is* haunted ground. In Shakespeare's time there was a charnel-house in the graveyard, like that in *Romeo and Juliet* :

> Or shut me nightly in a charnel-house,
> O'er-covered quite with dead men's rattling bones,
> With reeky shanks and yellow chapless skulls.

In spite of the changes time has brought, no Elizabethan *revenant* would have any difficulty in recognising the features of the splendid collegiate building. There is the high wide nave, with broad clerestory above, and, beyond the tower crossing, the beckoning chancel. At the back of the nave is the broken bowl of the medieval font in which Shakespeare was christened. Up beneath the pulpit on the south side was the New Place pew in which the family sat ; on the other side the Cloptons lie in all their glory upon their gilded monuments. After the Reformation the chancel was boarded off : preaching became more important than the sacraments. In winter the wind rustled in the roofs and draughts played about the unwarmed, roomy nave :

> When all aloud the wind doth blow,
> And coughing drowns the parson's saw.

We pass through into the transept where Richard Hill, neighbour and honest woollen draper, lies :

> He did not use to swear, to glose or feign,
> His brother to defraud in bargaining ;

He would not strive to get excessive gain
In any cloth or other kind of thing :
His servant I this truth can testify,
A witness that beheld it with my eye.

We enter the chancel where are still all the original medieval stalls of the college of priests, with their carved misericords, knights and ladies, quarrelling peasants, mermaids and monsters, roses and shields. There, within the sanctuary rails, Shakespeare and his family are gathered together ; above, his figure looks serenely down upon it all, the laurels, the wreaths and flowers, the unending procession of pilgrims from all parts of the world.

The church stands away from the town in a little community of its own — Old Stratford ; the interest of this is that it was the site of the original Saxon monastery outside the bounds of the subsequent borough. All through the Middle Ages the town belonged to the see of Worcester ; the Reformation emancipated it. In 1539 the college of priests that served the church was dissolved ; their residence came into the hands of the Combes, from whom Shakespeare purchased a moiety of the tithes which had been part of the endowment. In 1547 the gild of the Holy Cross was dissolved —it was a near thing that the Chapel itself was not destroyed ; but with the parish church being out of the town, the Chapel was convenient for sermons and services, in particular for the grammar school next door. The town bestirred itself to purchase from the Crown the gild properties that had been nationalised, and this was the foundation of its new-found independence.

Stratford's new status was signalised by a grant of a charter in 1553, incorporating it as a borough, with a council of fourteen aldermen and fourteen burgesses, presided over by a bailiff elected annually. The corporation was given considerable powers to govern the town, make by-laws to this end, and manage the town's property and its revenues. The bailiff was the chief executive officer, who presided over council meetings, and also in the local law-court, the court of record, for which purpose he was to act as Justice of the Peace. A permanent officer on the spot was the town clerk. First of the line was Richard Symons, who held the office from 1554 to 1568 and wrote a good clerkly hand. Later on, Shakespeare's cousin, Thomas Greene of Middle Temple, became town clerk in 1603 ; to him there succeeded Francis Collins of Clement's Inn, an active attorney at Stratford, who wrote Shakespeare's will, was an overseer of it and was left twenty marks.

The accounts were vetted annually and submitted by two chamberlains from the corporate body. There were four constables to keep order in the town, with their complement of third-boroughs ; two ale-tasters and bread-weighers each year to ensure proper weight and quality of food and drink. The corporation took over the powers of a parish vestry to levy a poor-rate on the inhabitants for the aid of the poor. This became important in the years of depression after the great fires of 1594 and 1595. Grander officers, though less on the spot, were the stewards and recorders, who held something of an honorific position (but with a retainer) : their function was to provide some protection, to make interest in high places, in a litigious age. Henry Rogers, steward from 1570 to 1586, was also steward to Sir Thomas Lucy, who took a friendly interest in the town's affairs and was always available to help. From 1576 Stratford shared a recorder with Warwick in Edward Aglionby ; after him came Sir Fulke Greville of Beauchamp's Court, who was followed by his famous son, the poet, from 1606 to 1628.

The manor of Stratford, which had been granted to Ambrose, Earl of Warwick, was purchased after his death by the horrid Sir Edward Greville of Milcote. He kept trying to assert himself, putting his nose into the town's affairs, and enclose the town commons for his own benefit. Fortunately he suffered from increasing financial difficulties, was successfully resisted by the tough little corporation and parted with the manor to the still horrider Sir Arthur Ingram, the notorious Jacobean capitalist.[11] But the charter of 1610 completed the town's emancipation and prevented further interference with its rights. Within Shakespeare's lifetime Stratford attained its majority as a self-governing borough, sufficient to itself. It is pleasant to record that it still possesses its original mace of 1553, symbol of authority, and the bailiff's privy seal presented by Richard Quiney in 1592.

The town lived chiefly by trade, since it was a good focus of communications, its principal industry that of malting. Quiney wrote that it was 'ancient in this trade of malting and have ever served to Birmingham from whence Wales, Salop, Stafford, Cheshire and Lancashire also are served', for supplies of corn and seeds as well.[12] 'Our houses are made to no other use than malting' : one-third of the more substantial householders held stores of malt, including Shakespeare, who had ten quarters at New Place. The neighbouring gentry also held stores of malt in the town — it was clearly a good market for malt. In times of distress, as in the 1590's, the people attributed dearth to the maltsters buying up corn which might have been made into bread. We hear one of the poor folk crying 'God send my Lord of Essex down shortly, to see them hanged on gibbets at their own doors'. From which one sees too Essex's popularity with simple folk, and the foolish expectations they entertained of him.

Within the town this was a time of increasing activity and efficiency in organising trades and crafts — to control conditions of apprenticeship and uphold standards of craftsmanship, the better to carry weaker members and provide for the poor. The aim was to bring all the working members of a craft into some company or other — first the bakers : baking was under the direct control of the corporation, no baker could own more than one bakehouse, for obvious reasons. Then in rapid succession in the 1570's followed the smiths, next the weavers, whose early ordinances still survive, then the masons, joiners, carpenters and the trades involved in building formed one company. In 1578 the shoemakers and saddlers came together, in 1581 the drapers ; in 1604 there was a merger to form the biggest company, mercers, grocers, drapers and hatters. In 1606 there followed the glovers and whittawers, that is those who worked the softer, white skins, in contrast to tanners. The glovers reached their heyday in Shakespeare's lifetime ; there were seven or eight of them, some of them to the fore on the corporation, his father notably.

The vivacity of life in the little community was much increased by religious dissension — a pleasure open to all. Mary's burnings had had their quota of Warwickshire men, and the reaction against her gloomy régime was equally strenuous. Alderman Jeffreys, who had made himself too active a Catholic under Mary, took out a re-insurance with a pardon from Elizabeth for his doings. Schoolmaster Smart, who was in orders, could wait no longer than the Queen's coronation-day to take to himself a wife — thus giving a hostage to the new deal.[13] The corporation treated their Catholic vicar meanly, waiting for him to depart without paying him his stipend. Two of the neighbouring Catholic gentry, Sir Robert Throckmorton and Sir Edward Greville, intervened on his behalf, and the corporation paid him something on account. The Crown proceeded to present the indubitably Protestant John

Bretchgirdle, who had been brought up at heretical Christ Church. He was vicar from 1561 to 1565, and thus baptised burgess Shakespeare's son William. When Bretchgirdle came to die he hoped to be received into the heavenly kingdom only 'through the merits of our Saviour Jesus Christ', and he left a library of books to reveal his competence as a scholar and his interests : Cooper's revision of Eliot's Latin dictionary, a Greek lexicon, Sallust and Justin, Virgil and Cicero's *Offices*, Erasmus's *Encheiridion* and Josephus, Aesop, and the Psalms and Acts of the Apostles in English metre, with other singing books and school texts.[14]

He was succeeded by schoolmaster Smart, and next year Alderman Jefferys died, leaving his soul, in accordance with the more charming old formula, 'to be in joy with our Blessed Lady and with all the company of Heaven'. Smart's place as schoolmaster was taken by Bretchgirdle's pupil Brownsword, who had won fame as schoolmaster of Macclesfield and is mentioned by Francis Meres for his Latin poems. As we have seen, vicar and schoolmaster lived in close proximity in the Chapel precincts. Others of Brownsword's successors at the school had Catholic sympathies. In the crisis year of the Northern Catholic rebellion, 1569, schoolmaster Acton suddenly departed. So also the new vicar, *in animo Catholicus* ; while the curate took the opportunity to abscond, leaving wife and children behind. (Next year the stained glass windows were removed from the Chapel.) Simon Hunt, an Oxford man, was master from 1571 to 1575, when Shakespeare was yet young ; Hunt left for Douai in 1575, became a Jesuit and ended up by succeeding Father Parsons as English penitentiary in St. Peter's. Another Oxford man, Thomas Jenkins, succeeded as master (1575-9) during Shakespeare's chief years at school. Then came John Cottom, of a Lancashire Catholic family, whose Jesuit brother came from Rheims with a letter to John Debdale of Shottery ; was arrested, arraigned with Campion, and executed. Upon this Cottom resigned and returned to Lancashire, where he inherited the family property and became a firm recusant. Then came another Brasenose Lancashireman, Alexander Aspinall, who lasted a long time, from 1582 to 1624. In middle age he had the sense to marry Widow Shaw of Henley Street, who had inherited her husband's wool-business. This enabled Alexander — 'Great Philip of Macedon', as they called him — to be more than a mere dominie : he engaged in trade, buying and selling malt, he became burgess, alderman, chamberlain and head-borough of the ward Shakespeare lived in. He declined to take on being bailiff, but the council kept him on 'in regard of his sufficiency for his continual advice and great experience in the borough affairs ... and in regard he is an ancient Master of Art, and a man learned'.[15] Shakespeare apparently wrote a posy for him when he went a-wooing his middle-aged spouse with a pair of gloves :

> The gift is small :
> The will is all :
> Alexander Aspinall.[16]

We see the variegated pattern of relationships in this small society, cut across by religious and personal prejudices. Neighbours Badger and Barnhurst, both woollen-drapers, could not bear each other. Badger was well-to-do, had many children and obstinate Catholic convictions. He paid his recusancy fines and went to prison rather than to church, refused to obey orders at meetings of the corporation and was ultimately deprived of his alderman's gown. At the time of Gunpowder Plot he harboured Mass relics from Clopton, and ten years after had his house searched by candlelight, at a cost to the borough of 2d. for candles. Just below Badger lived his rival draper, Nicholas Barnhurst, who raged at Badger at council meetings, called him knave and rascal, was made to apologise and also was expelled from the aldermanry. Both suffered severe losses in the fires of 1595 : not even that reconciled them.

From the other end of the town, from the secularised College, we derive another revealing picture. In the days of Henry VIII, when the going was good, John Combe had grown rich by money-lending and acquiring monastic and church properties. Notwithstanding, he and his son were Catholics : the latter reported in 1564 to be 'an adversary of the true religion'. He left two sons, one of them William from whom Shakespeare bought land. This William's large estate came to his nephews, William and Thomas, who purchased the College in 1596 and died there in 1609. It was to this young Thomas that Shakespeare left his sword. More interesting was his bachelor uncle, John Combe, who lived at Welcombe and with whom Shakespeare had dealings over the tithes there. John Combe was a moneylender and a pious, grave Protestant. His will — like Shakespeare's, also made by Francis Collins — began by 'hoping and steadfastly believing that through the only merits of Jesus Christ, my alone Saviour and Redeemer,

I shall, after this life ended, be partaker of the life everlasting'.[17] He proceeded to make an extremely generous and public-spirited will : £10 to Francis Collins, £5 to Shakespeare, 20s. to Henry Walker, to Sir Francis Smith of Wotton Wawen £5 'to buy him a hawk and to the Lady Anne, his wife, £40 to buy her a basin and ewer'. And so on to many friends and relations. Then came the turn of the poor : ten black gowns to poor folk following him to the grave, each worth 13s. 4d., £20 to the poor of Stratford, to fifteen young tradesmen £100 on loan to help them in trade, £100 to three old servants, and 20s. annually 'to a learned preacher to make a sermon twice a year at Stratford church'.

He also left a large sum of money for a grand tomb for himself : an alabaster and marble recumbent effigy, like Shakespeare's made by Gerard Johnson in his Southwark workshop, and not far away on the north side of the chancel in Stratford church. In his will Combe had released a shilling in the pound to all his 'good and just debtors'. But this did not save him from people's tongues : upon his tomb they fastened an epitaph :

> Ten in the hundred the Devil allows,
> But Combe will have twelve he swears and avows.
> If anyone asks who lies in this tomb,
> 'Oh', quoth the Devil, 'tis my John a Combe.[18]

And, of course, people ascribed it to Shakespeare, so famous was he thus early.

In 1564, the year of Shakespeare's birth, the worst visitation of plague during Elizabeth's reign, brought back by the Earl of Warwick's army from Le Havre, reached Stratford. *Hic incipit pestis*, wrote vicar Bretchgirdle in the church register in July ; for the rest of that year the plague raged in Stratford. Whole households perished, mostly of poor folk, though all suffered — the town clerk lost two sons and a daughter, the vicar himself, worn out, died next year. One-sixth of the population was wiped out, a much higher proportion than in the more normal visitations of 1578, 1596, 1597, 1604. All the same, it was a near chance for the child in the cradle in Henley Street. The father attended meetings of the council held in the Gild garden — which he had secured for their use when chamberlain — for fear of infection : there amid the orchard-trees they voted money towards the relief of poor sufferers.

The crisis years, 1569 and 1570, have left their evidence in the minutes of the corporation. January 1569 has, 'for dressing of three goonnes' [guns].[19] January 1570 has, 'for dressing of harness, 11s. 6d. ; to Robert Lock, 3s. 4d. ; for dressing of harness another time, 3s. 4d. ; to the soldiers at their first muster, 4s. ; to Robert Joiner for a gunstock, 2s. ; to Simon Biddle for dressing of two pikes and a bow, 2s. 4d.'[20] Eight men from the town were dispatched north to serve under the Earl of Warwick. The more famous crisis of Armada year, 1588, has left fuller evidences. That wet and stormy summer, which brought the English fleet back from the coast of Spain and the Armada into the Channel, was reflected in the inland water of the Avon. The Welford church register says that the water rose a yard every hour, and three men were marooned on Stratford bridge, able to go neither forward nor back for the floods. The gentry of the county were called upon to furnish a hundred light horsemen for the army at Tilbury, and the general musters for the shire were held this year at Stratford. The town expended no less than £8 on coats for the soldiers, £6 on conduct money — to take them to the *rendezvous* at Tilbury. There were charges for swords, daggers and dagger-girdles — good business for the local saddlers ; for flasks, gunpowder and match ; for fetching and carrying the armour, and, an endearing item, 'for mending Robert Smith's piece, 6d.'[21] Above the council-chamber in the Chapel precincts, where the great chest with the town-moneys was kept, was the armoury. We remember

An old rusty sword ta'en out of the town-armoury.

Let us look at the town accounts for the year before the Armada, 1587, for the characteristic comings and goings in the busy little place, the amenities and refreshments.[22] Sermons were coming to be regarded as a pleasure, and increasingly so until their upshot in the Civil War and Commonwealth, when the country had a perfect orgy of them. Thomas Oken left a bequest for an annual sermon on election day for the aldermen and burgesses. This year it was preached by vicar Barton, who had been presented to the living by the Earl of Warwick in 1584 and gave satisfaction to the growing Puritan inflection of the corporation. Barton was one of the few incumbents in the county to win the whole-hearted approbation of the censorious Puritans — he must have been one of them himself : 'a preacher learned, zealous and godly, and fit for the ministry. A happy age if our church were fraught with many such.' [23] His efforts were highly appreciated by the Council, who made him many gifts beyond his stipend in order to keep him ; but not even this warm appreciation prevented him from moving on to a richer benefice.

On leet-day three quarts of claret wine and a quart of sack were provided to wet their whistles over manorial business. One sees that some amenities went with membership of the council. There was wine and sugar when Sir Thomas Lucy sat on the commission against tipplers ; wine again for the preacher, and 5s. for the players over and above their collection for performing. Wine was provided for those redoubtable Puritans Mr. Job Throckmorton and Mr. Cartwright who preached in the Gild-Chapel ; for the curate, faithful Sir William Gilbert, who for years made himself useful to the corporation, a jack of all trades running their errands — merely liquor, and whipcord. But there was wine and sugar for my Lord's steward, Mr. George Turville — that is, the interesting writer, George Turberville, who translated books from the Italian, the Eclogues of Mantuan, wrote poems and epigrams and a verse description of Russia, the manners and customs of the people. His celebrated Book of Falconry or Hawking he dedicated to the Earl of Warwick.

One sees what a cultivated circle there was around the Dudleys — Leicester and his nephew, Philip Sidney, were the greatest literary patrons of the age — in addition to Leicester's consistent, and politic, patronage of the Puritans. Sometimes Majesty herself passed by on the horizon on her summer visits to the Dudleys at Warwick and Kenilworth. In 1572 she was there, with the French ambassador, La Mothe Fénelon, in her train. On her way back to Woodstock she halted at Sir Thomas Lucy's at Charlecote ; the town paid its modest quota towards the provision of her household. This was the regular form, as on the Queen's first visit in 1566, when twenty oxen had been consumed at a breakfast, so great was the train.[24] The Mayor and aldermen of Coventry had been entertained at dinner, and presented with thirty bucks from Kenilworth's spacious parks for distribution. The bells were rung in the churches as she passed by, and Stratford contributed loyally to her carriage towards Woodstock. The summer of 1575 saw the most memorable visit of all, when Elizabeth stayed over a fortnight at Kenilworth, where Leicester had built on lodgings grand enough to house her and the Court, and three or four thousand people from round about crowded the Castle precincts every day to watch the entertainments and catch a glimpse of her.

During all these years the players came regularly to Stratford, in addition to what pastimes the townsmen or boys of the grammar school put forward. The drama in various forms was a nation-wide activity. In towns of any size the local gilds of craftsmen put on their own shows at Whitsuntide or Corpus Christi, as at neighbouring Coventry where their traditional plays were famous. In schools of any size, like Shrewsbury or Merchant Taylors, Westminster or St. Paul's — all celebrated for their plays — the drama was a regular feature in performance no less than in instruction, in what they read and studied. All over the country there were mummings at Christmas. Then there were the professional troupes of players, who took the badge and livery of some noble, or the Queen herself, for countenance and protection. At Stratford evidence remains in the town accounts of a show put on by townsmen in 1583, when 13s. 4d. was paid to 'Davy Jones and his company for his pastime at Whitsuntide'. Now Davy Jones married first a daughter of Adrian Quiney, and secondly Frances Hathaway.[25] It is not surprising to find Shakespeare recalling in an early play, *Two Gentlemen of Verona* :

At Pentecost
When all our pageants of delight were played.

Of the professional companies of players touring the country and performing at Stratford during these years, the Earls of Worcester's and Leicester's were the most to the fore.[26] In 1569, when John Shakespeare was bailiff, the Queen's men were given a reward of nine shillings, Worcester's one shilling — this would be in addition to their collections at performances. In 1573 Leicester's men, led by James Burbage, were at Stratford ; they came again in 1576 and in 1587. The Earl of Warwick's players came in 1575, Worcester's no less than six times between 1569 and 1587. In addition there were visits from Lord Berkeley's, Lord Strange's, Lord Derby's, the Countess of Essex's, the Earl of Essex's, Lord Chandos's, the Queen's — usually two, sometimes three, companies a year. The peak was reached in this same year, 1587, when no less than five troupes are rewarded in the town accounts : the Queen's, Leicester's, Essex's, Lord Stafford's and an anonymous company. Worcester's men already had Edward Alleyn as their star. The Queen's men had been reconstituted in 1583 with twelve of the best players drawn from other companies, including the country's most popular actor of comic parts, Richard Tarleton. When the Queen's men came to Stratford in this very year, 1587, they were lacking an actor, who had been killed by one of his fellows on their way through Oxfordshire.[27] Some of Leicester's players were also missing, out of the country : they had accompanied their patron to the Netherlands, where he headed the English army in 1585. There they joined in the festivities in his honour and went on to serve the King of Denmark for three months. Their star-comedian received the highest pay at Elsinore ; thence they trekked back through Germany. At home Leicester's men, reduced in number, toured the south and west, Canterbury and Dover, Southampton, Marlborough, Oxford, then Bath and Exeter, turning back to reach Stratford and Coventry in July, into Lancashire to perform at the Earl of Derby's, Lathom House, and back to Coventry in August. On Leicester's death in 1588 his company broke up, and three of its leading men, Kemp, Bryan and Pope, joined that of Lord Strange, the Earl of Derby's heir. When we reflect that both Burbage and Kemp had been Leicester's men, and that they and Pope became leading associates for years along with Shakespeare in the Lord Chamberlain's company, remembering too Leicester's close connection with the county, do we have to look far for a natural channel of recruitment to the theatre for a promising young man from Stratford ?

At the end of it all, not long after that prodigious career was over, Dugdale was ready to cite it as a principal distinction of the town : 'one thing more in reference to this ancient town is observable, that it gave birth and sepulture to our late famous poet William Shakespeare'.[28]

CHAPTER III

Family : School : Church

WE are fortunate to know so much as we do about the early years of Shakespeare. Of other Elizabethan dramatists we do not know anything like so much — with the possible exception of Marlowe ; of some of them we know hardly a thing. Take the case of Ben Jonson, the outstanding personality among them all, whose later years we come to know in more detail than any other's.

And yet for the early years of Jonson's life there have been found none of those definite records which exist with unusual completeness (contrary to popular belief) for Shakespeare. Many documents have survived concerning Shakespeare's parents, but not even the names of Jonson's father and mother. Precise dates can be given for Shakespeare's baptism at Stratford, his marriage licence at Worcester, the christenings of his three children, his residence in the parish of St. Helen's, Bishopgate, in Southwark, and in Silver Street. The biographers of Jonson, on the other hand, have been unable to tell when and where he was born, when and where he was married, what was the name of his wife, or the number of his children.[1]

That we know all this about Shakespeare is not without significance : it is due to the rootedness of his family in the neighbourhood of Stratford, his father's prominence in the public life of the little town, and his own exceptional attachment to the place of his birth.

The Shakespeares lay thick on the ground in those villages north of the river, especially in the parish of Rowington. Shakespeare's grandfather, Richard, came to Snitterfield to take a farm some time before 1529. He rented his house, with land that reached down to the brook that still flows through the village, from Robert Arden of Wilmcote. It is probable that Robert Arden was a sprig of that clan of Warwickshire gentlefolk, since he owned land and left a houseful of goods — there was no clear-cut division between the status of prosperous yeoman and small gentleman. What is more, we find in his inventory that, in addition to the solid oak furniture, the copper pans, brass pots and candlesticks, his house had no less than eleven painted cloths : five in the chamber adjoining the hall, two in the hall, four in the bedrooms above.[2] That marks a standard of taste above that of the ordinary farmer. He left a number of daughters : Joan, who married Edmund Lambert of Barton-on-the-Heath ; Margaret, who married Alexander Webbe of Bearley. His youngest daughter Mary was as yet unmarried. Robert Arden left her 'all my land in Wilmcote called Asby's and the crop upon the ground sown and tilled as it is, and £6. 13. 4 of money to be paid or ere my goods be divided' ; and she was made an executor of the will. Mary Arden proved the will in 1556 and shortly after married Richard Shakespeare's son, John.

John would have been born, then, some time before 1540 and was brought up in the parish of Snitterfield, where such teaching as he acquired he would get from the vicar — he never found it necessary to learn to write. (His son more than compensated for that.) Richard Shakespeare had friends in Stratford, for one of them, Thomas Atwood, clothier and vintner, bequeathed him 'my four oxen which are now in his keeping'. And he apprenticed his son John in the town. It was this small move that had such consequences, for it gave John's son his chance to go to school.

John was already a householder in Henley Street by 1552, for in April he was fined for making a dungheap in the street instead of at the end, under the trees : nothing demeaning in that, it was just part of the give and take of neighbourly government. In 1556 John Shakespeare bought a house and garden in Henley Street, and another in Greenhill Street. Sued for a debt of £8, he won his case, was made arbiter in another suit and brought a third against Henry Field over eighteen quarters of barley. He was often involved in cases in the court of record — the usual change of small town life. In September 1557 he was made an ale-taster of the borough, the first step in an active career of twenty years in its affairs.

That year he married Mary Arden, pretty certainly at her parish church of Aston Cantlow — still standing there with its squat, square tower with the turret that may have been intended to carry a light for travellers along the causeway over the flooding water-meadows of the Alne. Within is the Gild-Chapel of Mary's patron-saint, a pulpit she would recognise, and the same medieval bell that may have clanged her to church : *Ad laudem clare Michaelis do resonare*. That year John paid his fine for absence from three sessions of the court as ale-taster : he had other courting to do.

His marriage, with the comfortable dowry his wife brought him, land as well as ready money, increased his respectability and advanced his status. He became a burgess on the town council, in 1558 and 1559 one of its four constables, witnessing the minutes of the leet-court with his mark, a pair of glover's compasses. No-one was so prominent in the town's affairs for many years : from 1561 to 1565 he was the active chamberlain of the borough, overseeing the accounts and signing them with his mark. In the latter year he was made alderman in place of the unpleasant William Bott, who, as the agent of the Cloptons, had forked himself into New Place and made himself disagreeable to the corporation. Henceforth it was 'Master' Shakespeare, who, in his black furred gown — such as we see on brasses or tombs today — took his place with his fellow aldermen in procession to church on Sundays or on public business about the streets. Such was the status of the father the children grew up with.

In September 1558 a first child was born and shortly died — Joan, called after Mary Arden's sister. In the winter of 1560–1 old Richard Shakespeare died, leaving goods to the value of £38 : 17s., evidently a respectable, prosperous yeoman. Alexander Webbe took over the Snitterfield farm ; his son Robert — William Shakespeare's first cousin — succeeded in buying up the shares of various properties, including one of his aunt Mary Arden's, and did well out of it. An uncle, Henry Shakespeare, lived on in Snitterfield, and died with money in his coffers, corn and hay in his barn.[3] They were all inching their way up.

In Henley Street a second child was born in 1562, called Margaret after another Arden aunt. In April 1564 the eldest son, William ; in 1566 another son, christened Gilbert on 13 October, and named for neighbour Gilbert Bradley. A second Joan was baptised on 15 April 1569, and this one survived her eldest brother who left her in possession of the old home in Henley Street. Another girl was given an Arden name, Anne, and died at the age of seven in 1578. To complete the family there were Richard, born in 1574, and Edmund, who followed his eldest brother into the profession of player, born in 1580.

Meanwhile, John Shakespeare in his municipal *cursus honorum* progressed to chief place as Bailiff in the crisis year 1569, with friend

Wheeler as his deputy. Together they were 'escorted from their houses to the guildhall by the serjeants bearing their maces before them. They were waited on by these buff-uniformed officers once a week to receive instructions, and accompanied by them through the market on Thursdays, through the fair on fair-days, about the parish bounds at Rogation, and to and from church on Sundays'.⁴ The town's chief officer, John Shakespeare, presided as a J.P. at the monthly sessions of the court of record, where, aided by the steward, he dealt with cases of debt, breaches of the by-laws, and handed out warrants of distraint or arrest. He presided at council meetings, sealed leases, saw to the town properties, was in charge of its interests, and received instructions from the Privy Council regarding larger matters — musters, recalcitrant Catholics, the rebellion in the North. This was a year of crisis, and a busy time he had of it.

In September 1571, after his year as Bailiff was over, John was elected chief alderman and deputy to the new Bailiff, Adrian Quiney. Together they were commissioned to go up to London on the town's business — matters at variance with the lord of the manor, the Earl of Warwick. While in London John Shakespeare took the opportunity to recover a debt of £50 from a Banbury glover at the Court of Common Pleas in Westminster. In the same Court he was sued for a debt of £30 by a former steward of Stratford ; he did not pay up, for in 1578 he was sued again. During these years he was leasing meadows from the former Clopton estate, and in October 1575 he bought two more houses, with gardens and orchards, in the town for £40. He leased a house to a William Burbage, but some years later it was agreed that Burbage should be released from the bargain and receive the £7 he had already paid. He seems never to have got it. Some years before, John Shakespeare had stood surety for an acquaintance at Shottery, Richard Hathaway, for two debts which were paid when harvest came in.

In several other instances one finds Alderman Shakespeare willing to stand surety for other people's debts, and in one instance having to pay the forfeit. One gets an impression of his being easy-going about money matters, and there is no doubt that he neglected his own business for the town's. He had large ideas ; for about this time, 1575 to 1576, he took steps to apply to the Heralds' College for a grant of a coat of arms. Master Shakespeare, who could not write his name, would a gentleman be.

William Shakespeare

Something happened to cause the application not to be proceeded with : it is not difficult to see what. From his election as Bailiff up to the end of 1576 he attended every council meeting ; after that, never again (except for one single occasion) in all the years of his life. His brethren of the corporation went out of their way to be lenient to him : they reduced his tax for equipping soldiers from the town, they remitted his fines for absence from meetings, they let him off paying towards poor-relief. It was not until ten years of entire non-attendance had passed that the council elected another alderman in his place. Later, we have evidence that he absented himself from church for fear of process for debt being served on him. There can be no doubt that his prosperity had ended, that he had fallen on evil days financially, and that the town's most active alderman was forced into complete withdrawal. What can the council's exceptional forbearance towards him mean but a recognition that he had injured his own affairs by devoting himself to the town's ?

At the time when this blow fell — not a catastrophe, but still a blow to pride and status — the alderman's sharp and sensitive eldest son was a boy at the unlucky age of thirteen.

We know so much more now about Shakespeare's education, as the result of the detailed study in our time of the way in which the whole process is reflected in his plays.[5] And this to a surprising degree — it is extraordinary that the completeness of the description should not have been recognised till our day ; though perhaps we should be the less surprised when we consider how fully, and with how representative a balance, the plays reflect the life of the age.

The grammar school at Stratford was characteristic of the numerous schools throughout the country which were founded or refounded in the second half of the sixteenth century — a marked consequence of the Reformation impulse and the increasing efficiency of society. The charter of 1553 provided for a grammar school, the master to receive the generous remuneration of £20 a year with a house in the Gild-precincts, where the school was, himself to provide an usher for the lower school. There was some elementary teaching at Stratford, prior to the grammar school. This was for the petties, the small children below seven or eight, to learn to read and write, to learn their numbers and the elements of religion from the Catechism, grace

34

before and after meals, the psalms in metre. They learnt this from
a horn-book, or an ABC book, of which few specimens survive,
since they would be used to bits by so many small hands over
the centuries. Shakespeare has several references to the Absey
book with its rows of letters and syllables, the first row beginning
with a cross — hence 'Christ-cross row' for the alphabet — and
the Lord's Prayer. An early play, *The Two Gentlemen of Verona*,
has,

>To sigh, like a schoolboy that had lost his ABC ;

In *Richard III*, King Edward, suspicious of his brother George,

>from the cross-row plucks the letter G.

There are reflections of the elementary learning process, of reading
by rote while one yet could not spell ; the form of catechism,
blunt question and answer, appears constantly, though most frequently in the earlier plays. In *Much Ado* Hero says,

>how am I beset !
>What kind of catechising call you this ?
>*Claudio :* To make you answer truly to your name.

The first question of the Catechism, as we all remember, is :
'What is your name ? '

At about seven, having learnt to read and write, a boy was
ready to enter grammar school, where the whole of one's education
was based on Latin. Grammar meant Latin grammar, learned
from Lily's text-book, which was prescribed for use throughout
the nation. (Think what an effect that must have had in inducing
common modes of thought and speech.) From contemporary
books we can see exactly what was expected of the boy. He was
'to say his prayers in the morning, wash and dress and comb his
hair, say "Good morrow" to his parents, take his satchel of books,
and be in his place at school before the small bell of the chapel,
which was probably rung for a quarter of an hour, ceased, at six
o'clock in summer and seven in winter. School opened, as it
closed, with devotions — a reading from the Bible, singing of a
psalm, and prayer.' [6] When one thinks of those early hours, of
birdsong and dawn in summer, the streets of Stratford still dark
in winter, cold and numb, one sees with some sympathy,

>the whining schoolboy, with his satchel
>And shining morning face, creeping like snail
>Unwillingly to school.

Shakespeare memorised his Lily — quotations from it and references to it appear in all his earlier work. Sir Toby Belch opines, 'Not to be abed after midnight is to be up betimes, and *diluculo surgere*, thou know'st . . .' Sir Andrew Aguecheek, the silly, did not know. The tag was from Lily : '*Diluculo surgere saluberrimum est*, to arise betime in the morning is the most wholesome thing in the world'. In *The Merry Wives of Windsor* there is a complete parody of a lesson in Latin grammar from Lily. It is given by Sir Hugh Evans, the Welsh curate, to young William Page, with Welsh mispronunciations, play on words and the usual bawdy suggestions to make the audience laugh.

At seven, then, Shakespeare would enter grammar school in 1571, and spend his first three years in the lower school under the usher. Simon Hunt was master from 1571 to 1575 ; so that young William would get most of his education from the next master, Thomas Jenkins, who sounds a Welshman, and who held the post from 1575 to 1579. These masters were Oxford men, with degrees, and perfectly well equipped for their job. Among the pupils was Richard Field, the tanner's son : a couple of years older than Alderman Shakespeare's boy. Richard Field became one of the leading printers in London.

Along with their grammar the boys learned from a Latin phrase-book, such as Drayton mentions :

> And when that once *Pueriles* I had read
> And newly had my *Cato* construèd . . .

These books provided phrases for conversing in Latin though we need not suppose that the boys got very far in that art. In *Love's Labour's Lost* we are given a parody of such a conversation, with schoolmaster Holofernes, Nathaniel and Armado, exchanging these tags and trying to make discourse out of them. The phrase-books, with simple texts like Aesop and Cato, served a further purpose : they provided the moralising tags which were such a feature of Elizabethan education and life. Everywhere one has evidences of their sententiousness, not only in their works, but painted up in church, on the walls at home, on the brain. It was an effective way of moral instruction for a young, vigorous, undisciplined people. All this appears in the Plays, while quite a lot of Shakespeare's animal-lore goes back to Aesop at school. The boys began Latin poetry with Mantuan, a recent sixteenth-century poet whose Christian *Bucolica* was more suitable for (young) boys'

ears than the pagan ambivalence of Virgil. Holofernes is made
to quote the first eclogue :

> Fauste, precor, gelida quando pecus omne sub umbra
> Ruminat . . .

and sighs, 'Ah, good old Mantuan! . . . Old Mantuan, old Mantuan!
who understandeth thee not, loves thee not.' It sounds as if not
only Holofernes but Shakespeare is speaking — he certainly was
remembering his schooldays.

While still in the lower school the boys were introduced to
Terence and possibly Plautus : Shakespeare's first acquaintance
with classical drama, which provided the models and the inspiration for his first comedies. Another modern third-form author,
Palingenius's *Zodiacus Vitae*, provided the source for at least two
famous speeches on the theme of the Ages of Man : Jacques's
'All the world's a stage', and Antonio's exchange with Gratiano :

> *Antonio :* I hold the world but as the world, Gratiano —
> A stage where every man must play a part,
> And mine a sad one.
>
> *Gratiano :*   Let me play the fool.
> With mirth and laughter let old wrinkles come . . .
> Why should a man whose blood is warm within
> Sit like his grandsire cut in alabaster ?

As late as *The Tempest*, the memory of what he had imbibed in
learning the Zodiac of Life bore fruit in Prospero's farewell : it
is touching to think that at that moment Shakespeare should go
back in mind to his earliest schooldays.

In the upper school he went on to Ovid, and this was the love
of his life among Latin poets. Ovid made an overwhelming
impression upon him, which he carried with him all his days.
Four times he refers to him directly by name, five times to the
swan's singing at death as described in the *Heroides*. The story
of *Lucrece* comes from Ovid's *Fasti*. But it is the *Metamorphoses*
above all that echoes throughout his work : subjects, themes,
characters, phrases haunted his imagination. Along with the
Bible and the Prayer Book, Ovid made the most constant and
fertilising impression upon his mind. The bulk of his classical
mythology came from the *Metamorphoses*, which he used in the
original as well as in Golding's translation later. When he challenged critical opinion as a poet, with the first heir of his invention,

Venus and Adonis, he did it with a couplet from Ovid. Intelligent people saw the appropriateness and recognised him as an English Ovid. Francis Meres wrote, 'the sweet witty soul of Ovid lives in mellifluous and honey-tongued Shakespeare'.

Though he drew upon all the books, it was the first book of the *Metamorphoses* with which he was much the most familiar, and next to that the second. Here is something characteristic of him, a pointer both to his nature and perhaps to his restricted opportunities. In the Old Testament, similarly, he was far the best acquainted with the first chapters of Genesis, in the New Testament with the first chapters of St. Matthew's Gospel. His mind was not that of a scholar, pursuing these things as an end in themselves, or of an intellectual following the pursuit for the fun of it, but that of a poet adhering to his own instinctive affinities, the choice perhaps made by an unconscious tact. Very often it was the words themselves that got fixed in his mind, to come out again by a process of unconscious association. The phrase in Ovid, *rudis indigestaque moles,* fastened on his ear to pop out again at different times in his writing : Richard III is described as a

heap of wrath, foul indigested lump.

After the chaos of King John's reign, his son is hailed as born,

To set a form upon that indigest
Which he hath left so shapeless and so rude.

The plain fact is that Shakespeare had a fabulous aural memory — nothing like it in the whole of literature : he heard a phrase at school, like Quintilian's *universis . . . largitur* ; it comes out years later as 'largess universal'. It is not a common cliché, but an association ; it was the word, the phrase, that transfixed him. This is the first, though by no means the last, sign of the poet ; but no-one has ever had it as he had.

In addition to Ovid we should add a little Virgil and rather more Horace — the Horace of the Odes, not of the Satires. Even so, we must not overestimate the extent of his reading in these : much of it, especially in such a small school, would come through handy phrase-books and extracts. However, his education in and through Latin left an unmistakable impression upon his vocabulary. Dr. Johnson admitted, with the condescension of the eighteenth century, 'I always said Shakespeare had Latin enough to grammaticise his English'. But the point holds much further than this : there are not only numerous Latinisms in his vocabulary, but his natural instinct, grounded early, is always towards a Latin grandeur of word or phrase. The other side to this is his use of ludicrous etymologies, in the early plays when he was nearer his schooldays, to poke fun at the phrase-books used in schools and raise a laugh. We know that the school possessed a copy of Cooper's Latin dictionary, his *Thesaurus*, left by vicar Bretchgirdle, and it is obvious that it was in constant use. It is nice to think, however, that the boy sometimes played truant from all this and went off into the fields blackberrying. There is a tell-tale association of the word for playing truant, to 'mich' (we called it 'minch' in my time at a country school) : 'shall the blessed sun of heaven prove a micher and eat blackberries ? '

In the upper school one graduated to logic and rhetoric. The place of this in a grammar-schoolboy's education is as plainly discernible as the more elementary stages. Again and again we find Shakespeare's expertise in dialectical argument according to the text-books turned to use, especially in the earlier plays — the sentence by sentence question and answer, the line by line statement and rejoinder, passages of wearisome antiphony to our ears, hair-splitting about words which seems obsessive to us. It was drilled into him at school, it remained with him all his days ; the Eliza-bethans liked that sort of thing. It turned out extremely useful for a young dramatist, who could fill in the interstices of action with these exchanges at a time when life had not yet provided him with much experience by way of content.

Even more useful when he came to write was the training in rhetoric, so important to Elizabethans — and to which he took like a duck to water. There it all is easily recognisable : the high, low and medium styles ; the conscious use of epithet and synonym for purposes of varying — and of course he caricatures school-masters in Holofernes for too much varying without tact or sense. There is the business of narration, comparison, amplifica-tion upon a ground, comparable to the fa-burden with which musicians amplified their ground-melody. The text-book used at school for themes in rhetoric and modes of discourse was that of Aphthonius, where Ovid's story of Venus and Adonis was analysed as an example of narration.[7] It is another tell-tale associa-tion that the very next example in the book is the story of Pyramus and Thisbe, which Shakespeare guyed in Bottom's play in *Mid-summer-Night's Dream*. It was from this ready handbag that

Shakespeare picked up some of his blithe knowledge of Greek mythology or history — and used it with his marvellous capacity for making a little go a long way. He had a useful acquaintance with Quintilian ; while much of what the clowns say is based on the formulae of rhetoric, playing with them and turning them inside out.

Above all, Shakespeare rates invention highest, for these things were not ends in themselves to him, as they would be to a school-master : they all came in handy to the overriding aesthetic intentions of the poet and dramatist. Nor must we forget the set oration, which had its influence upon the famous soliloquies and formal speeches with which the plays are encrusted. Such orations were a feature of public life, and Elizabethans were fortunate to have an eloquent, well-educated ruler who could herself set a model. That Shakespeare heard her speak we need not doubt :

> there is such confusion in my powers,
> As after some oration fairly spoke
> By a beloved prince, there doth appear
> Among the buzzing, pleasèd multitude ;
> Where every something, being blent together,
> Turns to a wild of nothing, save of joy,
> Expressed and not expressed.

History was read in schools almost entirely for moralising purposes, the lessons taught by experience, the consequences of good and ill courses, of good and bad rulers, the comparisons to be drawn. Sallust and Caesar were universal in schools, the backbone of teaching, supplemented by some Livy. Shakespeare knew Livy's version of the Lucrece story, and Caesar ; and that is about all of school-history. But we find the underlying attitude towards history as moral tale pervasive in the plays. The moment the young dramatist gets to work on the story of the Wars of the Roses, with *Henry VI* and *Richard III*, it is not only the events, the drama, that interest him : these plays are held together by the moral of it all, which is as constantly enforced as any school-master could wish. So too with *Richard II* and *King John*, with *Henry IV* and *Henry V*, with *Julius Caesar* and *Coriolanus*, and at the very end with *Henry VIII*.

We should, in conclusion, emphasise that all Elizabethan education was built on training the memory — as the classical grind in our public schools was until yesterday. (It is a loss that modern education is not.) Immense attention was paid to memorising, since books were scarce and it was intended that what one learnt should stand one in good stead for life. Something had to be memorised every day, and there were regular repetitions of what one had learnt by heart — this is why the *first* books of Ovid, the *first* books of the Old and New Testaments made such an indelible impression upon the schoolboy. It is perfectly evident that he memorised his Latin grammar — the appropriate passages and allusions came spontaneously to mind years later when he wanted them. The value of the training was inestimable, for in addition to the passages, tracts, lines remembered, there they were available for imitation and invention — in the proper mind they were a spur to creation. That this was their real justification for him, who was the reverse of pedant and not interested in scholarship for its own sake, we have some corroboration from the lines :

> Small have continuous plodders ever won
> Save base authority from others' books.

All the same, simple as Elizabethan education was in method and content, it was sufficient to stand the world's prime dramatist in good stead all his life.

No less important than his education at school, for an Elizabethan boy, was that which he received from the church, from regular attendance at its services from earliest childhood, catechising, teaching, sermons, singing the psalms, saying the prayers. Nor is this any the less fully or clearly reflected throughout the Plays. Of all Shakespeare's 'sources' the Bible and the Prayer Book come first and are the most constant. Altogether there are definite allusions to forty-two books of the Bible, including the Apocrypha.[8] The story of Cain gripped his imagination. 'He refers to the story of this "primal" murderer not less than twenty-five times. Others seized on him with only less tenacity. Jephthah is the source or occasion of at least seven passages in his writings, Samson of nine, David of six, Goliath of three, Solomon of nine, Job of some five-and-twenty. . . . Judas of perhaps twenty-one, Peter of seven, Pilate of seven, the Prodigal Son of nine, Dives and Lazarus of seven, the Whore of Babylon of seven.'[9] It has been estimated that his Biblical range is five times that of Peele or Marlowe, far greater than that of any contemporary dramatist.

What is the reason for this ?

Quite clearly, in the first instance, regular attendance at church from childhood on. Study of Shakespeare's multitudinous allusions to the Bible shows that up to about 1596-7 versions from the Bishops' Bible predominate, and those are what he would commonly hear in church. After that date, readings from the Genevan version are more numerous. The evidence points to his possessing the Old Testament in this version bound up with Lawrence Tomson's revised version of the Genevan New Testament. Above all, he quoted the Psalms, or re-echoed their phrasing: 'from first to last there is not a play in the Folio entirely free from a suggestion of a use of the Psalms'.[10] But the phrasing is always that of the Prayer Book, and this is what he would have heard all his life in church.

So, too, with the services of the church: the phrases picked up by that retentive ear re-echo through all the Plays. When Hamlet holds out his hands to Guildenstern, calling them 'these pickers and stealers', it goes back to a phrase one is not likely to forget from the Catechism, when one answers that it is one's duty 'to keep my hands from picking and stealing'. (I well remember how the phrase made me blush at the proper age of five or so.) The phrase 'special grace' comes from the Catechism. When Shakespeare quotes the Commandments, he does so in the Prayer-Book form, not that of the Bible: 'thou shalt do no murder', or 'visit the sins of the fathers upon the children unto the third and fourth generation of them that hate me':

> Thy sins are visited in this poor child,
> The canon of the law is laid on him,
> Being but the second generation
> Removed from thy sin-conceiving womb.

Phrases from Morning and Evening Prayer are constantly echoed. Prince Henry says to Falstaff, 'I see a good amendment of life in thee'; Falstaff says to Bardolph, 'Do thou amend thy face, and I'll amend my life.' The phrase 'amend your lives' comes at Morning and Evening Prayer, in the Communion Service and in the Litany. At Communion the priest says, 'confess yourselves to Almighty God, with full purpose of amendment of life'. The point of these phrases would, of course, be redoubled with an audience that knew them and where they came from. And they would derive all the more amusement when Falstaff turns them round to his own lusty purposes. When the Prince sees a good amendment of life in him, the old rascal rejoins with — 'Why,

Hal, 'tis my vocation, Hal ; 'tis no sin for a man to labour in his vocation'. He has the whole Prayer Book with him : the Catechism enjoins the duty 'to labour truly to get mine own living' ; the Epistles tell us to give ourselves to some vocation ; the Homily against Idleness bids everyone 'in some kind of labour to exercise himself, according as the vocation whereunto God hath called him shall require'. This is by no means the end of the old reprobate's variations on themes from Prayer Book and Bible. 'Oh, if men were to be saved by merit . . .', he sighs : this goes back to St. Paul's Epistle to the Romans and justification by faith, not works, as the Homily on Fasting — a nice authority for a Falstaff — lays down. Or again we hear him preaching, with all sorts of reverberations from Scripture and the Collects :

> Well, God give thee the spirit of persuasion, and him the ears of profiting, that what thou speakest may move, and what he hears may be believed.

The phrase from the Litany, 'O God, we have heard with our ears', must have fastened itself in the mind of many an Anglican besides William Shakespeare. But out it comes with Sir Hugh Evans : 'What phrase is this, "He hears with ear"? Why, it is affectatious' — the joke being that it is a Welsh parson who does not recognise it. Anyone familiar with the Prayer-Book services will recognise in

> their best conscience
> Is not to leave't undone, but kept unknown,

the echo from the General Confession, 'we have left undone those things which we ought to have done' — a sentence we can never forget. There are similar phrases and echoes from all the services, from Baptism and Holy Matrimony — references to which are numerous — to the Commination Service and the Churching of Women. He had attended them all, many times. We learn that for him there were only two sacraments, Baptism and Holy Communion — not a trace of the Catholic teaching in which his parents had been brought up, nor had he any knowledge of the Vulgate. He was an orthodox, conforming member of the Church into which he had been baptised, was brought up and married, in which his children were reared and in whose arms he at length was buried.

'Hear what comfortable words our Saviour Christ saith', we hear in the Communion service ; these appear at a crisis in *Richard II*, 'For God's sake, speak comfortable words'. We must

43

remember, however, that in those days the word 'comfort' was a much stronger word, indeed, it meant to 'strengthen' — 'the Holy Ghost, the Comforter'. On the other hand, it is amusing to hear from Mistress Quickly that she is 'the weaker vessel'. Phrases like 'to weep with them that weep', to be 'in adversity', 'they know not what they do', may crop up anywhere in the Plays — the last does in different forms in several of them. Or the sensitive ear will hear Biblical echoes in many a line like

> Home art gone and ta'en thy wages.

It goes back to the Gospel according to St. Matthew — 'the labourer is worthy of his hire'. It is this further reference to another world of thought, as if what shadows we are, and what shadows we pursue, that adds another dimension to what we hear from him, and that, when we hear it, so searches the heart.

Above all, it was the Psalms Sunday by Sunday at Morning and Evening Prayer that made a lifelong impression on him. Psalm xc in the Prayer Book version has it : 'we bring our years to an end, as it were a tale that is told'. It is another of those phrases one does not forget — certainly not Shakespeare, with whom it becomes in years to come,

> Life is as tedious as a twice-told tale ;

or further on still, in *Macbeth*, that life

> is a tale
> Told by an idiot.

But the effects are sometimes, intentionally, comic. Psalm xcii has, 'They shall also bring forth more fruit in their age : and shall be fat and well-liking'. In *Love's Labour's Lost*, which has a wider range of Scriptural allusions than any other of the early plays, Rosaline describes the young men of the Court of Navarre, 'Well-liking wits they have : gross, gross : fat, fat'. It is the collocation of the words that clangs. Or when Dromio of Syracuse is all mixed-up, in *The Comedy of Errors*, and says, 'Nay, 'tis for me to be patient : I am in adversity', this would raise a laugh from an audience that regularly heard in church, 'that thou mayest give him patience in time of adversity'.

A regular feature at church in those days was the reading from the *Book of Homilies* when, as was often the case, there was no sermon. In *As You Like It*, there is a direct reference to this rather boring reading, when Rosalind says, 'O most gentle pulpiter, what tedious homily of love have you wearied your parishioners withal, and never cried, "Have patience, good people"?' Nevertheless, some of these homilies made a deep impress on Shakespeare's mind. That against Swearing and Perjury, in particular, elicited his attention and came to his mind several times at junctures in his plays : in it people were admonished against taking an unlawful or ungodly oath, or performing it. The gist of the homily is stated in two lines of 2 *Henry VI* :

> It is great sin to swear unto a sin,
> But greater sin to keep a sinful oath.

Shakespeare dwelt on this theme several times in the first half of his career, again in 3 *Henry VI*, in *Two Gentlemen of Verona* and in *As You Like It*.

Still more important is the extension given in the Plays to the political homilies : that on Obedience and that on Disobedience and Wilful Rebellion. I do not mean at this point to embark on the subject of Shakespeare's political views, but merely to point out that his views on these subjects go back to what he heard enforced in church all his life, that there is no doubt that he held them with entire conviction and expressed them consistently, and that he carried them forward into his plays with greater insistence and fulness than any other dramatist. We learn that 'Shakespeare outdoes every other important dramatist of his time in the number and variety of the allusions made to the divine right of the reigning monarch, the duty of passive obedience, enjoined on subjects by God, and the misery and chaos resulting from civil war and rebellion'.[11] These themes are touched on in no less than twenty plays, from the earliest to the last.

With these cogitations we approach the adult Shakespeare : it is hardly likely that the grammar-schoolboy, though boys were mature earlier then, plumbed their full significance. That came later. Nevertheless, the magnificent phrases would reverberate in this sensitive mind, to achieve their own expression in time. 'Almighty God hath created and appointed all things in heaven, earth and waters, in a most perfect order. In heaven he hath appointed distinct and several orders and states of archangels and angels. In earth he hath assigned and appointed kings, princes with other governors under them in all good and necessary order. The sun, moon, stars, rainbow, thunder, lightning, clouds and all the birds of the air do keep their order.' In short, order is the form, the key, to the universe. Some years on, this comes out in a famous oration :

> The heavens themselves, the planets and this centre,
> Observe degree, priority and place,
> Insisture, course, proportion, season, form,
> Office and custom, in all line of order.

But, warns the homily : 'Take away kings, rulers, princes, magistrates, judges and such estates of God's order, no man shall ride or go by the highway unrobbed, no man shall sleep in his own house or bed unkilled, no man shall keep his wife, children and possession in quietness, all things shall be common, and there must needs follow all mischief and utter destruction both of souls, bodies, goods and commonwealth.' This becomes, in *Troilus and Cressida* :

> Take but degree away, untune that string,
> And hark what discord follows . . .
> Strength should be lord of imbecility,
> And the rude son should strike his father dead . . .

The homilist elaborates on the consequences of rebellion : 'the brother to seek and often to work the death of his brother, the son of his father'. The image seized hold of the mind of the young dramatist, who in one of the very first of his plays, 3 *Henry VI*, has a scene :

> Alarum. Enter a son that hath killed his father, at one door ; and a father that hath killed his son, at another door.

All this does not exhaust the subject, indeed it but serves as illustration of what Shakespeare owed to his upbringing and going to church. For I am not dealing here with his reading of the Bible on his own account, either for the purpose of such a play as *The Merchant of Venice* or for his own interest and consolation. Here we are concerned simply with his upbringing and how it formed his mind, consciously, and perhaps even more, unconsciously. The rhythms of the majestic phrases of Bible and Prayer Book, heard all the days of one's youth, enter into the blood-stream : one cannot get them out of one's head, even if one would : they come back into the consciousness again and again unbidden, at every kind of juncture, in accordance with laws of association too subtle for description. And this is one aspect of a fundamental characteristic of Shakespeare's mind that

everyone recognises : the extreme range, subtlety and completeness of its power of association, largely unconscious. He picked
up everything. It was noticed in his own day that everything
came easily to him — though on the basis of that natural gift,
how he worked to make the most of it ! There can be no doubt
that the methodical training of the memory at Elizabethan
grammar school and church entered largely into it.

Close students of this particular subject conclude that it is
not likely that young William was grounded in the Bible at home :
there is no impregnation with doctrine, little interest in it even
later, no *parti pris*. He was grounded at church, and read the
Bible later. Of course, the Bible was the commonest and most
discussed book of the day : it was of all books the best seller,
especially the Genevan Bible with its handy size and low price —
this was the one to take home for reading. We must remember,
too, that the language of Bible and Prayer Book was modern
and newly minted for them, and made all the more fresh an impact
on their minds — where for us the effect is an opposite one, the
archaic language has a charm upon it and stirs further echoes,
less intellectual, more suggestive and mnemonic. The Elizabethans
it woke out of sleep — out of the long medieval sleep of the
mnemonic Latin of the Mass. The Bible sounded a trumpet-note
in their ears, until, with the Puritans, it became deafening. Shakespeare, *felix opportunitate vitae*, inhabited the providentially fortunate
years before the deafening crash became civil war. As yet, in the
Elizabethan age, these horrid developments were not even in sight,
and sensible people were in control. The Bible provided the
foundation and bed of popular culture ; everybody had to go to
church. Quotations, allusions, sentences, phrases, tags, sometimes
turned round to make jokes, would be almost as familiar to the
audience as to the author : they came out of the same bed. It is
impossible to exaggerate the importance, then, of this grounding
in childhood : for the adult writer the Bible and the Prayer Book
formed the deepest, most constant and continuing influence and
inspiration.

CHAPTER IV

Youth and Marriage

WE can build up a picture of the kind of youth Shakespeare was from the information he drops as to his choices and preferences in his writings, though we must watch for corroboration from external evidence. After all a writer writes about his own experience — he cannot exclude himself from his work, even if he would. Even with a dramatist, instinctive affinities, unconscious preferences are revealed by tone and frequency of reference. And there are overtones, recognisable enough, when the writer is speaking for himself through one of his creations.

For his environment, let us look at his father's shop. As a glover and whittawer John Shakespeare tawed the white skins of deer, sheep, goats, but not those of cattle and swine, which would fall to Richard Field's father, the tanner. Young William knew all about skins : he would have to help his father in the shop. When Aubrey got the information, for which he has been too much misdoubted, that the father was a butcher, he was not so far out : there is always something in what Aubrey tells us. The glover would take a hand in killing the animals, as neighbours used to help each other in the country village of my youth. Aubrey adds of the son : 'I have been told heretofore by some of the neighbours that when he was a boy he exercised his father's trade, but when he killed a calf he would do it in a high style and make a speech'.[1] But 'killing a calf' was an item in the repertory of popular entertainers [2] — and this may be the tale Aubrey got hold of and reported it literally.

Shakespeare refers to most kinds of skin that were dealt with at Stratford, skins of calf, sheep, lamb, fox, dog, deer and cheveril.

He knew that neat's leather was used for shoes, sheep's leather for a bridle. The poet was aware that horse-hair was used in bow-strings and calves' guts in fiddle-strings. He notices leathern aprons, jerkins and bottles, the 'sowskin bowget' or bag carried by tinkers. He

Youth and Marriage

alludes to 'flesh and fell', to the greasy fells of ewes and to the lamb's white fleece. He knew that the deer's hide was the keeper's perquisite. References to cheveril (kid-skin) are much to the point. On account of its softness and flexibility it was used in the making of finer qualities of glove. Shakespeare speaks of 'a wit of cheveril, that stretches from an inch narrow to an ell broad'. He mentions also a 'soft cheveril conscience', capable of receiving gifts if the owner will 'please to stretch it', and 'a cheveril glove . . . how quickly the wrong side may be turned outward . . .' Last but not least is Shakespeare's reference to a tool which he must often have seen in his father's hand. 'Does he not wear', asks Dame Quickly of Slender, 'a great round beard like a glover's paring-knife ?'[3]

No doubt all that made for a smell to emancipate oneself from. Shakespeare's juvenile senses were not so highly developed as they became with entry into a more sophisticated world : no doubt they were rustic and healthy enough. And so with other, more important tastes too. From a study of his imagery, it appears that ' Shakespeare's extreme sensitiveness about the quality, freshness and cleanliness of food developed rather late — possibly after experience of more delicate fare than that at Stratford, at the tables of his London friends. Up to about the age of thirty, we get little sign of it, and his references to hunger, appetite and surfeit are such as might be made by any healthy youth. From thirty onwards there is increasing evidence of fastidiousness.' [4]

Domestic images are common enough with Elizabethan playwrights, but Shakespeare has an unusually large number from the occupations of the kitchen — washing, scouring, wiping ; steeping, wringing, hanging out to dry ; dusting and sweeping ; sewing, mending, patching clothes ; above all, removing stains and smears from what has become sullied or spotted. There is the equipment of an old-fashioned kitchen, bellows, sieve and skillet ; the jugs and jacks for liquor, vessels of all sorts. The images are those of a dim light and an open smoky fire, with a noticeable one of a stopped oven that appears only in his early work :

> Sorrow concealed, like an oven stopped,
> Doth burn the heart to cinders where it is.

'This workaday kitchen is, next to the orchard or garden, the atmosphere in which Shakespeare's mind moved most easily, the concrete background from which he most readily selects objects for comparison or analogy.' [5] Naturally enough, for that is the simple background from which he came.

49

'One occupation, one point of view, above all others, is naturally his, that of a gardener : watching, preserving, tending and caring for growing things, especially flowers and fruit. All through his plays he thinks most easily and readily of human life and action in the terms of a gardener.' 6   Images from the garden come readily enough to most English poets, but apparently Shakespeare's interest is in the 'processes of growth, as his prime reaction to the body is to its movement and life, and in the human face to its changing expressions. Images are frequent of garden growth choked by weeds, buds shaken by rough winds, the canker in the flower ; while trees, their branches and roots are constantly allied in his mind with families, dynasties, kingdoms.'

Beyond the garden there are the out-of-door sports of the little town, of the pastures outside, or up on the Cotswolds. His references reveal that archery, a common enough sport in the town, was a favourite : he always writes about it with the feeling of personal acquaintance :

> In my schooldays, when I had lost one shaft,
> I shot his fellow of the self-same flight
> The self-same way with more advisèd watch,
> To find the other forth ; and by adventuring both,
> I oft found both.

Archery was much encouraged, both by the government and the town authorities, as a pursuit for the common people, useful for national defence. Bowling was a superior game, intended for the upper classes, and this was Shakespeare's prime favourite. 'Of all the game and exercises Shakespeare mentions — tennis, football, bowls, fencing, tilting, wrestling — there can be no doubt that bowls was the one he himself played and loved best. He has nineteen images from bowls, besides other references, or more than thrice as many as from any other game, and these all show close knowledge of the game and of the peculiar run of the bowl.' 7 Most other dramatists hardly so much as mention the game.

> Well, forward ! forward ! thus the bowl should run,
> And not unluckily against the bias.

Perhaps we may observe that it is a peaceable occupation, 'gentle' in both senses of the word.

The liming or snaring of birds, which was still a country-sport of my youth, never fails to bring out Shakespeare's sympathy for the poor creatures — as is usually the case with hunted animals, deer or hare, though not the fox.

> The bird that hath been limèd in a bush
> With trembling wings misdoubteth every bush . . .

Out in the stubbles, on the heaths to the north of the town, or high on the Cotswolds, there was coursing the hare :

> a brace of greyhounds
> Having the fearful flying hare in sight.

Shakespeare's early poem, *Venus and Adonis*, has a description of coursing the hare by someone clearly very familiar with the sport :

> And when thou hast on foot the purblind hare,
> Mark the poor wretch, to overshoot his troubles,
> How he outruns the wind, and with what care
> He cranks and crosses with a thousand doubles . . .
>
> Sometime he runs among a flock of sheep,
> To make the cunning hounds mistake their smell,
> And sometime where earth-delving conies keep,
> To stop the loud pursuers in their yell ;
> And sometime sorteth with a herd of deer.
> Danger deviseth shifts ; wit waits on fear.
>
> By this, poor Wat, far off upon a hill,
> Stands on his hinder legs with listening ear,
> To hearken if his foes pursue him still ;
> Anon their loud alarums he doth hear ;
> And now his grief may be comparèd well
> To one sore sick that hears the passing bell.
>
> Then shalt thou see the dew-bedabbled wretch
> Turn and return, indenting with the way ;
> Each envious briar his weary legs do scratch,
> Each shadow makes him stop, each murmur stay.
> For misery is trodden on by many,
> And being low never relieved by any.

So too with the deer — his sympathy is with the hunted animal :

> the poor frightened deer, that stands at gaze,
> Wildly determining which way to fly.

All the same — and these things are not mutually exclusive — he liked following the chase, there was the excitement and the spectacle. He knew all about hounds, down to points like 'the hound

that runs counter and yet draws dry-foot well', or the observation
that

> coward dogs
> Most spend their mouths when what they seem to threaten
> Runs far before them.

All animals get a good word from him, except the fox and the dog.

He loved horses and wrote of them with either fellow-feeling
or sympathy :

> As true as truest horse that yet would never tire.

An early sonnet brings him very close to us :

> The beast that bears me, tired with my woe,
> Plods dully on, to bear that weight in me,
> As if by some instinct the wretch did know
> His rider loved not speed, being made from thee :
> The bloody spur cannot provoke him on
> That sometimes anger thrusts into his hide,
> Which heavily he answers with a groan
> More sharp to me than spurring to his side.

But this is the adult player speaking : he has crossed the river
that leads to London, the theatre and fame.

The river provides the most frequent images — natural enough
for a poet who lived all his early years beside the Avon, came
back to it to spend some part of most summers, and eventually
retired to live his last days beside it. River-images are negligible
with his contemporaries, except for Spenser — only the ocean
was sufficient for Marlowe. But it was the river in flood that
chiefly impressed Shakespeare's imagination, particularly the movement of water, stirring the flags on the banks as it passed, or the
life of the current :

> As through an arch the violent roaring tide.

There is a current with an eddy beneath one of the arches of the
bridge at Stratford, though the word 'tide' would indicate the
arches of old London Bridge where the current was much more
violent and became a familiar spectacle to one living and working
by the Thames.[8]

Still, the underlying ground of his imagery indicates that he
was a countryman through and through. 'One interest above
all others stands out : this is the life of the countryside and its
varying aspects : the winds, the weather and the seasons, the sky
and clouds, birds and animals.'[9] This was his countryside, the

Avon flowing down to the Severn, bounded by the forest of Arden and the wide sweep of the Cotswolds to the south. Indications of his acquaintance with Cotswold country appear in the plays, especially in *2 Henry IV* where Justice Shallow inhabits recognisable Gloucestershire. When his man inquires of him, 'Shall we sow the headland with wheat?' Shallow answers, 'With red wheat, Davy.' Apparently red wheat was sown in August or September on Cotswold into the eighteenth century.[10] Shakespeare was familiar with the western escarpment going down to the Severn. Davy says, 'I beseech you, sir, to countenance William Vizor of Woncot against Clement Perkes of the Hill'. Woncot is probably Woodmancote near Dursley, which for centuries had a family called Vizor or Vizard. On Stinchcombe Hill there lived long ago a family of the name of Perkes, and from the Hill one sees Berkeley Castle, as in *Richard II* : Northumberland says,

> I am a stranger here in Gloucestershire :
> These high wild hills and rough uneven ways
> Draws out our miles and makes them wearisome . . .

Percy points out,

> There stands the castle by yon tuft of trees —

exactly as it is today.

In a town like Stratford there were dramatic entertainments for a clever grammar-schoolboy to take part in or enjoy as a spectator, mummings, the regular St. George's play common all over England, pageants, disguises. As it happens we have only one recorded, Richard Davy's play at Whitsuntide 1583, because the corporation contributed towards the expenses. In one of the earliest plays Shakespeare wrote, we find :

> At Pentecost,
> When all our pageants of delight were played,
> Our youth got me to play the woman's part,
> And I was trimmed in Madam Julia's gown,
> Which servèd me as fit, by all men's judgments,
> As if the garment had been made for me. . . .
> And at that time I made her weep agood,
> For I did play a lamentable part :
> Madam, 'twas Ariadne passioning
> For Theseus' perjury and unjust flight :
> Which I so lively acted with my tears
> That my poor mistress, movèd therewithal,
> Wept bitterly.

How then did Shakespeare speak?

We can tell from his highly idiosyncratic spellings, and it is not surprising that he spoke as a Warwickshire man would, with that country flavour — as Tennyson spoke with a Lincolnshire inflexion, and Wordsworth with a North Country burr. In Elizabethan times disparities of speech were much wider, local dialects stronger, the patterns richer and more diversified. Grandees at Court spoke with the accents of the regions they came from — as they continued to do up to the end of the Victorian age. It is familiar knowledge that Sir Walter Ralegh 'spake broad Devonshire to his dying day', and that is corroborated by his peculiar spellings. His not well-educated Lady, Elizabeth Throckmorton, wrote largely by ear : in her phonetic spellings we can hear the accents of her voice.[11]

Characteristic of old Warwickshire was the deeper 'u', which we saw reflected in the corporation accounts in the spelling 'goones' for 'guns'. Shakespeare said 'woonder', where we say 'wonder', and so with that sound consistently : 'woone' for 'won', or 'one'. The word 'smother' is spelt 'smoother'. Several of the vowel-sounds are deeper, as in Warwickshire or Staffordshire dialect today : one said 'smoake' not modern, rather too refined, 'smoke', and, more heavily, 'sturre' for 'stir'. On the other hand there was the light Midlands 'u', an inversion of southern usage : it seems from his spelling that Shakespeare said 'kuckoo', as proper Midlands folk still do. Other vowel-sounds were deeper, especially the long 'a' : Shakespeare said auncient and daunger, inchaunt and awnser.[12]

Another feature was the stronger enunciation of consonants indicated in Shakespeare's spellings, shedde, kisse, mistresse, chidde, comming, musique, starre, farre, jarre — the 'r' being rolled. The terminal 'y' had more value as we see in spellings like legacie, perjurie, solitarie. One excellent vowel-sound has been lost from modern standard English, though one still hears it among old-fashioned provincial people in words like 'fruit', pronounced by them 'friwt', as the Elizabethans did. This vowel-sound appeared in words like 'truant' and 'fuel', spelt by Shakespeare 'trewant' and 'fewell'. Then there is the 'er' sound that was pronounced broadly 'ar' in that age : we still preserve it in words like 'serjeant' and 'clerk'. Altogether, the language as Shakespeare spoke it had a much stronger and warmer sound. With a broader range and more emphatic enunciation, it was better suited to dramatic declamation : compared to our modern speech, having more character, at once more masculine and more truly poetic. It would be good to hear a Shakespeare play once more as the Elizabethans heard it.

Meanwhile, Alderman Shakespeare's affairs were going downhill, his financial difficulties increasing. He was already in debt to his brother-in-law Edmund Lambert when, in November 1578, he mortgaged to him a house and fifty-six acres in Wilmcote, part of his wife's inheritance, to raise £40 in ready cash. At Michaelmas 1580, John Shakespeare was unable to repay the money, and the property remained in the hands of the Lamberts. This led to a family quarrel and a lawsuit in which William Shakespeare's name was joined as his father's heir. John Shakespeare claimed that, in return for another £20 promised, the Lamberts might have full title to the property. The Lamberts denied the claim. Some ten years later John Shakespeare offered to repay the £40, but then it was refused, since the lease on the property was nearly expired and it would let for a higher rent. Notice that this was in 1597, when William had recouped the family fortunes in London. But this part of his mother's property never was recovered.

In that same November 1578 John and Mary Shakespeare conveyed another considerable section of their property in Wilmcote, some eighty-six acres, to a Webbe relative for a period of years and then to revert to them or their heirs. The point of this was to bring in an immediate sum of money, evidently needed. Next year they sold their ninth share in property in Snitterfield for another £40.[13] In the following year, 1580, John Shakespeare was fined £20 in Queen's Bench for not appearing to find surety for keeping the peace, and another £20 as a pledge for a Nottingham hatmaker ; two others were fined £20 as pledges on Shakespeare's behalf. There is no record that these fines were paid, nor is their interpretation certain ; but it looks as if John Shakespeare were in aggressive mood towards his creditors and might break their heads. Certainly he went in some fear, for two years later, in 1582, he petitioned Queen's Bench for sureties of the peace against four men named, 'for fear of death and mutilation of his limbs'.[14]

In spite of his own difficulties John Shakespeare was willing, perhaps improvidently, to come to the aid of others. In 1586 he became surety for his brother Henry, and was next year sued in consequence by Nicholas Lane, was driven to obtain bail from good-natured Alderman Hill and to sue out a writ of Habeas Corpus for his own protection. At Coventry the same year he gave bail for a Stratford tinker accused of a felony, and when the tinker, a Welshman, did not appear John Shakespeare forfeited £10, quite a sum in those days. Perhaps he was improvident, easy-going about money — it would seem so. It was for the son to learn by his father's experience and rectify the fault ; in time he did. In 1592 Master Shakespeare's name appeared on a list drawn up by the J.P.s of Warwickshire of those who did not attend church : he was one of those who absented themselves 'for fear of process for debt'. It was understandable, for he had never paid the debt and damages recovered against him by William Burbage in 1589. When he failed to appear in the Court of Common Pleas in April 1592, the judges ordered the sheriff to execute the judgment against him. It was reasonable not to appear in church on Sunday, for that offered a good opportunity for the sheriff to nab him ; but it was a sad contrast from the days when he sat in his furred gown in the front pew, or processed through the streets with the town's officers before him.

Is it to be supposed that these things, going on over a long course of years, during the whole of his adolescence and young manhood, had no reaction upon the sensitive, observant son ?

Unfortunately, he was himself adding to the family difficulties.

Towards the end of August 1582, at the mature age of eighteen, he got Anne Hathaway with child, a spinster eight years older than himself. She was of a respectable parentage and had to be married. Her father Richard Hathaway was an old acquaintance of Shakespeare's father, who with his usual obliging good nature had stood surety for a debt of Hathaway's back in 1566.[15] Hewlands farm at Shottery, where the Hathaways lived, was not more than a mile from Stratford church : the situation of the place — romanticised now as Anne Hathaway's Cottage — is exactly described in the lines :

> West of this place down in the neighbour bottom,
> The rank of osiers by the murmuring stream,
> Left on your right hand brings you to the place.

Here Richard Hathaway died in September 1581, leaving Anne, the eldest daughter by his first wife, and several other children. Anne was left 10 marks, that is, £6 : 13s. : 4d., as her dowry — a fairly usual sum for a girl of her class ; otherwise, she had no property of her own, unlike Shakespeare's mother.

After her father's death Anne had moved out of the old home, to her relatives at Temple Grafton or to Stratford — at any rate more accessible to the attentions, the 'sportive blood', of the youth so much her junior. By November, at least, it was clear that she was pregnant, and at the end of the month young William and two friends of hers rode off to Worcester, where the diocesan registry was, to obtain a licence to marry. For Shakespeare was a minor — so that the consent of his parents was necessary ; and there had to be two sureties on behalf of the bride to look after her interests — two neighbours, friends of her father. All was above board, but there was need for some hurry for Advent was about to begin, when there was a close season for marriages, without a special and expensive licence, and after Septuagesima fell a similar inhibited season until April, when Anne would be eight months gone with child. So after only once calling the banns, William and Anne were married on 30 November or 1 December, either at Worcester or more probably at Temple Grafton.

When Rosalind tells us how 'Time travels in diverse places with diverse persons', there is a flavour of personal experience. 'Marry, he trots hard with a young maid between the contract of her marriage and the day it is solemnized : if the interim be but a sennight, Time's pace is so hard that it seems the length of seven year.' Anne Hathaway, twenty-six years old and fatherless, had done well to involve herself with the boy of eighteen, could she but foresee the future. Apart from his youth and the depressing circumstances of his family, the marriage was a perfectly proper one socially : the Hathaways and the Shakespeares were of the same social standing and the families known to each other all their lives. It was not to be thought of that the youth would go back on his word to the (rather mature) woman, or that his parents would refuse to give their consent, in the circumstances. It does not seem that young William had any regrets : normal, and in this respect like ordinary folk — one reason why his work has always appealed to them — he writes gaily of the marriage-bed and marriage-night, even if in his case he had anticipated it :

> O let me clip ye
> In arms as sound as when I wooed, in heart
> As merry as when our nuptial day was done
> And tapers burned to bedward !

Back to Henley Street they went, to live under his parents' roof, where their first child was born, and baptised Susanna by vicar Barton at church on Trinity Sunday, 26 May 1583.

Twenty months later, twins were born to the young couple (at least the father was young) : baptised Hamnet and Judith, 2 February 1585, after neighbours Hamnet and Judith Sadler of High Street, the godparents.

But here was a family to provide for, just when his father's circumstances were most discouraging.

How are we to suppose that the young man contributed to the upkeep of the family ? No doubt he helped in his father's shop and with his business. But John Aubrey heard later from one of the family of Christopher Beeston, the actor, who had been in a position to know, that Shakespeare 'understood Latin pretty well, for he had been in his younger days a schoolmaster in the country'.[16] There is no reason at all to reject this : it is rather corroborated by Shakespeare's facetious interest in schoolmasters and their habits in the early Plays, and it would give him time to store up some of the reading that went into the writing of them later.

Still, there was no future in being an usher, with his ambitions and responsibilities. By nature he was a poet, and one fine day in the later 1580's — the opportunities were specially inviting in the year 1587, with five companies visiting Stratford, including Leicester's and the Queen's, the former below strength and the latter wanting a man — he took the road to London.

CHAPTER V

London : The Armada Years

THERE could not be a more exciting, a more inspiring, moment for a young man to arrive in London than in the year or so before the Armada. Not to be there was not to be there on St. Crispin's day. To be there was to be in at the birth of modern England — the first demonstration, with the victory over imperial Spain, that a new power had come into the front rank of European powers.

The inspiration of nationalism, the surge of self-confidence, the thrill of pride through the veins are expressed in a thousand places. In the books they wrote, in the ships they built and the names they gave them : the *Ark Royal*, the *Elizabeth Bonaventure* (in which Drake performed the exploit of 'the singeing of the King of Spain's beard'), the *Elizabeth Jonas*, the *Triumph*, the *Revenge*. It is to be seen in the incitements they urged, the future they saw for the language, the pride they expressed for everything English, their unparalleled Queen, the heroic exploits of the seamen, the oceans penetrated, in which the flag of St. George had been shown for the first time ; in their fighting men, the fame of Drake and Black John Norris, of Philip Sidney and Sir Richard Grenville, the soldierly Veres. It is to be seen, no less, in the extension of good works with prosperity, the noble foundations of grammar schools throughout the land, the philanthropy of the merchant class, their civic and eleemosynary foundations ; in the conspicuous panoply of the nobles in their new-built palaces ; in the thrill of music, the new spirit billowing through the poetry and the drama ; in a modest professional pride even in their actors.

Looking through the state-papers of the time one gets a whiff of the dangers and excitements. The plots against the Queen's life had reached their climax with Babington's, which at length brought Mary Stuart to book. Yet this January of 1587 the secretary to the French ambassador confessed to a plan to kill the Queen, either by laying a train of gunpowder, poisoning her stirrup or shoe, 'or some other Italian device'.[1] All this, of course, only raised people's devotion to their Queen, this precious, irreplaceable person, to new heights. In February one of the Catholic Ardens escaped from custody, and there was a rumour of Mary's escape from Fotheringhay. The government were taking no risks, even if the Queen could never make up her mind to the execution of a royal person. Burghley took control and forced her hand : the end of Mary's career came on the scaffold at Fotheringhay on 8 February. Mary was nine years younger than Elizabeth ; when the Spanish invasion took shape there would now be no candidate available to take Elizabeth's throne.

Eight days later Sir Philip Sidney's body was borne through the streets of London with great solemnity and 'all possible moan', to his burial in St. Paul's.[2] There was a rumour of a plot to burn his uncle Leicester's mansion at Wanstead : one, Fishwick, had knowledge of inflammable oils for burning houses and making mortal poison and perfumes, 'such as Baron Bell experienced at Oxford'. Actually, Leicester was in some disgrace with the Queen for his ill-success in the Netherlands, beseeching her 'to behold with the eyes of her princely clemency his wretched and depressed estate, and to restore him to some degree of her Majesty's former grace and favour'. Drake was at Plymouth in early April, waiting to pounce on Cadiz : 'there never was in any fleet more likelihood of a loving agreement'. Spanish preparations were immense, and he wrought havoc in Cadiz harbour, burning and sinking provision ships. He could not penetrate the defences of Lisbon, where the Armada was preparing ; but he postponed its sailing for a year. From Warwickshire, as from other Midland counties, bands were levied to serve under Leicester in the Netherlands — the county's contingent this year was a band of 150 foot.[3]

That spring the whole country had been put into a state of preparedness ; instructions rained down upon the local authorities as to what they were to do. Two armies were to be formed : one at St. James's for the defence of the Queen's person, the other at Tilbury to oppose any landing. On 1 April the Council instructed the Earl of Warwick, as Lord-Lieutenant, to have the forces of the shire levied and trained, and he appointed George Turberville as Muster Master to train them.[4] The Warwickshire levies were some 600 foot ; when the Spaniards were expected in July, they were among those summoned up to St. James's to protect the Queen.

Of all this martial activity and excitement Shakespeare was a
spectator like any other, perhaps a participant. Just outside
Bishopsgate, where we first hear of him lodging, lay the open
space of Artillery Yard, recently enclosed by a brick wall (it still
is), where the gunners of the Tower came to do their weekly
practice with their brass ordnance against a great butt of earth.[5]
At Mile End the armed bands of the city did their training, as
Justice Shallow recalled : 'I remember at Mile End Green, when
I lay at Clement's Inn, there was a little quiver fellow, and 'a
would manage you his piece thus ; and 'a would about and about,
and come you in and come you in. "Rah, tah, tah", would 'a
say ; "Bounce", would 'a say ; and away would 'a go, and again
would 'a come. I shall ne'er see such a fellow.' And among the
mouldy lot of recruits whom Falstaff mustered to make the theatre
laugh, we must not forget Feeble's good spirit : 'By my troth,
I care not ; a man can die but once ; we owe God a death. An't
be my destiny, so ; an't be not, so. No man's too good to serve's
Prince.'

There is the very voice of England in those years.

This mood of national pride and self-confidence provides the
impulse that carried the theatre, and with it Shakespeare, upwards
into the nineties. Shakespeare was its most sensitive register and
expression, even exponent with his first plays on English history.
He caught the mood and made himself the mouthpiece, as we
learn from Nashe's tribute ; hence his earliest success.

But, first, there came his apprenticeship in the theatre as a
player and, along with that, as a reader of the new literature coming
forth at last, after a long winter, in such profusion and promise.
About this we can infer a good deal, by reading back from what
appears in his work. It is obvious that he had a lot of leeway to
make up, as a country lad who had not had the advantage of a
London background like Thomas Lodge and Thomas Kyd, or of
years at the university like Lyly and Peele, Greene and Marlowe
and Nashe. When one thinks that Peele wrote plays while still
at Oxford, that Marlowe had *Tamburlaine* produced on the London
stage while he still was only twenty-three, one sees the considerable handicap Shakespeare suffered from compared with them.
Actually Marlowe and he were the same age, Shakespeare only
a couple of months junior. The fact that he ultimately went
beyond them all is a tribute in the first place to his greater capacity

for development, and in the second to his determination and industry, no less than to his genius. But there is no doubt about the handicap or that he was conscious of it : so far from appearing precocious, he was some time in getting going.

It is hardly likely that Shakespeare did not make contact with his Stratford acquaintance, Richard Field, now established in London. Field, too, was an ambitious young fellow, a couple of years senior to Shakespeare. He had come up to London in 1579 and served his apprenticeship as a printer with Thomas Vautrollier, a French Huguenot who had won a leading position by the quality of his printing. When Vautrollier died, Field married his widow and succeeded to the business in Blackfriars. He was already comfortably established by Armada year, ready to launch out with an interesting list of publications, including Shakespeare's own first narrative poem, *Venus and Adonis*, in 1592. It is clear that their acquaintance was close.

When we examine the list and the nature of Field's publications in these years, we perceive how much they mean in Shakespeare's continued education and reading.[6] For the first book Field printed on his own was Puttenham's *Arte of English Poesie*, the prime Elizabethan work of literary criticism which summed up all that had been achieved in the past thirty years and pointed the way to the future. Apart from particular echoes, it is noticeable how closely Shakespeare agreed with Puttenham in his intellectual attitude, tone and temper. The book must have chimed with Shakespeare's own instinctive preferences, indeed helped to give them form and authority for a young man without guidance, on his own.

Puttenham had an independent mind, with the freedom of approach, the strain of hedonism, of an aristocrat.[7] He was all for enjoyment and laughter, for 'pleasant and lovely causes' ; he was in favour of pageantry and tradition, and appreciated the place of ceremony in society. He was a middle-of-the-road man, when 'grass must have grown on the *via media* in Elizabethan times'.[8] He had, indeed, a rare point of view, a philosophic and humane naturalism, at a time when so many people were urging their own ugly perfectionism and offering to impose it on everybody else. He thought that God himself suffered 'some few evils to prefer many goods'. In later years one finds Shakespeare expressing just this cast of mind, the temperate view that good and evil are inextricably mixed, that good is found along with evil, may sometimes come out of it. This inflexion went along with a humane and tolerant spirit, wise and understanding ; but anyone who knows the Elizabethan age will know how rare it was and how it went down before the fanatics in the end.

Nature and common reason were Puttenham's authorities : he thought common sense a better guide than either authority or received opinion. He refused to constrict poetry to a merely moralising function : he thought of it as the expression of the whole range of human interests and needs, the legitimate expression of human instincts. Of course, he was writing for a cultivated circle, for the Court, indeed for the Queen herself, who was the person who stood out most manfully in all her kingdom for just this point of view : she effectively hated the precisians. Now and again Puttenham had written poems encouraging her in her stand, and imploring her not to give way to their habit of seeing things in black and white, their rigid schematism, the shadow she had combated with some success — to give a blessed intermission before the Civil War. The inhibiting Puritan attitude in religion and art meant an impoverishment in civil life ; it grudged all that margin necessary for proper cultivation ; there was no scope for traditional decencies ; it took away

> from old relics reverence,
> From public shows magnificence.

It was an attempt to wed the practically impossible to the aesthetically undesirable.

> Princess, it is as if one take away
> Green woods from forests, and sunshine from the day.

His literary approach was in keeping : a clever man — indeed, far subtler than the precisians — his mind had been intently watching the actual course of the language over the past thirty years. It was a course of extraordinary expansion to match the needs of expression of a people who in those decades were experiencing, in action as well as in the realm of the mind, more than ever before or since. That moment of extreme sensibility and flexibility in the language itself, of expansiveness and readiness to experiment — that moment, too, was never known before or since. As Lyly wrote, 'it is a world to see how Englishmen desire to hear finer speech than the language will allow'.

Here, too, Puttenham was wise — and Shakespeare after him

— to follow, more subtly, their feeling for language, the instinctive tact of ear and eye. Neither of them was a theorist ; indeed they were both allergic to theory. They moved in keeping with the inner nature of the language, dictating its own rhythms, proprieties and uses. Puttenham, like Shakespeare after him, wrote prose naturally, with an easy sequence of clauses, with a loose, not strict, finish. But, though Puttenham had a copious vocabulary, he was actually a stickler for linguistic exactness ; he laid stress on fastidious discrimination — with the result that the words he adopted into the language, like Shakespeare's, have survived. Then, too, he was all for the proper organisation of customary usage and bringing it under rules, instead of laying down the law as to what should exist. He concentrated on rhetoric, rather than barren logic, for this was the climax of the rhetorical movement that contributed so much to the flowering of Elizabethan literature. All Shakespeare's early plays are rhetorical plays. 'What is the figure ? What is the figure ?' says Holofernes, in *Love's Labour's Lost.* Having absorbed all rhetoric had to teach, they could afford later to dispense with it. 'More matter, with less art', says the Queen in *Hamlet* to old-fashioned Polonius.

With entire self-confidence Puttenham had faith in the native capacities of the language and their natural fulfilment in the literature now under way, particularly as shown by the Court poets, Sidney and Dyer, the Earl of Oxford and Ralegh, and 'that other gentleman who wrote the late *Shepherds' Calendar*'.[9] The new words danced like fire-flies for them all — for no-one more than the ingenuous young man from Stratford. How fascinated he was by all this we see in his early work, while it reaches its crest with *Love's Labour's Lost.* Now in London he was in the swim, young and eager to learn ; Field's shop was a useful place to meet, particularly the authors coming there about their books. In the end Puttenham was a patriot, like Shakespeare, to whom this national pride was a foremost inspiration in his work, very obvious in all the English-history plays, but with reverberations to the very end. Puttenham had undertaken his work in the conviction 'that there may be an art of our English poesy, as well as there is of the Latin and Greek'. The poets were now proving him right : after a long winter of discontent, here was spring.

Field presented this masterly work to Lord Treasurer Burghley, with an upstanding and not at all sycophantic dedication, in May-time of 1589. He addressed the mighty minister as man to man in a well-written preface.

> This book (right honourable) coming to my hands with his bare title without any author's name or any other ordinary address, I doubted how well it might become me to make you a present thereof, seeming by many express passages in the same at large that it was by the author intended to our sovereign lady the Queen, and for her recreation and service chiefly devised . . . Perceiving besides the title to purport so slender a subject as nothing almost could be more discrepant from the gravity of your years and honourable function, whose contemplations are every hour more seriously employed upon the public administration and services. . . .

Anonymity was, of course, common form with an aristocratic author : it did not necessarily mean that he was unknown to Field. The young printer from Stratford made a good job of his first independent publication, and we find that Sir John Harington, courtier and wit, the Queen's godson, wished it to be taken for a model in the printing of his translation of Ariosto's *Orlando Furioso*.[10] This was only two years later, in 1591, while Shakespeare was still in close association with Field and before they moved apart.

What the young countryman learned from Field's shop, in the intervals from his acting, may be placed beyond doubt when we consider some of Field's other publications during these years. There were several pamphlets dealing with topical French affairs, in which the King of Navarre, the Duc de Longueville, the Duc de Mayenne and Biron are to the fore. These are the names of characters in *Love's Labour's Lost* ; while Mistress Field's name, Jacquinetta, is used for the country girl. From the first Shakespeare had the art of making a little go a long way. In 1586, before Field had taken over from Vautrollier, they had printed Timothy Bright's *Treatise on Melancholy* : it is recognised that Shakespeare drew on this when he came to write *Hamlet* — or perhaps he had unconsciously stored away, in his instinctive frugal manner, what he had learned in the days of his association with the shop in Blackfriars. The firm had enjoyed a monopoly of the publication of some of the classical school-texts familiar to Shakespeare : Ovid, Cicero, Manutius's Phrases, Plutarch's Lives. In 1592, Field published a translation of Du Bartas, *The Divine Weeks and Works*, which has left its trace on Shakespeare. His few Italian phrases all came from the *Campo de Fior*, which the firm had published as a hand-book for learning Italian and French.

Blackfriars — to the south-west of St. Paul's, south of Ludgate hill, and between Fleet ditch and the Thames — was at this time an aristocratic *enclave* within the precinct of the former friary. The great church had been pulled down after the Dissolution, and with it the parish church.[11] In Mary's reign the lessee, Sir Thomas Carwarden, Master of the Revels, was made to provide a church out of part of the friary buildings. Into this conveniently walled-off close there came a number of well-to-do residents, led by that loquacious tartar, the Dowager Lady Russell — aunt of Robert Cecil and the Bacons — along with a number of foreigners serving the luxury trades, goldsmiths and jewellers. Along with these had come Vautrollier, the printer. Already in the 1580's, and for some time before, a portion of the friary premises, the old frater, had been used by the Children of the Chapel as a theatre — the first Blackfriars theatre.[12] Here Lyly had produced his plays under the patronage of the Earl of Oxford. There was a good deal of dispute about the leases, and theatrical performances came to an end about 1585–6. However, the tradition hung about the premises — to be taken up a decade later, when they were bought by James Burbage. In 1600, the Children of the Chapel resumed playing here 'under the name of a private house' ; in 1608, the partners in the Globe theatre, Shakespeare among them, took over the Blackfriars as their winter house. Blackfriars, thus early familiar ground, played a considerable part, one way and another, in his career.

These same years, the later 1580's, saw a dramatic activity — the companies themselves, theatres, players and playwrights — reach a crest and achieve the form by which it is recognised as one of the supreme moments in the world's drama. There was no indication of this in the first two decades of the reign, any more than there was that the rather pedestrian level of verse and the extraordinary prevalence of doggerel would achieve such a florescence of poetry. Take one of the better of the earlier writers, Jasper Heywood's prologue to his translation of Seneca's *Thyestes* :

> In Lincoln's Inn and Temples twain,
> Gray's Inn and others mo,
> Thou shalt them find whose painful pen
> Thy verse shall flourish so

That Melpomen thou wouldst well ween
  Had taught them for to write,
And all their works with stately style
  And goodly grace t'endight . . .[13]

Think of the difference between this and the soaring, majestic verse of Marlowe's *Tamburlaine*, written in the year before the Armada ! Heywood's trotting verses serve to point to the continuing influence of the Inns of Court in the dramatic movement, in providing poets no less than audiences, either at the theatres or at performances on grand nights in their halls. He celebrates, too, the earlier writers and their works, Sackville's Sonnets, Norton and Yelverton's ditties, Baldwin's *Mirror for Magistrates* and old Barnaby Googe — but O the difference to us !

What was it that made the drama become poetical in the 1580's, that brought about the fusion of drama with poetry at such a high level and with increasing tension and power ?

The answer cannot be given only in literary terms, but must be historical also — in terms of society, in terms of the historic situation, the readiness, the mounting excitement, the inspiration of the moment. The drama was a nation-wide activity reaching into the farthest recesses of the country ; everybody, however remote, had a chance of being in touch with it, either through visiting players, or players retained by the local nobility or gentry, through the performances put on in so many towns by the crafts or gilds, by mummers in the countryside, or traditionally through the church. Now the organisation of travelling troupes into companies under some lord's name improved standards and competition, and this became still more so with the establishment of permanent theatres in London from 1576. This gave the leading companies the stable headquarters, the security, necessary for the best standards in acting. Professionalism was, then, a factor. From 1583, with the establishment of the Queen's men, London was never without a professional company with the highest standards. 'Touring the country town in the summer, rehearsing and performing the new plays in the autumn in the London suburbs, in the winter moving nearer to the heart of London, and with that shining goal before them — the glory and the profit of acting before the Court itself, they were more in touch with the nation at all levels of taste and intelligence, and in all classes of society, in City, Court and Country, than any English actors at any other time.'[14] This integration, I may add, reflected the heightened integration, and sentience, of the country during the twenty years' conflict with Spain.

There is, in addition, the importance of the audience which equally provided an integral cross-section of society, from the appreciative Queen to the enthusiastic apprentice and loose women on the look-out, in that blessed moment of time while things yet held together. 'The drama reached its peak when the audience formed a great amalgam, and it began its decline when the amalgam was split in two.' [15] This was the audience to which Shakespeare was conditioned early and 'for which he never ceased to write. It thrived for a time, it passed quickly, and its like has never existed since'. How fortunate Shakespeare was in hitting just that moment — how lucky he was, once he got over his earlier lack of fortune and got going ! And how providential seems the conjunction of just that man with the moment ! There was the extraordinary responsiveness and excitability of an Elizabethan audience, which bound players and spectators into a unity, like the antiphonies of a ritual. The audience weep at *Henry VI*, or 'they take up a wonderful laughter and shout altogether when they see some notable cousenage practised'. What did Shakespeare himself see when he looked from the stage in one of the 'kingly parts' he favoured, as the Ghost in *Hamlet* or old Adam in *As You Like It* ? —

> Nay, when you look into my galleries,
> How bravely they're trimmed up, you all shall swear
> You're highly pleased to see what's set down there :
> Storeys of men and women mixed together,
> Fair ones with foul, like sunshine in wet weather ;
> Within one square a thousand heads are laid
> So close that all of heads the room seems made ;
> As many faces there filled with blithe looks
> Show like the promising titles of new books
> Writ merrily, the readers being their own eyes,
> Which seem to move and to give plaudites . . .

There was, also, the range from the sophisticated nobles and Court-gallants, or the clever young men from the Inns of Court, to the simpletons who so much annoyed Ben Jonson by preferring drolleries or slap-stick to his classical tragedies, *Sejanus* and *Catiline*. All these people were far more educated by ear and memory than we are, quicker in the uptake, more susceptible emotionally, not any stupider for being more direct and *naif*, more retentive in memory and far more able to quote in consequence. There obviously grew up a *rapport* between the players and their faithful audience, those who came again and again to see their favourite stars, Tarleton and Will Kemp, Ned Alleyn and Burbage, the leading comedians and tragedians of the age. Clearly this *rapport*, this instinctive understanding, would be of the greatest value and help to that player who was also their favourite playwright.

For, lastly, come the literary factors, the language and the poetry. Mulcaster, the famous headmaster of Merchant Taylors' School, who, himself, regularly produced his boys in plays at Court and strongly advocated acting for its good effect on their bearing, 'behaviour and audacity', bears witness : 'this period in our time seemeth to be the perfectest period in our English tongue . . . there is in our tongue great and sufficient stuff for art'.[16] While Heywood, in his *Apology for Actors*, claimed that the proper enunciation of the stage, propagating good standards of speech, had played a part in this. The moment, then, at which the professionals turned to gifted young university men, trained in classical poetry and drama, to write their plays sparked off something unprecedented. (Observe that Shakespeare, owing to his father's troubles, was not one of them.) The fusion of the intellectual standards of the universities, exemplified first by Lyly and Peele from Oxford, then by Greene and Marlowe from Cambridge, with the native vigour of the popular tradition going back wide and deep into the Middle Ages, gave birth to the Elizabethan drama. Before the end of the 1580's Marlowe was writing, in accents that even now make the heart stand still with expectancy :

> If all the pens that ever poets held
> Had fed the feeling of their masters' thoughts,
> And every sweetness that inspired their hearts,
> Their minds and muses on admirèd themes ;
> If all the heavenly quintessence they still
> From their immortal flowers of poesy,
> Wherein as in a mirror we perceive
> The highest reaches of a human wit —
> If these had made one poem's period,
> And all combined in beauty's worthiness,
> Yet should there hover in their restless heads
> One thought, one grace, one wonder, at the least,
> Which into words no virtue can digest.

It was a world, in such minds, intoxicated with beauty, passion, the desire for life at its most intense and glorious, for knowledge, power and infinity. Such was the world that Shakespeare had entered ; here was its characteristic, unforgettable voice.

Though nothing of the ultimate harvest could have been foreseen, yet it turned out that all the proper preparations had been made for it. By a certain historic propriety Leicester's was the first important company ; we find it in existence from the beginning of the reign and it continued until his death in the month after the Armada had passed by. James Burbage was one of Leicester's men, and it is with his sons that Shakespeare was associated through most of his career. The father had been a joiner, but found it more profitable to become a player. He it was who took the decisive step of building the first permanent playhouse in 1576, when hitherto the players had performed in the yards of such famous inns as the Red Lion, the Bull, the Bel Savage, the Cross Keys, in the City. Burbage borrowed the money to put up the Theatre out in the fields beyond Bishopsgate, in the precincts of the former Holywell priory — another nice illustration of the Reformation progress from the next world to this.

James Burbage was a stubborn fellow — no doubt he needed to be, and no doubt also he found his craft as joiner came in handy in setting up the Theatre, as later in demolishing it and making use of the materials to build the Globe on the south bank of the river. He was also not particularly honest : he was supposed to have his own secret key to the box in which the gatherers kept their takings, defrauded his partners by withdrawing some of the cash, and was observed to deposit it in his own bosom. In one of the brawls about a right to a moiety of the profit, his son Richard — Shakespeare's fellow — makes his first appearance, in 1590. He was seen with a broomstaff in his hand, and when a participant asked ' "What stir was there ?" he answered in laughing phrase, "Huh, they come for a moiety. But," quoth he, holding up the said broomstaff, "I have, I think, delivered him a moiety with this, and sent them packing." ' [17] It makes a pleasant entrance for the famous actor upon our stage.

Within a few months a second theatre was built quite near the first, in the liberties of Shoreditch : the Curtain. Meanwhile one of the inns, the Red Lion, was made over into a permanent playing place ; and in 1580 another theatre was built at Newington Butts, less than a mile out from London Bridge on the south side of the Thames. The success of these ventures led the rumpus from preachers, Puritans and City fathers to rise to a crescendo of protest. 'Will not a filthy play, with a blast of trumpet, sooner call thither a thousand than an hour's tolling of a bell bring to the sermon a hundred?' [18] The speaker was the preacher at Paul's Cross, obviously an interested party. The Lord Mayor and his brethren were constantly protesting to the Privy Council, now against 'the unchaste, shameless and unnatural tumbling of the Italian women', now against the performances of the Children of her Majesty's Chapel, 'the lascivious writhing of their tender limbs, and gorgeous decking of their apparel', and other uses to which they were put.[19] Again and again the City fathers tried to suppress plays, but found themselves up against a stone-wall somewhere ; only when there was plague and danger of infection did they get their way. They then resorted to the argument that 'to play out of plague-time is to draw the plague by offendings of God upon occasion of such plays'. As for the players, 'if they were not her Majesty's servants, they should by their profession be rogues'.

There was the snag ; there was their stone-wall. Nothing that these people thought or did had any effect with the Queen : that clever, cultivated woman was not likely to give way to these frightful kill-joys. And the interesting thing is that, much more sophisticated and subtle than these *bourgeois*, her tastes were also more in keeping with average human nature. Not the least of the debts that English-speaking people owe to this remarkable woman is her encouragement of the Elizabethan drama and her holding the line against its enemies. Think of it — there might have been no Globe or Fortune or Blackfriars, no *Midsummer-Night's Dream* or *Hamlet* or *Othello*, no Lance or Dogberry or Bottom, no Lady Macbeth or Cleopatra, no Harry Hotspur or Falstaff ! In place of the Renaissance richness of the Elizabethan age, we might have had the dreary life of Puritan New England : plenty of John Cottons, and Cotton Mathers, and Increase Mathers, but no Marlowe or Shakespeare or Ben Jonson.

A decisive reply to these people was made by the formation of the Queen's company in 1583, sponsored by the government. Twelve of the best players from other companies were selected to wear her livery as her servants, to prepare themselves for her recreation and solace with plays at Christmas-time and Shrove-tide (always a trump-card to play against Lord Mayors and such), for the rest to act at the theatres now hemming in the City and to tour the country. Two, among these players, were outstanding :

Robert Wilson, 'for a quick, delicate, refined, extemporal wit, and Richard Tarleton, for a wondrous, plentiful, pleasant, extemporal wit : he was the wonder of his time', wrote Stow later. 'He lieth buried in Shoreditch church. He was so beloved that men use his picture for their signs.' [20] Tarleton's appearance was one impossible to forget : people began to laugh the moment he peeped out his head. He was stocky and squat, with a broad nose and a squint, curly hair and moustache, always with a cap, tabor and pipe. It was remembered of him how he 'played the God Luz with a flitch of bacon at his back, and how the Queen bade them take away the knave for making her to laugh so excessively as he fought against her little dog, Perrico de Faldas, with his sword and long staff, and bade the Queen take off her mastic'.[21] He was greatly gifted, famous for his ballads and jests no less than his jigs — some of the music for his jigs still remains. Many pamphlets and ballads attest his fame. Then he died, in Armada year, in a Shoreditch house 'of a very bad reputation'. We have a letter from him, written on his deathbed, to Walsingham imploring his protection for his little son of six, a godson of Sir Philip Sidney after whom he was named.[22]

The Queen's men dominated the 1580's, till Tarleton's death, a blow from which they never recovered. In the same year Leicester's company came to an end with his death. The next four or five years, in consequence, were a period of confusion among the companies, of kaleidoscopic changes of personnel, of companies combining temporarily for a season or longer, breaking apart again, of players moving from one to the other, so that it is difficult to establish continuity or certainty. This is the period when Shakespeare came into the theatre, and it is one reason for our lack of knowledge of his whereabouts, though we have a fair idea of what he was doing. The confused state of affairs left the chances wide open for new people to come up. First and foremost, the Lord Admiral's company, which took his livery in 1585 : this troupe had at its disposal the genius of Edward Alleyn as a tragic actor, along with his gifts as manager and producer, the financial backing of his stepfather-in-law, Philip Henslowe, and Marlowe's plays.

It certainly looked as if the future were with the Admiral's men. So it was — but only secondarily : for another, quite unexpected and even more successful, combination turned up out of the welter. The alliance of Henslowe with Alleyn gave the Admiral's men strength and stability over the next two decades. Henslowe was not a theatre-man by origin, but a dyer. He married his master's well-to-do widow, and about this very time, from 1587, began to invest in theatrical enterprise. It so happens that his papers and account-books remain, a chief source of our information as to Elizabethan plays and playwrights. If only the accounts and correspondence of the Burbages remained ! — we should know about their business dealings with Shakespeare, so much the more about him.

It is usual to regard Philip Henslowe as a hard-fisted capitalist, but I find a certain gruff kindness in the man. After all, one had to be careful with these improvident playwrights, frequently not up to time with their assignments, or with one like Robert Greene, who sold a play to one company and, when it went on tour in the provinces, sold the same play to another company playing in London. Henslowe's correspondence with Alleyn reveals a family-life of complete trust and affection ; one finds the elder man, by no means hard-hearted, leaning on the younger in his troubles. He writes to son Ned, on tour in Sussex : 'I desire rather to have your company and your wife's than your letters. .. . Now to let you understand news : I will tell you some, but it is for me hard and heavy. Since you were with me I have lost one of my company, which hurteth me greatly. That is, Gabriel ; for he is slain in Hogsden Fields by the hands of Benjamin Jonson, bricklayer. Therefore I would fain have a little of your counsel, if I could.' [23] This was in 1598, and it is Ben Jonson's first appearance on our stage. He was not wholly to be blamed, for Gabriel Spencer was a fighting fellow who had previously killed his man. Actors were no worse than others, though, if possible, even more high-spirited : this was what their world was like.

Edward Alleyn, a couple of years younger than Shakespeare, had the advantage of having been born in London, in Bishopsgate, and bred from youth a player. At sixteen he was one of the Earl of Worcester's men, and subsequently joined the Admiral's. In 1592 he married Henslowe's stepdaughter Joan, and with 'father' Henslowe behind him he made the largest theatrical fortune of the age, to which we owe his munificent foundations at Dulwich. His letters to his wife when away on tour are full of charm : ' my good sweetheart and loving mouse', and 'farewell, micho mousin and mouse and farewell Bess Dodipoll'.[24] Or he writes her instructions how to keep infection away in the plague of 1593 :

'therefore use this course : keep your house fair and clean, which I know you will, and every evening throw water before your door and in your back-side, and have in your windows good store of rue and herb of grace'. He asks her to forward letters to Lord Strange's players, with whom he is touring, 'and thus, sweetheart, with my hearty commendations to all our friends I cease, from Bristol this Wednesday after St. James's day, being ready to begin the play of *Harry of Cornwall*'.

If only we possessed similar letters home to Henley Street ! — but there is no evidence that Shakespeare's wife could read.

Alleyn became the leading tragedian of his age, with Richard Burbage not far behind. When Alleyn retired from the stage about 1597, he was called back again for a time by the express wish of the Queen. There were many tributes to him : Nashe says of him that ' his very name was able to make an ill matter good'. He was at his best in 'majestic parts', such as those he created, Tamburlaine, Barabas in *The Jew of Malta*, and Faustus. Having made a fortune, Alleyn was bent on becoming, and living the life of, a gentleman. The purchase of the valuable manor of Dulwich made this clear, though at the time of his death he was hoping for 'some further dignity' — evidently a knighthood (not so easy to come by in those days, before inflation in such things). Alleyn's withdrawal and immersion in business left the way open for Richard Burbage to achieve foremost place as a tragedian, as Marlowe's early death in May 1593 left the foremost place as playwright for another to fill.

The emergence of Burbage and Shakespeare, with the group around them who became their fellows, in a few years to form the first, most stable and successful company of the time, is more difficult to trace. We may legitimately infer that their coming up was slower and by a harder way than Alleyn's with Marlowe's plays to perform. We know that James Burbage and Kemp had been Leicester's men, and so may Bryan have been, since he was one of the English actors at Elsinore in 1586-7, presumably sent thither by Leicester from the Netherlands. John Heminges is thought to have started as a Queen's man. All this group, most of whom entered into the famous companionship of the Lord Chamberlain's men in 1594, are intermediately to be found in the company of Ferdinando, Lord Strange, heir to the Earl of Derby : Richard Burbage, Augustine Phillips, Thomas Pope, William Sly, John Heminges, George Bryan.

Lord Strange not merely gave his name to the company but was personally very keen on the players. He married the strong-minded Alice Spencer, whom we still see extended in all her glory on her marble four-poster, curtains and all, in the church of Harefield in Middlesex. In a couple of years or so, in 1594, he was dead. In the intervening years there was every kind of change and chance. In the winter of 1591–2 we find Alleyn and his fellows playing along with Strange's men, a rich combination of talents which put all other companies in the shade.

Meanwhile, it now seems recognised, Shakespeare was associated with Pembroke's men, for whom he wrote his earliest plays. But the company was beaten by the plague conditions of 1592–3 — a crisis in Shakespeare's life, as we shall see. They returned from a country tour in the summer of 1593, broken, as Henslowe reported to Alleyn on 28 September : 'as for my Lord of Pembroke's which you desire to know where they be, they are all at home and have been these five or six weeks ; for they cannot save their charges with travel, as I hear, and were fain to pawn their apparel for their charge'. [25] These circumstances may well bear upon Shakespeare, and be referred to in Sonnet 90, of this date :

> Then hate me when thou wilt ; if ever, now ;
> Now, while the world is bent my deeds to cross,
> Join with the spite of fortune, make me bow,
> And do not drop in for an after-loss . . .

It has been inferred from the absence of his name from dramatic records in 1592 and 1593 — when his name was at last known as a dramatist — that he was not playing, but writing his poems. Two such poems as *Venus and Adonis* and *The Rape of Lucrece*, deliberately challenging the claim to be taken as a poet, express his prime literary ambitions. In accordance with the Elizabethan scale of values Shakespeare's dearest wish was to be, and to be taken for, a poet. But he was an outsider : as he complained bitterly, fortune had not provided better for his livelihood

> Than public means which public manners breeds :
> Thence comes it that my name receives a brand.

Popular as leading members of the profession might be, it was not quite respectable to be an actor. However, acting earned bread, and thereby independence.

CHAPTER VI

Apprenticeship

WHAT then would Shakespeare have been doing in these early years in London, besides acting, touring in the country, making acquaintances, probably helping Field with his book-business ?

One thing we can be certain of : he was reading, going on with his self-education. A modern student of this particular subject tells us that 'Shakespeare was at some time in his life an avid reader, especially in English books'.[1] We learn, too, that he was a rapid reader, who could tear the heart out of a book for what he wanted, and that it is surprising, later, what little use he made of some of the books he looked at. By then he was an exceedingly busy, hard-worked man ; it is to these early years that we must look for his laying in a stock of reading that served him to such good purpose. As to this we have evidences from the work itself.

In 1587 there came out the second, and much enlarged, edition of Holinshed's chronicle history of England, of which Shakespeare made such splendid use during the rest of his life. This was the edition that he used, for he followed it mistakes and all. It opened up for him a new world of his country's past, untaught at school ; it provided him not only inexhaustible material for plays, but inspiration : it fed that love of his country which was an abiding theme in his work, an apprehensive, didactic concern such as no other dramatist displayed. This concern with the importance of unity and good government, the disaster of dissension, the chaos, anarchy and cruelty that ensue from the breakdown of government in civil war, is unique with him and makes him the most *Elizabethan* of dramatists. This theme was reinforced by his reading of Hall's Chronicle, the main thesis of which was the ending of the feud between Lancaster and York in the Tudor dynasty. The Wars of the Roses had a particular interest for a Midlands man, and in *Henry VI*, Warwickshire is brought well to the fore. Holinshed himself took the trouble to go from Bramcote to see Bosworth Field, for he is able to tell us that 'it was a great marish then, but at this present, by reason of ditches cast, it is grown to be firm ground'.[2] Shakespeare follows this detail, in *Richard III*, with 'the enemy is past the marsh'.

It has been noticed how strongly literary a quality pervades all Shakespeare's early work — natural enough in any young writer ; but in this case it has a special significance, for it is rather contrary to his true nature as it subsequently developed. One gets the impression of a young man, much on his own, having to pick up his education from books and make the most of what he can get. Not for him the intellectual companionship of the university wits — of the Oxford group from which Peele, Lyly and Lodge emerged, or the Cambridge groups of Spenser and Harvey, Greene, Marlowe and Nashe. And though he clearly was reading Sidney and Spenser, he did not belong to their circle, the *conoscenti* of Leicester House. He had had none of their opportunities, so he had to pick up such sophistication as he could from literature, and for the rest trust to his own native endowments, a shrewd, exact, country observation, a marvellous gift for language, a memory that registered everything and made the most of it.

Nevertheless, to a young man of literary ambition these were exciting years, dominated by new figures and the new poetry. 'He arrived in London during the great florescence. . . . The speed of development in the art of poetry at the time was greater than England has ever known before or since. Shakespeare was no theorist — indeed one of the least theoretic minds that could be imagined — but he could learn from such masters as Marlowe and Spenser by the direct method. . . . When he abandoned the learned models, it was to go back to popular and unassuming traditions and transform them. His humility may not have been without some modest self-assurance behind it.'[3] He lived 'at a moment in the tide of time when the current of speech flowed strongly, and like a strong swimmer rejoicing in his art, he swam with the stream of common speech. Here he rejected the doctrine of decorum, which restricted the vocabulary to fitting terms.' But this was when he had found his own nature and had the confidence to follow it. We shall watch him discovering it in the course of his apprenticeship.

One element in his schooling which he continued to develop and which became of prime importance in his early plays was that of rhetoric, in the technical, not the pejorative, sense of the term. We can be sure that he read Thomas Wilson's best-selling *Arte of Rhetorique*. Wilson has a translation of Erasmus's epistle to persuade a young gentleman to marry, with reasons and arguments — he is the only hope of continuing his family, the single state agrees ill with man's nature, and so on. This argument becomes the opening one of the Sonnets in a few years' time. Wilson held the congenial view that practice was more important than theory, for 'rhetoric was first made by wise men, and not wise men by rhetoric'.[4] We are given examples of rhetorical devices which Shakespeare uses over and over. There is *descriptio*, for instance, as applied to nations : 'the Englishman for feeding and changing of apparel ; the Dutchman for drinking ; the Frenchman for pride and inconstancy ; the Spaniard for nimbleness of body and much disdain ; the Italian for great wit and policy ; the Scot for boldness ; and the Boeme for stubbornness'.[5] Characters to become familiar to us appear in sequence in Wilson's pages : Timon, 'a deadly hater of all company', Portia, Brutus's wife, Lucretia and others.

Rhetoric had sharp direct modes as well as the rotund and elaborate.[6] Line for line exchanges are frequent at intervals in the early plays and evidently audiences delighted in them — very suitable for taunts between opponents in the Wars of the Roses, and no less for the banter between those other opponents, men and women in love. Another kind of delight that Shakespeare provided for his early audiences was that of amplification, piling up speeches with metaphor, until we have an oration like that of Queen Margaret on the battlefield of Tewkesbury (*3 Henry VI*, V. iv) with nearly forty lines on the theme of shipwreck, so vivid that many have been driven to conclude that Shakespeare had experienced one. If that isn't a tribute to rhetoric's prime object of persuasion ! Even the language of love was deliberate and artificial. Contrary to modern ideas, this heightened the emotions : with the Elizabethans verbal artifice corresponds with a rise in the emotional temperature. We are not to read backwards from the subsequent dominance of blank verse to disapprove the large elements of rhymed verse, of sonnet forms, stanzaic speeches ending in a rhymed couplet, quatrains that proliferate in all the early plays. A large part of three scenes of *1 Henry VI* is in heroic couplets. Frequently in all three parts he ends a scene, or even a short speech, with a rhymed couplet.

Here was the poet, first and foremost, at work — though it does not stand in disjunction from the dramatist : as a player he would know how it sounded ; it was designed to vary and try out the effect. We cannot over-estimate the importance of Shakespeare's being an actor : he learned the exact tone of speech to hold a large and varied audience. Here is the difference between school-rhetoric and the real art of persuasion : engaging the sympathy of an audience.

That Shakespeare was reading the poets and trying his hand at poetry in these formative years we may infer from the fact that from the moment he breaks upon public attention, with plays no less than with poems, his verse is fluent, practised, facile. He was a rhyming poet — and all through his life his natural ear for rhyme, his facility for it, comes cropping up in places where it is not needed, sometimes where it is not wanted, in the middle of blank verse lines as well as at the end.

In this year 1587 there was a reissue of Arthur Brooke's *Tragical History of Romeus and Juliet*, first printed in 1562. It is the basis of *Romeo and Juliet*, but even earlier various *motifs* and incidents appear in *The Two Gentlemen of Verona*, one of Shakespeare's first comedies. For the difference between early Elizabethan poetry and what it has become by 1590, as also for a borrowing characteristic of Shakespeare all through, let us compare Brooke's lumbering fourteeners :

> The proverb saith unminded oft are they that are unseen.
> And as out of a plank a nail a nail doth drive,
> So novel love out of the mind the ancient love doth rive.[7]

For such verses Brooke should have been drowned. (He was : going over to serve at Le Havre in 1563.) In early Shakespeare the lines become :

> Even as one heat another heat expels,
> Or as one nail by strength drives out another,
> So the remembrance of my former love
> Is by a newer object quite forgotten.

There is the difference between someone who is trying to write poetry without any gift for it, and a born poet.

Perhaps in these years Shakespeare was closest to the humble, charming Daniel. His own instinct agreed with Daniel's conviction that poetry depicted nature, and he was influenced by Daniel's example both in form and diction, in purity of style and in naturalness of expression.[8] In 1592 Daniel published *The Complaint of Rosamond*, along with his Delia sonnets. This poem is directly imitated by what we must take to be Shakespeare's first piece, his prentice-work, *A Lover's Complaint*. The subject is much the same — the loss of her virginity by a maid who has allowed herself to be overborne by a lover who proved false. The poem has a country setting, as it might be the Cotswolds :

> From off a hill whose concave womb re-worded
> A plaintful story from a sistering vale . . .

The young woman appears,

> Upon her head a platted hive of straw,
> Which fortified her visage from the sun . . .

> Oft did she heave her napkin to her eyne,
> Which on it had conceited characters . . .

She proceeds to tell her story, a sexy one of the kind that never ceased to appeal to Shakespeare, and of her treatment at the hands (and not only the hands) of a handsome youth whose like we recognise in the Sonnets as in *Venus and Adonis* : long, hanging curls, hardly any hair as yet upon his chin :

> His qualities were beauteous as his form,
> For maiden-tongued he was, and thereof free ;
> Yet, if men moved him, was he such a storm
> As oft 'twixt May and April is to see,
> When winds breathe sweet, unruly though they be . . .

> Well could he ride, and often men would say,
> 'That horse his mettle from his rider takes !'

(From even this much we see that Shakespeare had by now read some Chaucer as well as some Spenser.) Such a youth was too much for the poor young woman :

> That he did in the general bosom reign
> Of young, of old, and sexes both enchanted,
> To dwell with him in thoughts, or to remain
> In personal duty, following where he haunted :
> Consents bewitched, ere he desire, have granted,
> And dialogued for him what he would say,
> Asked their own wills and made their wills obey.

We recognise the characteristics of the young man of the Sonnets.[9] The play on the word 'will' is repeated in those : the secondary meaning, to an Elizabethan, was something essentially feminine, and it was this precious citadel that the young man breached.

> So many have that never touched his hand
> Sweetly supposed them mistress of his heart.
> My woeful self that did in freedom stand
> And was my own fee-simple, not in part,
> What with his art in youth and youth in art
> Threw my affections in his charmèd power,
> Reserved the stalk and gave him all my flower.

There follow certain moral reflections :

> But, ah ! whoever shunned by precedent
> The destined ill she must herself assay ?
> Or forced examples, 'gainst her own content,
> To put the by-past perils in her way ?
> Counsel may stop awhile what will not stay ;
> For when we rage, advice is often seen
> By blunting us to make our wits more keen.

Shakespeare had already had enough experience of life, with Anne Hathaway, to know the truth of that ; however, like a gentleman, if at some sacrifice, he had made an honest woman of her. And it could be pleaded, as he does again and again in the Sonnets :

> All my offences that abroad you see
> Are errors of the blood, none of the mind.

From the first Shakespeare was a magpie, an inveterate borrower. It is true that there was a lot of language — phrases, images, citations — that formed a common stock among these poets, still more among the dramatists ; and there was much borrowing to and fro. But Shakespeare is the most generous borrower of them all ; he picks up right and left, makes use of whatever he lays his hand on — naturally enough with his early restricted opportunities. Over and above that it was his nature — chameleon-like, except that he improved the colours he took on. There is the genius : the most adept at annexing from all sources, the most adaptive and absorptive, sucking up everything that comes his way, he yet leaves his own personal stamp upon it : it is absorbed and transmuted.

He drew upon Daniel's *Civil Wars*, four books of which appeared in 1595, for *Richard II*. A poem in Watson's *Hekatompathia* inspired the passage on Time in *The Rape of Lucrece*. Sidney and Daniel are echoed in the Sonnets ; the Robin Hood ballads inspired the outlaws in *The Two Gentlemen of Verona* and contributed to the forest theme of *As You Like It*. This last play was suggested by Lodge's *Rosalynde*, which appeared in 1590. The plot of *The Winter's Tale* was taken from Greene's *Pandosto*, which first came out in 1588, so that Shakespeare could have read it in these early reading years and been reminded of it when it was reprinted in 1607. The names of *The Winter's Tale*, Leontes, Antigonus, Cleomenes, Archidamus and Mopsa, all come from Sidney's *Arcadia* ; Pericles is the Pyrocles of the *Arcadia*. The story of the Paphlagonian unkind king, which provided the sub-plot of *King Lear*, is also adapted from the *Arcadia*, which Shakespeare could have been reading at any time since it came out in 1590. The name Menaphon he got from Marlowe's *Tamburlaine*, or he could have got it from Greene's *Menaphon*. For he lifted names from all over the place — like Dickens, except that Shakespeare's came from books and from history, not from the lower-class streets of London.

By far the closest and most exciting influence upon the young Shakespeare was that of Marlowe — one would say that it was overwhelming, except that Shakespeare stood up to it and came through it still himself. For, in fact, his own nature and temperament were very different from Marlowe's. Marlowe's stormy, fractured personality and his aspiring genius made an astonishing impact upon the theatre and the minds of the young writers during the brief period of his ascendancy, the years 1588 to 1593. Even to Heywood, writing in the reign of James I, Marlowe was still

the best of poets in that age.

What would he not have achieved if he had lived ! — his was perhaps the greatest of all losses to English literature.

Shakespeare did not belong to Marlowe's circle, but he naturally admired his genius. Indeed he acknowledged his equality as a poet, for we shall find subsequently that there is no reason now for doubting that Marlowe was the rival poet of the Sonnets, and that Shakespeare's fortune was far more closely entangled with Marlowe's in the last months of his life than anyone has hitherto suspected.[10] We shall find that Marlowe was on the way to ousting Shakespeare in his patron's favour, or at least taking first place ; that there is every reason to think that *Venus and Adonis* and Marlowe's unfinished *Hero and Leander* were written in rivalry for that favour ; and, most surprising of all, that *Venus and Adonis* was a length ahead—the influences here that used to be thought to be Marlowe's upon Shakespeare are seen to be the other way round, or at least mutual. In this atmosphere they would have seen each other's work in progress. Shakespeare's was published in the spring in which Marlowe perished miserably in the tavern at Deptford, leaving *Hero and Leander* a fragment, not published till five years later.

Shakespeare had every reason for never forgetting *Hero and Leander*. The subject is mentioned again and again in later plays, sometimes somewhat ruefully, as in *As You Like It*, which also has the direct reference to Marlowe :

> Dead shepherd, now I find thy saw of might :
> '*Who ever loved that loved not at first sight ?* '

This is a quotation from Marlowe's poem, but we find other phrases from it sinking into Shakespeare's mind, to come to the surface years later : Marlowe's —

> A kind of twilight break . . . this false morn
> Brought forth the day before the day was born —

comes to life again in Shakespeare's song :

> Take, O, take those lips away,
> That so sweetly were forsworn ;
> And those eyes, the break of day,
> Lights that do mislead the morn.

It is touching to find Marlowe's words,

> where all is whist and still,
> Save that the sea, playing on yellow sand,

echoing still in Shakespeare's ear at the end of his career, in *The Tempest* :

> Come unto these yellow sands,
> And then take hands :
> Curtsied when you have and kissed
> The wild waves whist . . .

One could cite more ; but Marlowe's dramatic impact was more powerful still.

'Shakespeare's was a harder way than Marlowe's, with his six to seven years at the university ; but though Marlowe was more learned than Shakespeare, somehow Shakespeare acquired as much of the culture of his age as was necessary to him as a poet.'[11] Still, in the circumstances of the age, those years gave Marlowe a long lead ; moreover, his arrogant temperament was that of a leader, where Shakespeare was content to follow, humbly enough but more wisely, learning all the time. The tremendous impact of Marlowe's starry genius is seen all through Shakespeare's early work. Aspiring, ambitious figures like Tamburlaine and the Duke of Guise are followed up, and improved on, with Richard III and Macbeth. The weak king Mycetes of *Tamburlaine* is echoed in the character of Henry VI, at length in the third part with an inner sympathy of which Marlowe was incapable, with such a type. Barabas the Jew is first echoed in Aaron in *Titus Andronicus*, and then with so much deepening in Shylock, and at length in that final portrait of villainy in Iago. Marlowe's Edward II is taken up and improved on, again with more sympathy and compassion, in Richard II. There are direct echoes of Faustus in several plays, in *Romeo, Troilus and Cressida, The Merry Wives*. In a sense Prospero is Shakespeare's Faustus, and we need not think of it as so remote a flowering since Marlowe's extraordinary play held the stage through all these years.

Though there are verbal echoes from Marlowe through all the plays, we must confine ourselves here to Shakespeare's apprenticeship. The *First Part* of *Henry VI* begins in Marlowe's style, popularised by *Tamburlaine*, with his planetary imagery :

> Hung be the heavens with black, yield day to night !
> Comets, importing change of times and states,
> Brandish your crystal tresses in the sky,
> And with them scourge the bad revolting stars
> That have consented unto Henry's death !

The very literary speech at the end of Act I reflects not only Tamburlaine's grief for Zenocrate but Marlowe's very rhythm :

> A statelier pyramis to her I'll rear
> Than Rhodope's or Memphis' ever was.

The *Third Part* of *Henry VI* continues to echo Marlowe :

> How sweet a thing it is to wear a crown,
> Within whose circuit is Elysium,
> And all that poets feign of bliss and joy.

The particular poet in mind here was Marlowe, and the famous lines we have quoted on the power of poetry. The passage also catches up Tamburlaine's

> Is it not passing brave to be a king
> And ride in triumph through Persepolis ?

It is fairly clear that Shakespeare was echoing those particular lines of Marlowe's, which end with

> One thought, one grace, one wonder, at the least ;

for, a scene or two later, Shakespeare comes out with

> Now are they but one lamp, one light, one sun.

There is a world of difference in their cast of mind revealed in those few words : Marlowe's mind more abstract and general, dedicated to intellectual power, Shakespeare's concrete and visual, but with the alliteration that is instinctive with a natural poet.

In the next Act, at the end of a fine speech of Gloucester's, looking forward to *Richard III*, we have two Marlowe references in two lines. They come after a few lines of classical inspiration which display the young Shakespeare showing off his school-learning, bent on making an impression even if he had not been to a university like the 'wits' :

> I'll play the orator as well as Nestor,
> Deceive more slily than Ulysses could,
> And, like a Sinon, take another Troy.
> I can add colours to the chameleon,
> Change shapes with Proteus for advantages,
> And set the murderous Machiavel to school.
> Can I do this and cannot get a crown ?

One line refers back to the *Massacre at Paris*, which was about the Machiavellianism of the Guise — a subject very congenial to Marlowe's political, amoral mind ; the other to *Tamburlaine*. Yet this same speech shows Shakespeare's difference : it has the imagery of a countryman, quite foreign to the urban Marlowe.

> And I, like one lost in a thorny wood,
> That rents the thorns and is rent with the thorns,
> Seeking a way and straying from the way . . .

And earlier, one detects a reflection of an experience when on tour, particularly when one finds it again in the Sonnets :

> Like one that stands upon a promontory,
> And spies a far-off shore where he would tread,
> Wishing his foot were equal with his eye,
> And chides the sea that sunders him from thence.

One cannot but think that this is Dover, looking across to France, for we know that Shakespeare's company several times visited Dover. There is a larger reflection of it all in *King Lear*.

Shakespeare already has his own grand language, different from Marlowe's, his lordly Latinised words and 'high terms'. Naïve as they are, they are effective, for they have his instinctive tact behind them. In his earliest work we hear of 'intermissive miseries' (note the hidden alliteration and the chime) : 'loathsome sequestration' (alliterative again) ; 'rehearse the method of my pen' ; 'particularities and petty sounds' ; 'my words effectual' ; 'and prove the period of their tyranny'. Or

> These eyes, like lamps whose wasting oil is spent,
> Wax dim, as drawing to their exigent.

Or

> But now the arbitrator of despairs,
> Just death, kind umpire of men's miseries,
> With sweet enlargement doth dismiss me hence.

It is all very grand and youthful, quite unlike Marlowe, already characteristically Shakespeare.

The three *Henry VI* plays show him to us very recognisably : no real writer can disguise himself in his work, though he may lose himself in it, and the young Shakespeare peeps out at us again and again. All through the early plays there is Shakespeare's passion for hunting the deer, and not merely in the imagery. Both the *Third Part* of *Henry VI* and *Titus Andronicus* have deer-hunt scenes :

> Under this thick-grown brake we'll shroud ourselves,
> For through this laund anon the deer will come,
> And in this covert will we make our stand,
> Culling the principal of all the deer.

Coming upon the wandering king, the keeper says,

> Ay, here's a deer whose skin's a keeper's fee.

In these plays the country and country sports are never far away ; there is falconry, the greyhounds

> Having the fearful flying hare in sight ;

taking woodcock in the gin, conies in the net. There is country lore in

> But when the fox hath once got in his nose,
> He'll soon find means to make the body follow,

as there is in this,

> like the owl by day,
> If he arise, be mocked and wondered at —

as happened still in the country days of my childhood.

These plays have a good deal of snake-imagery — perhaps they were written at home in full summer :

> Or as the snake, rolled in a flowering bank,
> With shining checkered slough, doth sting a child.

Images of swans bring the Avon, or the Thames, to mind :

> as I have seen a swan
> With bootless labour swim against the tide,
> And spend her strength with over-matching waves.

In *Titus Andronicus* Aaron says,

> For all the water in the ocean
> Can never turn the swan's black legs to white,
> Although she lave them hourly in the flood.

This reverberates a few years later in

> Not all the water in the rough, rude sea
> Can wash the balm from an anointed king.

We see Shakespeare on the way to becoming his own chief 'source', constantly re-handling, re-shaping, refining, improving. And yet Ben Jonson, the intellectual, was crude enough to say that Shakespeare 'wanted art'. This was never so, from the very beginning : always the instinctive artist, but of his own kind, not somebody else's.

Whether in London, or in the country, we can see him watching a bear-baiting :

> Or as a bear, encompassed round with dogs,
> Who having pinched a few and made them cry,
> The rest stand all aloof and bark at him.

We are very near to Stratford in the slaughter-house references that run all through these plays, with their tone of personal experience :

> And as the butcher takes away the calf,
> And binds the wretch, and beats it when it strays,
> Bearing it to the bloody slaughter-house . . .
> And as the dam runs lowing up and down,
> Looking the way her harmless young one went,
> And can do nought but wail her darling's loss . . .

There is pity in that, as there is always in Shakespeare ; not in Marlowe.

Pleasanter it is to think of Cotswold morris-dancers :

> I have seen
> Him caper upright like a wild Morisco,
> Shaking the bloody darts as he his bells . . .

or of such images as—

> like the night-owl's lazy flight,
> Or like a lazy thresher with a flail . . .

and we come upon the shepherd 'blowing of his nails'. This takes a more perfect form in a year or two's time :

> When icicles hang by the wall,
> And Dick, the shepherd, blows his nail.

While the line,

> Let Aesop fable in a winter's night,

brings to mind the thought of a schoolboy poring over his book many a winter's night in Henley Street.

Certainly Warwickshire is given a good show in the *Henry VI* plays. In the first part Sir William Lucy of Charlecote — he was actually sheriff of Warwickshire in Henry's reign — is brought on in two or three scenes, spiritedly fighting in France. Joan of Arc says,

> I think this upstart is old Talbot's ghost,
> He speaks with such a proud commanding spirit.

That ought to have pleased the neighbours out at Charlecote — it was a characteristic neighbourly gesture. In the *Third Part* of the play, Warwick the king-maker naturally has an important rôle, but Shakespeare goes out of his way to bring the opposing forces to 'a plain in Warwickshire', 'a camp near Warwick', King Edward's challenge and entry into the city of Coventry. Familiar places in the neighbourhood are all brought in. The Earl of Oxford has arrived at Dunsmore : it is the heath that the road skirts between Dunchurch and Coventry. Warwick's brother has reached Daintry 'with a puissant troop' : this is, of course, the proper pronunciation of Daventry. There enters Sir John Somerville — of another Warwickshire family — of whom the Earl asks, 'How nigh is Clarence now ?' Somerville replies, 'At Southam I did leave him with his forces'.

These early plays add some strokes to our personal portrait of him, consistent with what we learn of him all through. There is the insistent concern with gentility. It is true that this is in keeping with the characters speaking, but when it is insisted upon over and over we may conclude that it means more for the author.

> Let him that is a true-born gentleman,
> And stands upon the honour of his birth . . .

> We grace the yeoman by conversing with him . . .
> Spring crestless yeomen from so deep a root ?

These are aristocrats speaking ; but we find that kind King Henry and unkind Jack Cade have the same opinion of the common people as a mob :

> Look, as I blow this feather from my face,
> And as the air blows it to me again,
> Obeying with my wind when I do blow,
> And yielding to another when it blows,
> Commanded always by the greater gust :
> Such is the lightness of you common men.

While Cade says, 'Was ever feather so lightly blown to and fro as this multitude ?' It is always the Cades who know best the facts of popular psychology.

In these Cade scenes of *2 Henry VI*, Shakespeare first finds the comic voice of the people, and one of his own most authentic voices : 'dost thou use to write the name, or hast thou a mark to thyself like an honest plain-dealing man ?' (Did Shakespeare think of his own father when he wrote those lines ?) 'Is not this a lamentable thing, that of the skin of an innocent lamb should be made parchment ? that parchment, being scribbled o'er, should undo a man ? Some say the bee stings ; but I say, 'tis the bee's wax, for I did but seal once to a thing, and I was never mine own man since.' How that must have made the merry young men from the Inns of Court laugh ! An unfortunate peer is charged by the rebels : 'Thou hast most traitorously corrupted the youth of the realm in erecting a grammar school ; and whereas, before, our forefathers had no other books but the score and the tally, thou hast caused printing to be used ; and, contrary to the king, his crown and dignity, thou hast built a paper-mill. It will be proved to thy face that thou hast men about thee that usually talk of a noun and a verb, and such abominable words as no Christian ear can endure to hear.' How through and through this man of the people knew the people ! The wonderful thing is that he did not hate them for their stupidity, as Ben Jonson did. But then Shakespeare saw through everybody equally. John Holland — it is the name of one of the actors whose name has come through from the original manuscript — is given the sentence : 'Well, I say it was never merry world in England since gentlemen came up'. The audience would catch the reference to the famous saying of the reactionary old Duke of Norfolk, who thought it was never merry England since the new learning came up. We may cry quits : there is truth and rough justice in it all.

In these early plays, 'the unlearned man from Stratford was an adept at concealing ignorance'.[12] He does not know any English history outside the chronicle he is following ; if the chronicle makes a mistake he follows that too. What history he knows is classical, coming from Stratford grammar school. To impress the audience he quotes Latin tags, naïvely enough :

> Integer vitae, scelerisque purus,
> Non eget Mauri jaculis nec arcu.
> O, 'tis a verse in Horace : I know it well :
> I read it in the grammar long ago.

Of course, Elizabethan audiences were more easily impressible. Nevertheless, the poet was there above all, obvious in his earliest manner, full of quibbles and conceits, of word-play and rhetoric, visual images and imaginative tropes, verbal sensibility and tact shaping the lines for him.

Then, too, there was the sympathy of his nature, such as Marlowe never had. Marlowe must have had fascination and intellectual glamour ; his strong personality exerted an attraction for some, repulsion for others. Small strokes in passing betray the gentleness of Shakespeare's nature :

> for when a world of men
> Could not prevail with all their oratory,
> Yet hath a woman's kindness over-ruled.

It is Talbot that is speaking, but it is true Shakespeare all through — the line is unthinkable for Marlowe.

So, too, with the inner affection that he ultimately develops for the character of Henry VI. In the first two plays of the trilogy he is not much more than a lay-figure, a young weak king who is no good at ruling. But in the *Third Part*, Shakespeare already shows his capacity for portraying the growth of a character — where Marlowe's are static, sprung fully grown from the brain of Athene. Henry's long speech on the battlefield of Towton must have been as surprising in its way, though an absolute contrast, as one of Tamburlaine's splendid ranting orations. The spirit of it is pastoral, the theme the superiority of simple country life to that of kings.

> O God ! methinks it were a happy life,
> To be no better than a homely swain :
> To sit upon a hill as I do now,
> To carve out dials quaintly point by point,
> Thereby to see the minutes how they run . . .
> So many hours must I tend my flock ;
> So many hours must I take my rest ;
> So many hours must I contemplate ;
> So many hours must I sport myself ;
> So many days my ewes have been with young ;
> So many weeks ere the poor fools will ean ;
> So many years ere I shall shear the fleece . . .

Here one sees the devices of school-rhetoric passing over into poetry.

> Ah ! what a life were this ! how sweet ! how lovely !
> Gives not the hawthorn bush a sweeter shade
> To shepherds, looking on their silly sheep,
> Than doth a rich embroidered canopy
> To kings, that fear their subjects' treachery ?

One cannot imagine such sentiments from Marlowe, with his self-identification with the ambitious and aspiring, with Tamburlaine and Faustus. Shakespeare, like all writers, has his moments of self-identification. Here is one of them, and it has a characteristic ambivalence. As an actor, he came to take kingly parts ; again and again one observes this inner sympathy with the burden of kingship, with Richard II, with his opponent, Henry IV, and with Henry V. Underneath the deference, the humility, he knew that he was as good as any king : the ambivalence, we shall see, is given direct expression in the Sonnets.

The patriotic theme, which became Shakespeare's particular concern as a dramatist, is already announced with *Henry VI*.

> *Hastings :* Why, knows not Montague, that of itself
> England is safe, if true within itself ?

Montague : Yes, but the safer when 'tis backed with France.

Hastings : 'Tis better using France than trusting France :
Let us be backed with God and with the seas
Which he hath given for fence impregnable,
And with their helps only defend ourselves.

This sentiment received more mature expression a few years later with *King John*, but we may not realise how precisely the passage expresses the actual situation in the years immediately after the Armada. In 1591 Elizabeth accepted the necessity of coming to the aid of Henry of Navarre, with France divided from top to bottom between the Catholic League backed by Spain, and the Protestants and Politiques behind the king. Sir John Norris was sent over with an expedition to Brittany, where the Spaniards were entrenched, and the gallant young Essex got his way to lead another to Normandy. He was the darling of the London mob, always popular whatever he did. The invasion of Normandy brought back a surge of memories of the fighting in France in the Hundred Years War, of brave Talbot, with whose name French peasants frightened their children to bed.

It was this surge of patriotic feeling, the memories of past triumphs, the sense of crisis, the excitement, that the *Henry VI* plays expressed. They were intended to match the mood and hence their popularity. Talbot once more walked the stage. 'How it would have joyed brave Talbot, the terror of the French', wrote Nashe, 'to think that after he had lain two hundred years in his tomb, he should triumph again on the stage and have his bones embalmed with the tears of ten thousand spectators at least — at several times — who, in the tragedian that represents his person, imagine they behold him fresh bleeding.' Nor were their expectations of Essex entirely neglected : it was given to Sir William Lucy in the play to bear away the bodies of Talbot and his companions, and

from their ashes shall be reared
A phoenix that shall make all France afeared.

Recent scholarship is at last reaching firmer ground as to the nature of Shakespeare's earliest work in the three plays of *Henry VI* — as against the mad disintegrators of his text — and very important conclusions flow from this as to his career, how he was occupying himself in the unknown years prior to 1592, and his relationship to Marlowe, that of rivalry and mutual influence.[13]

We can now see more clearly how the three parts of *Henry VI* fit into a general design on the part of their ambitious actor-dramatist, their aim being to dramatise a large tract of the English past. We see their inspiration as coming directly from the surge of national feeling that arose from the supreme test for the English of Armada year. 'The Johannes Factotum set himself and achieved the ambitious task of staging, in his country's finest hour, its quasi-Biblical story, from the original sin of Henry IV to the grand redemption of the Tudors.' [14]

Perhaps this is going a little far in one leap : it is more likely that the incipient dramatist saw the possibilities of making plays out of the English chronicles, was out to make best use of his material, and then that the design grew in the course of doing it. And that — the natural way of doing it, after all — also helps to account for inconsistencies, slips and occasional contradictions. (Some of these are simply due to his sources.) We are at length at liberty to stay our minds on the massive common sense of Dr. Johnson, who himself knew the ways of authorship better than textual critics : 'the diction, the versification, and the figures are Shakespeare's', and again, with regard to the crudities of these first plays, 'in the productions of genius there will be irregularity'.[15] With regard to *2 Henry VI* he wrote, 'it is apparent that this play begins where the former ends, and continues the series of trans-actions, of which it presupposes the first part already known. This is sufficient proof that the second and third parts were not written without dependence on the first.' Modern scholarship now ratifies this in regard to *1 Henry VI* : 'the play bears the stamp of a single mind in the organisation of material, in its adapta-tion to the exposition of a grand central design extending beyond the play itself'.

More intimately to our purpose is to notice how Shakespeare's earliest play bears out our portrayal of his education. One of his recognised sources in it is Cooper's *Thesaurus*, the book which vicar Bretchgirdle left to the school at Stratford. 'All the figures and devices of classical rhetoric, the Senecan stichomythia, the soliloquy, classical similes and allusions' of his schooling appear in profusion through all three *Henry VI* plays, while the imagery and verse-techniques — in spite of understandable *naïvetés* and lapses — are unmistakably his.[16]

The subject itself has all the *naïveté* and simplicity of the national feeling of 1588. *1 Henry VI* is, as an American scholar notes, 'a play about courage, prowess, and assumed righteousness of the English as represented by such loyal and able leaders as Salisbury, Bedford, Warwick, and above all Lord Talbot ; and about the opportunism, treachery and fox-like successes of the French as represented by the fraud and moral depravity of La Pucelle'.[17] It *is* very *naïve* ; but nationalism is nationalism, and there was the inspiration — though at the time the English were fighting Spain, not France.

This brings us to the question of date. All three *Henry VI* plays reflect Shakespeare's reading of the first three books of Spenser's *Faerie Queene*, published in December 1589. It is very probable that the first *Henry VI* play belongs to 1590 and the other two to 1591, when Essex's expedition to Normandy would redouble the appeal of the subject and lead to a demand for more. With these chronicle-plays the actor-dramatist invented something original : though influenced by *Tamburlaine*, they were quite different from that, with its concentration on one character. These plays were episodic, with no one dominant character ; they were like an Elizabethan serial, with all the appeal of action, hand-to-hand fighting, cannon-shot, deaths, funerals, processions, spectacle and pageantry. Plenty of drums and trumpets — there was never any doubt of their popular appeal.

And so, in return, Marlowe — the intellectual dramatist, the poet, no actor — was influenced by his junior, the rising actor-playwright. *Edward II* follows the model of *Henry VI* with a weak, undominant character at the centre of the action, and it is full of Shakespearean echoes. *Edward II* was the one play of Marlowe's performed by the transitory Pembroke's company — as were Shakespeare's *Henry VI* and others of his earliest plays. When he capped the *Henry VI* trilogy with *Richard III*, it was Shakespeare who was influenced by Marlowe. As again, after Marlowe's death, *Edward II* has its influence upon the germination of Shakespeare's *Richard II* : 'it is curious to think that in contemplating *Edward II*, he may have had in mind also its indebtedness to himself'.

These early relations and interactions are thus subtle, and Shakespeare's emergence from the wings, once so dark a matter, is now becoming clear. In any case it is a mistake to read backwards before reading forwards, and to find *1 Henry VI* unworthy of the author of *Hamlet* and *The Tempest*. The *First Part* of *Henry VI* is just such a play as an actor commencing author might write.

Even so, Shakespeare was no longer young, though a tyro as a playwright. He was twenty-six in 1590, twenty-five in 1589 if that is when he began contemplating it. His slow development at first, his comparatively late arrival at his powers as a writer, turned out an immense advantage not only in the long run — it became evident as soon as he got really going. It enabled him to take in, to observe and absorb so much before he started to write — where the more brilliantly precocious man, moving faster and maturing earlier, absorbs less. And this relates to, may have been a condition of, the particular kind of genius Shakespeare had : mimetic and imitative rather than intellectual, exploratory and searching, always reaching towards new expressions of his art ; adaptive and absorbing, following the form of things, the patterns of life, instead of imposing his own will on them — except in the idiom of his art ; ambivalent, capable of holding contraries within a single impression ; at once romantic and realist, poet and drama-tist, growing to the last. The fact that he began late meant all the more experience and latent energy accumulated in previous years, all the greater pressure to pour forth in torrential profusion when he came to it. Two things are most remarkable, though hardly ever remarked on ; they are indeed linked — the late start and long apprenticeship, the speed, pressure and unrivalled creative energy once started.

CHAPTER VII

Reputation

SUDDENLY, in September 1592, the obscurity in which we have been so long wandering, with Shakespeare, is illuminated by a flash of light : Robert Greene's attack on him, written when dying, bitter words that tell us a good deal about Greene himself, the rising dramatist of whom he was envious, and the literary life of Elizabethan London. This first reference to Shakespeare in London used to be taken as the starting point of his career as a dramatist. In fact, it is a recognition that he has arrived, that his apprenticeship is virtually behind him, that he is beginning to be well known. He now has a body of work to show. By 1592 he has accomplished the three chronicle plays of *Henry VI*, *The Comedy of Errors* and *The Two Gentlemen of Verona*.

Robert Greene, six years older than Shakespeare, was the most talked-about figure in literary life, especially in its Bohemian reaches — he saw to that, for he was always writing about himself. His appearance was no less familiar, with his long red beard, peaked like the spire of a steeple, says Nashe, which 'he cherished continually without cutting, whereat a man might hang a jewel, it was so sharp and pendant'.[1] He was the most prolific and versatile of them all, pouring out prose romances, pamphlets in the vein of social realism, plays and poems of some charm. Thus he made his living, and was prodigal of it. Literature was his trade — a rather modern type, an all-round literary journalist.

His first work, *Mamillia*, was written after the model of Lyly's *Euphues*, which had such an influence as a manifesto of the new refinement in culture. Greene's finest prose-romance, *Pandosto*, was taken by Shakespeare, ironically enough, years later for the story of *The Winter's Tale*. There followed a succession of pamph-lets on the ways of low life in town, the arts of coney-catching, or cheating at cards, of cross-biting, or blackmail of men pursuing whores by their husbands, real or supposed. This opened up a rich vein, which Greene exhausted with half a dozen tracts for the times. He then turned to plays — a poor imitation of *Tamburlaine* with his *Alphonsus*, and a more successful one of *Dr. Faustus* with his *Friar Bacon and Friar Bungay*. This gave more scope for his own comic vein, as did another play *James IV*. Greene was at his best as a writer when most himself.

An East Anglian, like Nashe, he was born at Norwich in 1558 and went up to Cambridge. He took his M.A. at both universities, a fact of which he was vain and blazoned it on all his works. He married a gentlewoman, spent her dower and then deserted her for a loose life in London. Henceforth a constant theme in his writing was that of the deserted wife, the devotion of a good woman to an unworthy man. Repentance was rather his forte, and he turned that to good use, too, in his writings. Now, in September 1592, he was dying, after that last fatal banquet of Rhenish wine and pickled herring with Nashe. He was dying in the house of the kind-hearted woman who kept him, the mother of his base-born son, Fortunatus. When he was dead, his woman crowned him with a garland of bay leaves : he was thirty-four, and was buried in the churchyard next Bedlam.

He left behind him a time-bomb which has gone on reverberating ever since. The printer, Chettle, who later became a playwright, saw Greene's last writing through the press. It contained a vehement warning to three playwright acquaintances of his — Peele, Marlowe and Nashe — against the players, one of whom in particular was taking it upon him to become a dramatist, and successful too, for he could turn his hand to anything. They were fools, all three of his acquaintance, if they would not be warned by Greene's experience and the misery in which he was dying :

> for unto none of you, like me, sought those burrs [the players] to cleave : those puppets, I mean, that spake from our mouths, those antics garnished in our colours. Is it not strange that I, to whom they all have been beholding, is it not like that you to whom they all have been beholding, shall — were ye in that case as I am now — be both at once of them forsaken ? Yea, trust them not : for there is an upstart crow, beautified with our feathers, that with his 'Tiger's heart wrapped in a player's hide', supposes he is as well able to bombast out a blank verse as the best of you, and being an absolute Johannes Factotum, is in his own conceit the only Shake-scene in a country.[2]

To those who know the devious ways of Elizabethan controversy, and the usual technique of insult, this is crystal clear.
For the line that is twisted to apply to Shakespeare is the famous
cry from York's dying curse upon Queen Margaret in *3 Henry VI* :

> O tiger's heart wrapped in a woman's hide.

We learn from this that the new man was an upstart, or considered
so by Greene ; that he was a player, who thought himself as well
able to turn out blank verse as any of those dramatists, the university wits ; that he was not beyond beautifying himself with
their feathers, making use of their work ; that they should take
warning, for he had a good conceit of himself and was ready to
turn his hand to anything.

This famous attack has been scrutinised *ad nauseam*, yet perhaps
not all the significance has been wrung out of the player's 'tiger's
heart' — if we are to take it seriously and not put it down to a
dying man's delirium. It looks as if Greene had some personal
reason for resentment against Shakespeare. There is also the
charge of plagiarism, the mere actor beautifying himself with
their feathers, that belonged to the playwrights. That it was
taken to mean this is clear both from Chettle's apology, and from
the defence of Greene that followed it, by R. B. in *Greene's Funerals*,
published in February 1594 :

> Greene is the pleasing object of an eye :
> Greene pleased the eyes of all that looked upon him.
> Greene is the ground of every painter's dye :
> Greene gave the ground to all that wrote upon him.
> Nay more, the men that so eclipsed his fame
> Purloined his plumes : can they deny the same ?

But 'tiger's heart' — in what way can Shakespeare have given
Greene reason for such bitterness ? The gravamen of his charge
is that the players, who were beholden to him, had left him to
die in misery. What wonder, after his expressed opinion and
treatment of them ? Had he any particular reason to expect help
or succour from Shakespeare ?

That Shakespeare much resented the imputations upon him
we know from Chettle's apology in the preface to his *Kind-Heart's
Dream*, of December that year, 1592. Marlowe also took offence,
for he had been described recognisably, if anonymously, as an
atheist and Machiavellian. Chettle made no apology to him, but
merely replied that he had cut out from Greene's tract yet another

charge, which 'had it been true, yet to publish it had been intolerable'. This was an obvious reference to Marlowe's homosexuality : he considered that 'all that loved not tobacco and boys were fools'. Chettle was a fat, easy-going, good sort, but he had no desire to know Christopher Marlowe.

> With neither of them that take offence was I acquainted, and with one of them I care not if I never be. The other, whom at that time I did not so much spare as since I wish I had ; for that . . . I might have used my own discretion, especially in such a case, the author being dead. That I did not, I am sorry as if the original fault had been my fault : because myself have seen his demeanour no less civil than he excellent in the quality he professes. Besides, divers of worship have reported his uprightness of dealing, which argues his honesty, and his facetious grace in writing that approves his art.

What a lot this tells us about Shakespeare, and how it fits in with what we gathered from Greene ! It is borne out, too, by what Aubrey learned of the direct tradition coming down through Beeston, the player. Shakespeare was 'the more to be admired *quia* he was not a company-keeper'.[3] He 'lived in Shoreditch, wouldn't be debauched, and, if invited to, writ — he was in pain'. With his honesty impugned by Greene's charge of plagiarism, he had taken the trouble to present a certificate as to his uprightness of dealing from 'divers of worship'. That shows us that the company Shakespeare preferred, the acquaintance he already had, was of good class and breeding, rather than the literary riff-raff of London. Chettle himself did not know him, but had obviously received a polite protest, and now was able to bear witness to his excellence in his profession as player, as well as to the attractive grace of his art as playwright.

Greene's attack brings out all the more clearly that Shakespeare was not one of *them*, but an outsider. He was neither a university wit, nor a literary journalist, nor a hanger-on of the Court. He was just a player. No-one could have foreseen that in that degradation lay his fortune as a dramatist : he was so much the more professional. And Greene's outburst announced the approaching end of an epoch, of the domination of the drama by the university wits.

We have seen that the years 1592–4 were years of theatrical disorganisation, and for an ill reason — both 1592 and 1593 were a period of severe plague, the theatres were closed most of the time, open only for short spells, the companies forced to travel in the worst conditions, some of them broken by their experience. The tradition comes through Sir William Davenant that before Shakespeare became an actor he took charge of horses at the play-house-door and that he was good with horses. Why, indeed, not? We know from the Sonnets that he *was* good with horses; we can also glimpse that he had a struggle to establish himself. Gentle-men would need horses to reach the Theatre or Curtain out in the fields. He would not have been acting much in the plague years 1592–3, though we may infer from the Sonnets that he was at some time on tour. We may conclude that he devoted himself much more to writing, when we consider the amount of work that emerged from those years. The marked success of the *Henry VI* plays made an encouraging start. To these years *Richard III*, *Titus Andronicus*, and the *Comedy of Errors* are assigned. It seems that we must place *Titus Andronicus* before *Richard III* on grounds of the greater maturity of the latter — indeed, in a sense, *Titus* is still school-work. To these early years we have also to allot *The Two Gentlemen of Verona* and *The Taming of the Shrew*. Then, too, 'the plague years gave opportunity for the development of literary ambitions outside the range of the drama, which took shape in the narrative poems of *Venus and Adonis* (1593) and *Lucrece* (1594).'⁴ What a pile of work to have accomplished, in addition to many of the Sonnets! We know that he worked with ease and rapidity, but no wonder he was not a company-keeper and did not accept invitations to go out on the loose.

Chambers thinks it possible that Shakespeare may have been writing for three companies in the hard and shifting circumstances of 1592–4. When *Titus Andronicus* was published in 1594, in a good text almost certainly from the author's manuscript, the title-page says, 'as it was played by the right honourable the Earl of Derby, Earl of Pembroke and Earl of Sussex their servants'. This seems to imply performance by those three companies in succession. Pembroke's men may have been a troupe splitting off from the main grouping of Alleyn's and Strange's men. These took the name of Henry Herbert, second Earl of Pembroke, whose wife was the celebrated Mary Sidney, Sir Philip's sister, herself a writer of distinction and a patron of conviction. This group did not last long, but during its brief spell it acted *Titus Andronicus*, *2* and *3 Henry VI* and *The Taming of the Shrew*; it is probable enough that Shakespeare acted with them. What is more surprising is that Marlowe's *Edward II* was acted by Pembroke's men ; it is generally agreed that in this case Marlowe was responding to the influence, and the challenge, of Shakespeare's *Henry VI* plays.

The influence of Kyd is second only to that of Marlowe upon the new actor-dramatist.

Thomas Kyd was four or five years senior to these two, having been born in November 1558, a fortnight before the Queen ascended the throne. The son of a London scrivener, he was educated at Merchant Taylors school. He did not go on to the university : his knowledge of the classics, like Shakespeare's, was that of a clever schoolboy, improved by his own reading. He was well read in Seneca, the translations of whose tragedies, by Thomas Newton, were appearing at intervals from the beginning of the reign, and this became the leading influence upon his drama. He was not the equal of his brilliant juniors as a poet, but he was a born dramatist, with a gift for contriving strong situations and bringing to the full all the existing resources of the theatre.

He won his reward with the resounding success and inexhaustible popularity of *The Spanish Tragedy*. It had been written in the year or so before the Armada, yet now in 1592 it was still in the full tide of popularity at the Rose, along with *The Jew oj Malta*. *The Jew of Malta* and *Tamburlaine*, indeed, were perhaps indebted to Kyd's influence, as also were Shakespeare's *3 Henry VI* and, most of all, *Titus Andronicus*. *The Spanish Tragedy*, with its revenge-motif and old Jeronimo acting mad, its tantrums and its curses, was the most famous of all the dramas of this earlier period. The cry for revenge that rang through the theatre is echoed in *3 Henry VI* :

Warwick, revenge ! brother, revenge my death !

Shakespeare parodies the bathos in the play to which he owed so much, but not unkindly, when he came to write *Hamlet* :

For if the King like not the comedy,
Why then, belike, he likes it not, perdy.[5]

Kyd then was in his mind, for Kyd was in all probability the author of the lost *Hamlet* on which the greater was based.

In May of this year 1593 Kyd fell into fearful trouble. The times were distempered, plague was raging — some two hundred deaths a week in the city — and there was agitation against alien immigrants, with libels being posted up inciting the mob to violence against them. In the search for their authors Kyd's rooms were raided, and incriminating papers were found denying the 'truths' of the Christian religion. Kyd was arrested, and tortured in Bridewell. In panic he made damaging revelations against Marlowe, dissociating himself from him and his opinions, and shifting the blame. Two summers before they had been writing in the same chamber, and the papers that were found shuffled together with Kyd's were Marlowe's — fragments of some Socinian treatise. But Kyd had never liked or approved of Marlowe, so he said, for 'he was intemperate and of a cruel heart', nor had he himself been a member of his atheistical circle with 'Hariot, Warner, Royden and some stationers in Paul's churchyard' (*i.e.* Edward Blount), and he disclaimed Marlowe's 'monstrous opinions'.[6] Marlowe was ordered to appear before the Privy Council a week later, but by the end of the month he was dead.

Kyd gave evidence that Marlowe was engaged in persuading men of quality to go to the King of Scots, 'where, if he had lived, he told me when I saw him last he meant to be'. Evidently, in the last months of his life Marlowe was in a very excited frame of mind. Kyd said that his first acquaintance with Marlowe was because he bore the name of servant to 'my lord', in whose household Kyd had served for the past six years. But Marlowe's attachment was simply in writing for his players, 'for never could my Lord endure his name or sight, when he had heard of his conditions'. We do not know who this discriminating, or conventional, lord was : all we know is that Marlowe's public plays were performed by the Lord Admiral's men, except for *Edward II*, which was performed by the Earl of Pembroke's. On his release, Kyd spent a winter's week in translating Garnier's *Cornelia*, and dedicated it to the new Countess of Sussex, asking her to excuse its imperfections 'with the regard of those so bitter times and privy broken passions that I endured in the writing it'.[7] He promised to do better next summer with a translation of Garnier's *Portia*, but before then he was dead, aged thirty-five.

Shakespeare learned greatly from this first tragedian touched with genius to appear in the Elizabethan theatre. It is Kyd's model that is followed in the dramatic use of rhetoric that is so dominating an element in the early plays — all the passionate exchanges between Lancastrians and Yorkists in *2* and *3 Henry VI*. Queen

Margaret in *Richard III* counts over the toll of her dead enemies, just like Andrea's Ghost in *The Spanish Tragedy*. So, too, the scene where Jeronimo dips a napkin in the blood of murdered Horatio is copied in that where Queen Margaret offers York a napkin stained with the blood of his son Rutland. *King John* has touches from *The Spanish Tragedy* : when Falconbridge quarrels with the Duke of Austria wearing a lion-skin taken from Cœur-de-Lion, he says,

> You are the hare of whom the proverb goes,
> Whose valour plucks dead lions by the beard.

This is a reminiscence from Kyd :

> He hunted well that was a lion's death,
> Not he that in a garment wore his skin.
> So hares may pull dead lions by the beard.[8]

Shakespeare seems to have read *Cornelia*, for the dialogue there between Cassius and Decimus Brutus anticipates *Julius Caesar*, while the character of Cassius owes some touches to Kyd's translation.[9] Some notorious passages from *The Spanish Tragedy* are poked fun at in *The Taming of the Shrew*. We do not know all that *Hamlet* owes to its predecessor, but we do know that Shakespeare owed the idea of a revenge-play to Kyd, and with *Titus Andronicus*, written probably in the year of Kyd's troubles, the plague-year 1593, we have a play completely following the model of its famous prototype.

The verbal parallels and the thoughts in Shakespeare's mind link *Titus* definitely with *Lucrece*, which was published in 1594 and was written therefore in 1593 or, at latest, in the winter of 1593–4. *Titus* is the first of his Roman plays ; while writing it his mind was filled with the memories of his school-reading. It is a Senecan tragedy, but there are numerous allusions to Ovid. Titus's little grandson is turning over the leaves of Ovid's *Metamorphoses*, and together they come to the terrible tale of Tereus, who raped his wife's sister Philomela and cut out her tongue so that she could not tell. This is the inspiration of the play, though the prentice Shakespeare goes one better with the horrors. Titus's daughter Lavinia is raped by the sons of the Gothic Queen, Tamora, who has married one of the last, decadent Roman Emperors — herself the lover of Aaron the Moor. Lavinia is mutilated, out of revenge, and sent back with her hands cut off. So, too, her father sacrifices his right hand. These things were not remote or unconvincing, when we reflect that in 1579 John Stubbs, the Puritan pamphleteer, had had his right hand cut off, to satisfy the fury of Queen Elizabeth at his impertinent comments on her private intentions with regard to the Anjou marriage.

Besides Seneca and Ovid, there are Virgil and Horace ; there are direct references to Tarquin and Lucrece, at this time in his mind — his mind was much running on sex, particularly on rape. There is Cornelia, no doubt fresh from his reading of Kyd's translation. Above all, there is Coriolanus : the situation of Titus is very much that of Coriolanus, a returned Roman general who has deserved well of the state in the war against the Goths :

> People of Rome, and people's tribunes here,
> I ask your voices and your suffrages :
> Will ye bestow them friendly on Andronicus ?

They wish him to take over rule, but he makes the mistake of standing down for the legitimate claimant, the son of the late Emperor. From that flow the disastrous consequences. Titus is a martial type, too simple and honourable for the treacheries of the world of politics. With our theme of Shakespeare as his own chief source, we see how this enters into the character and the situation of Coriolanus later, with whom they receive their full development. The play points forward also to Othello's tragic simplicity, while Aaron is analogous to Iago ; to Lear, with whom anger and inflexibility lead to tragic consequences, as with Titus ; to Hamlet, with whom, as with Titus, the feigned madness is so near the real thing that it is all the more terrible to watch.

Titus is a well-constructed play on a tight and somewhat rigid scheme, for the craftsman is imitating someone else. We observe that his own inner nature and sympathies are not engaged, that the tragedy has a curiously external attitude to its horrors, a kind of barbaric classicism not really natural to him. Dr. Johnson, with his usual penetration, observed that comedy in a way came more naturally to this author, and one certainly gets this impression in the first half of his career. For another thing, there is a curious disjunction between the horrors of the action and the country observations that are scattered all through — as if it were a school-piece written in the country, in absence from London during the closing of the theatres. Only once do we penetrate beneath this hard surface with the wonderful line :

> When will this fearful slumber have an end ?

Yet the play was immediately successful and long remembered, as we know from Ben Jonson's envious comment. Years later, Middleton also recalls the 'lamentable action of one arm, like old Titus Andronicus'.[10] In the civilised Victorian age the play could not be performed because it could not be believed. Such is the horror of our own age, with the appalling barbarities of prison camps and resistance movements paralleling the torture and mutilation, the feeding on human flesh, of the play, that it has ceased to be improbable. We have the worst of reasons for understanding how effective it was with the Elizabethans. A year or two ago, in London again after nearly four centuries, the play was all too effective, with people having to leave the theatre mentally and physically sick. Even in this early piece Shakespeare saw further into the true nature of human beings, their capabilities for evil as well as good, than optimistic rationalists hugging their illusions against the evidence. In one way, the Elizabethans had a more mature, because more tragic, sense of life : they knew there was no point in setting one's hopes, or having one's thoughts, in flagrant contradiction with how things are.

The contrast between the enclosed atmosphere of the play and the country life going on all round is a refreshing one. There is a deer-hunt, and we hear of 'lodges' in the pleasant chase.

> The hunt is up, the morn is bright and grey,
> The fields are fragrant and the woods are green.
> Uncouple here and let us make a bay.

The meads of Stratford are all around :

> One hour's storm will drown the fragrant meads . . .

>   behold our cheeks
> How they are stained, like meadows yet not dry,
> With miry slime left on them by a flood.

> O, let me teach you how to knit again
> This scattered corn into one mutual sheaf.

Shakespeare certainly knew a lot about deer :

> Seeking to hide herself, as doth the deer
> That hath received some unrecuring wound.

While the expert knowledge revealed in this couplet —

> What, hast not thou full often struck a doe,
> And borne her cleanly by the keeper's nose ? —

almost persuades one that there may have been something in the old tradition of his having been involved in a deer-stealing escapade in a park near Stratford. Why not ? — it was fair game to spirited young fellows near by who lived outside park-pales.

Perhaps it is not fanciful, either, to catch a glimpse of him travelling about the country with an eye open for monuments of antiquity :

> from our troops I strayed
> To gaze upon a ruinous monastery,
> And as I earnestly did fix mine eye
> Upon the wasted building . . .

It reminds us of the sonnet from just about this time :

> Bare, ruined choirs, where late the sweet birds sang.

Lastly, though the play is not yet fully mature, the characters still orating to an audience rather than talking with each other, it yet has Shakespeare's 'typical concern both in the first and in the fifth act with civil order and the forces which threaten to overthrow it'.[11] At the end all is made well with a new beginning, Titus's son Lucius succeeding to rule :

> Thanks, gentle Romans : may I govern so,
> To heal Rome's harms, and wipe away her woe.

The agitation against immigrants of 1593 — it sprang up at other times during these years, as it had done in the famous 'Ill Mayday' riots in 1517, when Sir Thomas More was under-sheriff of London — suggested a topical subject for a play round More's life. This was an awkward, not to say dangerous, subject to tackle in any case. But a play was sketched out by Anthony Munday in collaboration with Dekker and Chettle, which came before Edmund Tilney as Master of the Revels for censorship. In a society without a standing army or anything efficient in the way of police, the authorities had to keep their ears to the ground. The play is of some literary interest to us, for there seems little doubt that Shakespeare was called in to revise the riot-scene, and the balance of opinion among the experts is that this addition in the manuscript is written in his own hand. It is certainly written with ease, conviction and speed, the author pausing occasionally for a second thought as he went along. What makes it convincing is not only the style, the superiority in the writing, but the co-herence in the position taken, the character of the thought, its very inflexions, with what Shakespeare wrote elsewhere on the subject. As Greg saw, 'these hasty pages have individual qualities which mark them off sharply from the rest of the play. There is wit in the humours of the crowd, there is something like passion in More's oratory.' [12] It is the combination of the two that is so arresting ; their affinities are with the Jack Cade scenes in *1 Henry VI*, and with the crowd-scenes in *Julius Caesar* and *Coriolanus* to which they point forward.

This revised scene in *Sir Thomas More* gets going at once, with the vivacity and humorous delineation of the people we know so well. The mob is objecting to the strangers, *i.e.* immigrants.

Lincoln : Our country is a great eating country ; argo, they eat more in our country than they do in their own.

Clown : By a ha'penny loaf a day, troy weight.

Lincoln : They bring in strange roots, which is merely to the undoing of poor prentices, for what's a sorry parsnip to a good heart ?

[Parsnips, by the way, were just being introduced from abroad.]

William : Trash, trash : they breed sore eyes and 'tis enough to infect the city with the palsy.

Lincoln : Nay, it *has* infected it with the palsy ; for these bastards of dung — as you know, they grow in dung — have infected us ; and it is our infection will make the city shake, which partly comes through the eating of parsnips.

It is recognisable Shakespeare, with its bawdy *double-entendre* in the last line.

What More has to say is what Shakespeare enforces in play after play : the necessity of order and obedience if there is to be any civilised life in the land. If they had succeeded in overthrowing the laws and driving the wretched immigrants with their babes at their backs to the ports and out of the country,

> What had you got ? I'll tell you : you had taught
> How insolence and strong hand should prevail,
> How order should be quelled, and by this pattern
> Not one of you should live an agèd man.
> For other ruffians as their fancies wrought,
> With self-same hand, self reasons and self right,
> Would shark on you, and men like ravenous fishes
> Would feed on one another.

(Observe the typical Shakespearean alliteration and the images paralleled elsewhere.)

More goes further to qualify their disobedience to the king and his laws as disobedience to God :

> For to the king God hath his office lent
> Of dread of justice, power and command,
> Hath bid him rule, and willed you to obey.

What did they mean by rebelling ? —

> You'll put down strangers,
> Kill them, cut their throats, possess their houses,
> And lead the majesty of law in liom
> To slip him like a hound.

Suppose the king, to punish their offences, were to banish them, so that they in turn became strangers begging for admission to other countries,

> Would you be pleased
> To find a nation of such barbarous temper
> That, breaking out in hideous violence,
> Would not afford you an abode on earth,
> Whet their detested knives against your throats,
> Spurn you like dogs ? . . .
> What would you think
> To be thus used ? This is the stranger's case
> And this your mountainish inhumanity.

> *All :* Faith, a says true : let's do as we may be done by.

We observe the authority with which this is written, the neatness dramatically with which it is rounded off. It is exactly the treatment Shakespeare always metes out to the mob. He knows so well what fools they are, but that they have not bad hearts, their generous impulses can usually be appealed to. Not so with the leaders of the mob, like the tribunes in *Coriolanus*, whom he treats as they deserve for their bitterness and unrelenting spite. (He might be writing of *Tribune* leaders today.)

Another addition to the draft may well be Shakespeare's though it is not in his hand :

> It is in heaven that I am thus and thus,
> And that which we profanely term our fortunes
> Is the provision of the power above,
> Fitted and shaped just to that strength of nature
> Which we are born with . . .[13]

This is very much Shakespeare's line of thought — as in *Othello* and elsewhere :

> 'Tis in ourselves that we are thus or thus.

In the line —

> Which might accite thee to embrace —

we have the rare word 'accite', which affords a link with *Titus Andronicus* :

> He by the senate is accited home.

This, though a small indication in itself, helps to support a date for the play close to *Titus* and the anti-immigrant agitation of 1593.[14] Further, after Shakespeare's establishment with the Chamberlain's men in 1594, we do not find him co-operating with other dramatists. In any case, the play was not proceeded with — too dangerous ground. But we may conclude that no government need fear that Shakespeare, unlike Marlowe, would ever be subversive of order.

Marlowe's death this year could not but have a decisive importance for Shakespeare's career : it cleared the way for him. But it is an exciting thought what might have been if these two had continued in competition and mutual stimulus, challenging each other's genius to ever greater achievements.

Their social origins were much alike in that they were middle-class, though Marlowe's went further back in the town-life of Canterbury, where Shakespeare was but a generation away from country husbandry. Marlowe's people for generations had been vintners, ropers, fullers, tanners, when suddenly they produced this sport.[15] His father was a cordwainer, or shoemaker, who rose to be a prosperous townsman. The boy, Christopher, was baptised at St. George's, a couple of months before William Shakespeare at Stratford ; he became a King's scholar at the King's school and went on to Corpus Christi College, Cambridge, in 1580, where he became Archbishop Parker's scholar. There he remained for some seven years, at the end of which he would be expected to take holy orders. No more unlikely candidate can have entered the gates of that ancient house of learning. He was brilliantly gifted, but his gifts were all for poetry, for Ovid — that sensuous, stimulating influence upon them all — for Virgil and Lucan whom he translated ; supposed to be reading theology, he was more excited by cosmography, the borderlands of psychology and witchcraft, and, more dangerous, politics and contemporary affairs.

Before finishing with Cambridge, at twenty-three, he had already been employed by the government in intelligence-work abroad — at Rheims, presumably to watch the activities of the Catholic exiles there in the years before the Armada. Already a certain ambivalence of mind was announced, suitable to the shady circle of spies and government agents who formed one part of his acquaintance, poets, publishers and intellectuals the other. For, when informed against in 1593 by Richard Baines, a Catholic informer with a sinister record at Rheims, Marlowe was said to think that 'if there be any God or any good religion, then it is in the Papists'', because the service of God is performed with more ceremonies, 'as Elevation of the Mass, organs, singing men, shaven crowns, etc. And that all Protestants are hypocritical asses.'[16] This ties in with what we know of Marlowe's religious views. Bertrand Russell described himself once as a Low Church unbeliever; Marlowe belonged to the more familiar type, among aesthetes, of the High Church unbeliever.

Marlowe was heterodox all round, not only with regard to religion, but also sex — perhaps the two were connected, as they certainly were in his strange, original genius. Homosexual affection had a natural attraction for him as a subject.[17] His earliest work, *Dido*, has an elaborate treatment of the dalliance between Jupiter and the wanton boy, Ganymede. Henri III and his minions appear in *The Massacre at Paris*, in *Hero and Leander* the passion is regarded from the woman's point of view, while we are treated suggestively to Neptune disporting with Leander. The relations of Edward II with Gaveston are a main subject of the play.

> The mightiest kings have had their minions :
> Great Alexander loved Hephaestion ;
> The conquering Hercules for Hylas wept ;
> And for Patroclus stern Achilles drooped.
> And not kings only, but the wisest men :
> The Roman Tully loved Octavius,
> Grave Socrates, wild Alcibiades.

He clearly knew all about it; perhaps his Cambridge classics, when he should have been reading theology, had gone to his head.

Of his religious heterodoxy Marlowe was a proselytiser : it was said that whatever company Marlowe came into he would persuade men of the absurdity of Christian beliefs. And some of the things that he added, about the relations of Jesus with St. John, the disciple whom he loved, are a little unmentionable in detail even today.[18] Clearly, a kind of Elizabethan Voltaire, who used his original mind and sharp dialectical wits to question all received ideas and create alarm and despondency among the right-thinking : it was a very unedifying development for Archbishop Parker's scholar.

Nor was the company he kept much better. The first thing we hear of him in London is of his being involved in the quarrel of the poet Watson with one Gilbert Bradley. One day in September 1589 Bradley and Marlowe were fighting in Hog Lane, when Watson intervened and killed Bradley. Marlowe fetched up for a fortnight in Newgate, where he learned from a fellow prisoner about coining and mixing metals — the knowledge is put to better use later in *Doctor Faustus*. The next years are filled with crowded achievement, the rapid succession of his plays — though we may notice that, under the licence of dramatic form, he exposed each of the three world-religions of his time one after the other, Christianity, Jewry, Mohammedanism. He expressed what he thought through one of his characters :

> I count religion but a childish toy,
> And hold there is no sin but ignorance.

His own real religion was that of the pursuit of knowledge and beauty as power :

> Still climbing after knowledge infinite,
> And always moving as the restless spheres,
> Wills us to wear ourselves and never rest.

If he had any God, it was an abstract deity

> that sits on high and never sleeps,
> Nor in one place is circumscriptible,
> But everywhere fills every continent
> With strange infusion of his sacred vigour,
> . . . in endless power and purity.

With the prophetic power of the true poet, Marlowe may have had some foreknowledge of his fate. In the Epilogue to *Faustus* he writes :

> Cut is the branch that might have grown full straight.

But we may doubt whether with him it would ever have grown straight — his would always have been an aberrant, deviating genius. And one cannot imagine where he could have gone to from *Faustus* — yet that is only another tribute to his genius, for it is a quality of it to make the conquest of new unimagined territory seem but the next step.

He was last seen in doubtful company with which he was dangerously familiar. At the centre of it was Robert Poley, a Catholic who was in on both sides, a recognisable type from that underworld. Poley had been married by a seminary priest, and placed by his co-religionists in Sir Philip Sidney's household to listen in to the movements of his father-in-law, Walsingham, Secretary of State. But, on behalf of Walsingham, Poley won Babington's confidence — to whom Poley was 'Sweet Robin' — and betrayed him to the Secretary. Poley boasted that the Secretary was more beholden to him than he was to the Secretary ; but it was this that introduced him to Walsingham's cousin, Thomas Walsingham, Marlowe's patron. The irresistible Poley next seduced a young Mistress Yeomans and induced her to elope with him. He was evidently a fascinating, false person such as an equivocal society throws up in the conflict of beliefs and ideologies.

Thomas Walsingham's servant, Ingram Frizer, invited Marlowe to feast at a tavern at Deptford Strand with their friends Nicholas Skeres and Robert Poley on 30 May 1593. There they had dinner and remained quietly in talk and walking in the garden till supper at six in the evening. After supper Marlowe and Frizer quarrelled about the reckoning, and Marlowe, rising up from the bed on which he was lying, drew Frizer's dagger from the back and wounded him. Frizer struggled to get back his dagger, with which he gave Marlowe a mortal wound above the right eye, driving the steel two inches into the brain. Thus perished so much genius.

In *As You Like It*, in which Shakespeare paid tribute to the 'dead shepherd' and quoted Marlowe's famous line — so that he evidently had him in mind — he makes Touchstone say : 'when a man's verses cannot be understood, nor a man's good wit seconded with the forward child Understanding, it strikes a man more dead than a great reckoning in a little room'. It seems a clear reference to the great reckoning in the little room at Deptford.

Marlowe was the kind of person who was dear to those who were fond of him and understood him, disliked by those who could not respond to him or understand him, detested by those who disapproved. It was impossible to be indifferent to him. Edward Blount, in dedicating *Hero and Leander* to Sir Thomas Walsingham — to think of that wonderful poem unfinished ! — goes out of his way to take farewell of that 'beloved object, yet the impression of the man that hath been so dear to us, living an after-life in our memory'. Drayton, so different a spirit, quiet and reflective, paid a fine tribute in declaring that Marlowe

> Had in him those brave translunary things
> That our first poets had : his raptures were
> All air and fire.

Peele wrote his epitaph as 'the Muses' darling',

> Fit to write passions for the souls below.

But the tribute from which we learn most is that which young Nashe paid under the guise of Aretine in *The Unfortunate Traveller*, which he finished on 27 June this year.[19] (Marlowe had been buried on 1 June.) Nashe wrote : 'Destiny never defames herself but when she lets an excellent poet die. . . . It was one of the wittiest knaves that ever God made. . . . His pen was sharp-pointed like a poniard ; no leaf he wrote on but was like a burning-glass to set on fire all his readers. Learning he had, and a conceit [*i.e.* conceptual power] exceeding all learning, to quintessence every-thing which he heard. His tongue and his invention were fore-borne ; what they thought, they would confidently utter. . . . His life he contemned in comparison of the liberty of speech.'

That last sentence penetrates to the heart of Marlowe's tempera-ment.

Shakespeare's grand tribute to Marlowe was *Richard III* — a play so Marlovian in inspiration that one is inclined to think of it as written in the year of his death, with him in mind — and yet perhaps with the unconscious feeling of release that the way was now forward for Shakespeare to be himself. For in spite of its concentration upon one character, in the manner of *Tamburlaine* or *Faustus*, it is yet very different. Without Marlowe's self-identification, there is room for the comic spirit, for an irony echoing through the grim vaults of the play. Unlike Marlowe's heroes, Richard is many-sided, mock-humble as well as audacious, plausible and adroit — he can get away with anything up to the last nemesis upon him — histrionic and yet introspective, perfectly self-aware and convincing, with a kind of gaiety in villainy that sweeps the action forward and has always swept the theatre with it. Among the most popular of Shakespeare's plays in his day, it has never ceased to be so. Though it does not plumb the spiritual depths of the last act of *Faustus* and the poetry is less majestic, *Richard III* is even better theatre, more rounded and complete. This is not apprenticeship, this is mastery ; the apprentice who has been humble enough to learn from wherever he could, and over so long a course, is at length surpassing his masters.

Long as this play is — it is the longest of all, save *Hamlet* — there is nothing superfluous in it, none of those prentice-bits sewn on as in *Henry VI*. The whole thing is of a piece, starts and bounds away like a shot, a long shot straight to the finish. The overwhelming impression one gets is that of genius finding itself, confident in its exercise and joying in its play. Nothing he ever wrote was written with more gusto ; one can imagine him laughing as he penned Richard's pious line :

O, do not *swear*, my Lord of Buckingham ;

or the wink that he practically gives the audience with

'Tis death to me to be at enmity ;

or the glee with which Richard treats fools with the humbug they ask for and receive. Irony is the ubiquitous element in which the play is blown along, which gives an exhilarating effect to a train of action essentially sinister. Though called a tragedy, in contemporary terms, it is really an historical melodrama. The full-blown development given to the character of Richard is something new, and yet it is suggested by Aaron : a stage-villain. In his first speech, Richard informs us,

I am determinèd to prove a villain ;

as Aaron says,

Even now I curse the day . . .
Wherein I did not some notorious ill.

Though we know that a play on Richard was envisaged before Shakespeare finished writing *3 Henry VI*, the play turned out very differently. The character of Richard took possession of him — with the result that *Richard III* stands in marked contrast with those plays. Where they are chronicle-plays, dispersed, disparate, with no concentration on any one character, *Richard III* is monodic, all of one piece, of a concentrated dramatic effect. One cannot but be struck by the contrast, or by the astonishing speed with which Shakespeare's genius was unfolding — under the influence at last, as we shall see, of friendship and love.

With this play history tends to pass, if not completely, into tragedy, 'becoming less of a fateful pageant and more the adventure of an individual soul'.[20]   The energy that is released into it is tremendous — not unlike *Macbeth* in its force, though that is only half as long ; again there is joy in the creation of *Richard III*, of a master triumphing in his new-found strength.   The sources Shakespeare read up for material were Holinshed and Hall's chronicle, *The Union of the Two Noble and Illustre Families of Lancaster and York*, the theme of which is expressed in the title and made a strong impression upon Shakespeare's mind : the conflict and anarchy of the Wars of the Roses being brought to an end by the union of the two houses in the Tudor dynasty. It was a commonplace of Tudor propaganda, nevertheless Shakespeare's uninstructed mind, so far as English history was concerned, owed a great deal to this book.   Behind that was Sir Thomas More's version of the events of Richard III's reign — the suggestion of Richard's sardonic humour came through More, directly or indirectly : Shakespeare seized upon it, in his devouring way, and elaborated it into a prime feature in Richard's personality.

The atmosphere of the play is haunted with guilt and night-terrors, there are no less than four dreams, while the word ' blood' runs as a *leit-motif* through it.   Shakespeare evidently read Nashe's *Terrors of the Night* in manuscript at this time, in progress 'from one scrivener's shop to another . . . becoming so common that it was ready to be hung out for one of their signs'.[21]   There he would read, 'the Night is the Devil's black book wherein he recordeth all our transgressions ; when we are shut separately in our chambers he keepeth his audit in our sin-guilty consciences. The only peace of mind he hath is despair.   There be them that think every spark in a flame is a spirit.'   In the night before Bosworth, when the ghosts of his victims appear to Richard and he dreams that he is in dire need of another horse and for his wounds to be bound up —

> O coward conscience, how dost thou afflict me !
> The lights burn blue. It is now dead midnight . . .

Nashe wrote, 'any terror, the least illusion is a cacodaemon unto him'.   The rare word is caught up in that mind that missed nothing : 'Thou cacodaemon', Queen Margaret calls Richard.[22]

For the suggestion of a deeply moving passage, Clarence's dream the night before his murder in the Tower, Shakespeare was indebted to Sackville's poem, 'The Complaint of Buckingham', in the ever-popular *Mirror for Magistrates*. We do not have to look abroad to Seneca for those ghosts and apparitions, personifications of Revenge and such like : they were a regular feature of the old moralities and the popular drama in which Shakespeare, like every other Englishman, had grown up.[23] Only he enriches these things with his imagination, into which a thousand things are caught up, so many fish gleaming silver in the net. Clarence dreamed that he was drowning — as he was to drown in a butt of malmsey :

> Lord, Lord ! methought what pain it was to drown :
> What dreadful noise of water in mine ears !
> What sights of ugly death within mine eyes !
> Methought I saw a thousand fearful wrecks ;
> A thousand men that fishes gnawed upon ;
> Wedges of gold, great anchors, heaps of pearl,
> Inestimable stones, unvalued jewels,
> All scattered in the bottom of the sea.
> Some lay in dead men's skulls ; and in those holes
> Where eyes did once inhabit, there were crept,
> As 'twere in scorn of eyes, reflecting gems . . .

Many years later, at the end of Shakespeare's writing life, that was to find perfection and conciseness of expression with

> Those are pearls that were his eyes.

It is thought that this imagery was suggested by the capture of the richest carrack ever to come to these shores, the *Madre de Dios*, in just these years, the autumn of 1592, as we shall see an unmistakable reflection in the contemporaneous *Comedy of Errors*.[24]

This episode of Clarence's last night in the Tower foreshadows greater things to come — *Richard II* and the haunted atmosphere of *Macbeth*. A modern commentator of democratic convictions says perceptively, if somewhat innocently, 'a time like our own that has out-Machiavelled Machiavelli, has turned intoso ber realism much in this play that to a reader of forty years ago sounded like sheer invention. The world is forever catching up with Shakespeare — only to fall behind him again. . . . The play is a sort of biography of force, of the tyrannical, or, as we call it, the totalitarian principle. . . . It is a pity our age did not take warning from him.' [25] But, of course : it should not have been necessary. The play's 'general moral intention and upshot are as sound as those of the later tragedies'. True, the simple orthodox morality of the early plays is in marked contrast with Marlowe, whose mind was more torn and troubled. The moral of this play is that of all Shakespeare's political plays : out of conflict and dissension comes anarchy, out of anarchy despotism ; upon the crimes that are committed comes nemesis. Early as it is, '*Richard III* remains one of the most powerful presentations of the idea of nemesis in any literature'.

We need say little of its literary characteristics, they are crystal-clear. There is the same dramatic use of rhetoric, even more effective than before, the sharp exchanges between opponents taking up each other's words and flinging them back with a different inflexion : it all makes for trenchant dialogue, if somewhat overdone, and still a little naïve, to our ears. There is the functional use of rhymed couplets we have noticed in the previous plays to punctuate a period, a speech or a scene. In the end, Richard's last night on earth, real tragedy breaks through :

> I shall despair. There is no creature loves me ;
> And if I die, no soul will pity me.

Then, with a quick return :

> Nay, wherefore should they, since that I myself
> Find in myself no pity to myself ?

And we observe that the whole speech is hinged upon Shakespeare's characteristic reflexive conceit.

The humours of the people, as usual, provide a little fun. One of Clarence's murderers jibs at his job : 'I'll not meddle with it; it makes a man a coward ; a man cannot steal, but it accuseth him ; a man cannot swear, but it checks him ; a man cannot lie with his neighbour's wife, but it detects him. . . .' This looks forward to Hamlet's most famous speech, the same thought expressed in a line :

> Thus conscience doth make cowards of us all.

The theme of gentility is sounded, though its use by Richard is dramatic and perhaps ironical :

> Since every Jack became a gentleman
> There's many a gentle person made a Jack.

Is it fanciful to suggest an increase of social awareness with Shakespeare's entry into the Southampton circle ? — there is plenty of evidence of it elsewhere in Shakespeare :

> He capers nimbly in a lady's chamber
> To the lascivious pleasing of a lute . . .
>
> I'll be at charges for a looking-glass,
> And entertain a score or two of tailors.

We have not come upon such touches in the previous plays. We begin to have references to his own profession, with increasing familiarity and confidence, with Buckingham's,

> Tut, I can counterfeit the deep tragedian,
> Speak and look back, and pry on every side,
> Tremble and start at wagging of a straw,
> Intending deep suspicion : ghastly looks
> Are at my service, like enforcèd smiles ;
> And both are ready in their offices,
> At any time, to grace my stratagems.

Indeed, there is a good deal of play-acting within the play, the farce put up by Richard and Buckingham over the offer of the crown and again for the benefit of the Lord Mayor and citizens, as in a good deal of Richard's behaviour : he was, among other things, a consummate actor.

It is this that contributed to the play's immense popularity in its own day and ever after, and to the appeal of Richard's part for actors. Richard's last cry —

> A horse ! a horse ! my kingdom for a horse ! —

has never been forgotten. In his day Richard Burbage was best known for this rôle he created, so much so that in the next generation the guide who took people over the field of Bosworth confused his name with Richard's :

> For when he would have said, King Richard died,
> And called 'A horse ! A horse !' — he Burbage cried.[26]

And a tale went round London, reported by a barrister of Middle Temple, John Manningham : 'when Burbage played Richard III, there was a citizen grew so far in liking with him that, before she went from the play, she appointed him to come that night unto her by the name of Richard III. Shakespeare, overhearing their conclusion, went before, was entertained and at his game ere Burbage came. Then, message being brought that Richard III was at the door, Shakespeare caused return to be made that William the Conqueror was before Richard III.' [27]

Perhaps we can now sum up the more serious contrasts between Shakespeare and the writer of genius to whom he owed so much in inspiration and challenge.

By the end of the year of Marlowe's death Shakespeare had written not only the three parts of *Henry VI*, *Titus Andronicus* and *Richard III*, but *The Comedy of Errors*, *The Two Gentlemen of Verona* and *The Taming of the Shrew*. That is to say, Shakespeare's was a dual, ambivalent nature, as good for comedy as for tragedy, altogether more *ondoyant et divers*, where Marlowe's was more unitary and homogeneous, more restricted and intellectual. As yet, Marlowe's is the more splendid poetry, scaling loftier heights, searching greater depths. But already with the comedies of these years Shakespeare is moving in a totally different world from Marlowe, quite unlike his interests or genius.[28] Shakespeare regards the vagaries, the fooleries, of human beings with a sympathetic eye — too sceptical and wise to seek after the correction of manners. For the full comedy of life women have to play an equal part with men, and in Shakespeare's comedies women are gallantly given precedence — an inflexion unthinkable for Marlowe.

Marlowe had wit and an ironic cast of mind, with a cruder sense of comedy; his laughter was not sympathetic, it was that of an intellectual, contemptuous, with a sardonic twist. It is like the irony of life that Marlowe, who was so much more of a rationalist, should have died quarrelling not very rationally over a tavern reckoning; while Shakespeare, who did not attach so much importance to reason, should have conducted his life altogether more reasonably. Shakespeare had not yet the advantage of a world of high breeding, yet he had far greater instinctive courtesy and tact, a *politesse du cœur*. 'The delightful *bravura* of Marlowe's mocking wit', we are told, 'was all-pervasive; but Shakespeare still had some heavy provincial Warwickshire loam sticking to his boots.' [29] As a poet, Shakespeare was more ingenuously taken with figures of speech, his images simpler and more visual where Marlowe's were magnificent and general, planetary or even cosmic, as if he wrote much by night. Shakespeare's was a less academic intelligence, Marlowe's more instructed, more intellectually controlled, more philosophic. Yet Shakespeare's social disadvantage was ultimately an immense literary advantage, especially for a dramatist. Where Marlowe had other interests and perhaps ambitions, Shakespeare was an actor. The theatre was his home and that meant team-work — in touch with a wider spread of human nature, the discipline to subordinate himself to other natures, the mimetic faculty, that was second nature with him, to see others' natures from within.

Connected with this is Shakespeare's eminent sense of society, of men's kinship with each other, their responsibilities to each other, the necessity of ties and affections, the recognition of order and degree, of authority. His was from the first a social, a family, vision of mankind ; Marlowe's individual, independent, arrogant, alone. Shakespeare's view was orthodox : he made a simple identification, being no intellectual, of Machiavellianism with what ordinary people had always called Evil.[30] His orthodoxy, however, went along with a sceptical temperament : he knew instinctively the uselessness of much speculation. Marlowe, the heterodox rationalist, an intellectual sceptic, had a less sceptical and more positive temperament, assertive and daring. He was not afraid to say everything that he thought : few have been so brave, but I fear he was not wise. And the interesting thing is that it is the other cast of mind that goes further — more open to the sun, more flexible, capable of a larger development.

Marlowe had the wit to see that men's beliefs have no absolute validity and their conventions no inner authority ; but, himself on the margin of society, not rooted in it, he did not perceive that these things are indispensable to the society's existence. He saw that they were put across by authority to keep men in order and obedience, but, without Shakespeare's normal social sense, he did not allow that some of these things — loyalties, obligation, kindness, social bonds — might even be good things in themselves. He was out to scoff and deride, more deeply, to search and question, himself troubled, possessed with the desire to find what was true, what one *could* believe. He thought little of life, according to Nashe, compared with the liberty of speech. And he was only twenty-nine when he died.

The power of Marlowe's genius is all the more testified when one reflects how alien a spirit his was to Shakespeare's, gentle and conforming, natural and sound — until deepened and perturbed by the experience of love and treachery, suffering and abnegation.

CHAPTER VIII

The Early Comedies

By the year of Marlowe's death, we have seen, Shakespeare had written not only some four plays on English history but probably his first three comedies. It is not certain in what order they were written, but there is fair agreement that *The Comedy of Errors* came first ; it would seem to me that *The Two Gentlemen of Verona* came next, which is very close in character and texture, and *The Taming of the Shrew* third, on ground of its maturer characterisation, force and imaginative realism. Other playwrights had shown diversity in their output, particularly Peele, who had produced pastoral, a topical play, a Biblical tragedy, a history play and, in *The Old Wives Tale*, a mixture of fairy enchantments with some literary satire. But in Shakespeare thus early we see a deeper, more significant, duality, which reflects the ambivalence, the two-sidedness, of his nature.

The tutelary deity who presided over this side of his develop-ment — as Marlowe and Kyd over the other — and from whom Shakespeare learned with all the ardour of his nature for learning everything from everybody, was John Lyly.

It would be difficult to exaggerate Lyly's influence in the 1580's and for a little later — in setting a model with his *Euphues and his England*, a novel-discourse of manners, with its appeal to women, its refinement of sensibility, its fashionable affectation. His comedies set another model, with their exquisiteness after the coarseness of early Tudor comedy, their courtliness, their moonlit grace and fantasy — so well considered for the Children of the Chapel whom he trained to act them : a dream-world that never quite came alive. Above all, there was his share in the refinement of the language, the achievement of style. This was what Shakespeare instinctively sought for : though he had not yet attained the conversation of the world of high breeding, he had natural good manners —

Sir, I commend you to your own content.

The early comedies show him to us aspiring to the world of elegance and taste, from which circumstances had excluded him, though it was in keeping with his own nature. In entering it, he found himself.

Lyly was ten years senior to Shakespeare, having been born at Canterbury in 1553 or 1554. He had the immense advantage of birth into a cultivated family — his grandfather was the celebrated William Lily, from whom Shakespeare and all England learned their Latin grammar.[1] His father was Registrar of the diocese — the son was able to boast, in *Euphues*, of the majesty of Canterbury cathedral, the background of his childhood. At fifteen he was sent to Magdalen College, Oxford, with Burghley's aid — and that great man was never over-generous in assisting anybody, outside his own family. At Oxford Lyly rather wasted his time, as bilious Gabriel Harvey informs us later, in 'horning, gaming, fooling, and knaving'. He came away without a degree and, like others who have made little of their time at Oxford, went on to attack the university in his best-seller, *Euphues*.

On going down, Lyly landed on his feet as secretary to Burghley's son-in-law, the Earl of Oxford. This talented young peer was a trial to all who knew him. Immensely aristocratic — he was the seventeenth De Vere Earl — he was a gifted aesthete, taken up by the Queen at first, self-indulgent and quarrelsome, hopelessly extravagant, intolerable, in the end perhaps a little mad. Burghley, who had been his guardian, snobbishly married his plain daughter to the Earl, who became a frightful headache to him ever after. For the Earl treated his wife abominably — in any case, his inclinations were otherwise ; what was worse, he ran through all his estates, and ended up a pensioner of the Crown.

Life in the proximity of the Earl of Oxford was far from smooth, and in the end Lyly left his service — sooner or later, one always quarrelled with Edward de Vere. Meanwhile, Lyly had the *entrée* to Court, and produced his plays there, most of them before 1590. All his life he aimed at becoming Master of the Revels, in control of the Court entertainments ; but he got no further than to train the Children of Paul's, which was more in keeping with his talents as a producer of boy-actors. Perhaps, 'a little fellow', he never fully grew up himself ; his plays would give one to suppose that he remained an adolescent at heart. Even so, his career received a grievous blow : an inhibition was placed upon the boy-actors, for the part they had taken in the Martin Marprelate controversy, and Lyly's Children of Paul's and the Children of the Chapel were stopped from acting throughout the years 1591 to 1599. Like other men of taste without genius, a man of many talents, ingenious and clever but without force or passion, Lyly turned sour and despondent. His last petitions to the Queen were bitter protests at his frustration ; the removal of the inhibition came too late for him : he wrote only one more play, and died in 1606.

Lyly's plays were nearly all published in the 1590s — naturally, when they were not being performed. And Shakespeare learned any number of things from them — his first comedies show clearly his growing familiarity with contemporary literature. There are direct echoes, as usual. A passage from *Campaspe* is taken up from prose and put into verse in *Richard III* ; while the lines,

> . . . the lark so shrill and clear :
> How at heaven's gate she claps her wings,
> The morn not waking till she sings . . .

are echoed in a sonnet about this time :

> Like to the lark at break of day arising
> From sullen earth, sings hymns at heaven's gate.

And there are others, direct or indirect, conscious or no.

It seems to have been Lyly's first play, *Campaspe*, that made such an impression on Shakespeare, opened his mind to the possibilities in this vein : it provided just what his genius needed here and at this moment. Here were the wit-combats, as it were in inverted commas, the lightness of touch indispensable in high society, above all for a Court audience. This certainly did not mean that the exchanges were not sharp and biting : the converse. Some of these early seeds sown had their most brilliant and sinister flowering much later : the character of Diogenes in *Campaspe* and his unsparing exchanges with Alexander are reflected years later in the personalities and rôles of the cynical misanthropes, Thersites and Apemantus, in *Troilus and Cressida* and *Timon of Athens*.

In these first years, in comedy, Shakespeare picked up as much from Lyly as he had from Marlowe and Kyd in tragedy and melodrama. Lyly afforded a deft model in weaving a sub-plot into a unified dramatic structure, while all was held together in a balance skilfully maintained between groups symmetrically

William Shakespeare

opposed.[2]   Then, too, there was a different kind of courtship from that of visits to Shottery — an upper-class world in which the women held the men at bay, and exacted their price, by their greater skill in words.   Here lay the way forward to the leading place of women in Shakespeare's comedy, and to what a sequence of characters !

Shakespeare had nothing to learn from Lyly in character-drawing : Lyly's figures were rather cut-flowers, where Shakespeare's grew out of the soil of life, out of experience and instinctive knowledge.   Here from quite early we detect his own idiom developing — which can best be described, perhaps, as that of romantic realism.   But in the mode in which to express his own vision of people and things, Shakespeare learned something from his senior : in the use of a colloquial prose, amusing and natural ; and specifically in the comic exploitation of popular proverbs, folk-sayings, the absurd *clichés* in which ordinary people conduct their conversation, display their collective wisdom.

It is the general model that matters : of a courtly world of polished manners and natural ease, the lightness of touch, sparring in place of the deadly exchanges of the tragic history plays, the urbanity of high society, if only a mask for such people's relation-ships.   Courtiers were interested above all in love, but it was in manner very different from the simplicities of ordinary folk — getting a girl into trouble, having to marry her and there an end.[3] These accidents sometimes happened at Court, but at the climax of the chase : it was all a game, with its hazards (as Leicester, Essex, Ralegh, Southampton all found).   They needed to be adepts at keeping several balls in the air at once ; there were the delights of gossip, malice, scandal, the joy when someone came down with a crash. It was a heartless world. Shakespeare, like every-body else, was very anxious to enter it, for it was 'the world, the power and the glory' ; but, we perceive, he entered it both on sufferance yet also on his own terms, retaining that essential, silent independence of his — so much greater in reality than the much self-advertised independence of Ben Jonson.   In the end, he left it, turned his back on it noiselessly, without a word, for the familiar endearments — so much truer and more rewarding to the soul, if not to the intelligence — of Stratford.

The Comedy of Errors is the shortest of the plays, and would serve therefore for performance after dinner of an afternoon, or after supper in the evening, in some great house or hall or at Court.

It was performed, though not necessarily for the first time, both at Court and at Gray's Inn during the Christmas festivities of 1594. It was played by the Lord Chamberlain's men, the author among them, before the Queen at Greenwich on Innocents' Day, and the same day at night — we may imagine the players in their barge coming up the river with the tide — in the hall of Gray's Inn, where Christmas was being celebrated with elaborate revels through the holidays. We need not go into the high-spirited nonsense of the law-students, the entertainment of an 'embassy' from the Inner Temple on the second Grand Night, 28 December, the crowding of the dais so that the offended Templarians left in a huff and all was confusion. After dancing with the ladies invited, 'a comedy of Errors (like to Plautus's *Menaechmi*) was played by the players. So that Night was begun and continued to the end in nothing but confusion and errors ; whereupon, it was ever afterwards called "The Night of Errors".' 4 It was evidently long remembered : John Manningham of Middle Temple wrote in February 1602, 'at our feast we had a play called *Twelfth Night*, or *What You Will*, much like the comedy of Errors or *Menaechmi* in Plautus'. Some nights after the performance of the play, to conclude the festivities, the Lord of Misrule presided over some exercises — the young lawyers speaking on themes such as war, the study of philosophy, the achievement of fame by buildings and foundations, virtue and government. These were written by Francis Bacon, with whom such subjects were a characteristic concern, and who lived in chambers in the Inn in these years.5

The plot is highly artificial and symmetrical ; where Plautus has one pair of twins, Shakespeare has two, thus doubling the mistaken identities until the head reels at the confusion of it all, as those of the characters did. They thought they were either bewitched or dreaming — one more tribute to the Lyly-like atmosphere ; and the Dromios get their names from Lyly's *Mother Bombie*. No doubt Shakespeare was rather twin-conscious, with his own burden to support ; the wife of Aegeon is

> almost at fainting under
> The pleasing punishment that women bear.

The play 'leaves the impression that its author must have possessed this quality of ingenuity above all others. Yet ingenuity — not that he ever lacked it — is one of the last things we associate with the mature Shakespeare. It is an attribute of talent, not of genius.

. . . He continued to make use of the popular appeal that lies in the ingenious plot and theatrical situation, but he subordinated these things progressively to other ends or transmuted them to something higher.' [6] We see thus early his artistic and literary ambition, his fidelity to the standards of art he set himself, the achievement he purposed and meant — an aspect of him which ceased to be understood in his own lifetime, with the criticism and the conceptions of Ben Jonson, which prevailed in the succeeding centuries.

We are not concerned here to 'evaluate' the play — blessed word so forward on the lips of those whose pretentiousness is only equalled by their literary insensibility. Let us traverse the play, more humbly, to learn what we can of the author, his nature, environment and concerns.

The scene, for all the foreign names, is London : the proximity of the port, the readiness of shipping, the merchants and their affairs, the enmity with Spain. The abbey, behind the walls of which one of the characters takes refuge, is no doubt Holywell priory, where both the Theatre and the Curtain were, near which Shakespeare lived and worked. Syracuse and Ephesus are at war, like England and Spain ; and we are given a reference to the sea-war in the description of an unwanted woman's nose, 'all o'er embellished with rubies, carbuncles, sapphires, declining their rich aspect to the hot breath of Spain, who sent whole armadoes of carracks to be ballast at her nose'. This is pretty far-fetched, high-spirited and youthful. A reference to the Lapland sorcerers, who were supposed to enchant sailors away from their coast, may mean that Shakespeare was reading Hakluyt, where this information appears ; Hakluyt's immense collection of voyages, *The Principal Navigations*, had appeared in 1589 and we know that Shakespeare read in it later.

Among the characters we have Doctor Pinch, a schoolmaster, who is disparagingly described :

> a hungry, lean-faced villain,
> A mere anatomy, a mountebank,
> A threadbare juggler, and a fortune-teller,
> A needy, hollow-eyed, sharp-looking wretch.

Perhaps he was played by the actor Sinckler, who looked like that. With the play's fourth line only we have an inflexion that bears the unmistakable stamp of Shakespeare :

> I am not partial to infringe our laws.

Ephesus has decreed against Syracuse

> To admit no traffic to our adverse towns.

The phrases have his recognisable ring — the naturalness, where other writers at this time were apt to be wooden, along with a certain lordliness. Not only does the style reveal him, but the situation is familiar to him. Here he is. The situation, the sinking ship, the separation, that appealed to his prentice imagination at the beginning, remained to inspire him to the end with *The Tempest*.

> I'll view the manners of the town,
> Peruse the traders, gaze upon the buildings,
> And then return and sleep within mine inn,
> For with long travel I am stiff and weary :

it is not fanciful to see him there, for he describes himself in a sonnet, when on tour doing just that.

The humour of the play is frequently arranged with the help of school-rhetoric :

> The capon burns, the pig falls from the spit ;
> The clock hath strucken twelve upon the bell ;
> My mistress made it one upon my cheek :
> She is so hot, because the meat is cold ;
> The meat is cold because you come not home . . .

But the scene is always recognisably one of contemporary life. The man who newly comes to town says,

> They say this town is full of cozenage :
> As nimble jugglers that deceive the eye,
> Dark-working sorcerers that change the mind,
> Soul-killing witches that deform the body,
> Disguisèd cheaters, prating mountebanks,
> And many such-like liberties of sin . . .
> I greatly fear my money is notsafe.

This is London, as the young man from the country sees it.

Watching, as we must, each play to extract the personal, for touches of the man, since every writer portrays himself in his writing, we come upon something that speaks out of context in this artificial comedy :

> He that commends me to mine own content
> Commends me to the thing I cannot get :
> I to the world am like a drop of water
> That in the ocean seeks another drop
> Who, falling there to find his fellow forth,
> Unseen, inquisitive, confounds himself.

Surely there is a personal note there ? — it is the very rhythm and accent of the Sonnets, and the experience described in them was to provide the answer.

Considering how much of this play is invented rather than imagined, it is noticeable that one strand stands out with a certain reality from the fabric of invention. It is the theme of the relation between man and wife : who was to be top dog ? Two women discuss the ways of husbands, Adriana and Luciana. One says,

> A man is master of his liberty :
> Time is their master, and when they see time
> They'll go or come.

To which the other replies :

> Why should their liberty than ours be more ?

Answer :

> Because their business still lies out-o'-door.

This is the answer given in *The Taming of the Shrew*, and by Luciana here :

> Why, headstrong liberty is lashed with woe :
> There's nothing situate under heaven's eye
> But hath his bound in earth, in sea, in sky :
> The beasts, the fishes, and the wingèd fowls
> Are their males' subjects and at their controls.

Much more men,

> Indued with intellectual sense and souls.

This language, put into the mouths of women, may have just a shade of irony to grace it ; but it would be a mistake to interpret it out of its age, as so many modern critics do : this is what Elizabethans thought. The husband stays away from home and dinner ; the wife complains :

> His company must do his minions grace,
> Whilst I at home starve for a merry look :
> Hath homely age the alluring beauty took
> From my poor cheek ? . . .
> Are my discourses dull ? barren my wit ?

The situation is dramatic, so that there can be no crude transference from the dramatic to the biographical ; all the same, a writer does not write *in vacuo*, he writes from his own experience and what he knows about. Nothing of Anne Shakespeare's discourses has come down to us ; nothing to indicate wit, or education, or anything but a housewife keeping house for the errant player who chose life in London.

> My decayèd fair
> A sunny look of his would soon repair ;
> But, too unruly deer, he breaks the pale,
> And feeds from home.

A writer is never more himself than when referring covertly to his own delinquencies :

> I know his eye doth homage otherwhere,
> Or else what lets it but he would be here ?

This is the situation to be revealed shortly in the Sonnets.

Adriana turns round on the supposedly errant husband :

> How dearly would it touch thee to the quick
> Shouldst thou but hear I were licentious ! . . .
> Keep then fair league and truce with thy true bed.

We shall see how this theme worked out in Shakespeare's own life ; here we may note that he has already developed a characteristic of his to a degree we may describe as distinguishing him — such entire awareness, such self-awareness, such a sympathy with both sides of the question. It is this faculty in Shakespeare that is miraculous, and makes all who understand him love him beyond reason. Even when himself is in sin — no excuses, no self-illusion : he understands the situation perfectly, and the other's point of view, indeed those of all the others. The following advice to the supposed-false husband is written not without knowledge :

> Look sweet, speak fair, become disloyalty :
> Apparel vice like virtue's harbinger :
> Bear a fair presence, though your heart be tainted,
> Teach sin the carriage of a holy saint,
> Be secret-false : what need she be acquainted ?

Lyly's influence is still more visible in *The Two Gentlemen of Verona*, and not only in the symmetricality of structure, two lovers with two mistresses, two servants and opposing fathers. It has had its effect on the theme, the conflicting claims of friendship and love, in the emphasis on friendship as in *Euphues* where one is as much a leading subject as the other. Euphues and Philautus are friends, and famous friendships are several times cited — an emphasis which must have been appreciated in the exotic entourage of the Earl of Oxford. From this time on friendship occupied a prominent place in Shakespeare's mind. It is the primary subject of his Sonnets, where others' were dedicated solely to the passion of love, and it recurs through his work — with Romeo and Mercutio, Antonio and Bassanio, Brutus and Cassius, Hamlet and Horatio.

Shakespeare found his story, the loves of Proteus and Julia, in Montemayor's *Diana*, either from Bartholomew Young's translation in manuscript, or a French version, or an earlier play performed at Greenwich before the Queen. What matter? Sources are but a peg to hang the matter on : it is the content that counts, the seed from which it all germinates. More important is the way this play proliferates in Shakespeare's own mind, and flowers into more finished forms with *Romeo and Juliet, As You Like It* and *The Merchant of Venice*. In no play are there so many premonitions of later ones, so many devices given fuller development.

The Comedy of Errors was, in a sense, a schoolpiece, based on his school-reading of Plautus. But with *The Two Gentlemen*, first of romantic comedies, he opens up a vein he made peculiarly his own — crossed love, disguised heroines, flight and exile. The character of Julia receives fuller growth in Rosalind and Portia, that of Silvia in Juliet. Valentine looks forward to *As You Like It*, as does the theme of flight from an angry father to the forest. Life in the forest, the good-hearted outlaws who take Valentine for their leader, are suggested by the old Robin Hood ballads, to which there is a direct reference, as again in the later play :

> By the bare scalp of Robin Hood's fat friar,
> This fellow were a king for our wild faction.

Shakespeare remained always romantic about Warwickshire and the forest of Arden.

The leading theme is the conflict of love and friendship. Valentine's humble, confiding praise of his friend Proteus may be compared with Shakespeare's of his young friend in the Sonnets :

> His years but young, but his experience old :
> His head unmellowed, but his judgement ripe :
> And, in a word, (for far behind his worth
> Come all the praises that I now bestow)
> He is complete in feature and in mind,
> With all good grace to grace a gentleman.

Unfortunately, this gentleman proves a cad, and steals his friend's girl away from him. The *dénouement* is reached with,

> Thou common friend, that's without faith or love,
> For such is a friend now : treacherous man,
> Thou hast beguiled my hopes ; nought but mine eye
> Could have persuaded me : now I dare not say
> I have one friend alive : thou wouldst disprove me.

And then, on Proteus' shamed repentance, Valentine gives up his girl to him :

> Who by repentance is not satisfied
> Is nor of heaven nor earth : for these are pleased :
> By penitence th' Eternal's wrath's appeased.

This doctrine of the absolute value of repentance, and the moral obligation to accept the repentant, appears again and again in the plays right up to the end with *The Winter's Tale* — never more wonderfully than there, where it is the main theme. Whereupon Valentine makes an act of abnegation on behalf of his friend :

> And that my love may appear plain and free,
> All that was mine in Silvia I give thee.

This recalls the abnegation in the Sonnets :

> Take all my loves, my love, yea, take them all.

It is friendship carried to the last extreme, and it has greatly bothered the critics as either intolerable or improbable.[7] Nevertheless, in the way nature has of imitating art, this was what came about in the relation between Shakespeare, his young friend and the poet's mistress : suffering followed by abnegation.

That the dramatist was not without irony in the portrait of this gentleman we may surmise from his naming him Proteus, with its overtones, for the Greek Proteus was able to change appearances at will. Yet we know that Shakespeare genuinely held aristocratic qualities in esteem and pursued them. His unconscious may have been at work, for his conscious thought was all in favour of the social order and its natural hierarchy. His sense of truth-to-nature told him what the facts were and that only intrinsic value was any good, wherever it came from. Perhaps his unconscious mind was exacting retribution for his having been placed where he was by birth — we know how much he resented it — not by his nature, which deserved better. Such are the rewards that come to a writer who trusts his nature, does not go contrary to it or force it, allows it fulfilment to bring up from the depths of the unconscious, the repository of life's experience, the riches that are not to be found on the cerebral surface.

Launce, the kind-hearted clown, has more sense and natural intelligence than all the gentlemen in Verona, and his brief summing up of them — of Proteus, 'a kind of knave' — offers the sound comment of nature upon a world of artificiality. He has infinitely more humour, too — indeed they have none. In the scene of Launce's conversation with his dog we hear the authentic voice of the people, which Shakespeare was unsurpassed in rendering. Here it all is, to set beside Jack Cade and Clarence's murderers, thus early :

> He thrusts me himself into the company of three or four gentlemen-like dogs under the duke's table : he had not been there (bless the mark !) a pissing-while, but all the chamber smelt him. 'Out with the dog,' says one. 'What cur is that ?' says another. 'Whip him out,' says the third. 'Hang him up,' says the duke. I, having been acquainted with the smell before, knew it was Crab, and goes me to the fellow that whips the dogs. 'Friend,' quoth I, 'you mean to whip the dog ?' 'Ay, marry, do I,' quoth he. 'You do him the more wrong,' quoth I, "twas I did the thing you wot of.' He makes no more ado, but whips me out of the chamber. How many masters would do this for his servant ?

Shakespeare was irresistible at this kind of transcript from below-stairs life ; nothing so real had as yet appeared in the theatre : it must have delighted the audience.

Other touches bring him home to us : perhaps the Avon :

> The current that with gentle murmur glides,
> Thou know'st, being stopped, impatiently doth rage :
> But when his fair course is not hinderèd
> He makes sweet music with th' enamelled stones,
> Giving a gentle kiss to every sedge
> He overtaketh in his pilgrimage ;
> And so by many winding nooks he strays,
> With willing sport, to the wide ocean.

The extraordinary productivity of these years we must put down largely to the closing of the theatres and the time he would thus have on his hands ; it would be reasonable to suppose that with plague raging in London he would go home to Stratford, at least in summer when it was hottest, to write. The first lines of the play express the thought,

> Home-keeping youth have ever homely wits.

Valentine would rather

> see the wonders of the world abroad,
> Than, living dully sluggardized at home,
> Wear out thy youth with shapeless idleness.

Young men were off,

> Some to the wars, to try their fortune there ;
> Some to discover islands far away ;
> Some to the studious universities.

There was a summary of life in the early 1590's, but none of these were for him : a youthful accident had pre-empted his opportunities.

> Maids, in modesty, say No to that
> Which they would have the profferer construe Ay.

It is a thought that frequently recurs in Shakespeare, and so he had evidently found with Anne Hathaway.

We have already noticed the Cotswold background that Shakespeare gave *The Taming of the Shrew* — the ale-house on the heath, Marian Hacket the fat ale-wife of Wincot to whom Christopher Sly the tinker owes fourteen pence on the score for sheer ale, and

> Stephen Sly, and old John Naps of Greet,
> And Peter Turf, and Henry Pimpernell.

The play was performed in June 1594 at Newington Butts by the newly formed Chamberlain's men on their return from touring the provinces. It had come to them from Pembroke's men on their breaking up, so that the play would have been written originally in 1593. One cannot but mark the greater maturity and conviction of characterisation of the chief persons Kate and Petruchio, as well as the perfection of the Induction. It would seem reasonable to place it third in the grouping of the early comedies.

There are still school-touches and school-tags about : there is the flicker of classical subject behind Gascoigne's adaptation of Ariosto's comedy, with the whole colouring and flavour now modern and Italian. When a character quotes Terence, he quotes it not from the original but as it appears in Lily's school grammar. Schoolmastering appears yet again, with the suitors

getting through to the desired Bianca as teachers, one to instruct
her in Latin, the other in fingering on the lute. The Latin that
is construed falsely is Ovid, of course, and Ovid appears again
and again. The verse is young, and still near to experience of
school :

> Let's be no stoics nor no stocks, I pray ;
> Or so devote to Aristotle's checks
> As Ovid be an outcast quite abjured.

The play is full of fascinated report of Italy, placed in an Italian
setting, with touches from the *commedia dell' arte* — the popular
Italian vaudeville with stock figures of doctor and pantaloon —
and larded with simple Italian phrases such as a beginner would
use who did not know the language but wanted to make a cultivated impression. These could have been picked up in Field's
shop, or from the company of John Florio, at this time tutor in
Southampton's service : 'con tutto il cuore ben trovato', 'al la
nostra casa ben venuto, molto honorato signor mio Petruccio'.
All very simple : sufficient to give flavouring.

> O, this learning, what a thing it is !

Both the Adonis and the Lucrece themes were present to his
mind when writing this play :

> Adonis painted by a running brook,
> And Cytherea all in sedges hid.

> For patience she will prove a second Grissel,
> And Roman Lucrece for her chastity.

Shakespeare was chiefly indebted to the earlier Elizabethan dramatist George Gascoigne — an unrespectable, gamesome poet in
his day — whose *Supposes* he read for material. To this there is
a direct reference, with a Chaucerian-Spenserian word thrown
in for the sake of a rhyme — ingenious young man ! —

> While counterfeit supposes bleared thine eyne.

But the main theme of the play — conflict between husband
and wife as to who is to come out on top, the taming of a shrew
— is the dramatist's own, with the full and high-spirited characterisation of the two protagonists, Kate and Petruchio.

This theme has given modern critics (and producers) much
trouble, particularly with the revolution in the status of women.
Here it is useful to maintain an historical perspective and not to
regard the play anachronistically. It is true that Shakespeare

was gallant and chivalrous about women, and that he did not hold any doctrine of male superiority. But all sixteenth-century people held, as their institutions and laws bore out, that in marriage the man was to exercise external control : at home, within the household, was the province of wife and mother. Petruchio's taming of the bad-tempered, cross-bit Kate is not brutal — and nothing could be more crude or improper than the old Victorian habit of equipping him with a whip. For, observe, he never once beats her ; she once, at the beginning, beats him. Then she receives her lesson, by way of ridicule : his 'mad' conduct holds up a mirror to her own bad behaviour, and shows her what it looks like from outside. Even so, the taming is conducted in the language of love, for in fact he loves her in spite of herself ; in the end, the sense of this transpires to her, and brings her not only to her senses, and civilised conduct, but to love of him. It is, of course, knock-about farce, but with much psychological sense in it. It is hardly likely that Shakespeare was wrong in the matter and those who think themselves more exquisitely sensitive about women right.

The concluding speech of the play meant what it said : we are to take it simply and directly, if with a smile, not ironically as is sometimes suggested by anachronistic moderns. It is Kate speaking, a happy and loved wife, instead of a cross, unloved Shrew :

> Thy husband is thy lord, thy life, thy keeper,
> Thy head, thy sovereign : one that cares for thee
> And for thy maintenance ; commits his body
> To painful labour both by sea and land ;
> To watch the night in storms, the day in cold,
> Whilst thou liest warm at home, secure and safe ;
> And craves no other tribute at thy hands
> But love, fair looks and true obedience.

The play is full of high spirits and country lore. Petruchio's wedding is a farcical elaboration of the uncouth merriment that accompanied many a tying of the knot :

> when the priest
> Should ask if Katherine should be his wife,
> Aye, by gogs-wouns, quoth he, and swore so loud,
> That all amazed the priest let fall the book,
> And as he stooped again to take it up,
> This mad-brained bridegroom took him such a cuff,
> That down fell priest and book, and book and priest.

We see the picture of man and wife, riding on one horse on a cold wet evening and coming to grief in the mire going down a hill. They arrive at the manor-house, with serving men in blue liveries and white stockings, strewing rushes and laying carpets on the tables. We hear of

> Six score fat oxen standing in my stalls,

hear the roasted chestnuts bursting in a farmer's fire, take the bawdy suggestion of 'I knew a wench married in an afternoon as she went to the garden for parsley to stuff a rabbit'. Plenty of sound, hearty bawdy in the play: Hortensio teaching Bianca the lute teaches her 'fingering', and Petruchio pursues Katherine with jokes and puns, 'what, with my tongue in your tail', and he will be her 'combless cock, so Kate will be my hen'. The Induction has a bit of equivocal sex-appeal to the audience, when drunken Sly says to the page dressed up to pretend to be his wife:

> Servants, leave me and her alone.
> Madam, undress you and come now to bed.

The boy has to entreat that this pleasure may be put off 'yet for a night or two':

> I hope this reason stands for my excuse.
> *Sly :* Aye, it stands so that I may hardly tarry so long.

We observe the continual ambivalence of the Elizabethan stage — all the women's parts taken by pretty boys, dressed up as women, disguised back as youths, the women's and young men's parts frequently exchanged.

The play provides us with further hints of social awareness with increasing acquaintance with high society, where they would

> burn sweet wood to make the lodging sweet . . .
> Let one attend him with a silver basin
> Full of rose-water and bestrewed with flowers,
> Another bear the ewer, the third a diaper,
> And say, will't please your lordship cool your hands?

This was how it was in a great house. Perhaps there were twinges still about the university: 'While I play the good husband at home, my son and my servant spend all at the university'.

There is a virtuoso piece about horse-flesh: Petruchio's horse is 'possessed with the glanders, and like to mose in the chine; troubled with the lampass, infected with the fashions, full of wind-galls, sped with spavins, rayed with the yellows, past cure of the fives, stark spoiled with the staggers, begnawn with the bots; swayed in the back, and shoulder-shotten; near-legged before, and with a half-cheeked bit, and a headstall of sheep's leather', etc. There are terms from the poet's favourite falconry and bowls, and a no less virtuoso piece about hounds:

> Brach Merriman, the poor cur is embossed,
> And couple Clowder with the deep-mouthed brach.
> Saw'st thou not, boy, how Silver made it good
> At the hedge-corner, in the coldest fault? . . .

with a good deal more such knowing talk. We are more moved by the arrival of the players at this lord's house.

> This fellow I remember,
> Since once he played a farmer's eldest son —
> 'Twas where you wooed the gentlewoman so well —
> I have forgot your name . . .

They are taken to the buttery, and given meat and drink.

It must have happened to Shakespeare just like that; and he must often have been shown, like a servant, into the buttery.

CHAPTER IX

Friendship

IN these years Shakespeare found a patron, a friend and, at length, love. It has been observed that his mind was becoming increasingly obsessed with the theme of friendship and love, and the conflict of their claims. Well it might be : the theme had now emerged in full force in his own life. He was to give unprecedented and unique expression to it in his writings, leaving imperishable traces in the world's literature.

We have watched the long apprenticeship of this self-made countryman, the hard struggle to establish himself — where others, like Lyly and Marlowe, had found places waiting for them and had had the luck of immediate success — the energy and industry he had put into the plays, with which he was now more than catching up with them. Now, in 1593 and 1594, he was ready to challenge fame as a poet with the two splendid narrative poems he put forth in those years. We may assume with fair certainty that the first of these, *Venus and Adonis*, was written in 1592, and *The Rape of Lucrece* in 1593. Those were the plague years that gave him time, away from the theatre and in the country, for those ambitious compositions. In the dedication of the first he speaks of devoting 'all idle hours' to them. In fact, we are astonished by his tumultuous, easy productivity in these crowded years, greater than at any other time, in the effort to establish himself. For, in addition, there were the sonnets he was writing, which belong to the early 1590's, as we shall show. All in all, it was an almost unexampled burst of creative activity, into which an element more important even than patronage entered, that of the inspiration given by intense emotional experience.

Shakespeare's patron, the only recipient of his dedications, was the young Earl of Southampton.

This youth, Henry Wriothesley, had been born in October 1573 and was therefore between nine and ten years Shakespeare's junior. He came of a Catholic family that had nevertheless done well under Henry VIII and been ennobled by him. His father had spent some time in the Tower as an obstinate supporter of Norfolk and Mary Stuart, while his mother, daughter of Viscount Montague, belonged also to a family of Catholic *dévots*. Not even this unity in religion kept the pair together, however, and before his early death the husband had quarrelled with the wife and was living separated from her. He left an extravagant and rather cruel will, keeping his wife from custody of their daughter : which the Queen decently set aside. An immense sum was left to provide tombs in Titchfield church, upon one of which we see the new boy-Earl kneeling at a *prie-dieu* in full armour, the tall obelisks symbolising eternity all round.

The boy was eight when he succeeded his father. He had been baptised and brought up a Catholic, but he now came to the guardianship of Lord Burghley as a state-ward. Burghley sent him to his own college, St. John's, at Cambridge ; the boy turned out to be talented, precocious, with a desire to distinguish himself, somewhat fantastic and wayward, and, as he grew towards manhood, extremely handsome in a feminine vein with golden hair falling over his shoulder. Two other young earls were also Burghley's wards, as the Earl of Oxford had been before them — Rutland and Bedford ; the old man sought to tie them to himself by marriage into his family.

In 1590 the Lord Treasurer resolved to provide for his granddaughter, Lady Elizabeth Vere, the unfortunate Oxford's daughter, by marrying her to Southampton. They were much of an age — the young Earl not yet seventeen, the girl two years younger : what more suitable ? Southampton belonged to the new nobility, would be marrying a De Vere, gaining the protection of the Lord Treasurer for his regrettably Catholic family, as such in need of cover in high places.

Unfortunately marriage was far from the young man's mind or taste. No notice was taken of Lord Burghley's expressed wishes, and he began to grow suspicious whether some other were not intervening to land such a catch. He called upon Sir Thomas Stanhope to explain himself, who replied :

> my lord, I confess that, talking with the Countess of Southampton thereof, she told me you had spoken to her in that behalf. I replied she should do well to take hold of it, for I knew not where my lord, her son, should be better bestowed. Herself could tell what a stay you

would be to him and his, and for perfect experience did teach her how beneficial you had been to that lady's father, though by him little deserved [i.e. the incorrigible Oxford]. She answered I said well, and so she thought, and would in good faith do her best in the cause ; but, saith she, 'I do not find a disposition in my son to be tied as yet. What will be hereafter, time will try, and no want shall be found on my behalf.'[1]

And so the summer passed, with no further sign from the reluctant young Earl. At the end of it Lord Burghley called the grandfather, Lord Montague, into consultation and prevailed upon him to put pressure upon the inexplicable youth, so little awake to his opportunities. And this was what Lord Montague and his daughter came back with.

> We have laid abroad unto him both the commodities and hindrances likely to grow unto him by change ; and indeed receive to our particular speech this general answer — that your lordship was this last winter well pleased to yield unto him a further respite of one year, to ensure resolution in respect of his young years. I answered that this year which he speaketh of is now almost up, and therefore the greater reason for your lordship in honour and in nature to see your child well placed and provided for : whereunto my lord gave me this answer and was content that I should impart the same to your lordship. And this is the most as touching the matter I can now acquaint your lordship with.[2]

This is the time to which we must date Shakespeare's early sonnets, of which the first eighteen are addressed to this theme and — as we shall see unmistakably later — to this very subject, this young man.

Anyone who studies the portrait made of Southampton when he was nineteen will see how striking his beauty was. There are the familiar golden tresses, which he retained for some years more, falling over his left shoulder, the haughty aristocratic look on the face, a perfect oval, delicate features, lightly arched eyebrows, sensitive nostril, small mouth. It is a feminine appearance, yet there is a certain indefinable masculinity in the assertive stare of the eyes. For another thing, though it is a face to arrest attention anywhere and it might be anyone's fate to come under its spell, there is something that gives an unfavourable impression — a touch of obstinacy and fixation, in the eyes and pouting lip, a look of self-will.

This is that under whose spell Shakespeare came, an experience to which he owed inspiration and fulfilment, and so much else :

the discovery of himself and his own true nature, through which he revealed his nature to us in all its range of sympathy, humility, abnegation — a capacity for suffering, while understanding all that was happening to him, in a word, his own lovableness, which is an element in our never tiring of him.

But all this was not yet. Indeed the story that unfolds as the Sonnets proceed, the character of the relationship, its strangeness, considering that it was between a young patron and his poet — everything is unprecedented and unlike anything else. This, again, is why the Sonnets were essentially private, and, unlike other sonnet-sequences, not intended for publication.

They begin, conventionally enough, if not quite conventionally, with a series of sonnets to persuade the young man to marry, to perpetuate his looks and carry on the family. This was his plain duty, and it is put to him as such. Reading the Sonnets continuously and closely, one cannot fail to notice the tutorial element in Shakespeare's attitude, solicitous and apprehensive — after all, the young man had no father to direct him. I think it probable that the poet was called in by the family, perhaps by the mother, to aid in their campaign to incline the youth to marriage. For the Sonnets began as duty-offerings of a poet to his patron, and that character continues throughout, with the proper deference of the writer to one so much above him in social station.

At the beginning the tone is rather literary, and not yet engaged : the poet is making an argument, and though the circumstances are unusual, the situation is not unrecognisable. Then the imagination of the poet — one of the most subtly suggestible in literature — is caught by the personality, the position, the peerless looks of the young peer : a new world of the imagination opens out for the actor-poet, hitherto starved of all this. No wonder everything in him leaped to the chance : *this* experience of a new way of life is what made the difference between the *Henry VI* plays and the first comedies on one hand, and *A Midsummer-Night's Dream* and *Romeo and Juliet* on the other.

So far from thoughts of marriage, in 1591 Southampton's mind was full of the approaching campaign in Normandy, and his desire was to hitch himself to the star of Essex. Essex was six years his senior, now becoming the Queen's first favourite : the decade was to be dominated by his doings and misdoings, his unsteady ascendancy, his decline and catastrophe — in all of which his young follower remained faithful to him, nearly sharing his fate in the end.

The first sonnet announces the theme that dominates the first section, some twenty-six of these poems :

> From fairest creatures we desire increase
> That thereby beauty's rose might never die,
> But as the riper should by time decease,
> His tender heir might bear his memory.

But Southampton showed no inclination to beget an heir :

> But thou contracted to thine own bright eyes,
> Feed'st thy light's flame with self-substantial fuel.

The poet warns him, in traditional fashion,

> When forty winters shall besiege thy brow
> And dig deep trenches in thy beauty's field,
> Thy youth's proud livery, so gazed on now,
> Will be a tattered weed, of small worth held.

From which we learn that this handsome young ornament of Court and peerage was already much admired and gazed on.

> Look in thy glass, and tell the face thou viewest
> Now is the time that face should form another.

His mother had been a beauty and, as we shall see, she was not averse to marrying again.

> Thou art thy mother's glass, and she in thee
> Calls back the lovely April of her prime.

Gradually we learn more about the youth : he was ambivalent about music :

> Music to hear, why hear'st thou music sadly ?
> Sweets with sweets war not, joy delights in joy.
> Why lov'st thou that which thou receiv'st not gladly,
> Or else receiv'st with pleasure thine annoy ?

Southampton was at this stage not only much admired, but much made up to : we may well wonder whether all this adulation did not turn his head. There was something of a narcissistic strain in him — the image itself occurs at the end of *Venus and Adonis* — and we later have reason to think that it was not good for him.

> Grant, if thou wilt, thou art beloved of many,
> But that thou none lov'st is most evident.

So far all seems disinterested enough, but at the end of this Sonnet 10, Shakespeare has the first reference to himself and the affection between the two of them.

> Make thee another self, for love of me.

Sonnet 12 seems to have been written away in the country in autumn :

> When I behold the violet past prime,
> And sable curls all silvered o'er with white ;
> When lofty trees I see barren of leaves,
> Which erst from heat did canopy the herd,
> And summer's green all girded up in sheaves,
> Borne on the bier with white and bristly beard . . .

The tone becomes warmer and more engaged this winter :

> O, that you were yourself ! but, love, you are
> No longer yours than you yourself here live :
> Against this coming end you should prepare,
> And your sweet semblance to some other give.

This sonnet concludes with a reference to his dead father :

> dear my love, you know
> You had a father : let your son say so.

The next two are winter-sonnets, written when prognostications for the next year came out, of plagues and dearths, the seasons' weather, predictions whether it would go well with rulers. But the young Earl was at the top of his fortune :

> Now stand you on the top of happy hours,
> And many maiden gardens, yet unset,
> With virtuous wish would bear your living flowers
> Much liker than your painted counterfeit —

that is to say, his portrait, perhaps the very one painted in 1592.

With early summer we have the first sonnet to become very famous, Sonnet 18, and appropriately Shakespeare's first expression of belief in his own poetry and its destiny to live :

> Shall I compare thee to a summer's day ?
> Thou art more lovely and more temperate :
> Rough winds do shake the darling buds of May,
> And summer's lease hath all too short a date . . .
>
> But thy eternal summer shall not fade,
> Nor lose possession of that fair thou ow'st ;

Nor shall Death brag thou wander'st in his shade,
When in eternal lines to time thou grow'st :
So long as men can breathe, or eyes can see,
So long lives this, and this gives life to thee.

After long waiting and suppression of himself, after such humble willingness to learn from everyone and pick up hints from every quarter, this new note strikes like a trumpet-call.

With Sonnet 20 we come to the clue to the Sonnets as a whole, the nature of the young man's personality and of Shakespeare's love for him.

A woman's face with Nature's own hand painted
Hast thou, the master-mistress of my passion ;
A woman's gentle heart, but not acquainted
With shifting change, as is false women's fashion ;
An eye more bright than theirs, less false in rolling,
Gilding the object whereupon it gazeth ;
A man in hue, all hues in his controlling,
Which steals men's eyes and women's souls amazeth.

That is to say, the young man possessed a feminine beauty which attracted men's eyes to him as much as it did women's hearts ; and it was with this beauty that Shakespeare, susceptible to the loveliness of all things in nature, had fallen in love. But as to the nature of his love, Shakespeare could not be more clear ; it was not homosexual — it was not sexual at all, but ideal and all the more enthralling of heart and mind :

And for a woman wert thou first created ;
Till Nature, as she wrought thee, fell a-doting,
And by addition me of thee defeated,
By adding one thing to my purpose nothing.
But since she pricked thee out for women's pleasure,
Mine be thy love, and thy love's use their treasure.

What could be clearer than that ? — No need whatever for most of the embarrassed argument that has raged around and about the Sonnets. There is not the slightest trace of homosexuality in Shakespeare or even interest in the subject — as there was in Marlowe and in Bacon. There is no trace of it in the plays, with the single exception of the relationship of Achilles to Patroclus in *Troilus and Cressida*, there treated with disapprobation.[3] Shakespeare's attitude towards women was perfectly normal, or perhaps more than normally appreciative. But these considerations do not exhaust the complexity or the subtlety of such a nature. There

was a great deal of the feminine in Shakespeare's make-up : hence
the duality of his understanding, the duplicity (in the good sense)
of his sympathies, his double meed of comprehension.⁴ As it
happened, Southampton's nature as he grew older affirmed itself
as dominantly masculine ; and yet we have later evidence that
he was not merely ambivalent, but ambidextrous.⁵ Such is the
duplicity of things.

With the deepening of emotion, for friendship has passed
over into love, Shakespeare tells us all about himself, simply and
naturally, without any reserve — as indeed we know he was, for
Ben Jonson has told us the first and the last thing about him.
Even Ben, apt to be so crabbed and jealous, was reduced to shining
generosity by that golden nature : the first thing about Shakespeare, he tells us, was that he was ' of an open and free nature' ;
the last thing was his surpassing genius. In Sonnet 22 we see
Shakespeare looking at himself :

> My glass shall not persuade me I am old,
> So long as youth and thou are of one date ;
> But when in thee time's furrows I behold,
> Then look I death my days should expiate.
> For all that beauty that doth cover thee
> Is but the seemly raiment of my heart,
> Which in thy breast doth live, as thine in me :
> How can I then be elder than thou art ?

In this year, 1592 — when Shakespeare was writing *Venus and
Adonis*, and these early sonnets with it — he was twenty-eight,
the youth not yet nineteen. Elizabethans aged earlier than we,
ran through more of life in shorter space ; and the truth is, as
we find Shakespeare does not disguise from himself, that he was
no longer young.

The next sonnets tell us more about himself, and specifically
about his profession. He compares himself to a nervous actor
who is over-burdened with his part and with too much feeling,
so that he cannot express himself in person : his poems must
speak for him. There is veracity in this : for all the passion in
the poems, the poet does not step beyond the proper bounds of
deference in addressing someone so very much his superior. It
is true that Shakespeare regarded himself as a gentleman, though
he had hardly yet achieved the external status ; but the young
man was a noble — and this great difference is observed concord-
antly in the Sonnets. The remarkable thing is that he should

have got so far — the whole story of the Sonnets is quite unlike anybody else's ; but we can be sure that, to put on the other side of the balance, Shakespeare had not only his genius, but wit and charm, instinctive breeding now refined by his acquaintance in such circles, though — it must never be forgotten, he does not forget it himself — as an inferior.[6]

> As an unperfect actor on the stage,
> Who with his fear is put beside his part,
> Or some fierce thing replete with too much rage,
> Whose strength's abundance weakens his own heart,

so Shakespeare feels

> O'ercharged with burden of mine own love's might.
> O, let my books be then the eloquence
> And dumb presagers of my speaking breast,
> Who plead for love, and look for recompense,
> More than that tongue that more hath more expressed.

And so Shakespeare reveals his own feeling about himself, his birth and want of fortune in this unequal, and therefore ultimately doomed, friendship.

> Let those who are in favour with their stars
> Of public honour and proud titles boast —

nothing of all that for him —

> Whilst I, whom fortune of such triumph bars,
> Unlooked for joy in that I honour most.

We see again the humility in the phrase 'unlooked for' — the unexpected good fortune that had befallen him to be taken notice of, and made a friend of, by someone of such a rank. This is better fortune than that of

> Great princes' favourites their fair leaves spread
> But as the marigold at the sun's eye,
> And in themselves their pride lies burièd,
> For at a frown they in their glory die.
> The painful warrior famousèd for fight,
> After a thousand victories once foiled,
> Is from the book of honour razèd quite,
> And all the rest forgot for which he toiled.

It is obvious — though it has not been noticed — that what put this in mind was Ralegh's spectacular fall from favour this summer, for his seduction of and secret marriage to Elizabeth Throckmorton, and this corroborates still more firmly the date 1592. The phrase 'once foiled' even echoes Ralegh's own, 'once amiss hath bereaved me of all' — a phrase that reverberated at Court and would be picked up by Southampton.[7]

This summer, while Ralegh was in the Tower, the Queen went on progress attended by Burghley, Essex and Southampton. At Oxford the Earl was incorporated as Master of Arts ; we do not know if Shakespeare was in attendance on his patron at Oxford, but from a passage written not long after in *A Midsummer-Night's Dream* it would certainly seem so. The Duke is speaking, as it might be the Queen herself, and what he says gives an amusing and veracious report of just such a reception of her by the dons :

> Where I have come, great clerks have purposèd
> To greet me with premeditated welcomes ;
> Where I have seen them shiver and look pale,
> Make periods in the midst of sentences,
> Throttle their practised accent in their fears,
> And in conclusion dumbly have broke off.

In absence Shakespeare sent him a testimony of his duty, while Southampton had accepted the dedication of *Venus and Adonis* composed this year. Others have noticed how closely the language of Sonnet 26 approximates to that of the prose dedication of the poem. 'Lord of my love', Shakespeare salutes him — and anyone who knows Elizabethan usage intimately will recognise that this is to be taken in both senses, that the recipient is not only figuratively a lord, but in fact :

> Lord of my love, to whom in vassalage
> Thy merit hath my duty strongly knit,
> To thee I send this written embassage,
> To witness duty, not to show my wit.

Observe the emphasis on duty in this passage. The sestet goes on to express the hope that his work will justify his patron's confidence, the feeling of apprehension that many writers have felt on the appearance of their first book :

> Till whatsoever star that guides my moving,
> Points on me graciously with fair aspect,
> And puts apparel on my tattered loving,
> To show me worthy of thy sweet respect :
> Then may I dare to boast how I do love thee,
> Till then not show my head where thou mayst prove me.

We have seen one or two signs already in the plays that Shakespeare's imagination was much taken with the themes of Venus's vain pursuit of Adonis, and Tarquin's ravishment of Lucrece : both very suggestive themes, one of the torment of desire frustrated by an adolescent's chastity, the other of the suffering endured by chastity forced. Both very Renaissance, of course — neither very much appreciated by the Victorians ; indeed it is rather comic, as it is absurd, to think how little of the full Shakespeare, rounded and whole, how little of Shakespeare in depth, comes through in the English convention — a somewhat shadowy, two-dimensional silhouette behind his plays, and not all of them.[8]

A group of sonnets dealing with Adonis and Venus, under her name of Cytherea, was pirated along with other sonnets and poems of Shakespeare by Jaggard and published in *The Passionate Pilgrim*. We have reason to be grateful, for otherwise they might have been lost ; they must have been among the ' sugared sonnets ' which, Meres noted, were handed round among his private friends. It is unlikely that the more intimate sonnets written to Southampton were. And indeed these gay, naughty pieces about Venus offer a contrast with the respectful chastity of the sonnets to the young man. They provide a frank and natural eroticism, against a country background, which is quite delightful. The little poems are variations in attitudes, sketches for the large diploma-piece to come. Here is Venus, sitting by a brook as usual in the Renaissance pictures of her, with Adonis in captive attendance :

> She told him stories to delight his ear ;
> She showed him favours to allure his eye ;
> To win his heart she touched him here and there —
> Touches so soft still conquer chastity.

Alas, not with Adonis :

> Then fell she on her back, fair queen, and toward —
> He rose and ran away — ah ! fool too froward.

In the next sonnet, on a summer morning — pure Shakespeare — when had

> scarce the herd gone to the hedge for shade,

Venus waits to spy on the handsome youth stripping to bathe in the brook :

> Anon he comes, and throws his mantle by,
> And stood stark naked on the brook's green brim ;

The sun looked on the world with glorious eye,
Yet not so wistly as this queen on him :
He, spying her, bounced in whereas he stood :
'O Jove', quoth she, 'why was not I a flood !'

A third sonnet foreshadows the tragedy, Adonis' mortal wounding by the boar.

'Once', quoth she, 'did I see a fair sweet youth
Here in these brakes deep-wounded with a boar,
Deep in the thigh, a spectacle of ruth !
See, in my thigh,' quoth she, 'here was the sore.'
She showed hers ; he saw more wounds than one,
And blushing fled, and left her all alone.

In 1593 the long poem, for which these were but preliminary sketches, appeared : on its title-page, 'imprinted by Richard Field, and are to be sold at the sign of the White Greyhound in Paul's Churchyard'. The motto, taken from Ovid, advanced a lofty claim to be regarded as a pure poet — no mere playwright :

Vilia miretur vulgus : mihi flavus Apollo
Pocula Castalia plena ministret aqua.

Let the populace admire base things, but for him let the god minister cups filled with water from the purest Castalian spring. Or, as Ben Jonson translated it later :

Kneel hinds to trash : me let bright Phoebus swell,
With cups full flowing from the Muses' well.

Let the populace admire the base indeed ! — if it were not for the populace his plays would not have been written or performed, nor himself have made a living. However, this was but a manner of speaking, and he dedicated the poem to Southampton in his grand gentlemanly manner :

Right Honourable, I know not how I shall offend in dedicating my unpolished lines to your Lordship, nor how the world will censure me for choosing so strong a prop to support so weak a burden. Only, if your Honour seem but pleased, I account myself highly praised ; and vow to take advantage of all idle hours, till I have honoured you with some graver labour. But if the first heir of my invention prove deformed, I shall be sorry it had so noble a godfather, and never after ear so barren a land, for fear it yield me still so bad a harvest. I leave it to your honourable survey, and your Honour to your heart's content, which I wish may always answer your own wish, and the world's hopeful expectation. Your Honour's in all duty, William Shakespeare.

How beautifully phrased it is, with its instinctive tact and courtesy, the stylish balanced phrases — and yet so perfectly natural, with its recurrence to a country image. If the poem fails, he will never after 'ear', *i.e.* plough, so barren a land. There is, too, the proper deference, and the subscription 'in duty', for the poet is under obligation to the young peer as his patron. The poem was licensed for publication by the Archbishop of Canterbury with his own hand, the stern Whitgift — we can only suppose by Southampton's influence. We may perhaps wonder if the celibate Archbishop read so Renaissance, so erotic, a work ; and, if so, we can admire his tolerance still more and thank our stars that the horrid Puritans were not in a position to suppress it.

Nothing was wanting to make the poem a success, and it succeeded beyond the poet's dreams — ten or eleven editions in his own lifetime, twenty before the Civil War winged culture. Shakespeare himself saw the poem through the press, and Field made a good job of it from the poet's manuscript. It was conceived to make its appeal to the cultivated, to the Court and fashionable society, and here it found a delighted audience, especially with the young men of the Inns of Court and the universities, who were ready to take it to bed under their pillows and must have found it stimulating. 'The style,' an academic authority chastely says, 'so much richer and more glowing than that of the earliest histories and comedies, suggests either a new literary discipleship or some recent enrichment of personal experience.' [9] Certainly the latter ; but from the more strictly aesthetic point of view, Shakespeare, with his attested literary ambitions, is entering a new field of endeavour, flexing his muscles, enjoying new-found strength and skill. There is no doubt about the saucy ingenuity ; the poem is wanton, witty and sympathetic, like himself, sparkling and ever fresh with its enchanting background of country and country scenes and sports. There is the dramatist's gift of vivid characterisation and speed, or not, at will, with diversity and variation in place of the enamelled perfection of *Hero and Leander*.

For, like that, this was a fashionable Ovidian poem, for which Shakespeare not only used Golding's translation of the *Metamorphoses*, but read up the *Fasti* and the *Ars Amatoria* in Latin. As usual he drew upon several sources, but as usual he fused them in his imagination and made them entirely his own. The effect of the poem is highly personal, for Shakespeare's sympathies are

very much engaged. The situation is Southampton's, that of
the handsome youth who will not allow a woman to possess him
— for the whole thing is seen essentially from the woman's point
of view. The poet's sympathy is all in favour of the pleasures of
sex, with coupling whether in man or beast — though all is expressed with a suggestive delicacy, with wit and evident enjoyment.
Beneath this, as our authority perceives, the inspiration provided
by emotional disturbance 'urged Shakespeare to fresh verbal flights
and was one cause of the freedom, wit, allusiveness and elegance
which accompany the emotional enrichment of the next plays'.[10]

Desire raises its head from the first stanzas, the desire of a
passionate woman for an adolescent —

> With this she seizeth on his sweating palm —

so right a physical symptom for a young man. But it does not
answer :

> She red and hot as coals of glowing fire,
> He red for shame, but frosty in desire . . .

> Backward she pushed him, as she would be thrust,
> And governed him in strength, though not in lust.

(Had the Archbishop even read thus far ?) Soon we come to
the very same arguments advanced in the early Sonnets, and in
much the same phrases :

> Is thine own heart to thine own face affected ?

There follows a reference to Narcissus, and a warning as to the
effects of narcissism.

> Upon the earth's increase why shouldst thou feed,
> Unless the earth with thy increase be fed ?
> By law of nature thou art bound to breed,
> That thine may live when thou thyself art dead.

Venus herself offers him all her delights — who could possibly
resist ?

> 'Art thou a woman's son and canst not feel
> What 'tis to love, how want of love tormenteth ?' . . .

> 'Fondling,' she saith, 'since I have hemmed thee here
> Within the circuit of this ivory pale,
> I'll be a park and thou shalt be my deer :
> Feed where thou wilt, on mountain or in dale ;
> Graze on my lips, and if those hills be dry,
> Stray lower where the pleasant fountains lie.

> Within this limit is relief enough,
> Sweet bottom grass and high delightful plain,
> Round rising hillocks, brakes obscure and rough,
> To shelter thee from tempest and from rain :
> Then be my deer, since I am such a park,
> No dog shall rouse thee, though a thousand bark.'

We see again how delightedly Shakespeare's mind strayed to deer-parks ; but it was this kind of thing that made the poem's fortune with the younger generation.

Next comes the splendid episode of the horse, paralleled in Marlowe's poem, and still more stimulating :

> But lo from forth a copse that neighbours by,
> A breeding jennet, lusty, young and proud,
> Adonis' trampling courser doth espy,
> And forth she rushes, snorts and neighs aloud :
> The strong-necked steed being tied unto a tree,
> Breaketh his rein, and to her straight goes he.

There is a virtuoso description of the horse, which, even if based on the Latin, nevertheless bespeaks the enthusiastic countryman :

> Round-hoofed, short-jointed, fetlocks shag and long,
> Broad breast, full eye, small head, and nostril wide,
> High crest, short ears, straight legs and passing strong,
> Thin mane, thick tail, broad buttock, tender hide . . .

The 'kind embracements' of horse and jennet supply Venus with further ammunition.

> Hot, faint and weary with her hard embracing,
> Like a wild bird being tamed with too much handling,
> Or as the fleet-foot roe that's tired with chasing,
> Or like the froward infant stilled with dandling :
> He now obeys, and now no more resisteth,
> While she takes all she can, not all she listeth . . .

> Now is she in the very lists of love,
> Her champion mounted for the hot encounter.
> All is imaginary she doth prove ;
> He will not manage her, although he mount her.

And so the poem goes on to the sad end foreseen by the goddess, Adonis' death by the boar's tusk — symbol of male potency : a kind of nemesis.

Throughout the poem there are all sorts of subsidiary delights, especially those of country life. There is the endearing descrip-

tion of coursing the hare we have already noted,[11] and things such
as Shakespeare constantly noted in nature :

> Like a dive-dapper peering through a wave,
> Who being looked on, ducks as quickly in . . .

> Like a milch-doe, whose swelling dugs do ache,
> Hasting to feed her fawn, hid in some brake . . .

> Or as the snail, whose tender horns being hit,
> Shrinks backward in his shelly cave with pain,
> And there all smothered up in shade doth sit,
> Long after fearing to creep forth again.

Other passages suggest him to us no less personally, if more
sophisticatedly. There is a passage about painting which reminds
us of that about Apelles in the *Shrew*, and indicates increasing
sophistication and the wider cultural interests of high society :

> Look when a painter would surpass the life
> In limning out a well proportioned steed,
> His art with nature's workmanship at strife,
> As if the dead the living should exceed . . .

If only we had a portrait of him limned by Hilliard !
  Occasionally one hears him speaking in his own voice :

> Things out of hope are compassed oft with vent'ring —

he had certainly found it so in his own life, now achieving recognition with success — and he adds, what is no less revealing,

> Chiefly in love, whose leave exceeds commission.

We seem to see him,

>   as one on shore
> Gazing upon a late embarkèd friend,
> Till the wild waves will have him seen no more,
> Whose ridges with the meeting clouds contend.

And indeed the frequency of references to sea and sea-shore, storm
and shipwreck, in these early works would seem to indicate some
personal experience. In the lines,

> But now I lived, and life was death's annoy ;
> But now I died, and death was lively joy,

my ear detects an echo from Chideock Tichborne's lines,

> And now I die, and now I was but made . . .
> And now I live, and now my life is done :

written in the Tower while awaiting execution for his part in the Babington conspiracy. Southampton would have known him : a Hampshire neighbour and a Catholic. A reference to the plague and to the almanac-makers with their prophecies for the ensuing year (wrong, alas) anchors these lines to the end of 1592 :

> To drive infection from the dangerous year :
> That the star-gazers, having writ on death,
> May say, the plague is banished by thy breath.

In the year 1594 Shakespeare fulfilled his promise of accomplishing some 'graver labour' for Southampton with *Lucrece*, and dedicated it to him in terms which, as everyone has noticed, went quite beyond the formal language usual in dedications to express deep devotion : [12] 'The love I dedicate to your Lordship is without end ; whereof this pamphlet without beginning is but a superfluous moiety. The warrant I have of your honourable disposition, not the worth of my untutored lines, makes it assured of acceptance. What I have done is yours, what I have to do is yours, being part in all I have, devoted yours. Were my worth greater, my duty would show greater ; meantime, as it is, it is bound to your Lordship, to whom I wish long life still lengthened with all happiness. Your Lordship's in all duty, William Shakespeare.' We note here the increase of assurance — Shakespeare, fortified by the success of *Venus and Adonis*, is confident of the acceptance of *Lucrece*. Once more his 'duty' to his patron is doubly acknowledged.

In the interval Southampton was being increasingly made up to by other poets. Peele included a tribute to him in *The Honour of the Garter*, and shortly after disappeared from view :

> Gentle Wriothesley, Southampton's star,
> I wish all fortune that in Cynthia's eye,
> Cynthia the glory of the western world,
> With all the stars in her fair firmament
> Bright may he rise and shine immortally.[13]

These verses enable us to appreciate, if nothing else, the contrast between the poetry of this university wit, a star at Christ Church, and the self-made man from Stratford. Young Nashe also tried to insert himself into the charmed circle of Southampton's patronage, by dedicating *The Unfortunate Traveller* to him. 'Long have I desired to approve my wit unto you', he wrote jauntily. 'A dear lover and cherisher you are, as well of the lovers of poets as of the poets themselves. Your Lordship is the large spreading branch of renown from whence these my idle leaves seek to derive their whole nourishment.' [14] He was unsuccessful : no response, and the dedication was dropped from the next edition.

Lucrece was preceded by a prose argument, in the proper Latinised style appropriate for such a classical piece, and quite different from any other prose we have from Shakespeare's pen. It only goes to show that he could turn his hand to anything. Let us cite, by way of an example, a passage which is curiously not made use of in the poem.

> During which siege [of Ardea] the principal men of the army meeting one evening at the tent of Sextus Tarquinius, the King's son, in their discourses after supper everyone commended the virtues of his own wife ; among whom Collatinus extolled the incomparable chastity of his wife Lucretia. In that pleasant humour they all posted to Rome, and, intending by their secret and sudden arrival to make trial of that which everyone had before avouched, only Collatinus finds his wife, though it were late in the night, spinning amongst her maids ; the other ladies were all found dancing and revelling, or in several disports. Whereupon the noblemen yielded Collatinus the victory, and his wife the fame.

It all reads like a page of Livy. Actually Livy was one of the sources Shakespeare read for his story, along with Chaucer's *Legend of Good Women*, but above all Ovid, with some strokes from the *Aeneid* of Virgil. The poem was published by John Harrison, to whom Richard Field assigned it, though the latter printed it and made a fine job of it.

This poem stands in marked contrast to the other. The dark, grave gloom of *Lucrece* is appropriate to the subject : it is a night-poem, with a brooding, fearful atmosphere, conscience-stricken and guilt-laden. In this it chimes with the Sonnets about Shakespeare's relationship with his mistress, and the story they reveal. The poem is, above all, and profoundly, psychological. The conflict of conscience within Tarquin is well exposed at the beginning ; he is completely self-aware, and knows quite well what the consequences may be for himself and everyone else. The common sense of the eighteenth century was affronted by the lines,

> That for his prey to pray he doth begin,
> As if the heavens should countenance his sin.

> But in the midst of his unfruitful prayer,
> Having solicited th' eternal power
> That his foul thoughts might compass his fair fair,
> And they would stand auspicious to the hour . . .

Those who are better acquainted with the facts of sin and guilt know that this is psychological truth.

There is clearly a deepening experience behind this poem, a greater knowledge of the shadowy side of life, the exploration of sin and remorse, the full realisation of consequences, as always with him. However, he was himself engaged at the time in exploring the dark night of the soul ; and this had its rewards in the realm of art. Considerable passages reflect the inspiration of school-rhetoric, with amplifications in moralising : the contrast between innocence and lust, hospitality and betrayal, chastity and uncontrolled desire. Several times we are reminded of the famous sonnet :

> The expense of spirit in a waste of shame
> Is lust in action . . .

Tarquin reflects :

> What win I if I gain the thing I seek ?
> A dream, a breath, a froth of fleeting joy.
> Who buys a minute's mirth to wail a week,
> Or sells eternity to get a toy ?

Sometimes the moralising comes straight out of a text-book of rhetoric ; but when Shakespeare comes to his own variation upon the sentence he found, we get this :

> So that in vent'ring ill we leave to be
> The things we are, for that which we expect ;
> And this ambitious foul infirmity,
> In having much, torments us with defect
> Of that we have : so then we do neglect
> The thing we have, and all for want of wit,
> Make something nothing by augmenting it.

The sheer understanding of life that lies behind that ! — it applies not only to the ordering of life but to the conduct of one's investments. How did he arrive at such understanding ? I suppose by the way of humility and observation, watching everything, summing up everything, forcing nothing, following experience open-eyed, aware of everything and with a great capacity for suffering and charity.

Tarquin was the son of a king ; his treachery — his action was a kind of treason towards one who was his follower — had the consequence of bringing the rule of kings in ancient Rome to an end. Lucrece says,

> Thou art not what thou seem'st, and if the same,
> Thou seem'st not what thou art, a god, a king :
> For kings like gods should govern everything.

And, first of all, himself is the implication. How this points forward to the history plays, and the ill consequences that flow from monarchs who know not how to rule themselves and therefore not others — to *Richard II*, shortly to come. On a deeper level, there is Shakespeare's life-long concern, preternaturally sharpened by his being an actor, between being and seeming, his passionate hatred of false-seeming, and yet how to tell the reality from the dream, whether we are not all insubstantial shadows dreamed in the mind of a poet ?

All is at a deeper level in *Lucrece*, more revealing of him morally, less so on the surface. We occasionally glimpse the countryman, even in the night-gloom of this Roman palace, in images of limed birds, birds' fear of the falcon's bells, and always the deer :

> He is no woodman that doth bend his bow
> To strike a poor unseasonable doe.

There are references to the stage :

> To see sad sights moves more than hear them told,
> For then the eye interprets to the ear
> The heavy motion that it doth behold,
> When every part a part of woe doth hear.

The line,

> Black stage for tragedies and murders fell,

reminds us that the stage was hung below with black when tragedies were performed. We observe his interest in painting in the long and literary description of the scene of the destruction of Troy :

> A thousand lamentable objects there
> In scorn of nature, art gave lifeless life . . .

> To this well-painted piece is Lucrece come,
> To find a face where all distress is stelled . . .

> In her [15] the painter had anatomized
> Time's ruin, beauty's wreck, and grim care's reign.

His constant consciousness of monuments and antiquities is attested :

> To fill with worm-holes stately monuments,
> To feed oblivion with decay of things,
> To blot old books and alter their contents,
> To pluck the quills from ancient ravens' wings,
> To dry the old oak's sap and cherish springs,
> To spoil antiquities of hammered steel,
> And turn the giddy round of fortune's wheel.

He is no less conscious of heraldry and coats of arms, and their social significance :

> Yea, though I die the scandal will survive
> And be an eye-sore in my golden coat ;
> Some loathsome dash the herald will contrive
> To cipher me how fondly I did dote :
> That my posterity shamed with the note
> Shall curse my bones.

Lucrece is, in the nature of things, a much less appealing and popular poem than *Venus and Adonis*. Where the earlier reflects the spring-time of his love for Southampton, the later belongs with the guilt-laden and remorseful Sonnets, the tormented and shameful relationship with the dark mistress. *Lucrece* is more laboured, and without the sparkle of *Venus and Adonis*. From the artistic point of view, it is right that it should be so : for the poem is deeply serious, where the earlier is not or only half-serious, and this is concerned with grave moral issues. We may concede that Shakespeare, no longer a youthful poet as his critics suppose, knew better than they what he was about. The intensity of his moral sensibility, deepened by the experience he was himself going through, here first achieves full expression and points forward to the later tragedies. There is a deep emotional disturbance in the poem ; it is the greater susceptibility to the anguish in life and the world's suffering, allied to the capacity to give it final expression, that places such spirits as Aeschylus and Shakespeare, Dante and Milton, apart. They are of

> those to whom the miseries of the world
> Are misery, and will not let them rest.

Lucrece is 'but an earlier manifestation of that tragic disgust and revulsion which appear in various forms in *Hamlet*, *Lear* and *Timon*, and underlie so much of Shakespeare's later work. . . . The murk of *Macbeth* is not without its reminiscence of Tarquin stalking his prey, and in *Cymbeline* Iachimo's penetration of Imogen's bed-chamber becomes almost a deliberate allusion to the early work. These are incidental and external parallels, but they indicate the deeper continuity of Shakespeare's sensibility' — and perhaps more.[16]

The success of the poems was undoubted, and the response of the public itself offers an interesting index. Where *Venus and Adonis* had some ten editions in Shakespeare's life-time, *Lucrece* had five ; where the former had twenty before the Civil War, the latter had eight. References to the poems are frequent in contemporary literature.[17] The curious, rather mystifying book, *Willoughbie his Avisa,* refers to *Lucrece* in the year of its publication:

> Yet Tarquin plucked his glistering grape,
> And Shakespeare paints poor Lucrece' rape.

Next year, 1595, William Covell, Fellow of a Cambridge college, annotates : 'All praiseworthy : Lucretia sweet Shakespeare . . . Wanton Adonis. Watson's heir.' It would have been music to Shakespeare's ears to be regarded as the poetic heir to the scholarly and gentlemanly Watson, as much admired for his Latin as for his English verse. Francis Meres, in 1598, writes : 'the sweet witty soul of Ovid lives in mellifluous and honey-tongued Shakespeare : witness his *Venus and Adonis*, his *Lucrece*, his sugared Sonnets among his private friends, etc.' In the same year a younger poet, Richard Barnfield, paid him a welcome tribute :

> And, Shakespeare, thou whose honey-flowing vein,
> Pleasing the world, thy praises doth obtain :
> Whose *Venus* and whose *Lucrece*, sweet and chaste,
> Thy name in fame's immortal book have placed.

In the following year John Weever has another tribute from Cambridge :

> Honey-tongued Shakespeare, when I saw thine issue,
> I swore Apollo got them and none other,
> Their rosy-tainted features clothed in tissue,
> Some heaven-born goddess said to be their mother :
> Rose-cheeked Adonis with his amber tresses,
> Fair fire-hot Venus charming him to love her,
> Chaste Lucretia, virgin-like, her dresses,
> Proud lust-stung Tarquin seeking still to prove her.

Observe that the epithet for Shakespeare is always 'sweet' ; but the word had a stronger meaning in those days : it meant not 'saccharine', but sweet as honey tastes or as roses smell, and was without its modern sentimentalising connotation : a description of fact.

The young men at Cambridge expressed their devotion to his poetry, rather than his plays, in their own *Parnassus* trilogy : 'O sweet Master Shakespeare ! I'll have his picture in my study at the Court. Let me hear Master Shakespeare's vein.' There follow verses in imitation of *Venus and Adonis*, of course ; and then 'let this duncified world esteem of Spencer and Chaucer, I'll worship sweet Master Shakespeare, and to honour him will lay his *Venus and Adonis* under my pillow'. The dons were more discriminating, as we see from Gabriel Harvey, Spenser's friend : 'the younger sort takes much delight in Shakespeare's *Venus and Adonis* ; but his *Lucrece* and his tragedy of *Hamlet, Prince of Denmark*, have it in them to please the wiser sort'.

This, from the university, was recognition at last.

CHAPTER X

The Story of the Sonnets

THE Sonnets of Shakespeare have hitherto presented the greatest problem in our literature : there has been no certainty recognised as to the person for whom they were written, the nature of the relations between Shakespeare and that person, the story they reveal, the identity of the rival poet and the part he played in the story, or even as to the character and dating of the Sonnets, where they come in Shakespeare's life, or whether they belong together, to one period or not. Yet the answers to these questions are of fundamental importance not only to Shakespeare's life, but to our conception of him ; and the Sonnets are documents of the first importance, for they are the most autobiographical ever written.

It is here that historical method is indispensable : there can be no certain answer to these questions without a firm dating and chronology, and only historical method can give it. Hitherto, it has been the habit with literary men to reach down here a sonnet, or there another, and try to think up the circumstances of time that may fit it and apply that as a key to the rest. In consequence they have been all over the place, any and every date suggested from the Spanish Armada to the death of Queen Elizabeth : no certainty, and a vast deal of nonsense.

Now, for the first time, certainty as to dating has been achieved and the consequences are immeasurable : a flood of light pours in, all the main problems of the Sonnets receive their solution, the questions are answered — with the one exception of the identity of the dark mistress, and this, though it would be fascinating to know, does not affect the essence of the situation or the story.

The solution of these age-long problems has come through the historical method of following what Shakespeare wrote, humbly line by line, watching at every point the internal consistency of what he says for its coherence with what is going on contemporaneously in the outside world. Only the historian can do that with firmness and achieve certainty.

I must ask the reader then to follow me patiently, with critical attention, sonnet by sonnet, while the picture builds up gradually, inescapably, to certainty and conviction.

It is extraordinary to think, after long groping in the dark, that we are suddenly faced with an almost embarrassing outpouring on the part of Shakespeare about himself. We can be quite sure that it was no aristocrat who wrote the Sonnets : there is no aristocratic reserve, as there is, for example, with Sir Philip Sidney even in the most intimate expression of his feelings towards Stella. With Shakespeare, there is nothing that he does not tell us about himself; everything is exposed : his humiliations, the indignities he suffers, his fears and apprehensions of the loss of love ; the sin he commits in his adulterous relation with his mistress, his remorse and yet his weakness, his inability to free himself from subjugation. There are the suspicions he endures about both friend and mistress, his submission and willingness to bear the joint burden of his own and his friend's faults. There is the gathering disillusionment with the golden youth's character as he grows older in the world's ways and takes its stains. Yet the older man, with no illusions about his age and recognising that separation had always been inevitable, forgives him everything. It is this moral quality, arising out of an equivocal situation that strips all three naked and from which none can escape with rectitude or honour, that paradoxically lends the Sonnets in the end their dignity. For they speak the simple human truth about the inmost concerns of the human heart, and only a man of the people could have written them.

Their fate has been no less strange. For, after all, it is extraordinary that the most splendid sonnets in the English language should have been written to one man by another — very few of those who speak the language have still any conception that this is so. And when we come to the woman, 'there is nothing like the woman of Shakespeare's Sonnets in all the sonnet literature of the Renaissance'.[1] So far from being ideal, this is a completely realistic portrait, with no illusion whatever, shocking in its candour. Indeed, the consistent realism about sex, exposed in the Sonnets as in the plays, has not been at all palatable to the modern English. How have they managed to idolise him ? By leaving out much that is essential to the portrait of the man. But it is only in our own time that we have come to understand at all appreciatively that Renaissance woman, the Queen herself — the Victorians had a very unappreciative, not to say disapproving, attitude towards her.

With Shakespeare, the sheer poetry of the Sonnets conquered — but disparately, taken one by one, anthologised, not linked up and considered for the story they reveal, their significance as a whole or in his life. And yet the influence of their poetry has been immeasurable. Whenever poets writing in the language turn to writing sonnets, one hears the rhythms of his voice. They cannot escape it : these shape and form the very idea of the sonnet in the language, laid up in a Platonic heaven, the model for as long as the language recognisably lasts. It is strange, again, that he should have had, amid all his apprehensions and dubieties, a prophetic sense of the eternity of their appeal.

But, then, poets are the only true prophets.

When we take up the Sonnets again, after the first section, we find that Shakespeare is absent from his friend. And, indeed, absence is the normal condition of their relation. It would hardly have been possible for them to have shared their lives, with the difference in their social station, the 'separable spite' that kept them apart. Absence is all the more stimulating to the mind of a lover, and with a poet all things go to the imagination. Like other poets, Shakespeare was also in love with the idea of being in love : this was unexplored territory for him, inspiration for his art, the subject of all verse, a revelation of himself to himself, in the end, of the possibilities and powers of life.

Sonnet 27 shows him travelling in the country, probably on tour, for the theatres were closed through most of 1592 and 1593.

> Weary with toil, I haste me to my bed,
> The dear repose for limbs with travel tired ;
> But then begins a journey in my head,
> To work my mind, when body's work's expired.

One sees him sleepless, his thoughts journeying after his friend 'from far where I abide'. Weariness and work, the melancholy of absence, plunge him into depression.

> When, in disgrace with fortune and men's eyes
> I all alone beweep my outcast state,

And trouble deaf heaven with my bootless cries,
And look upon myself and curse my fate,
Wishing me like to one more rich in hope,
Featured like him, like him with friends possessed,
Desiring this man's art and that man's scope,
With what I most enjoy contented least.

This was but a mood, and yet it shows us what he genuinely thought about himself: it is the reflex of long and arduous struggle, the resentment at not having been better circumstanced in life. Remember that he had not yet achieved the confirming success of *Lucrece*, nor the security of the re-establishment of the Chamberlain's men with himself as their dramatist: that was to come in 1594.

This melancholy mood inspired a sonnet that has become famous, that commemorating earlier friends now dead:

When to the sessions of sweet silent thought
I summon up remembrance of things past . . .
Then can I drown an eye, unused to flow,
For precious friends hid in death's dateless night.

The next sonnet is a kind of chime to this one. And here we should notice that these poems often go in couples, antiphonally: the first is suggested by a direct thought or experience of the friend, the second sonnet is suggested by the first, takes it up, expands it or replies. The effect is that of an interior dialogue; and the poet is more often communing with himself than with his friend — who has other occupations, and pre-occupations, does not suffer the obsessions that go with genius.

There are the usual ups-and-downs in such a relationship, and next a cloud comes between them:

Even so my sun one early morn did shine,
With all-triumphant splendour on my brow;
But, out, alack! he was but one hour mine,
The region cloud hath masked him from me now.

But when this cloud has passed over, a more serious state of affairs is revealed between them: Southampton has committed a breach of friendship, though once more he makes up to the poet.

'Tis not enough that through the cloud thou break,
To dry the rain on my storm-beaten face,
For no man well of such a salve can speak,
That heals the wound and cures not the disgrace:

> Nor can thy shame give physic to my grief;
> Though thou repent, yet I have still the loss:
> The offender's sorrow lends but weak relief
> To him that bears the strong offence's cross.

What had happened between them? There can be little doubt, as we know from the later Sonnets — later in numbering, not necessarily in time; indeed, those sonnets, written to Shakespeare's mistress, overlap these written to his friend. The fact is — and it might be expected from what we learn later about his character — that she had got hold of the young man. It is so like the irony of life that this should be the form the handsome, reluctant youth's initiation into sex should take. The boy was repentant, and Shakespeare forgives him, as always, everything:

> No more be grieved at that which thou hast done:
> Roses have thorns, and silver fountains mud . . .
> All men make faults, and even I in this,
> Authorising thy trespass with compare,
> Myself corrupting, salving thy amiss,
> Excusing thy sins more than thy sins are.

Shakespeare takes the fault upon his own shoulders, and defends the young man against himself:

> For to thy sensual fault I bring in sense —
> Thy adverse party is thy advocate —
> And 'gainst myself a lawful plea commence:
> Such civil war is in my love and hate
> That I an accessory needs must be
> To that sweet thief which sourly robs from me.

Nevertheless, this new factor forces the older man to review their whole relation, and this he proceeds to do with the unselfishness that is a charm in him:

> Let me confess that we two must be twain,
> Although our undivided loves are one:
> So shall those blots that do with me remain,
> Without thy help, by me be borne alone.

He accepts the necessity to recognise their separateness through the immense difference in their social station: thus early we see signs of that philosophy of acceptance which became Shakespeare's ultimate wisdom — though again, after long and intense inner struggle.

> In our two loves there is but one respect,
> Though in our lives a separable spite,
> Which though it alters not love's sole effect,
> Yet doth it steal sweet hours from love's delight.

That means that they were kept apart by their different ways of life, though they took much pleasure in each other's company when they could meet — as who would not ? On the other hand, he recognises his own guilt in his infatuation with a mistress of no good fame, that this is publicly known and may do harm to Southampton's reputation :

> I may not evermore acknowledge thee,
> Lest my bewailèd guilt should do thee shame,
> Nor thou with public kindness honour me,
> Unless thou take that honour from thy name.

In the antiphon, or echo, to this (Sonnet 37), Shakespeare expresses again his resentment at the ill-fortune that divides him from his friend, but takes comfort in the thought of the latter's gifts and golden qualities, his wit as well as his rank, and is content to add his love to those.

> So I, made lame by fortune's dearest spite,
> Take all my comfort of thy worth and truth ;
> For whether beauty, birth, or wealth, or wit,
> Or any of these all, or all, or more,
> Entitled in thy parts do crownèd sit,
> I make my love engrafted to this store.

Observe the word 'entitled' — once more there is the characteristic double meaning, the literal as well as the ordinary general use : everything to show that the recipient of the Sonnets bore a title ; there is no disguise about it but an honest pride in the fact, natural to any Elizabethan. And the next sonnets express Shakespeare's sense of gratitude at having such a subject for his verse :

> How can my Muse want subject to invent,
> While thou dost breathe, that pour'st into my verse
> Thine own sweet argument, too excellent
> For every vulgar paper to rehearse ?

Any poet might indeed be grateful for such a theme ; it was the poet in Shakespeare as much as the man, if the two are separable, that caught at the inspiration, the golden chance.

Nevertheless, the underlying fact of the situation remained

that the young man had captured Shakespeare's mistress, or rather'
been captured by her.

> Take all my loves, my love, yea, take them all ;
> What hast thou then more than thou hadst before ?
> No love, my love, that thou mayst true love call ;
> All mine was thine before thou hadst this more.

What could be sadder, or more generous, than that ? — though
I fear that into this genuine spirit of self-abnegation, such is the
equivocal subtlety of things, there entered still the deference due to
their difference in condition, the poet's dependence upon his patron.

Besides, Shakespeare well understands the temptations the
younger man is subjected to

> When I am sometime absent from thy heart . . .
> For still temptation follows where thou art.
> Gentle thou art, and therefore to be won,
> Beauteous thou art, therefore to be assailed ;
> And when a woman woos, what woman's son
> Will sourly leave her till she have prevailed ?

We remember how that practically repeats the lines from *Venus
and Adonis* :

> Art thou a woman's son, and canst not feel
> What 'tis to love, how want of love tormenteth ?

Well, at length a woman had prevailed on Adonis, and in what a
guise ! Shakespeare could not but rue it :

> Ay me! but yet thou mightst my seat forbear,
> And chide thy beauty and thy straying youth,
> Who lead thee in their riot even there
> Where thou art forced to break a two-fold truth :
> Hers, by thy beauty tempting her to thee,
> Thine, by thy beauty being false to me.

We next are given clearly, without any disguise, what Shakespeare's attitude was to one and the other of his loves :

> That thou hast her, it is not all my grief,
> And yet it may be said I loved her dearly ;
> That she hath thee, is of my wailing chief,
> A loss in love that touches me more nearly.

The next sonnets, from 43 to 55, are written in absence, in the
country or on tour ; once more, as at the beginning, Shakespeare

consoles himself at night-time by summoning up his friend's image :

> All days are nights to see till I see thee,
> And nights bright days when dreams do show thee me.

When Shakespeare left his room in London,

> How careful was I, when I took my way,
> Each trifle under truest bars to thrust . . .
> But thou, to whom my jewels trifles are,
> Most worthy comfort, now my greatest grief,
> Thou, best of dearest and mine only care,
> Art left the prey of every vulgar thief.

Shakespeare saw, as others have done—in his case with so much more humility and charity — his young friend growing away from him.

> Against that time, if ever that time come,
> When I shall see thee frown on my defects . . .
> Against that time when thou shalt strangely pass,
> And scarcely greet me with that sun, thine eye,
> When love, converted from the thing it was,
> Shall reasons find of settled gravity.

Here is the saddest thing in the world : when love is gone and a bare, nodding acquaintance takes its place, a matter of rational convenience without heart in it any more.

In the next sonnets Shakespeare is still travelling wearily about the country, measuring the miles that take him further from his friend. Absence only sharpens his appreciation of 'the seldom pleasure' of being with him. No doubt : such meetings are rare feasts,

> Since, seldom coming, in the long year set,
> Like stones of worth they thinly placèd are,
> Or captain jewels in the carcanet.

What is the secret of Southampton's magnetism ?

> What is your substance, whereof are you made,
> That millions of strange shadows on you tend ?
> Since every one hath, every one, one shade,
> And you, but one, can every shadow lend.
> Describe Adonis, and the counterfeit
> Is poorly imitated after you ;
> On Helen's cheek all art of beauty set,
> And you in Grecian tires are painted new.

I think this gives us the answer : it was the appeal of this peerless youth, in all the flourish of his spring and beauty, to the imagination. These were men of the Renaissance, and they were infinitely more sensitive to physical beauty, whether in women or men, since it was so much more brief and shone all the more clearly against that variegated background, where the ravages of time could not be disguised. Evidently the perfection of that first spring, the unblemished innocence of youth, appealed to the poet's imagination, along with beauty, rank and (in those days) the concomitant splendour — qualities of which his early life had been starved and with which he had now come into such unexpected intimacy. What a strange turn of fate ! Confidence in his own powers welled up in him when he contemplated it :

> Not marble, nor the gilded monuments
> Of princes, shall outlive this powerful rhyme.

Strangely enough, that turned out true too.

All the same, we must never forget the terms of the intimacy accorded : it adds a further dimension to the relationship, complicating it, making it the more difficult to get quite right and to interpret the language in which it is expressed. In Elizabethan terms the poet of a noble patron was his servant, and in fact was a dependant — fairly certainly dependent on Southampton for a meed of support in these difficult years. Through many of the sonnets, certainly beyond half way, there appear the notes of apprehension, anxiety, resentment against the circumstances in which he has been placed by fortune. There was always this limiting condition in the relationship ; in view of this it is all the more remarkable that Shakespeare should have maintained such independence-in-dependence. It is another facet of that elusive, easily withdrawn mind, so hard to pin down.

Here, for example, is the servant as well as the friend, dependence along with devotion :

> Being your slave, what should I do but tend
> Upon the hours and times of your desire ?
> I have no precious time at all to spend,
> Nor services to do, till you require.

One must not take that too simply — there is the slightest shadow upon it : one must not go so far as to say even a shade of irony — just a sigh. Then :

> Nor dare I chide the world-without-end hour
> Whilst I, my sovereign, watch the clock for you,
> Nor think the bitterness of absence sour,
> When you have bid your servant once adieu.

We see the poet kept waiting by his young lord, or dismissed casually enough. Nothing strange, in the circumstances, in that ; what was strange was the extent to which they became emotionally involved — no doubt more on the poet's part, to whom this was a new world opening like a flower.

All the same —

> Nor dare I question with my jealous thought
> Where you may be, or your affairs suppose,
> But, like a sad slave, stay and think of nought
> Save, where you are, how happy you make those.

And the next sonnet goes on to imply a gentle rebuke :

> O, let me suffer, being at your beck,
> The imprisoned absence of your liberty ;
> And patience, tame to sufferance, bide each check,
> Without accusing you of injury . . .
> I am to wait, though waiting so be hell,
> Nor blame your pleasure, be it ill or well.

There is the double relationship : poet-servant, patron-friend, which makes it so subtle a matter precisely to catch the tone of what is being said, and how to take it.

For one thing, the element of duty, the expectation of offerings in praise of the poet's patron, has not been sufficiently recognised ; yet this is their context. It is probably a dim perception of this that made some Victorian commentators think that the sonnets were a mere literary exercise ; whereas the subtlety is that, though there is an element of that in them, they are also sincere and true, expressing a real situation, real feelings and emotions. Shakespeare is expected to write these poems in praise of his lord, a cultivated and spoiled young peer avid of such praise ; at the same time there is no doubt about the sincerity of what the older man feels, alone at night, away from him, his mind possessed with the image of him :

> For thee I watch, whilst thou dost wake elsewhere,
> From me far off, with others all too near.

However, Shakespeare blames himself, not the young man — it is just as well — for neglect and casualness. There is the inevitable difference between them, and Shakespeare, always conscious of the march of time, recognises himself as growing older :

> But when my glass shows me myself indeed,
> Beated and chopped with tanned antiquity . . .

The simple reflection on what time ruins — the theme of a long poem by Spenser — produced the magnificent Sonnet 64 :

> When I have seen by Time's fell hand defaced
> The rich-proud cost of outworn buried age ;
> When sometime lofty towers I see down-razed,
> And brass eternal slave to mortal rage . . .

We observe once more Shakespeare's feeling for the past : he was, in truth, a backward-looking man, historically minded, with a dream of an antique world at heart — shortly to be marvellously expressed in a speech in *Romeo and Juliet* — of what an older England had been like. He must have been affronted, as he went about the country, by the scars left by the Reformation and the rapacity of Philistines — the bare ruined choirs, the lofty towers down-razed, the splendid medieval brasses ripped out to turn into cash.

> When I have seen the hungry ocean gain
> Advantage on the kingdom of the shore,
> And the firm soil win of the watery main . . .

The frequency of these passages about the sea brings him before us as a player on tour along the south coast towns from Dover to Plymouth, and perhaps earlier in his career, up the western side from Bristol to Lancashire. Plenty of ruins from the Middle Ages on the way.

When Shakespeare returns to the thought of Southampton, after an interval, with Sonnet 69, it is with a reproach : his name is being slandered by people outwardly friendly :

> Then churls, their thoughts, although their eyes were kind,
> To thy fair flower add the rank smell of weeds :
> But why thy odour matcheth not thy show,
> The soil is this, that thou dost common grow.

As usual, Shakespeare excuses him :

> That thou art blamed shall not be thy defect,
> For slander's mark was ever yet the fair.

The mood of these next sonnets becomes increasingly one of farewell. The very next one we have all known since childhood, without knowing the experience that lay behind it ; nor is this the place to expatiate on the way it has chimed in the minds of other poets, in the sonnets of Christina Rossetti and in *In Memoriam*.

> No longer mourn for me when I am dead
> Than you shall hear the surly sullen bell
> Give warning to the world that I am fled
> From this vile world, with vilest worms to dwell.

Back in London, he was able to enjoy his friend's company, if only contingently, on sufferance :

> Now proud as an enjoyer, and anon
> Doubting the filching age will steal his treasure ;
> Now counting best to be with you alone,
> Then bettered that the world may see my pleasure :
> Sometime all full with feasting on your sight,
> And by and by clean starvèd for a look.

Sonnet 77 is an *envoi* to the preceding score of sonnets ; Shakespeare presents his friend with a glass, a pocket-dial and a volume containing these poems :

> Thy glass will show thee how thy beauties wear,
> Thy dial how thy precious minutes waste ;
> The vacant leaves thy mind's imprint will bear
> And of this book this learning mayst thou taste.

Now a danger looms ahead — a rival poet offering his praises to Southampton. Shakespeare meets it with his usual modesty, admitting that the young Earl

> Deserves the travail of a worthier pen.

Yet, for all the gifts of the rival poet, his verses can but describe the qualities that are already in his subject :

> He lends thee virtue, and he stole that word
> From thy behaviour ; beauty doth he give,
> And found it in thy cheek.

Nevertheless, Shakespeare feels discouraged by the competition, since it comes from 'a better spirit' :

> O, how I faint when I of you do write,
> Knowing a better spirit doth use your name,
> And in the praise thereof spends all his might,
> To make me tongue-tied, speaking of your fame !

It now appears that the rival poet is taking Shakespeare's place in Southampton's favour :

> But since your worth wide as the ocean is,
> The humble as the proudest sail doth bear,
> My saucy bark inferior far to his,
> On your broad main doth wilfully appear.

Then, with a feeling of apprehension :

> Your shallowest help will hold me up afloat,
> Whilst he upon your soundless deep doth ride ;
> Or, being wrecked, I am a worthless boat,
> He of tall building and of goodly pride.
> Then if he thrive and I be cast away,
> The worst was this : my love was my decay.

This announces a situation of crisis for Shakespeare. If the rival succeeds in ousting him from Southampton's favour, all is up with him : he will be 'cast away'. As we shall see, the doubt lasted for some time, and was resolved in the end only by a tragic event. Meanwhile, Shakespeare affirms a proper confidence in his own verse, if not in himself :

> Your monument shall be my gentle verse,
> Which eyes not yet created shall o'er-read,
> And tongues to be your being shall rehearse,
> When all the breathers of the world are dead.
> You still shall live — such virtue hath my pen —
> Where breath most breathes, even in the mouths of men.

Yes, indeed ! — 'eyes not yet created shall o'er-read', 'tongues to be your being shall rehearse'. It is very curious, this contrast between the humility of the man, and the prophetic confidence of the poet. Sometimes one thinks of him as possessed by a spirit greater than he knew ; but this too he seems to have known — such are the rewards of relying on inspiration, the intuitive, the psychic, the whole gamut of nature.

> I grant thou wert not married to my Muse,

but where his competitors have devised

> What strainèd touches rhetoric can lend,
> Thou truly fair wert truly sympathised
> In true plain words by thy true-telling friend.
> And their gross painting might be better used
> Where cheeks need blood ; in thee it is abused.

This tells us that Shakespeare thought his rival's verses strained and rhetorical, while he set store by his own naturalness and sincerity. Nevertheless for a time he withdraws — until his patron complains of his silence :

> This silence for my sin you did impute,
> Which shall be most my glory being dumb ;

> For I impair not beauty being mute,
> When others would give life and bring a tomb.
> There lives more life in one of your fair eyes
> Than both your poets can in praise devise.

From this we learn that the rival poet had been received: he was now on an accepted footing along with Shakespeare.

In these circumstances of doubt and anxiety for the future it was spirited of Shakespeare to tell the young man:

> You to your beauteous blessings add a curse,
> Being fond on praise, which makes your praises worse.

There is a direct hit, such as again only a man of the people would make: well-deserved, no doubt, though not very tactful; showing, underneath everything, a proper spirit of independence, that love had not corrupted sound judgment.

Actually Shakespeare found himself daunted, his Muse 'tongue-tied', in comparison with his rival, whose

> comments of your praise, richly compiled,
> Reserve their character with golden quill,
> And precious phrase by all the Muses filed.

He can only cry 'Amen', like an unlettered clerk,

> To every hymn that able spirit affords,
> In polished form of well-refinèd pen.

Who was the rival whose superiority of spirit Shakespeare was so ready to acknowledge? Sonnet 86 makes it quite clear, once we grasp the chronological fact that this is still 1593, and the information we are given as to the rival is of the utmost importance:

> Was it the proud full sail of his great verse —

there was only one contemporary to whom those words could possibly apply —

> Bound for the prize of all too precious you,
> That did my ripe thoughts in my brain inhearse,
> Making their tomb the womb wherein they grew?

The meaning is plain: was it the fact that the splendid verse his rival was writing to Southampton froze his own inspiration and his rival profited by his silence?

> Was it his spirit, by spirits taught to write
> Above a mortal pitch, that struck me dead?
> No, neither he, nor his compeers by night
> Giving him aid, my verse astonishèd.

I think this tells us that the rival poet dabbled with the spirits —
nothing surprising in that, considering his strange make-up —
and to that he owed his more than human inspiration. We are,
with this, in the world of Doctor Faustus, and the attendant spirit
that waited on him by night. But Shakespeare speaks up for
himself in his own realm with proper courage : his poetry was
not put out of countenance either by him or his night-companions.

> He, nor that affable familiar ghost
> Which nightly gulls him with intelligence,

— this would seem fairly certainly to refer to Mephistophilis in
the play, though it would be more piquant if it referred to a dead
crony, like Watson or Greene —

> As victors, of my silence cannot boast ;
> I was not sick of any fear from thence :
> But when your countenance filled up his line,
> Then lacked I matter : that enfeebled mine.

The tense of this is the past ; but in the sonnet immediately preceding, the rival is referred to in the present. There is only one
possible rival who could be described in terms such as Shakespeare
describes him, and that is Marlowe. It would be a fair inference
that in the interval between the two sonnets, he had met his end,
and that this is Shakespeare's valediction on him. We may conclude, too, that by 1593 Shakespeare was not afraid even of
Marlowe's rivalry as a poet : it was only when Southampton
inclined his favour to Marlowe, that Shakespeare feared for himself.

The information that all this gives us about Marlowe is as
precious as that it gives us about Shakespeare. It would seem
to confirm that it was *Faustus*, not *Edward II*, that was his last work.
The splendid verse Marlowe was engaged on when he died was
Hero and Leander, and it is clear that it was being written in competition with *Venus and Adonis*. *Hero and Leander* begins with
a pleasant salute to the rival theme : upon Hero's wide green
sleeves is embroidered a grove,

> Where Venus in her naked glory strove,
> To please the careless and disdainful eyes
> Of proud Adonis that before her lies.

But what do we find when we come to Leander ?

> His dangling tresses that were never shorn,
> Had they been cut and unto Colchos borne,
> Would have allured the vent'rous youth of Greece
> To hazard more than for the Golden Fleece.

Long unshorn tresses were not characteristic of a Greek youth, but they were a distinguishing mark of Southampton by which all his early portraits know him. We are at liberty to suspect that this was a compliment to the young man, as is the description that follows, even more responsive physically to his beauty than Shakespeare's more chaste appreciation :

> His body was as straight as Circe's wand,
> Jove might have sipped out nectar from his hand.
> Even as delicious meat is to the taste,
> So was his neck in touching, and surpassed
> The white of Pelops' shoulder —

Southampton was very fair and pale in complexion. And next we find complete agreement with Shakespeare as to the feminine cast of his looks :

> Some swore he was a maid in man's attire,
> For in his looks were all that men desire,
> A pleasant smiling cheek, a speaking eye,
> A brow for love to banquet royally,
> And such as knew he was a man would say,
> Leander, thou art made for amorous play :
> Why art thou not in love — and loved of all ?
> Though thou be fair, yet be not thine own thrall.

There is the first theme of the Sonnets.

The parallels between these two poems have often been noticed, but it has always been supposed that Shakespeare was the debtor. There is the fine passage about Adonis's horse, which Shakespeare developed at some length. In *Hero and Leander* this is contracted to :

> For as a hot proud horse highly disdains
> To have his head controlled but breaks the reins,
> Spits forth the ringled bit, and with his hooves
> Checks the submissive ground : so he that loves
> The more he is restrained, the worse he fares.

Shakespeare's comparison with Narcissus,

> Narcissus so himself himself forsook,
> And died to kiss his shadow in the brook,

is taken up by Marlowe :

> Those orient cheeks and lips, exceeding his
> That leaped into the water for a kiss
> Of his own shadow, and despising many,
> Died ere he could enjoy the love of any.

And so with other comparisons and themes, for example, that
of use and usury. Where Shakespeare says,

> Foul cankering rust the hidden treasure frets,
> But gold that's put to use more gold begets,

Marlowe expands into :

> What difference betwixt the richest mine
> And basest mould, but use ? for both, not used,
> Are of like worth. Then treasure is abused
> When misers keep it : being put to loan
> In time it will return us two for one.

Notice that we are back with the theme of the Sonnets.

There are other parallels, too, between the poems, but we
have seen enough to prove how close they are in inspiration.
From the conjunction of the facts that Marlowe's poem was unfinished when he died and that he does not appear as the rival
poet until not long before that event — at any rate, some time
after the beginning of the Sonnets — it seems most probable that
Venus and Adonis came first. After all, it was ready for publication
in the month before Marlowe's death. No doubt manuscripts
passed from hand to hand, each other's poems were read aloud,
in the cultivated circle of the young Earl. But this lets in a flood
of light on the relations between Marlowe and Shakespeare.

We are all the more teased by the question, what *would* have
happened had Marlowe lived ? Would he have captivated the
young Earl ? Was he on the way to doing so when he died ?
It would seem so from what Shakespeare tells us.

The next sonnet is valedictory, an *envoi* to this section : a
masterpiece technically, with nearly all the lines ending in feminine
rhymes, present participles — like the beginning of *The Waste
Land* — and creating a haunting cadence of farewell :

> Farewell ! thou art too dear for my possessing,
> And like enough thou know'st thy estimate :
> The charter of thy worth gives thee releasing ;
> My bonds in thee are all determinate . . .
> Thyself thou gav'st, thy own worth then not knowing,
> Or me, to whom thou gav'st it, else mistaking ;
> So thy great gift, upon misprision growing,
> Comes home again, on better judgment making.
> Thus have I had thee, as a dream doth flatter,
> In sleep a king, but waking no such matter.

The word 'misprision' means mistaking ; perhaps Southampton, being young, had made a mistake in his man when he gave his love to his servant, the poet. Though, likely enough, the young aristocrat knew his own value. Very well, that value, his own worth, releases him ; he has no obligation to Shakespeare, who has no claims upon him. There is heart-ache in every line.

At this point one sees the young man withdrawing. Shakespeare was ready to fall in with his wish, whatever it was :

> knowing thy will,
> I will acquaintance strangle and look strange ;
> Be absent from thy walks ; and in my tongue
> Thy sweet belovèd name no more shall dwell,
> Lest I, too much profane, should do it wrong,
> And haply of our old acquaintance tell.

This coldness came at a bad time for the poet, who was undergoing 'crosses' in his career ; that is, the closure of the theatres which was practically continuous, not only in 1592, but now in 1593 ; and perhaps the failure of Pembroke's company, which had been performing his plays.

> Then hate me when thou wilt ; if ever, now ;
> Now, while the world is bent my deeds to cross,
> Join with the spite of fortune, make me bow,
> And do not drop in for an after-loss . . .
> If thou wilt leave me, do not leave me last,
> When other petty griefs have done their spite,
> But in the onset come : so shall I taste
> At first the very worst of fortune's might.

Nevertheless, if Southampton should desert him at this ill juncture, he will be his for the term of the poet's life. And there follows a sonnet, the seriousness of which has never been appreciated ; for Shakespeare tells us that, at this crisis of his fortunes, his life depends on Southampton's love and support.

> But do thy worst to steal thyself away,
> For term of life thou art assurèd mine ;
> And life no longer than thy love will stay,
> For it depends upon that love of thine.

Things were as serious with him as that.

> Then need I not to fear the worst of wrongs,
> When in the least of them my life hath end.
> I see a better state to me belongs
> Than that which on thy humour doth depend :

> Thou canst not vex me with inconstant mind,
> Since that my life on thy revolt doth lie.
> O, what a happy title do I find,
> Happy to have thy love, happy to die !

We have seen all the way through how deeply Shakespeare means what he says ; and we have to take this literally. After all, in these very years 1592 and 1593, there was nothing remote in the idea of the death of a poet. In May 1593 Marlowe had died ; in 1592 both Watson and Greene had died, only a few years older than Shakespeare ; in the winter of 1593–4 Kyd died. It was a fine clearance of the poets — what matter if one more were added to them ? But that one might have been William Shakespeare — like Keats, before he had accomplished his work. We have an external indication later that Southampton came to Shakespeare's support ; and that would be assumed in the relations at that time between patron and poet. There was a dependency : in return for singing the patron's praises, there was a meed of support. What would have happened had Marlowe lived to supplant Shakespeare in Southampton's favour ? It may have been a very near thing. In view of all this, the underlying tone of independence with which Shakespeare writes, in spite of emotional (and probably financial) dependence, is all the more admirable. It is borne out in the conduct of his life.

Nevertheless, relations could not be what they had been at the first ; disillusionment creeps in :

> So shall I live, supposing thou art true,
> Like a deceivèd husband ; so love's face
> May still seem love to me, though altered new :
> Thy looks with me, thy heart in other place.

That is, Shakespeare had to accept a certain falseness in the relation and live with it ; the time comes when one has to accept the second-best. There follows a sonnet of acute psychological interest ; not easy, yet not obscure :

> They that have power to hurt and will do none,
> That do not do the thing they most do show,
> Who, moving others, are themselves as stone,
> Unmoved, cold, and to temptation slow :
> They rightly do inherit heaven's graces
> And husband nature's riches from expense ;
> They are the lords and owners of their faces,
> Others but stewards of their excellence.

There is a cutting edge to this, but its meaning is quite simple : those people who do not give themselves away, who do not bare their hearts, but are cold and unmoved and leave it to others to do so, they are the types who remain in control of themselves and of others : they inherit the earth. This is, in fact, the governing, political type ; poets do not belong to it. Southampton became, in the end, a politician and — God save the mark ! — something of a Puritan. This is what life does with people.

At this time, the year 1593, Southampton is beginning to be spotted with ill report :

> How sweet and lovely dost thou make the shame
> Which, like a canker in the fragrant rose,
> Doth spot the beauty of thy budding name !
> O, in what sweets dost thou thy sins enclose !

What are people saying of him ?

> Some say thy fault is youth, some wantonness ;
> Some say thy grace is youth and gentle sport ;
> Both grace and faults are loved of more and less :
> Thou mak'st faults graces that to thee resort . . .
> How many gazers mightst thou lead away,
> If thou would'st use the strength of all thy state !
> But do not so ; I love thee in such sort,
> As thou being mine, mine is thy good report.

It cannot but be said that Shakespeare tried to exert a good influence on the young man — quite different from what Marlowe would have done ; and from this point of view, his family, in particular his mother the Countess, would have no reason but to welcome the association. Nevertheless, the young Earl would not marry and settle down : he was out to have a good time. Early in 1594 a marriage was proposed for the Earl of Rutland's daughter, Lady Bridget Manners, either with the eligible Bedford or Southampton. But this sage young lady would have neither of them, 'for they be so young and fantastical, and would be so carried away . . . she doubteth their carriage of themselves, seeing some experience of the like in this place', *i.e.* at Court.[2]

The winter of 1593 is approaching, and away in the country, in absence, Shakespeare is in reminiscent, nostalgic vein — as are the sonnets of this section, following Sonnet 97, and as such they help to corroborate the dating of these poems as a whole. This sonnet is very familiar :

> How like a winter hath my absence been
> From thee, the pleasure of the fleeting year !
> What freezings have I felt, what dark days seen,
> What old December's bareness everywhere !
> And yet this time removed was summer's time . . .

But with him absent,

> Yet nor the lays of birds, nor the sweet smell
> Of different flowers in odour and in hue,
> Could make me any summer's story tell.

It is probable that *A Midsummer-Night's Dream* was now germinating, for, as we shall see, its first performance was on Mayday next year, 1594.

With Sonnet 102 Shakespeare goes back in mind to the beginning of their relationship :

> Our love was new, and then but in the spring,
> When I was wont to greet it with my lays ;
> As Philomel in summer's front doth sing,
> And stops her pipe in growth of riper days.

Shakespeare is writing less to Southampton now than in those days of their first delighted acquaintance with each other, though apparently the lordly patron still expects his due meed of praise.

> To me, fair friend, you never can be old,
> For as you were when first your eye I eyed,
> Such seems your beauty still.   Three winters cold
> Have from the forests shook three summers' pride,
> Three beauteous springs to yellow autumn turned
> In process of the seasons have I seen,
> Three April perfumes in three hot Junes burned,
> Since first I saw you fresh, which yet are green.

We are now in a position to read the chronology of this with some certainty, and we learn from it that the acquaintance began three winters ago, that is, in the winter of 1591–2 ; the seasons that follow, then, are those of 1592, 1593, 1594. The Sonnets are addressed to Southampton, and to no-one else :

> Since all alike my songs and praises be
> To one, still such, and ever so.

We have another means of confirming these dates, if any more were necessary, with Sonnet 107, which has given insuperable difficulty to commentators.   Yet there is no necessity : it falls in place simply and directly — Shakespeare did not write his sonnets with the idea of providing inextricable puzzles for posterity, as one might suppose from the heavy weather the professors have made of them. Completely contrary to the truth and directness, the openness, of his nature. And he wrote, like anyone else, in an actual historical environment, with the events of the day going on around him, making their impact as we saw with the fall of Ralegh in 1592. Now we come to the events referred to in this :

> Not mine own fears, nor the prophetic soul
> Of the wide world dreaming on things to come,
> Can yet the lease of my true love control,
> Supposed as forfeit to a confined doom.

So far all is general, expressed in the poet's lordliest language : neither Shakespeare's own apprehensions, nor future events in the outer world, can yet bring his love to an end, though it must come to an end some day, like all things human. Now for two references to contemporary events, the conjunction of which fixes and confirms our dating for us :

> The mortal moon hath her eclipse endured,
> And the sad augurs mock their own presage ;
> Incertainties now crown themselves assured,
> And peace proclaims olives of endless age.

There is no real difficulty here either. Many people have appreciated that the second couplet refers to the coming about of peace in France, the ending of the long religious wars that had distracted the country for decades — all Shakespeare's life, in fact. And this is correct. Henri IV — Henry of Navarre, to the English — had made his submission to the Roman church in July 1593, as an indispensable preliminary to peace. In March 1594 Paris at last submitted to him and the country was open to complete pacification. The long religious wars were over, and perhaps pointed the way to a general peace.

And what about the previous couplet ? —

> The mortal moon hath her eclipse endured,
> And the sad augurs mock their own presage.

All Elizabethan scholars of any judgment recognise that 'the mortal moon' refers to the Queen : she is always Cynthia, the chaste deity, the 'terrene moon', the 'mortal moon' with all the poets. She has come through an eclipse — as indeed she had that winter with the Lopez conspiracy. This made an immense sensation at the time ; for Dr. Lopez, a Portuguese Jew, was her personal physician in close attendance on her, and was found to be in correspondence with Spain with the idea of poisoning her, for a sufficiently large reward. The Queen herself, never wanting in courage, would not believe it ; but he was an intelligence-man, in on both sides, and in a position to carry it out. It was too dangerous a matter to leave uninvestigated, and Essex engaged his honour to bring Lopez to book. The government investigators found that 'he was her Majesty's sworn servant, graced and advanced with many princely favours, used in special places of credit, permitted often access to her person and so not suspected, especially by her, who never fears her enemies nor suspects her servants'.[3] Lopez' treasonable correspondence about the project was brought to light, and he never was able to explain it satisfactorily. He may not have intended it seriously, but who was to know ? It was clearly too dangerous to leave him alive in his position ; Essex pressed the matter to a conclusion, and Lopez was executed in March 1594.

That was the grave threat to her life that the Queen had come through. The prognosticators of woe had been proved wrong.

With the next sonnets we return to Shakespeare, and these are most revealing of how he thought of himself. It was now his turn to apologise for being away from his patron :

> O, never say that I was false of heart,
> Though absence seemed my flame to qualify . . .
> Never believe, though in my nature reigned
> All frailties that besiege all kinds of blood,
> That it could so preposterously be stained,
> To leave for nothing all thy sum of good.

We strike a deeper note of resentment at the way he is forced to earn his living :

> Alas, 'tis true I have gone here and there,
> And made myself a motley to the view —

that means, a jester, for players were still only a superior sort of vagrants —

> Gored mine own thoughts, sold cheap what is most dear,
> Made old offences of affections new :

which means, perhaps, that he had made objectionable new ties.
If anyone thinks his resentment was not sincere, a bitter sonnet
follows :

> O, for my sake do you with Fortune chide,
> The guilty goddess of my harmful deeds,
> That did not better for my life provide
> Than public means which public manners breeds.

All the evidence shows that, in spite of adversity and long frustration, Shakespeare always had, and set store by, the standards of
a gentleman : they were in accordance with his own nature ;
he had, moreover, the extreme sensibility we have observed.
How could he be expected to like going about exposing himself
to the public view, selling cheap what he held dearest, wounding
his own inner thoughts, making himself a jester, subjecting himself to a way of life that bore a common stamp and bred common
manners ? This was the way of life fortune had provided for
him — it had provided no better. If anyone thinks that he appreciated having been born a glover's son in a country town, it was
not what William Shakespeare thought, after experience of life
in the Southampton circle.

For fuller measure, the next sonnet tells us that his profession
as player had marked him with a vulgar scandal : the use of the
odd, invented word 'o'er-green' seems to refer back to Greene's
attack upon him as a plagiarist. Southampton had been then,
as now, his only protection :

> Your love and pity doth the impression fill
> Which vulgar scandal stamped upon my brow ;
> For what care I who calls me well or ill,
> So you o'er-green my bad, my good allow ?

It seems that now his patron was complaining of his neglect of
his duty, and of his being about with other people :

> Accuse me thus : that I have scanted all
> Wherein I should your great deserts repay,
> Forgot upon your dearest love to call,
> Whereto all bonds do tie me day by day :
> That I have frequent been with unknown minds,
> And given to time your own dear-purchased right . . .

'Dear-purchased' : that means that Shakespeare was under an
obligation to his patron and, I think, a handsome one.

The next movement in their relations shows Shakespeare at fault, or rather both at fault, and Shakespeare full of remorse — the more poignant because love has returned and welled up in him more strongly than ever :

> And ruined love, when it is built anew,
> Grows fairer than at first, more strong, far greater.

But all is made more complex and tortured by the presence of the woman in the background, or, rather, between them :

> What potions have I drunk of Siren tears,
> Distilled from limbecks foul as hell within,
> Applying fears to hopes and hopes to fears,
> Still losing when I saw myself to win !
> What wretched errors hath my heart committed,
> Whilst it hath thought itself so blessèd never !
> How have mine eyes out of their spheres been fitted,
> In the distraction of this madding fever !

He always speaks of his relation to this woman as a fever.

Once, at the time when Southampton had been unkind, Shakespeare felt it bitterly ; and now,

> Needs must I under my transgression bow,
> Unless my nerves were brass or hammered steel :
> For if you were by my unkindness shaken,
> As I by yours, you've passed a hell of time.

In the next, Shakespeare speaks up with spirit in firm defence of himself :

> 'Tis better to be vile than vile-esteemed,
> When not to be receives reproach of being,
> And the just pleasure lost, which is so deemed
> Not by our feeling, but by others' seeing.

That seems clear enough : it is better to enjoy oneself, whatever other people think ; even if one is not being vile, they will think one is ; then one loses one's just pleasure, if pleasure has to be rated not by one's feeling, but by how other people view it. That Shakespeare was giving himself to pleasure, and the pleasures of sex, we see from what follows :

> For why should others' false adulterate eyes
> Give salutation to my sportive blood ?
> Or on my frailties why are frailer spies,
> Which in their wills count bad what I think good ?

Then comes a downright affirmation of himself, as no better than he should be, but no worse than others :

> No, I am that I am, and they that level
> At my abuses reckon up their own :
> I may be straight, though they themselves be bevel ;
> By their rank thoughts my deeds must not be shown.

In fact, he regards himself as straighter than they are : they are not straight (*i.e.* 'bevel'), and he refuses to have his actions judged by their rank thoughts.

Sonnet 122 shows that the commerce between the two was an intellectual one, for it refers to a note-book, with Southampton's thoughts in prose or verse, which he had given Shakespeare, and which the latter had given away. It seems rather a curious thing to have done, but anyway it provided matter for a sonnet, an excuse in verse :

> Nor need I tallies thy dear love to score :
> Therefore to give them from me was I bold,
> To trust those tables that receive thee more :
> To keep an adjunct to remember thee
> Were to import forgetfulness in me.

This section of the Sonnets, the first one hundred and twenty-six, written to and for Southampton, come to an end with an affirmation of the constancy of Shakespeare's love. It is not subjected to injurious time :

> No, it was builded far from accident ;
> It suffers not in smiling pomp, nor falls
> Under the blow of thrallèd discontent,
> Whereto the inviting time our fashion calls . . .
> But all alone stands hugely politic.

Nor is it external, a matter of social pride :

> Were't it aught to me I bore the canopy,
> With my extern the outward honouring . . .

These and other state-images at the end of the Southampton sonnets, with their political references, the canopy borne above a person of state, serve to remind us, at the end as at the beginning, to whom and for whom they were written. Moreover, they confirm and clinch our dating. In October 1594, Southampton had attained his majority, and now had to pay for his virtual breach of promise to marry the Lord Treasurer's grand-daughter.

From the Jesuit, Henry Garnet, we learn that Southampton had to pay an immense fine, and we know that from this time he was financially much constricted.[4] Shakespeare's sonnet affirms that his love is not dependent on circumstance. Other circumstances of the time are referred to, which anchor the sonnet at this end of the relationship to the winter of 1594–5. For at this period the government's campaign against the Jesuits reached its climax with the execution of a larger number than for the rest of the reign — among them such men as John Cornelius, Robert Southwell, Henry Walpole. This is what is referred to at the end of Sonnet 124 :

> To this I witness call the fools of time,
> Which die for goodness who have lived for crime.

These men died as martyrs for religion, but the government's view was that Jesuits in particular, involved as some of them were in conspiracy against the state in time of war, were traitors. We find, as we should expect, Shakespeare reflecting the point of view of the country at large in this matter and at this juncture.

The last sonnet in the Southampton series is complex and suggestive, of a philosophical cast of reflexion, appropriate to the conclusion of so strange, so chequered a relationship. For some time we have watched them drawing apart, and Shakespeare's increasing independence from his patron, his own concerns taking him away. Now we have a summing up, a final reflection on the friendship so momentous for our literature.

> Were't aught to me I bore the canopy,
> With my extern the outward honouring . . .

If there were the slightest doubt, as there is not, as to the person to whom the Sonnets were addressed, here is sufficient confirmation : he was a person of state, a peer of the realm, to whom Shakespeare was engaged to do outward honour. But the poem goes on to say that that had meant little to Shakespeare, he had seen too much of hangers-on of the great, throwing away all they had for dubious expectations. That was not Shakespeare's conception of their relation :

> No, let me be obsequious in thy heart,
> And take thou my oblation, poor but free,
> Which is not mixed with seconds, knows no art
> But mutual render, only me for thee.

At the end, Shakespeare's offering to Southampton is 'poor but free' : his independence is established. It is psychologically revealing that just at the moment of this affirmation his mind goes back to his country origins : his oblation is not 'mixed with seconds', *i.e.* the second-class flour after the best has been used. And he conceives of the relationship only on a basis of mutual equality, 'only me for thee'.

After this the Southampton sonnets, and perhaps the closeness of the relationship, came to an end. The final sonnet in the sequence, Sonnet 126, is an *envoi* summing up what may be regarded as the dominant theme of them all : Time and its ineluctable destruction of beauty, and by implication, of love too. However, the expression of it all in art remains.

We now come to the other side of the story, with the sonnets concerned with Shakespeare's mistress. It is impossible to suppose that most of them were sent or shown to her, when we consider how very candid, often disobliging and damaging in effect, they are. They were for Southampton, like all the other poems Shakespeare was writing in these years when his patron would be helping to support him, especially when things were at their worst in 1593. And Shakespeare's friend was as deeply concerned in these sonnets, and appears in them almost as much, since the dark lady became his mistress too. It is the equivocal position among these three, but still more the feeling that the woman was corrupting the goodness, as she had seduced the innocence, of the young man, that partly accounts for the trouble of mind they express.

They begin pleasantly enough with a couple of sonnets describing her. To the Elizabethans fairness was the height of beauty — as with the contemporary Venetian painters : blue eyes, golden or red-gold hair. But Shakespeare's mistress was dark, raven-black hair and eyes, and yet beautiful in his sight :

> Therefore my mistress' brows are raven black,
> Her eyes so suited, and they mourners seem
> As such who, not born fair, no beauty lack,
> Slandering creation with a false esteem :
> Yet so they mourn, becoming of their woe,
> That every tongue says beauty should look so.

She likes music and performs on the virginals; we have a picture of the poet standing at her side as she plays :

> How oft, when thou, my music, music play'st
> Upon that blessed wood whose motion sounds
> With thy sweet fingers, when thou gently sway'st
> The wiry concord that mine ear confounds,
> Do I envy those jacks that nimble leap
> To kiss the tender inward of thy hand,
> Whilst my poor lips, which should that harvest reap,
> At the wood's boldness by thee blushing stand.

It is a charming conceit, and the tone makes it clear that it was a lady — not necessarily a Court-lady — who was performing on the keyboard.

But the next thing is that we are in the midst of revulsion, with the famous sonnet about lust — veracious enough, even if we allow for the poet's impulse to exaggerate, and an element of literary inspiration :

> The expense of spirit in a waste of shame
> Is lust in action ; and till action, lust
> Is perjured, murderous, bloody, full of blame,
> Savage, extreme, rude, cruel, not to trust.

We notice how all this tallies with what he says in *The Rape of Lucrece* : almost the very same word, 'trustless'.

One cannot imagine the next sonnet being read by the lady, though it may have given amusement to Southampton :

> My mistress' eyes are nothing like the sun ;
> Coral is far more red than her lips' red :
> If snow be white, why then her breasts are dun ;
> If hairs be wires, black wires grow on her head.

The literary motive is obvious : it is a skit against the idealisation of women that prevailed among the Court-poets, with all their Celias and Delias and Caelicas and Dianas. Who remembers who they were ? But this woman, the unknown Dark Lady — would we knew her name, but we shall never know it — has never been forgotten. There is an absolute reality about her, with all her faults and her bad character. The sonnet goes on :

> I have seen roses damasked, red and white,
> But no such roses see I in her cheeks ;
> And in some perfumes is there more delight
> Than in the breath that from my mistress reeks.
> I love to hear her speak, yet well I know
> That music hath a far more pleasing sound :
> I grant I never saw a goddess go,
> My mistress, when she walks, treads on the ground.

Here the intention to point a contrast between himself and the Court-poets is quite explicit. The women in their verse were goddesses ; but — there are such revenges — by the same token they were not women. Shakespeare grants that he has never seen a goddess walk : his mistress *treads* on the ground — as she has continued to do ever since.

She is a real woman, and Shakespeare is not the less, but all the more infatuated. It is not her beauty that holds him — other people cannot see that she has any : it is simply, sex. And what do others think of her ?

> Yet, in good faith, some say that thee behold,
> Thy face hath not the power to make love groan.

He, himself, has no illusions about her :

> In nothing art thou black save in thy deeds,
> And thence this slander, as I think, proceeds.

Others can resist her ; Shakespeare cannot : he is under her spell, or whatever it is that she has :

> Thine eyes I love, and they, as pitying me,
> Knowing thy heart torments me with disdain.

Again we see that he has no illusions about what she feels for him : no love, scorn rather ; no doubt she was his social superior and not really attracted by the actor-poet.

Such a woman would have no hesitation in getting between him and his friend, if she could — especially if the friend was a so much better proposition : a handsome young Earl against a poor player and playwright. And this is what she did. Sonnets 133 and 134 therefore overlap those sonnets precisely one hundred before in numbering, Sonnets 33 and 34, in which we first learn of the cloud between Shakespeare and his friend, and over what, the shame and the loss. We are now looking at the situation from the point of view of Shakespeare's relation to his mistress :

> Beshrew that heart that makes my heart to groan
> For that deep wound it gives my friend and me !
> Is't not enough to torture me alone,
> But slave to slavery my sweet'st friend must be ?

She has got hold of the young friend whom at this time, for we are back in the earlier days of the relationship, Shakespeare regards as his better self :

> Me from myself thy cruel eye hath taken,
> And my next self thou harder hast engrossed —

that means, he himself is therefore all the more in her toils —

> Of him, myself, and thee, I am forsaken :
> A torment thrice threefold thus to be crossed.

The next quatrain tells us how it came about :

> But thou wilt not, nor he will not be free,
> For thou art covetous, and he is kind ;
> He learned but surety-like to write for me,
> Under that bond that him as fast doth bind.

This tells us that Southampton had been called in to write on Shakespeare's behalf — so that it was his fault that the young man had been entangled, and they were both now in fast.

> Him have I lost ; thou hast both him and me :
> He pays the whole, and yet am I not free.

The next sonnet is frankly bawdy — and it is psychologically true that it should be : a very natural reaction to the situation Shakespeare is caught in. It is no very esoteric knowledge that, to the Elizabethans, the word 'will' meant — a secondary implication from the meaning 'desire' — the sexual organs, male or female. With that in mind it is not difficult to understand what follows :

> Whoever hath her wish, thou hast thy will,
> And will to boot, and Will in overplus ;
> More than enough am I that vex thee still,
> To thy sweet will making addition thus.

But he wants to continue his relations with her ; he wishes her to accommodate him too :

> So thou, being rich in will, add to thy will
> One will of mine, to make thy large will more.

No lady could relish being told the following, in the next sonnet that continues to play on this regrettable word :

> In things of great receipt with ease we prove
> Among a number one is reckoned none.

Let us hope that, in this acutely uncomfortable situation, the poet and his friend occasionally had a laugh, in the indignity of it all.

191

In truth, it was no laughing matter : it not only searched
out all the secret places of the heart and created disturbance of
mind and conscience, but it awoke all the unquiet uncertainties
in him we have noticed as peculiar to him, in such a degree :
between seeming and being, between appearance and reality,
shadow and substance, the dream and what is.

> Thou blind fool, Love, what dost thou to mine eyes,
> That they behold, and see not what they see ?

Why should the heart prompt him to regard as his individual
own that which his mind very well knows is open to all ?

> Why should my heart think that a several plot
> Which my heart knows the wide world's common place ?

A few lines further on occurs the phrase, 'false plague', to remind
us where we are : in the plague years.

Next follows a sonnet of acute psychological perception in
analysing the hypocrisies in which they were thus involved.

> When my love swears that she is made of truth,
> I do believe her, though I know she lies,
> That she might think me some untutored youth,
> Unlearnèd in the world's false subtleties.

No doubt she came from a superior social class to Shakespeare
and felt that she could look down on him.

> Thus vainly thinking that she thinks me young,
> Although she knows my days are past the best,
> Simply I credit her false-speaking tongue :
> On both sides thus is simple truth suppressed.

And then, with a return to his native truth of temperament, his
inability to blind himself as to the facts :

> But wherefore says she not she is unjust,
> And wherefore say not I that I am old ?
> O, love's best habit is in seeming trust,
> And age in love loves not to have years told.

That is to say, he accepts again : he has come to terms and settled
for a second-best. Better to go on seeming to trust, if one is to
have any relations at all :

> Therefore I lie with her and she with me,
> And in our faults by lies we flattered be.

There is a characteristic double-meaning in the word 'lie' : it is to be taken in both senses.

And Shakespeare would rather have her on her own terms, so humiliating for him, than not at all :

> Tell me thou lov'st elsewhere ; but in my sight,
> Dear heart, forbear to glance thine eye aside :
> What need'st thou wound with cunning, when thy might
> Is more than my o'er-pressed defence can bide ?

I think this corroborates again his sweetness of nature and also the normality of his sexual impulse — he is so dependent on a woman for its satisfaction. He considers his attitude towards her, with an equal candour :

> In faith, I do not love thee with mine eyes,
> For they in thee a thousand errors note ;
> But 'tis my heart that loves what they despise,
> Who, in despite of view, is pleased to dote.

The next quatrain is brutally candid — he has his return for the humiliation he endures :

> Nor are mine ears with thy tongue's tune delighted,
> Nor tender feeling, to base touches prone,
> Nor taste, nor smell, desire to be invited
> To any sensual feast with thee alone.

And yet, he is enslaved : in thrall to sex :

> But my five wits nor my five senses can
> Dissuade one foolish heart from serving thee.
> Only my plague thus far I count my gain,
> That she that makes me sin awards me pain.

Here is a perverse satisfaction : they are in sin, and he is glad to be made to feel the pain of it. This further reference to the plague — it would be interesting to count how many there are altogether — serves to remind us once more where we are in time.

Sonnet 142 is another famous one : on the consciousness, and the consequences of sin.

> Love is my sin, and thy dear virtue hate,
> Hate of my sin, grounded on sinful loving :
> O, but with mine compare thou thine own state,
> And thou shalt find it merits not reproving.

This is expressed with such compression, so much emotional pressure behind it, that it is not immediately easy to follow ; but it means that both are in sin, her state is no worse than his and calls for no more reproving :

> Or, if it do, not from those lips of thine,
> That have profaned their scarlet ornaments
> And sealed false bonds of love as oft as mine,
> Robbed others' beds' revenues of their rents.

One is as bad as the other : both are adulterers.

The next sonnet lets up the emotional pressure, with a rather comic country picture of their situation. A housewife, chasing after one of her chickens, puts down her child to run after the chicken and catch it ; the child runs after her, crying because it cannot catch her. Each is after that it cannot get. (Where did he get this image from ? Quite likely, it is piquant to think, from home-life in the country. How much of all this going on in London, did his simple country-wife know ? At this time, the eldest child was ten, the twins eight.)

> So runn'st thou after that which flies from thee,
> Whilst I, thy babe, chase thee afar behind ;
> But if thou catch thy hope, turn back to me,
> And play the mother's part : kiss me, be kind :
> So will I pray that thou mayst have thy will,
> If thou turn back and my loud crying still.

We may infer from this that Southampton was trying to get away from her, and the next sonnet suggests that Shakespeare was not sure of their relations, and in much anxiety as to where they all were.

> Two loves I have of comfort and despair,
> Which like two spirits do suggest me still :
> The better angel is a man right fair,
> The worser spirit a woman coloured ill.

His uncertainty now about the relations between these two, in this phase, was a torment :

> And whether that my angel be turned fiend
> Suspect I may, yet not directly tell ;
> But being both from me, both to each friend,
> I guess one angel in another's hell :
> Yet this shall I ne'er know, but live in doubt,
> Till my bad angel fire my good one out.

The last sonnets devoted to his mistress are full of unrest, disturbance of mind and conscience, desperation, remorse :

> My love is as a fever, longing still
> For that which longer nurseth the disease ;
> Feeding on that which doth preserve the ill,
> The uncertain sickly appetite to please.

His reason condemns him, and, since he cannot follow its commands, has left him. The humiliation worsens, for now she is reproaching him — having perhaps lost the young peer ; for at the end, Shakespeare and his mistress are together again :

> Canst thou, O cruel ! say I love thee not,
> When I against myself with thee partake ?
> Do I not think on thee, when I forgot
> Am of myself, all tyrant for thy sake ?
> Who hateth thee that I do call my friend ?
> On whom frown'st thou that I do fawn upon ?

At the end, he is left questioning what power it is in her that so dominates him against his reason. It is like the extraordinary case of Benjamin Constant, most intelligent of men, understanding what was happening to him at every move, always fluttering his wings to escape — and yet totally unable to get away from his thraldom to Madame de Staël. It is always difficult to understand the weakness of men, especially clever ones, towards women.

> O, from what power hast thou this powerful might
> With insufficiency my heart to sway ? . . .
> Whence hast thou this becoming of things ill,
> That in the very refuse of thy deeds
> There is such strength and warrantise of skill,
> That, in my mind, thy worst all best exceeds ?

At this point, one's sympathy fails :

> Who taught thee how to make me love thee more,
> The more I hear and see just cause of hate ?

The last sonnet in this series is full of self-accusation and reproach :

> In loving thee thou know'st I am forsworn,
> But thou art twice forsworn, to me love swearing :
> In act thy bed-vow broke, and new faith torn,
> In vowing new hate after new love bearing.

No doubt she was a married woman, but the 'bed-vow' here would seem to refer to the vow she had given Shakespeare when in bed with him. This quatrain implies that after a breach between them, they had made it up — as we can also infer from the course of the sonnets. Now she had broken word again, and after their reconciliation had torn their renewed faith, broken with him once more.

> But why of two oaths' breach do I accuse thee,
> When I break twenty ! I am perjured most,
> For all my vows are oaths but to misuse thee,
> And all my honest faith in thee is lost.

All the time he had known the truth and yet not been able to help himself :

> For I have sworn deep oaths of thy deep kindness,
> Oaths of thy love, thy truth, thy constancy ;
> And, to enlighten thee, gave eyes to blindness,
> Or made them swear against the thing they see.

And that was his final comment on the affair.

Or was it ? For at the end of all the sonnets, as a kind of *envoi*, there is a pair, only loosely attached, about Cupid and the power of the Love-god. They seem to tell us something about the poet, sick with love's distemper, going to Bath for the cure :

> I, sick withal, the help of bath desired,
> And thither hied, a sad distempered guest,
> But found no cure : the bath for my help lies
> Where Cupid got new fire — my mistress' eyes.

It reads like some real experience, a tail-piece to all that he had undergone.

We may now sum up the true nature of Shakespeare's sonnets and the solution of their problems. Hitherto they have provided an unsolved problem. Many scores of books have been addressed to it, proposing this or that thesis ; the Sonnets have been re-arranged, disarranged, deranged, in the interests of one thesis or another. Suggestions have been made at random as to the identity of the rival poet, ranging from Marlowe down to the common-place Markham. Those who have seen that the poet whose equality Shakespeare fully recognised, in sonnet after sonnet, wrote of 'the proud full sail of his great verse', could only be Marlowe turn out to be right, though hitherto there could be no certainty for want of a firm, established chronology.

In the absence of this, every kind of speculation has run rife — as to when the Sonnets were written, whether they were written over one long period or at wider intervals, whether they belong together, to whom they were written. The most massive of Shakespearean scholars in our time thought, with curiously little insight, that they were written to Lord Herbert, later Earl of Pembroke, who in 1592 was aged twelve ! Sir Edmund Chambers was, of course, bemused — as the whole discussion has been bedogged — by the publisher's inscription of the volume when it came out, years later, to the 'Mr. W. H.' who got him the manuscript. (We shall come to this in a moment.) All kinds of wild-cat notions have been proposed as to the identity of the Dark Lady. In fact we do not know, and are never likely to know, who she was ; nor is this a matter of much importance — of more sentimental interest, than scholarly. All that we can say of her for sure is that she was a dark lady well known to the intimates of the Southampton circle.

It is of little interest compared with the establishment of the date, the true character of the Sonnets and their place in the life and work of the world's poet. Here also the discussion has been wide open — no certainty where to place the Sonnets from 1588 to 1603, or even later. (Of all suggestions the idea that 'the mortal moon hath her eclipse endured', referred to the Spanish Armada is now seen to be, as it always was, the craziest.) Actually, a better literary perception should have seen that the earlier sonnets are anchored to *Venus and Adonis*, as the later ones are to *The Rape of Lucrece*.

All this mare's nest has been due to a radical defect of method, or, rather, absence of method. It is hopeless to proceed by picking out here a sonnet and there a sonnet, arriving at some preconceived idea as to what it might refer to and then applying it as a kind of thesis to which the rest must fit — then closing the ears to reason. This is no method at all, and I am only astonished that so many literary scholars have lent themselves to what was, after all, only a game. The game has now come to an end, for good and all.

After all, Shakespeare did not write his sonnets to provide a puzzle for posterity : he wrote them simply and directly, straightforwardly and rapidly, in the heat of emotions many and varied. The only way to tackle the problem has been that of sound, reliable historical method : watching the Sonnets carefully for every internal indication of date and circumstance, keeping in mind what was happening in the external world and noticing how far these are consistent, confirm each other, hang together. In that way, all the outstanding problems fall into place and receive their solution. I am not proposing yet another thesis : the problem is solved, as is clear for all to see.

The Sonnets were written in the years 1592–5, though they mostly belong to the two plague years, years of crisis in Shakespeare's career while the theatres were closed : 1592 and 1593. And they all belong together, in a rational order as we have received them. It is obvious enough that the sonnets to the mistress overlap the later ones to the young man : as I have shown, Sonnets 133 and 134 to her coincide with Sonnets 33 and 34 to him, when the relations between his mistress and his friend begin to trouble Shakespeare's mind, and so onward. But it is best to read them in the traditional order in which we have received them, for then we can keep the very different relations between the poet and his friend, and between the poet and his mistress, separate in our minds in spite of the complexities among the three of them.

We all know the rapidity with which Shakespeare worked, with which his imagination carried him away. It is obvious that he wrote more at some periods, and then went fallow at others. Sometimes he may have written two sonnets in a day ; for we have observed how frequently they go in couples — the original idea suggesting either a literary amplification or a personal reaction, and so another. If they sometimes seem exaggerated to a modern taste, we must reflect that the Elizabethans were much more highly emotional, as well as emotionally expressive : they ran through more real experience in shorter time. And though there is an element of literary suggestion in the Sonnets, as with any writer who recognises a good subject when he sees one, there is no doubt that Shakespeare experienced it all : he was too direct and natural, too straight and true a writer for it to be otherwise. He says this himself — where

> every word doth almost tell my name,
> Showing their birth and where they did proceed.

We need say little more on this point except that their proper understanding adds the whole dimension of depth and reality to our grasp of his personality and life. It also adds something very important to our knowledge of Marlowe in his last phase, besides establishing a poignant reality to the relations between

Marlowe and Shakespeare. But it is almost inexplicable that his biographers should have written their biographies of Shakespeare without taking account of his autobiography — except that they were men of little imagination and I suppose they found the full story too uncomfortable.

For the Sonnets are the most autobiographical ever written. They are not finished, like the contemporary sonnet-sequences written for publication, precisely because they were not literary exercises. Some critics think that they are artistically inferior to the more perfect sonnets of Sidney and Spenser, as they are totally opposite to the marble perfection of Heredia. They are a world away from the shadowy worlds of Daniel and the earlier Drayton,[5] Greville and Constable, with their pale evocations of a Delia, a Caelica, or an Idea, where the critics have sometimes not been sure whether there was any lady at all or the personification of an idea. Shakespeare's mistress may not have been much of a lady, but she was a woman of flesh and blood and will.

So, too, with the young man : we know now, as it was fairly clear all along, that it was Southampton, his only patron, for whom alone he wrote, to whom alone he dedicated his poems,

> To one, of one, still such, and ever so.

It is worth recalling here that Southampton's family motto was 'Ung par tout, tout par ung', and this may have been intended, in the Elizabethan manner, to reflect it. Shakespeare, with all the directness and sincerity of his open nature, was during this time possessed by one of the most remarkable relationships recorded in literature. This is why the poems are so moving, at the beginning sparkling with pleasure, progressing into a clouded region of doubt and anxiety, becoming tormented and remorseful, with those to the mistress, running through the whole gamut of the emotions. And this is why they were not for publication : they were too intimate, too private, his patron's personal possession. It is so like the irony of life that these sonnets, in a way unliterary and not to be published when in the 1590's sonnet-sequences were all the rage, should in the end have exerted a greater influence in literature than any others.

Certainly Southampton got his money's worth. Before Shakespeare met him, the poet had long been waiting in the wings. He was not the man to fail to seize his chance with both hands when it came to him. Indeed, it was a matter of dire necessity, perhaps even of survival in 1592-3, when the death-rate among the poets was abnormally high. The young patron was as good as his word, and saw the poet through. We have reason to be grateful that such as Southampton — not wholly attractive in his life — ever existed, for the impulse that in his youth he gave to the world's poet. As for Shakespeare, underneath everything, his real reward, as any poet must feel, was the inspiration his genius had received.

And so the Sonnets were folded and put away, at Southampton House, whence they emerged into the light of day years later. We have reason to think that good relations subsisted between the poet and his patron's mother. In 1607 she died, and her third husband, Sir William Harvey, next year married Cordelia Annesley. The simplest and most direct explanations are almost always the best. It seems clear that it was he who handed over the sonnets for publication next year, in 1609 — when Shakespeare was famous and getting towards the end of his career — and to whom the publisher, Thomas Thorpe, acknowledged his indebtedness in a grateful, somewhat fulsome, inscription. There is no difficulty whatever in the brief description, 'Mr. W. H.' — to the Elizabethans, by the way, Mr. was always pronounced Master ; the Countess of Southampton, in her letters, addressed her second husband, Sir Thomas Heneage, as Master Heneage, and Sir William Harvey as Master Harvey — perfectly correct and proper usage. So the publisher's inscription of the book, which has led so many people *in vacuo* astray, need give us no trouble : 'To the only begetter of these ensuing sonnets, Mr. W. H., all happiness and that eternity promised by our ever-living poet wisheth the well-wishing adventurer in setting forth. T. T.'. There is no problem with the word 'begetter', though it has misled generations : Shakespeare himself uses it in the sense of to get or acquire. Hamlet bids the players : 'for in the very torrent, tempest, and, as I may say, whirlwind of your passion, you must acquire and beget a temperance that may give it smoothness'. The publisher had not much of a fist at writing — putting 'wisheth' alongside of 'well-wishing' ! — but he was anxious to express his gratitude, and did so rather clumsily. Sir William Harvey had married a young wife : nothing was more appropriate than the opening theme of the Sonnets :

> And nothing 'gainst Time's scythe can make defence,
> Save breed, to brave him when he takes thee hence.

CHAPTER XI

Romance and Reality

WITH the ending of the Sonnets the brilliant lighting of our stage from within which we have enjoyed for a space is at an end. On the other hand, we at last reach firm ground and a clear way forward in external matters.

The earliest tradition coming through Rowe from Sir William Davenant is seen, in the light of our new perspective, to be likely to be true. The most conservative of Shakespearean scholars has already accepted the likelihood : 'an Elizabethan patron was expected to put his hand in his pocket. Rowe tells us that Shakespeare met with "many great and uncommon marks of favour and friendship" from Southampton, and on Davenant's authority that the Earl "at one time, gave him £1000, to enable him to go through with a purchase which he heard he had a mind to". The sum named is quite incredible.'[1] I entirely agree ; anyone who knows Elizabethan values will accept the suggestion that 'probably a cipher has been added to the figures during the transmission of the story ; and some such amount as £100 Shakespeare may have spent on acquiring a share in the Lord Chamberlain's company, when it was formed during 1594'.

That was a handsome sum in those days — a generous and suitable reward for the dedications of two of the most admired poems of the age. We must add generosity to the other good qualities Shakespeare celebrated in his young patron, and to offset his later defects. What our literature owes to this famous friendship ! — for without it, we have seen, it was doubtful whether Shakespeare could have gone on. Now, with the purchase of a share in the new Chamberlain's company, he achieved security at last. It meant all the difference between the dreadful insecurity poor Greene and others had died of, and having firm ground under his feet.

He had come through the crisis of his life ; henceforth his

career was continuously successful, borne up by the unbroken prosperity of the Lord Chamberlain's, later the King's, men, to which he in turn contributed so largely. After this turn in his fortunes, he never wrote for any other company than his own. No need to depend on anyone else's humour, except the people's, and that never failed him. His company won the undoubted lead over the Admiral's men (their great dramatist now dead) ; before the end of the reign the Chamberlain's gave thirty-two performances at Court to twenty by the Admiral's and only thirteen by all others.[2] Shakespeare's status in the company is attested by the fact that at the end of this first winter season, in March 1595, he received the moneys for the plays given at Court on behalf of the company. His earlier plays, including any previously performed by other troupes, passed into the possession of the Chamberlain's. There came, too, from Strange's company five men who remained Shakespeare's fellows for years : William Kemp, Thomas Pope, Augustine Phillips, George Bryan, John Heminges — to the last of whom, alone with Henry Condell, our debt is incalculable. For after their colleague's death, with devoted care they published the great Folio volume of his plays, which he had never got round to bringing together.

This gave him the stable foundation upon which to accomplish his work — and what tremendous use he made of it !

But there is one other, and sadder, reflection. From the terrible crisis of those plague years he was the only one of the playwrights to come back into activity : Marlowe was dead at twenty-nine ; Greene at thirty-four ; Kyd at thirty-five ; Peele was shortly to die ; Lyly was frustrated of his private stage and wrote hardly anything more. From 1594 until the appearance of Ben Jonson — to whom Shakespeare, with characteristic generosity, gave his chance with the Chamberlain's men — he had the London stage, as dramatist, virtually to himself.

After long trial, the stars in their courses had fought for him.

With the way forward now clear, Shakespeare's natural high spirits soared ; gaiety returned to his heart. Release into the full flight of inspiration is to be seen in the lyrical spirit of the next four plays which, though each is different in kind, have this in common. We may take these to be *A Midsummer-Night's Dream*, *Love's Labour's Lost*, *Romeo and Juliet*, *The Merchant of Venice*. In these we watch not only a maturing of characterisation

but a progress in power, a rapidly matured grasp of life transmuted into poetry, a created world upon which real events impinge
and into which real people erupt. We know now to what he
owed this deepening, transforming sense of life — from the way
life had opened out for him, changing everything : his imagination, impregnated, flowered with it.

With *A Midsummer-Night's Dream* he achieved the first of his
undoubted masterpieces, a work approaching perfection. In
addition, there is the extraordinary originality of the work —
the thistledown and moonshine out of which it is made, the fairy-
lore he brought with him from his childhood in Warwickshire,
the country mechanics, the imperishably real Bottom the weaver,
the mixed-up lovers wandering in the forest. 'This device of
taking his characters away from Court and city into a freer, half
fairy-tale world (a device he was to employ again in *As You Like
It*, *The Winter's Tale*, and *The Tempest*), Shakespeare first fully
discovered in *A Midsummer Night's Dream*.' 3 Shakespeare may
be regarded as the creator of this fairy-tale genre, in which his
countryman Drayton and Ben Jonson immediately became his
followers. It has borne fruits in our literature right down to today.

There are more profound implications lightly suggested in
the *Dream*, the conviction that underlies the tragedies : 'that this
world of sense in which we live is but the surface of a vaster unseen
world by which the actions of men are affected or overruled.' 4
Then, too, 'the congruity, in spite of their differences, of *A Midsummer-Night's Dream* with *The Tempest* is one of the most striking
demonstrations of the continuity and integrity of Shakespeare's
genius that his works afford'. It is a singular confirmation of
this that in Keats's *Shakespeare* these are the two plays most thumbed
and most frequently read.

Though generally agreed that the play was written for a
wedding-ceremony, there has been no agreement as to the occasion and, without the advantage of a firm chronology, suggestions
have been oddly wide of the mark, ranging all round the 1590's
for a suitable occasion *in vacuo*. In truth, we do not have very
far to look.

Since her husband's death in 1581 the Countess of Southampton
had remained a widow. Now, with her son obdurate on the
subject of marriage, exposing himself to the resentment of the
Lord Treasurer — who had a genuine grievance, for Southampton
when young had let it be understood that he would marry

Burghley's granddaughter and had now kept the old man waiting for four years — the young man's mother decided to marry, if only for protection. She could not have made a better or more sensible choice.

Nearly twenty years the Countess's senior, Sir Thomas Heneage was a confidential servant of the Queen. He was Vice-Chamberlain of her household and Treasurer of the Chamber; he was Chancellor of the Duchy of Lancaster and, as Privy Councillor, an important member of the government. A reliable Protestant, the Queen had rewarded him richly, with many estates and properties, including Copt Hall where he proceeded to build a splendid house. The Southamptons needed protection in the highest quarter — that was something the Earl would not understand or, if he did, would not take the necessary steps to achieve. There was a vein of obstinacy in him, and we shall see him going over into the ranks of the opposition, to bring his life in danger. For the Southamptons were Catholics on both sides, the Montagues as well as the Wriothesleys; priests were constantly in and out of Montague House and Southampton House, the gentlemen-retainers served as go-betweens, the priests were secreted in their homes, with the usual train of spies and informers set on them. For these were war-years, full of dangers, plots, threats to the Queen's life, mob-hysteria against foreigners, papists, Jews.

In 1592 we find Heneage in constant touch with Robert Cecil about this kind of thing. The latter has been interviewing Marlowe's acquaintance, the insidious Robert Poley, and 'finds him no fool', only a few days before Marlowe's death.[5] 'The Queen is out of quiet, with her foreign foes and home broils.' Cecil much wants Heneage's company 'to participate vexations', which are good for nothing but to disquiet the Queen. Benjamin Beard alias Tichborne, the Catholic spy upon other Catholics — in this Graham Greene world — informs us that, though Sir Thomas Heneage was 'a man as earnest against Catholics as any other', he yet had some 'good men' planted on him as well as others. This included a mischievous young man called Roper, of indubitable Catholic family. The priest Butler was chamber-fellow with Mr. Harrington, gentleman in waiting to Lady Southampton; some eight years ago they lived in Southampton House in the next chamber to Robert Gage, executed for his part in the Babington conspiracy.[6] We see how dangerously honey-combed a world this was.

With her son doing nothing to protect the family's interests or even to carry it on, the Countess did the best she could by marrying Sir Thomas Heneage. The wedding took place on 2 May 1594.[7] We have no reason to doubt that *A Midsummer-Night's Dream* was produced to grace the occasion.[8] We have seen, from the Sonnets, that a 'summer's story' had been germinating in Shakespeare's mind. But the play is connected with Mayday, by the Duke's reference to the lovers :

> No doubt they rose up early to observe
> The rite of May ; and, hearing our intent,
> Came here in grace of our solemnity.

The Duke, Theseus, a grave and dignified figure, who knows all the ways and graces of government, is marrying his Hippolyta — they are outside the fooleries of the lovers, the depredations and quarrels of the fairies. They provide the framework of the play — an appropriate compliment to Sir Thomas and his bride when the play was, with fair certainty, performed the night before the wedding.

Heavy weather has been made by scholars over the Duke's disapprobatory words, in the very first scene, as to the unmarried state :

> To live a barren sister all your life,
> Chanting faint hymns to the cold fruitless moon . . .
> But earthlier happy is the rose distilled,
> Than that which withering on the virgin thorn
> Grows, lives and dies in single blessedness.

We ought to know by this time whom this refers to : no-one can say that the family poet did not do his best for the family's interests. Yet no-one has perceived that this is a reference to the young Earl who would not marry. Everyone has seen, absurdly, a reference to Queen Elizabeth, where a sense of tact should have told them that such words could not possibly have been uttered in her presence.[9] And that, *ipso facto*, would have excluded any wedding-ceremony at which she was present as the occasion for the production of *A Midsummer-Night's Dream*.

At the end of the play the fairies wend their way through the house :

> Through the house give glimmering light,
> By the dead and drowsy fire . . .
> Now, until the break of day,
> Through this house each fairy stray.

To the best bride-bed will we,
Which by us shall blessèd be . . .
With this field-dew consecrate,
Every fairy take his gait,
And each several chamber bless,
Through this palace, with sweet peace,
And the owner of it blest,
Ever shall in safety rest.

The Cambridge editor saw perceptively that these words 'were written for a performance in the great chamber of some private house, and the exit of the fairies at Oberon's command was arranged in such a way that they seemed to be departing on their mission of consecration from chamber to chamber. . . . The performance was at night : "the iron tongue of midnight hath told twelve".' [10]

This editor's suggestions as to revision are now strengthened by the support they receive from our now-ascertained historical framework.[11] The play was also publicly performed by the Chamberlain's men — hence the alternative endings Shakespeare provided which remain embedded in the text. For public performance it needed filling out, if possible with matter to give it more general interest to link it with topics of public discussion. The weather is always a perennial topic of interest in England, but never more so than after the disastrously wet summer of 1594. For the winter season Shakespeare made a feature of this with the long speech of Titania :

Therefore the winds, piping to us in vain,
As in revenge have sucked up from the sea
Contagious fogs : which, falling in the land,
Hath every pelting river made so proud
That they have overborne their continents.
The ox hath therefore stretched his yoke in vain,
The ploughman lost his sweat, and the green corn
Hath rotted ere his youth attained a beard.
The fold stands empty in the drownèd field,
And crows are fatted with the murrion flock,
The nine men's morris is filled up with mud,
And the quaint mazes in the wanton green
For lack of tread are undistinguishable.

It is a perfect picture of how things were in the country in that bad summer, even if the literary inspiration came from Goulding's Ovid.

A topic that gave amusement in London this year concerned the baptism of Prince Henry in Scotland at the end of August.

Everything Scottish was, of course, funny in London, especially when a triumphal car that should have been drawn in by a lion had to be drawn by a blackamoor for fear it would fright the ladies. This is made a point of in the comic rehearsal of Bottom's play of Pyramus and Thisbe. Bottom wants to play that part, too : 'I will roar, that I will make the Duke say, "Let him roar again, let him roar again"'. Peter Quince objects : 'An you should do it too terribly, you would fright the duchess and the ladies, that they would shriek, and that were enough to hang us all'.

It used, in the uncertainty as to dating, to be thought that the famous reference to

> The thrice three Muses mourning for the death
> Of learning, late deceased in beggary . . .

was to Spenser's death. It is now seen to be a reference to Robert Greene's death, which was once more a matter of public discussion with the controversial pamphlets being exchanged between Gabriel Harvey and Nashe. And this is rendered probable by Shakespeare's comment in the next lines on the unfitness of the subject for a wedding-feast :

> That is some satire, keen and critical,
> Not sorting with a nuptial ceremony.

He had not forgotten Greene's attack upon him.

These insertions all helped to strengthen what was in essence a private play with the general public. One more may refer back nearly twenty years to his own childhood and the famous entertainments of 1575 at Kenilworth. It is likely enough that as a boy of eleven he went over to the castle for these spectacular events, and remembered the promontory in the lake, the mermaid singing on a dolphin's back. With our greater knowledge of the way in which contemporary events were absorbed into his experience and made good use of, I think that the remembrance is made more probable by the reflection on Cupid's aim

> At a fair Vestal, thronèd by the west . . .
> But I might see young Cupid's fiery shaft
> Quenched in the chaste beams of the wat'ry moon :
> And the imperial Vot'ress passèd on,
> In maiden meditation, fancy-free.

More : this would seem to preserve the Warwickshire tradition that these splendid pageants were Leicester's last attempt to capture the hand, as he already had the heart, of the Queen.

Let us look at the play from the point of view of our own particular purpose : the light it throws on its author and his environment.

The question of sources, a rather secondary matter, need not detain us long. The character of Theseus, the Greek names in the play and something of the colouring Shakespeare got from Sir Thomas North's translation of Plutarch's *Lives* — his first use of what was to become a prime source for his Roman plays. His second source was Chaucer's *Knightes Tale*, for the contrast between staid married happiness and the plight of younger unhappy lovers, as also for the name Philostrate. The Pyramus and Thisbe story came from Golding's translation of the beloved Ovid, though the name Titania came directly from Ovid ; Oberon from either the *Faerie Queene* or the romance *Huon of Bordeaux*. Bottom's transmogrification was suggested by Richard Adlington's popular translation of Apuleius' *Golden Ass*. It seems, too, that Shakespeare read the like-minded, tolerant Reginald Scott's *Discoverie of Witchcraft*. He hardly needed to read much about Robin Goodfellow and Puck and the fairies : as Q. says, 'it is even more likely that he brought all this fairy-stuff up to London in his own head, packed with nursery legends of his native Warwickshire. When will criticism learn to allow for the enormous drafts made by creative artists such as Shakespeare and Dickens upon their childhood ? '[12] Q. was himself a real writer, and he knew.

The historian here would make only a slight emendation : it seems that Shakespeare never lost touch with his native Warwickshire. The mechanics, for example, are straight out of the streets and occupations of Stratford, just the kind of people we found the whittawer and glover John Shakespeare, and tanner Field and blacksmith Hornby, hobnobbing with in an earlier chapter. Nick Bottom, the world knows, was a weaver, Peter Quince a carpenter, Francis Flute a bellows-mender, Robin Starveling a tailor, Snout a tinker and Snug a joiner. A further subtlety with this double-minded man is that these names indicate their trades : a bottom is the core of skein upon which the weaver's yarn is wound, quince refers to the 'quines' or wooden wedges of the carpenter, snout for a nozzle is appropriate for a tinker mending kettles. I think we may say that, though Shakespeare resented the disadvantages of having been born a glover's son, what his imagination owed to his background was incalculable, and his sense of this kept him always loyal to it.

STRATFORD: THE CHURCH WAY

HOLY TRINITY CHURCH,
STRATFORD:
INTERIOR

THE GILD CHAPEL: INTERIOR

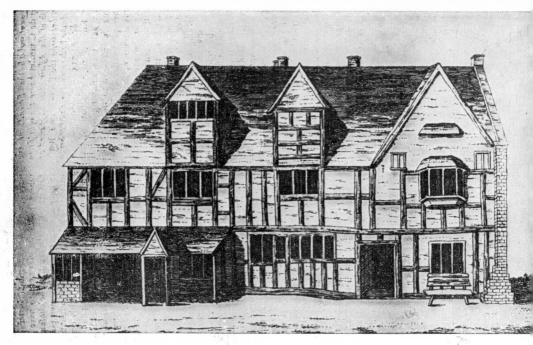

SHAKESPEARE'S BIRTHPLACE

SIR THOMAS LUCY OF CHARLECOTE

THE SCHOOL QUAD AT STRATFORD

HEWLANDS FARM AT SHOTTERY

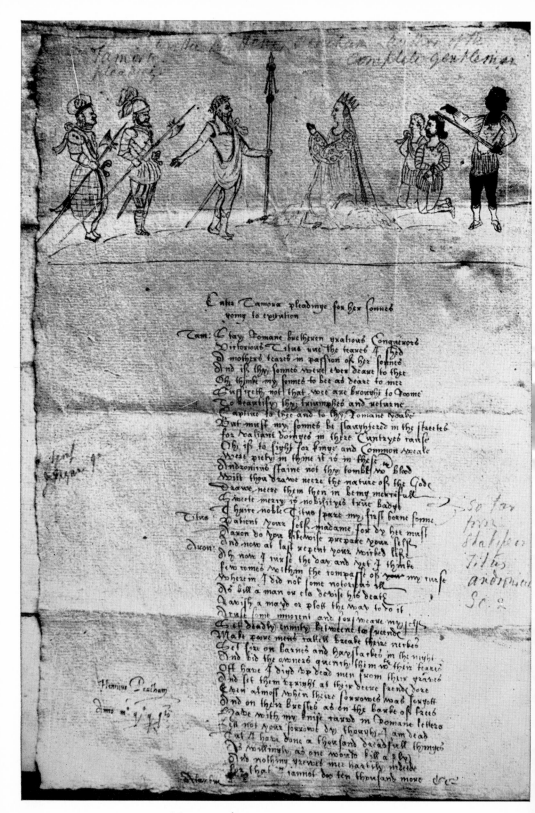

A SCENE FROM *Titus Andronicus*

VENVS
AND ADONIS

Vilia miretur vulgus: mihi flauus Apollo
Pocula Castalia plena ministret aqua.

LONDON

Imprinted by Richard Field, and are to be sold at
the signe of the white Greyhound in
Paules Church-yard.
1593.

RICHARD BURBAGE

BEN JONSON

SOUTHAMPTON
AT THE PERIOD
OF THE SONNETS

SOUTHAMPTON'S
MOTHER

LONDON

S. PAULES CHURCH

THAMESIS

FLUVIUS

South warke

THE BRIDGE

BANKSIDE

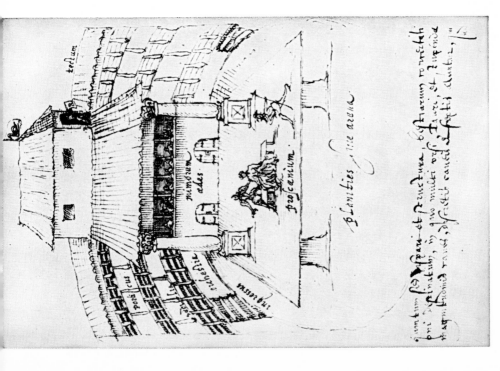

THE SWAN THEATRE

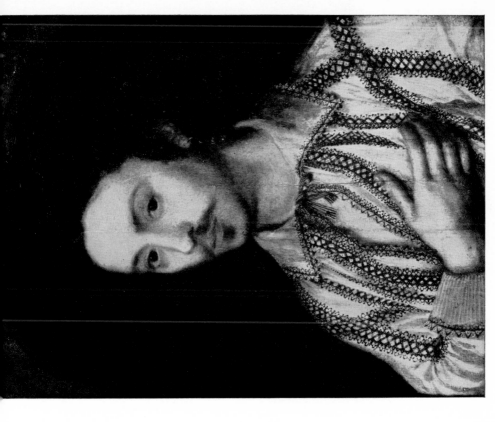

AN ELIZABETHAN PLAYER

SOUTHAMPTON
AS A YOUNG MAN

SOUTHAMPTON
IN THE TOWER

HONI SOIT QVI MALY PENSE

The most noble ROBERT
Earle of Essex and Ewe, Earle
Marshall of England Vicount Hereford
and Bourghier. Lord Ferrers of
Chartly L.Bourghier. and Louayn
and her Maiesties lientenant and
Gouernour generall of the
Kingdome of Irlant.
1600.

William ky ex.   Robert Boisard.

HIC TVVS ILLE COMES, GENEROSA ESSEXIA NOSTRIS,
QVEM QVAM GAVDEMVS REBVS ADESSE DVCEM.

THE EARL OF ESSEX AS LORD GENERAL

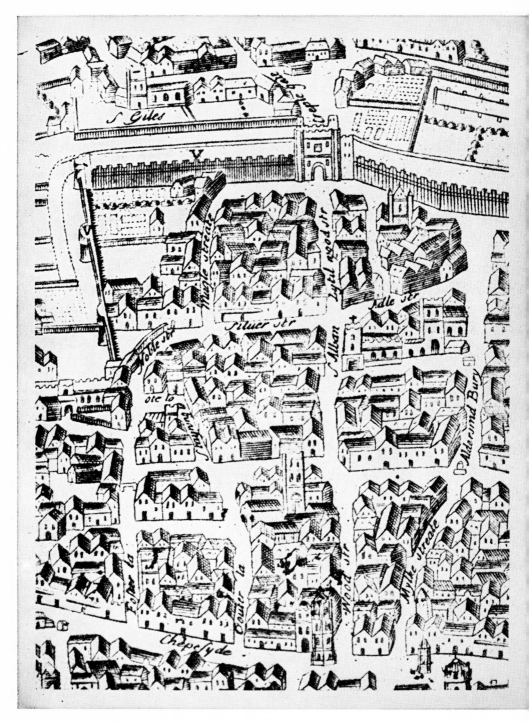

WHERE SHAKESPEARE LODGED WITH THE MOUNTJOYS

From Aggas map, c. 1560

The house at the corner of Silver Street and Monkswell (Mugle) Street

ENGRAVED PORTRAIT OF SHAKESPEARE BY DROESHOUT

SHAKESPEARE'S
MONUMENT IN
STRATFORD
CHURCH

THE
GILD CHAPEL
AND THE
SITE OF
NEW PLACE

The perpetual inspiration of his own countryside is at its height in this play. In it we have his finest tribute to the music of the hounds : they are given a Greek habitat, but they belong to the Cotswolds, just as Theseus is an English gentleman. He says :

> My love shall hear the music of my hounds.
> Uncouple in the western valley, let them go . . .
> We will, fair queen, up to the mountain's top,
> And mark the musical confusion
> Of hounds and echo in conjunction . . .
> My hounds are bred out of the Spartan kind :
> So flewed, so sanded ; and their heads are hung
> With ears that sweep away the morning dew,
> Crook-kneed, and dewlapped like Thessalian bulls ;
> Slow in pursuit ; but matched in mouth like bells,
> Each under each. A cry more tuneable
> Was never hollaed to, nor cheered with horn.

A good deal of loving knowledge out on those hills has gone into that. So too with images, like that of sound

> More tuneable than lark to shepherd's ear,
> When wheat is green, when hawthorn buds appear ;

or the following,

> As wild geese that the creeping fowler eye,
> Or russet-pated choughs, many in sort,
> Rising and cawing at the gun's report,
> Sever themselves, and madly sweep the sky.

Country beliefs and lore are still more important : this play is largely compounded of them. Ghosts visit by night, but with the dawn —

> At whose approach, ghosts, wandering here and there,
> Troop home to churchyards : damnèd spirits all,
> That in crossways and floods have burial.

Suicides used to be buried at the crossroads.

> Now it is the time of night
> That the graves, all gaping wide,
> Every one lets forth his sprite,
> In the church-way paths to glide.

One cannot but think of the leafy church-way, still called so, at Stratford.

Puck, or Robin Goodfellow, is a leading character, if that is the word, in the play. In true traditional fashion he mixes things up all right :

> are you not he
> That frights the maidens of the villagery,
> Skim milk, and sometime labour in the quern,
> And bootless make the breathless housewife churn,
> And sometime make the drink to bear no barm,
> Mislead night-wanderers, laughing at their harm ?

This kind of thing was faithfully believed by country folk all over England ; it added interest to their simple lives, was stimulating, and sometimes comforting, to the imagination. Puck admits the indictment :

> And sometime lurk I in a gossip's bowl,
> In very likeness of a roasted crab,
> And when she drinks against her lips I bob,
> And on her withered dewlap pour the ale.
> The wisest aunt, telling the saddest tale,
> Sometime for three-foot stool mistaketh me :
> Then slip I from her bum, down topples she,
> And 'tailor' cries, and falls into a cough ;
> And then the whole quire hold their lips and laugh,
> And waxen in their mirth, and neeze, and swear
> A merrier hour was never wasted there.

At the same time Shakespeare gentles the fairies : whereas they remain mischievous, they are not positively malevolent. Towards humans they are in a way indifferent ; this gives Puck the distance from which to offer the first, if not the last, word on human beings and their affairs :

> Lord, what fools these mortals be !

Endearing touches of Elizabethan life appear here and there with Helena and Hermia as girls working at a sampler together — such a piece of work as we still have examples of in museums, and even in some private houses — 'sitting on one cushion, warbling of one song'. The regular Elizabethan interest in heraldry appears with the image :

> Two of the first, like coats in heraldry,
> Due but to one and crownèd with one crest.

More enlightening is Helena's bitchy description of her girlhood friend :

> She was a vixen when she went to school :

an indication that some girls did go to school, to the petty rather than the grammar-school.

Shakespeare's own beliefs and sympathies are revealed here and there. He uses the fairies to illustrate his view of love as an enchantment that alienates men's minds to a kind of madness — how much that chimed with his own experience we can now appreciate. There is his natural courtesy in the grace with which the Duke gives welcome to the mechanicals :

> I will hear that play,
> For never anything can be amiss
> When simpleness and duty tender it.

Elizabeth throughout her reign had often had to take that attitude, though bored enough. A modern commentator says, 'if Shakespeare intended a compliment to someone at Court he did it very pleasantly'.[13] As we see more clearly now it was a courtly compliment to a courtier — Heneage.

The playwright's reactions to his own profession come out increasingly clearly. Bottom's play is a 'most lamentable comedy' : Shakespeare always laughed at the conventional stock classifications of drama — just as an historian of genius, Macaulay, poked fun at 'the dignity of history' upon which dull, third-rate historians insist.[14] The Prologue to 'Pyramus and Thisbe' and the explanations are about as long as the play itself — it is a take-off of the dumb-shows and their clumsy, ham-handed presenters, rather like the school prize-givings of today. Even so, there is a divine comment from Theseus when Hippolyta says how silly the poor players are : 'the best in this kind are but shadows, and the worst are no worse, if imagination amend them'.

There we have Shakespeare, speaking on his art, directly to our hearts.

It used to be thought that *Love's Labour's Lost* was a very early play ; we know better now, and indeed there are several reasons to place it alongside of *A Midsummer-Night's Dream*. There is no knowing whether it came before or after the *Dream*, but we know that Shakespeare was thinking of that in 1593, that it was produced in May 1594, and this inclines me to think that it was the earlier, as it is also the less sophisticated. In any case the events of 1593-4 are again very much present in the mind of the writer. *Love's Labour's Lost* has this in common with its predecessor that it is made up of diverse, disparate strands — an invention of its author, in this case without any source-plot at all. The plays are alike in their high spirits, their lyricism and poetry — much of it in rhyme. But their tone and temper are different : where one is magical, the other is intellectual ; where one appeals to the heart and is ever popular, the other appeals to the head and has gone out ; where the *Dream* looks to the past, *Love's Labour's Lost* is topical, and that always dates. On the other hand, it has a peculiarity of its own, for it is a piece by a clever intellectual against intellectualism. If this were all, it would never have survived ; but its other theme is the rejection of love and the confounding of those who reject it. And that ties in closely with Shakespeare's experience and redeems it ; one of the characters, Berowne, might be speaking for Shakespeare : he gives voice to the poet's recognisable sentiments.

A recent editor comments, 'of all Shakespeare's plays this is the most personal ; a solution of the puzzle he has set here (and I had better say at once that I cannot provide it) would not only satisfy the most rabid detective ardour but illuminate Shakespeare's own early life and the conditions that shaped his career and his first plays — an essential background of which at present absolutely nothing is known'.[15] We have had reason to see that this is too defeatist a view.

Love's Labour's Lost is made up of two main strands, linked and interwoven. One is the theme of the rejection and validation of love, with its dependent interest of oath-taking and oath-breaking. This is pegged upon the King of Navarre and his associates, for obvious reasons. They were much in the public mind just now : Henri IV was England's Protestant ally, and his conversion to Catholicism deeply disturbed English minds. The Queen was so much upset that it forced her, for once, to console herself with long consultations with her Archbishop. The English public were fortified in their view that there was no faith in Frenchmen. Their favourite Henry of Navarre had broken his oath — just as Ferdinand of Navarre in the play, where all was moved on to the plane of love, has done. In the realm of actual affairs, Henry of Navarre was made to wait some period before the Church gave him absolution ; in the play, Ferdinand of Navarre has to go into solitary retreat for a year before his Princess absolves him. Henry of Navarre was notorious for his love-affairs : to present him and his gallants as shy of ladies was in itself a good joke.

The second element was suggested by the furious literary quarrel between Gabriel Harvey and Nashe which raged in just these years. Pamphlets, insults, provocations, rejoinders flew back and forth, providing mirth for everybody in the know with a seat at the ringside of these sparring intellectuals. 'At the present day, when literary activity is so widely spread and so diverse,' says McKerrow, 'it is difficult for us to realise the interest which, in the far more limited circle of Elizabethan writers and readers, such a quarrel could arouse.' [16] Is it so ? — one still finds literary quarrels, particularly when one of the combatants is a venomous don, capable of arousing amusement. In the end, the poor Archbishop had to be called in once more to put a stop to the fracas and suppress the publications.

It was all a quarrel among Cambridge men, and seems to have gone back to Robert Greene's aspersion on the three Harvey brothers. One of them, with astrological pretensions, had made himself ridiculous by prognostications which did not come off. The most redoubtable was Gabriel Harvey, a leading exponent of the new criticism at Cambridge, a figure certainly tinged with megalomania and probably persecution-mania. Harvey was not a bad man, he had been a friend of Spenser and the modern poets ; but he was an acutely uncomfortable bed-mate at Cambridge, anguished by a sense of social inferiority on one side and even greater intellectual superiority on the other. He was very much of a modern in his tastes, with ambitions totally beyond his capacity to achieve. Once, when he had been presented to the Queen, with his wizened mahogany complexion she took him — or pretended to take him — for an Italian ; and this compliment completely turned his head. He was no fool, he was well read, he had a passion for literature ; but he was insufferably conceited, vainglorious, fatuously patronising — really an ass.

The play then was originally written, like *A Midsummer-Night's Dream*, for a special audience, the circle at Southampton House who would recognise all the hits and skits, some of which are lost to us. The key which has hitherto been missing is that it is a skit on the circle by one of its intimates, the family poet. That this was the audience it was written for is supported by this consideration : when, in 1605, the Earl entertained King James at Southampton House, the play he chose to entertain the royal party with was *Love's Labour's Lost*. It had a particularly personal reference. In between, there was a performance at Court before Queen Elizabeth ; and once more, as with the *Dream*, Shakespeare revised his play and inserted passages improving and strengthening it.

From the beginning of the play Berowne is opposed to Navarre's idea of abjuring the society of women to concentrate on their masculine studies without distraction. This idea — which used to be that of the universities — he does not think a good one :

> Why, all delights are vain, but that most vain
> Which with pain purchased doth inherit pain :
> As painfully to pore upon a book
> To seek the light of truth ; while truth the while
> Doth falsely blind the eyesight of his look . . .
> Small have continuous plodders ever won
> Save base authority from others' books.

Nevertheless, Shakespeare's acquaintance with university terminology — he must have been acquainted with Oxford, constantly passing to or from Stratford — is witnessed a few lines on :

> Proceeded well, to stop all good proceeding !

This refers to proceeding to one's M.A. degree, as Greene and Marlowe had done, Shakespeare not.

In order to hold themselves fast to their studies the King and his friends take an oath to keep away from women. But was this not very much Southampton's line ? We may properly infer that he was the inspiration of the part of the King. They plan to create something of an academy — as Navarre actually had done in France : it is a topical idea. Their plans are disrupted by an embassy of ladies, headed by the Princess of France — just like the two embassies Marguerite de Valois had made to Navarre, in 1578 and 1586, concerning her dowry, with all her ladies — *l'escadron volant*. Among the ladies in the play Berowne falls for a dark lady, Rosaline. The King says that she is 'black as ebony'. To this Berowne replies :

> Is ebony like her ? O wood divine ! . . .
> No face is fair that is not full so black.

Navarre answers :

> O paradox ! Black is the badge of hell,
> The hue of dungeons and the school of night.

This is a hit at a rival circle, addicts of night-thoughts, of which George Chapman had just declared himself an upholder with his poem, *The Shadow of the Night.*   These were self-esteemed, somewhat sombre, intellectuals — Chapman, Roydon, Hariot, who looked to Ralegh, Essex's enemy, as their patron.   Berowne replies :

> O, if in black my lady's brows be decked,
> It mourns that painting and usurping hair
> Should ravish doters with a false aspect ;
> And therefore is she born to make black fair.

We recognise the very language of the Sonnets, and that in portraying Rosaline Shakespeare was inspired by his dark mistress.

At the end of the play, its moral — the hopelessness of excluding women, the valuelessness of knowledge without them — is proclaimed in a fine speech by Berowne :

> But love, first learnèd in a lady's eyes,
> Lives not alone immurèd in the brain,
> But, with the motion of all elements,
> Courses as swift as thought in every power,
> And gives to every power a double power,
> Above their functions and their offices.
> It adds a precious seeing to the eye ;
> A lover's eye will gaze an eagle blind ;
> A lover's ear will hear the lowest sound ;
> Love's feeling is more soft and sensible
> Than are the tender horns of cockled snails.

Here once more are the cockled snails of *Venus and Adonis.* Berowne concludes :

> From women's eyes this doctrine I derive :
> They sparkle still the right Promethean fire ;
> They are the books, the arts, the academes,
> That show, contain and nourish all the world.

We realise that Berowne is speaking for Shakespeare : this was his religion at this time.   Shakespeare is always on the side of women — and perhaps this bespeaks the feminine side of his nature : like Tolstoy, he understood them from the inside.

With Berowne thus speaking for him, it is as well to look at him through Rosaline's eyes :

> but a merrier man,
> Within the limit of becoming mirth,
> I never spent an hour's talk withal.
> His eye begets occasion for his wit ;
> For every object that the one doth catch
> The other turns to a mirth-moving jest,

> Which his fair tongue (conceit's expositor)
> Delivers in such apt and gracious words
> That agèd ears play truant at his tales,
> And younger hearings are quite ravishèd,
> So sweet and voluble is his discourse.

Writers often, consciously or unconsciously, portray themselves. Here he has given us a pen-picture of himself. In this circle he is Berowne, with his dark mistress, evidently known to them all. This realization throws a flood of light on Berowne, for it is Shakespeare laughing at himself. His characteristics are well recognized: his fondness for women and for good cheer, his good humour and merry spirit. In addition to studying for three years,

> There are other strict observances,
> As: not to see a woman in that term —
> Which I hope well is not enrollèd there.

The audience would appreciate that joke at himself —

> And one day in a week to touch no food,
> And but one meal on every day beside —
> The which I hope is not enrollèd there,
> And then to sleep but three hours in the night,
> And not to be seen to wink of all the day —

that is, at anyone —

> When I was wont to think no harm all night,
> And make a dark night too of half the day . . .

another joke at his own amatory tendencies —

> Which I hope well is not enrollèd there.
> O, these are barren tasks, to hard to keep,
> Not to see ladies, study, fast, not sleep!

There we have him before us, as no doubt he played the part himself.

When we come to the second theme of the play, Don Armado is a fantastic, conceited, fatuously condescending person —'I love not to be crossed', 'it fitteth the spirit of a tapster', and so on. The transference from an Italianate type to a Spaniard was an obvious one to make, and he certainly was a don all right, for his language is Harvey's. It was a good joke to make this respectable, bachelor don fall for a slut of a country wife, who was no better than she should be. (Jaquenetta, by the way, has the name of Richard Field's wife.) 'I am sure I shall turn sonnet. Devise, wit ; write, pen ; for I am for whole volumes in folio.' This is a skit on Harvey's own words : 'a famous deviser in folio'. Throughout the play Don Armado talks in Harvey's absurdly inflated language : 'give enlargement to the swain, bring him festinately hither'. Again and again there are skits on Harvey's literary oddities and usages. There was his addiction to the use of an *envoi*, of which he was so proud and for which Nashe had already ribbed him. 'Some enigma, some riddle : come, thy l'envoy ; begin.' And then, after a lot of Harveyesque nonsense — 'the heaving of my lungs provokes me to ridiculous smiling : O, pardon me, my stars !' — Don Armado adds 'There's the moral : now the l'envoy.'

For, believe it or not, this is the way this Cambridge don — he has his successor (*mutatis mutandis*) — wrote. One of Harvey's characteristics was to write by donnish question and answer : 'What the salvation of David George ? a nullity ; what the deification of N. H. ? a nullity ; what the sanctification of Browne ? a nullity.' And so on. Don Armado's love-letter is written in this style : 'Who came ? the king ; why did he come ? to see ; why did he see ? to overcome. To whom came he ? to the beggar ; what saw he ? the beggar ; whom overcame he ? the beggar.' And so on, with variations, for a whole page. One of Harvey's silly verbal quibbles is repeated : where he had written, 'but to let titles and tittles pass, and come to the very point indeed', Don Armado writes, 'What shalt thou exchange for rags ? robes ; for tittles ? titles ; for thyself ? me'. When schoolmaster Holofernes appears he also talks in Harvey's language, pedantic distinctions piled up as in his writings, and both drag in Latin school-tags *ad nauseam*.

There is more to the same effect, but this is enough to make it clear that don Harvey contributed something to Don Armado, though in this play which most takes after Lyly Don Armado also derives some suggestion from Sir Tophas in Lyly's *Endimion*.[17] There is a good deal of further quibbling on the words pierce and pennyworth : Nashe had come out with his *Pierce Pennyless* in 1592, to which Harvey had replied with his *Pierce's Supererogation* in 1593. All this pamphlet warfare would have been much enjoyed by the wits of the Southampton circle. In the play Don Armado has an attendant spirit, young Moth.[18] From the moment he enters Moth is referred to three or four times over as 'tender

Juvenal'. This was the nickname for the young satirist Nashe, three or four years Shakespeare's junior : Greene refers to him as 'young Juvenal' in his famous attack on the players, others refer to him as 'gallant young Juvenal'. Shakespeare is not unkind to Nashe in the play ; after all, he and Nashe were on the same side against both pedants and intellectuals.

Since the play is so much a domestic product of the Southampton circle, no doubt his Italian tutor, Florio, also contributed something to the character of Don Armado. Perhaps we should see him as a conflation of Florio and Harvey.

And what about Holofernes ? Who is he that we should commend him ?

Perhaps the heaviest weather of all has been made about him — every conceivable suggestion. Just as the mistake about the Sonnets has always been to approach them from the wrong end and invent some putative Mr. W. H., so the mistake here has been to think up some possible figure to fit Holofernes and then use the invention as a clue to the play — as if the play were written, any more than the Sonnets, to provide a puzzle. Observe that Holofernes talks Don Armado's language. They are but two facets of the same concept : one stands for the don or tutor's pedantry, the other for the schoolmaster's. Notice too that Shakespeare has a kind word for the schoolmaster at the end, gives him the last word after his baiting by the callous young gallants of the Court : 'This is not generous, not gentle, not humble', and is accompanied out by the sympathy of a woman, the Princess : 'Alas, poor Maccabaeus, how hath he been baited'. Shakespeare knew a lot about schoolmasters : I think the tradition true that he had been one.

The play is a manifesto in favour of life and love, spontaneity and naturalness, against intellectualism, pedantry and affectation. It hardly needs demonstration that when it comes to the point the upholders of the first are far cleverer, of the second apt to be great asses. There may be other strokes in the play intended for other people.

> Beauty is bought by judgment of the eye,
> Not uttered by base sale of chapmen's tongues,

may well be meant as a reference to Chapman, whose *The Shadow of the Night*, of this same year, was intended as a manifesto of the opposite school of thought.

We can usually hear the overtones when Shakespeare is speaking for himself :

> A jest's prosperity lies in the ear
> Of him that hears it, never in the tongue
> Of him that makes it.

Again, how clever he was, apart from anything else : he seems to have understood everything. A reference to the plague shows us that we are still not far away from those terrible years :

> Write 'Lord have mercy on us' on those three ;
> They are infected, in their hearts it lies ;
> They have the plague, and caught it of your eyes.

These details help to build up a firmer frame for our dating. The pageant of the Nine Worthies, with Costard as Great Pompey, keeps us close to Bottom's play in the *Dream* ; and, though not as good as that unforgettable fooling, it is funny enough. Sir Nathaniel, the curate, is put out of countenance by the ragging of the courtiers and forgets his part. Costard apologises for him : 'There, an't please you : a foolish mild man ; an honest man, look you, and soon dashed ! He is a marvellous neighbour, faith, and a very good bowler ; but for Alisander — alas, you see how 'tis — a little o'erparted.'

The yokels have more real *politesse de cœur* than the grandees — as indeed they often have in life.

The play is dismissed, and the characters got off the stage, with a couple of marvellous songs, the Cuckoo Song and the Owl Song, which, for all their farcical intent, take us back to reality : the country, meadows in spring, frost and ice in winter, the realities of country life :

> When shepherds pipe on oaten straws,
>   And merry larks are ploughman's clocks,
> When turtles tread, and rooks, and daws,
>   And maidens bleach their summer smocks . . .

> When icicles hang by the wall,
>   And Dick the shepherd blows his nail,
> And Tom bears logs into the hall,
>   And milk comes frozen home in pail . . .

> When all aloud the wind doth blow,
>   And coughing drowns the parson's saw,
> And birds sit brooding in the snow,
>   And Marian's nose looks red and raw,

When roasted crabs hiss in the bowl,
Then nightly sings the staring owl :
Tu-whit,
Tu-who, a merry note,
While greasy Joan doth keel the pot.

The heart turns over at the reality and truth of the evocation.

On 6 October 1594 Southampton came of age : there were his affairs to settle, the inheritance of his estates, obligations to clear. Anxious to shine, avid of praise and distinction, he had not yet taken any appropriate step to ingratiate himself with the Queen, and he had earned the disfavour of the Lord Treasurer. The young man was an addict of poetry and plays, and he had with him in his household the Italian Jew, John Florio, to instruct him in Italian. Florio spent several years in his service, and in the dedication of his Dictionary in 1598 was able to pay him a tribute, 'being at home so instructed for Italian as teaching or learning could supply that there seemed no need of travel, and now by travel so accomplished as what wants to perfection ?'[19] In Southampton's immediate circle Shakespeare was certain to be acquainted with Florio ; if he needed anything for the Italian colouring of his plays there was a source of information at hand. The next two plays from this period, *Romeo and Juliet* and *The Merchant of Venice*, have a stronger Italian flavour than any.

At the moment of attaining his majority the Earl was in some trouble through a shocking murder committed by his friends, Sir Charles and Sir Henry Danvers, also friends and followers of Essex. Down in Wiltshire where the Danvers estates were, there was a feud between the Danvers and Long families, of which this was the culmination.[20] On 4 October 1594 these young swordsmen, the Danvers brothers, with nearly a score of their armed followers, entered a house at Corsham where the two Longs were sitting at dinner with Anthony Mildmay and others, and began an altercation and a scuffle in which Henry Long was killed. The two Danverses then fled across country to Southampton, whence to escape to France. Near Southampton they took refuge at one of the Earl's lodges near Titchfield and sent to him for help. He sent his servants with food and necessaries for them to make their getaway, and the day after his birthday he went over with half a dozen of his followers to sup with them and stayed with them all night. The brothers made their escape to France, whence they wrote to Essex vowing him their eternal service. They were exiles for some years; but they came back to keep their word — and Sir Charles Danvers was beheaded for his part in the Essex rebellion, when Southampton's death-sentence was commuted on grounds of his youth. Meanwhile, down in Wiltshire, John Aubrey, who knew everything about his native county, tells us that the father of these young men, 'a most beautiful and good and even-tempered person, was of a mild and peaceable nature, and his sons' sad accident brake his heart'.[21] True it is that the father died before the end of the year.

If Southampton had not given the Danvers brothers all possible aid they might not have got away. Their horses were taken into the Earl's stables, and then put out to graze in the park at Titchfield until their masters got a vessel to take them across Channel. One of the Earl's stablemen recognised Sir Henry Danvers's maidenhair-coloured velvet saddle all bloody. When the Sheriff of Southampton was passing over Itchen Ferry to inquire into the circumstances of the affair, a couple of the Earl's servants threatened to throw him overboard: one of them was 'Signor Florio, an Italian'.

It was time to make a reckoning with the young Earl — now that he had attained his majority and entered upon his estates — for his refusal to marry Burghley's granddaughter. After all, it amounted to breach of promise, and now the Lord Treasurer had a better match in view. Ferdinando, Lord Derby, better known to us as Lord Strange, patron of players, had died in April 1594, bewitched, as he thought. His brother succeeded as Earl, unmarried and a great catch. Lord Burghley entered immediately into negotiations for his despised granddaughter, who was accepted. Then the widow of the late Earl proved to be with child; the marriage was put off, until it was seen whether the issue was a boy — in which case the earl would be un-earled. The child turned out to be a girl, and the wedding went forward. At last the Lady Elizabeth Vere was safely and most grandly married to the Earl of Derby at Court at Greenwich, in the presence of the Queen. A knowledge of historical circumstances shows that it is impossible for Shakespeare to have written *A Midsummer-Night's Dream* for *that* marriage.

The Earl of Southampton now had to face the music. We have seen that the Jesuit, Henry Garnet, reported that the Earl had to pay £5000 immediately.[22] Whether this was the precise sum or no, it provides sufficient reason why the case of his inheritance came before the official attention of the Lord Treasurer.[23] From this we learn that the Earl's estates were worth 2000 marks a year, or some £1340, from which there would be considerable outgoing to his mother — a widow usually enjoyed one-third, while his father had been far too liberal with his legacies. At any rate, on attaining his majority the young man was faced with the financial facts of life, and for several years ahead found himself in considerable difficulties. It was a good thing, on the personal side, that Shakespeare was now safely established, only just in time. Politically, it was perhaps only to be expected that Southampton would line up with Essex against the Cecils — though that did him no good either ; after all, he had had the best of chances and disobligingly rejected it.

The Danvers-Long feud, with its issue in murder, made a sensation at the time, for these young men were at the top of society, followers of Essex who was involving himself more and more in what became a feud against Cecil and Ralegh. Essex exerted himself to recommend the Danvers brothers to Henri IV, who received them well.

Shakespeare's next play, written most probably in 1595, dealt with the familiar subject of love in the unfamiliar atmosphere of feud and family hatred, duelling and death.[24] He found his story in Arthur Brooke's *Romeus and Juliet*, which we have reason to think he had known for some time. This was already one of the best known of European stories ; but Shakespeare's genius had received a stimulus which drove his imagination forward at high pressure and with a single impulse to create a masterpiece. Critics have been quick to seize upon some contradiction between the theme of fate as determining the tragedy, and that of character — whether the lovers did not precipitate their fate by the rash unadvisedness of their passion : as Friar Lawrence points out to Romeo,

These violent delights have violent ends.

It may be admitted that there is some inconsistency between the traditional idea of tragedy he had inherited as due to fortune, and the insight, which became fundamental with him later, that people's tragedies are due to their own faults of character. The latter view he already glimpses in *Romeo and Juliet*, and it makes for some little disaccord with the theme announced in the Prologue, with its emphasis on the 'star-crossed' lovers condemned by their families' feud —

> From ancient grudge break to new mutiny
> Where civil blood makes civil hands unclean.

We need only reflect that here the idea of tragedy is *developing* in him, is not yet fully achieved, and that in any case it is never any stumbling-block to an audience ; for the play is perennially popular, it has so much lyrical beauty, such poetry and pathos.

Shakespeare followed his source very closely, in incident and sometimes in word and phrase — he was working rapidly as usual, carried forward by the subject, and this was the speedy way to get the play done. Again it is revealing to note what is entirely his own invention — the character of Mercutio, Romeo's devoted friend, fascinating, mercurial and bawdy, the young swordsman who falls by the sword. Tybalt on the Capulet side is a far less attractive specimen of the same type : a professional swordsman, as Mercutio describes him : 'he fights as you sing prick-song — keeps time, distance, and proportion ; he rests his minim rests — one, two, and the third in your bosom'. Mercutio describes himself, however, in teasing his friend Benvolio : 'thou art like one of those fellows that, when he enters the confines of a tavern, claps me his sword upon the table and says, "God send me no need of thee" ; and by the operation of the second cup, draws him on the drawer, when indeed there is no need'. There is a great deal more to the same effect, and Mercutio concludes, 'Nay, an there were two such, we should have none shortly, for one would kill the other'.

And this is what happens among these young fighting fools. Mercutio provokes Tybalt and is killed by him ; Romeo is practically forced by his friend to fight Tybalt and kills him. This precipitates the catastrophe, for Romeo is then banished. There is no doubt where the poet's sympathies lay in all this feuding among the young bloods — he had evidence enough of its fatal consequences among his acquaintance : what about Bradley ; what about Marlowe ? And now here was the Danvers affair within Southampton's immediate circle. Himself, a quiet, observant man, taking in everybody and everything that passed on the scene, was no swordsman.

Mercutio may have had a poet's imagination, but the poet was Shakespeare : I have always thought that the magical long

speech — quite unnecessary to the action — in which he expresses
the dream of an older England is the stuff that Shakespeare had
most at heart.

> O, then I see Queen Mab hath been with you.
> She is the fairies' midwife, and she comes
> In shape no bigger than an agate-stone
> On the forefinger of an alderman —

well, we may reflect, he had reason to know what belonged to
aldermen.

> Her waggon-spokes made of long spinners' legs,
> The cover of the wings of grasshoppers,
> Her traces of the smallest spider-web,
> Her collars of the Moonshine's watery beams . . .
> Her chariot is an empty hazel-nut,
> Made by the joiner squirrel or old grub,
> Time out o' mind the fairies' coachmakers.

It is the stuff out of which *A Midsummer-Night's Dream* had been
made, and looks as if it was material that had been left over, for its
sole purpose is to fill a gap at this point. It is no less securely
grounded in the life of the countryside than in its traditional lore.

> Sometime she gallops o'er a courtier's nose,
> And then dreams he of smelling out a suit —

this was the regular phrase in use for searching out some advantageous grant or office —

> And sometime comes she with a tithe-pig's tail
> Tickling a parson's nose as 'a lies asleep,
> Then dreams he of another benefice . . .
>   This is that very Mab
> That plats the manes of horses in the night,
> And bakes the elf-locks in foul sluttish hairs,
> Which once untangled much misfortune bodes :
> This is the hag, when maids lie on their backs,
> That presses them and learns them first to bear,
> Making them women of good carriage.

Here is the quintessence of Shakespeare, this dream of the English
country, which yet belonged as much to the real world as to the
world of dream, on which his imagination fed all his life from
earliest days to *The Tempest* ; to which in real life the alderman's
son remained loyal, never losing his hold of Stratford and Arden
and Cotswold, coming home each year in the summer to refresh

the spirit with these sources of inspiration, at length to be buried within the sound of the Avon washing the banks of the churchyard.

The churchyard appears again as in the *Dream*; the Count Paris comes with flowers to lay by Juliet in the tomb of her ancestors:

> Under yond yew-trees lay thee all along,
> Holding thine ear close to the hollow ground;
> So shall no foot upon the churchyard tread,
> Being loose, unfirm with digging up of graves,
> But thou shalt hear it.

The little page answers, as many a Stratford boy must have felt:

> I am almost afraid to stand alone
> Here in the churchyard, yet I will adventure.

Naturally, there is much less of country life in this intense and urban play; but falconry appears in Juliet's image,

> O for a falconer's voice
> To lure this tassel-gentle back again!

The Nurse's reference to an earthquake has been much pressed to yield a date for the play earlier than all the rest of the evidence supports, or is indeed possible.

> 'Tis since the earthquake now eleven years,
> And she was weaned — I never shall forget it —
> Of all the days of the year, upon that day:
> For I had then laid wormwood to my dug,
> Sitting in the sun under the dove-house wall . . .
> 'Shake', quoth the dove-house.

Everyone has noticed the earthquake of 1580; but there was, in fact, an earthquake on the Continent in the spring of 1584, which may have produced a tremor in England.[25] Nothing much rests upon that, though it would make eleven years to 1595, for that is the probable date for the play in any case.[26]

It is still not far away from the words and themes of the Sonnets: what is love? —

> A madness most discreet,
> A choking gall and a preserving sweet.

Romeo's first love, Rosaline, is vowed to chastity:

Romeo: O, she is rich in beauty, only poor
  That, when she dies, with beauty dies her store.
Benvolio: Then she hath sworn that she will still live chaste?

Romeo : She hath, and in that sparing makes huge waste :
For beauty, starved with her severity,
Cuts beauty off from all posterity.

We have now heard enough of what we may call the Southampton theme : it will shortly cease to apply to him.

There are pleasant references that speak to us of contemporary life below stairs, and above in the great chamber — as it might be at Hardwick or at Hatfield. The serving-men give us hints of their expertise : 'away with the joined-stools, remove the court-cupboard, look to the plate — Good thou, save me a piece of marchpane ; and, as thou loves me, let the porter let in Susan Grindstone and Nell — Anthony and Potpan !' Saving him a piece of marzipan, and letting in their wenches — Shakespeare knew it all, and the servants' complaints too. 'You are looked for and called for, asked for and sought for, in the great chamber.' To which the reply is, 'we cannot be here and there too' — and how often have we not heard that ?

One or two touches light up Shakespeare's own profession again and contribute to the considerable information he gives us as to his views on this and that aspect. Romeo and his friends come into the Capulet feast as masquers :

Romeo : What, shall this speech be spoke for our excuse ?
Or shall we on without apology ?

Benvolio : The date is out of such prolixity :
We'll have no Cupid hoodwinked with a scarf,
Bearing a Tartar's painted bow of lath,
Scaring the ladies like a crowkeeper :
Nor no without-book prologue, faintly spoke
After the prompter, for our entrance.

And it is from the prologue to the first Act that we learn the usual duration of an Elizabethan play :

the two hours' traffic of our stage.

We have seen enough now to persuade us that Shakespeare wrote, like other writers, not *in vacuo* but in an actual environment the events of which stimulated his imagination along with his reading and his memory. And, after all, this is but a matter of common sense. But scholars have put more energy and scholarship into exploring his 'sources' in his reading, than to giving attention to the personal associations, the events going on around them, which provide as much stimulus to a writer. Writers differ in their response to one and the other ; and I am the last person to reduce Shakespeare to the level of the topical : his own inner imagination is the creative force with him. However, it operated in and responded to the environment of a real world ; and here the historian has something to offer to the understanding of Shakespeare, making both him and his work more real to us.

Curiously enough, a little contrary to appearances perhaps, to no play are these observations more applicable than to *The Merchant of Venice*.

What are its themes ? Love and romantic friendship once more — Bassanio's love for Portia is less important in the play than his and Antonio's devotion to each other : it is on account of his love for Bassanio that Antonio engages himself in the bond to Shylock which brings his life in danger. The bond to Shylock, engaging a pound of flesh, the character of the Jew, the issue of Jew versus Christian, are more powerful elements in the play. An issue of practical interest and constant comment to Elizabethans is that of usury. The play takes place in an atmosphere of sea-argosies, captures and losses of ships, booty, a casket of jewels. Shakespeare looked up a good story, again a well-known one, upon which to hang his play ; but what were the events in the world that stimulated his interest, drew him to look for an appropriate story, having in mind also the public's interest in contemporary happenings ?

One indication of public excitement over the Lopez affair, and a pointer to how the theatres naturally reacted to the public's interest, was the revival of Marlowe's old play, *The Jew of Malta*. People were so keen that it was performed no less than fifteen times between the Lopez trial and the end of the year 1594. Marlowe's play belonged to the Admiral's men ; it was only natural for the Chamberlain's men to reply with another. We can see more clearly now what a motive it was with Shakespeare to go one better than his rival. Everyone notices that this is the most powerful part of *The Merchant of Venice*, not the conventional love-story. Even in its own day, when the play was entered for publication by James Roberts in 1598, it was referred to as ' *The Merchant of Venice* or otherwise called *The Jew of Venice* '.

The young men in Essex's following were spoiling for action, in particular Southampton, who had had as yet no opportunity of distinguishing himself or winning honour. Early in 1596

Calais was besieged by Parma, the brilliant soldier who commanded the Spanish army in the Netherlands. It was a grave threat to England's security and a powerful fleet was formed under the Lord Admiral at Dover to go to the rescue. In March Southampton went down and was received by Lord Admiral Howard on board his flagship, the *Due Repulse*.[27] In April the Queen sent her instructions with leave for certain peers to serve on the expedition, but ordering the young lords Southampton, Derby and Mountjoy to return.[28] (Her reason would be that they had no heirs as yet and she would not allow them to risk their lives.) Then Calais fell — a great blow. The objective of the fleet was changed to Cadiz, and the combined-operations expedition that brilliantly accomplished its capture was set in train.

All the young men were on edge to go, and at this time Thomas Wilson brought out his translation of Montemayor's *Diana* with a dedication to 'the Earl of Southampton, now upon the Spanish voyage with my Lord the Earl of Essex'. But it does not appear that he was permitted to go after all. And, if so, he missed the most dazzling achievement of the whole war, Essex's foremost part in which was celebrated by Spenser :

> Great England's glory, and the world's wide wonder
> Whose dreadful name late through all Spain did thunder
> And Hercules' two pillars standing near
> Did make to quake and fear . . .

All that Southampton had to console himself with was an attempt, along with the Earl of Derby, to make a deal with the interested parties to buy Sir Anthony Ashley's booty — evidently prize goods. [29] We learn later of rich spoil taken at Cadiz being stowed away secretly in the town of Southampton, and Sir Anthony Ashley, who was keeper of the Queen's jewels, was disgraced for appropriating a rich casket of jewels that should have come to her.[30]

Two flagships of the Spanish fleet were captured at Cadiz, one of them the vice-admiral, the *St. Andrew*. There is a reflection of this in *The Merchant of Venice* :

> I should not see the sandy-hour glass run,
> But I should think of shallows and of flats,
> And see my wealthy *Andrew* docked in sand,
> Vailing her high-top lower than her ribs
> To kiss her burial.

This helps to corroborate the date 1596 for the play.

What makes the play memorable is not the conventional love-interest, which Shakespeare could turn out with his left hand at any time, but the character of Shylock and the disquieting thoughts he gives rise to. He is real : as Charles Lamb saw, there walks in among the puppets on the stage a real man. Though he appears in only five scenes, he dominates the play and is the centre of its interest. We are given a clue, in Shakespeare's manner, as to where he came from, the creative spark that leaped into a flame in this play and gave it life :

> thy currish spirit
> Governed a Wolf, who hanged for human slaughter,
> Even from the gallows did his fell soul fleet,
> And whilst thou layest in thy unhallowed dam
> Infused itself in thee ; for thy desires
> Are wolvish, bloody, starved, and ravenous.

The idea of the Wolf and the wolvish would be sufficiently clear to the Elizabethans, though the whole play would appeal to the public's interest in Dr. Lopez, for the Latin form of the name, *lupus*, means wolf.

We hardly need to be reminded, after the appalling anti-Semitism that has disgraced this century, that with the Elizabethan mob a Shylock was a villain. And so his creator meant him to be — then Shakespeare's indefeasible human sympathy took over and the villain becomes a human being. Unlike Marlowe's complete villain, Barabas : an improbable Machiavellian monster with his creator's gift of magnificent speech. Here, not for the last time, we see the contrast between Shakespeare and his master : the humanity and sympathy of the one, the intellectuality of the other ; the diversity and variety of Shakespeare, the tragic power and concentration of Marlowe.

We see this more clearly than ever, for all the Shylock part of *The Merchant of Venice* is modelled on *The Jew of Malta*.[31] It was Shakespeare's way of writing to lay his hand on whatever fed his imagination ; not to bother with originality — that fetish of writers of the second rank — but to pit himself against a model and then surpass it. This is what he did now with Marlowe once more. Shylock is conceived after the model of Barabas, and they have much in common : both are possessed with resentment at their treatment at the hands of Christians and are filled with the desire for revenge.

I learned in Florence how to kiss my hand,
Heave up my shoulders when they call me dog,
And duck as low as any barefoot friar ;
Hoping to see them starve upon a stall,
Or else be gathered for in our synagogue,
That, when the offering-basin comes to me,
Even for charity I may spit into 't.

This is Barabas speaking, but it might equally be Shylock : some
of the phrases are echoed by Shakespeare's catching ear — the
advantageous ear of an actor. It is Barabas who expresses the
principle of the action :

It's no sin to deceive a Christian ;
For they themselves hold it a principle,
Faith is not to be held with heretics :
But all are heretics that are not Jews.

One hears the iron, implacable note of Marlowe's temper : what
he wants to say is that all people are fools in their religious beliefs ;
this is his way of expressing so dangerous a sentiment.

Shakespeare was not interested in these intellectual issues, nor
had he Marlowe's formidably educated mind. He is interested
in the human issues, the drama and the poetry. Here, too, he
follows Marlowe. Both Barabas and Shylock have a savage,
sardonic twist of humour ; both are led by their passion to a
cynical disregard of consequences. Each had an only daughter
he loves, who deceives her father for love of a Christian and
becomes converted. Even in details, Shakespeare once more
follows the master : both Jews discuss the self-multiplication of
money ; even in phrases : Barabas's phrase, 'sufferance in ease'
to watch for an occasion of revenge becomes Shylock's

patient shrug,
For sufferance is the badge of all our tribe.

Shakespeare has also taken over Barabas's comic confusion between
love of his daughter and love of his lucre :

O my girl,
My gold, my fortune, my felicity . . .
O girl ! O gold ! O beauty ! O my bliss !

This becomes Shylock's cry :

My daughter ! O my jewels ! O my daughter !

Both fathers are plunged into despair at their daughters' apostasy
and discountenance them.

For all Shakespeare's basing himself upon the master, there is a great difference between them : it is the difference between his temperament and Marlowe's. And this makes for a world of difference in atmosphere : as Q. saw so well, setting is an external matter, atmosphere is internal, a particular emanation of genius. Marlowe's Barabas is a total Machiavellian, ready to undertake any devilish stratagem, to experiment in genocide, kill off the sick — not unfamiliar in our time — engineer casualties for both sides at war, poison whole communities by poisoning wells. (Marlowe got this last idea from the Catholic informer Baines, who informed against him in the end.) [32]

There is nothing of this in Shakespeare : both a gentler nature and a better dramatist, he makes Shylock's desire for revenge understandable, he gives him cause, he holds the balance more persuasively. Antonio was ready to spit on him — and then borrow his money :

> Thou call'dst me dog before thou hadst a cause,
> But since I am a dog beware my fangs.

Antonio has wronged Shylock, only because he is a Jew : and 'hath not a Jew eyes ? hath not a Jew hands, organs, dimensions, senses, affections, passions ? fed with the same food, hurt with the same weapons, subject to the same diseases, healed by the same means, warmed and cooled by the same winter and summer, as a Christian is ? '

There is the ultimate difference between Shakespeare and Marlowe : in a word, sympathy and human understanding.

Other differences exist : Shakespeare has an ethical quality entirely lacking in Marlowe. One cannot imagine the latter writing Portia's famous speech, so much beloved by the Victorians :

> The quality of mercy is not strained,
> It droppeth as the gentle rain from heaven
> Upon the place beneath : it is twice blessed,
> It blesseth him that gives, and him that takes.

Then, too, the moonlit atmosphere of Belmont has no place in the grim *Jew of Malta*, though there is an approximation to Marlowe once more with —

> In such a night
> Stood Dido with a willow in her hand
> Upon the wild sea-banks, and waft her love
> To come again to Carthage.

In Shakespeare's associative, almost psychic, way this scene con-
nects up the immediate past of his own imaginative life with the
future :

> In such a night
> Did Thisbe fearfully o'er-trip the dew . . .
> In such a night
> Troilus methinks mounted the Troyan walls,
> And sighed his soul toward the Grecian tents,
> Where Cressid lay that night.

Marlowe's more educated intellect must have exerted its influence in ways now hardly decipherable, though it could have
given corroboration to Shakespeare's natural scepticism, both
with regard to people's pretensions and their convictions :

> In religion
> What damnèd error, but some sober brow
> Will bless it, and approve it with a text,
> Hiding the grossness with fair ornament ?
> There is no vice so simple but assumes
> Some mark of virtue on his outward parts.

We catch recognisable glimpses of himself and his experience in

> All things that are
> Are with more spirit chasèd than enjoyed ;

or in his obvious devotion to music :

> The man that hath no music in himself,
> Nor is not moved with concord of sweet sounds,
> Is fit for treasons, stratagems, and spoils,
> The motions of his spirit are dull as night.

In his own art, we note 'his usual economy in borrowing from
himself : the discussion of the suitors between Portia and Nerissa
being but an improvement on Julia's talk with Lucetta in *The
Two Gentlemen of Verona*'.[33]   Once more we observe that this
comedy, with its mingled atmosphere of tragedy, romance and
realism, shows Shakespeare at his game of defeating the categories
beloved of dull people.

All in all, I find this a truly personal play, along with
A Midsummer-Night's Dream and *Love's Labour's Lost* : it marks
a further stage in his progressive realisation of himself, and in his
revelation of himself to us.

CHAPTER XII

England's Past

It may be out of fashion now to recognise the fact, but William Shakespeare was a patriot. This was in keeping with his love of the country in and for itself, of the soil — wold and forest and stream — its sights and sounds, its customs and its lore. Patriotism, properly speaking, is an extension of just that : built upon that ground, rich in inspiration, the life of the spirit, drawing upon the sediment accumulated by the generations that have gone before. Not to be able to recognise what we owe to the vanished generations is an impoverishment of the soul ; to be unwilling to recognise it betokens meanness of spirit. Neither was characteristic of William Shakespeare — and he received his reward in inexhaustible inspiration, subjects, themes, characters, stories, legends, memories and associations, every kind of lore.

But also he lived at the fortunate moment of the culmination of the Elizabethan age, when the English felt they were living in golden hours, coming through the test of the struggle with Spain and all her empire, experiencing more, expanding more in action and in the realm of the mind, more speedily and vitally than ever before or since. It is only natural, since his plays are the most lasting expression of that age, that the impulse should be directly expressed in them.

This theme, then, is the main inspiration running through the English history plays that chiefly occupied the next five years, 1595 to 1599. We might almost say that their one hero is England ; though the story is the contemplation of the past, in its various guises, the tone and temper are contemporary, and there are many more reflections of the Elizabethan world than have been altogether appreciated.

Shakespeare was fortunate, too, in the publication, on the threshold of his career, of the *Chronicles* of Holinshed, 'the father of many plays', the second edition of which, in 1587, Shakespeare used to such effect. 'For the book, inspired by the new-found sense of national unity and purpose which was the mainspring of Elizabethan activity in every field, immensely quickened that sense in thousands of English playgoers by providing the dramatists of the day with material for a corpus of drama which mirrored the history of England with scarcely a break from before the Conquest to the defeat of the Spanish Armada.'[1] Indeed, in that day itself Nashe recognised the source of the inspiration of so many plays : 'the subject of them for the most part . . . is borrowed out of our English chronicles, wherein our forefathers' valiant acts, that have lain long buried in rusty brass and worm-eaten books, are revived and they themselve raised from the grave of oblivion, and brought to plead their aged honours in open presence'.[2]

In these last years of the reign Ireland came to be one chief focus of attention ; the other was the succession to the throne. The Spaniards managed to occupy a base on the west coast of Brittany, and the main strategic danger shifted away from a direct blow at England to an invasion of Ireland, where the last native prince, the O'Neil, Earl of Tyrone, was waiting to welcome them. In the end he broke out into rebellion, something approaching a national resistance, which proved a running sore, exhausted the Crown's resources, brought the career of Essex down in ruins and was not finally extinguished until the Queen was on her deathbed. Then there was all the doubt and anxiety as to the succession — the Queen never would declare a successor — as to what would happen on her death, with a feverish jockeying for position between the factions, becoming increasingly bitter, at Court.

Shakespeare was not the kind of man to write merely topical plays as such, but he was sensitive to what was in the air about him — needs must be, to catch what was interesting the public. He neither could nor would write a play dealing directly with the question of the succession, nevertheless it was very much in people's minds ; it is an important theme in *Richard II*, and runs a scarlet thread through its successors, *Henry IV* and *Henry V*. Ireland is quite important to the action of *Richard II*, while in *Henry V* there is a salute to Essex, sent over with full powers and an army to suppress the rebellion. People were conscious of a comparison at the end of the reign with that of Richard II, and of Essex as a potential Bolingbroke. Certainly the Queen was conscious of it, and of Essex's cultivation of popularity, like Bolingbroke's. Not the least of her objections to Essex was that, after her own lifetime of endeavour for the state, he was robbing her of the devotion of her people.

Naturally the governing circle was most aware of this disquieting reminder : to be, or not to be, one of King Richard II's men was a regular phrase. Lord Hunsdon wrote, 'I never was one of Richard II's men', that is, a flatterer of the monarch.[3] When on the Islands Voyage of 1597 with Essex, Ralegh wrote back to Cecil that Essex was 'also wonderful merry at your conceit of Richard II'. What was the joke among them on this equivocal subject ? Only a few years later, on the eve of Essex's attempted *coup d'état* on February 1601, one of his supporters procured a performance of *Richard II* at the Globe Theatre to put the audience in a proper frame of mind. When all was over, the Queen herself said angrily, 'I am Richard II, know ye not that ?', and complained, 'this tragedy was played forty times in open streets and houses'. We need hardly take her angry expostulation literally, but it was asserted at Essex's trial that he was 'often present at the playing thereof . . . with great applause giving countenance and liking to the same'. No wonder the government was sensitive on the subject, and when the play was printed in 1597 the deposition scene had to be omitted, while all reference to the deposition had to be left out of the *Henry IV* quartos until after the safe accession of James I.

The play was written in 1595, for it draws on Samuel Daniel's poem, *The Civil Wars between the two Houses of Lancaster and York*. At the end of the year, it had a private performance before a very select audience : Sir Edward Hoby, son of the translator of Castiglione's *Il Cortegiano*, invited the Secretary of State, Sir Robert Cecil, to sup with him on 9 December at his house in Canon Row, 'where, as late as it shall please you, a gate for your supper shall be open, and King Richard present himself to your view'.[4] The invitation was endorsed 'Readily' — so we may presume that the great little man was able to satisfy himself of the play's political reliability. Other special performances were not less interesting : the Chamberlain's men played it before the Queen at Whitehall the day before Essex went to the block. A rather more endearing occasion was off Sierra Leone in September 1607, when the ship's company of the East Indiaman, the *Dragon*, performed it — earlier that month they had played *Hamlet*.

In writing the play Shakespeare was once more pitting himself against Marlowe, in this case *Edward II*, in which Marlowe was following Shakespeare in exploring the English chronicles for a subject.[5] The subject of Edward II had a particular appeal for Marlowe — the king's infatuation for Gaveston — and he goes into their relations in sympathetic detail. Nothing of this in Shakespeare's *Richard II*. Our leading authority tells us, 'he certainly knew Marlowe's play and he may have known it the better from having acted in it'.[6] Both plays are studies of weakness in a ruler and its consequences. 'In both characters there is change, but the change is not so much in them as in our feelings to them, as we see them passing from the cruelty and selfishness of power to the helplessness and suffering of powerlessness. But the similarities between these two plays are superficial. It is an altogether grimmer world into which Marlowe takes us, a world of evil and corruption deeper and darker than that of *Richard II*.'

Once more it is the world of difference between the temper and genius of Christopher Marlowe and of William Shakespeare.

There is no alleviation in Marlowe's tragedy : in his masterful way, he never lets up on the horror ; it was not in his nature. 'Compassion did not come easily to Marlowe, and there is a cruelty in these last scenes which we do not find in Shakespeare. In *Richard II* there is every sort of alleviation.'[7] There is the gentle leave-taking from his Queen : they love each other, unlike Edward II and the she-wolf of France, who shares the guilt of his murder. Richard's last hours are lightened by his faithful groom who talks to him about Roan Barbary, his favourite horse — and that is so much more appealing dramatically too. Marlowe 'does not feel deeply the sacredness of royalty, the tragedy is in the main a personal tragedy without wider repercussions'. But, then, Marlowe was a rationalist, not a sacramentalist, about royalty.

Shakespeare, in spite of the awkwardness of the subject, could always be trusted to be politically reliable. With his wiser sense of the folly of human nature, he was too sceptical and sensible to wish to upset the social order : he knew too well what would ensue. This is the lesson that emerges from all his historical plays, whether English or Roman. It is significant that the less highly educated man, less intellectual and more in touch with average human nature, should have a far better sense of the 'wider repercussions'. He accepts, without illusion, the necessity of an aura with which to invest the monarch, if he is to fulfil his function in society :

> Not all the water in the rough, rude sea
> Can wash the balm from an anointed king.
> The breath of worldly men cannot depose
> The deputy elected by the Lord.

In the Deposition scene, Richard says,

> yet you Pilates
> Have here delivered me to my sour cross,
> And water cannot wash away your sin.

It was a sin, it struck away the constitutional basis of government in England, it left the road wide open for the naked conflicts of power, into which public life consequently degenerated. It released a stream of blood, as Richard prophesied :

> The blood of English shall manure the ground,
> And future ages groan for this foul act . . .
> And, in this seat of peace, tumultuous wars
> Shall kin with kin and kind with kind confound ;
> Disorder, horror, fear, and mutiny
> Shall here inhabit, and this land be called
> The field of Golgotha and dead men's skulls.

This was no very inaccurate description of the Wars of the Roses, to which Richard's deposition ultimately gave rise — the grim drama which Shakespeare had already depicted with his *Henry VI* and *Richard III* sequence. From the first, this countryman had a far greater sense of political responsibility than the Cambridge intellectual.

This did not mean that he had any illusions about Richard : he was both unjust and wantonly irresponsible, two radical defects in a king. Bolingbroke was much the better man for the job — Shakespeare lets us make no doubt about that. But Henry can never recover from the stain that branded him from the manner of his gaining the crown, by force and murder. However much he tries to be a good king — and he was an able one — other people feel that they have as much right to raise their hand against him as he had against Richard. It is a fascinating dilemma psychologically, of which Shakespeare made the utmost throughout these plays, right up to the start of *Henry V*.

His imagination was evidently engaged by the character of

Richard — something in him appealed to his own nature. Shakespeare read up his sources with more than usual care — Holinshed and Hall, Berners' *Froissart* in addition to Daniel and perhaps a French chronicle ; then his imagination bounded away, to write the play with one impulse, with one continuous tone running through it of lyrical pathos, pageantry and poetry, no clowning, no deviation from the aesthetic effect. In this respect it is close to *Romeo and Juliet*, as it is in time ; in versification also, for there is a good deal of rhyming in it. What spoke specially to Shakespeare in Richard was what seemed to strike him so much in life itself — the contrast between being and seeming, shadow and substance, between the world of appearances and the real world.

All his days Richard had been surrounded by ceremony and obeisance : he had lived his life in a realm of fantasy. When he comes back from Ireland to face Bolingbroke and find he is without an army, he reacts with —

> Is not the king's name twenty thousand names ?

When he finds that that is not so, he relapses into despair : he takes no active steps to recover the position, but sinks into the poetry of self-pity.

> Cover your heads, and mock not flesh and blood
> With solemn reverence, throw away respect,
> Tradition, form, and ceremonious duty,
> For you have but mistook me all this while.

But it was not they who mistook ; it was himself. One would suppose that his course was a progressive awakening from the reign of illusion to the rule of fact (no-one was ever more a man of fact than Henry IV). Richard consoles his Queen with the words,

> Learn, good soul,
> To think our former state a happy dream,
> From which awaked, the truth of what we are
> Shows us but this : I am sworn brother, sweet,
> To grim Necessity, and he and I
> Will keep a league till death.

But he is still playing a part, hypostatising necessity, rather than seeing the truth about himself. As is the case even with his own grief :

> The shadow of my sorrow — ha ! let's see :
> 'Tis very true, my grief lies all within,

And these external manners of lament
Are merely shadows to the unseen grief,
That swells with silence in the tortured soul.
There lies the substance.

He himself is intelligent enough to perceive that

they well deserve to have,
That know the strong'st and surest way to get.

Such a type is a puppet in time of revolution, when only a Bolingbroke knows how to navigate and is thus borne up by circumstances
to the highest place, whether he designs it or no. History is strewn
with such shattered puppets of illusion, from Richard II to Charles
I and James II, from Louis XVI to Nicholas II; and there have
been more recent examples.

The character of Bolingbroke is not developed in this play —
he is too busy making the most of circumstances; not until the
Henry IV plays does he gain the dimension of depth. But it is
worth noticing the one characteristic he had in common with
Essex: nothing else, for in the roots of his character Essex was
much more of a Richard, a *fantaisiste*. Richard had

Observed his courtship of the common people,
How he did seem to dive into their hearts,
With humble and familiar courtesy,
What reverence he did throw away on slaves,
Wooing poor craftsmen with the craft of smiles . . .
Off goes his bonnet to an oyster-wench,
A brace of draymen bid God speed him well,
And had the tribute of his supple knee,
With, 'thanks, my countrymen, my loving friends.'

Bolingbroke was a politician — he would do quite well in a
democracy; Richard was, and should have been no more than,
an aesthete. In the cultivation of popularity, Shakespeare had
Essex much in mind: it was observed of him how careful he was
to doff his hat to the people and never fail to court their favour.
Naunton says that he had 'a kind of urbanity or innate courtesy,
which both won the Queen and too much took upon the people'.[8]
Like Bolingbroke, he used it as a political instrument. But at this
date Shakespeare could not have seen how little of Bolingbroke
there really was in Essex: all the hopes of Southampton and his
friends were placed on him.

Old York has a speech which expresses the commonplace of

239

sixteenth-century Englishmen, like Ascham, about the decadent influences coming in from the Continent :

> Lascivious metres, to whose venom sound
> The open ear of youth doth always listen,
> Report of fashions in proud Italy,
> Whose manners still our tardy apish nation
> Limps after in base imitation.

In the State Papers of the time one notes the constant drain upon manpower and money to get Ireland under control : thousands of recruits received their coat-and-conduct money to march away to western ports and find their graves in Ireland. In the last phase of the war with Spain, when the English government had a full-scale Irish war besides on its hands for four years, it did not know where to turn for money. The Irish war cost a million of money to the Elizabethans ; the Crown was forced to sell vast quantities of land that were never recovered to its revenues. This is reflected in the play : on hearing of John of Gaunt's last illness, Richard hopes that

> The lining of his coffers shall make coats
> To deck our soldiers for these Irish wars.

The Duke of York, left in charge of the administration, while Richard was careering about in Ireland as futilely as Essex later, does not know where to turn :

> What, are there no posts dispatched for Ireland ?
> How shall we do for money for these wars ?

The play has a scene based on the extended image of England as a garden, now in a state of neglect :

> When our sea-wallèd garden, the whole land,
> Is full of weeds, her fairest flowers choked up,
> Her fruit-trees all unpruned, her hedges ruined,
> Her knots disordered, and her wholesome herbs
> Swarming with caterpillars.

This may be set against old Gaunt's ideal conception of England, which, though hackneyed by too much quotation, yet represents what Shakespeare thought and felt at the summit of his age, when the war with Spain was in its last phase :

> This fortress built by nature for herself
> Against infection and the hand of war,
> This happy breed of men, this little world,

This precious stone set in the silver sea,
Which serves it in the office of a wall,
Or as a moat defensive to a house,
Against the envy of less happier lands.

It is a vision that subsisted continuously right up to Kipling. It once was true. Alas, no longer.

Coming to more personal inflexions, we note once more favourable notice taken of bowls, unfavourable of dogs. As to Shakespeare's own art as a player, we have the following observation :

As in a theatre the eyes of men
After a well-graced actor leaves the stage,
Are idly bent on him that enters next,
Thinking his prattle to be tedious.

So, too, with coats of arms and the insignia of gentility : Bolingbroke complains that Richard's low-born minions had

From my own windows torn my household coat,
Razed out my imprese, leaving me no sign,
Save men's opinions and my living blood,
To show the world I am a gentleman.

The phrase 'as I am a gentleman' was no doubt common enough on people's lips, but it is very frequent in the plays of Shakespeare. He would shortly take steps to place his own gentility beyond doubt.

If people were conscious of a comparison between the end of Elizabeth's reign and of Richard II's, they might well have been aware of a more extended analogy between the main theme of her reign, her long struggle with the Papacy, and King John's similar conflict with Rome. In his reign, England had been placed under papal interdict ; in hers, she was excommunicated and her subjects absolved from their allegiance. Thus, the Cambridge editor thinks of *King John* as a topical play : 'it is the only occasion on which Shakespeare deals directly with the main issue of his age, the religious question and the conflict between the English monarchy and the Papacy'.[9] As we should expect, he handles these issues with tact and prudence ; unlike *Richard II*, *King John* gave the authorities no disquiet. And yet the play as faithfully represents his own point of view, and with regard to contemporary issues is even more revealing of how he felt and thought.

King John is obviously close to *Richard II* in character, and we shall not be far wrong if we place its writing in 1596-7. There is a tell-tale reference that helps with its dating, when King Philip says,

> So, by a roaring tempest on the flood,
> A whole armado of convicted sail
> Is scattered and disjoined from fellowship.

All commentators have taken this as a reference to the Armada of 1588. It is not: it refers to the armada Philip II dispatched in the autumn of 1596, which was scattered and dispersed by a great storm in the Bay of Biscay before ever it got to the Channel.[10] And we have seen enough now of the way in which Shakespeare's experience of life enters into his work to descry the expression of grief for a lost child. His only boy died, and was buried at Stratford on 11 August 1596. Turning to *King John* we find:

> Grief fills the room up of my absent child,
> Lies in his bed, walks up and down with me,
> Puts on his pretty looks, repeats his words,
> Remembers me of all his gracious parts,
> Stuffs out his vacant garments with his form . . .

Knowing Shakespeare better now, as we do, we need only say that it is likely that he had Hamnet much in mind in this year. The boy was eleven. Constance, Arthur's mother, says,

> I have heard you say
> That we shall see and know our friends in heaven:
> If that be true, I shall see my boy again.

Bereaved parents console themselves with just such thoughts and hopes.

Though cognate with *Richard II*, it is not an inspired play like that. Our Cambridge editor suggests that it was 'one of those plays which he originally wrote to supply the needs of his company for a special occasion, while his mind was engaged elsewhere'. There was plenty to engage his mind elsewhere that year. What, in these circumstances, was it best to do? The evidence points to the play having been rapidly written, and for greater speed Shakespeare seems to have taken an earlier play, *The Troublesome Reign of King John*, as a basis to improve on. The best authorities are agreed that 'he followed the earlier play for the most part scene by scene and incident by incident', and even, as Chambers notes, in 'the logical run of many of the dialogues'. But 'of course he rewrote throughout'.[11]

If that is so, it provides a unique example for us of how Shakespeare set about his work. He took over the framework and a good deal of the content of the action, along with phrases and words attaching to it, but never the poetic diction. In other words, he put the commonplace draft, which has none of Shakespeare's characteristic imagery, into his own language. It is at every point, dramatic effect that he is out for, not just historical accuracy, which he is always ready to sacrifice : the play's the thing. We catch him at work in the swift compression of the earlier exchanges between King John and his mother into a couple of lines, far more pointed in effect :

> *Elinor :* A strange beginning : 'borrowed majesty' !
> *King John :* Silence, good mother ; hear the embassy.

His most important departures from the Protestant tradition of John Bale's *King Johan* and *The Troublesome Reign*, not to mention Foxe the martyrologist and Holinshed, are most relevant to what we are pursuing : a portrait of the man and his way of thinking. Protestant tradition had made a hero of King John, on account of his struggle with the Papacy. He is no hero to William Shakespeare, who portrays him as an equivocal, unheroic character, instigator of the blinding of his nephew Arthur. So like himself, Shakespeare tones down all this, makes Hubert, touched by compassion for the boy, let him off the blinding and hide him away from his uncle. Then Shakespeare takes pains to rid the play of the anti-Catholic bias of its predecessor and cut out long scenes depicting the Bastard's unseemly adventures with the monks and nuns. The poisoning of the King at Swinstead abbey is omitted, and 'there are no clergy of any kind among his dramatis personae, except the legate, Pandulph, whose activity is strictly political'.[12]

In fact, Shakespeare has written not a religious play, but a patriotic one. It is only incidentally about the conflict with the Papacy — all that is played down. There is none of the Protestant rant of Bale or *The Troublesome Reign*. It is a Laodicean play ; Shakespeare himself spoke through the ambivalent character of the Bastard, who is the real hero of the play — so far as there is one. And *he* is not at all ambivalent about one thing : the necessity for unity, patriotism. We need not impute this to the Catholic flavouring of Southampton House, though it would be not disagreeable there. It is no doubt the way Shakespeare himself thought about the religious issue, it is completely in keeping with what the Queen thought on the subject : unsectarian, unfanatical, hoping to unite as many as possible on their prime duty to their country.

The main subject of *King John*, then, is that of relations with a foreign power, in this case, France. And that Shakespeare's mind was still reverberating to the stimulus of contemporary events — the blow of Henri IV's conversion, the question whether his word could be relied on, whether the alliance with France would now hold — is perfectly clear. The Legate from Rome, Pandulph, pronounces :

> And blessèd shall he be that doth revolt
> From his allegiance to an heretic —

Henri IV had now been received and absolved —

> And meritorious shall that hand be called,
> Canonisèd and worshipped as a saint,
> That takes away by any secret course
> Thy hateful life :

this was Elizabeth's position, proscribed by the Bull of 1570. The question is posed, with France in mind,

> And shall these hands, so lately purged of blood,
> So newly joined in love, so strong in both,
> Unyoke this seizure and this kind regreet ?
> Play fast and loose with faith ? so jest with heaven,
> Make such unconstant children of ourselves,
> As now again to snatch our palm from palm,
> Unswear faith sworn . . .
> And make a riot on the gentle brow
> Of true sincerity ?

This was how the Elizabethans saw Henri IV's defection, and how they put the issue to him :

> Bethink you, for the difference
> Is purchase of a heavy curse from Rome,
> Or the light loss of England for a friend :
> Forgo the easier.

In his own manner Shakespeare generalises the considerations that rule in the world, not only in the world of politics, in the Bastard's magnificent speech on Commodity. Commodity means more than convenience ; the Elizabethans used the word for the percentage paid on a loan, the profit a lender made on the transaction ; so it meant the advantageous calculation of one's own self-interest, in a word, expediency as opposed to principle. This is what prevails in the world :

> That broker that still breaks the pate of faith,
> That daily break-vow, he that wins of all,
> Of kings, of beggars, old men, young men, maids,
> Who, having no external thing to lose
> But the word 'maid', cheats the poor maid of that,
> That smooth-faced gentleman, tickling Commodity :
> Commodity, the bias of the world . . .

One cannot but think that this long oration would have a strong impact on Elizabethan ears, for they knew the word so much better than we do — though we know the thing well enough, and the truth of the speech. The immediate frame of reference to the situation abroad would not commend it any less to the audience :

> And this same bias, this Commodity,
> This bawd, this broker, this all-changing word,
> Clapped on the outward eye of fickle France,
> Hath drawn him from his own determined aid,
> From a resolved and honourable war,
> To a most base and vile-concluded peace.

Naturally, the English thought this, because they feared the French would desert the alliance against Spain, as they did with the Peace of Vervins in 1598.

Shakespeare commends the Bastard Faulconbridge — natural son of Cœur de Lion — even more to us, with his cynical turn at the end of the speech :

> And why rail I on this Commodity ?
> But for because he hath not wooed me yet.

Shakespeare always loathes humbug : the Bastard's cynicism is better than most people's sincerity : in fact it is sincere and true. And so it is given to him to pronounce the final words of the play, which enshrine its moral, and the message of all these plays :

> This England never did, nor never shall,
> Lie at the proud foot of a conqueror,
> But when it first did help to wound itself.
> Now these her princes are come home again,
> Come the three corners of the world in arms,
> And we shall shock them : nought shall make us rue,
> If England to itself do rest but true.

I suspect that this represents the mood of the winter of 1596, after the splendid triumph of the capture of Cadiz and the dispersal by storm of the armada of that autumn had increased war-weariness in Spain, and that it was a welcome home to Essex, Lord Admiral Howard and their valiant peers.

It is also possible that the expedition itself was glanced at in these lines — they were true enough to the circumstances :

> And all the unsettled humours of the land,
> Rash, inconsiderate, fiery voluntaries,
> With ladies' faces and fierce dragons' spleens,
> Have sold their fortunes at their native homes,
> Bearing their birthrights proudly on their backs . . .
> In brief, a braver choice of dauntless spirits
> Than now the English bottoms have waft o'er
> Did never float upon the swelling tide,
> To do offence and scath in Christendom.

There is little more to detain us, from our particular point of view. Shakespeare's familiarity with Dover, from touring — the Chamberlain's men paid it yet another visit in 1597 — may be reflected in the lines :

> that pale, that white-faced shore,
> Whose foot spurns back the ocean's roaring tides
> And coops from other lands her islanders . . .

The Cambridge editor is of the view that the play well fitted the Chamberlain's company for which it was written : Burbage playing the part of the Bastard, a big bluff man, while his legitimate brother, tall and thin-faced, would be taken by the comic actor, probably John Sinckler, who appears again as Holofernes, Slender, Aguecheek. The boy who played Constance needed vigour and a command of invective, the one who played Arthur, charm and pathos. Did Shakespeare, with his *penchant* for 'kingly parts', play King John ?

We have a reference to the theatre in —

> these scroyles of Angiers flout you, kings,
> And stand securely on their battlements,
> As in a theatre, whence they gape and point
> At your industrious scenes and acts of death.

The other side of Shakespeare's background is recalled in an image, depicting the soldiery fighting their way into the town like 'a jolly troop of huntsmen'. Another image is that of the 'muzzled bear', familiar from the bear-baiting not far away on Bankside, at Paris Garden. The Goodwin Sands, notorious for wrecks, appear once again as they had done in *The Merchant of Venice*. Are we to take the following as an indication of what Shakespeare thought —

his pure brain,
Which some suppose the soul's frail dwelling-house ?

This was doubtfully in keeping with contemporary orthodoxy. Was it one more fleck from the intellectual influence of Marlowe ?

With the two parts of *Henry IV* we reach Shakespeare's full maturity, the summit of his achievement in the English history play. By any count these are superlative plays ; but when we consider the scale of the achievement, that together they form one great chronicle-play of ten acts, with a continuous vitality and one aesthetic intention running through the whole, we may conclude that the endeavour was unprecedented. The example that comes closest to it had been Marlowe's *Tamburlaine*. But that was really a very different affair : the first part of it had been conceived as a complete and self-sufficient play ; it was such a success that a second had been called for, which had not been envisaged and was merely a sequel. The two parts of *Henry IV* are conceived as one canvas.

The popular interest in these plays was, and always has been, in and around the character of Falstaff, his cronies and their disreputable doings. That is quite right, so far as it goes, for Falstaff is the greatest of comic creations, the archetype of all such endearing rogues in which our literature has abounded. In his totally different way, he has been to English literature what his contemporary, Don Quixote, has been to Spanish — a patriarchal archetype, immensely fertile and progenitive. The difference between the two is the difference between the two minds and national temperaments, between England and Spain, the age of Elizabeth and the *siglo d' oro* of Philip II with its exhaustion of Spain's resources, living on a crazy, impoverished, fanatical chivalry.

The intellectual interest of the *Henry IV* plays is political, and for this people have much less capacity. It demands not only maturity of judgment, but a specific understanding of politics such as many otherwise intelligent people do not command and have not enough humility to know in what they are wanting. The proper understanding of politics is closely allied to historical understanding. Very few literary critics have either. Yet, the most important respect in which the twentieth century has extended its understanding of Shakespeare, improved on previous generations' estimation of him, is precisely in the realm of politics.

Not the least wonderful thing about him was the degree of his political intelligence. Where did he get it from ? I can only reply that it was not merely another facet of his extraordinarily perceptive intelligence in general, but that he had just the right combination of qualities for understanding politics as such. The combination of common sense with imagination, of an indefeasible sense of reality along with intuitive perception, is a very strong one for the purpose — far more so than any clever doctrinairism. Scepticism, absence of doctrinal prejudices apt to blinker the perception are further qualifications ; he clearly was not taken in by anyone's pretensions or pretences or by any humbug :

> As who should say, 'I am Sir Oracle,
> And when I ope my lips let no dog bark !'

But this is not enough, or it might imply a mere political cynicism. In addition, there must be an element of ethical idealism, devoid of illusions, but ready always to do duty in its vocation, to sacrifice the self for an overriding cause. Shakespeare found this, as the Queen herself did, in the love of their country.

These plays then are about kingship : its tests, temptations and trials, its unavoidable burdens, the cruel necessities it is subjected to, the treasons by which it is surrounded, the inadequacies of the man in the office, the inhuman demands made upon him ; the need for him to subordinate personal interest and look always to the well-being of the whole, to develop justice of mind, to exemplify mercy when compatible with security. The word 'kingship' in itself is not exclusive. In Shakespeare's time and before, and for long after, monarchy was the normal mode by which societies were governed. But these things apply just as much to any ruler at any time. In his day they were exemplified very notably in a great political leader who was no king, but was leading the revolt of his people against his legitimate monarch — namely, William the Silent, Prince of Orange. These things apply just as much to any President or ruler of a state today, for Shakespeare's treatment of them is universal : these plays are about government.

Shakespeare seems always to have had this understanding,

for it is present amid all the immaturities of the *Henry VI* plays. But it must have developed greatly with life in London — also a leading theme of these plays, with his lengthening acquaintance with the circle of Southampton and Essex, his constant proximity to the Court, in a front stall for seeing all that was going on, with no necessity, as a mere player and playwright, to commit himself.

It is probable that the *First Part* was written in 1597 — while Southampton was away with Essex on the Islands Voyage — for production that autumn, when they were back. It is well known that Falstaff was originally called Sir John Oldcastle in both parts of the play — so that the *Second Part* was written soon after the first, and that the new Lord Cobham took objection to the name and it had to be changed. There is more in this matter than meets the eye. The actual Sir John Oldcastle of Henry IV's reign had been sometimes known as Lord Cobham by virtue of his marriage. He was a Lollard, took refuge in Wales during Glendower's long national resistance, was captured, hanged and burnt. At his trial he gave witness that his youth had been given up to pride, gluttony and lechery. He had been cast off by the King after early favour. Catholic tradition was very unfavourable to him — naturally, for he was a Lollard and orthodoxy had burnt him. Naturally, too, the Protestant tradition coming down through Bale and Foxe was favourable.

It was not religious considerations that made the eleventh Lord Cobham object to the portrayal of a remotely attached member of his family as a glorious and gluttonous great tun-bellied buffoon. Something touched him more sensibly : Cobham was the brother-in-law of Sir Robert Cecil and friend of Ralegh ; he belonged to the party in power to which Essex and Southampton were violently opposed, and this uproarious portrayal of a Cobham in Sir John Oldcastle came straight out of the enemy's camp. The character was immensely popular and carried certain overtones to an Elizabethan audience. The new Lord Cobham was himself a great fool — perhaps that gave all the more point to it, but he objected and his representations had to be attended to. Traces of the original name of Oldcastle remain in the text and it long survived in people's memory. At the end of the *Second Part*, Shakespeare had to insert an explicit disclaimer : 'for Oldcastle died a martyr, and this is not the man'. When Shakespeare had to search for a new name for his old rogue, he fetched up from his memory the cowardly knight, Sir John Fastolfe, from *Henry*

VI, and so he arrived at Falstaff. One facet of this protean character
is that he was a favourite with the Essex and Southampton circle.
Early next year, in February 1598, Essex sent word to Cecil to
tell Sir Alexander Ratcliff that 'his sister is married to Sir John
Falstaff' — it would seem that they meant Lord Cobham, presumably he was as fat as he was fatuous.[13]   Next year, 1599 Southampton's wife wrote to him in Ireland : 'all the news I can send you that
I think will make you merry is that I read in a letter from London
that Sir John Falstaff is by his mistress, Dame Pintpot, made
father of a goodly miller's thumb, a boy that's all head and very
little body ; but this is a secret'.[14]   Evidently there was someone
whom the circle recognised as Falstaff, or Shakespeare's creation
was virtually a creature of the circle.

Shakespeare duly read up his sources, in this case a straight-
forward matter, resting mainly on Holinshed, with modifications
from Daniel's treatment of the subject, some touches from Stow.
For Falstaff, on the basis of those hints from the original Oldcastle
in his unregenerate days, he gave full rein to his imagination —
with what results ! We have already seen him combining history
with humour in *Henry VI*, but now these are interwoven with a
link through the dual presentation of Prince Hal as Falstaff's crony,
and as heir to the throne. (Historically there had been this duality
in the nature of the Prince — instead of being a stumbling block
to critics since the time of Hazlitt, it should have presented all the
more psychological interest.) The successful fusion of historical
fact with invention has made these plays the parents of the prodigious progeny of the historical novel in the world's literature.

Striking new developments were given to the characters of
Glendower and Hotspur : they became real men, re-created
sympathetically. When Shakespeare began writing the play,
and for the first two Acts, he accepted the usual English attitude
towards Glendower and the misrepresentations of the Welsh
coming down from the English Chronicles.[15] The poem in *The
Mirror for Magistrates* by Thomas Phaer, a Welshman, describing
Glendower, did nothing to change this for he subscribed to the
dominant English view of things. Then something happened
to change Shakespeare's tone and treatment. No doubt it was
partly due to the law we observe in the working of his imagination :
from an outer picture of the character to the inner man, and then
his power of sympathy lights up and displays the nature. We
see this operating from the extrovert Bolingbroke to the inwardly

troubled Henry IV, and again with Henry V.

In addition to the usual deepening as he gets inside a character, a good deal of Welsh lore and sympathies are collected around Glendower as the play proceeds. Glendower's daughter, Lady Mortimer, speaks on four occasions in Welsh, her father translates one of her speeches, she sings a Welsh song. (Perhaps there was a Welsh boy in the company for the part?) But where did Shakespeare get his Welsh material — as also the character of brave Fluellen? It has often been suggested that he had his eye on the famous Netherlands soldier, Sir Roger Williams, who was a Welshman and devoted to Essex. But Essex had a considerable Welsh following, of which the leader was Sir Gelly Meyrick, a constant intimate of Essex House, for ever egging the Earl on to rash courses.[16] Among the lesser followers was Captain John Salusbury, a ready swordsman, one of the numerous clan of Llewenny, with which we know Shakespeare was acquainted. For, only a couple of years after, in 1601 Shakespeare contributed his poem 'The Phœnix and the Turtle' to the volume, *Love's Martyr*, got up in honour of Sir John Salusbury, head of the family and an Esquire of the Body to the Queen. While a younger member of the family wrote lines to Heminges and Condell commending the Folio.

With this background it is the less surprising that Shakespeare tells us things about Glendower that only the Welsh would know. They regarded the leader of their national resistance as a fulfilment of prophecy, whose coming had been foretold. Glendower insists to Hotspur :

> at my nativity
> The front of heaven was full of fiery shapes,
> Of burning cressets.

The practical, hard-headed North Countryman cannot bear such mystical moonshine : 'Why, so it would have done at the same season, if your mother's cat had but kittened, though you yourself had never been born'. Glendower, though affronted, replies patiently and with absolute assurance :

> The heavens were all on fire, the earth did tremble.

Hotspur pooh-poohs it all, and explains it away in practical terms — almost a stage Englishman. But the curious thing was that the onset of Glendower's rebellion had coincided again with these phenomena, either a meteor or Northern lights, and these things were factors in the Welsh belief in him as their leader. The very weather, unseasonable rains and floods, fought for him and frustrated Henry IV's campaigns against him. In fact, Glendower survived Henry, though to this day no-one knows where he was buried. Glendower was a *Mage*, and it was extremely impolitic of Hotspur to challenge the roots of his power with his people in this rude way.

When Glendower, who is himself a true leader, warm and generous, with a proper admiration for Hotspur's courage, elaborates on the Welsh prophecies, Hotspur replies : 'I think there's no man speaks better Welsh. I'll to dinner.' This scene marvellously focuses the difficulties the Welsh and English have had in understanding each other through the centuries, what the Welsh have had to put up with at the hands of the English, what the English in turn dislike in Welsh nonsense. The Earl of Worcester points out the political defectiveness of such an attitude, the danger to their joint alliance against the King :

> Defect of manners, want of government,
> Pride, haughtiness, opinion, and disdain :
> The least of which haunting a nobleman
> Loseth men's hearts.

It is this that explains and justifies Prince Henry's contempt for Hotspur, in spite of the latter's better record against his own : Hotspur had no political intelligence, he was just a fighting man.

Prince Henry was, in spite of appearances and his irresponsible, wild youth, a political type — as he needed to be. This is what his critics have either not understood, or disliked, about him. Yet this was indispensable, to be any good as a king — as his father was, and Richard had not been. It is the contrast between brain and gallant courage, between political intelligence and the easy sentimental appeal of weakness and misfortune. The adult mind should understand more sympathetically the greater range of responsibilities and the strains of the former. As Shakespeare wonderfully does in his portrait of Henry IV. He was not far away from the Henry of history, either — as one sees him on his tomb in Canterbury cathedral, just across from Richard's father, the Black Prince. Henry was a strong, stocky man, not tall, square-faced with a thick beard of deep auburn. Brave, energetic, devout, all through his life he was self-controlled and pure — in contrast to the effeminate, neurotic Richard, who was wanton and luxurious. Henry was naturally more merciful — until constrained by sheer political necessity; he was politic and moderate, with a sharp tongue, intelligent and able, calculating as such a man should be. Where Richard was an aesthete, Henry delighted in the conversation of men of letters and had a curious liking to discuss points of casuistry: he combined a retentive memory with an uneasy conscience. Sleeplessly active, full of energy and initiative, how much superior as a king he was to Richard !

And, indeed, what is to be done with types like Richard II, and Edward II, and Charles I, except to get rid of them ?

In a fine scene between the King and his son, Shakespeare shows us how well he understands the inwardness of the situation, reveals to us the *arcana imperii*. Henry reproaches his son with behaving as Richard had done, with common irresponsibility, so that the loyalty of the people fell away from him :

> The skipping king, he ambled up and down
> With shallow jesters and rash bavin wits . . .
> Mingled his royalty with capering fools,
> Had his great name profanèd with their scorns . . .
> Grew a companion to the common streets.

How had he, Bolingbroke, manœuvred Richard off the pitch ? —

> By being seldom seen, I could not stir
> But like a comet I was wondered at :
> That men would tell their children, 'This is he' ;
> Others would say, 'Where ? which is Bolingbroke ?'
> And then I stole all courtesy from heaven,
> And dressed myself in such humility
> That I did pluck allegiance from men's hearts.

Such men, not the meek, are they that inherit the earth. Henry enforces the lesson to his erring son that he is going the way, like Richard, to lose the throne, underlines the contrast between Hotspur, admired by all for his courage and sobriety, and his own reprobate youth sullied by the company he keeps. Such is Shakespeare's sense of decorum that the King never names the Prince's companions.

The Prince is touched and repentant, and says movingly :

> Do not think so : you shall not find it so . . .
> I will redeem all this on Percy's head,
> And in the closing of some glorious day
> Be bold to tell you that I am your son —

as he proceeds to do on the battlefield of Shrewsbury, with which the play concludes. Shakespeare's grand design looks beyond this play to the next, to the Prince's conversion, away from the pleasures, escapades, and companions of his youth, to the assumption of the serious burdens of his life, the succession to the throne, kingship. Just as it had happened to the Prince in real life. This ultimate end Shakespeare has in view from the beginning, so that there is no justification for any critical complaint of inconsistency in the presentation of the Prince : he says,

> I know you all, and will awhile uphold
> The unyoked humour of your idleness :
> Yet herein will I imitate the sun,
> Who doth permit the base contagious clouds
> To smother up his beauty from the world,
> That when he please again to be himself,
> Being wanted, he may be more wondered at.

In the midst of all his madcap enterprises, Shakespeare always saves the Prince's dignity : the Prince returns the money that was robbed at Gadshill to its proper owners ; in all his exchanges with Falstaff, the Prince retains his distance, he is always controlled, whatever the fun afoot. One hardly needs to claim that this was a process of princely education in the ways of human nature, the knowledge of all sorts and conditions of men, for, in the end, the Prince's change was something far more interesting : it was, as it truly had been in history, a conversion.

New territory is opened up in these plays with Shakespeare's wonderful evocations of the life of London and its vicinity — it had evidently grown on him in the years there. The scenes at the Boar's Head tavern in East Cheapside, the conversation and character of Mistress Quickly, the talk of the carriers in the innyard at Rochester — all is positively Dickensian. 'Heigh-ho ! An't be not four by the day I'll be hanged : Charles's Wain is over the new chimney, and yet our horse not packed. What, ostler !' Shakespeare's care for horseflesh comes out : 'I prithee, Tom, beat Cut's saddle, put a few flocks in the point ; the poor jade is wrung in the withers out of all cess'. And then, the second carrier : 'I have a gammon of bacon and two razes of ginger to be delivered as far as Charing Cross'.

There is very little of the countryside in these plays, hardly a country image. In *1 Henry IV* we find only,

> his chin, new reaped,
> Showed like a stubble-land at harvest-home —

and one thinks of the stubble-land as one has seen it down the slopes from Wilmcote into Stratford. Or we have :

> The southern wind
> Doth play the trumpet to his purposes,
> And by his hollow whistling in the leaves
> Foretells a tempest and a blustering day.

Or,

> He was but as the cuckoo is in June,
> Heard, not regarded.

All the same, Warwickshire is loyally given a good show as it was in *Henry VI*. We meet Falstaff, on his way to Shrewsbury, on a public road near Coventry. 'Bardolph, get thee before to Coventry ; fill me a bottle of sack : our soldiers shall march through : we'll to Sutton Coldfield tonight. . . . Bid my Lieutenant Peto meet me at the town's end.' Peto was a good Warwickshire family name. And then, his soldiers were such a ragged scum, 'I'll not march through Coventry with them, that's flat. There's but a shirt and a half in all my company . . . and the shirt, to say the truth, stolen from my host at St. Alban's, or the red-nosed innkeeper of Daventry.' The Prince comes in on the scene : 'What, Hal ! How now, mad wag ! what a devil dost thou in Warwickshire ?'

Besides the tavern and road scenes, evidences from contemporary life peer through the canvas ; there is Hotspur's contempt for a recognisably contemporary type of foppish aristocrat :

> He was perfumed like a milliner,
> And twixt his finger and his thumb he held
> A pouncet-box, which ever and anon
> He gave his nose, and took't away again . . .
> To be so pestered with a popinjay . . .
>   made me mad
> To see him shine so brisk and smell so sweet
> And talk so like a waiting-gentlewoman
> Of guns, and drums, and wounds — God save the mark ! —
> And telling me the sovereign'st thing on earth
> Was parmaceti for an inward bruise.

No doubt this apparition was familiar enough at Court, as was ballading in London. Falstaff threatens, after the exposure of his cowardice at Gadshill : 'An I have not ballads made on you all, and sung to filthy tunes, let a cup of sack be my poison'. Hal's guess is that Falstaff's pockets are filled with 'memorandums of bawdy-houses' — a convincing touch. There is little enough, apart from the whole play, to bespeak Shakespeare personally, except Dame Quickly on Falstaff and Hal impersonating an interview between the King and his son : 'O Jesu ! he doth it as like one of these harlotry players as ever I see !'

Perhaps, too, we may detect the personal beneath the scepticism of Falstaff on the subject of honour on the battlefield : 'Honour pricks me on. Yea, but how if honour prick me off when I come on ? how then ? Can honour set to a leg ? — No. Or an arm ? — No. Or take away the grief of a wound ? — No. Honour hath no skill in surgery then ? — No. What is honour ? — a word. What is that word, honour ? — Air. A trim reckoning ! Who hath it ? — he that died o' Wednesday. Doth he feel it ? — No. Doth he hear it ? — No. It is insensible, then ? — yea, to the dead. But will it not live with the living ? — No. Why ? — Detraction will not suffer it. Therefore I'll none of it : honour is a mere scutcheon ; and so ends my catechism.' This is hardly different from Prince Hal's epitaph on Hotspur, now food for worms :

> Fare thee well, great heart !
> Ill-weaved ambition, how much art thou shrunk !
> When that this body did contain a spirit,
> A kingdom for it was too small a bound ;
> But now, two paces of the vilest earth
> Is room enough.

I think we may conclude that Shakespeare, sensible man, would not have been one to risk his life for honour.

Shakespeare went straight on to write the *Second Part* of the play, fairly certainly in 1598. Rumour, painted full of tongues, speaks the Induction :

> I speak of peace, while covert enmity
> Under the smile of safety wounds the world.

This was appropriate to the year 1598, which saw peace concluded between Spain and France and some promise of a general peace to include England and the Netherlands. This did not eventuate, however ; instead, rebellion on an almost national scale flared up in Ireland.

> And who but Rumour, who but only I,
> Make fearful musters and prepared defence,
> Whiles the big year, swoln with some other grief
> Is thought with child by the stern tyrant war ?

Rumour turned out to be right, in spite of its easy appeal to the mob, about which Shakespeare spoke in unvarying terms :

> the blunt monster with uncounted heads,
> The still-discordant wavering multitude.

Archbishop Scroop says later,

> An habitation giddy and unsure
> Hath he that buildeth on the vulgar heart.
> O thou fond many ! with what loud applause
> Didst thou beat heaven with blessing Bolingbroke
> Before he was what thou wouldst have him be.

Now that Henry was grappling with the difficulties of government and an empty exchequer, popular favour was turning away from him, whoring after the memory of Richard. This holy, intriguing Archbishop of York led a renewed rebellion against the King.

Historically, Henry had surmounted the crisis of his reign with energy, had seized the initiative, unlike Richard, and crushed the rebels at the battle of Shrewsbury. But it left him a sick man, and after the execution of the sainted traitor, Archbishop Scroop, at whose tomb miracles flowed, the idiot people began to think the King stricken with leprosy in consequence. There is no doubt about his illness and exhaustion for the rest of the reign : to a modern mind it sounds like a series of strokes. And this adds pathos to the character in the *Second Part*, a poignancy to his relations with his son and heir.

The second play does not have the unity of the first, but it has even more psychological interest. The duality of the Prince's nature is brought out ; we see him much less in association with Falstaff and the way is prepared for his eventual repudiation of his boon companions. Falstaff is free to go his own way, to cheat Mrs. Quickly of her expectation of marriage and out of money for his keep and Justice Shallow out of a thousand pounds. The old reprobate is freed of all restraint, takes no account of moral law or social obligation, and so goes on to his downfall. This is envisaged from the first : he has to be put down — or society, on his lines, would dissolve into anarchy. This would run clean contrary to the moral of *Henry IV* and all the plays. But what a run Shakespeare gives him before he is ultimately, and quite properly, brought down ! In him the old Vice of the traditional moralities — the ensnarer of youth, the braggart, gluttonous, bibulous, lecherous — ceases to be an abstraction and is immortalised as an individual. The Falstaff scenes are as uproarious as ever, his behaviour even more discreditable ; the Cotswold scenes as nostalgic ; while the last scene between Henry and his son, when he thought his father dead and took away the crown, is one of the finest the master ever wrote.

The way the Prince takes his father's sickness indicates the unspoken struggle going on within him. He says to Poins, 'Marry, I tell thee, it is not meet that I should be sad, now my father is sick : albeit I could tell to thee — as to one it pleases me, for fault of a better, to call my friend — I could be sad, and sad indeed too.' The crude Poins does not believe him. 'By this hand, thou thinkest me as far in the Devil's book as thou and Falstaff for obduracy and persistency. Let the end try the man. But I tell thee my heart bleeds inwardly that my father is so sick ; and keeping such vile company as thou art hath in reason taken from me all ostentation of sorrow.' And why may he not weep ? Poins says that he should think him a hypocrite. That is indeed why the Prince will not show his grief : 'it would be every man's thought ; and thou art a blessed fellow to think as every man thinks : never a man's thought in the world keeps the roadway better than thine : every man would think me a hypocrite indeed'. The end is in view ; but from such people the Prince has learnt a lot about the facts of human nature.

Warwick consoles the King in his last illness with the belief that

> The Prince will in the perfectness of time
> Cast off his followers, and their memory
> Shall as a pattern or a measure live,
> By which his grace must mete the lives of others,
> Turning past evils to advantages.

On his father's death, he assures his nobles that he means

> To mock the expectation of the world,
> To frustrate prophecies, and to raze out
> Rotten opinion, who hath writ me down
> After my seeming.

The dying Henry IV had confessed to his son the truth about his own life and the sin that stained it :

> God knows, my son,
> By what by-paths and indirect crookt ways
> I met this crown, and I myself know well

How troublesome it sat upon my head :
To thee it shall descend with better quiet,
Better opinion, better confirmation ;
For all the soil of the achievement goes
With me into the earth.

At this point dramatic truth meets the truth of history : this is
as it had been.

From this perspective it is inconceivable that Falstaff should not
be repudiated. Himself and his miscreant cronies had the largest
expectations on the Prince's coming to the throne : Pistol says,
'sweet knight, thou art now one of the greatest men in this realm'.
And Falstaff, to reconcile Justice Shallow to the loss of his thousand
pounds : 'Master Robert Shallow, choose what office thou wilt
in the land, 'tis thine : Pistol, I will double-charge thee with
dignities. . . . Let us take any man's horses — the laws of England
are at my commandment.' And, on the new King passing into
the Abbey for his coronation : 'Stand here by me, Master Robert
Shallow, I will make the King do you grace : I will leer upon him
as 'a comes by, and do but mark the countenance that he will
give me'.

What else was possible than the discountenance he receives
from the anointed King, returning from his coronation ? — what
has been described as the greatest snub in literature :

I know thee not, old man. Fall to thy prayers . . .
Presume not that I am the thing I was,
For God doth know, so shall the world perceive,
That I have turned away my former self.

The whole long play, both parts of it, have led up to this moment :
there is no dramatic inconsistency in it. And yet generations of
critics have been revolted by it. Hazlitt started the tradition :
he found Henry V's conduct intolerable. He would. Much as
one may admire his literary genius, one can have no respect whatever for his political judgment. The radical intellectual, the
enthusiast for liberty who made Napoleon, trampler on the liberties
of Europe, his hero, had no use for Henry V. Henry was the
ideal hero-king to the Elizabethans : Hazlitt would have done
well to inquire why. But, of course, he had no historical judgment,
any more than the other literary moralists following in his steps,
from Swinburne and Bradley to Yeats and Masefield. For Hazlitt
had already given the game away for them when he added :

'perhaps Shakespeare knew what was best, according to the history, the nature of the times, and of the man'.

Having said as much for political sense, we are at liberty to enjoy Falstaff's frolics, in the city and in the Cotswolds, as much as anyone.

Shakespeare's observation of low life in London is, if possible, more convincing than ever. Says Mistress Quickly, 'thou didst swear to me upon a parcel-gilt goblet, sitting in my Dolphin chamber, at the round table, by a sea-coal fire, upon Wednesday in Wheeson week, when the Prince broke thy head for likening his father to a singing-man of Windsor, thou didst swear to me then, as I was washing thy wound, to marry me and make me my lady, thy wife. Canst thou deny it?' And Doll Tearsheet, 'come, I'll be friends with thee, Jack : thou art going to the wars ; and whether I shall ever see thee again or no, there is nobody cares'. She turns with venom on Pistol : 'you a captain, you slave ! For what? for tearing a poor whore's ruff in a bawdy-house?' But for Falstaff she had endearments : 'I love thee better than I love e'er a scurvy young boy of them all'. And the old rogue : 'what stuff wilt have a kirtle of? I shall receive money o' Thursday ; thou shalt have a cap tomorrow. Come : it grows late : we'll to bed. Thou'lt forget me when I am gone.'

Shakespeare was evidently well acquainted with the ways of such types.

Justice Shallow, in his pleasant house in the Cotswolds, remembers and embroiders on the good times when he was a student at Clement's Inn. 'There was I, and little John Doit of Staffordshire, and black George Barnes, and Francis Pickbone, and Will Squeal, a Cotswold man : you had not four such swinge-bucklers in all the Inns of Court again . . . Jesu ! Jesu ! the mad days that I have spent ; and to see how many of my old acquaintance are dead . . . How a good yoke of bullocks at Stamford fair?' 'O, Sir John, do you remember since we lay all night in the windmill in Saint George's fields? . . . Ha, it was a merry night. And is Jane Nightwork alive? . . . Nay, she must be old ; she cannot choose but be old ; certain she's old ; and had Robin Nightwork by old Nightwork before I came to Clement's Inn.' Silence : 'That's fifty five years ago.'

For all the amusement of this scene, it is filled with pathos — the pathos of old men remembering, or misremembering, their youth as the days close in upon them. There are a few more local references : Hinckley fair, and old Puff of Barson, or Barcheston in Warwickshire — in case anyone thinks the author of the plays was not acquainted with Warwickshire. Shakespeare's familiar reaction to the tolling of a bell comes out with —

> as a sullen bell
> Remembered knolling a departed friend.

While an unwonted, almost unique, reference to building operations reminds us that, having bought New Place in 1597, he was engaged in repairs there, as we know from the Borough Accounts :

> When we mean to build,
> We first survey the plot, then draw the model ;
> And when we see the figure of the house,
> Then must we rate the cost of the erection ;
> Which if we find outweighs ability,
> What do we then but draw anew the model
> In fewer offices, or at last desist
> To build at all.

Falstaff had to be killed off, though it was natural enough that people should wish him to go on for ever. Shakespeare was too good an artist to allow that, as a modern serial-writer would do. But the Queen's express command had to be obeyed : she wished to see the fat knight in love, and the result was *The Merry Wives of Windsor*. The tradition has come down to us through the dramatist, John Dennis : 'this comedy was written at her command, and by her direction, and she was so eager to see it acted, that she commanded it to be finished in fourteen days : and was afterwards, as tradition tells us, very well pleased at the representation'. We have no reason to doubt the tradition : there are so many circumstances to confirm it, and there are evidences of haste throughout the play. It is nearly all in prose, which made for speed in composition ; it is clearly directed to a Court audience, probably for a Garter feast at the Castle ; it is full of Windsor lore — and one thing that emerges is that Shakespeare knew his Windsor well ; it ends with a graceful compliment to the Queen.

The balance of opinion places the play between *Henry IV* and *Henry V*. That is common sense, for *The Merry Wives* takes up Falstaff where the former left him, with Justice Shallow in a rage at having been cheated of his thousand pounds. Historical circumstances also converge upon this dating, 1598, as we shall see. The play is full of topical stuff and references, some of which

give us clues, some lost ; it is fadged up hurriedly around the
showing up of the lecherous old knight by the respectable citizens'
wives, Mistress Page and Mistress Ford. We are given a Welsh
curate, Sir Hugh Evans, for a schoolmaster, and a French doctor,
Dr. Caius, to raise laughs by murdering the English language and
getting enraged with each other. Like all Shakespeare's school-
masters, Sir Hugh is both simple and a pedant ; he gives young
William Page a Latin lesson that takes us straight back to Stratford
grammar school. Dame Quickly is brought in to do duty once
more, so are Corporal Nym and Ancient (*i.e.* Ensign) Pistol ;
Bardolph's red nose makes its appearance in all four of these plays.
It is amusing enough, rough-and-tumble stuff ; if we were to
bother about categories, we might describe it as a farce, rather
than a comedy. It is redeemed by its atmosphere, which has
poetry in it, though there is little in the play, and even a residuum
of magic which has inspired composers in our time to turn it into
music.

The play is particularly provocative to the historian on account
of the personal clues and traditions clinging to it, and for its portrait
of social life, sports and manners. We are confronted in the very
first scene with a problem. Justice Shallow gives for his coat-of-
arms a dozen white luces ; in Evans's mouth, 'the dozen white
louses do become an old coat well ; it agrees well, passant ; it is
a familiar beast to man, and signifies love'. (The point of the
joke might be lost on a really nice mind : he means that this is
how it is caught.) But is this a skit on the Lucys of Charlecote,
who bore luces in their coat-of-arms, and does it relate to the very
old tradition, that goes right back to the seventeenth century, that
Shakespeare as a young man got into trouble with them for
poaching their deer ? A sharp-eyed editor comments, 'if we had
no tradition, what should we make of the coat-of-arms passage ?
It would be utterly unmeaning.'[17] Unimaginative precisians have
pointed out that Charlecote had no deer-park in Shakespeare's
time. Pshaw ! — as if there were not other deer-parks in the
vicinity : it need not have been Sir Thomas Lucy's — though
he apparently had one at Fulbrook — the sportive youth could
have come before Sir Thomas as J.P. We have seen enough to
know now that in his younger days Shakespeare was mad about
hunting the deer ; and what inclines me to think that there is a
hidden reference here is that later in the same scene Justice Shallow
says to Page, 'I wished your venison better : it was ill killed'.

The treatment of the skit, if that is what it is, is in perfect good humour, years after. Most good judges hold that there is something in the tradition, and I think there must be.

That the Cotswolds and his home neighbourhood were running in Shakespeare's mind in this scene we can see from Slender's question : 'how does your fallow greyhound, sir ? I heard he was outrun on Cotsall', *i.e.* Cotswold. Slender is described by Bardolph as 'you Banbury cheese', and by Nym as 'Slice' : apparently Banbury cheese was made in thin slices.[18]

Most of the contemporary references are fairly clear. There was a tiresome German, Count Mompelgart, who had visited the Windsor vicinity a few years before, taking up horses and failing to pay for them. Becoming Duke of Würtemberg, he pestered the Queen, who had been good to him and entertained him well, to be made a Knight of the Garter, until she ultimately consented in 1597. Perhaps his banner would have been hoisted in St. George's Chapel for the Garter Feast of 1598 — anyway, he was not forgotten : there is a skit on him as 'Cousin Garmombles', cozening people out of their money — at which, we may expect, Elizabeth laughed. There was a good deal besides to make her merry. There is a hit at courtiers which would not be disagreeable to her, in Mistress Quickly's exciting the interest of Sir John in Mistress Ford :

> you have brought her into such a canaries [*i.e.* quandary] as 'tis wonderful. The best courtier of them all, when the Court lay at Windsor, could never have brought her to such a canary. Yet there has been knights, and lords, and gentlemen, with their coaches ; I warrant you, coach after coach, letter after letter, gift after gift ; smelling so sweetly, all musk, and so rushling, I warrant you, in silk and gold. . . . And I warrant you, they could never get an eye-wink of her : I had myself twenty angels given me this morning ; but I defy all angels — in any such sort as they say — but in the way of honesty. And, I warrant you, they could never get her so much as sip on a cup with the proudest of them all : and yet there has been earls, nay, which is more, pensioners ; but, I warrant you, all is one with her.

The pensioners were the Queen's Gentlemen-Pensioners, her body-guard, of whom Sir Walter Ralegh was Captain ; but to rate them as above earls was a piece of ignorance that would raise a laugh. Thus incited, Falstaff was with child to get on terms with such a paragon of virtue.

Ralegh's interest in Guiana was much to the fore in these

years. After his voyage there in 1595 and the publication of his book, he sent his faithful servant back, Lawrence Keymis, who published a *Relation* of his voyage next year. In this year 1598, Ralegh had dispatched another man there to keep touch ; the news was that, discouraged with his lack of progress at Court, he contemplated another voyage to make sure of the gold-mines.[19] Falstaff's enthusiasm, on fire for Mistress Page as well as Mistress Ford, would make fun for a Court audience : 'here's another letter to her : she bears the purse too ; she is a region in Guiana, all gold and bounty. I will be cheators [*i.e.* escheators] to them both, and they shall be exchequers to me'. (The escheators put their funds into the Exchequer.) 'They shall be my East and West Indies, and I will trade to them both.' This was a hit at Ralegh's enthusiasm for Guiana, and his constant propaganda for it : 'after the first or second year I doubt not but to see in London a Contratation House of more receipt for Guiana than there is now in Seville for the West Indies'. The Queen thought this nonsense, and would have her laugh at Shakespeare's joke.

There seems to have been another little jab at the rival party at Court, once more at the fatuous Cobham. Master Ford, to play his prank on Falstaff, calls on him at the Garter Inn, in the guise of Master Brooke. This was the family name of Lord Cobham, who must have resented this too, for it was subsequently changed to Broome. The Queen would not be displeased either by a hit at Essex's cheapening the order of knighthood by creating too many knights when he was in command at Cadiz — the 'Knights of Cales'. When Mistress Ford opines that she could be knighted if she would but go to hell for a moment or so, *i.e.* if she would but go to bed with Sir John, Mistress Page replies, 'What ? Sir Alice Ford. These knights will hack', *i.e.* become cheap. The Queen was much offended that each time she put Essex in supreme command, he used his powers to reward his followers with knighthoods in plenty.

It has been noticed that there is some parallelism between *The Merry Wives* and Ben Jonson's *Every Man in his Humour*, which was accepted by the Chamberlain's men about this time and in which Shakespeare acted. With this play, which had a great success, Ben Jonson hoisted his flag : it was the first of a series delineating people according to their 'humours', or leading characteristics — a good satirical device which had immense influence, much easier to apply in general than Shakespeare's inimitable individuality. There seems to be a hit at this in the delineation of Corporal Nym — Jonson had been a soldier too, for a time in the Netherlands — who cannot open his mouth without using the word 'humour'. 'The good humour is to steal at a minute's rest.' 'The humour rises : it is good : humour me the angels.' 'I like not the humour of lying. He hath wronged me in some humours : I should have borne the humoured letter to her. . . . My name is Corporal Nym ; I speak, and I avouch 'tis true. . . . I love not the humour of bread and cheese ; and there's the humour of it.' Page protests, ' "The humour of it ", quoth-'a ! here's a fellow frights English out of his wits'. That might quite well be Shakespeare's comment on it : it was evidently levelled at somebody : was it at Ben's combination of positiveness and obsessiveness ? It is all good-humoured enough.

Jonson's satirical Humour plays started a stage-war between himself, and Dekker and Marston on the other side. Shakespeare's sympathies were all with the school of life against the schoolmen, and he was thought at Cambridge to have given Ben a pill at some point in this literary warfare. In the St. John's play, *The Return from Parnassus*, we find : 'Why, here's our fellow Shakespeare puts them all down, aye, and Ben Jonson too. O, that Ben Jonson is a pestilent fellow. He brought up Horace, giving the poets a pill ; but our fellow Shakespeare hath given him a purge that made him bewray his credit.'

The Arden editor thinks that with this play Shakespeare rather read Court and Town a lesson.

> If he was compelled to bring with him to the country his troop of swindlers and town corruptions, he would set them down where their surroundings would show them off to their discredit. Simplicity, ignorance, and folly there may be there, but there is also honesty and all the other virtues. That is the Windsor atmosphere. The foils and vices all come from town. There is nothing in any of the villagers' [sic] doings to their discredit. . . . In the end they are the people who come off best. . . . The country folks show him [Falstaff] what they think of him, and of the ways of such as he and his companions.[20]

There may be something in this, without pressing it too far. It became a traditional representation, the vices of the town against country virtues ; but it probably represented Shakespeare's own inflexion, with his romantic feeling for the country, in particular for his native Warwickshire. And beneath his conformity and courtesy, there was a real independence. In truth, there is often more independence of mind to be found among those who care most for tradition and have conservative views about society, than among professional progressives adhering to their 'line'.

Falstaff, for his sins, was tumbled out in the dirty-clothes basket into the ditch at Datchet mead. There was a muddy ditch there beside the Thames in Shakespeare's time all right. The scene of the duel that did not take place, between the hot-tempered Evans and Dr. Caius, was Frogmore, now enclosed within Windsor Great Park. Master Page hoped to marry his daughter, pretty Anne Page, to the well-off nit-wit, Slender, at Eton ; it could have been at the parish church, or in those days, apparently, in the College chapel. Mistress Page hoped to marry her to rich Dr. Caius at the Deanery, attached to St. George's Chapel. Neither got her, but pleasant young Master Fenton. Herne's oak and the saw-pit, where Falstaff, expecting an assignation, was pinched and tormented by the fairies instead — Mistress Page and her children dressed up for the part — existed until the end of the eighteenth century. Shakespeare must have known it all quite well ; performances when the Court was at Windsor would have made him familiar with it.

And so the play comes to an end with the great bell of Windsor striking twelve, reverberating round the courts of the Castle, in and out the buttresses of St. George's Chapel, out over the little town clinging to those famed slopes, and away across the moonlit rides of the Great Park.

> Cricket, to Windsor chimneys shalt thou leap :
> Where fires thou find'st unraked and hearths unswept,
> There pinch the maids as blue as bilberry :
> Our radiant Queen hates sluts and sluttery . . .
> Search Windsor Castle, elves, within and out :
> Strew good luck, ouphes, on every sacred room,
> That it may stand till the perpetual doom,
> In state as wholesome as in state 'tis fit,
> Worthy the owner, and the owner it.

There follow the verses that make it fairly certain the play was written for a feast of the Order of the Garter, with its royal motto :

> The several chairs of order look you scour
> With juice of balm and every precious flower :
> Each fair instalment, coat, and several crest,
> With loyal blazon, evermore be blest !

> And nightly, meadow-fairies, look you sing,
> Like to the Garter's compass in a ring : . . .
> And *Honi soit qui mal y pense* write
> In emerald tufts, flowers purple, blue and white.

Just as *The Merry Wives* is more of a farce than a comedy, so *Henry V* is something different from the previous history plays in character. It has been described, with some disapprobation, as a pageant ; the Cambridge editor tells us that 'it is a play which men of action have been wont silently to admire, and literary men, at any rate during the last hundred and thirty years, volubly to contemn'.[21] It is the literary men here who are wanting in imagination, for when he came to it, Shakespeare found that the subject of Henry V demanded very different treatment. The history of the reign did not present the dramatic opportunities given by the conflict between Henry IV and his son, the contrast between Prince Hal and Hotspur, the Percy Rebellion. Everything concentrated upon the figure of the young king and the unbelievable victory, against such odds, of Agincourt, the conquest of half France. Henry V was the pattern of a hero-king to the Elizabethans, and could be treated only as such.

Two considerations converged upon Shakespeare to make this play something different, and new. In this year 1599 William Kemp, who had in all probability played Falstaff, left the Chamberlain's men. Shakespeare had promised his audience that they should see Falstaff again, serving — if that is the word — in the war in France. There is some evidence to indicate that in the first draft Falstaff did accompany Pistol, Nym and Bardolph across the Channel, and that it was Falstaff, not Pistol, whom Fluellen forced to eat the leek — far funnier if so, with the fat knight blubbering on his knees. The departure of Kemp that made it necessary to cut out Falstaff and kill him off meant the cutting down of the comic scenes and the increase of the serious element. This must have been agreeable to Shakespeare's artistic intention. All is still more concentrated upon the King, who completely dominates the play and gives the required unity. We have a number of set orations and soliloquies from him ; the episodes depicting the war in France, particularly the comic scenes, are properly subordinated so as not to detract from the effect ; the play is linked together by a unique development of the Chorus, speaking a prologue to each act and an epilogue to the whole. It is fairly clear from the personal, the proprietory, tone of these speeches that the Chorus was spoken by Shakespeare himself. The upshot was a new kind of play — of varied elements, mixed in kind, as always with Shakespeare, rather epic in tone. Let us call it an heroic play, and be grateful.

It was a good insight to suggest that where *Richard II* had been written at top speed, *Henry V* was written with more deliberation and with second thoughts. Once more, as with *Henry VI* at the beginning of the 1590's, so now towards their end Shakespeare had a stroke of luck with the mood of the moment to suit his play. The war was waking up, this time in Ireland with the emergency of Tyrone's quasi-national resistance, signalised by the gravest defeat English arms had ever suffered there with the disaster at the Yellow Ford in the summer of 1598. 'It seems hitherto to have been hardly realised how intimately associated with the Irish expedition the play as a whole must have been, both in inception and composition. . . . While he was at work upon it during the winter of 1598-9, the whole country was agog with the pressing and mustering of troops ; it was being finished about the time the expedition sailed ; and was certainly produced not long after.'[22]

In the prologues to the acts we have reflections of the excitement, the preparations, of the time — the armourers of the city :

> The armourers, accomplishing the knights,
> With busy hammers closing rivets up,
> Give dreadful note of preparation ;

the shipping for a large expedition — Essex led the largest army that had ever been sent to Ireland :

> Play with your fancies, and in them behold
> Upon the hempen tackle ship-boys climbing ;
> Hear the shrill whistle, which doth order give
> To sounds confused : behold the threaden sails,
> Borne with the invisible and creeping wind,
> Draw the huge bottoms through the furrowed sea.

In Henry V's triumphant return from Agincourt Shakespeare pre-figures the hoped-for return of a victorious Essex :

> But now behold,
> In the quick forge and working-house of thought,
> How London doth pour out her citizens —
> The mayor and all his brethren in best sort,

Like to the senators of the antique Rome,
With the plebeians swarming at their heels,
Go forth and fetch their conquering Caesar in.

We observe that that teeming brain simultaneously had *Julius Caesar* in mind, which begins with just this scene ; and then, with an immediate transition to the contemporary and Essex :

As by a lower but loving likelihood,
Were now the General of our gracious Empress,
As in good time he may, from Ireland coming,
Bringing rebellion broachèd on his sword,
How many would the peaceful City quit
To welcome him !

His faithful Londoners had given Essex such a send-off in March 1599 as he and his followers, including Southampton, moved out of the city : 'the people pressed exceedingly to behold him for more than four miles' space, crying out, "God save your Lordship, God preserve your Honour"', some even following him until the evening, only to behold him'.[23] So the play must have been written by June, by which time there was little 'likelihood' of Essex's returning a conquering hero : by then he had wasted all his chances of a successful issue. He left for Ireland like a Henry V, but he returned from it a Richard II, to stumble on to disaster. All the same, there is some flicker of Essex's gallant, chivalrous personality behind that of the hero-king. When Henry gives orders that in the English march through France nothing should be compelled from the villages, 'nothing taken but paid for, none of the French upbraided or abused . . . for when lenity and cruelty play for a kingdom, the gentler gamester is the soonest winner', this was very like Essex's known chivalry of conduct. By this lenity and courtesy at Cadiz he had won fame even throughout Spain.

It may be because of this inflexion that there is no known performance at Court in the Queen's time ; not until Essex's patron and supporter, James, was king was it performed there.

Kingship and patriotism are the twin themes of this play — not the internal trials of kingship that were the subject of *Henry IV*, but the external test of leadership in a foreign war. We need not embroil ourselves in the pros and cons of this war — to the medieval English their King's title as next heir to the French crown was a just one, and it would be anachronistic to view the matter from the so superior standards of the twentieth century. This does not mean that Shakespeare does not see the two faces of war — courage, loyalty, endurance, inspiration, happy valiancy, on one side ; on the other, sickness, wounds, death, devastation. He saw both sides very well — both much better than moderns who suppose themselves morally superior. War is a fact of human experience, because human beings are what they are ; Shakespeare is concerned with the facts of human nature, not with supposing them other than they are. We all wish they might be bettered, beginning with their intelligence.

In this context of the real world the prime function of a king is leadership, and Shakespeare probes wonderfully into the conditions of its exercise in the scene on the night before Agincourt, which Henry devotes to going about among his army disguised as a common soldier, encouraging, heartening, reassuring, finding out for himself what they are thinking. In this his earlier training in rubbing shoulders with common humanity stands him in good stead — he has not been divorced from it by his upbringing, as Richard had been. And the trick he plays on Williams by accepting the challenge of his glove, then giving it to Fluellen who finds himself challenged instead, is a prank that shows the old Prince Hal is not entirely submerged in the king. This scene with the common soldiers is of extraordinary interest as a revelation of Shakespeare's capacity for casuistry, for sheer intellectual interest : he argues as well as any lawyer, but concretely, imaginatively, without boring us.

Henry is inwardly concerned with the question what constitutes the difference between king and ordinary man, ceremony apart. They are all in grave danger together, vastly outnumbered and cut off. 'When he sees reason of fears, as we do, his fears, out of doubt, are of the same relish as ours are ; yet, in reason, no man should possess him with any appearance of fear, lest he, by showing it, should dishearten his army.' Williams directly confronts the king, unknown, with his responsibility for their lives : 'but, if the cause be not good, the king himself hath a heavy reckoning to make, when all those legs, and arms, and heads, chopped off in a battle, shall join together at the latter day and cry all "We died at such a place" . . . Now, if these men do not die well, it will be a black matter for the king that led them to it.' Henry's reply, briefly, is to accept the moral responsibility, while urging the individual to do his duty, be an upright man and therefore of good conscience : 'every subject's duty is the king's, but every subject's soul is his own'. *There* is the real equality ; not in responsibility : the responsibility of leaders is greater. There is a natural hierarchy in these matters.

Henry accepts this fully, and when he is alone there is a moment of most moving self-reflection — to those who understand its inwardness :

> Upon the king ! let us our lives, our souls,
> Our debts, our careful wives,
> Our children, and our sins, lay on the king !
> We must bear all.

This is not said in reproach, but in acceptance — and acceptance emerges as the deepest wisdom in Shakespeare's philosophy of life. It is like Elizabeth's moment of self-reflection in her last speech to Parliament, a woman grown old and weary in the service of the state : 'to be a king and wear a crown is more glorious to them that see it, than it is pleasure to them that bear it'. There follows a speech on Ceremony and its rôle in rule, which takes much the place of that on Commodity in *King John* — it is a clue to the meaning of the play.

> O Ceremony, show me by thy worth ! . . .
> Art thou aught else but place, degree, and form,
> Creating awe and fear in other men ? —
> Wherein thou art less happy, being feared,
> Than they in fearing.

It is Shakespeare seeing *through* everything, as usual. The speech that follows is very fine — all about the sleepless cares that keep a ruler awake when the simplest citizen may sleep sound in his bed. This theme seems to have had a special appeal to the writer — there were magnificent speeches on it in *Henry IV*. I wonder why ? — probably by the unconscious transference that lights up creative genius : he must have known that his imagination made him a king among men. No king ever bore rule over such a territory.

The upshot of these self-communings in the night is something recognisably true at all times and places. What is the difference between the king and his subjects, the ruler and his fellow-citizens ? It is that he is a representative man, who bears that capacity for them all. Henry passes on to prayer alone in the night — the Lancastrian House, unlike Richard, were all devout and orthodox :

> O God of battles, steel my soldiers' hearts,
> Possess them not with fear.

And then, with a return to the stain that rested on his House, though he had been a child at the time and bore no responsibility :

> Not today, O Lord,
> O not today, think not upon the fault
> My father made in compassing the crown ! . . .
> Though all that I can do is nothing worth,
> Since that my penitence comes after all,
> Imploring pardon.

To anyone who understands all that had gone before, and all the misery that was yet to come from that, it still moves one to tears : we are involved in the inextricable toils of human action, with its cruel necessities and culpabilities, the sins that are repaid unto the third generation. The best that can be said is what Shakespeare says, and what he always held :

> There is some soul of goodness in things evil,
> Would men observingly distil it out.

The inspiration, and the duties, of patriotism are a conjoint theme. After the hours of communing and intercession, on the morning of Agincourt all is clear in Henry's mind :

> This day is called the feast of Crispian :
> He that outlives this day, and comes safe home,
> Will stand a tip-toe when this day is named,
> And rouse him at the name of Crispian.
> He that shall live this day, and see old age,
> Will yearly on the vigil feast his neighbours,
> And say, 'Tomorrow is Saint Crispian' . . .

Henry is sure that Agincourt day will always be remembered in England, and those who fought there :

> We few, we happy few, we band of brothers.

It is all quite simple : this is why Henry was a hero-king to the Elizabethans. Nor is his appeal and that of the band of brothers confined in time to Shakespeare's day : those of us who lived through the Battle of Britain in 1940 and the heroic days of the liberation of Europe in 1944, and saw Shakespeare's sequence from Prince Hal and Falstaff to Henry coming home from Agincourt against the background of our own trial and long endurance, know that his scenes and words have not lost one whit of their power to move the heart.

Such is the overwhelming theme of Shakespeare's heroic-play. There remain a few indications of contemporary life, of personal preference, to yield us some information and add to our portrait. There is the seamy side to war, the rogues and criminals in the army no less than the decent fellows. Pistol and Nym get proper condemnation for the cowards and cutpurses they were. 'Why, 'tis a gull, a fool, a rogue, that now and then goes to the wars, to grace himself at his return into London under the form of a soldier. And such fellows are perfect in the great commander's names, and they will learn you by rote where services were done ; at such and such a sconce, at such a breach, at such a convoy : who came off bravely, who was shot, who disgraced, what terms the enemy stood on' . . . And so on : there were plenty of those in the streets and taverns of Elizabethan London.

As for Falstaff, there is Shakespeare's unforgettable description of his ending, and something like an apology for Henry's dismissal of him, put in the mouth of Fluellen : 'as Alexander killed his friend Cleitus, being in his ales and his cups ; so also Harry Monmouth, being in his right wits and his good judgments, turned away the fat knight with his great-belly doublet : he was full of jests, and gipes, and knaveries, and mocks : I have forgot his name.' That must have raised a laugh — as if any of Shakespeare's audience ever forgot the name of Falstaff !

In a virtuoso description of the desolation left by war across the fair face of France, the countryman speaks :

> Her vine, the merry cheerer of the heart,
> Unprunèd, dies : her hedges even-pleached,
> Like prisoners wildly overgrown with hair,
> Put forth disordered twigs : her fallow leas
> The darnel, hemlock, and rank fumitory
> Doth root upon ; while that the coulter rusts
> That should deracinate such savagery —

'Deracinate' — how like him ! —

> The even mead, that erst brought sweetly forth
> The freckled cowslip, burnet and green clover,
> Wanting the scythe, all uncorrected, rank,
> Conceives by idleness, and nothing teems
> But hateful docks, rough thistles, kecksies, burrs

Other touches speak to us of contemporary life — of the old English mastiffs and people's pride in them : 'their mastiffs are of unmatchable courage', says one. 'Foolish curs', says another, 'that run winking into the mouth of a Russian bear and have their heads crushed like rotten apples !' Shakespeare knew the bear-baiting well : it was a regular feature of Elizabethan entertainment all over the country, a rival attraction at the Bear Garden on Bankside. The famous bear, Sackerson, gets a mention in *The Merry Wives :* 'I have seen Sackerson loose twenty times, and have taken him by the chain ; but, I warrant you, the women have so cried and shrieked at it that it passed. But women indeed cannot abide 'em : they are very ill-favoured rough things.' No doubt they preferred Bucklersbury, smelling as it did in simple time — with Midsummer herbs.

It becomes clearer in this play that Pistol and Nym are caricatures, that Fluellen is modelled on some actual person. Fluellen is a friendly caricature, a spirited Welshman with a comic accent, who is well read in the art of war, has read Caesar's Commentaries, and knows all about Pompey and Alexander the Great. Nym continues to talk about humours : 'I would prick your guts a little in good terms, as I may, and that's the humour of it.' 'I cannot kiss, that is the humour of it.' 'The humour of it is too hot, that is the very plainsong of it.' Pistol is certainly a literary caricature : he speaks in the wooden, yet inflated language of earlier Elizabethan drama, from Gascoigne to Peele, stuck with alliteration and absurd figures of speech : the kind of thing that Lyly, Marlowe and Shakespeare had delivered the language from :

> Bardolph, a soldier firm and sound of heart,
> And of buxom valour, hath, by cruel fate,
> And giddy Fortune's furious fickle wheel,
> That goddess blind,
> That stands upon the rolling, restless stone . . .

Most personal, we come to Shakespeare's references to the stage, which mean so much to this unique play. The action covers a vast area, and he apologises again and again for the inadequacy of the stage to represent it : what he needed was the range of action of a modern film :

> Can this cockpit hold
> The vasty fields of France ? or may we cram
> Within this wooden O the very casques
> That did affright the air at Agincourt ?

It is exciting to think that the 'wooden O' meant, as used to be thought, the Globe, which was being built on Bankside in the early months of this year.[24] The Chamberlain's men henceforth had a theatre of their own ; it would be appropriate if we could think that they opened with *Henry V*. Before the battle we have a further apology for the inadequacy of the stage in representing heroic action :

> Where — O for pity ! — we shall much disgrace,
> With four or five most vile and ragged foils,
> Right ill-disposed, in brawl ridiculous,
> The name of Agincourt : yet sit and see,
> Minding true things by what their mockeries be.

The Epilogue, surely, makes it clear that the author himself spoke the Chorus :

> Thus far, with rough and all-unable pen,
> Our bending author hath pursued the story,
> In little room confining mighty men,
> Mangling by starts the full course of their glory.
> Small time, but, in that small, most greatly lived
> This star of England.

He goes on to refer to the story of Henry's child and heir, Henry VI, and the mismanagement of the inheritance :

> Which oft our stage hath shown : and for their sake
> In your fair minds let this acceptance take.

We shall not be wrong to see the 'bending author' himself in this, and in all productions of *Henry V* the opportunity should be taken to bring William Shakespeare in that part once more upon the stage.

CHAPTER XIII

The Late Nineties

WE must retrace our steps and return to Stratford for a little, where, as we have seen, Hamnet was buried in the August of 1596. In spite of this blow to Shakespeare's hopes of establishing a family of his name, he took up once more his father's old ambition of acquiring a coat of arms and this time pursued it to a successful conclusion. It is unlikely that the old man, within five years of his death, was behind this move ; it was a step up, a proper recognition of status, for the successful dramatist with a now assured position, the security of the good fellowship of the Chamberlain's company behind him, in which he was a sharer, the most important fellow after Richard Burbage himself.

From the documents we can tell that someone was stretching the bow. The heralds at the College of Arms were informed that the former bailiff of Stratford 'hath lands and tenements : of good wealth and substance, £500'.[1] That is an optimistic estimate of the wealth of the previously indebted John Shakespeare. On 20 October 1596 the king of arms made the grant of coat and crest to him, 'being solicited and by credible report informed' that his 'parents and late grandfather for his faithful and valiant service were advanced and rewarded by the most prudent prince, King Henry VII of famous memory, since which time they have continued in those parts, being of good reputation and credit ; and that the said John hath married the daughter and one of the heirs of Robert Arden of Wilmcote in the said county, esquire'. In the first draft Arden had appeared as but gentleman ; in his lifetime he was described as husbandman. The truth was that Robert Arden was a yeoman ; and this is the first we hear of any Shakespeare's service to Henry VII : it does not exclude the possibility of having carried a modest spear to Bosworth field. Someone was engaged in talking them up. After all, the son was a man of large ideas, and now he would be able to write himself, after long waiting, as the son of a gentleman.

The coat assigned by the College to John Shakespeare and his posterity bore these arms : 'Gold on a bend sables, a spear of the first steeled argent ; and for his crest or cognisance a falcon, his wings displayed argent, standing on a wreath of his colours, supporting a spear gold, steeled as aforesaid, set upon a helmet with mantles and tassels'. The motto : *Non sanz droict*. Never was motto more proudly deserved.

Three years later Shakespeare asked the heralds to confirm the family right to bear the arms of Arden impaled with their own. This got no further than a draft at the College, where a herald drew the coat of the Catholic Ardens of Park Hall, and then replaced it with arms borne by other Ardens. This draft went further to point back to a 'parent great-grandfather and late antecessor', of whom nobody has ever heard, and to state specifically that Henry VII had rewarded this ancestor with lands and tenements in Warwickshire. This may be as it may be : not for nothing was William Shakespeare a man of imagination. Three years later again there was trouble from the spiteful Ralph Brooke, who charged Garter king of arms with granting the Shakespeares arms which 'usurp the coat of the Lord Manley'. (Who was he ?) There was no usurpation and all was well : William Shakespeare *had* been born a gentleman.

This was a proper move : many hundreds of Elizabethans signalised their move up in society by acquiring a coat of arms. But I doubt if many of them took it out in their father's name to ensure, *ex post facto*, the gentility of their birth. We can now appreciate better all that it meant to Shakespeare with his extreme social sensitivity, the long struggle he had had to establish himself and by what means — as a player, the self-consciousness increased by life in the Southampton circle, rubbing shoulders (if no more) with the great, the attendances at Court. 'As I am a gentleman' is a phrase that appears again and again in the plays, and a modern scholar reminds us that gentlemanliness was what came naturally to the minds of Ben Jonson and Chettle, Heminges and Condell, when they thought of him.[2] Everyone pays tribute to 'gentle' Shakespeare ; to the Elizabethans this did not have its modern devitalised connotation — it meant a person of good bearing and breeding, of civil demeanour and decent behaviour, in short, a gentleman. No-one could have said 'gentle Marlowe', or 'gentle Ben Jonson'.

Our commentator draws attention to the various implications

of thus addressing Shakespeare — 'to recall his struggle to establish
his father's gentle rank ; to endorse the grant of the patent by
the College of Arms ; to recall the civil demeanour with which
he attempted to impress his gentility on his acquaintance ; and
to record how the gentle style had first distinguished his writing
from his rivals', and had remained his most supple strength.'
From the social point of view, '*Venus and Adonis* is a deliberate
first display of the gentle style. Addressed to young men, it must
be wanton ; but addressed by a gentleman to noblemen, it must
be free from crudity.' In it there is the instinctive tact of suggestion and of erotic transposition away from the too crude : what
is this but breeding ? It makes poetry out of gentlemanly occupations — hunting and horses, coursing and amorous discoursing.
While Shakespeare was interested only in the gentle side of his
lineage, he owed a great deal to the combination in him of the
gentle and the yeoman strains : he owed 'his energy to it, and
his success'. It is suggested that he carried this strain of gentleness
into the theatre and established it there definitely. Certainly there
was plenty of crudity there before.

At the end of Shakespeare's working life he can give expression
to his social self-consciousness with a very different assurance
from the early resentment against his profession, the

> public means which public manners breeds.

In *The Winter's Tale*, now fulfilled and successful, well off and
in harbour, he writes :

> As you are certainly a gentleman, thereto
> Clerk-like experienced, which no less adorns
> Our gentry than our parents' noble names.

The next thing was to move away from the constriction of
the little house in Henley Street, to something more in keeping
with the status he had won. Many who have not bothered to
take out a coat of arms have marked their social fulfilment by
moving from a humble home to a house more in keeping with
their position, their picture of themselves and, after all, their true
nature, the needs of the spirit. Nothing short of the best house
in the town was good enough for William Shakespeare : he
proceeded next year to buy New Place — just across the lane
from the Gild-Chapel he had attended as a boy — the capacious
house rich Sir Hugh Clopton had built for himself. It was a

handsome three-storeyed house with five gables, standing some-what back from Chapel Street with a little court before it.

He bought it from William Underhill, with two barns and two gardens, for £60. This sounds a very low price for such a property, but it may have been in some disrepair, for in 1598 we find Shakespeare selling a load of stone to the town. Or it may be that Underhill was in debt to him and Shakespeare had a lien on the property, for we must always remember that, among other things, he was a good, if good-tempered, man of business. A few years later he acquired a cottage across the lane from the garden of New Place — a convenience to the big house. Here he probably settled the family in the course of 1597, for early next year he is noted as a householder in Chapel Street ward, with the usual supply of malt for a substantial household. His wife 'no doubt looked after the brewing at New Place, and her daughters were soon old enough to help. Twenty bushels of malt belonging to Shakespeare were sold by some member of his household, at different times between March and May 1604, to his neighbour Philip Rogers, who borrowed two shillings besides.'[3] Rogers, the apothecary and tobacco-seller, was not good at paying his debts : Shakespeare had to put him in court to recover his money.

In this year, 1597, as a part of the plan of recovery and establish-ment — holding one's head high in one's native place — the Shakespeares made one more effort to regain Mary Arden's land in Wilmcote from their Lambert relations. But unbusinesslike, or unfortunate, old John had too much prejudiced the matter ever to get it back. His more businesslike son had to look else-where to invest the surplus cash now piling up.

In January 1598 neighbour Sturley was able to inform neigh-bour Quiney: 'our countryman Master Shakespeare is willing to disburse some money upon some odd yardland or other at Shottery or near about us ; he thinketh it a very fit pattern to move him to deal in the matter of our tithes. By the instructions you can give him thereof, and by the friends he can make there-fore, we think it a fair mark to shoot at and not unpossible to hit.' No doubt as boys they had all shot their arrows together at the butts down by the bridge ; now Shakespeare was mostly in London, though to them he is their 'countryman' still, *i.e.* their fellow Warwickshireman.[4] In October that year Alderman Quiney was in London upon the town's business, as Alderman Shakespeare had been years before : once more Stratford wanted more privileges and relief from taxes, after the disastrous fires of 1594 and 1595. Quiney found himself short of money, and wrote to Shakespeare from the Bell Inn near St. Paul's :

> Loving Countryman, I am bold of you as of a friend, craving your help with £30 upon Master Bushell's and my security, or Master Mytton's with me. You shall friend me much in helping me out of all the debts I owe in London, I thank God, and much quiet my mind which would not be indebted. I am now towards the court in hope of answer for the dispatch of my business. You shall neither lose credit nor money by me, the Lord willing, and now but persuade yourself so, as I hope, and you shall not need to fear ; but with all hearty thankfulness I will hold my time and content your friend, and if we bargain further you shall be the paymaster yourself. . . . From the Bell in Carter Lane, the 25 October 1598. Yours in all kindness, Ric. Quiney.

Quiney endorsed the letter : 'To my loving good friend and countryman Master William Shakespeare, deliver these'. It seems not to have been delivered, for it fetched up among Quiney's papers. Meanwhile, Quiney reported his hopes back to Sturley, according to the latter, 'that our countryman, Master William Shakespeare, would procure us money : which I will like of as I hear when, where, and how ; and I pray let not go that occasion if it may sort to any indifferent conditions'. I cannot but detect a note of dubiety in neighbour Sturley's letter — as if it were not an easy matter to extract money from their 'loving countryman'. And, come to that — Quiney's letter does not sound too confident, either ; yet the terms are those of affection and respect. The combination of a very careful business man with being a good fellow is a strong one.

It is nice to think that Quiney was successful after all in getting the town's remission from all the taxes and subsidies laid by the last Parliament. But it is maddening to reflect that his is the only letter addressed to Shakespeare that survives. If only we had some of Southampton's — there must have been some — or of the mistress's ! But perhaps that man, so prudent in his affairs, left no such imprudent testimonies behind him. His investments are recorded : a considerable acreage of land in Old Stratford in 1602, and a still more considerable purchase of tithes there and at Welcombe in 1605.

Meanwhile, in London, Shakespeare was living in the parish of St. Helen's, Bishopsgate, in 1596, for there he was assessed to pay 5s. for a second instalment on the subsidy, on goods valued at £5. This valuation was apt to be a rather formal figure : it betokens someone living in a fair state of middle-class prosperity, not like Greene or Nashe, Dekker or Chettle, or so many of Henslowe's poor playwrights. Bishopsgate was an interesting and variegated neighbourhood, straddling the main highway that led out of the city, through the Gate and across the ditch out to Shoreditch where the Theatre and the Curtain stood in the fields of Holywell. The whole neighbourhood was crowded with historic buildings and memories he relished.

At the bottom of the street going into the city was Crosby Place, where Richard III had lodged as Duke of Gloucester — it makes its appearance in the play. Next to it was St. Helen's priory church, packed with monuments — and we have noticed how much aware of them he was ; the latest of them was that to the financier Sir Thomas Gresham, whose big house stood opposite. Just before the gate stood the newly built conduit, and on either side 'divers fair inns, large for receipt of travellers', notably the Bull and the Angel with, outside, the biggest of them all, the Dolphin.5 Opposite this on the left hand, approached by a causey was Petty France, full of Frenchmen who had built their tenements right on the bank of the City ditch. Next to it was Bethlehem Hospital, or Bedlam, which speaks for itself, behind which were large open spaces, Moor Fields and Finsbury Fields, where Shakespeare could often have viewed the training of the Musters. Further along on the right was the brick enclosure where the cannoneers of the Tower did their training — still there as Artillery Yard. And so to Shoreditch and the theatres.

In the autumn of this year Shakespeare went across the river to live on Bankside, no doubt to be near the new theatre, the Swan, where the Chamberlain's men were playing. This fine theatre had been built recently, in 1594-5, by Francis Langley, the owner of Paris Garden : it was approached from the Garden stairs on the river just opposite Paul's stairs, at the bottom of the descent from St. Paul's. Fortunately we have a drawing of the interior of this theatre, so we know what it looked like, with its wide stage jutting right out into the open yard ; at the back of the stage two doors and the Lords'-room (or balcony) above, all under the shadow of a roof supported by columns some way out on the stage. Above this was the hut with the flag for a performance flying above the roof, and all round the three-storeyed galleries for the better-off spectators under shelter.

Francis Langley was having some trouble with an unpleasant Surrey Justice of the Peace, William Gardiner, this autumn and this indirectly involved Shakespeare. Gardiner was a predatory, bullying type — very unlike feeble old Justice Shallow. Early in November Langley appealed to the Surrey authorities for sureties of the peace against Gardiner and his stepson, William Wayte. Late in November Wayte sought sureties of the peace against Shakespeare, Langley, Dorothy Soer and Anne Lee — and that is all we really know of the matter.[6] Shakespeare did not remain for long living on the south side of the river, for by 1602, if not earlier, he was living with the Mountjoys, a French Huguenot family, in Cripplegate within the City. Evidently Bishopsgate had been his earlier residence for some time, for in 1598 the authorities again assessed him for taxation there, and once more his subsidy — this time 13s. 4d. — remained unpaid. Taxation seems to have caught up with him in the end : he must have paid, for he was not sued.[7]

In 1597 a satiric comedy, *The Isle of Dogs*, produced at the Swan, involved the player-folk in trouble. Begun by Nashe, the piece was finished by a formidable newcomer, Ben Jonson. It is a pity it is lost, for it must have been very rude about important people — and perhaps it brought Justice Gardiner on the stage, for a crop of actions for slander followed, on the part of Gardiner against Langley. The Privy Council suppressed the piece as slanderous, and an inhibition was clamped down on playing. Ben and the offending players were haled off to the Marshalsea, Nashe breezed off to Yarmouth for a holiday by the sea. The Chamberlain's men went on tour, in the course of which they visited Rye and Dover, Marlborough, Bath and were at Bristol at the end of September. The inhibition was removed early in October, in time to solace the Queen at Christmas : the Chamberlain's men performed at Court on St. Stephen's day, New Year's and Twelfth night, and at Shrovetide, 26 February 1598.

Shakespeare's established position with the public is reflected in an increasing spate in the publication of his plays from this time.[8] In 1597, Cuthbert Burby, who had already brought out a bad Quarto of *The Taming of the Shrew* in 1594, now produced a poor version of *Romeo and Juliet*, put together from memory. In those days an author had no copyright protection, so two years later Shakespeare had to content himself with issuing a good

version, 'newly corrected, augmented and amended', through
the same Burby. In 1597, too, Andrew Wise issued the popular
Richard III, probably printed with the concurrence of the Company from a playhouse manuscript ; five more editions of this
appeared before the Folio in 1623. Wise also published *Richard II*,
probably from the author's own manuscript, with his characteristic stage-directions, informal but graphic : 'The murderers rush
in . . . Here Exton strikes him down' ; 'He plucks it out of his
bosom and reads it.' 9 During Elizabeth's remaining years the
Deposition scene had to be omitted ; not until James was safely
on the throne was it restored, with the reprint of 1608. It is thought
that Burby produced a bad Quarto of *Love's Labour's Lost* in 1597,
which had to be offset by a good one in 1598, 'newly corrected,
augmented, and amended'. Early in 1598 Andrew Wise issued
1 Henry IV, 'probably within a few months of its production :
a desire to advertise the substitution of Falstaff for Oldcastle may
account for its early publication'. In July *The Merchant of Venice*
was entered to James Roberts, provided that it was not published
without licence first had from the Lord Chamberlain. This was
presumably a blocking entry on behalf of the players, though it
was published two years later. There was obviously a demand
from the reading public for those little sixpenny playbooks, read
to pieces in their time and now so precious.

The year 1598 marked a turning-point in the theatre. Since
the death of Marlowe, Shakespeare had enjoyed an ascendancy
unchallenged by anyone of comparable calibre. There now
entered a writer of the younger generation, Ben Jonson, who
with one play stepped into the front rank of dramatists, and started
upon a career of immensely rapid production and power. The
play was *Every Man in his Humour*, which Shakespeare must have
welcomed for his Company and in which he performed with his
fellows. In the folio of Ben Jonson's works we have the list of
the 'principal comedians' who performed it, and very valuable
it is for it is the earliest extant list of the famous Company. There
they all are together : 'Will. Shakespeare, Aug. Phillips, Hen.
Condell, Will. Sly, Will. Kemp, Ric. Burbage, Joh. Heminges,
Tho. Pope, Chr. Beeston, Joh. Duke'.

It is an old tradition that Shakespeare took Ben's play generously
under his wing and advanced Ben's interest, and one can detect
a note of gratitude in the extraordinary generosity of his tributes
after Shakespeare's death, especially when one considers that he

was the most pernickety and critical of men. For the Company, it was good business : nearly all the best of Ben's plays were written for it. I doubt if any sense of literary rivalry would have interfered with the good business judgment of that all-round man of the theatre, William Shakespeare. Of all the writers for the theatre he was the most professional : only a handful of the dramatists were actors as well. Out of these he is 'the only one who did not shift about from company to company, but maintained his close association with a single acting troupe for more than twenty years'.[10] Then, too, 'he is the only dramatist we know who owned stock in theatre buildings over an extended period. His income was derived from acting, from writing plays, from shares in dramatic enterprises, and from theatre rents. . . . He had more connections with the Company than any other man : he was actor, shareholder, patented member, principal playwright, and one of the housekeepers of the Globe ; even Burbage did not serve so many functions in the Company.' When he came to make his will, most of it is concerned with Stratford affairs, but turning his thoughts to his London life and associates, 'he singles out only three for a last remembrance. These men are John Heminges, Henry Condell, and Richard Burbage — all three actors, all three fellow-sharers in the acting Company of the King's men, all three fellow-stockholders in the Globe and the Blackfriars.'

Jonson stands in as marked contrast to Shakespeare, eight years his senior, as Marlowe had done earlier. Ben was of good Border stock, mettlesome and aggressive, though born in London in 1572, the posthumous child of 'a grave minister of the Gospel', who had lost all his worldly wealth under Mary.[11] The widow married a master-bricklayer, and Ben was put to school at Westminster, where he became devoted to Camden, the antiquarian, and laid the foundations of his copious learning. Instead of passing on to the university, he was early pressed into his step-father's business — he had that frustration in common with Shakespeare. Loathing bricklaying as much as Dickens did the blacking factory, Ben went off to the wars as a volunteer, killed his man and took his spoils. Returning in the early 1590's, he married a wife, 'a shrew yet honest', with whom he jogged along indifferently, later left her, and then returned. A very masculine type, broad-shouldered and muscular, with scarred, rugged face, fine eyes and a mass of black curly hair, he was not much interested in women.

One has difficulty in remembering a single attractive woman from his plays. Never a good actor, loud-mouthed and ranting, with a swashing energy, what a contrast he offers to Shakespeare's insinuating grace, that nature both sensitive and musical, prudent and detached ! No-one was ever more *engagé* than Ben ; his temperament, 'passionately kind and angry', divided people into warm friends and warmer opponents.

His mind, that powerful organ, was in equally sharp contrast with Shakespeare's. Ben's sympathies were not at all engaged by the literary romanticism that had formed Shakespeare. Ben considered that the *Faerie Queene* was 'writ in no language' : it was not to his taste, so much the worse for him. Nor were the pastoral romances, not even *Arcadia*, that breviary for Shakespeare's generation. Nor did Ben like any more the earlier drama with its disregard of classic rules of time and space — so he cannot much have liked the earlier Shakespeare. What, then, did he approve of ? Like a gifted writer of a younger generation, in the usual way he was defining his position by negatives. When he came to make his contribution, it would be very different, have a strong character of its own. What appealed to him was the satirical, lashing the age and its follies with ridicule ; the realistic, the manners, modes and foibles of society ; the analytical, scrutinising every profession according to type. In addition to this, Ben was a classic, with a scholar's veneration for classical standards ; a critic, with a powerful intellectual apparatus ; a poet, of a more restrained poetic, though not without a vein of fantasy and romance. Though so much of an intellectual, with a following among the wits and clever young men, he did have, thank goodness, creative genius.

Jonson's first play for Shakespeare's company made a sharp impact : it broke with the tradition of romantic comedy and yet had a marked success. Immediately afterwards Ben killed the actor Gabriel Spencer, no doubt in fair duel — Ben claimed with some complacency that his sword was ten inches shorter, pleaded clergy, was nevertheless branded with the Tyburn mark on his thumb, and was thrown into prison. There he was converted a Catholic by a visiting priest, thereby entering on another kind of danger. How more and more unlike the prudent life of Shakespeare ! Later the same year, Ben brought on *The Case is Altered*, a romantic comedy, with the revived Children of the Chapel — the beginning of his long connection with the private theatre :

it is curious to think of his sharp-edged satire delivered through those piping boys' voices. For these he wrote his personal satires, *Cynthia's Revels*, the *Poetaster* and his strangely effective farce, *Epicœne, or The Silent Woman*. For Shakespeare's company, in 1599, he wrote his *Every Man out of his Humour*, a still more daring breach with tradition. Shakespeare's willingness to take the risk — though he did not act in it — was so much evidence of Jonson's growing reputation with the town, particularly with the wits and students of the Inns of Court, to whom it is dedicated. The theme was the exposure of established City merchants, professional men, humbugs led into ridicule by two such young wits. Already Jonson was contributing to a cleavage in the older integrated Elizabethan public, between the gentlemen, to whom his work appealed, and the common sort, to whom it did not or only intermittently, when he got off his high horse and came down among them. Already, too, he was involving himself in warfare with his own profession, both players and fellow-dramatists, in particular Marston and Dekker, with whose outlook Shakespeare sympathised. Around Ben, who stood firm amid this torrential outpouring, there was uproar.

The Privy Council restricted the London companies to two : this left the Chamberlain's and the Admiral's at the Rose in direct rivalry. Disputes broke out : we find one of the Admiral's men following a suit against Thomas Pope, and Dekker, who wrote for Henslowe, under arrest by the Chamberlain's men. Actors and playwrights were no exception to the Elizabethan rule of vivacity. At the Theatre in Shoreditch the Burbages were having trouble with landlord and tenants as to the lease, and this winter of 1598–9 they decided to move the theatre, lock, stock and barrel, across the Thames to a new site on Bankside. Thus was the famous Globe arrived at — who thought of a name for it ? — and the Chamberlain's men had a permanent theatre of their own to play in. Under the new contract, 21 February 1599, the Burbages had one moiety of the interest ; the other moiety was shared by Shakespeare, Pope, Phillips, Heminges and Kemp. Shortly afterwards Kemp left the Company (to the demise of Falstaff), making his share over to the other four. So that Shakespeare had one-eighth interest in the Globe Theatre : a substantial and profitable investment.

Two years before, the Burbages had been frustrated in their endeavour to set up once more a permanent indoors theatre in the

Blackfriars. They bought the premises there that had served Lyly's Children for their performances, but now they were stymied by that redoubtable old tartar, the Dowager Lady Russell — aunt of Robert Cecil and the Bacons — who organised the inhabitants of the quiet precinct to petition the Privy Council against the nuisance. It would interfere with divine service, 'the same playhouse is so near the church that the noise of the drums and trumpets will greatly disturb and hinder both the ministers and parishioners in time of divine service and sermons' ; 'all manner of vagrant and lewd persons, under colour of resorting to the plays, will come thither and work all manner of mischief'. One sees their point: it 'will grow to be a very great annoyance and trouble, not only to all the noblemen and gentlemen thereabout inhabiting, but also a general inconvenience to all the inhabitants of the same precinct'.[12]

The inhabitants fell into these two classes : there were the nobility and gentry, and there were a number of craftsmen serving the luxury trades, a considerable proportion of foreigners. The first were headed by Lady Russell and the new Lord Hunsdon, who had not yet succeeded his father as Lord Chamberlain ; there were Henry Bowes, (of the family of the present Queen Mother, the Bowes-Lyons), and Stephen Egerton, (of the Ellesmere family whose papers form the original nucleus of the Huntington Library's manuscript collections). There follow a number of foreign names, and then, among the craftsmen, Shakespeare's earlier friend, Richard Field, the printer. It is little enough to go on, but it is odd that, after publishing *Venus and Adonis* in 1593, he should have assigned it over to Harrison and had no further dealings, so far as we know, with his companion at Stratford school.

All the foreigners who came to England at the turn of the century were struck by the London theatres, their gorgeous show, the quality of the acting, and the large resort to them. 'Nothing quite like them had been known in Europe since the days of the Roman Empire, and not for more than another two hundred years was there any other city which could show so many permanent theatres at one time.'[13] We know from Norden's map of just this date, 1600, the layout of the theatres on Bankside, and from Hollar's later drawing what the locality looked like.[14] To the south of London Bridge stood St. Mary Overy (now Southwark cathedral), beside it the great house of the bishops of Winchester, with its attendant, if lamentable, stews and the Clink prison in appropriate propinquity. Next along to the west, standing a little further away from the river was the new Globe. Next were the three older playhouses : the Rose, where the Admiral's men played in neighbouring rivalry, the Bear-baiting house which had formerly been the Hope, and the old Bear-baiting. This group of places for entertainment of all kinds stood some halfway between the Clink and the water-walks of Paris Garden with the Swan theatre at the eastern end. It was a naughty neighbourhood.

Since Bankside was in those days marshy, the Globe was built on piles, and, for all the interminable controversy of stage-experts, we know well enough what it looked like. Within the 'wooden O' — what does it matter whether it were an O, or so polygonal as to look as near as makes no difference like an O ? — were 'its penny and twopenny galleries and its twelve-penny rooms' : we may think of these as equivalent to modern boxes. The groundlings paid a penny to stand in the open yard ; one paid another penny for a seat in a gallery, another for a better seat. Towards the back of the stage were wooden pillars, painted or marbled, which upheld a roof-canopy, generally referred to as the Heavens ; this was painted with sun, moon and stars, heavenly bodies, what not. The back of the stage would have two doors, possibly an arras opening in the middle. At the back the Lords'-room looking down on the stage could also be used for balcony-scenes, like that in *Romeo and Juliet*, and for the musicians. Up above all the rest, was the hut which housed the hoisting and lowering machinery for the descent and ascent of gods ; externally the hut stood out on the skyline, with a flag flying to indicate a performance going on — the 'two-hours traffic' of the stage, usually concluded with a jig, or dance. Under the stage was Hell, with a trap door for the apparition or dismissal of demons, the 'cellarage' in which the voice of the Ghost in *Hamlet* was heard reverberating. A skirt of hangings right round the stage could conceal what went on below : plenty of room, for the stage was high. There were more scenic effects, greater variety of costume, more use of blood, above all more noise — clash of spears, drums, trumpets, occasionally cannon — than we usually conceive. And the whole thing had the Renaissance love of colour — a garish riot of colour — of the fantastic and ornate, of procession and symbol, violence and noise.

What Shakespeare thought of the acting we know exactly, for he has taken the trouble to tell us through the mouth of Hamlet. It is completely in keeping with what we should expect, and bears out our portrait of him : he is in favour of greater decorum and less noise, more subtlety and naturalness. 'Speak the speech, I pray you, as I pronounced it to you, trippingly on the tongue ; but if you mouth it as many of your players do, I had as lief the town-crier spoke my lines. Nor do not saw the air too much with your hand — thus; but use all gently, for in the very torrent, tempest and, as I may say, whirlwind of your passion, you must acquire and beget a temperance that may give it smoothness. O, it offends me to the soul, to hear a robustious periwig-pated fellow tear a passion to tatters, to very rags, to split the ears of the ground-lings, who for the most part are capable of nothing but inexplicable dumb-shows and noise.'

What could be clearer than that ? A prince is speaking ; but the prince was Shakespeare himself, speaking for himself, as he often does — as all writers do — through his characters. He goes on : 'Be not too tame neither, but let your own discretion be your tutor, suit the action to the word, the word to the action — with this special observance, that you o'erstep not the modesty of nature. For anything so o'erdone is from the purpose of play-ing, whose end, both at the first and now, was and is to hold as 'twere the mirror up to nature, to show virtue her own feature, scorn her own image, and the very age and body of the time his form and pressure.' How like him this is in every line, how it coheres with everything we know of him ; and what a reproof it is to those who have thought of him as no conscious artist ! He has reflected on his art to the greatest purpose — how could it be otherwise ? — and it is clear that he has the absolute con-ception of his art of the greatest dramatists, of Sophocles or Euripides or Ibsen : that the drama is coterminous with life and nature, of which it presents an image, and that in presenting the image the means should be appropriate and lifelike. Thus, 'the very age and body of the time' may be expressed in proper form — as certainly Shakespeare's own age was never more truly ex-pressed than in his plays.

As to the manner, he was a perfectionist : 'Now this over-done, or come tardy off, though it make the unskilful laugh, cannot but make the judicious grieve, the censure of which one must in your allowance o'erweigh a whole theatre of others'.

One sees that he was just as critical, just as exacting, as any intellectual like Ben Jonson ever was, but he kept his criticism in proportion and did not let it grow on him like a upas-tree, blighting all that was creative in its shade. Nor was he any less strenuous in condemnation : 'O there be players that I have seen play — and heard others praise, and that highly — not to speak it profanely, that neither having the accent of Christians, nor the gait of Christian, pagan, nor man, have so strutted and bellowed, that I have thought some of nature's journeymen had made men, and not made them well, they imitated humanity so abominably.' Was this, perhaps, the well-known 'purge' that Shakespeare administered to the so critical Ben ? Critics never much relish being given a piece of their own back, especially by someone who knows how to do the job far better than they do. And this passage is in keeping with what is known of Jonson's own acting, bellowing and strutting in parts like Jeronimo and Zulziman.

Shakespeare gives the target a last shot : 'O reform it altogether. And let those that play your clowns speak no more than is set down for them ; for there be of them that will themselves laugh, to set on some quantity of barren spectators to laugh too, though in the meantime some necessary question of the play be then to be considered. That's villainous, and shows a most pitiful ambition in the fool that uses it.' There's for plain speaking. And yet there are people who suppose that we know nothing of Shakespeare, what he was like, or what he thought. In these passages he gives us the upshot of his reflections, the benefit of his experience, as an actor over many years, now at the height of his powers. Nor can it be doubted that there enters into his criticism the fruits of his observation and judgment as a producer.

In the autumn of 1599 the Globe put on Shakespeare's new play, *Julius Caesar*. For Thomas Platter, a somewhat commonplace Swiss tourist, who could have told us so much more than he does, writes : 'after dinner on 21 September, at about two o'clock, I went with my companions over the water, and in the thatch-roofed house saw the tragedy of the first Emperor Julius with at least fifteen characters, very well acted. At the end of the play they danced according to their custom with extreme elegance. Two men in men's clothes and two in women's gave this performance, in wonderful combination with each other.'15 On Kemp leaving the Company, his place as leading clown was taken by Robert Armin, a hardly less distinguished comic actor, for whom Shakespeare wrote his finest Fool parts, those of Feste in *Twelfth Night* and the Fool in *King Lear*. The Chamberlain's men had now established an undoubted ascendancy, the result of the working together over a lengthening period of these men in good fellowship, Burbage, Shakespeare, Heminges and Condell, who became the lasting nucleus of the organisation. They performed at Court on St. Stephen's day 1599, on Twelfth Night and on 3 February 1600. On 6 March they were called in by their patron, the Lord Chamberlain, to entertain the Dutch envoy with a performance of *1 Henry IV*, to which the familiar name of *Oldcastle* still adhered. In May 1600 the Stationers' Company obligingly stayed the printing of three of Shakespeare's plays, presumably at the players' request. Within the year *Henry V*, in an abridged, unsatisfactory form, was pirated ; and then four plays — *Much Ado About Nothing, A Midsummer-Night's Dream, The Merchant of Venice* and *2 Henry IV* — were released by the Company, no doubt with the author's agreement, for they provide good texts and that was a measure of self-protection for an artist however busy and too much pushed for time to attend to unimportant details.

Meanwhile, what had been happening to Southampton and within the circle to which Shakespeare owed so much ?

In February 1597, proceeding on his misguided course, Southampton, now twenty-three, quarrelled with Essex's brother-in-law, the Earl of Northumberland. The young man does not seem to have been at fault, and Northumberland was a difficult, tetchy man, but Southampton sent him a challenge. The Queen, sensible woman, could not have two of her peers fighting and called them to order before her Council ; explanations were exchanged, and peace ratified. Sir Thomas Heneage had died in 1595, and the rumour in 1597 was that Southampton's mother would marry William Harvey, a follower of Essex who had been knighted at Cadiz. Still no move towards marriage on the part of her son, but in March he got leave to travel for a year, then changed his mind : instead he got leave to serve on the Islands Voyage, which Essex and Ralegh had combined to press on the Queen. Here was an opportunity for action, for which the young man evidently longed : he went as captain of the *Garland*. Before leaving from Plymouth he wrote to thank Cecil for 'your care of my good and love to me', with a tell-tale postscript : 'though my fortune was never so good as to enjoy any favour from her Majesty that might make me desire to stay in her Court, yet should I account myself infinitely unhappy if, with the loss of serving her, I should likewise lose her good conceit of me ; wherefore I pray you to study to preserve that, and I will direct the whole course of my life to do her service'.[16]

All the young men of Essex's following went — Rutland, Mountjoy, Sir Christopher Blount, William Harvey. The expedition narrowly missed, through Essex's fault, capturing the Spanish treasure-fleet and accomplished nothing. It led to a final breach between Essex and Ralegh, violent recriminations, and a settled determination on the part of the Queen that she would have no more such expeditions. Southampton was reported to have 'fought with one of the King's great men of war, and sunk her'.[17] I do not know if this was substantiated. That tempestuous autumn his mother was worried about him, and wrote, as everybody did with their troubles, to Secretary Cecil : ' yesterday's storm filled my heart with sourest thoughts'. The Queen sent her a favour, and followed it up with an order to pay over the large balance owed by Sir Thomas as treasurer of the Chamber. Money was scarce, the government did not know where to turn to finance the war ; the expedition had been a fiasco, a complete waste of men and resources. Essex returned to be received by the Queen with reproachful disapprobation and to find Cecil's position recognised openly as Secretary of State before old Burghley's death next year.

The year 1598 was a turning-point in Southampton's life : at last he was entangled with a mistress in the only way in which, like Ralegh, he could be made to marry — having given her a child. The lady was again one of the Queen's vulnerable maids-of-honour, Elizabeth Vernon, whose father, Sir John Vernon of Hodnet, was dead : a cousin of Essex, who took her under his wing. As long ago as three years before it had been observed at Court that 'my Lord Southampton doth with too much familiarity court the fair Mistress Vernon'.[18] But he was not proposing to marry the girl, who was virtually dowerless. Now in January 1598 he was at last, belatedly, embarking on his Continental tour, setting out with Secretary Cecil who was going to France to see if Henri IV could be prevented from making peace with Spain. Sir Robert Sidney's agent reports to him the news at Court : 'I hear my Lord of Southampton goes with Mr. Secretary to

France and so onwards on his travels, which course of his doth exceedingly grieve his mistress, that passes her time in weeping and lamenting'. The next we hear is of some unkindness between Southampton and his mistress, on account of some gossip about her put about by Ambrose Willoughby.

There followed a quarrel in the Presence Chamber late at night, after the Queen had gone to bed. Willoughby was an esquire of the Body and asked Southampton and Ralegh to give over playing at primero. Ralegh put up his money and went off, but Southampton 'took exceptions at him and told him he would remember it; and so, finding him between the Tennis Court wall and the garden, struck him and Willoughby pulled off some of his locks. The Queen gave Willoughby thanks for what he did in the Presence and told him he had done better if he had sent him to the porter's lodge to see who durst have fetched him out.' [19] Thereupon the Queen commanded Southampton away from Court: she obviously did not like him or approve of his conduct. 'My Lord of Southampton is much troubled at her Majesty's strangest usage of him. Somebody hath played unfriendly parts with him. Mr Secretary hath procured him licence to travel. His fair mistress doth wash her fairest face with too many tears. I pray God his going away bring her to no such infirmity, which is, as it were, hereditary to her name.' This refers to the celebrated elopement of a manly young Manners with Dorothy Vernon, earlier in the century, by which the Manners came by Haddon Hall.

Early in February, 'it is secretly said that my Lord of Southampton shall be married to his fair mistress', but, as he had done before, to such disadvantage to himself, 'he asked for a little respite'.[20] He shortly got leave to go abroad instead, and, raising a large sum of money for an intended two-year absence, departed with the Secretary, with his own train of ten servants and six horses. 'My Lord of Southampton is gone and hath left behind him a very desolate gentlewoman, that hath almost wept out her fairest eyes. He was at Essex House with 1000 [Essex] and there had much private talk in the court below.' In May, Southampton's mother, who had no such objection to the sacrament of marriage, was said to have married Sir William Harvey; but this was not yet.

From France, where Southampton was enjoying the company of the Danvers brothers, he intended to go on to Italy with them;

but the Queen suddenly pardoned them in June and they had to return, disrupting his plans. To Cecil he wrote, 'if I may not have the company of the younger, my voyage will be infinitely unpleasing unto me. . . . I cannot here imagine what may hinder him, but if any let should happen, I beseech you if you can, remove it, for I protest it will be an exceeding maim unto me, if I miss him.' [21] Evidently better him as a companion than Mistress Vernon. That poor lady's condition was now somewhat precarious : 'Mistress Vernon is from Court, and lies at Essex House ; some say she hath taken a venue under the girdle and swells upon it, yet she complains not of foul play but says the Earl of Southampton will justify it. And it is bruited underhand that he was lately here four days in great secret, of purpose to marry her and effected it accordingly.'

Of course, the Queen heard of Southampton's visit and bade her Secretary command him home. The news at Court was that when the Queen had learned of the new Lady Southampton and her adventures, her 'patience was so much moved that she came not to chapel. She threats them all to the Tower, not only the parties, but all that are partakers in the practice' (*i.e.* intrigue). [22]

Meanwhile, Sir William Harvey's name was rumoured for Comptroller of the Household, but Southampton had never gone the right way to advance his family connections in the Queen's good books. Nor does he seem to have appreciated the extent of his offence : he hoped, he wrote to Cecil, 'that as my offence is but small, so her anger will not be much'.[23] Essex was able to warn him as to that, and in reply Southampton poured out to him the financial troubles that hampered him : 'when I am re-turned, I protest unto your Lordship, I scarce know what course to take to live, having at my departure let to farm that poor estate I had left for the satisfying of my creditors, and payment of these debts which I came to owe by following her Court, and have reserved only such a portion as will maintain myself and a very small train in my time of travel'. He would have done better to marry Burghley's granddaughter long before, and have done with it ; now there was to be no Continental tour for him either.

Meanwhile, an intelligence agent wrote Cecil that the young man was gambling his substance away at tennis in Paris, wagering several thousand crowns on the game, that in a few days Marshal Biron had won 3000 crowns off him and that everyone was laughing at him. If Essex did not bring him back, he would

lose everything in France as well as in England and ruin himself
in a short time. This was what Shakespeare's 'lovely boy', 'Lord
of my love' and so on, had come to, it is sad to think : but so
like life. In November, 'the new Countess of Southampton is
brought abed of a daughter, and to mend her portion, the Earl
her father hath lately lost 1800 crowns at tennis in Paris'.[24] (But
had Southampton been over in England in the preceding March,
or in May — so that this might have been a seven-months child ?)
A couple of days later he was back, and was immediately committed to the Fleet. His punishment was not severe, and he was
shortly out and about.

Southampton signalised his release by quarrelling with his
mother about *her* marriage. Apparently he did not think Sir
William Harvey's station equivalent to hers, and he feared that
the match would have disadvantageous financial consequences for
himself. His mother was not pleased with her son, and with good
reason. Essex was called in to mediate, and represented to her
'how sad I found you, how the grounds of it were her unkindness,
the discomfort and discontentment you took in her marriage,
and scorn that Sir William Harvey should think to offer any
scorn to you'. Essex called Master W. H. to his presence, and
told him that 'I thought both she and he had not carried themselves towards your Lordship as they should have done. For by
their match, if it went forward, there was a certain mischief to
fall upon you, and they added to that unkind and unmannerly
carriage.'[25]

Evidently Southampton had succeeded in holding up the
marriage during the period of his disgrace : it had been rumoured
ever since May, and now the dowager and her young man were
going to the altar. The 'mischief' to her son was mainly financial :
he would not be getting all there was to come to him from his
mother. For Harvey it was a step up, and with Essex he stood
to his guns. Essex told him that 'he never had showed that respect
of you, since your coming over, that your favourable usage of
him heretofore did require, and that he had spoken carelessly,
as though he regarded not whether you were angry or pleased'.
To this Master W. H. spoke out : 'they that were angry without
cause must be pleased without amends'. The marriage went
forward and at the end of January 1599 the news came out : 'Sir
William Harvey's marriage with the Countess of Southampton
that hath been smouldering so long comes to be published'.[26]

This year, 1599, saw Essex in command of the English army in Ireland, his memorable send-off by London, Shakespeare's tribute to him in *Henry V*. Essex meant to pack the army with his own supporters — a contingent danger to the state. He proposed Southampton as Lord General of the Horse, which was expressly forbidden by the Queen; but when he got over there he used his powers as Lord Lieutenant to appoint him. The Queen commanded him to discontinue the young Earl from that office. There followed an angry exchange of letters, Essex, hysterical as usual, protesting hotly that if he had thought himself debarred from giving Southampton 'place and reputation some way answerable to his degree and expense', he would never have brought him over.[27]

The old woman of immense experience took up her pen to reply herself to all Essex's points, and — 'for the matter of Southampton, it is strange to us that his continuance or displacing should work so great an alteration either in yourself (valuing our commandments as you ought) or in the disposition of our army: where all the commanders cannot be ignorant that we not only not allowed of your desire for him, but did expressly forbid it, and being such a one whose counsel can be of little, and experience of less, use'.[28] One hardly knows what to admire most in this: the controlled irony, the judgment, the dignity or the style — for, of course, she was right, and with what power and edge it is expressed! She proceeds to carry the war into the enemy's quarters: as for Southampton's person, 'yea, such a one was, were he not lately fastened to yourself by an accident — wherein for our usage of ours we deserve thanks — you would have used many of your old lively arguments against him for any such ability of commandment. It is therefore strange to us, we knowing his worth by your report, and your own disposition from ourself in that point, will dare thus to value your own pleasing in things unnecessary, and think by your private arguments to carry for your own glory a matter wherein our own pleasure to the contrary is made notorious.'

That was that: Southampton was divested of his charge, and served as a plain captain. The atmosphere is already that of the Essex conspiracy, and when Essex had his futile, treasonable meeting with Tyrone at the ford, and discussed what should happen when the Queen was dead, Southampton was with him, 'charged to keep all men from hearing'.

From the letters his wife wrote Southampton while away it
is obvious that she was very much in love with the handsome
young man who had made an honest woman of her. She was
relieved that he was not 'troubled for my not being as, I protest
unto you, I infinitely desire to have been . . . and though I be
not now in that happy state yet I doubt not that in good time
and, for the infinite comfort of you and myself, God will bless
me with bearing you as many boys as your own heart desires
to have.' 29

Dear my love, you know
You had a father : let your son say so.

In every letter she prayed for his return and that 'most soon I
may enjoy the sight of you and ever your most faithful love,
which will make me know myself to be the happiest woman
of the world'. Evidently Southampton had a way with him,
to make people write of him thus. Service away at the wars
had other consolations, however. There was a tough fighting
captain in Essex's following, much favoured by him, one Piers
Edmonds. When Southampton was General of the Horse, we
learn later, Edmonds was made his Corporal General : 'he ate
and drank at his table and lay in his tent. The Earl of Southampton would cull and hug him in his arms and play wantonly
with him.' 30 Essex often had him ride in his coach with him.

After Essex's return from his humiliating fiasco in Ireland,
and the Queen had learned of his ominous contact with Tyrone,
he was placed under restraint at York House : he had become
a danger to the state. In his absence Essex's wife and sister, Lady
Rich — Sidney's Stella — with Southampton and his wife, kept
open house a little further along the Thames at Essex House, an
Opposition establishment. Then the ladies went down to the
country 'to shun the company that daily were wont to visit them,
because it gave offence at Court'.31 Left to their own resources,
'my Lord Southampton and Lord Rutland come not to Court
. . . they pass the time in London merely in going to plays every
day'. Among the plays to be seen in the winter of 1599–1600
would be *Henry V* and *Julius Caesar*, most political of all Shakespeare's plays, dealing with the assassination of a tyrant ; for
lighter fare, *Much Ado About Nothing* and *As You Like It*.

Like other unstable people in time of trouble, Essex saw the
light of revealed religion, and wrote to Southampton : 'I have
ceased to be a Martha caring about many things, and believe

with Mary . . . I wish you the comfort of unfeigned conversion. I was only called by divines, but your Lordship now has the call of one who knows the end of all this world's contentment. I have explained the way of salvation, and will never go to sleep or awake without prayer for you.' [32] The way of common sense, for both of them, would have been more to the point and saved them much suffering. The Queen was annoyed to hear that Southampton and others of Essex's party had gone to the house next to York House to converse with Essex as he took the air in the garden. She proceeded to order the Southamptons, Essex's intriguing mother, Lady Leicester, and others of the party out of Essex House. Southampton went into the country, where we hear of him staying at lovely Ramsbury — then a four-square, gabled Elizabethan house — with the young Lord Herbert, its owner, and the Danvers brothers. Lord Herbert, not yet twenty, had signalised his entry on the stage by getting another of those frail ladies, the maids-of-honour, with child — Mary Fitton. Cecil reported, 'we have no news but that there is a misfortune befallen Mistress Fitton. The Earl of Pembroke [in the interval Lord Herbert had succeeded] being examined confesseth a fact, but utterly renounceth all marriage. I fear they will both dwell in the Tower for awhile, for the Queen hath vowed to send them thither.' Actually Lord Pembroke fetched up in the Fleet — but he went on to make a much better marriage. He too was a great addict of plays, and became a famous patron of the theatre, a patron of the First Folio. In March 1600 we hear that 'all this week the Lords have been in London and passed away the time in feasting and plays'. It was at this moment that the Lord Chamberlain entertained the Dutch envoy with *Henry IV*. Dedications of books continued to be laid at Southampton's feet — among them a reminder of the past, a translation of a history of the union of Portugal with Spain, offered by Edward Blount, Marlowe's old friend.

The Queen was determined to subdue the Irish rebellion, and in Mountjoy, her own first candidate for the post, she found a really able commander to do the job. Southampton, thirsting for action and to achieve honour, accompanied him. In mid-March he was 'in very good hope to kiss the Queen's hand before going', but he was not accorded this honour.[33] His friend, Sir Charles Danvers, brought him along the road as far as Coventry, and in Ireland the young man did good service — he was not without courage. But no notice was taken of his desire for a command there. Cecil was a good friend to him, and Southampton asked for the Presidency of Connaught, 'in hope by that means to effect somewhat whereby to recover her Majesty's good conceit, which is my only end and all the happiness I aspire unto'. Nothing would effect that now, and Southampton left Ireland disgruntled for the Low Countries with other disaffected young men of Essex's following — to return for the most ill-conceived venture of all, the Essex Rising.

During these years Shakespeare was engaged not only on the two parts of *Henry IV* and *Henry V*, but in writing *Much Ado About Nothing*, *As You Like It* and *Julius Caesar*. There was plenty on the political scene to reflect about, if at a remove.

Much Ado may be dated to 1598-9; it is not mentioned by Meres in 1598, so it is subsequent. The plot appears to derive from Bandello through Belleforest's *Histoires tragiques* of 1582; there are hints that may come from Ariosto through Harington's translation of *Orlando Furioso*, as well as others from the *Faerie Queene*. Shakespeare *may* have remembered a lost play of the 1580's. But what does it matter about plot? Shakespeare was in the habit of economising on what interested him least, namely plot: any good story would do on the basis of which he could draw out the varieties and quirks of character, insert his own observations of human nature, wring out the drama, express it all in poetry, of which his prose is but another form. *That* was what interested him, elicited his imagination, gave scope to his genius. The search for sources, after all, is a tertiary academic exercise, of limited illumination. That attentive reader of Shakespeare, Charles I, summed up the main interest of *Much Ado* for us by inscribing for a title in his copy of the Second Folio at Windsor, 'Benedick and Beatrice'. For the subsidiary themes, it has been observed that Shakespeare played down the love-versus-friendship theme, important in all the other versions of the story: 'perhaps because he had used it in *The Two Gentlemen of Verona*, but more probably because it had become stale.' [34] We can perceive, a little sadly, that it meant less to him now.

Q. draws attention to Shakespeare's habit of repeating himself, his economy of invention, which went along at the same time with infinite variety, for 'it indicates no imaginative poverty, but a teeming wealth, and is of a piece with Shakespeare's genius for borrowing his plots from anywhere and everywhere'.³⁵ We should add to this that at each handling of the theme or story Shakespeare improves on it and deepens its meaning ; the plot of *Much Ado*, for instance, is re-echoed in *The Winter's Tale*, but with how much more poignancy in that wonderful play ! Not only is this true with regard to plot, Q. notices that it also applies to character, particularly the characters of the women : 'Rosaline shades into Beatrice, Beatrice into Rosalind, into Portia, and so into Imogen ; Cressida into Cleopatra ; Perdita into Marina, Miranda'. Q. concludes that 'we must allow them a family like-ness, indefinable, haunting us as family likenesses do in real life : so that Shakespeare's women . . . differ somehow, one and all, from the women of other Elizabethan playwrights and carry a common stamp of paternity'. I wonder whether there is not another factor : that in the masculine world of the theatre, with which Shakespeare was so wholly engaged, he would not have a wide variety of womenfolk under view ? They seem to me to be varieties on a restricted number of themes, when one com-pares them with the women of Balzac or Tolstoy ; and he would have to keep in view the capacities of the boy-actors to act the parts. One can very easily see boys in the parts of Rosaline, Beatrice, Rosalind or Portia ; or as Calpurnia, or Brutus's Portia, Constance or Hotspur's wife ; or Ophelia, Desdemona, Imogen, Miranda. One has known boys who would do very well as Cressida. But what about Lady Macbeth and Cleopatra ? One can only suppose that the emotional and intuitive potentialities of youths were more fully realised by the Elizabethans.

Q. enforces the view that 'all Shakespeare's "comedies" lie close to sorrow ; close at least to heart-ache, sometimes close to heart-break'.³⁶ If this sounds a little sentimental, we now know that there was plenty in his life to make it so. 'Even in *The Comedy of Errors* we have pathos induced upon Plautus, who knew it not : even in *Love's Labour's Lost* the shadow of death overcasts a revel. Portia, like the Princess of France, mourns a father, in the begin-ning of a play which sails very close to tragedy, and only fetches off by cleverness ; and so mourns Helena at the beginning of *All's Well that Ends Well*. In *Twelfth Night* Olivia and Viola mourn for brothers. No one can, under ordinary definition, make comedy of *Measure for Measure*. The half at least of *The Winter's Tale*, labelled a Comedy, is purely tragic. So *Much Ado* treads close, all the while, upon tragedy.' Perhaps we may add that this gathers upon Shakespeare with his deepening experience of life.

To scrutinise the play from our special point of view — we are immediately struck by the contemporary reference to

> favourites,
> Made proud by princes, that advance their pride
> Against that power that bred it.

This is an unmistakable reference to Essex, increasingly challenging the power of the Queen, and we see Shakespeare withdrawing his sympathy from that, in spite of his affiliation to Southampton and wishing well to Essex's campaign in Ireland. There is a reflection of the wars in this : 'a victory is twice itself when the achiever brings home full numbers' — it rarely happened, however, on land or sea in those days when more combatants died from disease than from combat. Beatrice has a nice image from contemporary actions at sea : 'I am sure he [Benedick] is in the fleet — I would he had boarded me'.

In 1598 Marlowe's *Hero and Leander* was at length published, to remind Shakespeare of him — not that he had ever forgotten, but there are phrases from him in both this and the next play. Here we have, 'Leander the good swimmer.' Beatrice's crossness reminds us of Kate's in *The Shrew*. Her long railing against marriage brings to mind Southampton's prolonged rearguard-action in actuality and the suggestion has been plausibly made that there may be an element of transference as in Proust and some other writers, where feminine characters owe some of their characteristics to masculine originals.

The country background is suggested with touches like Benedick's, 'why, that's spoken like an honest drover — so they sell bullocks'. Within a few lines we have a number of country references together : perhaps they were written there. There is the lapwing well-observed, that 'runs close by the ground'; and then —

> The pleasant'st angling is to see the fish
> Cut with her golden oars the silver stream,
> And greedily devour the tremendous bait ;

and last, the haggards of the rock that are 'coy and wild'. Best of all are the country humours of Dogberry and Verges, the constable and headborough. Aubrey tells us that Ben Jonson and Shakespeare 'did gather humours of men daily wherever they came', and that the humour of the constable was drawn from such a one at Long Crendon in Buckinghamshire — likely enough, the place is on a main road between Stratford and London.[37] Dogberry recites the formula : 'Are you good men and true ?' To which Verges replies : 'Yea, or else it were pity but they should suffer salvation, body and soul'. Dogberry continues with the catechism of his assistant : 'Five shillings to one on't with any man that knows the statutes, he may stay him — marry, not without the prince be willing, for indeed the watch ought to offend no man, and it is an offence to stay a man against his will'. Yet these wiseacres, when all is said, were not such great fools as Essex and Southampton.

The parts of Dogberry and Verges were taken by Kemp and Richard Cowley, for at one point their names appear in the text. Shakespeare clearly had them in mind while writing the parts, and it would seem that he had not yet decided what to call them. A couple of other possible names remain as fossils, Keeper and Andrew. It has been concluded, therefore, that Shakespeare's manuscript underlies the text, and that he composed the later scene in which these names appear before composing the earlier ones. If so, it would lead to the fascinating conclusion that Shakespeare did not necessarily compose a play straight on from beginning to end.[38]

Kemp left the company shortly after, to perform his famous dance for a wager all the way from London to Norwich in a month. Leaving London with much publicity on 11 February 1600, he arrived at Norwich on 11 March, where he hung his buskins up in the Gild-hall as a memento. 'I have danced myself out of the world', *i.e.* the Globe, he declared, and next went abroad to visit Italy and Germany. On his return in 1601 he joined Worcester's men, and died about 1603.

As to touches of personal taste and observation, we have monuments as usual. 'If a man do not erect in this age his own tomb ere he dies, he shall live no longer in monument than the bell rings and the widow weeps.' We have too —

> And on your family's old monument
> Hang mournful epitaphs, and do all rites
> That appertain unto a burial.

As in *Romeo and Juliet* we have a churchyard at night and a sepulchre. We note too, 'Pharaoh's soldiers in the reechy painting', and 'god Bel's priests in the old church window', and 'the shaven Hercules in the smirched worm-eaten tapestry'. When the parish officers appear at the gaol with their offenders, Verges says — an authentic touch from life : 'O, a stool and cushion for the sexton !'. The marriage-service, which made such an impression on Shakespeare's mind, appears again in the phrase — 'if his conscience find no impediment to the contrary'.

More personal still, perhaps, are the references to the unkindness it is 'to show a child his new coat and forbid him to wear it' ; or this :

> Be yet my nephew : my brother hath a daughter
> Almost the copy of my child that's dead.

And there is the thought we have had expressed before :

> what we have we prize not to the worth
> Whiles we enjoy it, but being lacked and lost,
> Why then we rack the value, then we find
> The virtue that possession would not show us
> Whiles it was ours . . .

There follows a passage filled with feeling :

> When he shall hear she died upon his words,
> The idea of her life shall sweetly creep
> Into his study of imagination,
> And every lovely organ of her life
> Shall come apparelled in more precious habit,
> More moving-delicate and full of life,
> Into the eye and prospect of his soul,
> Than when she lived indeed.

Whatever personal experience lay at the back of this, so charged with emotion and regret, it is the germ of *The Winter's Tale*.

In the same year, 1599, in which Shakespeare wrote *Henry V* and *Julius Caesar*, he wrote also *As You Like It*. At the height of his powers three plays a year seem to have been his maximum output. There is no difficulty with regard to the sources of this play : he boldly took over the story of Thomas Lodge's *Rosalynde*, changing the names and adding more characters for his own purposes : 'Le Beau, who adds a satirical touch to Duke Frederick's Court ; Touchstone, who provides a companion for the ladies on their journey to Arden and a satirical commentator on the other characters ; Amiens and Jacques who lend variety to the outlaws ; and Audrey and William — country folk after his own observation.'[39] There are changes, too, in the plot : the usurping Duke is made brother to the exiled Duke, and 'this provides a parallelism in the two plots, since Orlando, too, is cheated of his rights by a villainous brother, and both villains repent before the end of the play'. It is like Shakespeare to make the matter more complicated : this doubling of parts reminds us of *The Comedy of Errors* ; it not only varies the drama but enriches the aesthetic design.

It is the additions to his borrowed plots that we chiefly remember : impossible to keep straight in our head the banished dukes, the melancholy countesses, the aristocratic lovers, all the brothers lost and found. What we remember is what had life for him and to which he gave the life-blood of his imagination : Launce and his dog, Dogberry and Verges, Shallow and Falstaff, Bottom the weaver ; of the innumerable lovers we do remember Romeo and Juliet, Beatrice and Benedick ; but Shylock is printed more indelibly on our memory, and the incomparable portraits of kings, Richard III and Richard II, Henry IV and Henry V, Lear and Macbeth, and those princely characters, Hamlet, Othello, Prospero.

Lodge's *Rosalynde* had been published in 1590, with a dedication to Lord Hunsdon saying that, on a voyage to Terceira and the Canaries, 'to beguile the time with labour, I writ this book : rough, as hatched in the storms of the ocean, and feathered in the surges of many perilous seas'.[40] Apparently he had accompanied thus far the famous voyage Sir Richard Grenville made in 1585 to plant the first colony in Virginia. In 1591 Lodge went on the terrible second voyage of Cavendish, upon which he wrote *A Margarite of America* in the Straits of Magellan, around a story which he said he found in the Jesuits' library at Santos. Some six years Shakespeare's senior, an Oxford man and thus a university wit, Lodge was a friend of Greene. Together they collaborated in a couple of plays, the second of which had considerable success, *A Looking Glass for London and England*. Lodge's literary friends were Greene, Daniel, Drayton and Roydon, and behind *As You Like It* there lurks the unforgotten shade of Robert Greene.

Lodge may have known Shakespeare, though we have no evidence that they were acquainted. Shakespeare does not seem to have enjoyed the society of literary circles ; he was not a coterie man, and preferred to stick to his last. But there was a real sympathy of mind between the author of *As You Like It* and the author of *Rosalynde*. Lodge was a Catholic of good family — his father had been Lord Mayor of London ; he had the usual disabilities of a young intellectual of the time, lived a gay life and spent his inheritance fast. There was a note of recurring melancholy in Lodge's work, of unease with the world, reflecting his imperfect adjustment and dissatisfaction at ill-success. At this moment, in the years 1597-9, he was away at Avignon belatedly equipping himself for a profession as a doctor. In his earlier writings he had shown a charming lyrical gift, while *Rosalynde* had the nostalgia for pastoral romance that appealed to something deep in Shakespeare.

Q. reminds us that 'in play after play he gets his people into a woodland, or a wooded isle, where all are ringed around with enchantment, and escape the better for it. It is so in *A Midsummer-Night's Dream*, in *The Winter's Tale*, in *The Tempest*.' [41] And he adds, reasonably enough, that Shakespeare evolved the English Arden of *As You Like It* out of his childhood memories. Perhaps it would be going too far to say that there was an unconscious atavism that drew him back to Arden, but certainly there was an area there that his imagination turned back to fondly and fed upon.

Immediately, with Orlando's first speech, we are in the midst of what we may describe as the gentility-theme. Orlando is a younger brother, defrauded of his rights by the elder, who keeps him at home instead of educating him — or 'call you that "keeping" for a gentleman of my birth, that differs not from the stalling of an ox ? . . . He lets me feed with his hinds, bars me the place of a brother and, as much as in him lies, mines my gentility with my education.' Orlando reproaches his brother to his face : 'my father charged you in his will to give me good education : you have trained me like a peasant, observing and hiding from me all gentleman-like qualities'. When he takes to the forest he is attended by a faithful family-retainer, Adam, and by an old tradition this small part was taken by the dramatist. Of Adam, Orlando speaks lines that evidently spoke for Shakespeare :

> O good old man, how well in thee appears
> The constant service of the antique world,
> When service sweat for duty, not for meed !
> Thou art not for the fashion of these times,
> Where none will sweat but for promotion.

With the particular provenance of this play there is a good deal that reflects back to the literary life of the early 1590's. The well-known scene in which Orlando hangs his love-poems to Rosalind on the branches of the trees is a reminiscence from Greene's *Orlando Furioso* : Greene's shade might well gibber with ineffective anger once more at his junior's successful plagiarism. A mightier shade was called up with the publication of *Hero and Leander* the year before. *As You Like It* has the famous couplet with the line quoted from the poem :

> Dead shepherd, now I find thy saw of might :
> 'Who ever loved that loved not at first sight ?'

And there are other references to the poem Shakespeare had so much reason to remember. 'Leander, he would have lived many a fair year, though Hero had turned nun, if it had not been for a hot midsummer night. For, good youth, he but went forth to wash him in the Hellespont and being taken with the cramp was drowned, and the foolish chroniclers of that age found it was "Hero of Sestos". But these are all lies. Men have died from time to time, and worms have eaten them, but not for love.' This is not merely humorous ; there is disillusionment in it.

Of the many contemporary references with which this play abounds, we are naturally struck, in the circumstances of 1599, with one about treason :

> Treason is not inherited, my lord,
> Or, if we did derive it from our friends,
> What's that to me ?

The Irish troubles appear with the odious comparison, ' 'tis like the howling of Irish wolves against the moon' — and we recall that, to the Elizabethans, the moon was Cynthia, the Queen. The maritime interests of the time appear in : 'one inch of delay more is a South sea of discovery' ; 'thy loving voyage is but for two months victualled' ; 'my affection hath an unknown bottom, like the bay of Portugal'. We are reminded of the young men who sold their lands for foreign travel : 'then, to have seen much, and to have nothing, is to have rich eyes and poor hands'. It does not seem that this option was to Shakespeare's taste. So, 'farewell, Monsieur Traveller : look you lisp and wear strange suits ; disable all the benefits of your own country ; be out of love with your nativity, and almost chide God for making you that countenance you are ; or I will scarce think you have swam in a gondola'.

There is a comment on contemporary lawyers, calculated to give pleasure to the termers of the Inns of Court — like 'lawyers in the vacation : for they sleep between term and term, and then they perceive not how time moves'. An unattractive accompaniment of Elizabethan oratory is indicated : 'very good orators, when they are out, they will spit'. One remembers an interval in Parliamentary oratory in that age, when 'the House [of Commons] hawked and spat'. All kinds of contemporary modes and manners are glanced at in Jacques's — 'I have neither the scholar's melancholy, which is emulation [how true for the Harveys] ; nor the musician's, which is fantastical [true to the life of John Bull, or Dowland] ; nor the courtier's, which is proud [the whole Court bore evidence of the truth of that] ; nor the soldier's, which is ambitious [true for Essex, Ralegh and a hundred others] ; nor the lawyer's, which is politic' (witness Bacon and Coke). One sees how exactly Shakespeare had estimated Elizabethan social life, and the gilded individuals that swam in it.

It is Jacques who speaks Shakespeare's summing up of the human condition, with an edge on it, in terms of the stage :

> All the world's a stage
> And all the men and women merely players ;
> They have their exits and their entrances,
> And one man in his time plays many parts . . .

One recognises them well :

> the justice,
> In fair round belly with good capon lined,
> With eyes severe and beard of formal cut,
> Full of wise saws and modern instances.

Or the penultimate

> lean and slippered pantaloon,
> With spectacles on nose and pouch on side,
> His youthful hose, well saved, a world too wide
> For his shrunk shank, and his big, manly voice,
> Turning again toward childish treble, pipes
> And whistles in his sound.

All this may be based on a contemporary commonplace, one of the tropes of school-rhetoric ; but it is as individualised as Shallow.

The dominant mood of the play may be said to be the contrast between the life of the Court and that of the country, and, with our knowledge of Shakespeare's predilections now, we know which has his loyalty. Touchstone says, 'if thou never wast at Court, thou never saw'st good manners'. To which the shepherd Corin replies, 'those that are good manners at the Court are as ridiculous in the country, as the behaviour of the country is most mockable at the Court'. Nor is this any the less pointed because the joke would be appreciated at Court. Standing outside all social classes, as in the event he did, having made a diagonal cut across society from the glover's shop to the aristocratic circle of Southampton House with the *entrée* (if as a player) at Court, Shakespeare saw the foibles and follies of all classes and conditions. The wonder is that he retained his patience and good humour — except that he made his fortune out of them. He leaves the last word to the countryman : 'I am a true labourer. I earn that I eat, get that I wear, owe no man hate, envy no man's happiness, glad of other men's good, content with my own ; [42] and the greatest of my pride is to see my ewes graze and my lambs suck.'

This emphasis is enforced with some of the finest songs in the plays : 'Under the greenwood tree', 'Blow, blow, thou winter wind', and 'It was a lover and his lass'. One can hardly hear —

> Between the acres of the rye,
>   With a hey, and a ho, and a hey nonino,
> These pretty country folks would lie,
>   In the springtime —

without thinking of the acres of rye and the walks out towards Shottery ; or of the lines,

> If ever been where bells have knolled to church,
> If ever sat at any good man's feast,

without thinking of the bells of Stratford ringing out over those meads, the closely knit life of the little town in those days.

We may see a personal inflection in the way the lines go on :

> If ever from your eyelids wiped a tear,
> And know what 'tis to pity and be pitied,
> Let gentleness my strong enforcement be.

That is consistently Shakespearean — consistent with all we know of him. He reveals himself, too, in his dislike of intemperance, twice enforced in this play :

> For in my youth I never did apply
> Hot and rebellious liquors in my blood,
> Nor did not with unbashful forehead woo
> The means of weakness and debility.

Instead, we have the perfect fixation on deer-hunting that seems to rule in the first half of his career, and the lengthy piece of Jacques's philosophising over the wounded stag. A passage about hands is revealing :

> I saw her hand — she has a leathern hand,
> A freestone-coloured hand : I verily did think
> That her old gloves were on, but 'twas her hands :
> She has a huswife's hand . . .

I don't suppose that in earlier days Shakespeare had known any other — now, how different !

The Epilogue reveals, as does the title of the play itself, the easy confidence the master reposes in his audience — after all, they knew each other well now : 'I charge you, O women, for the love you bear to men, to like as much of this play as please you ; and I charge you, O men, for the love you bear to women — as I perceive by your simpering, none of you hates them — that between you and the women the play may please'.

While writing *Henry V*, Shakespeare already had *Julius Caesar* in mind, perhaps was reading Plutarch's Life of Antony for it, as we may guess from the reference forwards :

> Like to the senators of the antique Rome,
> With the plebeians swarming at their heels,
> Go forth and fetch their conquering Caesar in.

This comes from the Prologue to the last Act of *Henry V*, so that the first scene of *Julius Caesar* was already present in his mind. But what a contrast these two plays present ! The one an heroic English chronicle-play ; the other a classic piece, of perfect proportions and restrained simplicity, with everything subjected to the overriding aesthetic intention, not a single note of bawdy and hardly a touch of comedy, yet alive in every member. These two plays have this in common, that each is a masterpiece, and each is unique : *Henry V* is Shakespeare's one heroic poem, *Julius Caesar* is his most political play, exfoliating outwards from an abstract idea — the conflict between tyranny and liberty — as displayed in a world-famous event, the assassination of Caesar, through characters every one of whom is individualised and lives in his own right. It is an extraordinary achievement, by every test : no wonder Ben Jonson, with his classical ideals and claims, was jealous of this masterpiece by an outsider, when his own classical productions were dead, or never came alive.

The contrast between the character-drawing of Henry V and Caesar is illuminating. For one thing it is that between responsible, and irresponsible, power : the latter is the definition of tyranny :

> The abuse of greatness is when it disjoins
> Remorse from power.

Henry V was an English king subject to the rule of law, not a dictator whose wishes *are* laws : a man of a religious conscience, of an ultimate humility, as we saw on the night before Agincourt, as opposed to a semi-divinity, one hailed by the crowd as a god, who encourages the idea, and — though an exceedingly great man — whose weaknesses, as he is depicted, are self-adulation and a measure of self-deception.

The play had all the success it deserved, and made a marked impact. A couple of years later John Weever wrote of the Forum scene already famous :

> The many-headed multitude were drawn
> By Brutus' speech that Caesar was ambitious ;
> When eloquent Mark Antony had shown
> His virtues, who but Brutus then was vicious ?

Years later Leonard Digges wrote of it, comparing it with the failure of Jonson's frigid tragedies :

> So have I seen when Caesar would appear,
> And on the stage at half-sword parley were
> Brutus and Cassius — O, how the audience
> Were ravished ! With what wonder they went thence,
> When some new day they would not brook a line
> Of tedious, though well-laboured, Catiline.
> Sejanus too was irksome, they prizèd more
> Honest Iago, or the jealous Moor.

Sensible groundlings, who wouldn't ? — though it was not the judgment of the groundlings only, but of the whole theatre.

Jonson found this hard to take, and noted down in his notebook of Shakespeare : 'Many times he fell into those things could not escape laughter : as when he said in the person of Caesar, one speaking to him, "Caesar, thou doest me wrong" — he replied, "Caesar did never wrong, but with just cause." And such like : which were ridiculous.' In a play of his own, *The Staple of News*, Ben made fun of the passage and turned it into a joke. By the time of the Folio the original passage had been corrected to read :

> Know, Caesar doth not wrong, nor without cause
> Will he be satisfied.

Antony's words,

> O judgment, thou art fled to brutish beasts,
> And men have lost their reason,

are turned into fustian in *Every Man out of his Humour* ; and the famous '*Et tu, Brute?*' — Caesar's last words — are used nonsensically in the same play. Antony's speech is further ridiculed in a passage of *Cynthia's Revels*. Altogether Ben could not leave *Julius Caesar* alone : its success, against *his* classic rules, narked him.

While writing *Julius Caesar* Shakespeare was reading Daniel's fine poem *Musophilus*, which came out the same year. When Cassius says,

> How many ages hence
> Shall this our lofty scene be acted over
> In states unborn and accents yet unknown ! —

he is reflecting the stanza :

> And who, in time, knows whither we may vent
> The treasure of our tongue, to what strange shores
> This gain of our best glory shall be sent,
> To enrich unknowing nations with our stores ?
> What worlds in the yet unformèd Occident
> May come refined with the accents that are ours ?

It is pleasant to think that Shakespeare was struck with the prophetic sweep of this stanza, which has had its appeal to like-minded people since. From another echo we know that he was reading Sir John Davies' philosophic poem *Nosce Teipsum* of that year. These things add to our portrait : they show the popular dramatist reading the most intellectual works to come out at the time.

For his source Shakespeare was fortunate to have North's translation of Plutarch's *Lives,* the prose of which was so good that in all his Roman plays Shakespeare could adapt whole passages rapidly and easily into blank verse. For the rest he treated Plutarch as he had Holinshed, shaping it to present as good a play as possible, everywhere selecting and rejecting, combining incidents, foreshortening time, taking out the life of the matter to produce a convincing interpretation of the history. Some touches come from Marlowe's translation of Lucan's *Pharsalia*, while use was made of Kyd's translation of Garnier's *Cornelia*. Shakespeare did not cease to borrow the plumes of the intellectuals to dispose them to better purpose.

But the play's the thing. It may be a little enthusiastic to call it 'the most brilliant and the most penetrating artistic reflection of political realities in the literature of the world', and yet it is impossible to think of another that is more so.[43] Two things are astonishing about this play : the extraordinary penetration of the political understanding — such as one very rarely gets from a literary man : it is more like that of a profound political thinker, a Hume or Burke or De Tocqueville ; the other is 'that final impression of dramatic justice which all allow to be one of his chief claims to greatness'.

For notice how he holds the scales fairly between sides, even in regard to that which forfeits our sympathy. The play assumes the greatness of Caesar : he has no difficulty in asserting an ascendancy over all the remarkable men around him ; he towers easily over them : this is why they kill him. He is a potential danger to the liberties of the state, and to theirs. Not that, so far, he has overstepped the bounds ; but· he may do, for on his return to Rome, a conqueror, he is in a position to do so. Brutus admits,

> to speak truth of Caesar,
> I have not known when his affections swayed
> More than his reason.

Now this is the specific, and so rare, essence of the political type : this central judgment, capable of thinking in terms of the well-being of the state, apart from all private interests and affections. This is what, in Shakespeare's time, the Queen notably had, old Burghley and his son Robert Cecil ; Essex, Ralegh and the rest notably had not. Caesar has it in the play : just before he is murdered he rejects a petition that might have saved him :

> What touches ourself shall be last served.

Brutus also has this capacity — which is what makes him the natural leader the conspirators look to ; but he has no gift for ruling — as Caesar had supremely — and this is fatal. Brutus has the fatality of the idealist; he is defeated by the facts of human nature, about which he is wrong, as idealists always are. He has no understanding of what human beings really are like. Caesar had seen through Cassius at one glance, saw him for the restless, envious spirit he was, whose envy of another's greatness gave him no peace. Brutus falls in with his purpose, for the noblest reasons, but does not really understand him. And he makes every conceivable mistake, against Cassius's better judgment — allows Mark Antony to speak at Caesar's funeral and turn the Roman mob against the conspirators; allows the issue to be resolved against them in one last throw, on an unfavourable field of action. He quarrels with Cassius over the recruiting of resources from the provinces: his nobility leaves to others the job of collecting the cash. And yet everyone agrees that Brutus is noble. The ordinary man may well say, God save us from such nobility. One does not much admire this nobility which creates so much suffering for everybody. *Surtout point de zèle !*

On the other hand, Caesar has his weaknesses, and Shakespeare has put them in, partly invented them, to hold the scales more evenly. There is his deafness, his epilepsy, Cassius's story of his fear of drowning, his self-adulation, love of flattery: these also serve the purpose of reducing the semi-divinity to the level of the human. Underneath, there is Shakespeare's philosophic insistence that all men are fallible, that it is a mistake to put too much trust in any one being, system or idea. How did he come to have such a sceptical understanding of everything? I suppose from his hard experience of life, by the lonely course he had made across society so that he saw everyone defined and confined by his position in it — himself outside: an observer, watching everything and everybody.

Nevertheless, Caesar, Caesar's spirit, dominates the play. Those are superficial critics who have not seen that the play has an essential unity. The assassination is at the summit of the arch: everything before it leads up to it; the rest of the action flows from it, is its revenge. In fact, we have 'a plot which is supremely well-proportioned in its distribution of interest and wholly consistent in its development of character, and which seems inevitable in its chain of cause and effect'.[44] At this moment, in 1599, Shakespeare had under view the fatal chain of cause and effect in politics.

The action is accompanied, like a kind of chorus, by the voices of the people. Everybody knows what idiots they are. Even Cassius allows that Caesar

> would not be a wolf
> But that he sees the Romans are but sheep . . .
> What trash is Rome,
> What rubbish and what offal !

And what an exposure of the mob, its fickleness and gullibility, we have in the famous Forum scene. Brutus, like the noble ass he is, appeals to their reason : 'Censure me in your wisdom, and wake your senses, that you may the better judge'. He gets what he deserves, what might be expected — complete misunderstanding : the mob are so persuaded that they are ready to set this republican up for Caesar instead : 'Let him be Caesar'. When he actually pleads with the mob to give Mark Antony a hearing, Antony has no difficulty in gradually turning the mob. First, and an authentic touch : 'poor soul ! his eyes are red as fire with weeping'. Next : 'They were traitors : honourable men ! Villains, murderers.' The crowd had been neatly egged on with appeals to their curiosity and greed to know about Caesar's will. In the end they are so inflamed that they forget about the will ; Antony has even to remind them. They are then rendered so mad that they are ready for murder. They turn on poor Cinna the poet, simply because he has the same name as Cinna the con-spirator. No matter : 'Tear him for his bad verses.' 'Pluck but his name out of his heart.' 'Tear him.' 'Come, brands, ho ! fire-brands ! To Brutus', to Cassius', burn all.' Poor Cinna is left a mangled body : we have been given a spectacle not un-known in democratic communities — a mob-lynching.

What an exposure of human nature in politics it is ! Anyone who has had any experience of an electorate knows how true. In justice we must allow that some mobs are better than others, as some peoples are better than others. All, collectively speaking, are sheep ; but not all are carnivorous sheep. As to the facts, the last word has been said by a philosophic theologian, Bishop Butler : 'Things and actions are what they are, and the conse-quences of them will be what they will be : why then should we desire to be deceived ? '

In so classic a play there are few extraneous notes, or even personal flecks, apart from the whole. Conspiracies were familiar fare to Elizabethans, and this one has a contemporary flavour, when we see the conspirators' faces muffled in their cloaks, their hats plucked about their ears. It was the regular thing to seal such an undertaking with an oath — which Brutus rejects ; while Cassius uses the contemporary phrase for such a band, the 'knot' :

> So often shall the knot of us be called
> The men that gave their country liberty.

Touches of contemporary life appear : 'if the tag-rag people did not clap him and hiss him according as he pleased and displeased them, as they use to do the players in the theatre, I am no true man'. At the crowd-scene in the Forum Casca 'durst not laugh, for fear of opening my lips and receiving the bad air'. One other thing to remember about Elizabethan crowds — the smell !

Shakespeare could not write a play without some revealing, and endearing, glimpses of himself. There is sad experience behind,

> When love begins to sicken and decay,
> It useth an enforcèd ceremony ;

and in,

> A friend should bear his friend's infirmities.

We note the personal application of the lines,

> There is a tide in the affairs of men
> Which taken at the flood leads on to fortune:

Certainly Shakespeare had taken his, with the desired consequence. While, so consistently with this and with what he says ëlsewhere that we may regard it as personal conviction, we have :

> Men at some time are masters of their fates :
> The fault, dear Brutus, is not in our stars
> But in ourselves, that we are underlings.

CHAPTER XIV

Between Two Worlds

THE years 1600 to 1604 saw the great change : the figure that had dominated England and represented her in the eyes of the world for half a century passed from the scene. But not before she had surmounted the last and saddest crisis of the reign with the Essex Rising — the fringes of which touched the Chamberlain's men, and in which the Earl of Southampton was inculpated with Essex. In the theatre, a new period began in 1600 with the reopening of Blackfriars, after so many years, for the performances of the Children of the Chapel. This set up once more a rivalry between the private and the public theatre, of decisive importance for the future, and was accompanied by the outbreak of a stage-quarrel between Ben Jonson on one side, Marston and Dekker on the other, which touched rather more than the fringes of the Chamberlain's men and Shakespeare in particular. These were the years in which he wrote *Hamlet* and *Twelfth Night*, *Troilus and Cressida*, with *All's Well that Ends Well* and *Measure for Measure* — the disenchanted titles of which might well stand as epigraphs for the time.

The stage-quarrel that agitated the theatres began with a misunderstanding between Jonson and young Marston. Marston was a university wit of the new generation, an Oxford man of a satirical, moralising turn of mind, who was made to be Ben's disciple. He intended a flattering portrait of the master in *Histriomastix*, but unhappily this early effort read like a clumsy caricature. The master winced and retorted in kind. Upon which the disciple attacked. Thereupon Jonson portrayed both Marston and his companion Dekker in his next comical satire, *Cynthia's Revels*, the one as a 'light voluptuous reveller', the other as his shabby, foul-mouthed crony. This play was performed by the piping Children of the Chapel, now in competition with the newly revived Children of Paul's, and both in rivalry with the adult companies of the public theatres. *Cynthia's Revels* was a bid for the Queen's favour, with an overt apology for the severity of her treatment of Essex. How crude and tactless ! — perhaps it was intended to take the opportunity when Shakespeare could say nothing. How could he ? — when Southampton was as guilty as Essex and lay under a like condemnation for treason. The Chamberlain's men played at Court on 24 February 1601, the night before Essex was executed.

The quarrel around Ben went on. Marston portrayed him in *What You Will*, but was overborne by the arrogance and scorn of the *Poetaster* in which he was ridiculed as Crispinus. Many other people came under the lash, too, soldiers, lawyers and his fellow-players. Dekker was aroused to give Ben some of his own back in *Satiromastix*, which the Chamberlain's men produced. All this raised up only more enemies for Jonson, his defence of Essex's execution was unpopular — for Essex remained the idol of the people through thick and thin. Threatened with prosecution, Ben withdrew from the warfare and took to the colder climes of classical tragedy. He also withdrew somewhat from public life, left his wife from 1602 to 1607, and went to live on his patrons, Sir Robert Townshend and Esmé Stuart, Lord Aubigny, spending the summers agreeably with Sir Robert Cotton at moated Connington in Huntingdonshire.

At some point in these exchanges even Shakespeare was provoked. Jonson's assumption all through was that he alone stood for the cause of the intellect, for poetry and letters, and that everyone who cared for these things agreed with him. Happily there are different ways of caring for them. It is characteristic of the prudent, elusive Shakespeare that posterity has found it difficult to put its finger on just how and where he scored off Ben. The Cambridge *Return from Parnassus* of 1601 tells us that he did so, while we know that *Hamlet* was performed at both Oxford and Cambridge ; so it may well be that the strictures on loud-mouthed, rumbustious acting may, as I have suggested, have something to do with the case. And this seems to be corroborated by Ben's rueful words :

> Only amongst them [*i.e.* the players] I am sorry for
> Some better natures, by the rest so drawn,
> To run in that vile line.

It reads true to Ben's queasy relations with the older man : admiration, envy, some critical disparagement, independence, in the end an undying gratitude that came out in unexampled generosity when Shakespeare was dead, mingled with affection and some wonderment.

Hamlet was written in 1600–1, for it has references to these and other contemporary happenings — to the eclipses of the sun in these years, that were taken to portend the direful events on the way. It is thought that the lines —

> We go to gain a little patch of ground
> That hath in it no profit but the name —

refers to the siege of Ostend which began in the summer of 1601 : the struggle for those sand-dunes went on for three more years. When Shakespeare embarked on *Hamlet*, *Julius Caesar* was still echoing in his mind, as we see from the first scene :

> In the most high and palmy state of Rome,
> A little ere the mightiest Julius fell,
> The graves stood tenantless, and the sheeted dead
> Did squeak and gibber in the Roman streets ;
> As, stars with trains of fire, and dews of blood,
> Disasters in the sun ; and the moist star
> Upon whose influence Neptune's empire stands
> Was sick almost to doomsday with eclipse —

there were lunar as well as solar eclipses to upset people's nerves —

> And even the like precurse of feared events,
> As harbingers preceding still the fates
> And prologue to the omen coming on,
> Have heaven and earth together demonstrated
> Unto our climatures and countrymen.

That may stand for a description of the dominant mood in the year of *Hamlet* — the cloud over the public scene, with the people's hero in disgrace, withdrawn into an inner world of resentment, meditating treason, thinking of some dramatic *coup* to gain power, in touch with James, gathering his camp-followers from all parts to Essex House, yet for long undecided on any course of action until more impulsive natures, in particular Southampton, wondered whether he was ever going to make a move to right himself.

Such mountains of commentary have been piled on *Hamlet* that we must remind ourselves to keep within the bounds of sanity : it is, after all, a play like any other play. Its Cambridge editor tells us that, the longest of all Shakespeare's plays, it is 'the turning-point of his spiritual and artistic development'.[1] If this seems a large claim we can agree that it is the beginning of those profound searchings of the soul, those explorations of territories on the ultimate limits of human experience, which are the great tragedies. These we can place beside only such comparable, if comparable, works as the Sistine ceiling of Michelangelo, the dynamic Panzer-divisions marching in Beethoven's mind.

One reason for the depths that *Hamlet* plumbs, for the endless reverberations set going in the conscience and in time, is that the story is a primitive one, going right back to the early Middle Ages like a saga, reaching down to the roots of the unconscious in the natal areas of experience : the murder of a brother, the primeval curse of Cain, revenge, piety for the father laying an inhuman burden on the son, incest, the special disturbance when a sensitive son has reason to suspect his mother. All the elements of the story are already present in Saxo Grammaticus in the twelfth century, a contemporary of Geoffrey of Monmouth — to whom European literature owes so much of the Arthurian inspiration. By an interesting rhythm, and perhaps aesthetically aware of what he was doing, after so much of Italy Shakespeare turns to grimmer, more sombre Northern Europe ; as again, after *Othello*, he turns to legendary Britain with *King Lear* and *Macbeth* and *Cymbeline*.

There had already been an earlier play on the subject, now lost, on which Shakespeare based his, with touches from Belleforest. This earlier play seems linked in character and theme, as also by an uncertain but suspicious reference by Nashe, to Kyd and it goes back to Kyd's active period, about 1589, with unmistakable affinities to *The Spanish Tragedy*. A *Hamlet* was acted at Newington Butts in June 1594 ; it continued to hold the stage, for in 1596 Lodge has a reference to 'the ghost which cried so miserably at the theatre, like an oyster-wife, "Hamlet, revenge !" '[2] This phrase became a household word, and was picked out by Dekker in his burlesque of Jonson. So the original *Hamlet* was close to Shakespeare's : it was a revenge-tragedy with a ghost. To what a miracle of art — for it has everything in it — Shakespeare transformed the old play ! Shakespeare brought the ghost into the story, and made him Hamlet's father.

So much criticism of the play has related to the character of Hamlet that, though this is beside our purpose, it is well to remind ourselves that he is but a character in a play, bounded by the exigencies of the drama and to be understood in that context.

Though the subtlest of characters in the history of our stage, his interest is not illimitable and should be definable. He is, above all, an intellectual, not a man of action ; again, he is not really a political type — as his uncle Claudius well sees :

> being remiss,
> Most generous, and free from all contriving.

Yet he has a sacred injunction laid upon him by his murdered father to revenge him. It is an ultimate human situation like that of Orestes — and yet, so much more psychologically interesting and varied ; for Hamlet, as a modern, has free will and it is open to him to do it or not to do it. (Orestes is caught in the ineluctable curse upon the house of Atreus and has no choice.) Not being a man of action, Hamlet's first thought on receiving the fatal injunction is suicide :

> that the Everlasting had not fixed
> His canon 'gainst self-slaughter !

His second reaction is that the Ghost's story of murder needs corroboration, and this is what the inset-play, 'The Murder of Gonzago' achieves for him. Now he knows for certain : 'O good Horatio, I'll take the Ghost's word for a thousand pound.' But he chooses not to kill his uncle when praying in his closet and thus needs his dead father's renewed prompting :

> this visitation
> Is but to whet thy almost blunted purpose.

In his heart, Hamlet does not want to act :

> The time is out of joint : O cursed spite
> That I was ever born to set it right !

In the famous characterisation of him —

> The courtier's, soldier's, scholar's, eye, tongue, sword,
> The expectancy and rose of the fair state,
> The glass of fashion, and the mould of form,
> The observed of all observers —

he is really much more the scholar and courtier, than the soldier. Here, though I wish to preclude myself from the crudity of thinking that Hamlet was based on Essex, this does not exclude the possibility that a touch was drawn from Essex at this point, Essex too, was 'the observed of all observers'; all his friends thought of him as 'the rose and expectancy of the fair state'.

To gain time to make up his mind what to do Hamlet feigns madness, and this serves his purpose : it confuses his uncle for some time, until he, being a real political type, suspects danger behind it. Placing himself to overhear Hamlet's conversation with Ophelia, he concludes,

> what he spake, though it lacked form a little,
> Was not like madness. There's something in his soul
> O'er which his melancholy sits on brood ;
> And I do doubt the hatch and the disclose
> Will be some danger.

Feigned madness is in the tradition of revenge-tragedy, and we have seen Shakespeare's first attempt at it in *Titus Andronicus*. In Hamlet it is at a far higher voltage of power, reality and persuasiveness, and it immensely intensifies the excitement of the drama. Our excitement grows with his, until the terrible poignancy of his psychotic dialogue with Ophelia, for it has in it all the anguish of love betrayed — he thinks she has lent herself to the purposes of her father and the King against him — becomes almost unbearable. Hamlet's speech is brilliantly bitter — just like a clever man on edge with love denied and fancied betrayal.

Though there may be touches of Essex, there is far more of William Shakespeare in Hamlet. Everyone sees that he is the most autobiographical of all the characters : Shakespeare sees many of his creations from the inside — it is a prime gift — but he sees Hamlet in a special way, fondly, and cannot let go of him. No wonder the play goes on and on, probing ever further into the crevices of the heart. It is the first play, too, to exemplify the psychotic, and so authentic, reflexion of disgust with sex that becomes marked with Shakespeare in these years, with *Troilus and Cressida* and *Lear*, and perhaps *Measure for Measure* and *Othello*. 'Why would'st thou be a breeder of sinners ? I am myself indifferent honest, but yet I could accuse me of such things that it were better my mother had not borne me.' It is like Swift, and we know the madness in Swift's blood that made him think like that. When Hamlet comes to the scene with his mother —

> Nay, but to live
> In the rank sweat of an enseamèd bed,
> Stewed in corruption, honeying and making love
> Over the nasty sty ! —

it is no less terrible to see and hear than it is psychologically true. At the heart of his grievous experience of life, Hamlet has his creator's moral discrimination :

> Refrain tonight,
> And that shall lend a kind of easiness
> To the next abstinence ; the next more easy ;
> For use can almost change the stamp of nature.

To turn to our particular purpose, which is not dull analysis but illumination — the play has been described as 'the most topical in the whole corpus' : I am less sure of this than that, at a deeper level, it is full of political reflection.[3] Naturally, with such a theme in such a context. There is the theme of royal marriages, which had filled the century earlier with alarms and excursions — even today, apparently, they are not without interest to the public. Now Hamlet's :

> His greatness weighed, his will is not his own,
> For he himself is subject to his birth :
> He may not, as unvalued persons do,
> Carve for himself ; for on his choice depends
> The sanity and health of this whole state.

Therefore his choice has to be circumscribed by the voice of the body of which he is to become the head. Still more, his madness becomes a question of state ; as his uncle says,

> Madness in great ones must not unwatched go.

As much might be said of Essex, who was as temperamental and unbalanced, as hysterical and moody, as subject to melancholy, as Hamlet.

We may reasonably see a touch of Essex in the King's —

> How dangerous is it that this man goes loose !
> Yet must we not put the strong law on him :
> He's loved of the distracted multitude,
> Who like not in their judgment but their eyes ;
> And where 'tis so, the offender's scourge is weighed,
> But never the offence.

This was exactly the Queen's position with regard to Essex after his return from Ireland. She alone knew his treasonable contacts, what he had discussed with Tyrone at the ford, and had good reason to suspect his intentions. But she could not put her case to the people : the *arcana imperii* could never be discussed or brought into the light of day ; so her case went by default, and she was much blamed by the multitude for her punishment of their favourite. They were capable of seeing only 'the offender's scourge . . . but never the offence'. If this interpretation is correct, it shows once more Shakespeare's judgment on the matter, withdrawing his sympathy from the popular leader, with whom Southampton had completely thrown in his lot.

Nor do I think we need hesitate to see reflections of old Lord Burghley in old Polonius — not only in the fact that their positions were the same in the state, the leading minister in close proximity to the sovereign, in ancient smug security. Shakespeare had had plenty of opportunity to imbibe Southampton's unfavourable view of the prosy and meddling Lord Treasurer. It is not so much that there is question of the marriage of his daughter to the prince, but that his whole personality reflects the view of these young men, while there are certain specific references reflecting Burghley's known characteristics. Burghley had died in 1598, and it was safe enough to represent these in general terms. To the glittering gallants of the younger generation the Lord Treasurer had been a great bore, and no doubt he was, with his old-fashioned sententiousness and his moralising — still more with his unshakable hold on power. But they were incapable of appreciating his immense services to the state, the wisdom that lay behind the 'policy' of which he had reason to be proud.

Burghley had left a series of Precepts for his clever son Robert Cecil, which became famous for their combination of piety with worldly wisdom. Everyone in the circle of the Court would know them. Polonius gives his parting son, Laertes, a similar set which smack of the same character in their prosy prudence, moderation and self-interest.

> And these few precepts in thy memory
> Look thou character. Give thy thoughts no tongue,
> Nor any unproportioned thought his act.
> Be thou familiar, but by no means vulgar.

'Vulgar' in the Elizabethan sense meant courting popularity, as Essex had done. One clue to Burghley's power had been his intelligence-system : like Polonius he knew everything about everybody :

> Look you, sir,
> Enquire me first what Danskers are in Paris ;
> And how, and who, what means and where they keep,
> What company, at what expense . . .

And so on. Sober Polonius has one source of smug pride, that he is very politic : he thinks he has discovered the source of Hamlet's lunacy :

> or else this brain of mine
> Hunts not the trail of policy so sure
> As it hath used to do.

We have reason to think of *Hamlet* as the most autobiographical of the plays, in the sense that it is fullest of what Shakespeare himself thought about the theatre. We have already cited his criticisms of contemporary acting. He satirises the attachment of dull people to formal categories by putting them into the mouth of Polonius — *he* would be the person to attach importance to them : 'the best actors in the world, either for tragedy, comedy, history, pastoral, pastoral-comical, historical-pastoral, tragical-historical, tragical-comical-historical-pastoral, scene individable, or poem unlimited'. There is also Shakespeare's commentary on the revival of the private theatre, with the new popularity of the Children's performances taking away somewhat from the appeal of the adult companies. 'Their endeavour keeps in the wonted pace ; but there is, sir, an eyrie of children, little eyases, that cry out on the top of the question and are most tyrannically clapped for it. These are now the fashion, and so berattle the common stages — so they call them — that many wearing rapiers are afraid of goose quills and dare scarce come thither.'

'The common stages, *so they call them*' — the phrase shows a trace of resentment at being written down by the intellectuals of the private theatres, Ben Jonson in the van. It had been a recurring theme in Shakespeare's career, first to have been dis-considered by the earlier university wits, attacked by Greene for being too successful, almost pushed out of Southampton's favour by Marlowe. In these next years, 1600 to 1608, he was put on his mettle by the rivalry of the Blackfriars theatre, with its increasing appeal to fashion and wit — until the Globe itself was forced to take over the Blackfriars in self-defence. We shall see how superbly he responded to the challenge with his own experiment in comical satire, the intellectual comedies, the great tragedies, the Roman plays and the last romances. It seems that, as in the earlier years of his career, his genius achieved the more for having something to pit itself against.

Meanwhile, the private theatre, with its special line in satire and music in the act-intervals — which the public theatre was gradually forced to adopt in competition — was all the rage with wit and fashion. *Hamlet* gives us Shakespeare's first reaction to the new development. 'The least we know is that he was a real actor-author in a real public theatre ; and the least we may infer is that he was capable of evaluating himself and his situation. Does it not follow that he neither accepted nor viewed with indifference the judgment that the popular plays were inferior as a class ?'[4]

Meanwhile, 'what, are they children ? Who maintains 'em ? . . . Will they pursue the quality no longer than they can sing ? Will they not say afterwards, if they should grow themselves to common players — as it is most like, if their means are no better — their writers do them wrong to make them exclaim against their own succession ?' *There* is a touch of his characteristic prudence expressed in his no less characteristic grand language. Touchingly embedded in it are the very words he had used of himself years before —

> That did not better for my life provide
> Than public means which public manners breeds.

He proceeds to refer to the stage-quarrel : 'Faith, there has been much to-do on both sides ; and the nation holds it no sin to tarre [provoke] them to controversy. There was for a while no money bid for argument, unless the poet and the player went to cuffs in the question.' This shows that the stage-warfare had at least been a good draw. And, 'O, there has been much throwing about of brains'. This off-hand reference shows what Shakespeare really thought of the dog-fight — it was as good as throwing away brains on such stuff. Lastly, 'do the boys carry it away ?' 'Ay, that they do, my lord — Hercules and his load, too.' That is a comic reference to the Globe itself, with its sign of Hercules carrying the globe, and shows a fair confidence in its ability to survive.

How much of his dual experience as player and playwright has gone into this !—

> Is it not monstrous that this player here
> But in a fiction, in a dream of passion,
> Could force his soul so to his own conceit
> That from her working all his visage wanned :
> Tears in his eyes, distraction in's aspect,
> A broken voice, and his whole function suiting
> With forms to his conceit ? And all for nothing !

> For Hecuba !
> What's Hecuba to him or he to Hecuba,
> That he should weep for her ? What would he do
> Had he the motive and the cue for passion
> That I have ?

But Hamlet is only a player of no more substance than Hecuba :
we see once again this double reflexive, the ambivalence, that
runs through and through Shakespeare — using a player as if
outside the play, a person in real life, to comment on the player
within. Confidence in his craft could go no further. And such
is the power of his genius that we accept the creatures of his
imagination as real inhabitants of our own, with whom we live.
Here there is pride, too, in his profession : let the players be well
used, 'for they are the abstract and brief chronicles of the time ;
after your death you were better have a bad epitaph than their
ill report while you live'.

In this most autobiographical of the plays it is touching to
catch an echo from the earlier Sonnets :

> The canker galls the infants of the spring
> Too oft before their buttons are disclosed.

The 'hebona' with which Claudius poisoned Hamlet's father
came from Marlowe's likely imagination, out of *The Jew of Malta*.
It is thought that the Pyrrhus speech rehearsed by the players
before Hamlet may have come from an earlier piece of Shakespeare's written in competition with an earlier *Dido*, perhaps
Marlowe's, 'to show that he could better its style and criticise
it at the same time'.[5] Certainly a couple of lines of Marlowe's
Dido —

> Which he disdaining, whisked his sword about,
> And with the wind thereof the king fell down —

are guyed :

> But with the whiff and wind of his fell sword
> The unnerved father falls.

Hundreds of lines of the earlier drama Shakespeare seems to have
had in his head, many of them perhaps from playing in it.

How continuous, too, from his early days is his fondness for
grand language — a particular fondness for latinized adjectives
is one of the characteristics of his style :

> Nor customary suits of solemn black,
> Nor windy suspiration of forced breath . . .

> Let it be tenable in your silence still . . .

> The form of plausive manners.

He was specially addicted to adjectives ending in 'ive', like plausive, tortive, insistive, suspensive, defunctive, semblative, corresponsive, persistive ; though he also liked words such as waftage, or wafture, fraughtage, questant, insisture, vastidity, prolixious, concupiscible, adoptious, deceptious — many of them of his own coinage ; a rolling phrase like 'corporal sufferance', or 'prenominate in nice conjecture'.

His personal beliefs are bound to have left traces in the plays — sometimes in relation to the folklore he inherited and out of which he grew. On the cock crowing on Christmas Day :

> Some say that ever 'gainst that season comes
> Wherein our Saviour's birth is celebrated,
> The bird of dawning singeth all night long :
> And then, they say, no spirit dare stir abroad,
> The nights are wholesome, then no planets strike,
> No fairy takes, nor witch hath power to charm,
> So hallowed and so gracious is the time.

The comment on this comes very persuasively :

> So have I heard, and do in part believe it.

Claudius's self-reproach indicates his creator's values :

> In the corrupted currents of this world
> Offence's gilded hand may shove by justice ;
> And oft 'tis seen the wicked prize itself
> Buys out the law. But 'tis not so above :
> There is no shuffling : there the action lies
> In his true nature ; and we ourselves compelled,
> Even to the teeth and forehead of our faults,
> To give in evidence.

The scene in the churchyard gives opportunity for reflection on all conditions of men. One gravedigger comments on Ophelia's suicide : 'will you ha' the truth on't ? If this had not been a gentlewoman, she should have been buried out a' Christian burial.' Ophelia's death by drowning may have been suggested by an event that made an impression on the little community of Stratford when Shakespeare was a boy of sixteen. Katherine Hamlet was drowned in the Avon at Tiddington at the end of the year 1579. With Shakespeare the name Hamlet would be enough to bring it all back, and this is the more likely in that there had had to be a coroner's inquest in Stratford with twelve men of the jury to decide whether it was an accident or suicide.[6]

Hamlet is in his element among the skulls : 'this might be the pate of a politician, which this ass now o'er-reaches : one that would circumvent God, might it not ? . . . Or of a courtier, which could say, "Good morrow, sweet lord ! How dost thou, sweet lord ?" This might be my Lord Such-a-one, that praised my Lord Such-a-one's horse, when 'a meant to beg it — might it not ?' This was a regular gambit of the time. 'Why may not that be the skull of a lawyer ? Where be his quiddities now, his quillets, his cases, his tenures, and his tricks ?' The graveyard is a great leveller, and anyone who knows a country churchyard and the discourse of country sextons will recognise how authentic the gravediggers in *Hamlet* are. Hamlet was to have been sent out of the way into England. 'Why ? because 'a was mad : 'a shall recover his wits there ; or, if 'a do not, 'tis no great matter there. . . . 'Twill not be seen in him there : there the men are as mad as he.'

This must have raised a laugh ; but, like so much of the laughing in *Hamlet*, it was a bitter jest. In that year when the play was written, there was much in it — especially at the top of society, beginning with Shakespeare's noble acquaintance.

At the beginning of February 1601 Essex's crazily unstable career reached its term with the mad enterprise to seize the Court and the Queen's person, and force her to change her government. Such a *coup* would have been fatal to the monarchy, even if they did not mean to take her life — though Essex's stepfather, Sir Charles Blount, admitted that they would not have stopped short of shedding blood. Essex had called his followers from all parts up to London ; he meant to time his move with the arrival of James's ambassadors from Scotland. On 3 February a final meeting of the leaders was held in Southampton's lodgings at Drury House to decide on their plans : after the Court was surprised, the two Earls alone were to penetrate to the Privy Chamber into the Queen's presence. When the others drew back, Southampton, who egged Essex on, demanded in passion, 'shall we resolve upon nothing then ?' On 7 February some of the conspirators procured a performance of *Richard II* at the Globe to put them in a good frame of mind. Augustine Phillips gave evidence afterwards that 'Sir Charles Percy, Sir Jocelyn Percy and the Lord Monteagle with some three more spoke to some of the players to have the play of the deposing and killing of King Richard II to be played . . . promising to get them 40s. more than their ordinary to play it. Where this examinate and his fellows were determined to have played some other play, holding that play of King Richard to be old and so long out of use that they should have small or no company at it. But at their request this examinate and his fellows were content to play it the Saturday.'[7]

That evening the Council sprang the mine prematurely by summoning Essex to its presence. Next day he broke out into the City hoping to turn the credit of his popularity into the coin of treason. But London was not Paris, following a Duke of Guise against its sovereign, and the tumult sputtered out in fiasco and dismay. Within Essex House, a Welsh captain, Owen Salusbury, was killed and a footman of Southampton's. The discipline of the English state held good, and all was soon over ; there remained only the price to pay. Essex and Southampton were tried together by their peers in Westminster Hall, and both condemned to death. Essex went forward to die with dignity, and in the odour, if not the reality, of sanctity on the block.

Secretary Cecil was besieged by appeals for mercy from Southampton's wife and mother. The dowager Countess wrote, 'God of heaven knows I can scarce hold my hand steady to write and less hold steady in my heart how to write, only for what I know, which is to pray mercy to my miserable son. . . . It appeared to me many times his earnest desire to secure her Majesty's favour, his doleful discontented behaviour when he could not obtain it, how apt despair made him at length to receive evil counsel and follow such company.'[8] This was true enough — but then Southampton had never gone the way to deserve favour. Cecil was determined to save the young Earl's life : he went a condemned man to the Tower, ill and shaking with ague, but to imprisonment, not death. We have a grateful letter from his mother to Cecil : 'I could hate myself and sex that bars me from showing my love to you as most I would, yet, as I can, I desire to assure you that no alteration of time or fortune can make me forget my bond to you for me and mine, who under God breathe by your means'.

The government was moderate and humane in its treatment of the conspirators, executing only some half a dozen ; but among them was Sir Charles Danvers, Southampton's friend. The Earl spent the remaining two years of the Queen's reign in the Tower. We have a well-known portrait of him from this time, standing in front of his panelled window-seat there, looking sadder and older, as well he might be ; there are the fine expressive eyes and the long locks falling on both shoulders, but with moustache and belated incipient beard. He is soberly but richly dressed, gloved hand with love-knots, signet ring on the little finger of the bare left hand. On the window sill rests a finely bound book, embossed with coronet and coat-of-arms ; behind is perched his attendant black and white cat, very pert and more prudent than its master.

This year 1600-1, that had seen *Hamlet* written, the Essex conspiracy run its course and Southampton shut up in the Tower, also saw a very curious production to which Shakespeare contributed a unique poem, 'The Phoenix and the Turtle'. This has given trouble to almost all commentators, many of whom have found the poem unintelligible. Others have thought there was some elaborate mystification about the book, *Love's Martyr*, in which it appeared, or an allegory about the Queen and Essex. Not at all. Those who know the ways of the Elizabethan mind recognise that things are very often what they say they are — that there is a literalness about the foundation, a factuality, upon which there is constructed a fantasy, often so elaborate, as with their decorative schemes, that it overruns the basic pattern.

Love's Martyr was produced in 1601 by Robert Chester in honour of the long married happiness of Sir John Salusbury of Llewenny in North Wales and his wife Ursula Stanley, of the Derby family. Sir John was himself the son of the celebrated Katherine of Berain, daughter of a natural son of Henry VII. Salusbury was Esquire of the Body to his cousin, the Queen — so there is no mystery in the fact that they were all dramatists who contributed their tributes in a supplement to the book : Shakespeare, Jonson, Chapman, Marston. Naturally they would come in contact with Sir John in presenting plays at Court. The Vatum Chorus, probably Jonson, makes the purpose clear :

> To your high influence we commend
> Our following labours, and sustend
> Our mutual palms, prepared to gratulate
> An honourable friend . . .

The bulk of the book consisted of rambling poems by Robert Chester, probably a dependant of Sir John, who realised that the effort was rather beyond him and wrote disarmingly in the Preface, that 'if Absurdity like a thief have crept into any part of these poems, your well-graced name will overshadow these defaults'.[9] It had ; but we must be grateful to Robert Chester's absurd venture for recruiting to itself a poem of supreme beauty. For, given the place of honour in the Supplement of 'Poetical Essays . . . done by the best and chiefest of our modern writers' stands Shakespeare's 'The Phoenix and the Turtle'.

Everybody agrees that it is an extraordinary poem, 'uniquely beautiful', of an 'unearthly simplicity', 'high fantasy, verging on the nonsensical'.[10] Indeed it stands out like a sunset-irradiated peak above the commonplace foothills of the other poets, the lowlands of poor Chester's 'untuned stringèd verse'. A modern poet has a fine evocation of it in general terms : 'this poem gives to a flock of thoughts about the passing of truth and beauty the mystery and vitality of birds, who came from a far country, to fill the mind with their crying'.[11] But what is it about ? It is Shakespeare's variation on the set theme of the book, the chaste love of these two improbable birds, their immolation and identity in love and death, emblem of truth in love to eternity.

In writing this poem, on a theme trembling on the verge between fantasy and nonsense, something happened within Shakespeare's imagination, to call up the deepest associations and transmute them, give them a meaning hardly otherwise expressible. The subject became an emblem, and therefore a release for the deepest feeling, which could not be made too precise. For the subject is the death of love.

But it is also its celebration. With this release into a pure world of emblem-language, it was possible to state once more what had been its true nature, and to lay it up for ever in perfect, almost abstract, form.

It leads us into the heart of Shakespeare's genius, for it is pure inspiration, welling up from what depths, as if effortlessly, to achieve the perfection of a work of nature — a sea-shell with its whorls. Another modern poet has seen that 'in this curious poem, sprung from as curious a set of circumstances, we see the imaginative power which charges one after another of Shakespeare's mature plays with inexhaustible suggestions of meaning. Nowhere else, however, have we an opportunity to see this power at work in isolation and in so small a compass.' As for its un-strained, achieved technique, so natural as to appear hardly conscious, 'the poem shows unsurpassed musical imagination, in its passage from the quatrains of the first section to the tercets of the *Threnos*; as the mood is evoked and rises to its full intensity, the verse follows it, seems to climb and soar in flight'. It is in fact poetry pure, the essence of poetry, like Valéry's *Charmes* or Rilke's *Sonnette an Orpheus*. Mallarmé erected it into theory, but it is strange, almost psychically strange, that Shakespeare should have provided a specimen of it centuries before, with that organ of intuition unexampled in literature. It is, in short, a surrealist, rather than a metaphysical, poem.

But it is not, as many have thought, inexplicable. Something in the emblematic theme — the mysterious theme of birds, their song, their flight and death — spoke to the folk-memories in him that always fed his inner life. It is a funeral poem : the birds have gathered together to sing the requiem of the chaste lovers, united in death, the phoenix — a royal bird, and the dove, emblem of humble fidelity.

> Let the bird of loudest lay
> On the sole Arabian tree
> Herald sad and trumpet be,
> To whose sound chaste wings obey . . . .
>
> Let the priest in surplice white,
> That defunctive music can,
> Be the death-divining swan,
> Lest the requiem lack his right . . .

The second section consists of the anthem for dead love :

> So they loved, as love in twain
> Had the essence but in one :
> Two distincts, division none ;
> Number there in love was slain.

Where have we met this before ? In the *Sonnets* :

> Let me confess that we two must be twain,
> Although our undivided loves are one.

The anthem continues :

> Hearts remote, yet not asunder ;
> Distance and no space was seen . . .

So between them love did shine
That the turtle saw his right
Flaming in the phoenix' sight ;
Either was the other's mine.

And so to the *Threnos* :

Beauty, truth and rarity,
Grace in all simplicity,
Here enclosed, in cinders lie . . .

Leaving no posterity :
'Twas not their infirmity,
It was married chastity.

Truth may seem, but cannot be ;
Beauty brag, but 'tis not she ;
Truth and beauty buried be.

Need one doubt the experience that was transmuted into this
strange and remote poem ? Its theme was love, now dead, grieved
over, folded and laid away for good.

Everyone has noticed the melancholy music that overhangs
Twelfth Night, written at this time, and it is not to be wondered
at. That mood of the play is given in the very first lines :

If music be the food of love, play on ;
Give me excess of it, that surfeiting
The appetite may sicken, and so die.
That strain again ! it had a dying fall . . .

It is the last of the comedies. The lawyer John Manningham
saw it performed at the Middle Temple on 2 February 1602 :
'at our feast we had a play called *Twelfth Night*, or *What You
Will*, much like the comedy of Errors or *Menaechmi* in Plautus ;
but most like and near to that in Italian called *Inganni*'.[12] In January
1601 Valentine Orsino, Duke of Bracciano, visited the Queen
and contributed two names — Orsino for the Duke, Valentine
for his gentleman — to Shakespeare's incubating comedy. Other
contemporary references help to fix the date to 1601. The year
before there appeared the account of the Shirley brothers' visit
to the Shah of Persia, or Sophy as the Elizabethans knew him.
Shakespeare probably read it, for there are two references to it :
'I will not give my part of this sport for a pension of thousands

to be paid from the Sophy'. 'They say he has been fencer to the Sophy.' The 'icicle on a Dutchman's beard' probably formed on that of William Barentz, the Dutch navigator whose voyage to Nova Zembla was much talked about in the preceding couple of years. Maria's reference to Malvolio smiling his face 'into more lines than is in the new map with the augmentation of the Indies' refers to the rhumb-lines in the first English map to appear, drawn on the principles of projection. It was produced by Edward Wright, Richard Hakluyt and John Davis in 1600, and gave a much larger space to the New World, *i.e.* the Indies, than before. A snatch of song comes from Robert Jones's *First Book of Songs and Airs*, which came out in the same year.

We see the kind of things Shakespeare noticed among the new things appearing, and the spread of his alert interests.

He took his main plot from an Italian comedy, *Gl' ingannati*, which had much success all over Europe and was imitated by another play, *Gl' inganni* ; apparently he knew both of these. We have to think of him as more professionally aware of what was going on on the European stage, especially that of Italy, both the Commedia Erudita and the Commedia dell' Arte, which exerted such an influence on the theatre in all countries. And it would not have been difficult for this clever man, with his grounding in Latin, to pick up enough Italian. We know that in some cases — the source of *Othello*, for instance — he read the originals. As usual, it is not what he borrowed that is most interesting, but what he added : the character of Malvolio, those of Sir Toby Belch and Maria, Feste the fool. When that appreciative reader Charles I read the play he inscribed as a title for it, 'Malvolio'. And all that part is what is most real and remains in the mind.

Q. has spoken well of the play's mood of disenchantment. 'We are . . . at 1601, and are dealing with a Shakespeare thirty-seven years old ; with a playwright who has mastered the dramatic trick and can play with it at will ; with an artist on the verge of using his skill to conquer the new kingdom of Tragedy : with a man who (however we speculate on the cause of it) had somehow acquired, or was in process of acquiring, a distrust of men's loyalty and a suspicion alive to smell the fitch in woman's purity.'[13] What wonder ? Q. also notices that this Farewell to Comedy recapitulates with easy mastery all the tricks Shakespeare had learnt from the beginning.

We find it a tissue of incidents, of characters, of situations, which have been proved effective by previous stage-experiments. Confusion of identity has been worked in *The Comedy of Errors*, with the ship-wreck that leads to recognition, and the friendly ship-captain who goes to explore the strange town. This friendship of an elderly man for a youth reappears in *The Merchant of Venice*, and Antonio, the friend's name in that play, is Antonio again in this. Viola again — the boy-actor exchanging skirts for trunk-hose, revives Julia, and like Julia attends her chosen lover as a page — revives also Portia, Nerissa, Jessica, Rosalind — all by different ways working up towards Imogen, paragon of women in boy's attire. We all recognise Sir Toby and Aguecheek as sibs to Falstaff and Slender : the trick played on Malvolio is cross-cradle with that played on Beatrice and Benedick — and so on.

In fine, at this turning-point in his career, it is time for him to explore the new and grander territories opened up by *Hamlet*. *Twelfth Night* is in the nature of a coda.

A contemporary happening has been caught up by Shake-speare to create the most amusing episodes of the play. During these years there was a great deal of fun over the ridiculous figure of Sir Thomas Posthumus Hoby, who exposed himself in an absurd posture over a case he should never have brought.[14] He was the son of the egregious Lady Russell who had kept Shake-speare's company out of the Blackfriars in 1596. Undersized, spindle-shanked, hunch-backed and, as everybody said, impotent, he was married to an East Riding heiress who, poor lady, took to evangelical religion in a big way : hence the well-known Journal of holy conversation of the Lady Margaret Hoby. Sir Thomas was a good deal of a Puritan too — 'dost think because thou art virtuous there shall be no more cakes and ale ?' — and made himself obnoxious in Yorkshire by interfering with the jollities of his Catholic neighbours. In Posthumus's absence from home a party of these good fellows entertained themselves in his house, helped themselves liberally to his cakes and ale, especially the latter, made a perfect uproar all night and next day, much interfering with the devotions of his religious lady. Worst of all, they had made the little man ridiculous, and, spirited as a bantam, he did not cease to splutter and fume in the courts. This was better still : everybody appreciated the joke.

Sir Thomas Hoby — Sir Toby : the chime of name and the transference of character are very like Shakespeare. Malvolio is made something of a Puritan. 'O, if I thought that,' squeaks

Sir Andrew, 'I'd beat him like a dog.' Sir Toby: 'What, for being a Puritan? thy exquisite reason, dear knight?' With the players, any stick was good enough to beat a dog of a Puritan with. We have a further reference to Puritans from the lips of Sir Andrew: he hates 'policy': 'I had as lief be a Brownist, as a politician'. Robert Browne was the unattractive, ill-tempered, wife-beating founder of the Independents, who were to win (temporarily) with Oliver Cromwell. To the Elizabethans the word 'politician' had not the endearing overtones it has for us today. Malvolio's misfortune was to combine the disabilities of both: nobody loved him; smug and self-satisfied, a prude disapproving of others and a spoil-sport, he was easily made a laughing-stock of, as Sir Thomas Posthumus Hoby had been.

Of other contemporary touches there are some, as usual, to appeal to the young men of the Inns of Court. 'Still you keep o' the windy side of the law' may have been a common phrase: it has become proverbial. 'Scout me for him at the corner of the orchard like a bum-baily': the skulking bailiff, lying in wait to arrest for debt, was a familiar figure to law-students — as to John Shakespeare in his time. Rather than fight, cowardly Sir Andrew 'will have an action of battery against him [Sebastian], if there be any law in Illyria'. We have another of Shakespeare's frequent references to that familiar feature of social life — bear-baiting. Then there is the wise woman — 'carry his water to the wise woman', the suggestion being that Malvolio is bewitched — of whom there were many about the country in those times, nor has the breed altogether died out in ours. The spinsters and lace-makers have, however:

> The spinsters and the knitters in the sun,
> And the free maids that weave their thread with bones.

The name of Sir Topas probably comes from a favourite book of Shakespeare's, Reginald Scot's *Discoverie of Witchcraft*: much to Shakespeare's mind for the sceptical tolerance of its outlook, displeasing to Calvinist King James and Puritans for the same reason.

What a thousand pities it is that we have not Shakespeare's library left as we have Robert Burton's and Sir Arthur Throckmorton's, much of Ben Jonson's and Donne's!

For personal touches, it is charming to hear 'the bells of St. Bennet', whether from some old popular rhyme or in actuality —

for St. Bennet Hithe, Paul's Wharf, was just across the water from the Globe. We are reminded of Shakespeare's consistent hatred of ingratitude :

> I hate ingratitude more in a man
> Than lying vainness, babbling drunkenness,
> Or any taint of vice whose strong corruption
> Inhabits our frail blood.

These lines on marriage have, not unnaturally, been given a personal application :

> let still the woman take
> An elder than herself ; so wears she to him,
> So sways she level in her husband's heart . . .
> Our fancies are more giddy and unfirm,
> More longing, wavering, sooner lost and won,
> Than women's are.

We know where Shakespeare was living in London in 1602 : he was lodging in the house of Christopher Mountjoy, a French Huguenot tiremaker, or headdress-maker, at the corner of Silver Street and Monkswell Street in Cripplegate ward. This nook of the City was due north of St. Paul's, enclosed within the north-west corner of the City Wall, with bastions thrust strongly out into the moat. Immediately without was St. Giles', Cripplegate, where John Milton's bones were laid later in the century. Monks-well Street ran parallel to the Wall up to the well from which it took its name ; at the bottom corner the Mountjoys' little house looked across the street to large Windsor House and further down to the parish church of St. Olave. In this enclave were the halls of several City companies, the Haberdashers', Surgeons' and, at the top corner, the Bowyers' . Two foundations of almshouses testified to civic spirit : one in neighbouring Wood Street of the previous century, the other of recent foundation, 1575, 'wherein be placed twelve poor and aged people rent free, having of them seven pence the week, and once a year each of them five sacks of charcoals, and one quarter of an hundred of faggots'.[15] These almshouses Shakespeare would see as he went up the street on the right ; business would call him more frequently down Foster Lane or Wood Street to the chafferings of Cheapside or the commerce round St. Paul's, where the publishers had their book-stalls. St. Paul's churchyard might be said to be the centre of London's literary life : here he was not far away.

In 1604 Stephen Belott, a French apprentice, married his

master's daughter, Mary, and in this affair Shakespeare took a keen interest and played an important part. Some years later Belott quarrelled with his father-in-law about his wife's portion and brought a suit in 1612, when Shakespeare came down from Stratford to give evidence in the case. Other members of the household seemed to remember better than himself the part he had played. Joan Johnson deposed that Mountjoy 'did send and persuade one Master Shakespeare that lay in the house to persuade the plaintiff [*i.e.* Belott] to the said marriage'.[16] Daniel Nicholas said that 'he heard one William Shakespeare say that the defendant [*i.e.* Mountjoy] did bear a good opinion of the plaintiff and affected him well when he served him, and did move the plaintiff by him the said Shakespeare to have a marriage between his daughter, Mary Mountjoy, and the plaintiff. . . . Whereupon, and in regard Master Shakespeare had told them that they should have a sum of money for a portion from the father, they were made sure by Master Shakespeare by giving their consent and agreed to marry . . . and did marry.' This means that it was Shakespeare who betrothed or contracted the young couple, though 'giving each other's hand' has been deleted from the deposition.

When Shakespeare came to give his evidence in 1612 he is described as 'of Stratford upon Avon in the county of Warwick, gentleman, of the age of forty eight years or thereabouts'. He had known the parties for the space of ten years or so, *i.e.* from 1602. His opinion of Belott was that he was 'a very good and industrious servant in the said service'. He next gave evidence that it was Madame Mountjoy — likely enough — who had prevailed on him to promote the marriage : 'the said defendant's wife did solicit and entreat this deponent to move and persuade the said complainant to effect the said marriage'. When it came to the details of the portion promised or the legacy Mary Mountjoy should have from her father's will, Shakespeare could not remember. How like him ! — one does not know whether this was prudence again, or a genuine failure of memory. He did recall that 'they had amongst themselves many conferences about their marriage which afterwards was consummated and solemnized. And more he cannot depose.'

How much like one of his own plays it is, and what would we not give to know more of the background ! It was intended to press his memory further, for a second set of interrogatories was prepared for him, but he did not appear to answer them. The case came to the elders of the French church to arbitrate, and they noted 'tous deux, père et gendre, débauchés'. So we can hardly think that it was a very respectable household. What it indicates is that Shakespeare — though he had two brothers living in London — did not bring his family up from Stratford, but had two separate lives. He lived in lodgings in London, but went home to Stratford for the summers. Very convenient, and more stimulating to the imagination.

In May of this year Shakespeare carried through his first considerable purchase of land in Stratford, which he had had it in mind to make since he bought New Place in 1597. He invested £320 — a considerable sum in those days — in acquiring from William Combe 107 acres of arable and 20 acres of pasture in Old Stratford, that is at the end of the town by the church, along the road from New Place. So it was a very convenient purchase. He was not in Stratford on Mayday when the deed was sealed, so his brother Gilbert took seisin of it for him in the presence of neighbours Anthony Nash, William Sheldon (of the Catholic family of tapestry-makers), Humphrey Mainwaring, Richard Mason and John Nash.[17] Gilbert Shakespeare had the freedom of being a bachelor to live, like his brother, in both Stratford and London. In 1597 we find Gilbert, a haberdasher of St. Bride's, giving surety for a Stratford neighbour who was a clockmaker. This brother died and was buried at Stratford in 1612, at the age of forty-five. Brother Richard was buried there in 1613, aged thirty-nine. The youngest brother Edmund, who was also a player, had a base child buried at St. Giles', Cripplegate in 1607 and was himself buried in St. Saviour's, Southwark on the last day of that year ; he was only twenty-seven. Shakespeare had him 'buried in the church with a forenoon knell of the great bell' that icy winter's day when the Thames itself was frozen over. None of the Shakespeare brothers lived to be old.

That Shakespeare already had the story of Troilus and Cressida in mind for his next play we may infer from *Twelfth Night*, where the Fool tells Viola, 'I would play Lord Pandarus of Phrygia, sir, to bring a Cressida to this Troilus'. It was written, with fair certainty, in 1602 ; various factors converged to make it the unique play it is and to give it the strange character it has, brilliant, disquieting, disenchanted, leaving an effect of unhappiness, a bitter taste in the mouth. No doubt it was intended to do so : it was Shakespeare responding to the challenge of Ben Jonson with a satire on war and love, with an element of the mock heroic. The prologue glances at the words of Jonson's prologue to the *Poetaster* of the year before. In spite of the play's extreme brilliance, and some of his finest writing, one has the feeling that it went against the grain : his genius was not for pure satire, and once more he produced something that was not like anything else, part satire, part farce, part bawdy, but more that was deeply serious and contains his maturest reflection on the problems of society and government ; the whole written in a mood of utter disenchantment. One cannot miss the melancholy undertone running through it all.

The play has never been popular, and there is some doubt whether it was given public performance ; in its nature it is caviare to the general, who do not much care for satire, especially on themes so dear to its great good heart — love and war. It is a play for intellectuals, and probably was written for private performance, perhaps at an Inn of Court, where the scatological element along with the legal word-play would be appreciated. Certainly Shakespeare was responding to the challenge to write something new — though it seemed not to be to his liking, for he did not provide this mixture again, unless in the unfinished *Timon*. That proved even more uncongenial.

On the other hand, *Troilus and Cressida* is of the utmost intellectual interest. He could not but be reflecting on the shattering events of the past two or three years ; this theme gave him a safely remote mode of expression for all the anguish and bitterness, the disillusionment and anger that welled up in him when he contemplated the way things had gone. The general mood in these years was one of disenchantment, of war-weariness and longing for it to come to an end, no desire for any further futile heroics, after the sputtering out of the brightest luminary in treason. That had not put an end to the feuding and faction-fighting, the bitter intrigues at Court, sparring for position over the succession, for favour with the successor. Some people were sick of the love-talk, the flattery, that surrounded an ageing Queen, herself heartsick at having had to destroy the gallant figure that should have been the consolation of her last days. Everyone longed for the resolution of the uncertainty that was in the air. People's teeth were on edge. It was hardly likely that the most sensitive intuition at work in that age would fail to register all this : it is the mood of the play.

And more, it is its subject. Put all the faction-fighting of the last years, the war of which the heroic phase was long past, petering out in discontent, general malaise and disease, the romantic cult of love and love-poetry, put it all into the remote past of the Trojan war and it was possible to pass savage comment on the follies of the time they were passing through. 'A plague on both your houses' is the message of the play : 'fools on both sides' are its specific words. But the peculiar *grincement*, the setting of the teeth on edge, that is in it came from what is always the most difficult to swallow, the fact that the worst follies had been committed by his own side, by those who had been his grand friends. This is always the least bearable. There is no evidence that Shakespeare had any friendly feelings towards the Cecils, the government side, or any particular devotion to the Queen ; his affiliation was to the other side, which in the event had behaved with infantile irresponsibility, incompetence and folly. It is always worse when one's own side behaves like that : the more cause for anguish, disillusionment and withdrawal not only inevitable but perhaps the only way out to preserve one's sanity.

But the disillusionment was never complete, the scepticism never absolute. For, underneath everything, in spite of his equivocal experience of life, in spite of the ambivalence of his own nature, Shakespeare retained a conviction of moral law, imbibed in youth and which his dubious experience had not undermined, but rather fortified. He retained his belief in sense and reason, in prudence and loyalty, in accepting the obligations of society. Therefore his comment was not merely a destructive one on people's criminal folly, but a constructive one, pointing out the sensible, reasonable course it was always possible to follow. That is of the essence of this play : the very condemnation — far more severe than that awarded from any less moral point of view, by those who 'couldn't care less' — implies a rectification. Shakespeare did care, deeply : there was a right course to follow, even if people would not take it. This course is always expressed or implied by Ulysses, who sees well the folly of both sides, who

> esteem no act
> But that of hand ; the still and mental parts
> That do contrive how many hands shall strike
> When fitness calls them on, and know by measure

Of their observant toil the enemy's weight —
Why this hath not a finger's dignity.

Actually, this point of view, where 'the still and mental parts'
dominated, was that of Cecil's politic brain which inspired the
government; the irony was that Shakespeare understood it
perfectly, expressed it in all his plays, and yet personal loyalties
and obligations aligned him with the other side. What could
be more agonising? Nevertheless, given the genius and the will,
what more stimulating to creative purpose — if it can be borne
without breaking? The truth is, it can be borne only by passing
over to the other side — as Bacon did; or by withdrawal.

Of all Shakespeare's characters Ulysses is the one who most
completely expresses his creator's views: indeed he hardly speaks
anything else. It may be seen that this extraordinary, uncongenial,
but brilliant play has far more intellectual content than many
more popular and delightful ones. It is unpopular. Of course.
It has more to offer us, especially today, to all modern societies.

What is it about?

The endless Trojan war — like the endless war with Spain —
is drawing to its end. Both sides are weary, full of lassitude,
without energy or moral purpose, without public spirit: mere
collections of individuals madly intent on their own personal
ends, the scene of public life a mere bear-garden. 'Brainsick'
is the word for it all, and time and again brainsickness is diagnosed
as what they are suffering from.

> Since the first sword was drawn about this question,
> Every tithe soul 'mongst many thousand dismes
> Hath been as dear as Helen—I mean, of ours.
> If we have lost so many tenths of ours
> To guard a thing not ours, nor worth to us,
> Had it our name, the value of one ten,
> What merit's in that reason which denies
> The yielding of her up?

This means that of the Trojans the lives of one in ten had been
sacrificed for this bitch. Thersites sums up the quarrel accurately
enough, if nakedly: 'all the argument is a whore and a cuckold —
a good quarrel to draw emulous factions and bleed to death upon'.
There is no more illusion among the Greeks about the issue. Says
Diomedes:

> She's bitter to her country . . .
> For every false drop in her bawdy veins
> A Grecian's life hath sunk ; for every scruple
> Of her contaminated carrion weight
> A Trojan hath been slain ; since she could speak,
> She hath not given so many good words breath
> As for her Greeks and Trojans suffered death.

What idiots humans are to go to war about such trifles as they do !
In this play war is seen as mere folly, made and kept going by
the idiots on both sides — not by the intelligent, in so far as there
are any. Helen in no sense appealed to Shakespeare's imagination
— as she had done to Marlowe's (if only in imagination) — nor
is she allowed to appeal to ours ; it is the destruction of Troy,
on account of her, that awoke his sympathy : again and again it
appears as a symbol of wanton destruction. Something prophetic
of calamity in his genius here, as in that of the American poet
who prophesied the destruction of London in 'The Waste Land'.

That love is not worth it is enforced by the main story of the
play, for Troilus, who is genuinely in love, wins his way to
Cressida's favours through a bawd, her uncle Pandarus — eponym
for all panders — and is, of course, played false by her the moment
she finds a pair of Greek arms to take her. It is an interesting
side-light that Shakespeare puts into this tart's mouth his own
consistent view of love as past a man's control :

> for to be wise and love
> Exceeds man's might : that dwells with gods above.

He always thought that : it is amusing that the greatest of the
world's dramatists should have come close to Hollywood in thinking
of love as a natural force, a kind of calamity, no-one can resist.

The main intellectual interest of the play, then, is political :
in its comment on war and faction-fighting, on authority and the
necessity of order, degree and obedience, each man taking his
proper place and ready to accept the obligations of his station.
For the view that is enforced is thoroughly social :

> no man is the lord of anything,
> Though in and of him there be much consisting,
> Till he communicate his parts to others.

That thought is developed at length by Ulysses in trying to
persuade Achilles to stop sulking in his tent and come out and
play the man in ending the war. Consciously or unconsciously,

there is an element of Essex in Achilles : sulking in his tent, withdrawing from Court and duty when he did not get his way, had been Essex's regular method of bringing pressure on the Queen to give him what he wanted. We should not look in Shakespeare for any crude transcript of a whole character, any more than with the more familiar case of a novelist — hence the dispute over Mr. Casaubon in *Middlemarch* ; it is rather that elements of experience enter into the fabric, but are differently distributed, recombined and transmuted. It is only that Shakespeare is so far away that they are more difficult to trace ; but a good knowledge of the Elizabethan age helps — without it one can do nothing. He does not differ in essence from other writers in this respect : it is our ignorance only that makes us think it so.

One must be on constant guard against too crude a transcription. Nevertheless, there was something in the relationship of Essex and Southampton imaged in that of Achilles and Patroclus : we have seen them skulking in their tent together, sulkily withdrawing themselves from action and the life around them ; and their relationship was an emotional one, particularly on Southampton's side. Here is another well-known characteristic of Essex, with which he had frequently plagued the Queen :

> Things small as nothing, for request's sake only,
> He makes important.

A request of no great importance for a follower he would turn into an issue of confidence in himself.

> Possessed he is with greatness
> And speaks not to himself but with a pride
> That quarrels at self-breath : imagined worth
> Holds in his blood such swollen and hot discourse . . .

This exactly describes what had been the situation, so that in the end there was no coming to terms with him :

> He is so plaguy proud that the death-tokens of it
> Cry 'No recovery.'

That indeed had been the upshot of it all.

The consequences of his fall, and even of the premonitory signs of it, are also noted down :

> 'Tis certain greatness, once fallen out with fortune,
> Must fall out with men too. What the declined is
> He shall as soon read in the eyes of others

As feel in his own fall ; for men, like butterflies,
Show not their mealy wings but to the summer,
And not a man, for being simply man,
Hath any honour, but honour for those honours
That are without him — as place, riches, and favour,
Prizes of accident as oft as merit ;
Which, when they fall, as being slippery standers,
The love that leaned on them as slippery too,
Doth one pluck down another and together
Die in the fall.

What an exact observation of the Elizabethan political scene there
is in that ! The fact that it is given to Achilles strengthens the
view that something of Essex is in him. Francis Bacon had been
the first rat, understandably, to leave Essex's leaky vessel ; but
Robert Cecil's victory brought a crowd of Essex-supporters
over to him. Nor were they wrong to go : what sense in clinging
to a sinking ship ? It is merely that the human movement was
observed and registered for what it was worth.

On faction-fighting within the party Nestor has a comment :
'their fraction is more our wish than their faction. But it was
a strong composure a fool could disunite !' To which Ulysses
(or Shakespeare) points the moral : 'the amity that wisdom knits
not, folly may easily untie'. The appositeness of this to all political
parties is obvious, never more so than in our own time with the
Liberal party that destroyed itself, and the Labour party that
destroyed its chances for years, by internal faction-fighting. Their
leaders evidently rest under Shakespeare's condemnation for fools.
The point is an obvious one, which even a moderate intelligence
should be able to understand. But he understood something much
more subtle, the mysterious operation of government, which can
never be made fully explicit :

There is a mystery, with whom relation
Durst never meddle, in the soul of state,
Which hath an operation more divine
Than breath or pen can give expressure to.

It was a pity that circumstances and affections kept him away
from Robert Cecil's company : they would have understood
each other.

All these words of wisdom and political understanding are
placed in Ulysses' mouth, who stands rather outside the action,
a commentator on it all, disinterested in one sense but concerned

that things should go well, or at least take a better course. In his speeches, Shakespeare's conception of society is magnificently expressed : it is the summing-up of all that he had urged in previous plays, and — though the speeches are long — more concisely and richly. Order is universal : it runs through the planetary system as through human society :

> The heavens themselves, the planets and this centre,
> Observe degree, priority, and place,
> Insisture, course, proportion, season, form,
> Office, and custom, in all line of order.

But, if there is a breach in the order, earthquakes, tides, hurricanes, tempests, plagues, what devastation can ensue ! Similarly with human affairs :

> O, when degree is shaked,
> Which is the ladder of all high designs,
> The enterprise is sick !

We have more reason today than ever before to realise how true that is. Take away incentives to achievement, and naturally all high designs suffer. Take away the recognition of difference in human achievement, and the sense of quality is undermined. No wonder the enterprise is sick : no truer word was ever spoken. It is the political understanding revealed that is so extraordinary : so penetrating as to be a prophetic insight.

How can communities hold together, the speech goes on, without the sense of degree, different functions, unequal merits, different contributions ? Impossible to make a wall of thousands of equal pebbles to stand up ; but given stones of various shapes and sizes, a dry wall can be fitted together that will stand. Take degree and difference of function away, reduce everything to the same level, and only force prevails, no justice or protection for the weak or for minorities.

> Force should be right ; or rather, right and wrong,
> Between whose endless jar justice resides —

a very searching view that —

> Should lose their names, and so should justice too.
> Then everything includes itself in power,
> Power into will, will into appetite ;
> And appetite, an universal wolf,
> So doubly seconded with will and power,
> Must make perforce an universal prey,
> And last eat up himself.

Have we not seen precisely that happen in our day? The facts, and the truths, of political society do not alter, only the methods and the colouring. But it is rare to find a poet who understands: poets are apt to be natural Platonists, whereas Shakespeare may be described intellectually as an Aristotelian. It may seem paradoxical that a poet should be, but Shakespeare was that kind of poet, observant of how things are, at the opposite pole from a Plato or a Shelley.

He is no less observant of the method by which things are undone:

> the general's disdained
> By him one step below, he by the next,
> That next by him beneath; so every step
> Exampled by the first pace that is sick
> Of his superior, grows to an envious fever
> Of pale and bloodless emulation.

To the Elizabethans emulation meant envy and jealousy; a sick fever of emulation serves to describe the egalitarian society of England today.

These statements of fact are by no means the bitterest draughts of the play: those are put in the mouth of Thersites — whose name may have come from Chapman's Homer published in 1598. He curses the whole outfit: 'vengeance on the whole camp! or, rather, the Neapolitan boneache! [*i.e.* syphilis] for that, methinks, is the curse dependent on those that war for a placket', *i.e.* a drab. That was historically true, too: the wars of the sixteenth century spread syphilis, starting from Naples to which returning Spanish soldiers brought it back from the New World, all over Europe: it spread like wildfire in the wake of the armies; and nothing could arrest it. Some think that the force of Puritan feeling, constantly growing, owed something to this dread sanction. The playwrights made a joke of its ravages, as Pandarus, himself suffering from them, does in his epilogue:

> Good traders in the flesh, set this in your painted cloths:
> As many as be here of Pandar's hall,
> Your eyes, half out, weep out at Pandar's fall;
> Or if you cannot weep, yet give some groans,
> Though not for me, yet for your aching bones.
> Brethren and sisters of the hold-door trade,
> Some two months hence my will shall here be made.
> It should be now, but that my fear is this,
> Some gallèd goose of Winchester would hiss.
> Till then I'll sweat and seek about for eases,
> And at that time bequeath you my diseases.

The reference here is to the diseases caught in the stews on Bankside in the propinquity of Winchester House, on property belonging to that venerable see.

Where so much is personal and contemporary we hardly need look for any more. We have a reference to a sailor breaking ship's-biscuit into shivers with his fist, no doubt hard as a rock; and to

> the dreadful spout
> Which shipmen do the hurricano call.

We catch an echo again from Shakespeare's reading of Davies's *Nosce Teipsum* in the passage,

> nor doth the eye itself,
> That most pure spirit of sense, behold itself,
> Not going from itself; but eye to eye opposed
> Salutes each other with each other's form.

Marlowe's unfortunate sword-image does duty again :

> Even in the fan and wind of your fair sword.

We recognise the contemporary, yet perennial, social scene in the comparison of time,

> like a fashionable host
> That slightly shakes his parting guest by the hand
> And, with his arms outstretched as he would fly,
> Grasps in the comer.

That same wonderful speech of Ulysses on Time has many personal touches : Shakespeare's peculiar loathing of ingratitude — as if it were not to be expected from inferior natures !

> Time hath, my lord, a wallet at his back
> Wherein he puts alms for oblivion,
> A great-sized monster of ingratitudes.
> Those scraps are good deeds past, which are devoured
> As fast as they are made, forgot as soon
> As done.

The speech has a score of touches of epigrammatic wisdom, no doubt learned the hard way from experience : keep straight on ahead, for there are a thousand envious ones pursuing to push you aside :

> if you give way,
> Or hedge aside from the direct forthright,
> Like to an entered tide they all rush by
> And leave you hindmost.

348

He must have observed that often enough in life, and drawn his own conclusion.

> O, let not virtue seek
> Remuneration for the thing it was ;
> For beauty, wit,
> High birth, vigour of bone, desert in service,
> Love, friendship, charity, are subjects all
> To envious and calumniating Time.

It must have been hardest of all to have to admit that love and friendship were so subject.

No wonder this play was never popular : too near the bone. Human beings can bear very little of the truth about themselves at a time. The text of the play is a good one and evidently rests on an authoritative manuscript close to the author. Dekker and Chettle had produced a lost *Troilus and Cressida* for Henslowe, which may have stimulated Shakespeare to do something different : it turned out quite unlike even anything of his own. He based himself on Caxton's Troy histories, drawing on familiar Ovid for filling-in material. The play was already referred to in verse in 1603, so there must have been a private performance. James Roberts was conditionally licensed to print it in 1603, but did not do so. It seems that the Chamberlain's men, to whom it belonged, did not want it printed. When it came out first in 1609, the title-page saying that it had been acted 'by the King's Majesty's servants at the Globe' was cancelled, and a new preface added calling it 'a new play, never staled with the stage, never clapper-clawed with the palms of the vulgar'. The inference is that it was published against the wishes of the players. (Who got the publishers their copy ?) There is a suspiciously warm tribute to 'this author's comedies, that are so framed to the life that they serve for the most common commentaries of all the actions of our lives, showing such a dexterity and power of wit that the most displeased with plays are pleased with his comedies. . . . And believe this, that when he is gone and his comedies out of sale, you will scramble for them and set up a new English Inquisition. . . . And so I leave all such to be prayed for, for the states of their wit's healths, that will not praise it.'

It is very curious : it sounds as if there had been some obstacle to, or no enthusiasm for, its production. However, here was the playbook to be bought 'at the Spread Eagle in Paul's churchyard, over against the great North door.'

Shakespeare's next play, *All's Well that Ends Well*, is something quite different again. It is not a satire like *Troilus and Cressida* though it has satirical elements ; it is certainly not a romantic comedy like *Twelfth Night* — that had been the last in that *genre*. It is a strange hybrid of folk-tale and morality-play, placed in a realistic environment which permits a sharp, disenchanted comment on the manners and morals of the time. The only play that is like it is its twin, *Measure for Measure*, and in the resolution of their conflicts, if in nothing else — for nothing could be more different in atmosphere and mood — they point forward to the last morality-romances. We know how little Shakespeare cared about labelling plays, rightly, for so many of his are unique. It is more important to realise the organic unity, the integration, of his work as a whole, with its gathering rhythms like waves of the sea, each crashing more powerfully, resolved more perfectly until the rainbow-spray at the end ; with the repeated themes tried out in varying ways, until a greater satisfaction is found ; with all the chimes and reverberations of character and variations on theme ; with the internal connections and cross-rhythms binding the work together. The whole appearing in the end as one, division none : within which we can study the self-portrait of a mind.

There has been some doubt about the dating of the play : I do not see why : it visibly comes between *Troilus* and *Measure for Measure*, and it breathes the atmosphere of early 1603, that self-questioning, uneasy time when the Queen was sickening to her death, while the country waited, poised on the edge of they knew not what, certainly a new order, a new world, a younger generation in the ascendant. Once again we find Shakespeare apprehending infinitely more from the world of experience around him, and drawing on his own, than anyone has conceived — though the best commentator on the play has guessed it : previous views have not allowed sufficiently, he says, 'for the creative interplay between author and environment, the fact that the feelings of the author are a creative part of the climate of opinion in which he lives'.[18]

The play is something new, in some sense an experiment. It is an undeniably difficult, hardly a congenial, one ; but again it is packed with intellectual interest, far more so than more congenial ones. One has the impression that there is too much material, too much thought, in it. *All's Well* was certainly not written easily, with one rapturous lyrical impulse, like *Richard II* and *Romeo and Juliet*. There is no lyricism in it ; what music there is is rather tormented, uneasy music. It has been described as bitter and complex ; complex certainly, but I think disenchanted and searching, rather than bitter. He gave much thought to it and wrote it with more difficulty than usual — one can tell from the considered, contorted verse, among other things. But the work did not spark ; it did not set his imagination alight in the familiar fashion ; and so it is not resolved aesthetically with entire satisfaction, though his mastery of his medium is such that, when played with understanding, it is very effective drama. Not brilliant like *Troilus and Cressida*, but searching like *Measure for Measure*. Perhaps he was in an unhappy frame of mind, uncongenial to inspiration : there was plenty in the experience of these years to make him so, both politically and socially, and perhaps in his personal life.

The story came from Boccaccio, either through William Painter's *Palace of Pleasure* or through a French version ; or, as is now thought likely, both. It is a tale of primitive folk-lore — that of the king who is sick unto death and yet is magically cured. Into this there enters the theme of the magic potency of virginity, exemplified by the virtue of the orphan-girl Helen, who cures him. Thus she fulfils her task — a fairy tale theme — and, like Cinderella, marries her prince, in this case a count, Bertram. But Shakespeare has placed this in the realist setting of contemporary society. Helen is an honest girl of middle-class origin who is in love with the spirited young count, far above her station, and seeks to marry him, much against his will. (Where have we met that theme before ?) Shakespeare has set himself a perhaps insoluble problem, as artists sometimes do, to bring those totally divergent worlds together and fuse them. It is done by the king rewarding Helen with the hand of his young noble, who resents the marriage and refuses to consummate it. Helen has to entrap him by inserting herself in place of the young maiden he makes an assignation with in Florence. No doubt the bed-trick has a creditable medieval ancestry ; no doubt Elizabethan taste did not wince at a husband so procured — all was fair in love and war ; but nothing can make it congenial to a modern.

Granted this insuperable defect in one's sympathy, *All's Well that Ends Well* offers us special interest in its comment on the contemporary situation and society. He added the character of

Parolles, the braggart soldier, with the sub-plot and the knock-about farce of his well-merited exposure. The Braggart, like the Pedant, is a stock-figure from the tradition of Italian comedy, transplanted out all over Europe, but Shakespeare gives him a verisimilitude (if not veracity) of his own and he is very effective theatre. He is not created from within, like Falstaff; he is depicted, and exposed, like a Jonsonian type — tribute to the influence of the younger man upon the older for ever learning. Witness to Parolles' stagey effectiveness is that Charles I, better at literature than at politics, inscribed 'Monsieur Parolles' as his name for the play.

Its first theme is the conflict of virtue and nobility as exemplified in Helen and Bertram. Helen is all virtue ; we may assume that she has beauty too, but she is poorly born, the orphan child of a doctor :

> we, the poorer born,
> Whose baser stars do shut us up in wishes —

Shakespeare knew all about that. She, too, is hopelessly in love with a young count :

> That I should love a bright particular star
> And think to wed it ! He is so above me.

What remedy ? Well, as Shakespeare often says and had found for himself :

> Our remedies oft in ourselves do lie.

She proceeds to apply her talents, bravely goes to Court to heal the sick king.

This introduces a second theme, the conflict between the older and the younger generation, of whom Bertram is representative. The King, Bertram's mother, the Countess, Lafew 'an old lord', and Helen exemplify the values of an older world, more courteous and generous, virtuous and loyal. The King allows that the young courtiers are witty,

> but they may jest
> Till their own scorn returns to them unnoted
> Ere they can hide their levity in honour.

They might well take a lesson from the humility and kindness with which Helen's father, the eminent doctor — whom the King had known — treated those below him in rank :

> Such a man
> Might be a copy to these younger times.

He had been used to say,

> 'Let me not live
> After my flame lacks oil, to be the snuff
> Of younger spirits, whose apprehensive senses
> All but new things disdain ; whose judgments are
> Mere fathers of their garments ; whose constancies
> Expire before their fashions.'

The conflict between older and younger generations is typically exposed. There was a marked scission between the generations at Court at the end of the Queen's reign : these years were a turning point : it is Shakespeare grown older.

Bertram is young, above all immature — he will not accept the obligations of his station ; he is spirited, petulantly wilful, full of aristocratic pride, and does not want to be tied down in marriage. Nevertheless, very conscious of his nobility, he is dutiful towards his noble mother. Where have we met this combination before ? Anxious as I am to avoid the suggestion of crude transference of experience, I cannot but note that this was very much the situation of Southampton and his mother. All that we know of the dowager Countess shows her as tender, wise, kind and good, respected by the Queen and Cecil — never a word against her in the malicious environment of the Court ; and we know her solicitude for her unwise, *égaré* son. She was all that the Countess of Rosillion is in the play. This is the aristocratic circle with which Shakespeare was intimately familiar ; these were the people he had had under view.

Bertram will not marry Helen, though she has saved the King from death and it is his command :

> A poor physician's daughter my wife ! Disdain
> Rather corrupt me ever.

To which the King replies :

> 'Tis only title thou disdain'st in her, the which
> I can build up. Strange is it that our bloods,
> Of colour, weight, and heat, poured all together,
> Would quite confound distinction, yet stands off
> In differences so mighty.

This is a new emphasis in Shakespeare :

> From lowest place when virtuous things proceed,
> The place is dignified by the doer's deed.
> Where great additions swell' s and virtue none,
> It is a dropsied honour . . .

Honours thrive
When rather from our acts we them derive
Than our foregoers. The mere word's a slave,
Debauched on every tomb, on every grave
A lying trophy, and as oft is dumb,
Where dust and damned oblivion is the tomb
Of honoured bones indeed.

This is a pretty cutting comment on the grand tombs with which
the post-Reformation aristocracy filled the empty places where
the altars had stood in the churches. We are intrigued by the
new development in Shakespeare's mind. Earlier, glamourised
by first acquaintance with the aristocratic world, he had been
willing to take it on its own terms — perhaps that was the price
for admission to those delights. He now knew that the gilded
denizens of this world were no better than anybody else ; recent
events had exposed them as at least as great fools, and the more
blameable from their position and the chances they had had.
This led him to assert purely human values, that only virtue is
any good, and that is not inherited or handed down from the lies
inscribed on grand ancestral tombs.

Though Bertram has to marry Helen, he still will not make
her his wife : she is a wife only in name. So he receives a series
of blows to awaken him to the truth about himself and life : he
is disclaimed by his mother, who welcomes Helen with open arms
as her child instead ; the King disowns him in disapprobation
of his conduct ; Bertram is led to suppose the death of a nobly
virtuous wife ; he is disapproved of by his own companions, and
his only intimate, the empty Parolles — a kind of adventurer like
Pierce Edmonds — is cruelly unmasked and shown to be ridiculous. This is the bitterest blow of all, in Bertram's situation, for
Parolles is all that he has left to him. There is no kindness or
enjoyment in it as in the unmasking of Falstaff : we can only
suppose that Shakespeare's nerves were too much on edge. The
joy had gone out of life.

Our critic sees that the inner crux of the play is Shakespeare's
sense of the ineluctable injustice in the circumstances of our lives
thwarting, and sometimes destroying, the fulfilment of our own
true natures. His was not the more superficial conception of
the satirist — a Jonson, or a Shaw — watching the absurd effects
of social pressures on people's behaviour ; his is the deeper sense
of ' the injustice of life which prevents inner ideals from being

realised, the same injustice that appears in all his serious plays.' [19]
Helen surmounts the disability of her birth by her talents, her
very virtue and the astute use of her virginity — as William
Shakespeare had surmounted his initial obstacles and trials. But
the struggle had left him singularly *désabusé*, with no illusions
about life or human beings — perhaps the proper frame of mind
to enter upon the great tragedies : a realm where only true values
count in and for themselves, where men are face to face with their
own souls, as the murderer of Hamlet's father sees in his moment
of illumination :

> There is no shuffling, there the action lies
> In his true nature.

With *All's Well* and *Measure for Measure* we are entering the
Jacobean world ; gone are the heroism and inspiration of the
1580's in which Shakespeare had grown up, the ardours and enchantments of the 1590's which had borne him forward. There
is nothing esoteric about the difference in feeling in public life
between one year and another, to those who have the sensibility
to perceive it. All who remember it can tell the difference between
the atmosphere of Britain in 1939 and in 1940 ; others can sense
the difference, say, in the United States between 1960 and the
year 1962. Similarly there is no greater difficulty, to those aware,
in discerning the difference in mood between the year 1600 or even
1601, and that in which this play was written, the winter of 1602–3.

The Jacobean world was going to be both more complex and
morally coarser than the old ; a society richer and more ostenta-
tious, both more materialist and more ideological — above all, the
unity, the integration of the old was cracking. There would be
plenty of opportunity for men to live by their wits. Parolles,
when shown up, goes out in very symptomatic fashion.

> Simply the thing I am
> Shall make me live . . .
> Rust, sword ; cool, blushes ; and Parolles live
> Safest in shame ; being fooled, by foolery thrive.
> There's place and means for every man alive.

Several touches reinforce the date. A reference to Cressida —

> I am Cressid's uncle
> That dare leave two together —

points to *Troilus* being still in mind. With the Queen in her last
illness, the linked Puritan and Papist questions were popping up

their heads again : both had expectations. 'Young Charbon [*i.e.* charcoal] the Puritan and old Poysam [*i.e.* poisson = fish] the Papist, howsome'er their hearts are severed in religion, their heads are both one ; they may jowl horns together like any deer in the herd.' That is, they are both liable to being cuckolded. Again, 'though honesty be no Puritan, yet it will do no hurt ; it will wear the surplice of humility over the black gown of a big heart'. With an incoming Scotch Calvinist on the throne, the fatuous surplice-question was raising its dreary head again. A reference to the American Indians worshipping the sun is a tribute to all those voyages that had been a glory of the departing Elizabethan age, and comes out of Shakespeare's reading about them in Hakluyt :

> Thus, Indian-like,
> Religious in mine error, I adore
> The sun that looks upon his worshipper.

Parolles provides us with a pretty example of what Shakespeare told us, in *Henry V*, about how such returned soldiers talked : 'you shall find, in the regiment of the Spinii, one Captain Spurio, with his cicatrice, an emblem of war, here on his sinister cheek ; it was this very sword entrenched it. Say to him I live.'[20] Familiar Mile End, where troops did their training, appears : 'more of his soldiership I know not, except in that country he had the honour to be the officer at a place there called Mile End, to instruct for the doubling of files'.

For Shakespeare himself we have the consistent relativism of his observations : 'How mightily sometimes we make us comforts of our losses ! How mightily some other times we drown our gain in tears !' And the conclusion : 'the web of our life is of a mingled yarn, good and ill together ; our virtues would be proud if our faults whipped them not, and our crimes would despair if they were not cherished by our virtues'.

This, a consistent thought with him, would be made the theme of his next play, *Measure for Measure*.

On 24 March 1603, the eve of Lady day, the Queen died and James was King. At once all Essex's followers could look to the sun. Southampton was delivered out of the Tower, and went to meet the King on his journey south at Huntingdon, where he was privileged to bear the sword of state before the new sovereign. Essex's friend, and with *his* looks, was treated with marked favour by the susceptible James, and Southampton was awarded the privileged entrée to the Privy Chamber permitted to few. It was not long before there were rumours that he would be the favourite, but somehow the idea came to nothing — it was said to have been discouraged by Cecil, but perhaps Southampton at thirty was a little old for the part. At any rate, royal favour accomplished what nothing else had been able to do : he conformed at last, became a Protestant and went to church with the King. The rewards of commonsense at length flowed in fast and free : Keeper of the Isle of Wight for life, Keeper of the King's Game in the royal forests of Hampshire, joint Lord Lieutenant — with the young Earl of Pembroke — of the county, and Knight of the Garter. More important, he got the lucrative grant of the farm of sweet wines, the renewal of which Elizabeth had denied to Essex, to support his impoverished estate ; to this were added grants of lands and manors, grants of land even to his faithful followers.[21]

Next year the dowager Countess received a free grant of £600 out of the Exchequer. We find the new Queen standing godmother to Southampton's daughter Anne, christened in the royal chapel at Whitehall, and Southampton along with Cecil, now Lord Cranborne, feasting the Queen and her brother, the Duke of Holstein. The friendship with Cecil held good ; Southampton went hawking with him at Theobalds, and when this place was exchanged with James for Hatfield, Southampton went down with Cecil, now Earl of Salisbury, to decide on the site for the new house. Later we find Southampton along with Salisbury and Pembroke as sponsors for the founding of the Virginia Company. We hardly need follow his career in detail any further, out of Shakespeare's proximity and concern.[22]

It was observed that Shakespeare did not sing the Queen's praises at her demise, though expected to do so :

> You poets all, brave Shakespeare, Jonson, Greene,[23]
> Bestow your time to write for England's Queen.

His earlier acquaintance, Chettle, reproached him for this silence :

> Nor doth the silver-tonguèd Melicert
> Drop from his honeyed Muse one sable tear
> To mourn her death who gracèd his desert,
> And to his lays opened her royal ear.
> Shepherd, remember our Elizabeth
> And sing her rape, done by that Tarquin, Death.

His silence was not without significance : his affiliations were all with the opposition-party ; she had executed Essex and imprisoned his friend.

Moreover, James's accession meant a marked improvement in social status for the Chamberlain's men, and a considerable one financially. Fascinated by the English theatre — after the dreary preachings he had been subjected to in Scotland — the son of Mary Stuart took Shakespeare's Company under his own patronage. They became the King's men, with special licence to play in any town or university in the realm — no more interference from Lord Mayors and town authorities — and sworn as officers of the royal household as Grooms of the Chamber in ordinary. As such Shakespeare and his fellows received their regulation livery of 4½ yards of red cloth to walk in the royal procession on the King's reception by the City of London. One can imagine him there — the occasion itself was a very theatrical one, with the decorated arches set up at points along the route, themselves the most elaborate stage-sets yet contrived. Again in the summer of 1604, when the Spanish plenipotentiaries came over to make peace in London, Shakespeare and eleven of his fellows in their scarlet liveries were in waiting during the negotiations.

The one drawback in the general euphoria was that 1603 was a plague year ; the Court took to the country and in December was down at Wilton, Pembroke's house, where the King's men presented a play on the 2nd of the month. They came down from Mortlake and were paid £30, at the rate of three plays. The young Pembroke was host, and Southampton was there with the King — interesting to think of the player-dramatist in the wings after all that had passed. A lost letter that seems once to have been at Wilton spoke of 'the man Shakespeare' being there — correct enough : that was what he was to them. On their return the Company played at Hampton Court on St. Stephen's day at night, and on Innocents' day. In January they were paid £53 for their performances, with a bonus of £30 on account of the inhibition due to the plague. In February they played at Whitehall on the nights of Candlemas and Shrove Tuesday. The new King and Queen could not have enough of the English plays, and performances were put on to enable them to see famous pieces they had not been able to witness. In March came the coronation, with more pageants and masques,

the devices written by Jonson, Drayton, Webster, Daniel, Dekker
— all the dramatists but Shakespeare, who had other things to
do. Once more, the King's men were in the coronation procession ; and at the tilting Southampton won special commendation.

By the time of the arrival of the Queen's brother from Denmark
the royal family had seen most of the Company's repertory. For
the entertainment Southampton and Cecil designed, Sir Walter
Cope reported, 'I have sent and been all this morning hunting
for players, jugglers and such kinds of creatures, but find them
hard to find. Wherefore, leaving notes for them to seek me,
Burbage is come and says there is no new play the Queen has
not seen, but they have revived an old one called *Love's Labour's
Lost*, which for wit and mirth, he says, will please her exceedingly.
And this is appointed to be played tomorrow at my Lord of
Southampton's, unless you send a writ to remove the *corpus cum
causa* to your house in the Strand. Burbage is my messenger.'[24]

An interesting sidelight at this time is that in and around
Southampton House were taken up some £200 worth of Popish
books, which were burned in St. Paul's churchyard.[25] The Southampton household had never conformed under Elizabeth : this
was what favour could do. On the King's state-visit to Oxford
in the summer of 1605, Southampton was once more there, bearing
the sword. At St. John's college a device of Three Sybils saluting
Banquo appeared : 'these sybils now in the name of England and
Ireland saluted the King of Scotland as the fulfilment of the old
prophecy'. We are reminded of the witches in *Macbeth* and
Banquo, who was to be 'no king, but to be the father of many
kings'. Can Shakespeare have been in attendance, or passing
through Oxford on his familiar way home to Stratford ?

The King's men were in clover. Mary Stuart's son had no
idea of the value of money, and at Court every extravagance and
ostentation reigned. Shortly, the rate of remuneration for performances, which had been £10 under Elizabeth, was doubled ; at
£20 performances became more frequent. 'In the ten years before
they became the King's Company, their known performances
at Court average about three a year ; in the ten years after they
attained their new service their known performances at Court
average about thirteen a year, more than those of all other London
companies combined. They were officially the premier company
of London ; a good part of their time must have been devoted
to the preparation of command performances.'[26] These were

much more remunerative than public playing ; and the increasing importance of this sophisticated audience must have played its part in shaping the character of the new period in Shakespeare's dramaturgy — the great tragedies and the Roman plays. His plays had to appeal to both audiences, and in their nature, and universal scope, they did.

His prosperity was reflected in a third, and larger, purchase at this time. In 1605 he invested £440 in a lease of half the tithes — confiscated from the College of canons at the Reformation — of Old Stratford, Welcombe and Bishopton, along with some other parcels of tithe. It was a good investment, and brought in a steady income of £60 a year to this excellent man of business, the gentleman of New Place.

Meanwhile, in 1603–4, *Measure for Measure* was written and bears traces of just that time. In contrast to Elizabeth, James had a dislike of crowds and a fear of them — he had several times been surprised by tumults in unruly Scotland and subjected to *force majeure* by his undisciplined nobles. On his way south the nobility and gentry had flocked to the rewarding spectacle of their new ruler, out of loyalty, expectation, or mere curiosity. James quickly tired of being the target of people's gaze, and the plague of that summer gave a proper excuse for forbidding the access of crowds to view the new monarch. This is caught up in the new play, where the Duke, a wise, fatherly ruler, says :

> I love the people,
> But do not like to stage me to their eyes ;
> Though it do well, I do not relish well
> Their loud applause and Aves vehement.

This is immediately succeeded by a reflection back on Essex's cult of popularity :

> Nor do I think the man of safe discretion
> That does affect it.

In the next act, James's attitude — which was not much relished by the English, who were used to a popular monarchy — is given support with a graceful phrase :

> even so
> The general subject to a well-wished king
> Quit their own part, and in obsequious fondness
> Crowd to his presence, where their untaught love
> Must needs appear offence.

Measure for Measure is connected on one side with *All's Well that Ends Well* and on the other with *Othello*, of 1604. Shakespeare took his story from Cinzio's *Ecatommiti*, a collection of Italian *novelle*, from which he also got the plot of *Othello*. He seems to have looked at Cinzio's play *Epitia* for hints, and in English to have read George Whetstone's play, *Promos and Cassandra*, and the prose version in his *Heptameron*. There is evidence, as for other plays, of his turning over a number of versions of the story before deciding on how best to turn it to dramatic use. From *All's Well* the bed-trick is repeated. *In Measure for Measure* it is used to trick Angelo, the Duke's too self-righteous and morally severe deputy — who had condemned Isabella's brother Claudio to death for fornication and is willing to pardon him only if Isabella, passionately chaste and a religious novice, will go to bed with him — into bedding with his own jilted betrothed, Mariana of the moated grange. Her name also comes from *All's Well*. So we need not doubt the dating of this play or its place in relation to others.

The play is very close to *All's Well* and, like that, has been called a problem-play ; but it would be truer to call it problematical. Once more we have a story, having an element of ritual in it, placed in a realistic, not to say sordid, environment. The supposed retirement of the ruler, in order to watch how things go in his absence, to find out how things really are, is a traditional theme to be accepted as such and far from purposeless. The theme of the play, then, is justice, with consequential consideration of forgiveness and mercy. The Duke means to test it in the purpose of his deputy, Angelo :

> Lord Angelo is precise ;
> Stands at a guard with envy ; scarce confesses
> That his blood flows, or that his appetite
> Is more to bread than stone. Hence shall we see,
> If power change purpose, what our seemers be.

We know how much Shakespeare disliked seemers, especially those people who wanted to appear morally better than others — we have seen that all along.

Angelo was one such : self-satisfied and much under control, he stands for the severity of the law upon offenders and means to execute it. We know from the Sonnets what Shakespeare felt about the type :

They that have power to hurt and will do none . . .
Who, moving others, are themselves as stone,
Unmoved, cold and to temptation slow . . .

But Angelo is not a bloodless type, as others think :

> whose blood
> Is very snow-broth : one who never feels
> The wanton stings and motions of the sense ;
> But doth rebate and blunt his natural edge
> With profits of the mind, study and fast.

Naturally the people, who never understand anything, think
'this Angelo was not made by man and woman after this downright way of creation. . . . Some report a sea-maid spawned
him. Some that he was begot between two stock-fishes.' That
is the authentic voice of the people, and funny too. The truth
is that Angelo is a man under unnatural control : that is what
makes him inhuman. We have all known such types, and know
that going contrary to nature in *this* manner is stultifying, anti-
creative and makes them hypocrites. We know too that Shakespeare, no saint himself, had a dislike of thwarting nature : he
thought it hopeless, as well as undesirable in its effects. Nor is
Angelo a villain : he falls, as anyone else is liable to fall, and so
offends most gravely, is caught in the trap of his own sour severity.

Whatever critics may think, this is a very Shakespearean
situation : nothing artificial or forced, but one that spoke to him
personally. Why then try to screw up nature more than it will
stand ? Lucio expresses the view of the ordinary sensual man :
'Yes, in good sooth, the vice is of a great kindred ; it is well
allied, but it is impossible to extirp it quite, friar, till eating and
drinking be put down'. That must have raised a laugh in the
theatre, but one cannot doubt that the point had the sympathy
of William Shakespeare with it, as also in the naughty comment
that follows : 'why, what a ruthless thing is this in him, for the
rebellion of a codpiece to take away the life of a man'. The self-
righteous, unjust judge is brought down by the same sin, that
is, the same force of nature, for which he had condemned another
to death.

Walter Pater, among the best of critics — for he wrote from
an intellectual level on a par with what he was commenting on
— appreciated the fineness of *Measure for Measure*. 'The action
of the play, like the action of life itself for the keener observer,

develops in us the conception of this poetical justice, and the yearning to realise it, the true justice of which Angelo knows nothing, because it lies for the most part beyond the limits of any acknowledged law.'[27]   Ideal justice must be related to 'the recognition of that which the person, in his inmost nature, really is ; and as sympathy alone can discover that which really is in matters of feeling and thought, true justice is in its essence a finer knowledge through love.   It is for this finer justice, a justice based on a more delicate appreciation of the true conditions of men and things, a true respect of persons in our estimate of actions, that the people in *Measure for Measure* cry out as they pass before us ; and as the poetry of this play is full of the peculiarities of Shakespeare's poetry, so in its ethics it is an epitome of Shakespeare's moral judgments.'   That epitome had been stated in a sentence of Hamlet's before : 'use every man after his desert, and who should 'scape whipping ?'   There is really not much doubt what William Shakespeare thought, or how it arose, or what he thought of himself.

With Pater I find this an altogether more satisfactory play than its twin, *All's Well* : the theme sparked Shakespeare's imagination.   In consequence there is fine poetry, no sense of constraint or reluctant accomplishment of a task, and it makes an integrated impression.   I suspect that the many critics of the play have really found it not so much unsatisfactory as uncomfortable — doubly so, for though all can enjoy the unmasking of an external, superficial hypocrisy, it is painful to have the lie in the soul exposed before our eyes ; and others have found too much for them the sordid realism of the accompaniment — the brothel-madam, Mistress Overdone, Pompey the bawd and pimp, the whoremaster Lucio — of which there is more than in any other play.   Shakespeare was obsessed by the unpleasanter aspects of sex in these years : there is a lot of talk about lechery and brothels and disease.   One gets the impression that, living on his own in London, he was well-acquainted with this aspect of contemporary life.   'What with the war, what with the sweat, what with the gallows, and what with poverty, I am custom-shrunk', says Mistress Overdone.   That would have been written before peace was made in 1604, by the way ; the sweat refers to the plague of 1603, and that in itself kept people poor.[28]   All these people in low life are very real and convincing, Overdone herself (a Jonsonian name), Pompey her servant and bawd, Elbow the constable, Barnardine the drunken prisoner, Lucio the dissolute young gentleman. Q., who rather fails with this uncomfortable play, does not mistake on this point : he recognises that Shakespeare runs the whole gamut of human nature.[29] Why exclude the nastier sides ? Shakespeare certainly knew all about them from experience — and yet retained inner moral delicacy and discrimination.

His was an accepting — and, fairly certainly, a suffering — nature ; he was also deeply social in his convictions, however he lived his life — no cool intellectual withdrawal from society, as with Montaigne. The very first scene reiterates this, a note we consistently hear in his work, now from the mouth of the Duke, who clearly speaks for his creator :

> Heaven doth with us as we with torches do,
> Not light them for themselves ; for if our virtues
> Did not go forth of us, 'twere all alike
> As if we had them not.

Shakespeare's sympathy is all with following the course of nature, as against Angelo's denial of nature, but there must be moderation :

> As surfeit is the father of much fast,
> So every scope by the immoderate use
> Turns to restraint. Our natures do pursue,
> Like rats that ravin down their proper bane,
> A thirsty evil ; and when we drink we die.

In a number of the plays we are given a long set speech on a theme : it was a habit he learned from his early training in school-rhetoric, and it became part of his recipe for writing a play. Each speech gives us a clue, or relates closely, to the essence of the play. In *King John* it is the speech on Commodity, or expediency ; in *Henry IV* it is Kingship and its cares ; in *Henry V*, Ceremony ; in *As You Like It*, the Seven Ages of Man ; in *All's Well*, Virginity. In *Measure for Measure*, it is Death. On this theme, Shakespeare, speaking through the Duke, reveals his thoughts :

> Reason thus with life :
> If I do lose thee, I do lose a thing
> That none but fools would keep : a breath thou art,
> Servile to all the skyey influences,
> That dost this habitation where thou keep'st
> Hourly afflict . . .

> Thou hast nor youth nor age,
> But as it were an after-dinner's sleep,
> Dreaming on both — for all thy blessed youth
> Becomes as agèd, and doth beg the alms
> Of palsied eld : and when thou art old and rich
> Thou hast neither heat, affection, limb nor beauty,
> To make thy riches pleasant. What's yet in this,
> That bears the name of life ?

A recurrent thought in *All's Well* is the ravages of Time and Change ; there had been much in these tormented years between two worlds to bring the theme home to him.

The young Claudio puts the other side :

> Ay, but to die, and go we know not where,
> To lie in cold obstruction and to rot,
> This sensible warm motion to become
> A kneaded clod ; and the delighted spirit
> To bathe in fiery floods, or to reside
> In thrilling region of thick-ribbèd ice,
> To be imprisoned in the viewless winds
> And blown with restless violence round about
> The pendant world ! . . .

The affirmation of life was just as well, for Shakespeare was on the threshold of his most imperishable achievements with the great tragedies.

CHAPTER XV

The Great Tragedies

A CELEBRATED lecture has warned us against too direct and easy a transference from the facts of Shakespeare's life to the creations of his mind, or rather — since we know so much more about the latter — from his plays to his life. This offered a salutary corrective to the simple view that 'dramatists write tragedies when their mood is tragic, and comedies when they are feeling pleased with life'.[1] We, however, are not so simple : we perceive that the truth in this matter lies somewhere in between. A real writer understands better than a mere critic that there is some correlation between the experience of a creative artist and what he creates, even if it is a question only, at the least, of a mood. And it is a mistake to confuse any literary cult of melancholy with the undoubted *malaise*, for which there was reason, that chilled sensitive men's spirits at the turn of the century. Though literary creations are not to be confused with their creators' lives, they are some evidence : there is the indefinable feeling of interior autobiography in *Hamlet*, so strong that it has given encouragement and material to the psycho-analysts, where we refrain. Our critic allows that 'in *Hamlet* and *Timon* we are shown a genuine disturbance of the spirit'. Even the conservative Chambers thought that the great tragedies 'are not without evidence of mental strain and sometimes exhaustion'.[2] What wonder ? It is not improbable, after the hard experience of life, the pressures on the spirit of which we have seen evidence.

This issue is a question of balance and understanding ; it needs subtlety in the handling. Our critic says, 'it is in the main a question of the artistic problems which Shakespeare set himself, not of the problems which life set Shakespeare'. We may agree, and yet add that the two are not mutually exclusive. As in all significant work we have a convergence of factors, on the one side literary, on the other personal and environmental, or historical.

To the Elizabethans tragedy was supreme, and therefore the test of greatness in drama. When Shakespeare's work was complete it was with the greatest tragedians that Ben Jonson was able to compare him, Aeschylus, Sophocles, Euripides and Seneca. If Shakespeare were to compare with his younger rival Ben, he must do so now in tragedy. With the tragedies he was to make his grandest efforts, extend his powers to their fullest capacity, and thus fulfil his destiny as a writer. Throughout this book there is cumulative evidence that, so far from not caring about his fame and achievement as a writer, his ambition was of the highest. The argument has come full circle : here is a personal consideration.

Now, with the succession secure, a king on the throne even more favourable and more generous to the theatre than his predecessor, with Shakespeare's company in undoubted ascendancy and greater prosperity than ever, with peace made in 1604 and a general feeling of appeasement and security, his friends in favour, Shakespeare was free in mind to go forward to the challenge of the tragedies, explore his own mind and experience to ultimate depths. In this new perspective the personal argument works out rather differently from what has previously been thought : no simple correlation. Of course, the tragedies chimed with his experience of life : it had been sufficiently upheaved, we can now appreciate, with its early disappointments and set-backs, the long struggle and the personal crisis of the plague years, 1592-3 — with all that we now know of the emotional tensions of that time, the later crisis of 1601-3 with his friends involved in fatal courses — and his was a nature to register all this.

He was now free to release himself wholly and utterly in his work, transmute all this into his art, in the proper realm of tragedy. Inspiration returned : the first work of this time, *Othello*, rushes through breathless and inspired, from beginning to end, with one impulse. No difficulty, no chill upon mind and heart, as if working against the grain, as with *All's Well*, or even *Troilus and Cressida* and *Measure for Measure*. All the world recognises *Othello* as an inspired play, written with one continuous impulse like *Romeo and Juliet* a decade before — indeed it is the *Romeo and Juliet* of the later period. With it Shakespeare immediately re-established his popularity in the new reign, after the questioning and uncongenial sequence that had filled the interim.

Othello is close to *Measure for Measure* ; the story comes from the same source, Cinzio's book of *novelle*, which Shakespeare read in the Italian, and he may have got the suggestion of the magical origin of Desdemona's handkerchief from Ariosto in the original. He evidently knew enough of Italian, as of other things, for his purposes. But what a contrast between these two Italianate plays ! In *Measure for Measure* he altered the old story, in which Isabella's chastity was sacrificed in vain, in order to get a more moral effect : her virtue shines out, a beacon upon the unquiet, uneasy scene, and effects a kind of redemption. Nothing of that in *Othello* : all are agreed that it is the most painful of the plays in its total effect, in which an innocent young wife is done to death by a passionate and adoring husband, under a misapprehension fostered by a malignant spirit of evil in Iago. Nothing is spared us : the aesthetic intention of the play, its urge, possessed the mind of its creator and carries us forward ruthlessly, without the least let-up of tension or any deviation of sub-plot, to its thrilling and terrible end in almost ritual murder.

Othello is the most concentrated of the plays : no subsidiary focus of interest is permitted, all our attention is fixed upon the drama of the three characters, Othello, Desdemona and Iago. The conflict of good and evil, which is elsewhere dispersed — in *King Lear* and *Macbeth* throughout the entire worlds of those plays — is here at its simplest and most intense.[3] And Shakespeare darkens and enriches the atmosphere, like a Tintoretto, with perhaps conscious symbolism, by accentuating the racial conflict : for he makes Othello a splendid negro, as potent sexually as he was militarily. Desdemona's father had been bitterly opposed to the marriage, and Emilia, after the catastrophe, speaks out what had been her unconscious mind all along. Shakespeare — evidently as much beyond conventional racial prejudices with Othello as with Shylock — depicts him as the heroic soldier he is, 'great of heart', a leader of men who easily towers above his environment. The mutual passion of Othello and Desdemona surmounts all obstacles — to be shipwrecked in the event by the natal difference : Othello does not really understand her, and so his natural confiding trust and simplicity of nature can be worked upon and overthrown by the sinister suggestions and suspicions created by the evil mind of Iago. Hence the absoluteness of Othello's reaction, the priest-like murder, the native ferocity and tenderness.

Here we have Shakespeare, always trying something new,

creating something new indeed — prophetically foreshadowing one of the crucial issues of the modern world.

The real crux of the play is the devilish Iago, who wreaks all this cruel mischief. It is not that he is wholly unmotivated : he too is suspicious by nature :

> For that I do suspect the lusty Moor
> Hath leaped into my seat ; the thought whereof
> Doth, like a poisonous mineral, gnaw my inwards ;
> And nothing can or shall content my soul
> Till I am evened with him, wife for wife.

There is nothing in his suspicions, they grow out of his cankered heart ; for he is an utterly wicked man, one of those rare creatures who say, 'Evil be thou my good'. A complete cynic — also a rare thing in Shakespeare — he is an artist in moral obliquity : he does evil really for the sake of doing evil. He knows the truth quite well, about himself as well as others :

> The Moor, howbeit that I endure him not,
> Is of a constant, loving nature . . .
> A most dear husband.

For such a type, that is sufficient motive to wreck the marriage. Now the interesting thing is that, though everybody has regarded Iago as a monster, he is in fact a recognisable human type. There *are* such malignant people, with whom others' happiness is a sufficient motive to destroy it. Nowadays, we are apt to regard such types as psychotic and absolve them of responsibility for the evil they do. In the play Iago gets his deserts for what he is and has done. He is, of course, a Marlovian creation — but how much truer than Marlowe, and how much more subtly Shakespeare shuts up the secret of his nature : when all that he has wrought is discovered —

> Demand me nothing. What you know, you know.
> From this time forth I never will speak word.

Since this is an inspired work the action is expressed in splendid poetry, unlike the constricted bare verse of *All's Well*. We note a new development in the verse, the tendency to depart from the tyranny of the line-unit to end speeches and sentences in the middle of the line. This must have satisfied some deeply felt urge — for something new, to get away from what had become monotonous, or, more important, a response to some inscrutable psychological or even physical change. Though only forty, he was in the rich, sombrely glowing autumn of his life. In his first period there had been the regular five-stress line, unrhymed or rhyming, with the sense ending with the line ; in the second, more flexible blank verse, with the sense running on ; in this third, verse paragraphs ending in the middle of the line, with frequent half lines. We are on the threshold of the last period where the verse is often irregular, sometimes incapable of exact scansion : what the ear catches are strong rhythmic phrases of indeterminate length, much variety and flexibility, a slackening of intellectual control as in the late brushwork of great painters. This corresponds to physiological changes : the artist is ageing.

Many famous passages attest the rich poetry of this work :

> Not poppy nor mandragora,
> Nor all the drowsy syrups of the world,
> Shall ever medicine thee to that sweet sleep
> Which thou owedst yesterday.

There is the echoing simplicity of

> Put out the light, and then put out the light,

that sends a shiver down the spine ; or of Othello's epitaph upon himself :

> Speak of me as I am. Nothing extenuate,
> Nor set down aught in malice. Then you must speak
> Of one that loved not wisely, but too well ;
> Of one not easily jealous, but, being wrought,
> Perplexed in the extreme.

It has been well observed that in this play we see Shakespeare's verse at its most Miltonic.

Naturally, with such high-powered concentration, there is nothing extraneous for us to catch hold of for our special purpose, and little, where all speaks of its creator, that is specifically personal. We catch the inflexion of —

> But O vain boast !
> Who can control his fate ?

The other stroke of the pendulum to that from Othello is this from Iago : ' 'tis in ourselves that we are thus and thus. Our bodies are our gardens, to the which our wills are gardeners.' Shakespeare calculated both strokes, thought both things. It is

by a further subtlety that he puts into the mouth of Iago so much
of what he himself held to be true :

> Men should be what they seem ;
> Or those that be not [honest], would they might seem none !

> Good name in man and woman, dear my lord,
> Is the immediate jewel of their souls.

> But jealous souls will not be answered so ;
> They are not ever jealous for the cause,
> But jealous for they are jealous. 'Tis a monster
> Begot upon itself, born on itself.

We may not be wrong in inferring a personal inflexion in a famous
reference to drink : 'O God, that men should put an enemy in
their mouths to steal away their brains ! that we should with
joy, pleasance, revel, and applause transform ourselves into beasts !'
There is no bawdy in this play about marital chastity ; there is
one only of the now familiar jokes about venereal disease : 'why,
masters, ha' your instruments been at Naples, that they speak i'
th' nose thus ?'

In this ominously enclosed world, the window opens only
once on the outer world of Othello's travels :

> Wherein of antres vast and deserts idle,
> Rough quarries, rocks, and hills whose heads touch heaven,
> It was my hint to speak . . .
> And of the cannibals that each other eat,
> The anthropophagi, and men whose heads
> Do grow beneath their shoulders.

This is a specific reference to Ralegh's Guiana voyage of 1595
and to what he found there, written up in his book, *The Discovery
of the Large, Rich and Beautiful Empire of Guiana*, which Shakespeare had read, along with other voyages. The author of that
work, Essex's enemy, was now comfortably ensconced in the
Tower, having taken Southampton's place there later in 1603.

Othello was performed by the King's men in the banqueting
house at Whitehall on Hallowmas day, 1 November 1604. It
had probably been written earlier that year. Indescribable in its
effect of desolation and misery is the Willow Song sung by Desdemona just before her murder, like the scraps of traditional songs
sung by Ophelia before her suicide. The King's men must have
had a remarkable singing boy to perform these parts. Between

Advent 1604 and Lent 1605 several performances of Shakespeare's earlier plays were put on, including *The Comedy of Errors*, *Love's Labour's Lost*, *The Merchant of Venice*, which James and his Queen, avid of plays, had not seen.

Renewed, secure, inspired, Shakespeare went on to scale the highest summit he ever attempted, a Mount Everest of an achievement, *King Lear*. Of all the peaks he compassed we shall not be far out in considering *Hamlet* and *King Lear* as the twin summits : *Hamlet* for the interior drama of the soul, *Lear* for the relations of an heroic, outsize human being with others, its place in nature itself, a kind of cosmos, perhaps a cosmic drama. A modern critic says well that, compared with ancient Greek tragedies, its only peers, '*King Lear* suggests the Gothic order. Its form is irregular and organic, determined seemingly by a series of upward thrusts of mounting internal energy. There is even a Gothic element of the grotesque, as when mock-beggar, jester and king, reduced to common condition, hold their mad juridical proceedings in a storm-lashed hovel.' [4] Hazlitt's fine sentence on the play has been often quoted, but we cannot forgo it here : 'all that we can say must fall far short of the subject, or even what we ourselves conceive of it'.

For his story Shakespeare went back to the legendary pre-history of Britain. The unification of the island with the accession of a Scottish king brought this theme up to the surface of people's minds — gone was the self-sufficiency of Elizabeth's England, the England of *King John*, of John of Gaunt and the history-plays. Here, too, was a new world for the imagination to explore, and Shakespeare proceeded to explore it in *Lear*, *Macbeth* and *Cymbeline*. The legendary British king appears in the antiquarians, Camden and Carew, as well as in Holinshed. Shakespeare owed more to the old play of *King Leir*, in which he may have acted in the earlier 1590's, for there are close parallels, especially when Perillus is on the scene, which may have been his rôle. He read the story, too, in the *Mirror for Magistrates* and in the *Faerie Queene*, from which he got the form of the name Cordelia. He was much influenced by Sidney's *Arcadia*, whence he got the story of the Paphlagonian king for the sub-plot of Gloucester and his sons, with which he underlined a leading theme of the play — ingratitude.

Grief is the stone which finest judgment proves :

there are many verbal parallels and phrases caught up in Shakespeare's adhesive mind. The names of the fiends, and other crazy touches, come from Harsnett's recent *Declaration of Egregious Popish Impostures* (1603).

Of these diverse materials Shakespeare forged a white-hot unity ; though the structure is more complex than ever before, even than that of *Hamlet*, it is all closely welded and banded together in a superb aesthetic effort. As usual, it is more profitable to watch the changes the supreme artist made. He added age and stature, his Lear is older than any of the sources, he has furious energy, rage, epic grandeur. Then, too, Shakespeare made it infinitely tragic ; he knew from his experience with *Hamlet* how deeply moving madness is on the stage. He now gave up the centre of his play to a wild ballet of madness in storm across the heaths of southern Britain to Dover. He intensified the horror : 'Shakespeare alone and in defiance of precedent conducted Lear to ultimate misery. *Enter Lear with Cordelia in his arms. . . . He dies.* These directions enclose a scene which demonstrates beyond any other in tragic literature the intransigence of poetic art.' [5] No wonder the kind heart of Dr. Johnson found the fate of Cordelia unbearable. It *is* hard to bear, even in reading ; and to see it on the stage shakes one terribly. When Cordelia sees her father again, after the experiences he has gone through, and greets him — for the first time in the play — as 'your Majesty' and Lear replies,

> You do me wrong to take me out o' the grave —

the heart turns over. The exchange that follows is the most sorrowful in literature :

> *Lear :* I know you do not love me ; for your sisters
> Have, as I do remember, done me wrong.
> You have some cause, they have not.
> *Cordelia :*   No cause, no cause.

Shakespeare's infallible aesthetic instinct told him that his *Lear* could not but end in tragedy, anything else would be beneath the level of this sublime work of art. And yet there have always been people who thought that he did not care much about considerations of art ! The simple truth is that however much these were men of genius themselves — Ben Jonson, Dryden, Dr. Johnson, Voltaire, Tolstoy — they were not up to understanding the secret of it.

The story is a primitive one, like those of *Hamlet* and *Macbeth* ;

in this case, of the ingratitude of children towards the father, and like all such archetypes arouses the deepest searchings of heart and conscience. It becomes a kind of allegory of mankind, with a king as father-symbol, of man's discovery of the cruelty and malignancy in the world, well-nigh overwhelmed in the struggle — the human spirit for a time overthrown, but not extinguished — of the achievement of self-knowledge through suffering. That is a kind of redemption in purely human terms ; there is no happy ending, and attempts to reconcile this play with orthodox Christian values are beside the mark. It seems certain, however, that a fierce hatred of cold cruelty, hypocrisy and deceit, sheer wickedness, aroused Shakespeare to fury in this play, for everybody feels its intense sincerity. Where had he got this hatred from, and where had he seen these things exposed ? Evidently from life's experience, and in what he had observed upon the public scene. It is a significant pointer to his nature that he has much more charity for illusions : the source of Lear's troubles, after all, are his illusions —about himself, about others, about the facts of human life. Some of us may find it harder to entertain sympathy for such a frame of mind. Shakespeare is kinder and more morally discriminating : he reserves his artillery for the active forces of evil. But it is this fracture in Lear's nature that lays him wide open to these malign forces, and then he discovers how widespread they are — coterminous with life and nature. The elements themselves take a hand against man : the universe itself is at strife, imaged and symbolised in the only possible way.

Shakespeare was 'certainly in a ruthless mood when he wrote *King Lear*'.[6] It is a tragedy of parents and children, of hatred of the father ; of ingratitude, and retribution upon pride ; of kingship, and the inevitable consequence in the distortion of relationships, the uncertainty whether professed love is sincere : of hypocrisy and false professions ; of nausea for sex and breeding. Adversity alone brings the mighty down to the level of common humanity and sympathy with the poor, where there is less wickedness. Lear discovers their sufferings, which he had not felt before :

> Poor naked wretches, wheresoe'er you are,
> That bide the pelting of this pitiless storm,
> How shall your houseless heads and unfed sides,
> Your looped and windowed raggedness, defend you
> From seasons such as this ? O ! I have ta'en
> Too little care of this.

There are touches like this, and Lear's final meeting with Cordelia —

> We two alone will sing like birds i' the cage ;
> When thou dost ask me blessing, I'll kneel down
> And ask of thee forgiveness —

that point forward to the reconciliation, forgiveness, charity, of the last plays. In these, Christian values are affirmed, but with no metaphysical nonsense, which calls only for disbelief. Such values are the traditional and tried values by which mankind holds — or else 'chaos is come again' : hence their force. Irreparable disaster comes to Lear's wicked daughters and Gloucester's equally bad bastard who pursue only their own unscrupulous self-interest. Edmund is very like Iago in his calculation and hypocrisy, and that the character of Iago went on in Shakespeare's mind appears from Cornwall's description of the type :

> These kind of knaves I know, which in this plainness
> Harbour more craft and more corrupter ends
> Than twenty silly-ducking observants
> That stretch their duties nicely.

It is another pointer that Shakespeare, himself a rational calculating man, should turn against calculating rationalism as a guide to life. Evidently he thought it applicable to his external career and his investments, but no guide to the mystery and problems of life, where fate, or forces beyond rational calculation, take control.

In such a play we are naturally given insights into his values, his convictions, and preferences. As we have observed before, his native ambivalence — such an endowment for a dramatist — expresses itself in contrary strokes of the pendulum. Gloucester says, 'these late eclipses of the sun and moon portend no good to us : though the wisdom of nature can reason it thus and thus, yet nature finds itself scourged by the sequent effects. Love cools, friendship falls off, brothers divide ; in cities, mutinies, in countries, discord ; in palaces, treason ; and the bond cracked twixt son and father.' The bastard son's comment on this is the same as Iago's : 'this is the excellent foppery of the world that, when we are sick in fortune, often the surfeits of our own behaviour, we make guilty of our disasters the sun, moon, and stars'. The repetition of these contrary inflexions in play after play shows that they meant much to Shakespeare : between whose endless jarring justice resides. He leaves an open verdict : there may be something in the influence of the stars.   He sees the duplicity, the double-sidedness of things :

> I stumbled when I saw. Full oft 'tis seen,
> Our means secure us and our mere defects
> Prove our commodities.

We see the subtlety for, at the same time as he perceives the relativism of circumstance, he is no moral relativist.   He has so much surer a grasp of life than Tolstoy, who thought the primitive *King Leir* with its happy ending a greater work of art — and proved his percipience by himself stumbling, an old man, out into the world, another Lear, to die in despair.

This play continues the obsessive disgust with sex that is so characteristic of Shakespeare at this period that it must indicate something in his state of mind, if not of body.   Lear's mind, mad, dwells on the subject, as Ophelia's did :

> Adultery ?
> Thou shalt not die : die for adultery ! No —

we have seen that Shakespeare had had reason enough to be obsessed himself —

> The wren goes to't, and the small gilded fly
> Does lecher in thy sight . . .
>   Behold yond simpering dame,
> Whose face between her forks presages snow,
> That minces virtue and does shake the head
> To hear of pleasure's name ;
>   The fitchew nor the soiled horse goes to't
> With a more riotous appetite :
> Down from the waist they are centaurs,
> Though women all above.

Women are stripped of their pretences in these plays, one after another ; never were such harpies created as Goneril and Regan, and each lusting after the bastard Edmund.   On the other hand, there remains always Cordelia.   Edmund is a very different kind of bastard from earlier Faulconbridge, with his aggressive defence of his bastardy :

> Why brand they us
> With base ? with baseness ? bastardy ? base, base ?
> Who in the lusty stealth of nature take
> More composition and fierce quality
> Than doth, within a dull, stale, tired bed,
> Go to the creating a whole tribe of fops,
> Got 'tween asleep and wake ?

On this Shakespeare knew a thing or two.

Nor are we mistaken in seizing upon the applicability to his own case of the Fool's — 'he's a mad yeoman that sees his son a gentleman before him'. This may well be a saying of the time, but Shakespeare had seen to it that his father had been made a gentleman first. We have a description

> Of Bedlam beggars, who with roaring voices
> Strike in their numbed and mortified bare arms
> Pins, wooden pricks, nails, sprigs of rosemary,

which is in keeping with contemporary accounts of these horrors. They would be very familiar to him from the days when he had lived in Shoreditch and passed in and out the city through Bishopsgate, with Bedlam just outside. He reflects, through Edgar :

> When we our betters see bearing our woes,
> We scarcely think our miseries our foes.
> Who alone suffers, suffers most i' the mind ;

and we seem to hear his voice in the reflection,

> the worst is not
> So long as we can say 'This is the worst.'

We know that Shakespeare's company visited Dover on 4 October 1604 — they had been there previously in September 1597 ; so that Shakespeare's Cliff should be authentic enough :

> How fearful
> And dizzy 'tis to cast one's eyes so low !
> The crows and choughs that wing the midway air
> Show scarce so gross as beetles ; half way down
> Hangs one that gathers samphire, dreadful trade !
> Methinks he seems no bigger than his head.
> The fishermen that walk upon the beach
> Appear like mice, and yond tall anchoring bark
> Diminished to her cock, her cock a buoy
> Almost too small for sight. The murmuring surge,
> That on the unnumbered idle pebbles chafes,
> Cannot be heard so high.

Thoughts familiar to us now from so many plays come up, constants in his mind : with the bonds of morality broken,

> Humanity must perforce prey on itself,
> Like monsters of the deep.

There is his observation of moral relativism in the realm of fact, though he did not subscribe to it in the realm of principle : 'change places, and handy-dandy, which is the justice, which is the thief?' Again :

> Why dost thou lash that whore ? Strip thine own back :
> Thou hotly lust'st to use her in that kind
> For which thou whipp'st her.

It is the theme of, almost a quotation from, *Measure for Measure*. There are reminiscences from previous plays and reading : from *Troilus* with, 'none of those rogues and cowards but Ajax is their fool' ; from *Euphues*, from Chaucer, and back to his own *Titus Andronicus*, where the triangular relations of Aaron, Tamora, Saturninus resemble those of Edmund, Goneril, Albany. The scene of mad justice where Lear, the Fool and Edgar turn tables on ordinary mortals and judge them recalls Falstaff and Prince Hal playing the parts of the King and Prince ; only there is no joy in this, this is piteous.

Contemporary references traverse this spacious play, where they hardly penetrate the stifling, enclosed atmosphere of *Othello*. We have Kent putting down the foppish Oswald as a 'base football-player' — football was a low street-game in those days, played by boys rather than by overgrown adolescents. Oswald is an affected Court-fop, and we hear of 'Court holy water', *i.e.* flattery. Monopolies, which became increasingly unpopular and a subject of Parliamentary grievance after 1601, make their appearance : the Fool says, 'lords and great men will not let me ; if I had a monopoly out, they would have part on't'. We hear of a popular complaint : the 'mother' (the phrase still remains in remote places) or *hysterica passio*. A contemporary case of possession, relating to three chambermaids, is referred to by Edgar : this came from Harsnett, who was employed in exposing Catholic claims to have exorcised fiends from credulous women.

The oddest thing is the suggestive case of Sir Brian Annesley, only a year or two before Shakespeare tackled *King Lear*. In none of the versions of the story does the old king go mad. Sir Brian Annesley, who had been a gentleman-pensioner of Queen Elizabeth and may therefore have been known to the dramatist, did go mad ; and he had three daughters, the elder two of whom tried to get him certified as insane so as to get hold of his estate. This was resisted by the youngest daughter, called Cordell (or Cordelia), who considered that his services to the Queen 'deserved a better agnomination than at his last gasp to be recorded and registered a lunatic'.[7] It was this kind daughter who in 1608, after the dowager Countess of Southampton's death married her third husband, Sir William Harvey. How things come together !

The play was written in all probability, next after *Othello*, which would indicate the winter of 1604-5. We know that it was performed at Court on 26 December 1606, 'before the King's Majesty at Whitehall upon St. Stephen's night in Christmas holidays, by his Majesty's servants playing usually at the Globe on the Bankside'. In 1608 there appeared the celebrated Pied Bull Quarto — apparently a memorial reconstruction of the play by the actors. This version was that acted by Sir Richard Cholmeley's players at Candlemas 1610 up in Yorkshire at Gowthwaite Hall, a nest of Catholic recusants. It is not without interest that they were appreciators of Shakespeare.

Before these congenial happenings his Majesty received a great shock with the exposure of Gunpowder Plot, 5 November 1605, which was to have blown him and his family, with all the Lords and Commons assembled in Parliament, sky high at the hands of the extreme wing of young Catholic malcontents. These events are not only reflected in Shakespeare's next play, *Macbeth*, but I think it fairly clear that the conception of such a play was suggested by them. The reaction from the shock was one of immense relief (along, naturally, with horror at those who had intended to perpetrate it). The extirpation of the dynasty would have led to untold confusion, and there was a real movement of spontaneous feeling towards the King and his family. Shakespeare, ever-responsive to the public mood, was inspired to write a play to do honour to the dynasty's legendary forbear, Banquo, and thus to the King.

Greg's phrase that *Macbeth* was 'obviously designed to flatter King James' puts the matter a little crudely ; [8] but true it is that this work pays more tribute to the Scottish King than ever the dramatist had paid to the English Queen in all his previous works. Then, as we know, his affiliations had been with the opposition party, while King James's marked favour went to Shakespeare's friends. So in *Macbeth* we have tributes paid to Banquo, the mythical ancestor of the Stuarts, to his 'royalty of nature', the 'dauntless temper of his mind', the 'wisdom that doth guide his valour,' while we are constantly reminded of the prophecy that

Thou shalt get kings, though thou be none.

Similarly the King's personal interest in witches and demonology is catered for by the dominating influence exerted upon the action by the Weird Sisters, who are really incarnations of evil. James had written a book on demonology in Scotland, which Shakespeare read up for his play along with other Scottish lore : this Calvinist was very sure that witches and demons existed, where Queen Elizabeth, a sensible Erasmian, gave no thought to such matters. King James knew that it was witches who had raised up the storm that made his crossing the North Sea to marry Anne of Denmark so very unpleasant. There were further glances at James's powers, as an anointed king, of healing the King's Evil, which much flattered Mary Stuart's son, where Elizabeth had taken it in her stride. It is hinted that King James spoke with the power of inspiration, and this he was at no pains to disclaim, when put to him by venerable and religious bishops. Lastly, tribute was paid to James's aim at bringing about a universal peace — much the most respectable side of him.

The date, then, should offer no difficulties, though needlessly heavy weather has been made of it. In this perspective we see that it comes after Gunpowder Plot and the trial of the Jesuit Provincial, Henry Garnet, in March 1606, whose statements with regard to the use of equivocation made the worst impression. Garnet had been implicated in the Gunpowder treason, for he knew that something dastardly was afoot, though he may not have known the details, and said nothing about it. He also inculcated the doctrine that, under examination, rather than divulge what might be damaging one need not tell the truth : one could equivocate. This was strongly reflected in the direct reference to 'an equivocator that could swear in both scales against either scale, who committed treason enough for God's sake, yet could not equivocate to heaven'. Again, 'what is a traitor ?' asks young Macduff. His mother answers, 'why, one that swears and lies. . . . Everyone that does so is a traitor, and must be hanged.' Father Garnet was, properly, hanged ; it is not known whether he went to heaven, or not.

It seems certain that *Macbeth* was one of the plays given at Court on King Christian IV's memorable, if somewhat inebriated, visit to his sister and brother-in-law in 1606. There are references to *Macbeth* being acted at this time in Beaumont and Fletcher's *Knight of the Burning Pestle* and in *The Puritan*, perhaps by Middleton : in both cases it is the appearance of Banquo's ghost at table that made the impression. Middleton may have had a hand in revising the play for performance at the time of the Princess Elizabeth's wedding festivities in 1613, when Shakespeare had left the stage, and this may have resulted in some interpolations in the text. Shakespeare himself may have abridged the play, possibly for performance before Christian IV. The result is that it is much the shortest of the tragedies : in any case it always was a short play, of intense concentration.

It is closely connected with *King Lear* in kind ; not only in that the matter is drawn from the primitive world of Celtic Britain, but that it is a world haunted by the fact of evil. *Macbeth* is above all a triumph of atmosphere : a sombre realm of guilt, guilt for murder suggested, premeditated, accomplished, multiplied, and at length expiated. Evil is in the air. When the Weird Sisters prophesy to Macbeth that he will be king, he starts in fear, as Banquo notices. It is because his half-conscious ambitions are confirmed and given external voice. But are the voices altogether external ? They were to contemporaries and for long after ; but with our knowledge of psychology we are at liberty to reinterpret them as promptings of the unconscious. This, though strictly anachronistic, points to another wonder with Shakespeare, as with the world's greatest artists : that their scope offers a renewed interpretation for every age.

Was Lady Macbeth possessed, when she called on the powers of evil to unsex her, fill her full of cruelty and expel from her all signs of grace? Jacobean spectators would take this, like the Ghost in *Hamlet*, literally. Shakespeare leaves the question open. We are at liberty to interpret as we will, but there is no doubt about the fact of evil, the existence of the phenomenon. In our time we have seen Macbeth's fearful nightmare re-enacted in highest place on the public scene. Rule by murder gives no security : the moment Macbeth has the throne he begins to fear Banquo ; the moment he has had Banquo murdered, Macduff becomes a menace in his diseased mind and he has his family exterminated. We have seen the nightmare sequence carried out in both Stalin's Russia and Hitler's Germany. We may call it persecution-mania, but it does not cease to be evil and a crime against humanity. It was percipient of Professor Walter Raleigh, considering that he was bred in the civilised Victorian world, to smell 'the central fire which breaks through the thin crust of civilisation and makes a splendour in the sky above the blackness of ruined homes. Shakespeare knows how precarious is man's tenure of the soil, how deceitful are his quiet orderly habits and his prosaic speech. At any moment by the operation of chance, or fate, these things may be broken up, and the world given over once more to the forces that struggled in chaos.' We, too, know that — now.

The play portrays to us the temptation and fall of a noble character by the forces of evil — for Macbeth is in essence a noble Shakespearean hero ; we watch his overthrow, degeneration and destruction. All in a sphere of sombre, splendid poetry ; for his soul is a noble ruin, expressing itself in the finest Gothic verse :

> Methought I heard a voice cry 'Sleep no more !
> Macbeth does murder sleep '— the innocent sleep,
> Sleep that knits up the ravelled sleave of care,
> The death of each day's life, sore labour's bath,
> Balm of hurt minds . . .

In this Shakespeare was remembering Sir Philip Sidney's famous sonnet :

> Come sleep, O sleep, the certain knot of peace,
> The bathing place of wits, the balm of woe.

Or there is Macbeth's speech on hearing of his wife's death — nothing is spared him :

> She should have died hereafter :
> There would have been a time for such a word.
> Tomorrow, and tomorrow, and tomorrow,
> Creeps in this petty pace from day to day
> To the last syllable of recorded time,
> And all our yesterdays have lighted fools
> The way to dusty death . . .

And then, with a sudden transition of thought to Shakespeare's own life in the theatre :

> Life's but a walking shadow, a poor player
> That struts and frets his hour upon the stage
> And then is heard no more :

We are not far away from the death of the poor player, Shakespeare's young brother, and the knelling of the bell of St. Saviour's, Southwark for him.

There is little that is specifically personal or circumstantial for us to catch hold of in a play so concentrated as this. Macbeth sees himself as a bear being baited at the end :

> They have tied me to a stake ; I cannot fly,
> But bearlike I must fight the course.

We hear of Macdonald of the Western Isles, and his supply of kerns and gallow-glasses, who in fact had kept Ulster in turmoil in the last two or three decades.

> Her husband's to Aleppo gone, master o' th' Tiger —

there was a ship, the *Tiger*, that made the voyage to Aleppo in the 1580's ; Shakespeare was remembering it. There are several more references to the use of equivocation, such was the impression it made on people's minds : 'much drink may be said to be an equivocator with lechery : it makes him, and it mars him ; it sets him on, and it takes him off ; it persuades him, and disheartens him ; makes him stand to, and not stand to.' At the end Macbeth begins

> To doubt the equivocation of the fiend
> That lies like truth : 'Fear not, till Birnam wood
> Do come to Dunsinane' : and now a wood
> Comes towards Dunsinane !

And last there is the trick of relativism, that is a personal stamp of Shakespeare's :

> But I remember now
> I am in this earthly world : where to do harm
> Is often laudable, to do good sometime
> Accounted dangerous folly.

It is an indictment of the world and of our behaviour in it ; he did not agree that this was in truth the essence of the matter.

After these Gothic glooms, these sombre pinnacled edifices with their echoing vaults, their scenes by night and storm, back to the glowing autumnal colours of the Mediterranean world. *Antony and Cleopatra* is more Veronese-like than any of the plays, in its rich colouring, its exotic atmosphere, suggesting the panoply of the East. Back also to North's *Plutarch* and the classics for a source. The story of *Antony and Cleopatra* in a sense continues that of *Julius Caesar* : it is what happens to Antony afterwards — and, after all, Cleopatra had been mistress to both. There could hardly be a greater contrast in atmosphere : the controlled, chaste classicism of the one compared with the romantic richness, the lyric splendour of the other.

Once more Shakespeare produced something different, virtually unique ; and once more the critics have been put into a 'canary' as to how to label it. Bradley called it a history drama. The double tragedy, the deaths of Antony and Cleopatra at different times, imposed an unprecedented shape ; Cleopatra has the last act all to herself, but so far from this making for a declension of power, it inspired Shakespeare 'to compose a coda to the tragedy of Antony which many consider the most wonderful movement in any of his great symphonies'.⁹ Then, too, there was a whole world to suggest, the decisive world of Mediterranean politics from Rome to Athens, from Actium to Alexandria. During the first half of the play there is very little historical material or incident out of which to make drama, so that it is mesmerising to see with what acrobatic skill he keeps the interest aroused, curiosity alert. We are given a series of short episodic scenes, going to and fro between Rome, Athens, Alexandria, unlike anything else in Shakespeare — easy enough on the big, open Elizabethan stage, but setting a hard problem for modern production on a picture-stage. All these add cumulatively to our compelling interest in Cleopatra, but 'what confidence in his own mastery, what miraculous power, to have created this vast solidly constructed background and yet to have kept it as a background, with seemingly effortless ease !' ¹⁰ And over and beyond it all, there lurks an enigmatic smile — 'satirical' is too strong, too unsubtle a word : behind all the passion, the power and pathos, there is something enigmatical — as if in this story of a world well lost for love, Shakespeare had at last achieved detachment. For it is the smile of Leonardo.

If *Macbeth* is a triumph of atmosphere, so is *Antony and Cleopatra* — but how incomparable to be able to move, as apparently he did, straight from one to the other ! We have observed how frequently in his youth he had had to fall back on the art of making a little go a long way ; so now, too, at the later height of his career. There was little information about Egypt to go upon, almost nothing in Plutarch. So he made the utmost of the Nile,

its mysterious ebbing and flowing, its teeming mudbanks, croco-
diles and the flies of Egypt (from the Bible). There were the
pyramids, of course ; Isis seems to have been the only deity he
was aware of : he made the most of her. Following the early
habit of his old model, Marlowe, he regales us with the exotic
names of eastern potentates and kingdoms :

> He hath assembled
> Bocchus, the king of Libya ; Archelaus
> Of Cappadocia ; Philadelphos, king
> Of Paphlagonia ; the Thracian king, Adallas ;
> King Manchus of Arabia ; King of Pont ;
> Herod of Jewry ; Mithridates, king
> Of Comagene ; Polemon and Amyntas,
> The kings of Mede and Lycaonia, with a
> More larger list of sceptres.

How this must have rolled out in the theatre upon Octavius
Caesar's lips ! Shakespeare owed something here to the reading
of the Bible in church.

It may not have been observed how much the atmosphere
owes to the constant reiteration of the image of snakes — Shakespeare had always been very conscious of them — of serpents
and the idea of poison. More than a dozen times these connected
ideas appear, scattered from beginning to end of the play. According to Cleopatra Antony hails her,

> 'Where's my serpent of old Nile ?'
> For so he calls me. Now I feed myself
> With most delicious poison.

Infuriated with a mere messenger for bringing bad news, she turns
on him :

> Melt Egypt into Nile ! and kindly creatures
> Turn all to serpents ! Call the slave again.
> Though I am mad, I will not bite him.

Later in the same scene she wishes,

> So half my Egypt were submerged and made
> A cistern for scaled snakes !

The absurd Lepidus opines, 'Y' have strange serpents there . . .
Your serpent of Egypt is bred now of your mud by the operation
of your sun ; so is your crocodile'. (That is what the Elizabethans
thought.) And so also with the idea of poison : it echoes all
through the play.

At the very beginning when Charmian and Iras are having their fortunes told by a soothsayer, he foretells that Charmian will outlive her mistress. She is gratified: 'O, excellent! I love long life better than figs'. Commentators have appreciated the sexual impropriety here: they do not seem to have noticed the aesthetic propriety, whether unconscious or intended by the artist, for it looks forward to the end when death comes to Charmian, after her mistress, in a basket of figs.

Passages of famous poetry light up the scene with a Titianesque glow:

> The barge she sat in, like a burnished throne,
> Burned on the water. The poop was beaten gold;
> Purple the sails, and so perfumèd that
> The winds were love-sick with them; the oars were silver,
> Which to the tune of flutes kept stroke . . .

As for Cleopatra:

>   She did lie
> In her pavilion, cloth-of-gold, of tissue
> O'er-picturing that Venus where we see
> The fancy outwork nature.

I think this must be influenced by Renaissance pictures of Venus, or engravings of them which Shakespeare had seen — we know from *Timon*, as from elsewhere, how responsive he was to the art of painting. The enriched style of the poetry expresses the loose exoticism of the atmosphere:

> Eros! — I come my queen — Eros! — Stay for me
> Where souls do couch on flowers, we'll hand in hand,
> And with our sprightly port make the ghosts gaze;
> Dido and her Aeneas shall want troops,
> And all the haunt be ours.

The overriding impression that is left by *Antony and Cleopatra*, and what gives this play its peculiar glow, is the quite extraordinary virtuosity of the language. Just as there is a helter-skelter rush in the action, so there is a burning, hectic quality in the language: it there reaches a point beyond which not even Shakespeare could ever go. It is sometimes such as to make one doubt one's eyes or ears as one takes it in:

> Burn the great sphere thou mov'st in, darkling stand
> The varying shore of the world.

Now boast thee, death, in thy possession lies
A lass unparalleled. Downy windows close,
And golden Phoebus never be beheld
Of eyes again so royal.

The odds is gone, and there is nothing left
Remarkable beneath the visiting moon.

In this play, the lordliness towards language which had been in Shakespeare from the first reaches a pitch of virtuosity — a kind of playing with verbal magnificence — beyond which nothing could go, has ever gone, or can ever go so long as the language remains.

But what, in this realm where so much is mysterious, for we do not know, does it portend ? — writing under intense, nervous pressure, impending breakdown ?

When all is said, Cleopatra is the most wonderful woman in Shakespeare. She is the most complex, exotic and compelling to the imagination. It is essential to get her right. The Elizabethans had no comprehension that historically she was a Greek. To them she was an Egyptian, and gipsies were Egyptians. At the end Antony himself describes her as such :

Like a right gipsy hath at fast and loose
Beguiled me to the very heart of loss —

and 'fast-and-loose' was a gipsy game that was played with knots. So she was a tawny gipsy queen. She would dance 'forty paces through the public street', and recover herself, attractively breathless :

other women cloy
The appetites they feed, but she makes hungry
Where most she satisfies.

For she was infinitely various, changing from one iridescent mood to another, mercurial and bewitching, ready to rage and storm and beat her attendants. She well knew how to seduce Anthony's heart, and keep him tethered to her, himself a leading figure in the Roman world — for she was 'cunning past man's thought'. Brave and fearless of death, she could yet fly from the sea-battle at Actium never thinking that Antony would be such a fool as to follow her. For all her feminine gifts, she was a political type, who managed to outwit Octavius Caesar himself — who meant to show her off in triumph, upon the streets of Rome — by taking her own life. She was an enchantress, almost a sorceress, full of the lore of the East and its credulity, listening to fortune-tellers and soothsayers. And yet always, and improbably, she is regal, the descendant of many kings : she does not have to care about dignity. The politic brain of Caesar — such is the irony of things — understands her best, and pays her the last tribute :

> Bravest at the last,
> She levelled at our purposes, and being royal,
> Took her own way.

She is also the incarnation of sex, more so than any other woman in Shakespeare, and in a different kind. She is quite out-right about it :

> I take no pleasure
> In aught an eunuch has.

The opinion the ordinary common soldier has of her is in keeping, and describes Antony's infatuation for her in coarse enough terms :

> And is become the bellows and the fan
> To cool a gipsy's lust.
> The triple pillar of the world transformed
> Into a strumpet's fool.

Both Antony and Cleopatra think of their infatuation as *un grand' amor*, but in fact it is sex that confuses his brain and judgment — as Shakespeare knew all too well it was apt to do :

> Your presence needs must puzzle Antony,
> Take from his heart, take from his brain, from's time
> What should not then be spared.

It is this that makes him commit all the mistakes of judgment that lead to his overthrow :

> She once being luffed,
> The noble ruin of her magic, Antony,
> Claps on his sea-wing and, like a doting mallard,
> Leaving the flight in height, flies after her.
> I never saw an action of such shame.

Disaster, as usual, meant that some home truths were told : Antony himself told her :

> I found you as a morsel cold upon
> Dead Caesar's trencher. Nay, you were a fragment
> Of Cnaeus Pompey's, besides what hotter hours,
> Unregistered in vulgar fame, you have
> Luxuriously picked out.

And, in final defeat :

> Triple-turned whore ! 'tis thou
> Hast sold me to this novice ; and my heart
> Makes only wars on thee.

When they come to die, however, each dies magnificently with their last thoughts on each other.

No wonder there is an enigmatic smile on the face of the inscrutable author behind the play ! All the sex is in the language, however : there is very little love-making or embracing in the action, nothing, as has been pointed out very properly, 'which a boy could not act without unpleasantness or in fear of ridicule'. [11] Perhaps our sense of what is unpleasant is a little too discriminating. Shakespeare's company must have had a remarkable boy-actor at its disposal who could compass both Lady Macbeth and Cleopatra ; but perhaps the emotional range of adolescent boys was better appreciated in those days.

What are we to think of Antony ?

He is very highly spoken of in the play : are we to think of him as the old-fashioned lady did of the commodity that must be good, 'it is so highly spoken of in the advertisements' ? His words are very noble, but his actions are very foolish. At his first appearance he tells us :

> Let Rome in Tiber melt, and the wide arch
> Of the rangèd empire fall ! Here is my space.
> Kingdoms are clay ; our dungy earth alike
> Feeds beast as man. The nobleness of life
> Is to do thus [*Embracing*].

People in high place who think thus are apt to get what is coming to them : abdications ensue, and though it takes four acts to bring Antony to his end, the end is clearly foreseen. A key to his character, we are told, is magnanimity ; he is certainly generous — when Enobarbus deserts a leader so lost to reason, Antony sends his treasure after him. Rather a waste, in the circumstances. We know that he was good-looking, big and fine and sexy — Cleopatra tells us as much : he evidently gave satisfaction. He was very willing and amiable — intelligent enough at times to recognise his infatuation as 'dotage' and to know where his duty lay. But he was weak-willed and broke his promise to the young Caesar, besides insulting him by deserting his wife, Caesar's sister, for Cleopatra.

I must from this enchanting queen break off :
Ten thousand harms, more than the ills I know,
My idleness doth hatch.

But he cannot break off. It is always difficult to respect someone who, we are told, is a very fine fellow in this situation. And
the situation has its comic aspects too — as Shakespeare very
well knew ; it would have been aesthetically inappropriate in a
tragedy to give vent to these, so the smile remains latent, hardly
perceptible, except to those who know their Shakespeare. We
learn that Antony has been a great soldier in his time, much superior
to the young Caesar ; but we do not see it, he makes only a hash
of the two battles in the play. The clue to his character is that
he is a type of man who goes all out for the full enjoyments of
life, especially physical, and has all the equipment for the purpose.
Such men are not those that inherit the earth. We know that
he is growing older, perhaps somewhat losing his powers, for
we hear of his grizzled hair. Some may think of him as the most
splendid type in literature of the elderly lecher — he is certainly
rendered poetically sympathetic by his creator, who had reason
for a rueful fellow-feeling for him. Antony's much greater experience, his soldierliness, perhaps even his manliness, give him
a contempt for the young Caesar. Here he is wrong, and his
misconception is fatal.

We can admit that Antony has greater expanse of soul — I
will not say, as it is usual to, that he has a greater soul ; for greatness is not the same thing as largeness, or even for that matter
of breadth of response to life. Some forms of greatness demand
singlemindedness.

With Octavius Caesar we are brought up against the political
type again, whom nobody loves ; that may be as it may be, but
it is more important to understand it. Shakespeare does — and
there is no sly laughing, not the ghost of a smile, in his portrait
of him. Nor is Shakespeare unsympathetic, as people think ;
he is, in fact, just. Caesar is not without his own magnanimity ;
when he and Antony begin to fall apart —

Yet if I knew
What hoop should hold us staunch, from edge to edge
O' the world, I would pursue it.

In the politic hope of keeping them together, Caesar marries his
sister to Antony : but

> Let not the piece of virtue which is set
> Betwixt us as the cement of our love
> To keep it builded be the ram to batter
> The fortress of it ; for better might we
> Have loved without this mean, if on both parts
> This be not cherished.

In fact, Antony cannot stand up to the younger man in political discussion, and a soothsayer warns him against competing with Caesar, whose spirit overpowers Antony's :

> If thou dost play with him at any game,
> Thou art sure to lose ; of that natural luck
> He beats thee 'gainst the odds. Thy lustre thickens
> When he shines by.

In a moment of truth Antony realises that this is so :

> The very dice obey him ;
> And in our sports my better cunning faints
> Under his chance.

This draws our attention to a curious political phenomenon : in addition to all his other gifts under discipline and control, a leader has to command luck, too, to emerge as a great man.

Caesar is all that Antony is not, in discipline and self-control. Unlike Antony, who ends the second Act drunk, Caesar hates drink :

> I could well forbear't.
> It's monstrous labour when I wash my brain,
> And it grows fouler.

And he understands everything :

> It hath been taught us from the primal state
> That he which is was wished until he were —

what disillusioned observation there is in this —

> And the ebbed man, ne'er loved till ne'er worth love,
> Comes deared by being lacked. This common body,
> Like to a vagabond flag upon the stream,
> Goes to and back, lackeying the varying tide,
> To rot itself with motion.

It is this control of himself that gives Caesar control of others, indeed it is a necessity in a ruler : he is not likely to respond to Antony's challenge to fight out their quarrel in single combat :

> Yes, like enough high-battled Caesar will
> Unstate his happiness, and be staged to the show
> Against a sworder ! . . .
> > That he should dream,
> Knowing all measures, the full Caesar will
> Answer his emptiness ! Caesar, thou hast subdued
> His judgment too.

Yet, when Antony comes to his well-merited end, it is Caesar who is moved :

> > The death of Antony
> Is not a single doom : in the name lay
> A moiety of the world.

At the end of a Shakespearean tragedy, it is usual for one of the protagonists to speak the eulogium over the dead hero. Caesar speaks it here :

> > O Antony,
> I have followed thee to this ! But we do lance
> Diseases in our bodies. I must perforce
> Have shown to thee such a declining day
> Or look on thine : we could not stall together
> In the whole world. But yet let me lament,
> With tears as sovereign as the blood of hearts,
> That thou, my brother, my competitor
> In top of all design, my mate in empire,
> Friend and companion in the front of war,
> The arm of mine own body, and the heart
> Where mine his thoughts did kindle — that our stars,
> Unreconciliable, should divide
> Our equalness to this.

It is much what Ralegh thought about his enemy Essex, as he watched the scene of his beheading from a window within the Tower.[12] An inside knowledge of the faction-fighting upon the Elizabethan political scene has gone into the writing of *Antony and Cleopatra*. There was the striving for power, partnerships made and broken, friends deserting —

> > The hearts
> That spanieled me at heels, to whom I gave
> Their wishes, do discandy, melt their sweets
> On blossoming Caesar—

grief for the fallen enemy when he was safely under the sod, and the world, that had not been well lost for love, inherited by those that had heads to keep.

Little more need be said, except for a specific personal touch here and there. We are used by now to the signature-tune of the turn of relativism :

> We, ignorant of ourselves
> Beg often our own harms, which the wise powers
> Deny us for our good : so find we profit
> By losing of our prayers.

Here is another :

> There's a great spirit gone ! Thus did I desire it.
> What our contempts doth often hurl from us
> We wish it ours again ; the present pleasure,
> By revolution lowering, does become
> The opposite of itself.

Nevertheless, we must guard against the imputation of moral relativism : Shakespeare had an unshakably and profoundly moral view of life and experience. There is something more subtle and two-sided in his observation : his way of holding contraries together in his mind, and stating them as they balance out in life. This seems a reflection personal to him, too :

> I see men's judgments are
> A parcel of their fortunes, and things outward
> Do draw the inward quality after them,
> To suffer all alike.

Cleopatra foresees her story and Antony's balladed by rhymers on the streets in Elizabethan fashion :

> the quick comedians
> Extemporally will stage us, and present
> Our Alexandrian revels ; Antony
> Shall be brought drunken forth, and I shall see
> Some squeaking Cleopatra boy my greatness
> I' the posture of a whore.

There is a reflex vision, very characteristic of Shakespeare in that. What he says of the people is what he has always said :

> our slippery people,
> Whose love is never linked to the deserver
> Till his deserts are past . . .

While the following already trenches, in his manner, on his next play, *Coriolanus* :

> Mechanic slaves,
> With greasy aprons, rules, and hammers, shall
> Uplift us to the view ; in their thick breaths,
> Rank of gross diet, shall we be enclouded,
> And forced to drink their vapour.

We have seen how constantly interlinked Shakespeare's plays are, how one play betrays the thought of the next in his mind, or how the previous one is still re-echoing.   Thus, Macbeth says of Banquo :

> under him
> My Genius is rebuked, as it is said
> Mark Antony's was by Caesar.

Antony and Cleopatra was already in his mind before finishing *Macbeth* and would have been completed by summer 1607.   For in that year Samuel Daniel published a new edition of his *Cleopatra*, noticeably revised under the influence of the play.   Another play of 1607, Barnabe Barnes's *The Devil's Charter*, also took hints from the leading dramatist of the age.

Shakespeare's next undertaking was *Coriolanus*, and it would seem that he wrote it at home in Stratford some time in 1608. With his mind ever on the look-out for something new, with those sensitive antennae out to apprehend what was in the air, he produced something different again : a political tragedy.   For that is the character of the last of his great tragedies : the tragedy of a leader whose nature is in conflict with that of a society where he cannot but stand out, by his eminent services to the state, by his character, birth and position.   Coriolanus is a soldier and a patrician, caught in the toils of a society where to gain power it is necessary at least to talk humbug to the people.   He is a man of uncompromising integrity and cannot bring himself to do it ; his services therefore go unrewarded and are lost to the state ; he is driven out and goes over to the enemy, to bring defeat upon his native country and a tragic death upon himself.   It is evident that this play has much to say to us today.

There is in it a good deal of the social and political malaise of the time.   Peace had brought its problems, as post-war periods always do.   The striking achievements of the Elizabethan age had been due partly to the unifying effect upon the nation of the long struggle with Spain.   Now that the pressure was removed things tended to fall apart.   Class-feeling was certainly sharpened with the opulence and ostentation of the Jacobean age.   On the other hand, the poor were no better off, and were rendered the more conscious of their wants.   May 1607 saw a popular movement that almost attained the dimensions of a rising, shook the complacency of the governing class and disturbed men's minds : its centre was Northamptonshire, the area worst affected by the enclosures of arable by the gentry, but it spread to the neighbouring counties, including Warwickshire, where Shakespeare, now a landed gentleman, could not be indifferent to it.[13]

His friend, William Combe, wrote to Salisbury in June 1608 about the grievances of the people : '*videlicet*, with the dearth of corn, the prices rising to some height, caused partly by some that are well stored, by refraining to bring the same to the market out of a covetous conceit that corn will be dearer'.[14] The price of corn was at its highest that year. There is even a petition from 'the Diggers of Warwickshire', precursors of the Civil War Levellers, dating from the troubles of this time. Their grievance was enclosure of arable land for pasture, with consequent throwing out of the peasantry from their villages, and thus depopulation. It would be out of character to have dealt with this in a classical setting ; Shakespeare concentrates on the classic issue of dearth of corn. That issue, the class-issue, the pros-and-cons of peace and war, are the matter of the play, surging around the tragic personality of a war-hero who cannot adapt himself to peace, let alone democracy : Coriolanus.

People's attitude to this play has always been cooler and less appreciative than towards the other tragedies, precisely because it is political. They find it easier to understand the tragedy that enmeshed Othello and Desdemona, or Macbeth, or even King Lear, than that of Coriolanus where essentially political issues are involved. They find the atmosphere unappealing, for it has none of the golden glow of *Antony and Cleopatra*, the mad lyricism of *Lear*, the way the haunted atmosphere of *Macbeth* seeps into the crevices of guilt in every one of us. They think the play rigid, and there is a certain *raide* harshness about it. It is lacking in tenderness and warmth — what a contrast to *Antony and Cleopatra* ! Perhaps that was intended, for his mind moved by contrasting rhythms ; the subject appealed to his head, but hardly to his heart. The chaste, unwarm style is proper to the subject — one more evidence of Shakespeare's constant aesthetic decorum. The speeches naturally take on more of the nature of set orations, whether dealing with politics or war, since the whole thing has a political setting.[15] But Dr. Johnson, who understood politics, thought that the play has 'a very pleasing and interesting variety'. There is also a hard strain of realism in it, unlike the improbabilities and fantasies of *Lear* and *Othello*.

The subject is that of a leader in a political situation fatal to his nature, for it conflicts with his integrity, which is the rock his nature is built on. Coriolanus is a heroic soldier and a noble soul ; to us he is also a bit of a brute, who lives for fighting. We are not called upon to find him wholly admirable — evidently Shakespeare does not, though he made considerable changes from Plutarch, his chief source, in Coriolanus's favour. But Coriolanus is not insensitive : he cannot resist the appeal of his mother — a harsh type of Roman matron, a kind of female Cato — who has brought him up to be what he is and live by the values he has. Twice he succumbs to her appeal, and it is these very concessions to natural human feeling that lead to his ruin. Once, totally against his instincts, he consents to supplicate in traditional mock-humble form to the people for the consulship. The second time, when Rome lies at his feet as leader of her enemies, he spares the city at the intercession of his mother and wife, and goes back to die at the hands of his allies whose hopes of revenge he has betrayed with his own. It sometimes happens in politics that a man is ruined by his very virtues, by forbearance, by not being sufficiently ruthless.

Coriolanus's attitude to the people, though understandable, is intolerable : he never has a good word for them, not even one. He is filled with contempt for them ; and though that may be justified, it does not go with submitting oneself for election or confirmation by them. If he wants the consulship, the price of it is, as a citizen tells him, not unreasonably, that he should ' ask it kindly'. Coriolanus thinks that his eminent services to the state should be enough — as ideally they should be — and he will not expose his war-wounds to their vulgar curiosity or ask for their common sympathy. The situation is justly exposed by two officers of the Senate, speaking as a chorus. One says, 'there have been many great men that have flattered the people, who ne'er loved them ; and there be many that they have loved, they know not wherefore : so that if they love they know not why, they hate upon no better a ground'. The other says, as against Coriolanus, 'now, to seem to affect the malice and displeasure of the people is as bad as that which he dislikes, to flatter them for their love'. On which the first comments, 'he hath deserved worthily of his country ; and his ascent is not by such easy degrees as those who, having been supple and courteous to the people, bonneted, without any further deed to have them at all, into their estimation and report'. How true that is to the life, again, what political observation is in it !

Coriolanus's tragedy has been thought of as one of arrogant pride ; but this is not right — he displays no pride in relation to his own class, and towards his mother he is not only deferential but humble. His trouble is his integrity, his unbending honesty : he cannot say what he does not think :

> I will not do 't,
> Lest I surcease to honour mine own truth,
> And by my body's action teach my mind
> A most inherent baseness.

And then he goes and does it, at his mother's will — for no woman understands the inner core of a man's integrity (it is like Sir Thomas More's wife's incomprehension of his insistence on remaining in the Tower, rather than sell his soul). With Coriolanus's point of view, withdrawal from public life was the only sensible course. Poor man, having to solicit the asinine votes of the mob — anyone who has been through an election by his fellow-men knows the indignity, the humiliation, of it.

On the other hand, if one wills the end (Coriolanus had not really willed it, it was his mother who had), one wills the means. It was a fault in him not to treat the people as human beings, whatever he thought of them — and a politican would not have told them. He tells them outright. Even so, he goes through the humiliation of submitting himself and gets their vote—only to have it retracted by the odious tribunes of the people, mean unprincipled demagogues who well know how to work them up and how to take advantage of him —

> being once chafed, he cannot
> Be reined again to temperance.

His fellow-patricians give way before the popular tumult and he is banished, as Alcibiades was from Athens — to lead his native country's enemies in war against the faithless city. Coriolanus's soliloquy on being driven over to the enemy has a very Shakespearean turn of thought :

> O world, thy slippery turns ! Friends now fast sworn,
> Whose double bosoms seem to wear one heart,
> Whose hours, whose bed, whose meal and exercise
> Are still together, who twin, as 'twere, in love
> Unseparable, shall within this hour,
> On a dissension of a doit, break out
> To bitterest enmity.

And so, no less sadly, old enemies, for 'some trick not worth an egg' will grow dear friends by chance to make worthless common cause.

What can we descry of Shakespeare's personal attitude — since all writers leave trails of themselves in their writings — behind his consistent insistences, the changes he made from his sources to suit himself? Reading Plutarch's comparison of Coriolanus with Alcibiades in North's translation, he reversed Plutarch's judgment of them, and gives us a more favourable portrait of Coriolanus than was true historically. In historical fact the people of Rome had had more justification for their hostility. Shakespeare blackens the picture against them. He had always portrayed the mob from the very beginning, from the Jack Cade scenes of *Henry VI* onwards, with contempt but with an understanding good humour. There is no good humour towards them in *Coriolanus* : his attitude had hardened. The people had always been in his view beneath reason — and therefore not worth reasoning with ; inconstant and variable, changing with the slightest rumour, easy to panic ; but the mob had not been without generous impulses, too, if undependable. Now, there is not even a generous impulse in them, and so far from being spirited, if crack-brained like Jack Cade, he makes them cowards also.

At the beginning of the play the people are crying out about the dearth of corn, and so far from putting it down to natural causes they, as usual, regard the patricians as responsible : 'what authority surfeits on would relieve us. If they would yield us but the superfluity while it were wholesome, we might guess they relieved us humanely. . . . Let us revenge this with our pikes ere we become rakes.' But the dearth is a fact. This they will not accept : 'suffer us to famish, and their store-houses crammed with grain ; make edicts for usury, to support usurers ; repeal daily any wholesome act established against the rich, and provide more piercing statutes daily to chain up and restrain the poor'. Coriolanus tells them that their enemies, the Volsces, have plenty of corn : let them get it there. But when he gets them to the field of battle, they all turn coward :

> You souls of geese
> That bear the shapes of men, how have you run
> From slaves that apes would beat ! . . .
> Mend and charge home,
> Or, by the fires of heaven, I'll leave the foe,
> And make my wars on you.

There was plenty of this kind of thing in the armies of the time
— Falstaff's recruits were by no means unhistorical, merely exaggerated.

Naturally, Coriolanus cannot tolerate the idea that the state
should be ruled by such trash, or that their whims should be taken
into consideration :

> where gentry, title, wisdom
> Cannot but conclude but by the yea and no
> Of general ignorance — it must omit
> Real necessities, and give way the while
> To unstable slightness. Purpose so barred, it follows
> Nothing is done to purpose.

Here is the conservative Shakespeare speaking, as percipient as
Burke of the true facts of politics. What could be more prophetic
of the last state of democracy, the Welfare State, but that 'it must
omit real necessities', and that in the denial of the true purpose
of the state, 'nothing is done to purpose', or that in the end true
judgment is mangled, the state bereaved

> Of that integrity which should become 't,
> Not having the power to do the good it would,
> For the ill which doth control 't.

The end of the process is, we see in our time as Shakespeare fore-
saw, 'a falling fabric' :

> But now 'tis odds beyond arithmetic,
> And manhood is called foolery when it stands
> Against a falling fabric.

In the play the people are cock-a-hoop when the man who
told them such home-truths is banished :

> The people's enemy is gone, is gone !
> Our enemy is banished ! he is gone !
> Hoo-oo ! [*they all shout: and throw up their caps*]

It sounds like something out of the 1930's, when they went whoring
after Hitler in one country, after Mussolini in another, after Baldwin
and Chamberlain in a third. Coriolanus's comment might have
been Churchill's in the 1930's or in 1945 :

> I shall be loved when I am lacked.

Observe, from the literary point of view, that this phrase is
Antony's, carried on from *Antony and Cleopatra*. (There was a

touch of Ralegh in Coriolanus, if not consciously in the mind of the author.) Another reminiscence of the previous play comes into Shakespeare's mind with

> Not Afric owns a serpent I abhor
> More than thy fame and envy.

Shakespeare duly read up his source in Plutarch in the parallel lives of Coriolanus and Alcibiades, reserving in his mind the suggestion of the latter for his next play *Timon of Athens*. He derived something from Philemon Holland's translation of Livy, and some phrases from Camden's *Remains Concerning Britain* appear in Menenius's fable of the Belly and the Members, a commonplace analogue of the body politic. From North's splendid prose, Shakespeare could easily take over whole passages — they go straight into blank verse with little change. But one gets the impression that the play was carefully written and considered, not carried through in one rapid rush of lyrical inspiration. It was a thoughtful play. Once more, Shakespeare's conception of a classic play seems to have prodded Ben Jonson to mirth — his own were less successful: in *The Silent Woman* of 1610 he pokes fun at Cominius's irregular phrase :

> He lurched all swords of the garland.

Shakespeare may have derived some hints from a book of 1604, *Four Paradoxes or Politic Discourses* by Thomas and Dudley Digges.[16] The latter was stepson of Shakespeare's friend, Sir Thomas Russell, while his brother Leonard contributed verses to the First Folio : all probably acquaintances of Shakespeare. The book propounds the military virtues as against the ill-humours and dissensions of peace. Something of this is reflected in the play : the pros-and-cons of peace and war are discussed with as much sense by the serving men in Aufidius's house as they would have been by the Roman mob : 'Let me have war, say I ; it exceeds peace as far as day does night ; it's sprightly, waking, audible, and full of vent. Peace is a very apoplexy, lethargy ; mulled, deaf, sleepy, insensible ; a getter of more bastard children than war's destroyer of men' . . . 'Ay,' says another fool, 'and it makes men hate one another.'

The phrase, 'the coal of fire upon the ice', reflects the severe frost of the winter of 1607–8 when the Thames froze over and pans of coals were burnt in the fun-fair upon it. The prevalence of country imagery in an improbable play for it — and unlike the previous plays, from which it is absent — would suggest that it was written in the country :

> The shepherd knows not thunder from a tabor
> More than I know the sound of Marcius' tongue
> From every meaner man.

>   If I fly, Marcius,
> Holloa me like a hare.

> We have some old crab-trees here at home that will not
> Be grafted to your relish.

>   And that's as easy
> As to set dogs on sheep — will be the fire
> To kindle their dry stubble.

And here perhaps is Stratford :

>   the wounds his body bears, which show
> Like graves i' the holy churchyard.

Surely these two references to wedding-day in one play are personal reminiscences ? —

>   but that I see thee here,
> Thou noble thing, more dances my rapt heart
> Than when I first my wedded mistress saw
> Bestride my threshold.

And earlier in the play, though later that same day :

>   O let me clip ye
> In arms as sound as when I wooed ; in heart
> As merry as when our nuptial day was done,
> And tapers burned to bedward !

Do we see a reflection of old Stratford in summer in the simple passing phrase ? —

>   than boys pursuing summer butterflies,
> Or butchers killing flies.

The very full stage-directions, like those of others among the later plays, persuade scholars that these were likely to have been written away at Stratford, for they provide instructions sufficient for someone else in the company to produce the plays. The other end of his career, London, the King's men, the Globe theatre, are suggested to us in

> Like a dull actor now
> I have forgot my part and I am out,
> Even to a full disgrace.

Something of his personal dislikes may well appear in the outburst,

> I do hate thee
> Worse than a promise-breaker.

While the reflection,

> As if a man were author of himself
> And knew no other kin,

is not only consistent with what he always enforces about the nature of man in society but reflects what he would make the theme of a play, *Timon of Athens*.

In Shakespeare's life each play is a step. There has been some doubt where *Timon of Athens* comes, but, as with other matters, we may now feel ourselves on surer ground. This play belongs with *Coriolanus* and *Antony and Cleopatra*; when Shakespeare was reading his North's Plutarch for those, his eye lighted on the sections about Timon and Alcibiades which he decided to combine to make his next play. Actually these have nothing to do with each other, and they are given only the loosest connection in the play as Shakespeare left it. For it is unfinished : this is its fascination to us. In it we can observe, more clearly than in any other play, how he worked.

Timon was inserted in the First Folio to fill a gap, and it is somewhat remarkable that Shakespeare's fellows should have got hold of this manuscript when the play was never acted. (Did they get it from Shakespeare's family, who must have been co-operative over the editing of the Folio ?) Greg has observed that 'the drama has only half disengaged itself from the matrix of thought' — in that, like the late unfinished sculptures of Michelangelo, all the more revealing.[17] The stage-directions are curious, not even intended for the producer : 'Lord Timon, addressing himself courteously to every suitor', 'Ventigius, which Timon redeemed from prison' — evidently they are the writer reminding himself. The different spellings of names, Ventidius, Ventiddius, Ventigius, used to be taken as evidence of different hands in the play. Too silly — everyone who knows Elizabethan hands knows that people often did not bother to spell a name the same way twice in a paragraph. Often people did not spell their own surname the same way. In fact, the play is utterly Shakespearean from beginning to end.

But it is unfinished. There are loose ends left in the action : room is left for a sub-plot concerning Alcibiades and his grievance against Athens, which underlines and counterpoints Timon's, though the connection is left in the air ; or there could have been a comic underplot, for a Fool is introduced at one point, of whom no use is made. And the play is short. Shakespeare had not made up his mind about the characters, or their naming — though evidences of that remain in some finished plays.

What is riveting, is to see *how* he worked. There are, particularly in the speeches of Apemantus, the cynic, who plays towards Timon much the rôle of Lear's fool to him, chunks of prose intermingled with epigrammatic rhymed couplets. Like this :

> It grieves me to see so many dip their meat in one man's blood ; and all the madness is he cheers them up too.
> I wonder men dare trust themselves with men.
> Methinks they should invite them without knives :
> Good for their meat and safer for their lives.
> There's much example for't : the fellow that sits next him now, parts bread with him, pledges the breath of him in a divided draught, is the readiest man to kill him.

And so on. These are evidently jottings, and show the way Shakespeare's thoughts came to him : sometimes in a couplet, sometimes in a line or a prose sentence, to be worked over later. Often his thoughts came to him already pointed up in rhyme ; for late as well as early he was always a naturally rhyming poet. This play has a great deal of rhyme ; but all the plays have more rhyme than non-poets notice, for often it appears at irregular intervals in the body of the line, rather than at the end — even when it is not wanted : for this is the way things come into the heads of natural poets.

It is clear also that he sometimes wrote scenes as they occurred to him, not necessarily in the order of the play. This is particularly revealing of an actor-playwright, for he is visualising all the time, rather than following a unilateral line of development of plot. He did not compose in acts and scenes, and this reduces to its proper place the heavy going that has been made of his 'five-act structure' : these divisions were given later, not always convincingly, or even always sensibly. Shakespeare saw the play as a continuous stream of action, mounting, rising, pausing ; and within this, there are always shorter sections of action ended by a couplet in rhyme to mark it. And this goes from the beginning to the end of his work.

Why then did he not finish *Timon* ?

For the simplest of reasons — because he found it unsatisfactory, as we do. He worked mainly on the first Act and the last two, leaving the middle in a sketched-out state which he neither developed nor filled in. But it is neither chaotic, nor incoherent, as has been said : the bones are there, unclothed with flesh. The thought of the play is consistent, coherent, forceful, thoroughly Shakespearean, if uncongenial both to him and to us. For that seems the only conclusion to be drawn : it went against the grain with him, the play did not go well in his mind.[18] The truth is that Timon is not a really tragic character, and Shakespeare discovered in his handling of the story that he could not be made so. He had little enough to go on, not enough for a plot anyway : hence the combination of Timon's simple story with its doubling in that of Alcibiades. To what Shakespeare read in North's Plutarch he may have added his own reminiscence of a Latin dialogue of Lucian. The names in the play are mostly Latin — incongruously for Athens. There also seems to be a touch from his reading of the ever-sympathetic Montaigne.

It is impossible to make a hero like Lear or Macbeth, even Coriolanus or Antony, out of Timon. True, he has a noble soul and we are expected to be won by his boundless bounty, his largesse, his pouring out all that he had for the sake of his friends and in the name of friendship. (He has no wife, perhaps if he had he would not have been such a fool.) For these 'friends' are false : they are all out to sponge on him : they evidently think him a fool to be so free with his money and hospitality, his unrestrained giving. When he finds that he has ruined himself, and is in need of help, he discovers that he has no friends — only his faithful steward and the cynic Apemantus, who wants nothing of him, only the corroboration of his own view of what men are. He is equally percipient about Timon : 'the middle of humanity thou never knewest, but the extremity of both ends'. Timon passes at one bound from a too trustful confidence in human

beings and their professions of friendship — and this is difficult
to respect — to a too complete misanthropy, equally difficult to
respect. Though his situation is a sad one, and we can sympathise
with his disillusionment better than we can with his original illusions, it is not tragic. Nor is there a sufficient dramatic conflict
in the play — the last two acts are a succession of invectives against
humanity. So far from making a crude transference from these,
which are to be interpreted in the context of the play, one has
the feeling that they go against the grain with Shakespeare, or
at least that it is not his grain.

Nevertheless, Shakespeare's failures are more illuminating than
other people's successes, and, with these things understood, we
have a work which offers a searching comment on the time. The
background is that of the corruption of Athens ; senators and
patricians are alike unworthy of the benevolence of a good man.
The senators do not value his services ; his fellow-aristocrats
only make use of him so long as they estimate his prosperity to
last. This is very like the world of society, and the first scene
offers a convincing picture of the sycophantic hangers-on of a
great lord. In this case it is a poet and a painter, as Shakespeare
must often have seen them hanging round a patron like Southampton or in other great houses. Conversing before the patron
appears they talk the very language of intellectuals, the bogus
modesty, the envy beneath. The painter inquires of the poet,
'You are rapt, sir, in some work, some dedication to the great
lord ?' The poet replies, as one has so often heard :

> A thing slipped idly from me.

The poet flatteringly inquires about the painter's work in return,
and on being shown it : 'this comes off well and excellent'. The
painter disclaims such praise : 'indifferent', he says. The poet
enthuses, in verse :

> Admirable ! How this grace
> Speaks his own standing ! What a mental power
> This eye shoots forth ! How big imagination
> Moves in this lip !

The painter is moved to admit :

> It is a pretty mocking of the life.
> Here is a touch ; is't good ?

The poet assures him :

> I will say of it
> It tutors nature. Artificial strife
> Lives in these touches, livelier than life.

The atmosphere of hypocrisy is deftly established before Timon comes on the scene. So, too, is his overthrow foreshadowed :

> When Fortune in her shift and change of mood
> Spurns down her late beloved, all his dependants,
> Which laboured after him to the mountain's top
> Even on their knees and hands, let him slip down,
> Not one accompanying his declining foot.

Timon is not made like that :

> I am not of that feather to shake off
> My friend when he must need me.

He is to learn the hard way that that is just what people are like. He should have known it before, and then he would not have taken it so hard when the facts came home to him. It is difficult to sympathise with him. One recognises the truth of the general moral that is enforced, however, the sad truth that men are not to be trusted, not even those who call themselves one's friends. Apemantus has cynically accepted this : his view is at least based on a lifetime's disinterested observation. Timon is driven to accept it, though in his case there are two exceptions : his faithful steward and Apemantus, for what he is worth. That is about right. It has been observed that Shakespeare expresses his home-truths about life through not very nice people.

Timon's native generosity towards his own people — 'Th'art an Athenian, therefore welcome' — is completely reversed by the shock of his experience of the truth. We are told the truth about Timon's situation at the beginning : it is already undermined :

> What will this come to ?
> He commands us to provide and give great gifts,
> And all out of an empty coffer . . .
> His promises fly so beyond his state
> That what he speaks is all in debt ; he owes
> For every word. He is so kind that he now
> Pays interest for't ; his land's put to their books.

His faithful steward is hard put to it :

No care, no stop ! So senseless of expense
That he will neither know how to maintain it
Nor cease his flow of riot ; takes no account
How things go from him, nor resumes no care
Of what is to continue.

There are fools like that, and many a gentleman in the spend-thrift Jacobean age was forced to lament, in more English parlance :

To Lacedaemon did my land extend.

We recognise touches of the time : here is the insincere language of courtiers : 'might we have that happiness, my lord, that you would once use our hearts, whereby we might express some part of our zeals, we should think ourselves for ever perfect'. The clang of this is, to my ear, Jacobean rather than Elizabethan. Shakespeare puts a comment in the mouth of the painter : 'promising is the very air o' th' time : it opens the eyes of expectation. Performance is ever the duller for his act, and but in the plainer and simpler kind of people the deed of saying is quite out of use.' In Timon's set oration on Gold we observe not only Shakespeare's usual recipe for making a play in operation but also a comment on the time, the vulgarity, the moral coarseness, the exhibitionism of the Jacobean age, where gold could buy anything. It so happens that in the year 1608 there was a sudden gold-craze in Virginia : 'no talk, no hope, no work but to dig gold, wash gold, refine gold, load gold'.[19] The combination of this theme with that of digging for roots would seem to reflect this experience and support the date 1608 for the play.

Thus much of this will make black white, foul fair,
Wrong right, base noble, old young, coward valiant . . .
This yellow slave
Will knit and break religions, bless the accursed,
Make the hoar leprosy adored, place thieves
And give them title, knee, and approbation
With senators on the bench.

Timon reacts from his shock into a no less uncritical misanthropy, which is correctly estimated by Apemantus :

This is in thee a nature but infected,
A poor unmanly melancholy sprung
From change of fortune.

It is enough now for a man to be a fellow-Athenian for Timon to revile him with the foulest curses. Not all of these are convincing — they are too undiscriminating ; but some of them

are interesting commentary on the time. Alcibiades turns up
in Timon's desert solitude with a couple of whores : they receive
some sallies :

> Be a whore still : they love thee not that use thee.
> Give them diseases, leaving with thee their lust.
> Make use of thy salt hours. Season the slaves
> For tubs and baths ; bring down rose-cheeked youth
> To the tub-fast and the diet . . .
> > > > Plague all,
> That your activity may defeat and quell
> The source of all erection.

The savagery of this kind of thing, natural enough to Swift, is
not easy to Shakespeare.

We recognise more indubitably as his what I have described
as his turn of relativism :

> Raise me this beggar and deny't that lord :
> The senator shall bear contempt hereditary,
> The beggar native honour.

All men are flatterers,

> > for every grise of fortune
> Is smoothed by that below. The learned pate
> Ducks to the golden fool —

how often have we seen that in academics ! And the conclusion :

> > All's oblique :
> There's nothing level in our cursèd natures.

Do we detect a reflection from his own youth here ?—

> She is young and apt :
> Our own precedent passions do instruct us
> What levity's in youth.

For Timon there is nothing for it but withdrawal from the society
of men and a willing acceptance of death. Even his faithful
steward he dismisses :

> Come not to me again ; but say to Athens
> Timon hath made his everlasting mansion
> Upon the beachèd verge of the salt flood,
> Who once a day with his embossèd froth
> The turbulent surge shall cover. Thither come,
> And let my gravestone be your oracle.

It is already the atmosphere of the last period, of the romances
and, for a man thinking the thoughts we have diagnosed, of
increasing withdrawal.

CHAPTER XVI

The Romances

THE years 1608-9 mark the last significant turning-point in Shakespeare's career in the theatre, and a new (and last) period in his writing for it. Circumstances were changing in the theatre, as in the society for which it catered and which it expressed. The older cohesion of society was yielding to the pressure of new wealth, more complex strains. A new generation was coming up with other ideas and demands, and newer writers to please them. Old faces and friends were falling away.

Time was transforming the famous fellowship that had performed Shakespeare's plays since 1594. Kemp had been first to go, in 1599. Next of the sharers of the Globe was Thomas Pope. When young he had been one of the English actors to visit Denmark and Germany in 1586 and 1587. Coming from Lord Strange's men, he had joined the Chamberlain's company at its formation. Thus he had prospered and taken out a coat of arms, for it was complained that 'Pope the player would have no other arms but the arms of Sir Thomas Pope, Chancellor of the Augmentations'.[1] Retiring in 1603 he made a will, leaving considerable property, his interests in the Globe and the Curtain, and other legacies besides, to his fellow-actors Robert Gough and John Edmonds. Pope lived, in his own house in Southwark, apparently unmarried, and was not old when he died early in 1604. These actors did not have long lives. Next year, 1605, another of Shakespeare's close partners in the Globe died — Augustine Phillips, an especial friend. Coming from Strange's company to the Chamberlain's, he had prospered and risen to the consideration of 'gentleman'. He too aspired to a coat of arms, for Rouge dragon complained of him that 'Phillips the player had graven in a gold ring the arms of Sir William Phillip, Lord Bardolph'.[2] (Remember the three miscreants, Nym, Pistol and Bardolph.)

Augustine Phillips had purchased land and a house at Mortlake, wished to be buried in the chancel of the church like a gentleman and bequeathed £5 to the poor of the parish.[3] He left his wife and daughters well provided, and good legacies to other members of his family. Next he remembered his fellows : 'unto and amongst the hired men of the company which I am of— £5. To my fellow, William Shakespeare, a xxxs. piece in gold. To my fellow, Henry Condell, one other xxxs. piece in gold.' To his particular servant, Christopher Beeston, 30s. in gold ; 20s. in gold to each of his fellows, Laurence Fletcher, Robert Armin, Richard Cowley, Alexander Cooke, Nicholas Tooley. To his late apprentice, Samuel Gilborne, 40s and 'my mouse-coloured velvet hose and a white taffety doublet, a black taffety suit, my purple cloak, sword and dagger, and my base viol'. We see that Phillips must have ruffed it well in his coloured clothes. And he was a musician : at the time of his death he had another apprentice, James Sands, to whom he left 40s. and 'a cithern and a bandore and a lute at the expiry of his indentures'. Theatrical apprenticeship was on the same basis as that of other crafts. His executors were his fellows, John Heminges, Richard Burbage, William Sly and Timothy Whithorne, who was left the sum of £20 ; each of the executors to have a silver bowl worth £5. His sister Elizabeth had been married to one of the King's men, Robert Gough, at St. Saviour's, Southwark, in 1603 : she was left £10.

We observe how closely knit the fellowship was by marriages and relationships, as well as by their daily playing together for years, their sharing the proceeds of the theatre.

We have already noticed the death of Shakespeare's youngest brother in the frozen December of 1607. Next to follow, in the plague year 1608 and in August when the plague was at its height, was William Sly. Like Edmund Shakespeare he was unmarried and had an illegitimate son — buried in St. Giles's, Cripplegate, an infant a fortnight old, in 1606. He himself was buried in St. Leonard's, Shoreditch, on 16 August 1608. He left his house in Holywell Street to the daughter of Robert Browne.[4] We have met this player before in the correspondence of Edward Alleyn : originally a Worcester's man, he spent much of his time playing abroad in Germany. His family was wiped out by plague in 1593, but he married again : William Sly left him his share in the Globe, and made Browne's wife his residuary legatee. To

Phillips's apprentice, James Sands, Sly left the considerable sum of £40. This boy was evidently a musician — are we to think of him as singing the songs in the plays of these years? After making his will Sly bethought him of Cuthbert Burbage, and left him his sword and his hat; to the poor of the parish, 40s.

These wills confirm, what we have seen in Shakespeare's own career, that it was possible for a player to prosper — if he rose in his profession to become a sharer in the theatre. Mere players and playwrights were otherwise apt to have a lean time. As to the general standing of the King's men, pre-eminent in the profession, we have a tribute from their scribe, Ralph Crane, who must have transcribed Shakespeare's plays among others for the company, and may well have provided the manuscript for one or other of them for the First Folio :

> And some employment hath my useful pen
> Had 'mongst those civil, well-deserving men,
> That grace the stage with honour and delight,
> Of whose true honesties I much could write,
> But will comprise't, as in a cask of gold,
> Under the kingly service they do hold.[5]

The enforced leisure of these plague years enabled Thomas Heywood — one of the very few dramatists who were also actors — to write his persuasive defence of the profession, *An Apology for Actors*, published in 1612. Puritan feeling was growing constantly stronger now and detested the theatre, as it had not much use for other cultivated arts, sculpture, music, painting, architecture. We are on our way to the Civil War and the desecration of the churches, the destruction of stained glass windows, the smashing of monuments and mutilation of carving, the smashing of organs and other such delights in the name of purity and morals. Where, in Elizabethan days, the towns had welcomed the players, they now paid them to go away or refused to let them perform, and spent the money on the more civilised pleasures of sermons.[6] We are on the way to the Puritan closing of the theatres, with its ill consequences for English drama.

Heywood comes out with a strong case for the profession on patriotic as well as social grounds.[7] He naturally did not have the perspective to see the Shakespearean theatre as one of the chief distinctions of contemporary England in the eyes of foreigners, as it was; still less that it would one day stand alone beside the theatre of ancient Athens as one of the glories of the world's literature. He makes the patriotic point, if in a restricted sense : 'to turn to our domestic histories, what English blood seeing the person of any bold Englishman presented and doth not hug his fame, and honey at his valour, pursuing him in his enterprise with his best wishes, and as being rapt in contemplation, offers to him in his heart all prosperous performance — as if the personator were the man personated, so bewitching a thing is lively and well-spirited action that it hath power to new-mould the hearts of the spectators and fashion them to the shape of any noble and notable attempt'. And he specifically cites the instance of Henry V. The passage gives an insight, too, into the attitude of spectators at the uproarious, exciting public theatres.

He goes on to cite the value of theatrical training and observation in rhetorical delivery — hence the importance attached to it in schools and universities. 'It not only emboldens a scholar to speak, but instructs him to speak well and with judgment, to observe his commas, colons, and full points, his parentheses, his breathing spaces and distinctions, to keep a decorum in his countenance, neither to frown when he should smile, nor to make unseemly and disguised faces in the delivery of his words, not to stare with his eyes, nor draw awry his mouth, confound his voice in the hollow of his throat' — and so on, with all the other oddities of poor speakers. In regard to a speaker's action and gesture similarly, 'without a comely and elegant gesture, a gracious and a bewitching kind of action, a natural and a familiar motion of the head, the hand, the body, and a moderate and fit countenance suitable to all the rest, I hold all the rest as nothing. A delivery and sweet action is the gloss and beauty of any discourse that belongs to a scholar. And this is the action behoveful in any that profess this quality [*i.e.* acting], not to use any imprudent or forced motion in any part of the body, no rough or other violent gesture, nor on the contrary to stand like a stiff-starched man, but to qualify everything according to the nature of the person personated.' Observe that these are the sentiments expressed by Shakespeare in *Hamlet*.

Just as famous performers in the parts of the Commedia dell' Arte—doctors, pantaloons, harlequins—were celebrated by the Italians, so Heywood paid tribute to earlier English actors he had not known, Knell, Bentley, Mills, Wilson, Cross, Laneham. In more recent years 'I must needs remember Tarleton, in his time gracious with the Queen his sovereign and in the people's general applause, whom succeeded Will Kemp, as well in the favour of her Majesty as in the opinion and good thoughts of the general audience. Gabriel [Spencer], Sinkler, Pope, Phillips, Sly, all the right I can do them is but this that, though they be dead, their deserts yet live in the remembrance of many. Among so many dead let me not forget one yet alive in his time the most worthy famous, Master Edward Alleyn.' Alleyn, now retired, owner of Dulwich manor, founder of the school and almshouses, already stood out as the exemplar of the profession's respectability. 'Many amongst us I know to be of substance, of government, of sober lives and temperate carriages, house-keepers and contributory to all duties enjoined them, equally with them that are ranked with the most bountiful.'

The most important development in the theatre since 1594, with the formation of the Chamberlain's men (now King's), took place this year with their taking over the Blackfriars theatre for their winter performances. Its name and fame had been made by the boy-actors reaching back to Lyly and before, with their more intellectually sophisticated drama, their bent for satire and the latest literary fad, the place of music in their performances and their social *cachet*. Now for the first time a public company was taking over a private theatre, with its different type of audience, socially superior, more fastidious and selective, always looking for something new and exotic, more fantastic and fanciful, more exclusive and salacious, less receptive of the whole range of life that had made the greatness of Elizabethan drama.[8] It has been suggested that the tactical victory of Shakespeare's company was 'prophetic of the end of his kind of drama', and that the valedictory quality of his last plays reflects this changed situation.[9]

Actually Cuthbert Burbage had been the landlord of Black-friars since 1596 ; now in August 1608 the lease was made over to himself, Thomas Evans and five of the King's men, Richard Burbage, Shakespeare, Sly, Heminges and Condell. Shakespeare put down his share, an unknown sum, for the lease and agreed with the rest to pay his part of the rent, some £5 : 14 : 4. It would be a good investment. There was the convenience of being able to play indoors in the winter ; the Blackfriars *clientèle* paid much more for their seats, a basic 12d, and the takings were far higher than in the rougher conditions of the public theatre. The King's men now would make much more of their money from performances at Court and at Blackfriars than at the Globe. This

betokened a significant change ; the best days of the public theatre
were passing.

The consequences for the drama were even more signal. Quiet,
candlelit and smaller Blackfriars meant a quieter, subtler style of
acting. Plays for this audience brought in the fashionable cult
of the masque at the Jacobean Court. Shakespeare's last plays
reflect this with their masques or dumb-shows, and their greater
provision for music. It was the intervals for music in the private
theatre that brought about act-divisions, and these spread from
this time, with more music, to the public theatres. An aristocratic
audience liked to be at some remove from reality : it preferred,
on the one hand, fantasy and romance ; on the other, a more
cynical and satirical realism, hardly less removed from reality.

These conditions were propitious to the genius of the younger
writers, to Jonson, Marston, Middleton, but in especial to Fletcher
and Massinger, the inheritors of Shakespeare as the principal
dramatists of the King's men up to the Civil War. Jonson had
written nothing for the Company during the past three or four
years : he had been engaged principally on the Court masques
which had brought him a personal following among courtiers
and intellectuals. He was more fashionable than Shakespeare,
thought more highly of by the *conoscenti*, who often know
what is what less well than ordinary people : the literary allusions of
the time are twice as frequent to him as to Shakespeare, who was
perhaps beginning to be regarded (by them) as outmoded.

The Blackfriars audience always wanted new plays, and two
young stars were rising to give them what they wanted. These
were John Fletcher and Francis Beaumont : both of good family
and with a university background. Fletcher was a son of the
good-looking Bishop of London, whose second marriage to a
young woman Queen Elizabeth had so much resented : born
in 1579, John Fletcher was fifteen years Shakespeare's junior.
Beaumont was five years younger still : son of one of the Queen's
Judges, of an old Leicestershire family and an Oxford man. These
two set up bachelor lodgings together ; they were singularly
attuned to each other and the fruits of their affectionate co-opera-
tion were prolific. Aubrey writes in his life of Beaumont, that
'there was a wonderful consimility of phansey between him and
Mr John Fletcher, which caused that dearness of friendship between
them. . . . They lived together on the Bankside, not far from
the playhouse, both bachelors ; lay together . . . had one wench

in the house between them, which they did so admire ; the same clothes and cloak, etc. between them.' [10]   Later, in 1613, Beaumont married, unfortunately — for he died after only three years of it.

Fletcher found another collaborator in Massinger, another inheritor of one side of Shakespeare's work.   Shakespeare, as the Company's leading dramatist, must have given these young men a welcome, as he had done to Ben Jonson earlier — no doubt gladly, for he was tiring and the future of the company, in which he was so much concerned, had to be provided for.   Before their association with the King's men Beaumont and Fletcher had each had separately a failure, with the audience, over a good play : the first with *The Knight of the Burning Pestle*, and the second with *The Faithful Shepherdess*, presented by the Children of the Revels. But with their joint production *Philaster*, dating from just this period 1608-10, they had a resounding success which resulted in their association with the King's men and was most influential in fixing the fashionable new *genre* of pastoral romance.   These authors were *au courant* with the literary discussion on the nature of pastoral released by Guarini — the latest thing.   They were also sympathetic with Shakespearean themes, on which they drew for *Philaster*, and for their play *Bonduca* which explored the territory of legendary British history Shakespeare used for *King Lear* and *Cymbeline*.

On his side, as alive to what was in the air at the end of his career as at the beginning, Shakespeare was ready to respond to the new movement, to experiment with new modes and the richer scenic possibilities and techniques developing.   With his long experience and range of human appeal, his new plays could be expected to draw a response from both audiences, from his faithful public at the Globe, and also from Court and private theatre.   Nor was it surprising that, a tired man withdrawing more to Stratford — no doubt having ceased to act some time before — if he should need a helper, there was a disciple at hand in John Fletcher.

At Stratford, too, familiar faces were making way for new. In September 1608 Shakespeare's mother died, and was buried on the ninth of the month.   A fortnight later his nephew, Michael Hart, was brought from the old nest in Henley Street to be baptised ; and on 16 October Alderman Henry Walker's son was christened William, with Shakespeare as his godfather, either in person or by proxy. That summer he had had to institute proceedings against John Addenbroke for debt : next year verdict was given against this gentleman for the £6 due, with 24s awarded for costs and damages, but there seems to have been some difficulty in collecting it.

On 5 June 1607 Shakespeare's elder daughter Susanna, now twenty-four, was married to Dr. John Hall, the physician, eight years her senior. It was a respectable marriage : John Hall was the son of a doctor, born in Bedfordshire and a Cambridge man. Their child was conceived promptly and born in February 1608, christened Elizabeth on the 21st of that month. This was Shakespeare's only grandchild to survive, with whom his own family ended.

These years 1608-9 were plague years, and there cannot have been much acting in London until the plague abated in December 1609. This circumstance also operates to set a bound between Shakespeare's previous works, the tragedies, and the last period upon which he enters now with the romances. There seems to be a hiatus, a pause, if not something more, during these years. A convergence of indications persuades me that there may be something in Chambers's conjecture that 'an attempt at *Timon of Athens* early in 1608 was followed by a serious illness, which may have been a nervous breakdown. . . . Later in the year Shakespeare came to his part of *Pericles* with a new outlook. . . . There has been some mental process such as the psychology of religion would call a conversion. Obviously the philosopher of the tragedies is not a Christian philosopher, and in a sense that of the romances is.' 11

It is exceptional for the cautious Chambers to go so far, and I am not proposing to follow him wholly. But I am persuaded that the text of *Cymbeline* everywhere bears traces not only of literary experimentation, as is generally thought, but recognisable symptoms of nervous fatigue. And, indeed, what wonder ? Recovery seems to me to be indicated with *The Winter's Tale* and *The Tempest*, not only increased assurance in a new genre. Moreover, what made him willing to take up somebody else's indifferent play *Pericles* at this time and shape it up for the theatre, rather than write a new play of his own ? A few years previously he had been writing two and even three plays a year : now only one a year, if that. The rhythm of life was slackening.

On the threshold of the last period we are confronted with

the problem of *Pericles*. This play was excluded from the First Folio — perhaps as not wholly Shakespeare's. In the unhistorically-minded Augustan age it was considered an early play simply because of the inferiority of the text that has come down to us : I mention this only to illustrate the kind of confusion that comes from the absence of chronological order. Of course, all the affinities of *Pericles* are with the romances of the last period, of which it was the first and on which its success with the public had a perhaps decisive influence. A play of this name was seen by the Venetian ambassador, Giustiniani, during the period 1606-8 ; while at Candlemas 1610 it was performed along with *Lear* at Gowthwaite Hall in Nidderdale.

A Quarto text of the play was published in 1609 — the same year in which the Quarto of *Troilus and Cressida* was printed, and Thomas Thorpe came by the *Sonnets* and published them. *Pericles* was very popular with the reading public too : there were no less than six editions of the Quarto up to 1635. And this in spite of the inferiority of the text, for it is only a recon-structed report of the play. A play of 1609, *Pimlico, or Run Redcap*, testifies to its popularity :

> Amazed I stood to see a crowd
> Of civil throats stretched out so loud . . .
> So that I truly thought all these
> Came to see *Shore* or *Pericles*.

Ben Jonson was chagrined by the continued appeal of the play into the 1620's :

> No doubt some mouldy tale
> Like *Pericles* . . .
> May keep up the Play-club.

Opinion inclines befinitely to the view that, behind the text as we have received it, Shakespeare's hand is dominant in Acts III to V, while the hand of some other writer is to be discerned in Acts I and II. But I find evidence of Shakespeare's interven-tion among the very first lines of the first scene :

> For the embracements even of Jove himself —

'embracements' is a regular Shakespearean word. And the use of 'to glad' as a verb — 'to glad her presence' — is also like him. Similarly the prose dialogue of the Fishermen in Act II may well be his. A recent theory has been propounded that the differences between Acts I and II on one hand, and Acts III-V on the other, may be due as much to two reporters as to two authors.[12] This view is not so incompatible as the Cambridge editor thinks with his own view of the King's Men coming into possession of a play which Shakespeare rehandled, for we may agree that he interfered more with the last three Acts than the first two.[13] It is all very provoking : 'the majority of critics are surely right in saying that in these later Acts we are listening to Shakespeare, but equally surely we listen to him through an intermediary — someone who cannot quite render again the whole of the original, though to make good his shortcomings he does not try to re-create a metrical regularity such as is found in the early Acts'.[14]

The story obviously was taken from John Gower's *Confessio Amantis*, for Gower is used as a Chorus speaking archaic tetrameter couplets in rhyme. A second source was the antiquarian Laurence Twyne's *Pattern of Painful Adventures.* In 1608, stimulated by the popularity of the play, George Wilkins published a novel *The Painful Adventures of Pericles, Prince of Tyre*, which borrowed heavily alike from Twyne and from the play.

What emerges through the mist is a good deal of recognisably Shakespearean writing. More important are the themes and the atmosphere, which are those of a new period, a new vision. We find these themes re-echoing from play to play : reunion after long division, reconciliation, forgiveness. We are not at liberty to speculate on what these might mean in his own life : suffice it to say that they seem to well up from personal experience, as they move us personally, and these plays, for all their happy endings, are suffused with tears. Storm appears twice over at the source of the story, as if it were a symbol of the storm of life. There are children lost and found again, bringing together divided parents ; wife rejected and ill-used, restored again, as if from the grave. In *Pericles* there is the literal resurrection of Thaisa. The recurring myth of lost royalty recovered is curiously sounded. What can it mean psychologically ? — a lost authority or control upon which life was once pivoted : after much storm and stress one comes back to it by the way of forgiveness and reconciliation ? Shakespeare was always the most suggestive of writers : the last plays are haunted by symbol and suggestion, a world of meanings and wonder withdrawn within itself like the last quartets of Beethoven.

The impression one derives from *Pericles* is that of life's journeyings, of one bereaved and aimlessly navigating the sea, coming at length into harbour, the sense of trials and injuries endured, all made up in the end. The atmosphere, like that of *The Tempest*, is all of sea and music :

> The god of this great vast, rebuke these surges,
> Which wash both heaven and hell ; and thou that hast
> Upon the winds command, bind them in brass,
> Having called them from the deep !
>
> Well said, well said ; the fire and cloths.
> The still and woful music that we have,
> Cause it to sound, beseech you.

There are reflections from his earlier self :

> Like Patience gazing on Kings' graves and smiling,

recalls

> like Patience on a monument,
> Smiling at grief,

from *Twelfth Night*. The recognition of Marina by her father, Pericles, follows in the next lines :

Pericles :   What were thy friends ?
How lost thou them ? Thy name, my most kind virgin ?

Marina : My name is Marina.

Pericles :   O, I am mocked,
And thou by some incensèd god sent hither
To make the world to laugh at me.

It is the reunion of Lear and Cordelia.

In such a play one does not expect many touches of the contemporary scene. One such seems to have been missed by the commentators :

> Kings are earth's gods.

This was what King James had been telling Parliament in 1607, somewhat absurdly, and what Bacon had been sycophantically urging upon the courts. Shakespeare adds, with his independence of mind :

> in vice their law's their will ;
> And if Jove stray, who dares say Jove doth ill ?

This was rather pointed, if anyone made the application to James and the reigning favourite, young Carr.

The brothel scenes are recognisably Shakespeare, with their

references to disease that were such a joke to the Jacobeans : 'the poor Transylvanian is dead, that lay with the little baggage'. As for the Frenchman, Monsieur Veroles, 'he brought his disease hither : here he does but repair it. I know he will come in our shadow, to scatter his crowns in the sun.' We recognise that we are not far in time from *Timon*, and a world away from Constance and Arthur. This is the Jacobean age. There is all the veracity and realism of— 'faith, she would serve after a long voyage at sea', or 'what would you have me do ? go to the wars, would you ? where a man may serve seven years for the loss of a leg, and have not money enough in the end to buy him a wooden one ?' There is a reminiscence from the Falstaffian world of *Henry IV* : it seems ages ago.

Cymbeline, of 1609-10, is a tired man's play, slow-going and repetitive, though not without a reflective, moonlit beauty of its own.[15] Everyone notices that it is the most reminiscential of all the plays : there are repetitions in it from all over Shakespeare's work. When one observes the extent of this along with another feature, the large number of qualifying parentheses cluttering up the text like a stutter, it becomes clear that a literary explanation in terms of experiment is not enough : they are clear symptoms of nervous fatigue, perhaps recovery from breakdown or stroke.

Let us take the latter first — the nervous habit of qualifying every statement, when there is no purpose served by it. Within a short space we have, from quite different characters :

> He had two sons (if this be worth your hearing,
> Mark it).
> > Having thus far proceeded
> (Unless thou think'st me devilish).
> We count not worth the hanging (but none human)
> > Haply this life is best
> (If quiet life be best)
> My fault being nothing (as I have told you oft)
> > the which he hearing
> (As it is like him)
> Your daughter's chastity (there it begins) . . .
> > and wagered with him
> Pieces of gold 'gainst this (which he then wore
> Upon his honoured finger).

This is only a small number of examples of what runs all through the play. It is not so much the parentheses that matter as the *tic* of qualifying everything, explaining everything, that is a nervous symptom.

The repetitions from earlier work are also a symptom of fatigue, and they are numerous. The Arden editor of the play draws our attention to a number of reflections from *Venus and Adonis*, though the parallels with *Lucrece* are still more striking.[16] It is rather touching to think that he was re-reading his early poems and perhaps some of the plays, during this break, the years 1608-9. The motivation that sets going *Cymbeline* is that of *The Rape of Lucrece* repeated : the wager taken by a husband as to his wife's chastity during his absence. Lucrece was raped by Tarquin. In *Cymbeline* Iachimo gets into Imogen's bedroom in a trunk :

> Our Tarquin thus
> Did softly press the rushes, ere he wakened
> The chastity he wounded. Cytherea,
> How bravely thou becom'st thy bed ! fresh lily ! . . .
>   'tis her breathing that
> Perfumes the chamber thus . . .

This is a return to *Venus and Adonis*. Iachimo is Tarquin with a touch of Iago.

> She hath been reading late
> The tale of Tereus, here the leaf's turned down
> Where Philomel gave up.

This goes back to *Titus and Andronicus*.

> If she be furnished with a mind so rare,
> She is alone th'Arabian bird,

is a reminiscence of 'The Phoenix and the Turtle'. Here is an echo from *Hamlet* :

> Against self-slaughter
> There is a prohibition so divine
> That cravens my weak hand.

Two passages echo *Antony and Cleopatra* :

> Proud Cleopatra, when she met her Roman,
> And Cydnus swelled above the banks . . .

> the sword, whose tongue
> Outvenoms all the worms of Nile.

From *Troilus and Cressida* we have :

> Thersites' body is as good as Ajax'
> When neither are alive.

These verbal echoes are apart from repetitions of situation : the circumstances of foreign invasion, for example, are very like those of *Lear*. The Roman landing takes place, not at Dover, but at Milford Haven in *Cymbeline*. Why on earth, and so improbably, at Milford Haven ? Quite obviously, simply not to repeat Dover : no other reason, except possibly the romantic remoteness of the western fastnesses of Wales. The patriotic *leitmotiv* sounds more constipated and feebler than its expression in *Richard II* and *King John* :

> The kings your ancestors, together with
> The natural bravery of your isle, which stands
> As Neptune's park, ribbed and paled in
> With rocks unscaleable and roaring waters,
> With sands that will not bear your enemies' boats,
> But suck them up to th'topmast. A kind of conquest
> Caesar made here, but made not here his brag
> Of 'Came, and saw, and overcame.' With shame
> (The first that ever touched him) he was carried
> From off our coast, twice beaten : and his shipping
> (Poor ignorant baubles !) on our terrible seas,
> Like egg-shells moved upon their surges, cracked
> As easily 'gainst our rocks ·. . .

That has not the natural, enthusiastic eloquence of John of Gaunt back in the 1590's ; it is laboured work, complex and burdened with matter.

In all this, it is like Shakespeare reviewing his past work and picking up hints and echoes for the task before him.

The style is not only elliptical and compacted, as the critics say ; it is psychologically more interesting : it is the language of the last period of a great writer, who has written too much, who is now tied up from having too much to express, like late Henry James or the esoteric late Kipling :

> I will try the forces
> Of these thy compounds on such creatures as
> We count not worth the hanging (but none human)
> To try the vigour of them, and apply
> Allayments to their act, and by them gather
> Their several virtues, and effects.

Or,

> Can my sides hold to think that man who knows
> By history, report, or his own proof,
> What woman is, yea what she cannot choose
> But must be, will's free hours languish for
> Assured bondage ?

One sees what it means, but it is not immediately apparent. Even the prose-humour is roundabout and laboured : 'ay, and the approbation of those that weep this lamentable divorce under her colours are wonderfully to extend him ; be it but to fortify her judgment, which else an easy battery might lay flat, for taking a beggar without less quality'. It is thought that this last phrase intends to say the opposite of what it does.

All these indications, taken together, seem to point to one explanation.

Having said this, we can appreciate the art of the skilled hand trying out new ground, putting together a play from diverse sources and conducting the various strands to the final pattern knit up in the last Act. Shakespeare got the hint of his Cymbeline story from Holinshed, furbished it up from the two Guiderius tales in the *Mirror for Magistrates* and filled it out with matter from a Boccaccio story. Behind it all is the shadow of an old play, *Love and Fortune*, which he turned to use. The theatre audience wanted something new — the surprises, the improbable turns, the scenic spectacles, of romance. The old master, now in his later forties, labours hard to give it them, with a masque thrown in, an apparition of Jupiter descending in thunder and lightning, sitting upon an eagle, while the ghosts of the dead fall on their knees.

It must be admitted that the master pulled it off, with all his old virtuosity drawing an improbable number of threads together at the end. The play has never been a failure, and, suitably cut, can be presented a beautiful and affecting piece still.

In the poetry there is a certain slackening. It is at its most charming when he writes about flowers :

> I'll sweeten thy sad grave : thou shalt not lack
> The flower that's like thy face, pale primrose, nor
> The azured harebell, like thy veins ; no, nor
> The leaf of eglantine, whom not to slander,
> Outsweetened not thy breath.

On Imogen's breast there was

> A mole cinque-spotted : like the crimson drops
> I' the bottom of a cowslip.

Two images bespeak the life of the country : 'You know strange
fowl light upon neighbouring ponds'. Stratford and his life there
come graphically before us in these telescoped images :

> The cloyed will —
> That satiate yet unsatisfied desire, that tub
> Both filled and running — ravening first the lamb,

In the description of Imogen's bed-chamber an Elizabethan
great house, such as he had known at Southampton House, or
Wilton, or any of the royal palaces, Whitehall, Windsor or Greenwich, comes alive for us :

> The chimney
> Is south the chamber, and the chimney-piece,
> Chaste Dian, bathing : never saw I figures
> So likely to report themselves ; the cutter
> Was as another Nature, dumb : outwent her,
> Motion and breath left out . . .
> The roof o' the chamber
> With golden cherubins is fretted. Her andirons
> (I had forgot them) were two winking Cupids
> Of silver, each on one foot standing, nicely
> Depending on their brands.

Lastly, there is the Court, which he knew well from his particular
vantage-point :

> the art o' the court,
> As hard to leave as keep : whose top to climb
> Is certain falling : or so slippery that
> The fear's as bad as falling.

Essex was in his grave ; his great enemy, Ralegh, was spending
all these early years of James's reign, and until after Shakespeare
himself was dead, in the Tower.

With *The Winter's Tale* of next year, 1610–11, we have complete recovery, for it is a most beautiful and moving play. Even
so, good critics have seen evidences of tiredness in it. Doctor
Johnson was sorry that Leontes' recognition of his lost daughter,
Perdita, was not given a scene : 'it was, I suppose, only to spare
his own labour that the poet put this whole scene into narrative'.[17]

And Q. thought the play shows signs of inferior artistry : 'a huddled-up First Act and a hopelessly scamped and huddled-away situation in Act 5'. I cannot agree with these eminent critics on either point. With regard to the first, to have had a separate recognition scene for Leontes and his daughter would much detract from the force of the reunion with his wife Hermione, with which the play so wonderfully ends. On Q.'s other point, I find the First Act dramatically effective : Leontes is already jealous of his wife and his friend Polixenes, insanely jealous — for he is an unbalanced, psychotic character, as everybody else recognises. This does not need elaborating : a lengthy development of it would only spoil the effect. We should have the imagination to perceive that this has been simmering in his mind for some time, and we begin rapidly in the middle of things.

In the actual writing I perceive no signs of flagging ; though the style is compacted and full of matter, and there are many parentheses, they do not have any clogging effect, for the writing is direct and forceful. No-one can say that the poetry is inferior. The play makes a tremendous impact, harmonious and integrated, and though we do not experience the almost unbearable assault on the emotions of *Hamlet* or *Lear* or *Macbeth*, it searches out the crevices of the heart. One is moved to tears by the grief of it all, the insane way Leontes treats his unoffending wife, the punishment he suffers in the death of his only boy (not much younger than Shakespeare's son), his emergence from his mad jealousy into true repentance, Hermione's return as if from the grave, forgiveness and reconciliation. None of the plays has a more poignant atmosphere, more full of pathos and regret. Its affinities with *Pericles* and *Cymbeline* are obvious, but it is more touching in every scene and line.

It is pleasantly ironical that at the end of his career Shakespeare should have been indebted to poor Greene. For the story of *The Winter's Tale* Shakespeare rested entirely on Greene's early romance, *Pandosto*. This was republished in 1607 and that might have brought it back to mind, though it seems that Shakespeare used the original edition of 1588. He tightens up the story to make it dramatic and occasionally is able to transfer whole passages into verse from the prose of the older man who had been so vexed by his way of bringing it off. Greene would have been still more annoyed to hear that 'there are more verbal echoes from *Pandosto* than from any other novel used by Shakespeare as a source'.[18]

Nor is this all : for Autolycus's exploits in stealing clothes and picking the country clown's pocket Shakespeare was indebted also to Greene's cony-catching pamphlets. Several of the names in this Arcadian play came from Sidney's *Arcadia*, while there are reflections of Shakespeare's life-long devotion to Ovid and even echoes from Arthur Golding's translation. How things come together at the end !

What Shakespeare did was to give it all his genius : the wind of inspiration blows through the play and into every part of it. Into none more obviously than the pastoral scenes, which in other hands could be too unexciting from sheer absence of drama. The shearing-feast in *The Winter's Tale*, is as Q. says, beyond criticism, and even beyond praise. The country life of Arden and Cotswolds, that had inspired Shakespeare from the first and never ceased to do so, is given final expression here.

> When daffodils begin to peer,
>   With, heigh !, the doxy over the dale,
> Why then comes in the sweet o' the year,
>   For the red blood reigns in the winter's pale.

So sings Autolycus to himself, when the country clown enters. 'Let me see — every 'leven wether tods, every tod yields pound and odd shilling : fifteen hundred shorn — what comes the wool to ? . . . I cannot do't without counters.' [19] Many a Cotswold shepherd must have been in that pass — as is the economic historian today who has tods of wool to tot up. This country fellow has to buy the goods for the feast : 'three pound of sugar, five pound of currants, rice . . . I must have saffron to colour the warden pies, mace, dates none — that's out of my note — nutmegs, seven ; a race or two of ginger — but that I may beg ; four pound of prunes, and as many of raisins o' the sun'. The use of saffron, common in Elizabethan England, has rather died out, except in Cornwall where saffron-cake fortunately still retains a hold. Warden-pies were made of warden-pears or apples. The young shepherd's 'sister', Perdita, was to be mistress of the feast : 'she hath made me four and twenty nosegays for the shearers — three-man song-men all, and very good ones ; but they are most of them means and bases : but one Puritan amongst them, and he sings psalms to hornpipes'. Even that was something. Three-man songs were lively catches for men's voices, a regular feature of folk-music, as we gather from Carew's *Survey of Cornwall*.

We learn, too, about the Whitsun pastorals that were acted all over the country — as we saw from the Stratford town-accounts :

> Methinks I play as I have seen them do
> In Whitsun-pastorals.

Then there are the ballads that Autolycus dispenses : 'I love a ballad but even too well, if it be doleful matter merrily set down, or a very pleasant thing indeed and sung lamentably'. What the shepherd girls want to know is — 'is it true too, think you ?' and that is an authentic voice. We recognise across the centuries the figure of the country-wife :

> when my old wife lived, upon
> This day she was both pantler, butler, cook,
> Both dame and servant : welcomed all, served all :
> Would sing her song and dance her turn : now here,
> At upper end o' the table ; now i' the middle :
> On his shoulder, and his : her face o' fire
> With labour, and the thing she took to quench it
> She would to each one sip.

There is a lovingly observed detail from the homely life of the time. In these last plays, the struggle over, ultimate values peering through the stratification of society, there is a new note of equality — not that Shakespeare ever thought that one man was *better* for position than another :

> The selfsame sun that shines upon his court
> Hides not his visage from our cottage, but
> Looks on alike.

It is put into the mouth of Autolycus, the rogue, to reflect a little on the Court : 'whether it like me or no, I am a courtier. Seest thou not the air of the Court in these enfoldings ? hath not my gait in it the measure of the Court ? receives not thy nose Court-odour from me ? reflect I not on thy baseness Court-contempt ?' It is this play that has the passage I have already quoted on the

> Clerk-like experienced, which no less adorns
> Our gentry than our parents' noble names,
> In whose success we are gentle.

While Polixenes had a reflection that speaks for the flexibility that was always a strength of the old English class-system :

> We marry
> A gentler scion to the mildest stock,
> And make conceive a bark of baser kind
> By bud of nobler race. This is an art
> Which does mend nature — change it rather, but
> The art itself is nature.

Country reflections run all through the play. There is the churchyard of little Mamillius's unheard story :

> There was a man . . .
> Dwelt by a churchyard. I will tell it softly,
> Yon crickets shall not hear it.

There are the neighbouring ponds we heard of in *Cymbeline*, with the same sexy implication :

> And his pond fished by his next neighbour (by
> Sir Smile, his neighbour).

Best of all are the flowers that colour these late plays, as no doubt they did these last years (he was one who used to notice such things) :

> Here's flowers for you :
> Hot lavender, mints, savory, marjoram,
> The marigold, that goes to bed with the sun
> And with him rises weeping . . .
> daffodils
> That come before the swallow dares, and take
> The winds of March with beauty ; violets dim
> But sweeter than the lids of Juno's eyes
> Or Cytherea's breath ; pale primroses
> That die unmarried, ere they can behold
> Bright Phoebus in his strength : a malady
> Most incident to maids ; bold oxlips and
> The crown imperial ; lilies of all kinds,
> The flower-de-luce being one.

There are all the gardens and fields, the meadows and pastures, of Stratford in that.

In this world of pastoral romance we expect, and wish, little of contemporary incident to erupt. Hermione, we are told, was daughter of the Emperor of Russia — that means little, but probably reflects Shakespeare's reading on the voyages. Hermione's return to life is compared to a masterpiece of Julio Romano,

Raphael's disciple, whose epitaph Shakespeare seems to have read. Hermione has a contemporary explanation for Leontes' mad ill-usage of her :

> There's some ill planet reigns :
> I must be patient till the heavens look
> With an aspect more favourable.

I wonder if the theme of King Polixenes' overstaying his welcome at his friend Leontes' Court may not bear a touch of Christian IV's visit to his brother-in-law in 1606 ; and whether the theme of the baby to be consigned to the fire may not echo the contemporary story of the Darrells, by which the Pophams were supposed to have succeeded to their house, Littlecote ?

These are but suggestions ; in romance we can be more certain of atmosphere. In their youth the two kings had been fast friends :

> what we changed
> Was innocence for innocence ; we knew not
> The doctrine of ill-doing, nor dreamed
> That any did.

And they found what life could do to separate friends. The change that Shakespeare made in Greene's story shows what he wanted above all to enforce : 'nothing could better show his obsession with the themes of forgiveness and restoration than the way in which he transforms the ending of the story'.[20] Pandosto killed himself ; but Hermione is restored and Leontes forgiven.

We have reason to think that the play was popular. It was seen by Simon Forman, the astrologer, at the Globe on 15 May 1611, who gives us a good summary of the play and noticed especially the kind of thing that would appeal to one of his kind : 'remember also the rogue that came in all tattered like Coll Pixy, and how he feigned him sick and to have been robbed of all that he had, and how he cozened the poor man of all his money, and after came to the sheep-shear with a pedlar's pack and there cozened them again of all their money. And how he changed apparel with the King of Bohemia's son, and then how he turned courtier etc. Beware of trusting feigned beggars or fawning fellows.'[21] Perhaps that may stand as an example of what an exceptionally sharp-eyed member of a Jacobean audience saw in the play and was gripped by. He did not miss much.

It was acted at Court on Gunpowder Plot day, 5 November 1611, and was one of the plays performed during the wedding festivities of the Princess Elizabeth in the winter of 1612–13. Several times revived at Court after that, the play has always had its appeal to the hearts of the elect.

These years in which Shakespeare's imagination was taken with the themes of seafaring and shipwreck, storm and tempest at sea, were those of mounting national excitement over Virginia. Consciously or unconsciously people felt that the future of the nation was involved — as indeed it was. This was what the Elizabethans had fought Spain for, for twenty years — for a share in the New World, the opening of North America to English settlement. It was all Virginia to them, under the inspiration — sometimes with the financial interest — of the Virgin Queen. Within two years from the peace of 1604 the Virginia Company was founded, and almost everybody who was anybody took a share in it from the highest to the lowest.[22] (Shakespeare did not subscribe to lose his money.) Among those who appear in the Charter under which the colony at Jamestown was nursed along were the most powerful members of the government, Salisbury and Suffolk, with Southampton and Pembroke.

Southampton's interest in America went back to his years in the Tower, when in 1602 he was a chief backer of the voyage of Captains Gosnoll and Gilbert to explore the northern coast for suitable settlement. Three years later he was helping to fit out another ship for those climes, and in course of time American plantation became a leading interest with him. In the last years of his life he was made Treasurer of the Company, taking an active part with Sir Edwin Sandys in its controversial politics, and this brought him once more into opposition to the Crown.[23]

In addition to Southampton and Pembroke, a number of Shakespeare's acquaintance were interested in Virginia. There was Lord Carew of Clopton House, his grand neighbour at Stratford — both of them to become in a few years nearer neighbours in Stratford church. There were various friends of Shakespeare's acquaintance, one of whom he made overseer of his will, Thomas Russell, who lived out at Alderminster along the leafy road to Oxford and London. Chief among these was Russell's stepson, Sir Dudley Digges, whose younger brother Leonard wrote commendatory verses for the First Folio. The Diggeses in London were neighbours and acquaintances of Heminges and Condell in their parish of St. Mary, Aldermanbury.[24]

So that it is not at all surprising that Shakespeare should have had a sight of the news-letter sent home by William Strachey, describing the great tempest that drove the *Sea Venture* ashore upon Bermuda, with Sir George Somers aboard and colonists for Virginia — providentially with no loss of life. This letter provided the whole basis for *The Tempest*.

It was addressed to a 'Noble Lady' — and that means, in contemporary terms, the wife of a nobleman : we do not know which of them, Southampton's is as likely as any. Strachey had been on board the ship, going out to be Secretary for Virginia — a job poor undone John Donne had badly wanted. Strachey was a Cambridge man with mild literary aspirations, who had contributed a sonnet to the publication of Jonson's *Sejanus* in 1605, was a shareholder in the company of the Children of the Revels and was in and out of Blackfriars two or three times a week. In the background, withdrawn, less hard at work now, more at Stratford, was the elusive dramatist.

In his usual manner, he did not miss an opportunity that mattered to him. His imagination seized upon Strachey's news-letter : nothing that could be useful to the making of a play was missed. The *Sea Venture* had left Plymouth Sound on 2 June 1609 ; instead of taking the usual course of making for the West Indies and then, with the winds, up the American coast, she made straight for Virginia and ran into a hurricane. It is clear that that is what it was, for several aboard who had experienced severe storms before had never met anything like this. It is described vividly and in detail by Strachey, and it all appears, still better and more vividly, in riveting fashion in *The Tempest*. The action of the play is dominated by the storm and its consequences, is drenched with sea-spray and the noise of its surges. And there is more besides.

Strachey describes the phenomenon of St. Elmo's fire, 'like a faint star trembling and streaming along with a sparkling blaze half the height upon the mainmast and shooting sometimes from shroud to shroud . . . sometimes running along to the very end and returning'.[25] In the play this is Ariel's doing :

> Now in the waist, the deck, in every cabin,
> I flamed amazement : sometime I'd divide
> And burn in many places ; on the topmast,
> The yards and bowsprit would I flame distinctly,
> Then meet and join.

In the play, as in Bermuda, nobody was drowned :

Prospero :	But are they, Ariel, safe ?
Ariel :	Not a hair perished.

The colonists were convinced, with everybody of the time, that 'the still-vexed Bermoothes' were 'given over to devils and wicked spirits'. Shakespeare's island had Caliban for inhabitant, and there had been his witch-hag of a mother, Sycorax, now imprisoned in a tree. On coming upon Caliban, Stephano says, 'What's the matter ? Have we devils here ? Do you put tricks upon's with savages and men of Ind ?' (*i.e.* Red Indians).

In fact Strachey found the islands 'to be habitable and commodious as most countries of the same climate and situation', with abundance of fish, fowl, berries and roots to eat : not confined to the diet Prospero threatens Ferdinand with :

> Sea-water shalt thou drink ; thy food shall be
> The fresh-brook mussels, withered roots, and husks
> Wherein the acorn cradled.

The conspiracy against Prospero's life, engaged in by Caliban, the wicked Antonio, and the rest, comes straight out of Strachey. There were two or three attempts at mutiny and groups of men withdrawing from the little commonwealth, wandering off in the woods. At length there was a practice against the life of the governor, for which the guilty leader was condemned to be hanged : 'the ladder being ready, after he had made many confessions, he earnestly desired, being a gentleman, that he might be shot to death ; and towards the evening he had his desire, the sun and his life setting together'.

Strachey mentions the early description of the Islands by Gonzalo Ferdinando Oviedo — so that two names come from that source : Ferdinand, son to the King of Naples, and Gonzalo, an honest old councillor. The name of the heroine, as in these last plays with Marina and Perdita, which carry their own suggestions, is symbolic. Ferdinand, engaged in bearing logs at Prospero's behest — a fairy-tale task — breaks out :

> Admired Miranda !
> Indeed the top of admiration ! worth
> What'st dearest to the world !

Whence did Prospero get his magic, wonder-working name ?

Another great contemporary spirit is conjured up in *The Tempest* — Montaigne, whose essay on Cannibals, which Shakespeare read in Florio's translation of the *Essays*, is made use of. Gonzalo is describing his primitive, ideal commonwealth, the kind of Golden Age that has haunted the mind of man, I do not know why.

> I' the commonwealth I would by contraries
> Execute all things ; for no kind of traffic
> Would I admit ; no name of magistrate ;
> Letters should not be known ; riches, poverty,
> And use of service, none ; contract, succession,
> Bourn, bound of land, tilth, vineyard, none ;
> No use of metal, corn, or wine, or oil ;
> No occupation ; all men idle, all ;
> And women too, but innocent and pure ;
> No sovereignty . . .

It is like a more sophisticated version at the end of his career of Jack Cade's commonwealth at the beginning. What is the point of it ? It is a dream, a Utopia with which to cheat men's more sensible hopes of tangible progress.

> All things in common Nature should produce
> Without sweat or endeavour ; treason, felony,
> Sword, pike, knife, gun, or need of any engine,
> Would I not have ; but Nature should bring forth,
> Of its own kind, all foison, all abundance,
> To feed my innocent people.

It reads like the famous 'withering away of the State' of Marxist thought, so evident in practice in Communist Russia. Shakespeare puts it in proper perspective, brings us back to earth with Sebastian's question :

> No marrying 'mong his subjects ?

and Antonio's reply :

> None, man ; all idle : whores and knaves.

A major theme behind the play is the contrast between Art and Nature, between civilised and natural man. Montaigne, who had had quite enough for one lifetime of civilised men killing each other in the name of religion in the French civil wars, had reacted into primitivism, a somewhat idealised view of savages. It is a regular reaction that crops up, with sensitive persons, in the history of ideas. But it is not any the more sensible for that. Shakespeare, with his feet well on the ground, unlike an intellectual, knew that savages could be as bestial and cruel as the civilised, that blacks are not necessarily better than whites. In his unexampled creation of Caliban he puts this issue in an image concretely before us — and the picture is by no means wholly unfavourable to Caliban. He has had injustice done him : before the whites came the island was his and his mother's. He was not without the capacity for admiration, for affection ; he wanted something to worship, he recognised something above him :

> This island's mine, by Sycorax my mother,
> Which thou tak'st from me. When thou cam'st first,
> Thou stroked'st me and mad'st much of me, would'st give me
> Water with berries in it ; and teach me how
> To name the bigger light, and how the less,
> That burn by day and night ; and then I loved thee,
> And showed thee all the qualities of the isle,
> The fresh springs, brine-pits, barren place and fertile.

This has its pathos : what a parable there is in it of the relations between colonial powers and backward races ! And how prophetic a parable *The Tempest* is with the withdrawal of the whites, the island on their departure lapsing once more to its original owner, Caliban. (And what will he make of it ?)

Little enough had he made of it before, for he was a child of nature. Shakespeare had no more illusions about the state of nature than he had about civilised man. Caliban was capable of treachery, like any Caribs or American Indians : he had tried to rape Prospero's young daughter, and thus earned Prospero's changed treatment of him. His response was to try and murder Prospero. There is more sense in this picture than in whole volumes of Utopia.

The Arden editor tells us that 'Shakespeare's treatment of the theme has what all his mature poetry has, a richly analytical approach to ideas, which never reaches after a naked opinion of true or false'.[26] This is an attractive phrase, and it is applicable to poetry ; with ideas, regarded intellectually, the whole point is whether they are true or false, or how far true or false.

It is by a singular propriety that in his penultimate play Shakespeare, still looking for something new, should deal with a profound theme initiated in his time that yet fills the world with its reverberations today. Other contemporary touches occur :

> When we were boys,
> Who would believe that there were mountaineers
> Dew-lapped like bulls, whose throats had hanging at 'em
> Wallets of flesh ? or that there were such men
> Whose heads stood in their breasts ? —

that is from Ralegh's *Guiana* again —

> Which now we find
> Each putter-out of five for one will bring us
> Good warrant of.[27]

Such was the new world into which Shakespeare had lived.

We hardly need pause over the well-worn political tricks by which Prospero's brother installed himself in Prospero's place as Duke of Milan :

> Being once perfected how to grant suits,
> How to deny them, who to advance, and who
> To trash for over-topping, new created
> The creatures that were mine, I say, or changed 'em,
> Or else new-formed 'em ; having both the key
> Of officer and office, set all hearts i' the state
> To what tune pleased his ear. . . .

How truly this describes what Khrushchev has been at in our time, or Stalin before him ! — it is the common form of authoritarian politics : it is but Shakespeare's usual understanding of everything that goes on in political life. Here is just a touch in passing that reveals his observation :

> Ebbing men, indeed,
> Most often do so near the bottom run
> By their own fear or sloth.

That had been precisely true of Essex, havering and hovering, challenging and delaying, not making up his mind, pushed into action by his followers, too late.

On the personal side, more haunting is the theme that runs through all these last plays of finding what has been lost. Allied with this is that of innocence and youth threatened, endangered, then miraculously saved. The elders find what they have lost, though they have been transformed by the experience of loss and grief. Taught by suffering they make a better way clear for those coming after to succeed them ; these too learn from the knowledge of what their elders have endured. Patience, fortitude,

acceptance — and all may yet come well : such seems the thought
we are left with at the end of each of these plays.

At the beginning we have Prospero's reflection,

> I find my zenith doth depend upon
> A most auspicious star, whose influence
> If now I court not but omit, my fortunes
> Will ever after droop.

It is the recurring thought all through Shakespeare's experience
of life :

> There is a tide in the affairs of men
> Which, taken at the flood, leads on to fortune.

At the end we have — the moral of all the last plays :

> Yet with my nobler reason 'gainst my fury
> Do I take part : the rarer action is
> In virtue than in vengeance.

The language of *The Tempest*, though late, is direct and simple
— so different from *Cymbeline* ; the gaiety of humour, the sparkle,
have returned ; the poetry is equal to anything in the plays. But
the mood is one of farewell :

> Our revels now are ended. These our actors,
> As I foretold you, were all spirits, and
> Are melted into air, into thin air :
> And like the baseless fabric of this vision,
> The cloud-capped towers, the gorgeous palaces,
> The solemn temples, the great globe itself,
> Yea, all which it inherit, shall dissolve,
> And, like this insubstantial pageant faded,
> Leave not a rack behind.

From the exceptionally elaborate stage-directions — more so than
with any other play except his last, *Henry VIII* — it is inferred
that he wrote it down in the country, from which various images
come :

> like winter's drops
> From eaves of reeds.
> By moonshine do the green sour ringlets make
> Whereof the ewe not bites ; and you whose pastime
> Is to make midnight mushrooms, that rejoice
> To hear the solemn curfew.

We know that the play was performed on Hallowmas night
(*i.e.* 1 November) 1611 'at Whitehall before the King's Majesty'.

And apparently it found favour with the public, which had rejected Ben Jonson's *Catiline* in 1611, so that he wrote no more for the public stage for the next three years till *Bartholomew Fair* : in the Induction to which he said grumpily, 'if there be never a servant-monster (*i.e.* a Caliban) in the Fair, who can help it, nor a nest of antics ? He is loth to make nature afraid in his plays, like those that beget *Tales, Tempests,* and such like drolleries'. It was vexing that things that did not adhere to rule, particularly his rule, should have so much more appeal and, in the end, more life.

The play was performed again, along with five others by Shakespeare, among the fourteen given during the elaborate festivities for the Princess Elizabeth's marriage to the Elector Palatine of the Rhine. That proportion — out of fourteen, six from one dramatist — tells its own story. Hence the wedding-masque in its own proper style, rather formal and statuesque :

> A contract of true love to celebrate,
> And some donation freely to estate
> On the blest lovers . . .
> Honour, riches, marriage-blessing,
> Long continuance, and increasing,
> Hourly joys be still upon you !
> Juno sings her blessings on you.

And so forward into eternity.

What could be more appropriate than that for his last play Shakespeare should turn back to the English story in which he had begun and complete the cycle of his earliest plays on Henry VI and Richard III with one on Henry VIII and the birth of Elizabeth ? The wheel would thus come full circle and, with our fuller knowledge of his literary ambition, his inner aesthetic fidelity, we can see him, thus, bringing his life's work to its appropriate conclusion. One of the chief features distinguishing his work had been the appeal of history to his imagination : there would now be no less than ten plays inspired by England's past. And this in addition to the Roman plays, further evidence of the appeal of history to this most historical mind. For, as we have seen, historical imagination and political understanding walk hand in hand throughout his work.

Once more, then, a convergence of factors decided him. The

long-negotiated Protestant marriage of the Princess Elizabeth was very popular, and brought about a resurgence of national feeling such as had not been seen since the Stuarts descended upon England. The Princess was a god-daughter of the great Queen : her name alone was enough to make her loved in England, as she always was (the Winter Queen), whatever people thought of her father and her brother, Charles I. Elizabethan memories came surging back : Shakespeare, always sensitive to popular mood, would respond yet once more, for the last time. But also, there was the challenge of the subject : with internal unity achieved, Henry VIII's reign did not offer the dramatic conflict of civil war, of the struggle for the succession, of the earlier histories. Shakespeare would do something new : he would concentrate on the achieved Tudor peace, making his rhythms out of the falls of great person-ages — Buckingham, Wolsey, Queen Katherine — with a back-ground of splendid pageantry and processions, to echo the festive time, and making up for the absence of the old loved fisticuffs and fighting all over the stage by drums, trumpets and even cannon shot off.

Once more, and for the last time, the old master who had held the stage so long (in 1612 he was forty-eight) would accomplish something different. *Henry VIII* is not quite like any of the previous English chronicle-plays : a good deal of time had passed since those, and its tone and atmosphere align it with the other late plays. The trial of Queen Katherine has a close resemblance to that of Hermione in *The Winter's Tale*. The themes are again patience in adversity — the word 'patience' echoes like a bell through the play — spiritual achievement through earthly suffering.

Shakespeare read up his sources very carefully : there was the old faithful stand-by Holinshed and Hall's familiar Chronicle, he used Foxe's *Acts and Monuments*, looked into Speed and, for Wolsey's fall, used the life by his devoted servant, Cavendish. No more of the rapid scamping he had sometimes been reduced to in the rush of the theatre, all the pressures upon him, in earlier days : he had time now.

Naturally, he intended a serious play, as he tells us, the audience, in a very personal Prologue, which reminds us of that to *Henry V*. Assumed in it is a life-time's knowledge of his faithful following of the public theatres, of the Globe.

> I come no more to make you laugh ; things now
> That bear a weighty and a serious brow,

> Sad, high, and working, full of state and woe ;
> Such noble scenes as draw the eye to flow
> We now present.

Shakespeare's confident relationship with his audience is like Dickens's lifelong love-affair with his readers.

> Those that can pity, here
> May, if they think it well, let fall a tear :
> The subject will deserve it. Such as give
> Their money out of hope they may believe,
> May here find truth too.

He undertakes that those who only want to see a show or two shall have their money's worth 'richly in two short hours'.

> Only they
> That come to hear a merry bawdy play,
> A noise of targets, or to see a fellow
> In a long motley coat guarded with yellow,
> Will be deceived.

This may be a glance at a popular play turning Henry's reign into comedy round the figure of his famous jester, Will Summers. We have been warned not to expect any of that, and indeed there is little of it : only one comic scene with a little bawdy ; a grave, beautiful, reflective play, its rhythms rising and falling, with its own moving lyricism.

The Epilogue has an equally personal note, and perhaps a glance at the private theatres, whose staple fare was mocking at the bourgeois : some may have come

> to hear the city
> Abused extremely, and to cry 'That's witty,'
> Which we have not done neither.

Henry VIII has always been popular, for it provides two splendid rôles for actors and actresses in Wolsey and Katherine. The other parts give plenty of opportunity, too, for the characterisation is rich and the interest is dispersed, not concentrated as in high tragedy. The character of Henry, for instance, is of interest : Shakespeare has fastened on to a clue to understanding the actual man as he was — in his earlier years under the dominance of Wolsey, or at least prepared to leave him to carry the burden of the state, and only fully coming forward after his fall. Nevertheless, as king he is the source of power : he is the deciding influence upon people's lives, and as such plays something of the rôle of Prospero. The subordinate figures all have life, their salient characteristics seized upon and sketched with the old mastery : Buckingham's rash impulsiveness and lack of control ; Gardiner's testy impatience ; Cromwell's fidelity to his master ; Cranmer's gentle patience. Shakespeare has entered into sympathy with his characters, has notably enlivened Katherine and given a much more favourable portrait of Wolsey than Holinshed's. There is justice for everyone.

The play is carefully organised, with appropriate variations of pace and style, with its contrasts between crowd and processional scenes, between great personages seen in public splendour and the lonely souls at their end face to face with themselves. There are subtle juxtapositions like Anne's coronation and Katherine's death-scene. While the gentlemen talking together operate as a chorus commenting on the action, provide the sense of the nation in the background reacting to these dramatic historical events.

It is Wolsey who has chiefly come down from this play in the nation's tradition. This is not surprising, since his fall, from a height of such overweening pride and splendour, is the most dramatic. Shakespeare has made it deeply affecting : that this must have moved him most appears from the fact that Wolsey speaks the finest poetry : several splendid passages, which we all remember, attest this :

> Had I but served my God with half the zeal
> I served my King, He would not in mine age
> Have left me naked to mine enemies.

This theme appears again in Wolsey's famous soliloquy.

> Farewell, a long farewell, to all my greatness !
> This is the state of man : today he puts forth
> The tender leaves of hopes ; tomorrow blossoms
> And bears his blushing honours thick upon him ;
> The third day comes a frost, a killing frost,
> And when he thinks, good easy man, full surely
> His greatness is a-ripening, nips his root,
> And then he falls, as I do.

Observe that this recapitulates, in part, the rhetorical theme of the Seven Ages of Man, but in a country setting, with the imagery of the country life amid which it was written. The speech continues with the image of sea and river, a scene no doubt observed :

> I have ventured,
> Like little wanton boys that swim on bladders,
> This many summers on a sea of glory . . .

Now, weary and old with service, he is left 'to the mercy of a rude stream'. But, like Lear, Wolsey has at length, by the way of suffering, attained to self-knowledge :

> I feel my heart new-opened . . .

When Cromwell asks him how he does :

> Never so truly happy, my good Cromwell.
> I know myself now, and I feel within me
> A peace above all earthly dignities,
> A still and quiet conscience.

Similarly, Buckingham accepts his fate and learns resignation, calling on his friends —

> Go with me like good angels to my end ;
> And, as the long divorce of steel falls on me,
> Make of your prayers one sweet sacrifice,
> And lift my soul to heaven.

Katherine, for her virtue, receives spiritual consolation and is granted a vision of the spirits of peace. Her last moments are attended by a hand-maiden whose very name is Patience :

> Patience, be near me still, and set me lower.

These all emerge from personal suffering into peace ; so, though the play has in parts a tragic tone, it is not a tragedy, while the end merges into ritual and prophecy. And all things shall be well.

The accent is of farewell and departure, yet the end assures hope of the future. It has been noticed that the imagery of the play speaks often of sickness : Buckingham is sick with anger, Wolsey's deeds are pestilent, Henry is sick in conscience.[28] In a play where everything speaks to us of Shakespeare there are still specific touches that bring him personally before us. The 'soft cheveril' conscience goes right back to the glover's shop at Stratford. He had lived on into a new world :

> New customs,
> Though they be never so ridiculous,
> Nay let 'em be unmanly, yet are followed.

Friends fall away :

> for those you make friends
> And give your hearts to, when once they perceive
> The least rub in your fortunes, fall away
> Like water from ye, never found again.

He had often enough seen that in life. And his view of the people at the end remained what it had been at the beginning and all through :

> If we suffer,
> Out of our easiness and childish pity
> To one man's honour, this contagious sickness,
> Farewell all physic ; and what follows then ?
> Commotions, uproars, with a general taint
> Of the whole state ; as of late days our neighbours,
> The upper Germany , can dearly witness,
> Yet freshly pitted in our memories.[29]

This refers to the Peasants' Revolt and the brief experience of communism and anarchy in Germany in 1524–5 : it made the impression on the sixteenth century that the Bolshevik Revolution of 1917 made on the twentieth.

The only comedy comes with the crowd-scene before the christening of the Princess. Here is the recognisable old hand. 'You'll leave your noise anon, ye rascals : do you take the Court for Paris Garden ?' They are all pushing and jostling : 'we may as well push against Paul's as stir 'em'. 'Is this Moorfields to muster in ?' The scenes familiar to us throughout this book recapitulate themselves before our eyes, as before his. So many themes are resumed here — something Falstaffian comes at length, though placed in the new perspective of the Jacobean colonisation of Virginia : 'or have we some strange Indian with the great tool come to Court, the women so besiege us ? Bless me, what a fry of fornication is at door ! On my Christian conscience, this one christening will beget a thousand, here will be father, godfather, and all together.' This goes back to the good days of the Boar's Head in East Cheap, and Mistress Quickly and her profitless acquaintance. 'There is a fellow somewhat near the door, he should be a brazier by his face, or, o' my conscience, twenty of the dog-days now reign in 's nose.' This must be Bardolph, by his nose, who has come alive again for us at the end.

They have all come to the christening of the infant Princess Elizabeth. It is this that gave Shakespeare the opportunity to round off his life's work with that tribute to her he had not written when she died in 1603, and to sum up for us what he thought of the Elizabethan Age now for ever over — himself to become, improbably enough then, its greatest star to future ages :

> This royal infant — Heaven still move about her —
> Though in her cradle, yet now promises

Upon this land a thousand thousand blessings,
Which time shall bring to ripeness : she shall be . . .
A pattern to all princes living with her,
And all that shall succeed . . .
She shall be loved and feared ; her own shall bless her ;
Her foes shake like a field of beaten corn,
And hang their heads with sorrow. Good grows with her :
In her days every man shall eat in safety
Under his own vine what he plants, and sing
The merry songs of peace to all his neighbours.

The whole of this famous speech is full of imagery and suggestion from the Bible, heard Sunday by Sunday in church, and follows the form of Biblical prophecy. Where so much of all that has gone before is resumed, this is what those who had been born in and lived with the age thought of it now that it was all over.

At a performance of *Henry VIII* on 29 June 1613, the Globe was burnt down. Sir Henry Wotton, among others, tells us the news and that the production was staged with much pomp and spectacle.

Now, King Henry making a masque at Cardinal Wolsey's house, and certain cannons being shot off at his entry, some of the paper or other stuff wherewith one of them was stopped, did light on the thatch ; where, being thought at first but an idle smoke and their eyes more attentive to the show, it kindled inwardly and ran round like a train, consuming within less than an hour the whole house to the very grounds. This was the fatal period of that virtuous fabric, wherein yet nothing did perish but a few forsaken cloaks ; only one man had his breeches set on fire that would perhaps have broiled him, if he had not by the benefit of a provident wit put it out with bottle ale.[30]

Though the Globe had but two narrow doors to get out, and there was a full house for a new play, everyone got away without hurt. Ben Jonson celebrated the event :

Against the Globe, the glory of the Bank,
Which though it were the fort of the whole parish,
Flanked with a ditch and forced out of a marish,
I saw with two poor chambers taken in
And razed ere thought could urge this might have been !
See the World's ruins ! Nothing but the piles
Left.

This, too, for Shakespeare was an end. But, like a splendid coiled snake, glittering and richly iridescent — emblem alike of wisdom and immortality — his work lay about him rounded and complete.

CHAPTER XVII

New Place

THE Globe was rebuilt even finer than before, with no thatch to its roof. Meanwhile, the King's men went off on tour to familiar ground in Kent, where they have been traced at Folkestone, thence through the south country to Oxford and up to Shrewsbury.[1] It is unlikely that Shakespeare accompanied them, or that he had acted for some time. More and more he was at Stratford : his presence there is recorded in September 1611, October 1614, September 1615, in January, March and April 1616, when he died.[2] We know that in May 1612 he was in London to testify at the Court of Requests in Westminster Hall in the Mountjoy case, in which he did not appear again, as expected in June — so presumably he was back at Stratford. In March 1613 he was again in London. On 17 November 1614 Thomas Greene, steward and town clerk of Stratford, who was living at New Place in 1609, wrote of 'my cousin Shakespeare coming to town yesterday' with his son-in-law Dr. John Hall ; and Shakespeare was away from home still at Christmas.

These are snail-tracks upon the face of antiquated documents, but they serve to bring together the two sides of his life, Stratford and London, in evidence all through.

In 1611 we find him joining with the aldermen and leading townsmen to contribute towards forwarding a bill in Parliament for better repair of the highways. His name is added in the margin, perhaps after his return home ; few had had better experience of how much the highways needed it. That year his holding in Stratford tithe brought in a good income of £60 a year ; by 1625 when the family parted with it, it was worth £90 : evidently a nice, well-considered investment.

Another useful investment was made in March 1613 when he purchased the house over the great gate into the Blackfriars, 'abutting upon a street leading down to Puddle Wharf on the east part right against the King's Majesty's Wardrobe'.³ What could be more convenient if he wanted a London residence for himself? — on the spot for the Blackfriars theatre, down the street to the wharf and into a wherry across the Thames to the Globe. But those days were passing : the gate-house was no more than an investment. He paid Henry Walker, citizen and minstrel of London, £140 for it ; friends joining him in the indenture being John Heminges, John Jackson and William Johnson, citizen and vintner of London, no other than the host of the Mermaid in Bread Street. As in all these documents the dramatist is 'William Shakespeare of Stratford-upon-Avon in the county of Warwick, gentleman'. He had made it, *non sanz droict*.

The purchase led to some litigation, but more interesting are the associations of the house, for it had been a perfect nest for Catholic *intrigants* in Elizabeth's reign. It was inhabited by John Fortescue, in the service of his uncle, Master of the Queen's Wardrobe. This did not prevent him from being a Catholic, and his wife, a kinswoman of Southampton, was a regular *dévote* with priests constantly in and out of the old nest. It had 'many places of secret conveyance in it', communicating with 'secret passages towards the water'. In spite of the well-known activities of Mrs. Fortescue in aiding and abetting priests, her husband never lost his place in the Queen's Wardrobe — such was the intolerance of Elizabeth's rule ; their daughter married Francis Beaumont's brother, Sir John.

In this year Shakespeare and Burbage were asked to design an *impresa* for the Earl of Rutland, Southampton's friend. This meant a painted shield, with emblems and mottoes, for the Earl to carry at the tournament on the King's Accession Day, 24 March 1613. Burbage was known to have been a painter — he may have painted the portrait we have of him, with the intelligent eyes and arched brows, the trim-cut beard, at Dulwich. They were paid £2: 2s. each for their work. Sir Henry Wotton tells us that at the tilt, some of the emblems and mottoes were 'so dark that their meaning is not yet understood, unless perchance that were their meaning — not to be understood'.⁴

From this year, too, we have some of Shakespeare's last handiwork, his contribution to Fletcher's play, *The Two Noble Kinsmen*. When this play was published in 1634, as 'presented at the Blackfriars by the King's Majesty's Servants, with great applause', Shakespeare's name appeared along with Fletcher's on the title-page.

This in itself is no decisive evidence, for his name was made use of on other playbooks, with which he had no connection, to help to sell them. On the other hand, its exclusion from the First Folio is decisive, for in our time the honesty and fidelity of Heminges and Condell have been completely vindicated — nor need they ever have been questioned. What this means is that they did not regard *The Two Noble Kinsmen*, any more than *Pericles*, as wholly, or even mainly, by Shakespeare.[5]

Nor is it : the character of the piece — masque-like and processional, without real dramatic conflict — is unlike Shakespeare. These matters are ultimately a question of subjective impression, in the absence of external evidence ; nevertheless, one man's opinion is not as good as another's — most people's literary sensibilities are not subtle enough to be able to judge. My overriding impression of this play is of a voice and hand not Shakespeare's. This is contrary to the tendency of contemporary scholars to see more of Shakespeare in it than there is — it is very natural to wish that there were more from his hand, and the wish is father to the thought.[6] On the other side, we can agree that Shakespeare is present in the play, particularly in the invocations which no other pen was capable of inditing and which have obvious parallels in his own work. Such a passage is the prayer :

> Thou mighty one, that with thy power hast turned
> Green Neptune into purple, whose approach
> Comets pre-warn, whose havoc in vast field
> Unearthed skulls proclaim, whose breath blows down
> The teeming Ceres' foison . . .

We can recognise here his own phrases and words, like 'foison', the echo of the famous phrase from *Macbeth* :

> The multitudinous seas incarnadine,
> Making the green one red.

There are several traceable echoes in a passage like this :

>   O Queen Emilia,
> Fresher than May, sweeter
> Than her gold buttons on the bows, or all
> The enamelled knacks o' the mead or garden : yea,
> We challenge too the bank of any nymph
> That makes the stream seem flowers ; thou, O jewel
> O' the wood, o' the world, hast likewise blast a place
> With thy sole presence . . .

This echoes the masque in *The Tempest*.

Equally there are touches of him in the imagery, particularly in his well-recognised fondness for the rare word 'candied' :

> O my petition was
> Set down in ice, which by hot grief uncandied
> Melts into drops, so sorrow, wanting fortune,
> Is pressed with deeper matter.

Or there is the run-on imagery characteristic of him, where the punning association of the word suggests the idea :

> Palamon
> Has a most menacing aspect : his brow
> Is graved and seems to bury what it frowns on.

The play has some affiliations with *Henry VIII*, particularly in its processional character, but without the drama. Like it, however, it has a marked element in its imagery drawn from sickness and medicine : no less than seventeen such images have been detected. More important considerations, such as the inadequate characterisation, the failure of the figures to come to life, point to Fletcher.[7]

What can be agreed upon is that Shakespeare's hand *is* present, and that at the least he touched up the play of his admiring disciple, whose own work bears so many traces of the influence of the master. We may add that in Charles I's copy of nine Beaumont and Fletcher plays, including this one, the King has added a note at the end, 'All, by Beaumont and Fletcher'.[8] He was in the best position to know.

At Stratford in the summer of 1614, while Shakespeare was in residence at New Place, a third fire damaged the town, after the two disastrous fires of 1594 and 1595. Puritan preachers, on intimate terms with the deity, knew the explanation : 'and that which is most strange within these late years, a whole town hath been twice burnt, for the breach of the Sabbath, as all men judged'.[9] The preacher at neighbouring Evesham was able to be more specific : 'Stratford-upon-Avon was twice on the same day twelvemonth, being the Lord's day, almost consumed with fire : chiefly for profaning the Lord's Sabbath and for contemning his word in the mouth of his faithful ministers'. Unfortunately from their point of view the third fire happened on a Saturday. It consumed over fifty houses, with many barns and stores of grain, hay, malt, timber — the damage was estimated at £8000. These successive disasters considerably pulled down the active little town's prosperity. Nothing occurred to detract from that of the owner of New Place : in all three fires his luck held good, his property was untouched. That year one of the thirsty preachers was given entertainment at New Place, though the town provided the drink : 'for one quart of sack and one quart of claret wine given to a preacher at the New Place, 20d.'[10]

The names he had known all his life remained much unchanged, though a younger generation was coming up to take the place of the old. Next door to New Place now lived Henry Norman, a friend of Dr. John Hall. Across the way in the Chapel Quad schoolmaster Aspinall continued to hold sway, though no longer alone, for in 1611 the priest's house was converted into a vicarage for Vicar Rogers. 'Side by side lived vicar and schoolmaster in the quiet court ; and opposite in the old *camera* and rooms above the council chamber lived their assistants, the usher and the curate' ; these were now, in this year 1614, young men from Oxford, Richard Watts of Jesus and Edward Wilmore, a Bible clerk from All Souls.[11] When baker Allen made his will, witnessed by Shakespeare's nephew, Richard Hathaway, also a baker, it was sad to see Vicar Rogers indebted for a large amount of bread, 33s. 4d. Abraham Sturley died this year : he had never recovered his losses from the fire of 1594 and had been excused a second turn of duty as bailiff of the town for lack of means. He left two sons, whom he had sent to Oxford, beneficed clergymen at beautiful Broadway, the church on the broad slope of that splendid hill, and at Alcester, home of the Grevilles. Alderman Rogers, who had built the fine new house in High Street (now Harvard House) after the fire of 1594, had been allowed to resign from the council 'by reason of his great age and his grown unable through infirmity to bear the office of alderman . . . with great allowance of his good desert of this place'.[12] In 1611 his youngest daughter married William Harvard of Southwark : her sister had married the brother Robert Harvard at Stratford on 8 April 1605. It was their son John who was the founder of Harvard College.

At the corner of High Street and Sheep Street lived Shakespeare's old friends, Hamnet and Judith Sadler, in their new-built house, less prosperous than they had been. She died in 1614, and Sadler sold his business and house shortly after ; Shakespeare did not forget him in his will. Another friend lived in High Street, Henry Walker, whose little boy William was Shakespeare's godson : also remembered in his will. Walker's niece married a friend of the Halls, Matthew Morris : he was one of the trustees to whom the Blackfriars gate-house was transferred after the poet's death, to ensure the succession to his right heirs. The names of the Morris children, Susanna and John, confirm the friendship with the Halls.

Those quarrelsome old neighbours in Sheep Street, Badger and Barnhurst, Catholic and Puritan, who had so held up council meetings with their abuse of each other, had departed. Both had been turned out of the corporation and left the town. Julian Shaw, maltster and wool-dealer, an old neighbour from Henley Street days, had moved up in the world to become alderman and at length bailiff of the borough in 1615-16. He had followed Shakespeare to Corn Street, where he occupied a good, well-furnished house : he was one of the witnesses of Shakespeare's will. The Reynolds family, who were Catholics and lived in some style in both Corn Street and Old Stratford, were also friends. Early in James's reign, when Catholic hopes blossomed to be nipped by Gunpowder Plot, a Jesuit who was being pursued with hue and cry took refuge with them : disguised in green hose, white stockings and high-heeled shoes, muddied from a fall in his flight, he was last seen at the Reynolds's door laying his hand on the 'check-post'. The Reynoldses were good friends with their Protestant neighbours, the Combes, at Old Stratford and the Combes were the well-to-do family with whom Shakespeare had closest associations in his last years.

John Combe, a rich bachelor, died in 1614, leaving his friend at New Place £5 ; there were a large number of bequests, public and private, personal and charitable. His monument, with recumbent effigy, next along from Shakespeare's on the north wall of the chancel in the church, was made by Gerard Johnson of Southwark, and this no doubt prompted the poet's family to follow suit. His heir, William Combe, at once began to take steps to enclose the common fields at Welcombe and trouble ensued. Shakespeare was concerned, both as a freeholder owning land there and as farmer of part of the tithes. Thomas Greene, the town clerk, drew up a statement of the interests involved, at the head of which we find : 'Master Shakespeare, four yard-land, no common nor ground beyond Gospel Bush, nor ground in Sandfield nor none in Sloe Hill Field beyond Bishopton, nor none in the enclosure beyond Bishopton'.[13] Combe's agent agreed with Shakespeare to compensate him for any loss to his tithes. He apparently did not think the enclosure would be proceeded with, but he was protected anyway. We learn from Greene in London, on 17 November 1614, 'my cousin Shakespeare coming yesterday to town, I went to see him how he did. He told me that they assured him they meant to enclose no further than to Gospel Bush, and so up straight, leaving out part of the dingles to the Field, to the gate in Clopton hedge and take in Salisbury's piece ; and that they mean in April to survey the land, and then to give satisfaction and not before. And he and Master Hall say they think there will be nothing done at all.'

We see how well he knew those fields.

In spite of the opposition of the corporation and the local people, William Combe went forward with his plans. The town clerk noted in his diary, 'I also writ of myself to my cousin Shakespeare the copies of all our oaths made then, also a note of the inconveniences would grow by the enclosure'. Unfortunately his answer, if there were one, is missing. Combe defied the corporation and proceeded with hedging and ditching his intended enclosure. When some of the tenants set about filling in the ditches his men threw them to the ground, while Combe 'sat laughing on his horseback and said they were good football players'. The members of the corporation he called 'Puritan knaves and underlings in their colour'. Ill feeling mounted, and the people came out in numbers from Stratford and Bishopton to throw down his mounds and fill up the ditches. It seems that Shakespeare disapproved of the proceedings — as a quiet man he would ; for there is an entry in the town clerk's diary pointing that way : 'September. Master Shakespeare's telling J. Greene that he was not able to bear the enclosing of Welcombe.' And, in the event, William Combe was defeated.

The year before, 1613, there had been a piece of unpleasantness in Shakespeare's immediate family, when John Lane the younger slandered Susanna Hall, then thirty, saying that 'she had the running of the reins and had been naught with Ralph Smith at John Palmer's'.[14] I dare say she had the running of the reins, for she was the member of the family who possessed something of her father's spirit. (The utter silence about Shakespeare's wife is some indication of her place in the scheme of things — a housewife, and nothing more.) The slander was reported by Robert Whatcott, who was a witness to Shakespeare's will. John Lane was a young Catholic, nephew of Nicholas Lane whose effigy we see on his tomb in Alveston church. His sister Margaret was wife to John Greene, Shakespeare's cousin — so it was all in the family. However, Dr. Hall had the young man up before the consistory court in Worcester cathedral, where he was duly excommunicated. It does not seem to have done him much good, or Mistress Hall any harm.

Shakespeare's poor relations, his sister Joan Hart, lived on with her husband, the hatter, and their three sons — William, Thomas and Michael — in the old home in Henley Street. The husband, William Hart, died a few days before his brother-in-law, in April 1616. On 10 February 1616 Judith Shakespeare, at the ripe age of thirty-one, was married to Thomas Quiney, second son of her father's friend, Richard Quiney. It does not appear that Judith could write — she must have taken after her mother. There was some little trouble over the marriage, for, though the banns were properly called, it was celebrated outside the proper liturgical season. So they too were summoned before the consistory court at Worcester, did not appear, and Quiney was excommunicated. He did not take this to heart; he was a vintner.

More important were the provisions of Shakespeare's will, of which the first draft was drawn up in January. It was done by Francis Collins, the lawyer in whom Shakespeare and Stratford had entire confidence : an overseer of the poor, member of the town council, he had drafted John Combe's will; becoming clerk of the peace at Warwick in 1614, he was wanted back by Stratford to become town clerk in 1617. At the end of March Francis Collins was sent for and a second draft of the first page hastily substituted. Since this was mainly concerned with provisions for Judith, it would seem that it was her marriage that necessitated the changes. Shakespeare described himself then, on 25 March 1616, as 'in perfect health and memory, God be praised'.[15]

The first thing to note is that Shakespeare made his will in accordance with the regular Protestant formula : 'I commend my soul into the hands of God my Creator, hoping and assuredly believing through the only merits of Jesus Christ my Saviour to be made partaker of life everlasting'. This is important : one can always tell from the formula in these contemporary wills whether the person is dying a Protestant or a Catholic. Shakespeare died, as he had lived, a member of the Church of England.

There is some indication from the changes in the will that

he had not complete confidence in son-in-law Quiney, though the marriage lasted : he and Judith lived together all their days up to the Restoration. Their little boy, Shakespeare Quiney, baptised in November 1616, died next year : nothing in the ordinary family way seemed able to perpetuate his name. Her father left Judith £100 marriage-portion, with £50 more on giving up any claim to the cottage in Chapel Lane. Another £150 was settled on her conditionally, if living three years after the will ; meanwhile she was to receive only interest on the sum, until her husband settled an equivalent amount on her and her children. If Judith died without issue in the next three years, £100 was to go 'to my niece Elizabeth Hall' and £50 to Joan Hart and her children. The mistake 'niece' for 'grandchild' was very characteristic : he was thinking of the Harts, and his mind was running forward as in the 'run-on' imagery of his plays. In addition, Judith received a remembrance of a broad silver and gilt bowl. Joan Hart was left £20, all his wearing apparel and the tenancy of the old home in Henley Street for life ; £5 apiece to her three sons — Shakespeare could not remember the name of the third. To his grandchild Elizabeth Hall he left all his plate, except the big bowl that was for Judith. He thought of arranging a marriage-portion for this little girl, his only grandchild to survive, and then cancelled his provision since she was too young. He bequeathed nothing to his wife, except 'the second best bed with the furniture' : this has no significance, for the best bed would naturally go as an heirloom with the house. In spite of the nonsensical popular fixation on this point, it is of some significance that he left his wife nothing else, not even a ring. She was really left to the care of the Halls in whom he placed all his confidence.

For he left Susanna the bulk of his estate : New Place, the houses in Henley Street, the lands in Old Stratford, Bishopton and Welcombe, the house in Blackfriars. And this entailed estate was to descend to their male heirs (there were none), and in default to Judith's, who also had none, and so to his right heirs : thus the estate devolved upon Elizabeth Hall. All the rest of his goods, chattels, leases, plate, jewels, household stuff, he bequeathed, after the payment of specific bequests, to Dr. John Hall and Susanna jointly, whom he made executors. Leases would include his profitable shares in the Globe and Blackfriars theatres. 'To my fellows, John Heminges, Richard Burbage and Henry,

Condell 26s. 8d. a piece to buy them rings.' To the poor of
Stratford he left £10, to Thomas Combe his sword, to Thomas
Russell of Alderminster £5, to Francis Collins £13 : 6 : 8. He
left 26s. 8d. each to buy them a mourning ring to Hamnet Sadler
and William Reynolds, gent. ; to Anthony Nash, gent. of Welcombe 26s. 8d., to Mr. John Nash 26s. 8d., and 'to my godson
William Walker, 20s. in gold'. 'And I do intreat and appoint
the said Thomas Russell esquire and Francis Collins gent. to be
overseers hereof.' The witnesses to the will were Francis Collins,
Julian Shaw, John Robinson, Hamnet Sadler, Robert Whatcott ;
the date 25 March 1616, or, in old parlance, Lady day. It was
proved by John Hall in London on 22 June.

In the interval Shakespeare had died. The Restoration vicar
of Stratford noted down in his commonplace book half a century
later : 'Shakespeare, Drayton and Ben Jonson had a merry meeting
and, it seems, drank too hard, for Shakespeare died of a fever
there contracted'.[16] This kind of thing must not be taken too
literally ; on the other hand it may contain a kernel of fact. There
was nothing improbable in a meeting of these three. Ben Jonson
felt affectionately about Shakespeare ; even his grumpy remarks
about him are not ill-humoured. Drayton was a regular visitor
to Clifford Chambers nearby, though it was the summer that he
usually spent at the riverside house of his 'Idea', now Lady Rainsford. Shakespeare, we have seen, was not much given to drink
and disliked drunkenness ; that does not exclude the idea of a
'merry meeting'. There was even an occasion for it in Judith's
wedding in February.

He died on Tuesday, 23 April, St. George's day — the patron
saint of the medieval England in which he had found such inspiration. On Thursday the 25th, he was borne along the familiar
path to the church, fifty-two years almost to the day since he had
been carried there to be christened. A life had come full circle
along these ways, the leaves fresh and green upon the churchyard
elms, willows and alders in full flourish by the banks of the Avon, and
so in at the porch and up the nave to the resting-place in the chancel.

It was hardly likely — so much of his life had been secret —
that there was any there to remember his words, written twenty-
four years before :

> From you have I been absent in the spring,
> When proud-pied April, dressed in all his trim,
> Hath put a spirit of youth in everything . . .

Or was there anyone to say over the words ? —

> No longer mourn for me when I am dead
> Than you shall hear the surly sullen bell
> Give warning to the world that I am fled . . .

Alone to himself as his essential life had been lived, he had written the lines to be inscribed on his gravestone :

> Good friend for Jesus sake forbeare
> To digg the dust encloasèd heare !
> Bleste be the man that spares thes stones
> And curst be he that moves my bones.[17]

And, strangely enough, this wish has always been respected.

The family very properly bestirred itself — no doubt John Hall taking the lead — to give him a suitable monument, ordered like neighbour Combe's from Gerard Johnson's workshop. It is a worthy piece of Jacobean craftsmanship : a Renaissance arched niche with the bust of the poet in Cotswold limestone ; white marble surrounded with columns and panels of black touch. Above, flanked by cherubs symbolising Labour and Rest, is the panel with helm and crest in relief, and the famous coat of arms with the spear athwart it. Having attained to the rank of scholar, though no university man, he is given a Latin couplet :

> Iudicio Pylium, genio Socratem, arte Maronem :
> Terra tegit, populus maeret, Olympus habet.

These are large claims, but justified. Some rather good funerary verses follow :

> Stay passenger, why goest thou by so fast ?
> Read if thou canst whom envious Death hath placed
> Within this monument, Shakespeare, with whom
> Quick Nature died : whose name doth deck this tomb
> Far more than cost : sith all that he hath writ
> Leaves living art but page to serve his wit.

We can tell very well from the Droeshout portrait, which the bust corroborates, what he looked like. The whole impression is dominated by the magnificent domed forehead and bold cranium — very convincing, plenty of room for that capacious brain. He had evidently grown bald early : as early as *The*

Comedy of Errors there is a touch of self-consciousness about it :
'there's no time for a man to recover his hair that grows bald
by nature'. The eyes, under the well-arched brows, are all one
could hope for : luminous, full of intelligence, observation,
sympathy, but with puffy pouches under them. The face is of
a rounded oval shape, cheeks full, prominent nose, fleshy and
sensual, with refinement in the nostril. The lips confirm this
impression, sensitive and mobile, as became an actor, rather voluptuous, almost a Cupid's bow. Where the upper part of the head
is all intelligence, the lower is all sensibility and gives something
of a feminine impression, not weak but readily responsive. For
we can see under the mask-like expression of an inferior painter
that the moulded features, in their pallor, are very mobile, could
easily come alive with a smile that would communicate itself
to laughing, kindly eyes. The hair was worn moderately long
over the ears, with a little moustache and goatee beard on the
chin ; rather a hairless face. What indication we have of the
figure beneath the high starched ruff is of a rather slight, sprightly,
neatly made man. But, above all, one can never forget the splendid
dome of the head, candid and serene, yet retaining what secrets !

Among the tributes that began increasingly to come from
his fellow-writers only one made the point of his comparatively
early death :

> We wondered, Shakespeare, that thou went'st so soon
> From the world's stage to the grave's tiring room.[18]

Robert Armin, the principal comedian of the Company, for
whom he had written the fine parts of Feste and the Fool in *Lear*,
had died the year before him, in 1615. Next of the fellowship
to go was Richard Burbage himself in 1619 — perhaps unex-
pectedly, for he left a nuncupative will leaving everything in the
hands of his 'well-beloved' wife.[19] (The situation there was a
very different one from Shakespeare's, with an illiterate wife.)
Burbage's death was lamented as a great loss by his faithful public :

> He's gone and with him what a world are dead,
> Which he revived, to be revivèd so.
> No more young Hamlet, old Jeronimo,
> King Lear, the grievèd Moor, and more beside,
> That lived in him have now for ever died.

The best tribute was that of the Earl of Pembroke, who wrote
to Lord Doncaster of a grand entertainment being given to the

French ambassador, and himself stopping behind while the guests went to see a play, 'which I, being tender-hearted, could not endure to see so soon after the loss of my old acquaintance Burbage'.[20] If these were the feelings Pembroke entertained towards Burbage, Shakespeare was included, if less intimately, in that favour, as we know from the First Folio.

This great undertaking, the publication of all the plays in one volume, which came to fruition in 1623, must have been set in hand several years before. The idea probably dates back at least to 1619, when the publisher Jaggard, who had long had a rather dubious interest in Shakespeare's work, came out with 'a curious and rather shabby collection' of Shakespearean and non-Shakespearean plays under his name.[21] Many years before, as early as 1598 or 1599, Jaggard had put out a small book of verse, *The Passionate Pilgrim*, which included five poems only of Shakespeare's, and had put his name on the title-page. Thomas Heywood tells us of Shakespeare's displeasure at this : 'so the author I know much offended with Master Jaggard that, altogether unknown to him, presumed to make so bold with his name'.[22] Of the poems, 'he to do himself right hath since published them in his own name'. (Are we to infer from this, since two of them were sonnets, that Shakespeare was behind the publication of the *Sonnets* in 1609 ?)

After Burbage's death Heminges and Condell were the leading men in Shakespeare's Company and they gallantly dedicated themselves to producing a folio volume of all his plays, 'only to keep the memory of so worthy a friend and fellow alive as was our Shakespeare'.[23] Other subsidiary motives entered in : no doubt to defend his work from depredations or partial and inadequate presentation ; to give as good a text as they could of the plays. They may have been influenced by Ben Jonson's determination to produce a folio volume of his work to date in 1616 — he was only forty and his work was by no means complete. Jonson presented and edited his own works with the care due to a classic. Shakespeare had not bothered, and the task was bigger, more difficult and correspondingly more formidable.

It was also a risky undertaking as Heminges and Condell well realised. In their dedication they say, 'we are fallen upon the ill fortune to mingle two of the most diverse things that can be, fear and rashness : rashness in the enterprise and fear in the success'. There can be little doubt that these loyal colleagues took the initiative. To handle such a large volume a small syndicate of stationers came together : it seems that the Jaggards and Edward Blount, Marlowe's old friend, were the chief undertakers, joined by John Smethwick and William Apsley who both possessed rights in a number of the plays. These are the names given of those at whose charges the volume was printed ; but there may have been others taking a share in the background. But, Fripp asks pertinently, 'where was Richard Field? Why was he not in the undertaking ? He was high in his profession — Master of the Stationers' Company in 1619 and in 1622.'²⁴ If only we knew the story of the relations between these two Stratford men in London, their earlier association and then its complete end — something interesting is lost there. Altogether, a considerable work of organisation was involved : some nineteen of the thirty-seven plays exist in quarto form, good, bad and indifferent ; eighteen appear in the Folio for the first time. Think what we owe to the faithful Heminges and Condell, what we should have lost without them !

It was natural that they should dedicate their book to the brothers, the Earls of Pembroke and Montgomery, both ardent patrons of the theatre and in particular of the King's men ; for Pembroke was Lord Chamberlain, and as such continued the special relationship of his office to its affairs. They thus refer to Shakespeare as his 'servant,' and 'since your lordships have been pleased to think these trifles something heretofore, and have prosecuted both them and their author living with so much favour, we hope that they, outliving him and he not having the fate, common with some, to be executor to his own writings, you will use the like indulgence towards them you have done unto their parent'.

Such is their polite and proper tone towards their distinguished patrons. The address 'To the great Variety of Readers' that follows has a different tone, direct and humorous, rather hectoring: some have seen in it the pen of Ben Jonson, and indeed I think he must have had more of a hand in helping forward the work than he is usually credited with. Once more it is regretted that Shakespeare had not lived to see his own plays through the press. 'It had been a thing, we confess, worthy to have been wished that the author himself had lived to have set forth and overseen his own writings. But since it hath been ordained otherwise, and he by death departed from that right, we pray you do not envy his friends the office of their care and pain to have collected and published them.' That is a pretty good hint of the trouble it had caused to bring together the plays from the various sources to give the best result they could : from the prompt-books accumulated in the theatre's own library, from transcripts of the author's manuscript, from printed quartos compared and corrected, and, as we now know, from the author's own papers.[25] It had been a complicated and difficult job, impossible to accomplish with perfection or with the consistency that Ben Jonson had been able to achieve in the editing of his plays. But modern scholarship is agreed, as against earlier, in paying tribute to the fidelity and honesty of the editors' intentions and the remarkable accomplishment — within its own terms and considering all the difficulties that hampered them — of their task.[26]

They, themselves, claimed what we now know to be only their due — though meanly withheld from them by so many commentators without the imagination to see what the faithful pair of players accomplished : 'where before you were abused with divers stolen and surreptitious copies, maimed and deformed by the frauds and stealths of injurious impostors that exposed them : even those are now offered to your view cured and perfect of their limbs, and all the rest absolute in their numbers as he conceived them'. This famous passage has been discussed *ad nauseam*, and Heminges and Condell cross-examined in their graves as if they were impostors. All that they meant was — and this is the common-sense of the matter — that a number of the quartos, pirated publications of the plays or put together from the memories of actors that had played in them, offered thoroughly unreliable and inferior texts, some of them a travesty of what Shakespeare had written. And now his old fellows had done their best, within the limits of what was practicable and without being scholars like Ben Jonson, to give as good a text as they could.

They went on to a rough and ready indication of Shakespeare's way of writing, which has got them into more trouble. 'Who, as he was a happy imitator of nature, was a most gentle expresser of it. His mind and hand went together, and what he thought he uttered with that easiness that we have scarce received from him a blot in his papers.' Commonsense tells us that this is not the kind of thing meant literally or absolutely : it only means that Shakespeare wrote with the facility that everything goes to show he did, and that he did not make many of the corrections he might have done. Too busy, too pressed, the claims of the theatre, of acting, his mind besieged with thoughts of the next play : he did not belong to the type of the constipated and cramped or that kind of the critical. We have seen, everything in his work shows, what a keen, critical mind his was ; but with him criticism was not an end in itself, it was just a means to better acting, better plays. With him criticism was not allowed to cramp the creative : there were better things to do, his mind racing forward : hence a good deal of slipshod, of loose ends, bits not quite tied up. He does not seem to have minded much about that sort of thing.

The old players have their own reply on this, and an effective one : 'though you be a magistrate of wit and sit on the stage at Blackfriars, or the cockpit, to arraign plays daily — know these plays have had their trial already and stood out all appeals, and do now come forth quitted rather by a decree of court than any purchased letters of commendation'. However, there were verses in commendation, particularly the long critical and bio-graphical poem by Ben Jonson, from which we learn a great deal about both Jonson and Shakespeare. Shakespeare's portrait was engraved for the title-page, rather indifferently, by a young Fleming working in London, Martin Droeshout. Ben wrote the lines for it, with a note of apology :

> Wherein the graver had a strife
> With nature to out-do the life :
> O, could he but have drawn his wit
> As well in brass as he hath hit
> His face, the print would then surpass
> All that was ever writ in brass.

When we come to read Ben's 'ample' tribute — his own word — the first thing to notice is the affectionate tone of the inscription : 'To the Memory of my beloved the author, Master William Shakespeare, and what he hath left us'. When Ben looked back on the long years of association with his colleague and senior, the kindness he had received from him, the for-bearance with which he had been treated, the gentleness of nature and bearing — all feelings of grumpiness and envy fell away, and we are given a magnificent, an exemplary, tribute from one great writer to another. Full of generosity, Jonson's was not only laudation, it was a critical statement of what he believed — Ben was far too independent, too outspoken for it to be otherwise :

> While I confess thy writings to be such
> As neither man nor muse can praise too much :
> Tis true, and all men's suffrage . . .
>   Soul of the age !
> The applause, delight, the wonder of our stage !

Ben will commit him only with his peers,

> And tell how far thou didst our Lyly out-shine,
> Or sporting Kyd, or Marlowe's mighty line.

Observe how precisely this describes Shakespeare's progress : in each *genre* he had taken Lyly, Kyd, Marlowe, for model, learned from each one what he had to teach, and then gone on to surpass each and all of them.

> And though thou hadst small Latin and less Greek,

Ben proceeds to place him beside Aeschylus, Euripides and Sophocles ; nor is there anyone today to dissent. The too-much discussed line about 'small Latin and less Greek' only means that Shakespeare was not a classical scholar. It is unlikely that he had any Greek ; but we have seen that he had quite enough Latin for his purposes, and that he read French and Italian. (In that, his educational equipment was not unlike that of a clever modern grammar-schoolboy on the arts side — except that he made much more of less.)

It is pleasant to find that in his considered, deliberate judgment, as opposed to occasional outbursts against Shakespeare's too great facility and easy-going ways, Ben was concerned to pay a tribute to his art :

> Yet must I not give nature all : thy art,
> My gentle Shakespeare, must enjoy a part.
> For, though the poet's matter nature be,
> His art doth give the fashion. And that he
> Who casts to write a living line must sweat —
> Such as thine are — and strike the second heat
> Upon the Muse's anvil . . .

Such was Ben Jonson's critical credo, and his final judgment was :

> For a good poet's made, as well as born :
> And such wert thou. Look how the father's face
> Lives in his issue : even so the race
> Of Shakespeare's mind and manners brightly shines
> In his well-turnèd and true-filèd lines.

There was generosity, from a frequent critic. As for Shakespeare's place in his age :

> Sweet swan of Avon ! What a sight it were
> To see thee in our waters yet appear,
> And make those flights upon the banks of Thames
> That so did take Eliza and our James.

The conclusion of it all was, and how truly Ben spoke :

> He was not of an age, but for all time !

Young Leonard Digges, born in Armada year and stepson of Thomas Russell of Alderminster, was able to combine Stratford, Oxford and London in his tribute :

> Shakespeare, at length thy pious fellows give
> The world thy works : thy works, by which outlive
> Thy tomb thy name must : when that stone is rent
> And time dissolves thy Stratford monument
> Here we alive shall view thee still. This book,
> When brass and marble fade, shall make thee look
> Fresh to all ages.

Whatever element of commonplace there was in this has been far transcended by the fact. Hugh Holland, of Trinity College, spoke for Cambridge in his lines upon 'the famous scenic poet.' Seventeen years later, on the threshold of the Civil War, Digges summed up for us his memories of the theatre and the ever-popular reception of the plays :

> So have I seen when Caesar would appear,
> And on the stage at half-sword parley were
> Brutus and Cassius : O, how the audience
> Were ravished, with what wonder they went thence,
> When some new day they would not brook a line
> Of tedious, though well-laboured, Catiline.
> Sejanus too was irksome, they prized more
> Honest Iago, or the jealous Moor.
> And though the Fox and subtle Alchemist,
> Long intermitted, could not quite be missed . . .
> Yet these sometimes, even at a friend's desire
> Acted, have scarce defrayed the sea-coal fire
> And door-keepers — when let but Falstaff come,
> Hal, Poins, the rest you scarce shall have a room
> All is so pestered : let but Beatrice
> And Benedick be seen, lo, in a trice
> The cockpit, galleries, boxes are all full
> To hear Malvolio, that cross-gartered gull.

There we are : he has always had, as Jonson said, all men's suffrage.

At New Place Shakespeare's widow lived on — the silence unbroken, never a word — until the year of the Folio, when on 8 August 1623 she died. An old sexton of the church said that 'she did earnestly desire to be laid in the same grave with him', but 'not one, for fear of the curse abovesaid, dare touch his gravestone'.[27] Her slab was given the dignity of an inscription in Latin, presumably by her educated son-in-law, speaking for Susanna :

Ubera, tu mater, tu lac, vitamque dedisti . . .

At Oxford the year before there had died the Davenants, host and hostess of the Crown tavern, undoubtedly acquaintance of Shakespeare, and who may have been something more. For Aubrey, writing in only the next generation and in a position to know, gives us some interesting information from a close source in his life of Sir William Davenant, the dramatist and poet. 'His father was John Davenant, a vintner there, a very grave and discreet citizen : his mother was a very beautiful woman and of a very good wit, and of conversation extremely agreeable.'[28] There were three sons, Robert, William (was he perhaps named for the poet, after whom he turned ?) and Nicholas. 'Master William Shakespeare was wont to go into Warwickshire once a year and did commonly in his journey lie at this house in Oxon where he was exceedingly respected. I have heard parson Robert Davenant say that Master William Shakespeare has given him a hundred kisses. Now Sir William would sometimes, when he was pleasant over a glass of wine with his most intimate friends . . . say that it seemed to him that he writ with the very spirit that Shakespeare, and seemed contented enough to be thought his son.'

We may take this as we wish : at the very least it shows that a leading poet of the next generation thought it an honour to be taken as Shakespeare's offspring. What makes it likely enough is that Aubrey knew Sir William Davenant ; it is a convincing touch that the mother was both beautiful and witty, and 'of conversation extremely agreeable'.

At the end of 1624, at Bergen-op-Zoom, died Southampton and his eldest son, of a 'burning fever'. In 1607 when his mother had died, she left 'to my honourable and dear son, Henry Earl of Southampton, ten pieces of hanging of the story of Cyrus ; six pieces of hanging in which the months are described ; two pieces of hangings with gold wrought in them and Sir Thomas

Heneage's arms'.²⁹ She bequeathed him a scarlet bed with gold lace, a white satin bed, cushions, stools and chairs of cloth of gold ; basins, ewers and candlesticks of silver, and 'a ring of gold with a fair noble diamond in it, which Sir Thomas Heneage had of Sir Walter Ralegh'. After other legacies, 'all the rest of my goods and chattels, household stuff and estate, to my dear and well-beloved husband, Sir William Harvey, whom I make sole executor'. Thus, no doubt, along with other things had passed the manuscript of the Sonnets and 'A Lover's Complaint'.

Next year, 1625, Heminges and Condell headed the King's men in the funeral of King James. Two years before they had lost their fellow, Nicholas Tooley, who had also attained to the rank of gentleman and left a fair amount of money : £10 to Cuthbert Burbage's wife, 'in whose house I do now lodge as a remembrance of my love in respect of her motherly care over me' ; £10 to her daughter 'to buy her such things as she shall think most meet to wear in remembrance of me'.³⁰ He left more money to the women of the fellowship, Richard Burbage's sister and daughter, and to Condell's wife and daughter. He left a charitable stock of £80 for the poor of St. Leonard's, Shoreditch, for thirty-two penny wheaten loaves to be distributed every Sunday ; £20 for eight loaves weekly to the poor of St. Giles', Cripplegate. All the residue to Cuthbert Burbage and Condell. Condell died in 1627, leaving considerable property in land and tenements, making Heminges and Burbage overseers of his will and leaving them money for a piece of plate. To an old servant, Elizabeth Wheaton, he left 40s., a mourning gown 'and that place or privilege which she now exerciseth and enjoyeth in the houses of the Blackfriars and the Globe on the Bankside for life'.³¹ Heminges died in 1630, very well off and making Burbage overseer of his will.

We observe what respectability these players had attained to since the days of Tarleton and Kemp, and once more the closeness of the fellowship. They all provide a contrast with Shakespeare in one important respect : they made their lives and homes in London and built up their property there ; while he, though making his money in London, remained ever faithful to Stratford and transferred his gains to build up his patrimony in his native place. Not enough has been made of this pointed contrast and the significance it speaks.

John Fletcher died in 1625 in plague-time. He had been

invited into the country, but 'stayed but to make himself a suit of clothes, and while it was making, fell sick of the plague and died'.[32] Next year died the greatest of the actors, Edward Alleyn, who had made the largest fortune of them all. Two years younger than Shakespeare, he enjoyed his early retirement more than ten years longer. He had inherited Henslowe's wealth, and was thus able to bestow a munificent benefaction, some £10,000, in founding the school and almshouses on his estate at Dulwich. In 1623 he had lost his wife, the 'mouse' and 'Micho Mousin' and other endearments of his letters on tour as a young actor in the early 1590's.

At Stratford Dr. John Hall paid the fine of £10 rather than take up the knighthood proffered him for the coronation of Charles I. On 22 April 1626 Shakespeare's granddaughter Elizabeth, aged seventeen, went to church to marry Thomas Nash of Lincoln's Inn, nearly thirty-three, the son of her grand-father's old acquaintance, Anthony Nash of Welcombe. Dr. Hall was kept busy with a large practice among the country gentry round about and as far afield as Northamptonshire. He fulfilled his duty as church-warden in 1628–9, presenting the church with a carved Laudian pulpit. Too busy to attend to other duties in the town, he was reluctant to agree to become a burgess, and, when he consented, did not hit it off with the Puritan propensities of the corporation: they quarrelled vigorously and he was expelled. Fortunately for us he kept an account book recording the ailments of his patients and his prescriptions for them. There they all are — many of them Shakespeare's acquaintance, Combes, Nashes, Lanes, Underhills, Sheldons, Lady Rainsford of nearby Clifford Chambers, Drayton's patroness, whom he describes as well read in French and Italian. Lastly is the elderly poet laureate himself, 'an excellent poet, labouring of a tertian', for whom he prescribed an emetic of syrup of violets.[33]

Dr. Hall died in 1635, and Susanna in 1649. Buried beside her father and mother, she is described on her gravestone:

> Witty above her sex, but that's not all—
> Wise to salvation was good Mistress Hall:
> Something of Shakespeare was in that, but this
> Wholly of Him with whom she's now in bliss.

Her sister Judith had not been fortunate in her marriage: Thomas Quiney, the innkeeper, had turned out a tippler, and their two sons, Shakespeare's only grandsons, died in 1639.

There remained his granddaughter, Elizabeth Nash. Her father had left his 'study of books', which no doubt included Shakespeare's, to his son-in-law Nash 'to dispose of them as you see good. . . . As for my manuscripts . . . you may (son Nash) burn them or else do with them what you please.'[34] Nash died in 1647, leaving money to the Hathaways. Shakespeare's estate came to his granddaughter, who, a month before her mother's death, married again — a country gentleman, John Barnard, lord of the manor of Abington near Northampton. They lived on at New Place for a few years, until 1656 when they left it for Abington. At the Restoration Barnard was made a baronet; Elizabeth, Lady Barnard, died in 1670, leaving more money to the Hathaways at Stratford. Her property came to Sir John, who died in 1674, leaving to his family 'all the books', with pictures, 'old goods and lumber at Stratford-upon-Avon'.

There within the chancel they are gathered, Shakespeare and his wife, Susanna and John Hall, Thomas Nash — while all around, churchpath and churchyard, the willowy banks of the Avon, the narrow streets and lanes, New Place and Chapel precincts and along to Henley Street, over the level acres to Shottery, up the slopes to Wilmcote and across to Welcombe, back to the bridge that carries the road up into the Cotswolds and so to Oxford and London, all comes alive in the light of his imagination.

NOTES

Chapter I : ELIZABETHAN WARWICKSHIRE

[1] William Camden, *Britain*. Translated by Philemon Holland, 1610 ed., 567.
[2] R. H. Hilton, 'The Social Structure of Rural Warwickshire in the Middle Ages', *Dugdale Soc.*, Occasional Paper 9.
[3] *The Itinerary of John Leland*, ed. L. Toulmin Smith, II. 40 foll.
[4] And into my previous book, *Ralegh and the Throckmortons*.
[5] Camden, *ed. cit.* 561 foll.
[6] B. H. Newdigate, *Michael Drayton and his Circle*, vii.
[7] *The Works of Michael Drayton*, ed. J. W. Hebel, IV, *Polyolbion*, 275 foll.
[8] Mark Eccles, *Shakespeare in Warwickshire*, 89.
[9] Eccles, 77.
[10] *V.C.H. Warwick*, III. 209.
[11] *The Seconde Parte of a Register*, ed. A. Peel, II. 165 foll.
[12] Evidently at the time when it was expected that the Queen would marry Anjou, 1579–80.
[13] At the beginning of Elizabeth's reign there was, not unnaturally, perhaps a majority of Catholics among the gentry of south Warwickshire, with a fair number noted as 'indifferent in religion', cf. 'Letters of the Bishops to the Privy Council, 1564', *Camden Miscellany*, IX. South Warwickshire was in the diocese of Worcester.

Chapter II : STRATFORD TOWN

[1] Levi Fox, *The Borough Town of Stratford-upon-Avon*, 42.
[2] E. I. Fripp, *Shakespeare's Stratford*, 3, 8.
[3] *Ibid.* 22.
[4] Eccles, 39, 41.
[5] *Ibid.* 46.
[6] Fripp, 36-7.
[7] *V.C.H. Warwick*, III. 230.
[8] Fripp, 40.
[9] Leland, II. 49.
[10] It had, however, already been refaced.
[11] He did, however, build a palace of a house that is with us today — Temple Newsam, near Leeds.
[12] *V.C.H. Warwick*, III. 236, 239.
[13] *Minutes and Accounts of the Corporation of Stratford-upon-Avon*, transcribed by R. Savage, with Introductions and Notes by E. I. Fripp, I. xlv. These invaluable records (*Dugdale Society*, 4 vols., from 1566 to 1592) are the chief source for these details. It is a pity that they have not been proceeded with, at least to 1616.
[14] E. I. Fripp, *Shakespeare Studies*, 23 foll.
[15] Eccles, 57-8.
[16] I am the more inclined to accept this, which goes back to a seventeenth-century tradition, on account of the word 'will', a favourite one with Shakespeare, with its double meaning ; cf. below, p. 191.

17 E. I. Fripp, *Shakespeare, Man and Artist*, II. 803-4.
18 I have chosen Aubrey's form of the traditional verses as making better sense. Aubrey's *Brief Lives*, ed. A. Clark, II. 226. The Elizabethan statute permitted 10 per cent interest.
19 *Minutes and Accounts*, II. 22, 36. This spelling preserves the local flavour of pronunciation.
20 Biddle was a Stratford name ; Simon was a cutler, a kinsman of the Quineys.
21 *Minutes and Accounts*, IV. 39.
22 *Ibid.* 15-17.
23 *The Seconde Parte of a Register*, ed. A. Peel, II. 156 foll.
24 *Minutes and Accounts*, II. xii, xli.
25 Eccles, 83.
26 *Minutes and Accounts*, IV. xix foll.
27 Eccles, 82-3.
28 Dugdale, 523.

Chapter III : FAMILY : SCHOOL : CHURCH

1 Mark Eccles, 'Jonson's Marriage', *Review of English Studies*, XII. 257 foll.
2 E. I. Fripp, *Shakespeare, Man and Artist*, I. 31, 32.
3 Mark Eccles, *Shakespeare in Warwickshire*, 10.
4 Fripp, I. 43.
5 We owe this especially to the work of T. W. Baldwin, *William Shakespeare's Small Latin and Less Greek*, and *William Shakespeare's Petty School*, and E. I. Fripp, *Shakespeare, Man and Artist*, I. chaps. 8-12, on whom I rely chiefly for the following account.
6 Fripp, I. 84.
7 V. K. Whitaker, *Shakespeare's Use of Learning*, 8, 32, 38.
8 R. Noble, *Shakespeare's Biblical Knowledge*, 20, whom I follow for most of this account.
9 Fripp, I. 98-9, 100.
10 Noble, 47.
11 A. Hart, *Shakespeare and the Homilies*, 27.

Chapter IV : YOUTH AND MARRIAGE

1 Aubrey, *ed. cit.* II. 225-6.
2 E. K. Chambers, I. 17.
3 Fripp, I. 79-80.
4 C. F. E. Spurgeon, *Shakespeare's Imagery*, 121.
5 *Ibid.* 115.
6 *Ibid.* 86.
7 *Ibid.* 110.
8 In her endearing enthusiasm for Stratford Miss Spurgeon overlooked the more probable allusion.
9 *Ibid.* 86.
10 D. H. Madden, *The Diary of Master William Silence*, 85-7, 373.
11 Cf. my *Ralegh and the Throckmortons*, 164, 219.
12 Cf. Fripp, I. 379-85, II. 859-60.
13 Cf. Eccles, 30. But I prefer the figure of £40, as recorded in the fine of 1580; £4 is improbable.

[14] *Ibid.* 31.

[15] Professor C. J. Sisson gives us a vivid insight into the life of the Hathaways, the chief farming folk at Shottery along with the Burmans, in *Shakespeare Survey*, vol. 12, p. 95 foll. The Hathaways were the Earl of Warwick's tenants and Protestants, where the Burmans, like their landlord Francis Smith of Wootton Wawen, were really Catholics. This did not prevent the latter from getting justice from the Court of Chancery against the Protestant Earl.

[16] Aubrey, II. 227.

CHAPTER V : LONDON : THE ARMADA YEARS

[1] *Cal. S.P. Dom.*, *1581–90*, 379, 380.
[2] *Ibid.* 388, 391, 401, 457.
[3] *A.P.C. 1587–8*, 119.
[4] *A.P.C. 1588*, 17, 31.
[5] John Stow, *A Survey of London*, ed. C. L. Kingsford, I. 104.
[6] Cf. C. C. Stopes, *Shakespeare's Warwickshire Contemporaries*, 1-22.
[7] Cf. the admirable Introduction to Puttenham's *Arte of English Poesie*, by G. D. Wilcock and Alice Walker, to which I am indebted in the following paragraphs.
[8] *Ibid.* xcv-xcvi.
[9] *Ibid.* 63.
[10] W. W. Greg, 'An Elizabethan Printer and his Copy', *The Library*, Fourth Series, IV. 102 foll.
[11] Stow, *ed. cit.* I. 341.
[12] E. K. Chambers, *The Elizabethan Stage*, II. 495-7, 503-10.
[13] q. W. W. Greg, *A Bibliography of the English Printed Drama to the Restoration*, IV. 1191.
[14] F. P. Wilson, *Marlowe and the Early Shakespeare*, 7.
[15] Alfred Harbage, *Shakespeare's Audience*, 159, to which I am indebted in these paragraphs.
[16] q. F. P. Wilson, 10.
[17] E. K. Chambers, *The Elizabethan Stage*, II. 307.
[18] q. Alfred Harbage, *Shakespeare and the Rival Traditions*, 22.
[19] E. K. Chambers, I. 282, 287, 292.
[20] q. *Ibid.* II. 205, 344.
[21] *Cal. S.P. Dom. 1581–1590*, 541.
[22] *Ibid.*
[23] *Henslowe Papers*, ed. W. W. Greg, 48.
[24] *Ibid.* 34-6.
[25] *Ibid.* 40.

CHAPTER VI : APPRENTICESHIP

[1] F. P. Wilson, *Marlowe and the Early Shakespeare*, 111.
[2] W. G. Boswell-Stone, *Shakespeare's Holinshed*, 418.
[3] M. C. Bradbrook, *Shakespeare and Elizabethan Poetry*, 77, 78-9.
[4] Thomas Wilson, *Arte of Rhetorique*, ed. G. H. Mair, xx. 39, 47, 55.
[5] q. F. P. Wilson, 'Shakespeare's Reading', *Shakespeare Survey 3*, 14 foll.
[6] Cf. G. D. Willcock, 'Language and Poetry in Shakespeare's Early Plays', *Proceedings of the British Academy*, 1954, 103 foll.

7 q. H. R. D. Anders, *Shakespeare's Books*, 83.

8 Cf. John Buxton, *Sir Philip Sidney and the English Renaissance*, 192.

9 The fact that the poem was first published along with the Sonnets in 1609 indicates that it was in the Southampton *cache*, and was written for him, *v.* below, p. 463.

10 *v.* below, p. 172 foll.

11 F. P. Wilson, *Marlowe and the Early Shakespeare*, 112.

12 *The Third Part of King Henry VI*, ed. J. Dover Wilson, xiii.

13 I am much indebted to A. S. Cairncross's edition of *1 Henry VI* ('The Arden Shakespeare'), with whose argument I agree.

14 *Ibid.* xli.

15 *Ibid.* xxviii, xxxvii, liii.

16 *Ibid.* lv–lvi.

17 Alfred Harbage, q. *ibid.* xl.

Chapter VII : REPUTATION

1 q. J. C. Jordan, *Robert Greene*, 2, 6.

2 q. J. Dover Wilson, 'Malone and the Upstart Crow', *Shakespeare Survey 4*, 56 foll.

3 q. E. K. Chambers, *William Shakespeare*, II. 252.

4 *Ibid.* I. 61.

5 Cf. E. K. Chambers, *Shakespearean Gleanings*, 28.

6 F. S. Boas, *The Works of Thomas Kyd*, cviii–cx, cxix.

7 *Ibid.* 102.

8 Cf. J. Isaacs, 'Shakespeare's Earliest Years in the Theatre', *Proceedings of the British Academy*, 1953, 119 foll.

9 Boas, lxxxii foll.

10 Cf. *Titus Andronicus*, ed. J. C. Maxwell, 111.

11 *Ibid.* xxxvii.

12 A. W. Pollard, *Shakespeare's Hand in the Play of 'Sir Thomas More'*, 8.

13 q. Chambers, I. 514.

14 J. Bartlett's *Complete Concordance to Shakespeare* gives only two instances of this word, used in a slightly different sense, from *2 Henry IV*.

15 F. S. Boas, *Christopher Marlowe*, 2 foll.

16 *Ibid.* 251. But note that Boas corrected his account of Baines, 246 foll., in *Times Lit. Supp.*, 16 September 1949. The Baines who delated Marlowe was a priest at Rheims who, while there, was spying on his fellow-religious and reporting on them to Walsingham. He pointed out that by injecting poison into the well or the bath, the whole community could be carried off. Thus, 'Richard Baines can claim the credit of forestalling Marlowe's Barabas in Act III of *The Jew of Malta* in devising a plan for poisoning in one swoop an entire religious house'. It shocked Dr. Allen, later Cardinal, that while celebrating his Mass every day, this priest should be harbouring such thoughts. Later, he turns up in England, to inform against Marlowe : evidently a delator *de carrière*.

17 In this paragraph I follow Boas, 66 foll., 175 foll.

18 P. H. Kocher goes into them, in perhaps too much detail, in *Christopher Marlowe. A Study of his Thought, Learning and Character*, chapters 2 and 3.

19 Cf. L. and E. Feasey, 'Nashe's *The Unfortunate Traveller*', *English*, Autumn 1948, 125 foll.

20 P. Alexander, *Shakespeare's Life and Art*, 83.

21 q. Fripp, *Shakespeare*, I. 391.

22 These are the only instances of the use of the word in Elizabethan literature given by N.E.D.

[23] Cf. Howard Baker, *Induction to Tragedy*, 110 foll.

[24] *v.* below, p. 126.

[25] H. C. Goddard, *The Meaning of Shakespeare*, 36, 40.

[26] q. from Corbet's *Iter Boreale*, *The Oxford Shakespeare, The Histories and Poems*, 736.

[27] q. Chambers, II. 212.

[28] In these paragraphs I am much indebted to F. P. Wilson, *Marlowe and the Early Shakespeare*, 118 foll.

[29] M. C. Bradbrook, *Shakespeare and Elizabethan Poetry*, 62.

[30] N. Brooke, 'Marlowe as Provocative Agent in Shakespeare's Early Plays', *Shakespeare Survey 14*, 34 foll.

CHAPTER VIII : THE EARLY COMEDIES

[1] A. Feuillerat, *John Lyly*, 4 foll.

[2] Cf. G. K. Hunter, *John Lyly*, 241, 302, 318.

[3] Cf. M. Mincoff, 'Shakespeare and Lyly', *Shakespeare Survey 14*, 16.

[4] q. Chambers, II. 320, 327.

[5] J. Spedding, *Letters and Life of Francis Bacon*, I. 325.

[6] H. C. Goddard, *The Meaning of·Shakespeare*, 25, 27.

[7] Especially my old friend Q., with his Victorian romantic view of women ; cf. his Introduction to the Cambridge edition of *The Two Gentlemen of Verona*, xiii-xiv.

CHAPTER IX : FRIENDSHIP

[1] q. C. C. Stopes, *The Life of Henry, ·Third Earl of Southampton*, 36.

[2] *Ibid.* 37.

[3] Cf. for its admirable common sense, Edward Hubler, *The Sense of Shakespeare's Sonnets*, 97 foll.

[4] G. Wilson Knight, *The Mutual Flame*, 31 foll., is perceptive about this.

[5] Cf. Stopes, 199, and *v.* below p. 297.

[6] 'It is the strangest fact in Elizabethan social history.' Tucker Brooke, *Shakespeare's Sonnets*, 81.

[7] Cf. my *Ralegh and the Throckmortons*, 163.

[8] Cf. Sir Edmund Chambers, who writes in his standard biography (I. 543), 'a full treatment of the problems raised by Shakespeare's non-dramatic writings does not fall within the scope of this work'. Imagine writing the biography of Shakespeare without considering the Sonnets—of prime autobiographical importance ! Other Victorians, Sir Sidney Lee, for example, after much embarrassed wavering came to the conclusion that they were a literary exercise !

[9] *Narrative and Dramatic Sources of Shakespeare*, ed. Geoffrey Bullough, I. 161.

[10] *Ibid.* I. 164.

[11] *v.* above, p. 51.

[12] Except Sir Edmund Chambers, who says (*William Shakespeare*, I. 61-2) 'a super-subtle criticism detects a great advance in the poet's intimacy with his patron between the two addresses, which I am bound to say is not apparent to me'. It is pure want of imagination not to be able to see it. Cf. Tucker Brooke, *op. cit.* 81, 'there is no Elizabethan dedication like this'.

[13] q. D. H. Horne, *The Life and Minor Works of George Peele*, 253.

[14] *The Works of Thomas Nashe*, ed. R. B. McKerrow, II. 201-2.
[15] *I.e.* Hecuba.
[16] *The Poems* ('The Arden Shakespeare'), ed. F. T. Prince, xxxviii.
[17] Cf. Chambers, II. 192 foll.

Chapter X: THE STORY OF THE SONNETS

[1] Edward Hubler, *The Sense of Shakespeare's Sonnets*, 38.
[2] q. Stopes, 66.
[3] *Cal. S.P. Dom. 1591-1594*, 446.
[4] H. Foley, ed. *Records of the English Province of the Society of Jesus*, IV. 49. Garnet said £5,000, an improbably high figure.
[5] The later sonnets of Drayton, more moving and more real, were influenced by Shakespeare's.

Chapter XI: ROMANCE AND REALITY

[1] Chambers, I. 62.
[2] *Ibid.* I. 64.
[3] Madeleine Doran, Introduction to *A Midsummer-Night's Dream* ('The Pelican Shakespeare'), 18.
[4] Goddard, 74.
[5] *Cal. S.P. Dom. 1591-1594*, 222, 492, 502-3.
[6] This concatenation tends to support my suggestion of the echo of Chideock Tichborne's poem in Shakespeare's lines above, p. 153-4.
[7] Stopes, 63.
[8] We may dare then to correct the dating of a great scholar, Sir Walter Greg, *The Shakespeare First Folio*, 240, who gives 1595-6.
[9] Cf. The Cambridge Shakespeare edition of *A Midsummer-Night's Dream*, 105 : 'these are remarkable lines ; evidently written with Queen Elizabeth in mind. But phrases like "barren sister" and "withering on the virgin thorn" would surely have sounded harsh in her ears.' They would indeed !
[10] *Ibid.* 151.
[11] As against Greg's view, *loc. cit.* 242.
[12] Q., Introduction to *A Midsummer-Night's Dream* ('The New Cambridge Shakespeare'), xiv.
[13] Bullough, I. 369.
[14] 'There is a vile phrase of which bad historians are exceedingly fond, "the dignity of history".'
[15] Richard David, Introduction to *Love's Labour's Lost* ('The Arden Shakespeare'), xvii.
[16] McKerrow, *Nashe*, V. 65.
[17] G. K. Hunter, *John Lyly*, 317.
[18] A good deal of ingenuity has been expended on where the name Moth came from ; in 1592 Richard Field published *The French Alphabet* by one G. de la Mothe.
[19] q. F. A. Yates, *John Florio*, 190.
[20] Cf. the depositions in *Salisbury MSS.* (H.M.C.), V. 85 foll. For a summary of the previous misdeeds of the Longs against the Danverses, *v. Cal. S.P. Dom. 1595-1597*, 34.

[21] John Aubrey, *Brief Lives*, ed. A. Clark, I. 195.

[22] *v.* above, p. 187.

[23] *Salisbury MSS.* V. 553.

[24] I am glad to be in agreement with Sir Edmund Chambers in this dating.

[25] Cf. *Cal. S.P. Dom. 1581-1590*, 169.

[26] Perhaps I may point out a slight confusion in Mr. G. I. Duthie's Introduction to the Cambridge edition of *Romeo and Juliet*, xvi : it was not the earthquake, but Juliet's birth, that took place on Lammas Eve.

[27] *Salisbury MSS.* V. 102.

[28] *Cal. S.P. Dom. 1595-1597*, 203.

[29] *Salisbury MSS.* V. 158.

[30] *Ibid.* VI. 352 and *passim*.

[31] The comparison between the two is best made in Bullough, I. 454-7. It is hardly necessary, however, to look to the Portuguese Pretender, Don Antonio, for so common a name ; but Don Antonio is not to be confused, as on p. 445, with Antonio Perez, Philip II's exiled minister.

[32] *v.* above, p. 110.

[33] Introduction by Q. to the Cambridge edition of *The Merchant of Venice*, xxix–xxx.

Chapter XII : ENGLAND'S PAST

[1] J. Dover Wilson, Introduction to *King John* ('The Cambridge Shakespeare'), xv. I should like to pay tribute to Prof. Dover Wilson's editions of the History plays of this sequence, *Richard II, Henry IV, Henry V*, the historical approach to which is particularly appropriate and illuminating.

[2] McKerrow, *Nashe*, I. 212.

[3] q. Chambers, I. 353 ; II. 326-7.

[4] *Ibid.* II. 320-1.

[5] F. P. Wilson, *Marlowe and the Early Shakespeare*, 94.

[6] This is generally accepted now ; cf. H. B. Charlton and R. D. Waller, Introduction to Marlowe's *Edward II*, 8, 16–17.

[7] *Ibid.* 100, 102.

[8] Sir Robert Naunton, *Fragmenta Regalia* 'Arber's English Reprints', 51.

[9] J. Dover Wilson, Introduction to *King John* ('The Cambridge Shakespeare'), viii.

[10] Cf. my *Expansion of Elizabethan England*, 313.

[11] W. W. Greg, *The Shakespeare First Folio*, 248.

[12] J. Dover Wilson, *loc. cit.* lvii.

[13] q. A. R. Humphreys, ed. *1 Henry IV* ('The Arden Shakespeare'), xii.

[14] q. Chambers, II. 198.

[15] Cf. A. E. Hughes, *Shakespeare and his Welsh Characters*.

[16] Cf. David Mathew, *The Celtic Peoples and Renaissance Europe*, c. XVIII.

[17] H. C. Hart, Introduction to *The Merry Wives of Windsor* ('The Arden Shakespeare'), xxxiii.

[18] Slender is described, Act I, Sc. IV, as having 'a little yellow beard — a cane-coloured beard'. This has given trouble to the commentators. Could it not be a misreading for the familiar Elizabethan expression 'crane-coloured', meaning ash-coloured ?

[19] Cf. my *Ralegh and the Throckmortons*, 187, 211.

[20] *Ibid.* lvi-lvii.

[21] J. Dover Wilson, Introduction to *King Henry V* ('The Cambridge Shakespeare'), vii.

[22] *Ibid.* x.

[23] q. J. Dover Wilson, Introduction to *King Henry V* ('The Cambridge Shakespeare'), 9.

[24] I owe this point to Professor Richard B. Hosley.

CHAPTER XIII : THE LATE NINETIES

[1] Mark Eccles, *Shakespeare in Warwickshire*, 84 foll.

[2] H. Howarth, 'Shakespeare's Gentleness', *Shakespeare Survey 14*, 90 foll.

[3] Eccles, 91 foll.

[4] Cf. E. I. Fripp, *Master Richard Quyny*, 125.

[5] Stow, *Survey of London*, ed. cit. I. 174.

[6] L. Hotson, *Shakespeare versus Shallow*, 9.

[7] Chambers, II. 87 foll.

[8] His first plays to be published were *Titus Andronicus*, and the bad Quartos of *2 Henry VI* and *The Taming of the Shrew* in 1594.

[9] Greg, *The Shakespeare First Folio*, 236, 261.

[10] G. E. Bentley, 'Shakespeare and the Blackfriars Theatre', *Shakespeare Survey 1*, 38 foll.

[11] C. H. Herford and P. Simpson, *Ben Jonson*, I. 2 foll.

[12] E. K. Chambers. *The Elizabethan Stage*, IV. 319–20.

[13] C. W. Hodges, *The Globe Restored*, 15 foll.

[14] We must remember that in Norden's map the Rose is wrongly named the Star, and that in Hollar's drawing the names Bear-baiting and the Globe are accidentally interchanged.

[15] E. K. Chambers, *The Elizabethan Stage*, II. 365 ; I have emended the translation from the German.

[16] *Cal. S.P. Dom. 1595–1597*, 448.

[17] q. Stopes, 110, 111.

[18] q. *Ibid.* 86, 114.

[19] q. *Ibid.* 115, 116.

[20] q. *Ibid.* 116.

[21] q. *Ibid.* 121, 122–3.

[22] *Ibid.* 123, 124.

[23] q. *Ibid.* 126, 127.

[24] q. *Ibid.* 131.

[25] q. *Ibid.* 134–5.

[26] q. *Ibid.* 140.

[27] q. *Ibid.* 148.

[28] q. *Ibid.* 152–3.

[29] q. *Ibid.* 158–9.

[30] *Salisbury MSS.* XI. 94, 108. Mrs. Stopes amusingly suppressed this sidelight on Southampton, p. 199.

[31] q. *Ibid.* 173.

[32] q. *Ibid.* 174–5, 187.

[33] q. *Ibid.* 176, 178, 181.

[34] Kenneth Muir, *Shakespeare's Sources*, I. 53.

[35] Introduction to *Much Ado about Nothing* ('The Cambridge Shakespeare'), xxvi, xxvii.

[36] *Ibid.* xv–xvi.

[37] Aubrey, *Brief Lives*, ed. cit. II. 226. Aubrey actually says 'the constable in *Midsummer-Night's Dream*' : I assume he means Dogberry, unless, in his 'maggotty-headed' way, he meant Bottom the weaver.

[38] G. I. Duthie, *The 'Bad' Quarto of Hamlet*, 9–10.

[39] Muir, *op. cit.* 57.

[40] N. B. Paradise, *Thomas Lodge*, 35.

[41] Introduction to *As You Like It* ('The Cambridge Shakespeare'), x.

[42] I propose this emendation in the received text : 'content with my harm' is nonsense ; the proper apposition to 'glad of other men's good', is 'content with my own'. An Elizabethan compositor has slipped up and it seems to have escaped all textual critics hitherto.

[43] J. Dover Wilson, Introduction to *Julius Caesar* ('The Cambridge Shakespeare'), xv, xxxii.

[44] T. S. Dorsch, Introduction to *Julius Caesar* ('The Arden Shakespeare'), xiii.

CHAPTER XIV : BETWEEN TWO WORLDS

[1] J. Dover Wilson, Introduction to *Hamlet* ('The New Cambridge Shakespeare'), viii.

[2] *Ibid.* xx.

[3] *Ibid.* viii.

[4] Alfred Harbage, *Shakespeare and the Rival Traditions*, 294.

[5] J. Dover Wilson, *ed. cit.* 184.

[6] E. I. Fripp, *Shakespeare, Man and Artist*, I. 146-7.

[7] E. K. Chambers, *The Elizabethan Stage*, II. 205.

[8] *Salisbury MSS.* XI. 71-2 ; XII. 562.

[9] Robert Chester, *Love's Martyr*, ed. A. B. Grosart (The New Shakespeare Society), 4, 177.

[10] *The Poems* ('The Arden Shakespeare'), ed. F. T. Prince, xlii foll.

[11] John Masefield, q. *ibid.*

[12] q. P. Alexander, *op. cit.* 134 foll.

[13] Introduction to *Twelfth Night* ('The New Cambridge Shakespeare'), x, xv-xvi.

[14] Cf. my book *The English Past*, 29.

[15] Stow, *ed cit.*, I. 299.

[16] E. K. Chambers, *William Shakespeare*, II. 90 foll.

[17] Eccles, 101 foll.

[18] G. K. Hunter, Introduction to *All's Well that Ends Well* ('The Arden Shakespeare'), liii.

[19] *Ibid.* li.

[20] Cf. Gower's speech, *Henry V*, III. vi.

[21] *Cal. S.P. Dom. 1603–1610*, 2, 8, 19, 34, 58, 89, 106, 137, 162, 175.

[22] *Ibid.* 187, 203, 354, 515.

[23] Evidently this anonymous versifier thought Greene was still alive.

[24] *Salisbury MSS.* XVI. 415.

[25] Stopes, 289, 296.

[26] G. E. Bentley, 'Shakespeare and the Blackfriars Theatre', *Shakespeare Survey 1*, 40.

[27] Walter Pater, *Appreciations*, 189–90.

[28] Cf. J. W. Lever, 'The Date of *Measure for Measure*', *Shakespeare Quarterly*, X. 388.

[29] Cf. Q.'s Introduction to *Measure for Measure* ('The New Cambridge Shakespeare'), xxi.

CHAPTER XV : THE GREAT TRAGEDIES

[1] C. J. Sisson, 'The Mythical Sorrows of Shakespeare', *Proc. Brit. Academy*, 1934, 45 foll.

[2] Chambers, I. 85–6.

[3] Cf. G. E. Bentley, Introduction to *Othello* ('The Pelican Shakespeare'), 17.

⁴ Alfred Harbage, Introduction to *King Lear* ('The Pelican Shakespeare'), 18.
⁵ *Ibid.*
⁶ Kenneth Muir, Introduction to *King Lear* ('The Arden Shakespeare'), lviii.
⁷ *Salisbury MSS.* XV. 266.
⁸ W. W. Greg, *op. cit.* 389.
⁹ J. Dover Wilson, Introduction to *Antony and Cleopatra* ('The Cambridge Shakespeare'), xxxii.
¹⁰ J. W. Mackail, *The Approach to Shakespeare*, 89.
¹¹ H. Granville-Barker, *Preface to Shakespeare*, II. 126.
¹² Cf. my *Ralegh and the Throckmortons*, 220.
¹³ Cf. E. F. Gay, 'The Midland Revolt and the Inquisitions of Depopulation of 1607', *Trans.Roy.Hist.Soc.*, N.S. XVIII. 195 foll.
¹⁴ E. I. Fripp, II. 706.
¹⁵ Cf. H. J. Oliver, 'Coriolanus as Tragic Hero', *Shakespeare Quarterly*, 1959, 53 foll.
¹⁶ Cf. Kenneth Muir, 'The Background of *Coriolanus*', *Shakespeare Quarterly*, 1959, 137 foll.
¹⁷ Greg, 410.
¹⁸ I should like to pay tribute to the excellence of H. J. Oliver's Introduction to the play in 'The Arden Shakespeare', the most illuminating discussion of it I know.
¹⁹ Cf. my *The Elizabethans and America*, 192.

CHAPTER XVI : THE ROMANCES

¹ E. K. Chambers, *The Elizabethan Stage*, II. 334-5.
² *Ibid.* II. 333-4.
³ P.C.C. 31 Hayes.
⁴ P.C.C. Windebancke 75.
⁵ q. F. P. Wilson, 'Ralph Crane, Scrivener to the King's Players', *The Library*, 1927, 197.
⁶ Cf. Exeter in 1618, where the Mayor refused Daniel's Children of Bristol to play, and the significant comment, 'those who spend their money on plays are ordinarily very poor people'. J. T. Murray, *English Dramatic Companies, 1558-1642*, II. 6.
⁷ I quote from the edn. by R. H. Perkinson, *Scholars' Facsimiles and Reprints*, New York, 1941, without pagination.
⁸ Cf. G. E. Bentley, 'Shakespeare and the Blackfriars Theatre', *Shakespeare Survey*, I. 38 foll.
⁹ A. Harbage, *Shakespeare and the Rival Traditions*, 304.
¹⁰ Aubrey, *ed. cit.* I. 95-6.
¹¹ E. K. Chambers, *William Shakespeare*, I. 86.
¹² Cf. P. Edwards, 'An Approach to the Problem of *Pericles*', *Shakespeare Survey* 5, 25 foll.
¹³ J. C. Maxwell, Introduction to *Pericles* ('The Cambridge Shakespeare'), xxii.
¹⁴ P. Edwards, *loc. cit.* 38.
¹⁵ Just before Tennyson died, he was reading *Cymbeline* : his dead body lay with the moon coming into the room, with *Cymbeline* open beside him.
¹⁶ Cf. J. M. Nosworthy, Introduction to *Cymbeline* ('The Arden Shakespeare'), lxviii-lxxi.
¹⁷ Cf. Q., Introduction to *The Winter's Tale* ('The Cambridge Shakespeare'), xxiv, xxv.
¹⁸ Kenneth Muir, *Shakespeare's Sources*, I. 247.

19, This means, every eleven sheep yield a tod (*i.e.* 28 lb.) of wool.
20 Muir, I. 245.
21 q. Q., *loc. cit.* viii.
22 Cf. my *The Elizabethans and America*, 70–1.
23 Cf. *ibid.* 80–1.
24 Cf. L. Hotson, *I, William Shakespeare*, 222.
25 *Purchas His Pilgrimes*, MacLehose edn., XIX. 11 foll.
26 F. Kermode, Introduction to *The Tempest* ('The Arden Shakespeare'), xxxviii.
27 This was a contemporary mode of travel-insurance.
28 R. A. Foakes, Introduction to *Henry VIII* ('The Arden Shakespeare'), xxv.
Perhaps I may take the opportunity to say that I agree with this editor's argument
and see no reason for regarding the play as written in collaboration.
29 The received text says 'pitied', but surely 'pitted' is the meaning ?
30 *The Life and Letters of Sir Henry Wotton*, ed. L. Pearsall Smith, II. 32.

CHAPTER XVII : NEW PLACE

1 J. T. Murray, *English Dramatic Companies, 1558–1642*, I. 155.
2 Eccles, 131–2.
3 E. K. Chambers, *William Shakespeare*, II. 155 foll.
4 q. *Ibid.* II. 153.
5 Cf. G. E. Bentley, 'why Heminges and Condell did not include *The Two
Noble Kinsmen* in the Folio of 1623 is a puzzle', *Shakespeare : A Biographical Hand-
book*, 192. We see that it is no puzzle at all.
6 Cf. the discussion in Kenneth Muir, 'Shakespeare's Hand in *The Two Noble
Kinsmen*,' *Shakespeare Survey 11*, 50 foll.
7 Cf. E. K. Chambers, I. 531–2, with which I am mostly in agreement.
8 P. Simpson, *Studies in Elizabethan Drama*, 132
9 Eccles, 135.
10 Chambers, II. 153.
11 Fripp, 801.
12 *Ibid.* 791.
13 *Ibid*, 805 foll.
14 Eccles, 113.
15 Chambers, II. 170 foll.
16 *The Diary of John Ward*, ed. C. Severn, 183.
17 For once I keep to the original spelling, to be close to his own.
18 By J. M., probably James Mabbe, translator, of Magdalen College, Oxford ;
q. Chambers, II. 234.
19 P.C.C., Parker 38.
20 q. Bentley, 186.
21 Greg, 12.
22 q. *Ibid.* 9.
23 q. Chambers, II. 228 foll.
24 Fripp, 857.
25 Our leading authority sums up this complicated matter thus : 'despite the
diversity of materials directly or indirectly made use of by the printers, the great
bulk of our substantive texts are at no long remove from Shakespeare's autograph
versions, the majority of these texts, indeed, being for the most part immediately
derived from his "foul papers"'. Charlton Hinman, *Shakespeare Quarterly*, 1956,
97. Sir Walter Greg tells us that 'foul papers [*i.e.* author's manuscripts] come somehow into the picture in the case of twenty-one. Of the thirty-six plays in the Folio,
twenty-two were printed there for the first time, at any rate in a reputable text,

and in each instance from a playhouse manuscript.' Greg, *op. cit.* 430. The addition of *Pericles* makes thirty-seven in all.

²⁶ Cf. Greg's tribute : 'The Folio editors appear to have had a considerable amount of material at their disposal and to have given some thought to their choice and when they were in any way doubtful about the authenticity of the particular copy chosen, they endeavoured to remedy its defects . . . On the whole they performed their task in a reasonably conscientious manner and at times went to considerable trouble to provide their readers with what they believed to be an authentic text.' *Ibid.* 431.

²⁷ Fripp, 853.
²⁸ Aubrey, I. 204.
²⁹ Stopes, 334–5.
³⁰ P.C.C. 58 Byrde.
³¹ P.C.C. 18 Barrington.
³² Aubrey, I. 254.
³³ Fripp, 882.
³⁴ *Ibid*, 891, 908.

INDEX

Index